Manchester Medieval Sources Series

series advisers Rosemary Horrox and Janet L. Nelson

This series aims to meet a growing need among students and teachers of medieval history for translations of key sources that are directly usable in students' own work. It provides texts central to medieval studies courses and focuses upon the diverse cultural and social as well as political conditions that affected the functioning of all levels of medieval society. The basic premise of the series is that translations must be accompanied by sufficient introductory and explanatory material, and each volume, therefore, includes a comprehensive guide to the sources' interpretation, including discussion of critical linguistic problems and an assessment of the most recent research on the topics being covered.

THE PAPAL REFORM OF
THE ELEVENTH CENTURY

Published in our
centenary year
〜 **2004** 〜
MANCHESTER
UNIVERSITY
PRESS

D1545912

MedievalSources*online*

Complementing the printed editions of the Medieval Sources series, Manchester University Press has developed a web-based learning resource which is now available on a yearly subscription basis.

Medieval Sources*online* brings quality history source material to the desktops of students and teachers and allows them open and unrestricted access throughout the entire college or university campus. Designed to be fully integrated with academic courses, this is a one-stop answer for many medieval history students, academics and researchers keeping thousands of pages of source material 'in print' over the Internet for research and teaching.

titles available now at Medieval Sources*online include*

John Edwards *The Jews in Western Europe, 1400–1600*

Paul Fouracre and Richard A. Gerberding *Late Merovingian France: History and hagiography 640–720*

Chris Given-Wilson *Chronicles of the Revolution 1397–1400: The reign of Richard II*

P. J. P. Goldberg *Women in England, c. 1275–1525*

Janet Hamilton and Bernard Hamilton *Christian dualist heresies in the Byzantine world c. 650–c. 1450*

Rosemary Horrox *The Black Death*

Graham A. Loud and Thomas Wiedemann *The history of the tyrants of Sicily by 'Hugo Falcandus', 1153–69*

Janet L. Nelson *The Annals of St-Bertin: Ninth-century histories, volume I*

Timothy Reuter *The Annals of Fulda: Ninth-century histories, volume II*

R. N. Swanson *Catholic England: Faith, religion and observance before the Reformation*

Jennifer Ward *Women of the English nobility and gentry, 1066–1500*

Visit the site at *www.medievalsources.co.uk* for further information and subscription prices.

THE PAPAL REFORM
OF THE
ELEVENTH CENTURY
Lives of Pope Leo IX and Pope Gregory VII

selected sources translated and annotated
by I. S. Robinson

Manchester University Press
Manchester and New York

distributed exclusively in the USA by Palgrave

Copyright © I. S. Robinson 2004

The right of I. S. Robinson to be identified as the editor of this work has been asserted
by him in accordance with the Copyright, Designs and Patents Act 1988

Published by Manchester University Press
Oxford Road, Manchester M13 9NR, UK
and Room 400, 175 Fifth Avenue, New York, NY 10010, USA
www.manchesteruniversitypress.co.uk

Distributed exclusively in the USA by
Palgrave, 175 Fifth Avenue, New York, NY 10010, USA

Distributed exclusively in Canada by
UBC Press, University of British Columbia, 2029 West Mall,
Vancouver, BC, Canada V6T 1Z2

British Library Cataloguing-in-Publication Data
A catalogue record for this book is available from the British Library

Library of Congress Cataloging-in-Publication Data applied for

ISBN 0 7190 3874 x *hardback*
     0 7190 3875 8 *paperback*

First published 2004

13 12 11 10 09 08 07 06 05 04   10 9 8 7 6 5 4 3 2 1

Typeset in Monotype Bell
by Koinonia Ltd, Manchester
Printed in Great Britain
by Bell & Bain Ltd, Glasgow

CONTENTS

SERIES EDITOR'S FOREWORD

The eleventh century was a period of revolutionary developments in western European history which together made a Europe still recognisable today. Religious changes are particularly well-documented – in fact the explosion of partisan literature they evoked is something itself quite new in European history – yet they have proved particularly difficult to contextualise and explain. They were made possible by growing wealth in all sectors of the economy but there was nothing inevitable in their form or ultimate impact. Their most striking unifying feature, a focus on the papacy, was very definitely man-made. I. S. Robinson has devoted his scholarly career to analysing the aims and methods, the idealism and group-interest, of the papal reformers, the reactions they provoked, and the consequences their reform propelled. In this volume, he makes available to anglophone students, for the first time, the three central texts in which papal reformers represented critical phases of a contemporary history that they saw as growing out of the past: first the upbeat and 'dynamic' account of Pope Leo IX given by his biographer c.1060; then, from Lombardy, the cockpit of ideological and factional conflicts, Bishop Bonizo's rallying-cry in 1085/6 to supporters of the just-deceased and apparently-defeated Pope Gregory VII – a polemic framed in universal history; and third, in the relatively tranquil 1120s, Paul of Bernried's *Life* of Gregory, which provided the reformed papacy with its martyr and patron-saint. Two shorter pieces fill out the picture in very different ways: extracts from Benzo's diatribe against Gregory show what Bonizo was up against, while Bruno of Segni's retrospective on Leo IX as remembered by Gregory shows the construction of a coherent and necessarily historical defence of the two key protagonists of papal reform. I. S. Robinson is uniquely well-placed to present and clarify these sources: himself a leading expert, he also distils the wisdom of recent inter-national scholarship, most of it in German. The subject has long since been removed from the sterile confessional conflicts of the nineteenth century, but anglophone students have too often been denied the benefit of perspective. Now, thanks to Robinson, they have access to current interpretations, and, most important of all, they have the texts that record the authentic, passionate voices of papal reformers fashioning their case through the critical period from the 1060s to the 1120s. There is no better way to get inside these revolutionary decades: that authenticity, those interested passions, throw vivid light on why papal reform took hold, and why papal monarchy could change western Christendom.

Janet L. Nelson
King's College London

ACKNOWLEDGEMENTS

In compiling this collection of papal *Lives* I have been given most generous and valuable help. Professor Dr Horst Fuhrmann (Munich) has most kindly permitted me to see the Latin text of his forthcoming edition of Paul of Bernried's *Vita Gregorii VII papae*. My grateful thanks are also due to the Reverend Dr H. E. J. Cowdrey (whose massive work on Pope Gregory VII places all students of the papal reform in his debt) and to Professor Dr Rudolf Schieffer, President of the *Monumenta Germaniae Historica*, for their advice and help. Dr Detlev Jasper of the *Monumenta Germaniae Historica* was, as always, the most patient, generous and learned of correspondents. The staff of the Library of Trinity College, Dublin, especially my friends Ms Anne Walsh and Ms Mary Higgins, have been unfailingly helpful at a time of chaotic change in that famous library. Many friends have sent me important material from other libraries: my nephew Daniel Becker (Berlin), Dr Niall O Ciosáin (Galway), Dr Mark Humphries (Maynooth), Thomas McCarthy (Oxford), Jochen Schenk (Tübingen and Cambridge) and Douglas Carver (Washington). I am indebted also to Ms. Nuala Collins (Department of Medieval History, Trinity College) and to my research students Patrick Healy, Conor Kostick, Margaret Norton, Jeremy Quartermain and Maia Sheridan for their help and encouragement. Spouses are always thanked in prefaces but no spouse ever deserved the acknowledgement of her good advice and patient help more than Dr Helga Robinson-Hammerstein.

ABBREVIATIONS

CC	*Corpus Christianorum, series Latina*
CCM	*Corpus Christianorum, Continuatio Mediaevalis*
CSEL	*Corpus scriptorum ecclesiasticorum Latinorum*
Italia Pontificia	P. Kehr (ed.), *Italia Pontificia* 1–8 (Berlin, 1906–35)
JK / JL	*Regesta pontificum Romanorum* ed. P. Jaffé, W. Wattenbach, S. Loewenfeld, F. Kaltenbrunner, P. Ewald, 2 volumes (second edition: Leipzig, 1885)
MGH	*Monumenta Germaniae Historica*
Constitutiones	*Constitutiones et acta publica imperatorum et regum*
Libelli	*Libelli de lite imperatorum et pontificum*
SS	*Scriptores* (in Folio)
SS rer. germ.	*Scriptores rerum germanicarum in usum scholarum separatim editi*
MPG	J. P. Migne (ed.), *Patrologiae cursus completus. Series Graeca*
MPL	J. P. Migne (ed.), *Patrologiae cursus completus. Series Latina*
Sacra Concilia	J. D. Mansi, *Sacrorum conciliorum nova et amplissima collectio* 1–31 (Venice–Florence, 1759–98)

pgs. 1-17, intro material, background.

INTRODUCTION

The papal reform movement of the eleventh century is the best docu-
mented of a number of parallel movements dedicated to the reform of
ecclesiastical institutions. Some were concerned with monastic reform;
some were local reforming initiatives like that in the church of Milan.
An important influence was the notable acceleration in economic
growth in the eleventh century. Historians have traced in this period
a significant rise in population, territorial expansion, an 'agrarian
revolution', the extension of commercial activity and the 'rise of the
money economy'. In particular the century witnessed an increase in
the value of ecclesiastical property, especially in the developing urban
areas. As the Church grew wealthier, the struggle for control of ecclesiastical assets became more intense.[1] The churchmen who opposed
the claims of secular powers to control the Church's possessions did
so in the name of 'reform'.

By 'reform' they meant the restoration of the Church to the conditions
of an earlier golden age of prosperity and freedom. Abbot Desiderius
of Monte Cassino wrote of Pope Leo IX that 'all ecclesiastical affairs
were renewed and restored by him'; while the chronicler of Monte
Cassino described Desiderius himself as 'the restorer and renewer' of
his abbey.[2] Pope Gregory VII declared that his aim was 'to renew and
restore whatever has been long neglected in the Church through sin
... [and] through evil custom'. He would labour 'to lead holy Church
back to the condition of ancient religion'.[3] This former golden age was
the period from the beginning of the fourth to the end of the sixth
century: the three centuries following the conversion of Emperor
Constantine I and the Christianisation of the Roman empire.[4] It was
'that golden age in which [Pope] Leo [I] and [Pope] Gregory [I],
the lights of spiritual doctrine, shone more brightly than glass'.[5] The
Leo IX / Gregory VII namedaffer "golden age" popes

1 D. Herlihy (1958) pp. 23–37; D. Herlihy (1961) pp. 81–105; R. W. Southern (1970)
pp. 34–6; A. Murray (1978) pp. 55–67; R. I. Moore (1980) pp. 49–67.

2 Desiderius, *Dialogi* III, *prologus* p. 1143; *Chronica monasterii Casinensis* III, *prologus*
p. 362.

3 Gregory VII, *Registrum* V.5, p. 353; *Epistolae Vagantes* 2, p. 6.

4 This historical perspective is most clearly presented in Bonizo of Sutri, *Book to a
Friend* II, below p. 166.

5 John of Fécamp, *Letter to Leo IX*, *MPL* 143, col. 797B.

exemplary conduct of these great popes was remembered in the papal names of the reforming popes Leo IX and Gregory VII. Leo IX's biographer wrote that the pope 'imitated the character and life of Leo the Great, whose name he bore'. According to Paul of Bernried, 'the spirit of Gregory I truly rested' on Gregory VII.[6]

The adherents of the papal reform movement drew much of their picture of the golden age of the Church from the eighth-century forgery 'the Donation of Constantine' and the ninth-century Pseudo-Isidorean Decretals. The former document records the granting to the pope by the first Christian emperor of the Lateran palace in Rome, the imperial insignia, 'the city of Rome and all the provinces, places and cities of Italy and the western regions'.[7] The 'False Decretals' is a collection of 115 forged and 125 falsified letters ascribed to the popes of the first six centuries.[8] In these sources eleventh-century readers found a picture of a Church whose personnel and property were free from secular control. They also found a Church governed in all aspects of its life by the decrees of the pope, who was 'more exalted than all the priests of the whole world and foremost among them'.[9] Hence the reformer Peter Damian urged contemporaries to 'read the edict of Emperor Constantine, in which he established the principate of the apostolic see above all the churches in the world'.[10]

That golden age had been succeeded by an 'iron age', in which laymen usurped control of the Church and its property, blurring the all-important distinction between ecclesiastical and secular.[11] The aim of the papal reform movement was 'to reform this iron age to one of gold',[12] using the unique authority of the papacy. 'We command you by apostolic authority', wrote Pope Gregory VII to the clergy and laity of Ravenna, 'to snatch [your church] from servile oppression, or

---

6 *Life of Pope Leo IX* II.8, below p. 133; Paul of Bernried, *Life of Pope Gregory VII* c. 1, below p. 262.

7 *Constitutum Constantini* c. 14, 17, *MGH Fontes iuris germanici antiqui* 10, 87–8, 93–4.

8 H. Fuhrmann, *Einfluß und Verbreitung der pseudoisidorischen Fälschungen* 1 (Schriften der MGH 24/1: Stuttgart, 1972), 137–50.

9 *Constitutum Constantini* c. 12, p. 83.

10 Peter Damian, *Letter* 89 (*Briefe* 2, 546).

11 *Vita Adalberonis episcopi Wirziburgensis* c. 6, *MGH SS* 12, 131. See also J. Autenrieth, *Die Domschule von Konstanz* (Stuttgart, 1956) p. 87.

12 William, abbot of Hirsau, letter to anti-king Herman of Salm in *Briefsammlungen der Zeit Heinrichs IV.* p. 42. For the restoration of the golden age see Peter Damian, *Letters* 13, 20 (*Briefe* 1, 144, 201).

rather tyrannical slavery, and restore her to her ancient freedom'.[13]
This could only be achieved by the rigid separation of *ecclesiastica* and
saecularia. The reformers saw spiritual men, clergy and monks, as a
separate order *(ordo)* of Christian society, distinct from and superior
to the laity.[14] 'As clergy are separate from laymen in their habit and
profession, so they should also be separate in behaviour and conversation,' wrote the reformer Humbert of Silva Candida, 'so that
neither should seize for themselves the office or the hereditary condition of the other and both should pay attention to the limits set by
the holy Fathers and the orthodox emperors.'[15] The chronicler Bernold
of St Blasien applauded Gregory VII as 'a most strenuous defender of
ecclesiastical liberty', who wished that the clergy 'would tower above
[laymen] by virtue of the holiness of their conduct and the dignity of
their order'.[16]

Ensuring the freedom of the personnel and the property of the
Church entailed the eradication of the customs – the reformers called
them 'heresies' – of simony and clerical marriage (nicholaitism).
Simony, taking its name from Simon Magus, cursed for his unholy
ambition by St Peter (Acts 8:9–24) originally signified the sale of
priestly ordination by a bishop. By the eleventh century it had come
to mean the sale of the office of bishop or abbot by the secular ruler.
In the course of the century some reformers applied the term 'simoniacal heresy' to the feudal ceremony by which bishops and abbots
received investiture of their office from the hands of the king.
Humbert wrote that 'secular princes formerly sold and still sell
ecclesiastical offices under the false name of investiture'. He was the
leading proponent of the controversial view that simony invalidated
the sacraments, so that priests ordained by a simoniacal bishop were
not true priests and their ministrations were worthless.[17] Clerical
marriage or nicholaitism similarly invalidated the orders of priests:
'their blessing is turned into a curse and their prayer into a sin'.[18] In

13 Gregory VII, *Registrum* VIII.12, p. 532.

14 R. W. Southern (1970) pp. 36–9; I. S. Robinson (1988) pp. 264–5.

15 Humbert, *Adversus simoniacos* III.9, p. 208.

16 Bernold of St Blasien, *Chronicon* 1085, p. 444.

17 Humbert, *Adversus simoniacos* III.6, p. 206. On the economic implications of simony
see A. Murray (1978) pp. 87–90; R. I. Moore (1980) pp. 65–9. For the debate about
the validity of simoniacal orders, in which Humbert propounded the 'rigorist' view
and Peter Damian the opposite, 'Augustinian', view see below pp. 93, 203, 378.

18 Gregory VII, *Epistolae Vagantes* 32, p. 85.

the eleventh century 'priests were not ashamed to take wives; they married openly; they contracted impious alliances and gave them legal sanction'.[19] By the beginning of Gregory VII's pontificate married clergy – whether or not their marriages were valid in law and whether or not they had been contracted before ordination – had come to be described by reformers as 'those guilty of the crime of fornication'.[20] Nicholaites were guilty of the crime of incest, because their wives were also their spiritual daughters.[21] They also, as a later commentator observed, presented an economic problem. Married clergy produced children, 'who usually endanger the Church's wealth'.[22] The installation of the reform papacy in Rome marked the beginning of a relentless campaign against the 'heresies' of nicholaitism and simony.

Papal decrees against simony and clerical marriage had already figured in the history of the papal regime of 1012–46, dominated by the Roman family of Tusculani. In 1014 a synodal decree of Pope Benedict VIII anathematised the practice of purchasing churches and ecclesiastical offices.[23] In 1022 the council of Pavia, over which pope and emperor jointly presided, imposed the obligation of celibacy on the whole clergy.[24] These reform initiatives were, however, ignored by the papal reform movement, which represented the regime of the Tusculani popes as the antithesis of the reform papacy that succeeded it. The Roman aristocracy 'and especially the Tusculani, [laid] waste the Roman church ... [and] seemed to possess the papacy by hereditary right.'[25] 'For far too long,' wrote Leo IX, 'the holy Roman and apostolic see was possessed by mercenaries rather than pastors.' Leo described the Tusculan pope Benedict IX as an 'unjust pontiff'.[26] Peter Damian recorded c. 1060 that Benedict (whom in 1043 he had called 'my lord, the most holy pope') materialised after his death in the form of an ass. An 'unworthy' pope, he 'deserved after his death to have the

---

19 Bruno of Segni, *Sermon concerning Simoniacs* c. 1, below p. 377.

20 Gregory VII, *Epistolae Vagantes* 6, p. 14.

21 Peter Damian, *Letter* 61 (*Briefe* 2, 215).

22 Master Gratian of Bologna, *Decretum* D. 28 c. 13. On clerical concubines see R. I. Moore (1980) pp. 61–3.

23 K.-J. Herrmann (1973) p. 31; J. Laudage (1984) pp. 54, 82.

24 K.-J. Herrmann (1973) p. 37; J. Laudage (1984) pp. 83, 86–7.

25 Bonizo, *Book to a Friend* V, below p. 182.

26 Leo IX, *JL* 4333, *MPL* 143, col. 779C.

appearance of a beast, because [he] lived in a beastly manner'.[27] This vituperation was a measure of the reformers' fear of the resurgence of the power of the Roman aristocracy.

The Tusculani regime collapsed as a result of the crisis in the politics of Rome and the papacy that coincided with the first Italian expedition of King Henry III of Germany. The crisis began with a rising against Benedict IX in autumn 1044. 'He was cast out of the papacy,' records an early local source, 'and John, bishop of Sabina, to whom they gave the name Silvester, was appointed and wrongfully occupied the papal throne for forty-nine days. After he was expelled, Benedict recovered the papacy and held it for one month and twenty-one days. Then he himself gave it to John, archcanon of St John at the Latin Gate, his godfather, on 1 May [1045], to whom they gave the name Gregory [VI].'[28] Henry III, after initially recognising Gregory VI as pope, subsequently learned that he had acquired the papacy by simony: 'venality had intervened' when Benedict resigned in his favour.[29] Henry witnessed the deposition of Gregory VI by the synod of Sutri (20 December 1046), which also condemned Silvester III, while a subsequent synod in Rome (24 December) disposed of the claims of Benedict IX. This Roman synod elected Bishop Suidger of Bamberg as Pope Clement II, whose first official duty was to crown Henry as emperor (25 December).[30]

The events of December 1046 inaugurated the 'German papacy', a series of German bishops who owed their papal office to Henry III: Clement II (1046–7), Damasus II (1047–8), Leo IX (1048/9–1054) and Victor II (1054–7). Henry believed that he had obtained 'perpetual control over the election of the pope' by assuming the office of 'patrician of the Romans' after his imperial coronation.[31] The emperor's admirers attributed his intervention in December 1046 and the creation of the 'German papacy' to his zeal for reform. He was renowned as an opponent of simony.[32] Peter Damian applauded his

---

27 Peter Damian, *Letters* 4, 72 (*Briefe* 1, 110; 2, 337–8). This was an anecdote related to him by Cardinal Humbert.

28 Papal list of the abbey of Farfa: see R. L. Poole (1934) p. 188.

29 Peter Damian, *Letter* 72 (*Briefe* 2, 363). See K.-J. Herrmann (1973) pp. 154–6; H. E. J. Cowdrey (1998) pp. 22–3.

30 See below pp. 184–7.

31 Peter Damian, *Letter* 89 (*Briefe* 2, 547). On the office of patrician see below pp. 56–7, 174–5, 179, 182, 187.

32 Wipo, *Gesta Chuonradi II imperatoris* c. 8, p. 31. Cf. Ralph Glaber, *Historiae* V.25, p. 250.

conduct in Rome. 'After God it was he who snatched us from the
dragon's insatiable mouth, who cut off all the heads of the many-
headed hydra, simoniacal heresy, with the sword of heavenly virtue ...
Divine providence gratefully conferred on him what it had not
granted to very many of his predecessors: namely that the holy
Roman church should now be ordered according to his will and that
henceforward no one should elect a priest to the apostolic see except
by his authority.'[33] A generation later, in the light of his son Henry
IV's attempt to reconstruct his father's control over the papacy, the
adherents of Gregory VII would condemn Henry III for having
'seized the tyranny of the patriciate'.[34]

Twentieth-century commentators have questioned whether Henry III
was motivated by considerations of power politics rather than of
piety. In 1046 'Henry achieved what he had probably long planned: to
fill the Roman see henceforward with members of the German
imperial Church and so bring the papacy into his own hands'. Such an
interpretation was prompted by the fact that the German popes
retained their German bishoprics after their election to the papacy.[35]
If Henry III indeed aimed at 'the inclusion of the Roman church in the
system of the German imperial Church', such an aim was not incompatible with the reforming zeal attributed to him by his admirers.
It is unlikely, however, that Henry 'had long planned' his intervention
in the papacy. His principal concern in December 1046 was to be
crowned emperor by a pope whose title was not open to question. The
news of Gregory VI's simony and the existence of two other possible
papal claimants prompted him to take measures that had totally
unforeseen consequences.

The possibilities opened up by the inauguration of the reform papacy
first became apparent in the pontificate of Leo IX. In twelve papal
synods held in Rome, southern Italy, Germany and France, he legislated against simony and clerical marriage. In particular he emphasised the principle that 'no one should be promoted to ecclesiastical
government without the election of clergy and people'.[36] (This emphasis

---

33 Peter Damian, *Letter* 40 (*Briefe* 1, 501, 502). Cf. the praise of Humbert, *Adversus
    simoniacos* III.7, p. 206.

34 Bonizo of Sutri, *Book to a Friend* V, below p. 187.

35 P. Kehr (1930) pp. 50–1. See also W. Goez (1970) pp. 7–59; G. Frech (1991) pp.
    303–32.

36 Council of Rheims c. 1 in: Anselm of St-Remi, *Historia dedicationis ecclesiae sancti
    Remigii* c. 16, col. 1437A.

inspired his biographers to portray his own papal election as conforming to this principle.)³⁷ Leo recruited many distinguished reformers (especially from his Lotharingian homeland) to the service of the Roman church, their non-Roman origins proclaiming that the papacy was no longer the inward-looking, parochial institution of the Tusculani regime.³⁸ Foremost among his recruits was Cardinal Humbert of Silva Candida (formerly a monk of Moyenmoutier in Leo's old diocese of Toul). Humbert's most important contribution to the reform movement was the formulation of the doctrine of the papal primacy, 'the earthly and heavenly empire of the royal priesthood of the holy Roman see'.³⁹

His conception of the papal supremacy over the Church appears most clearly in the writings, including letters issued in the name of Leo IX, inspired by his legation to Constantinople in 1054. That was the ill-fated mission that culminated in the mutual excommunication of the papal legates and the patriarch of Constantinople and in the schism between the Greek and Roman churches.⁴⁰ In answer to the claim of the patriarch of Constantinople to equality with the pope, the patriarch of the West, Humbert declared that 'the holy Roman and apostolic church by a privilege of special authority, conferred by divine and human means, was made head of all the churches after Jesus Christ'.⁴¹ Humbert emphasised the judicial supremacy inherent in the papal primacy. 'As the door is ruled by the hinge, so the good of the whole Church is governed by Peter and his successors, and as the hinge remains unchanging while opening and closing the door, so Peter and his successors have free judgement over the whole Church, but no one may change their position because the highest see can be judged by no one.'⁴² Humbert linked this primacy with the pope's role as principal reformer of the whole Church. 'All men have such reverence for the holder of the apostolic office of Rome that they prefer to receive the holy commandments and the traditions of the Christian faith from the mouth of the head of the Church than from

37 See below pp. 33–5, 57, 131–3, 190, 379.
38 See below p. 191.
39 Leo IX, JL 4302, MPL 143, col. 752D.
40 See below pp. 146–9. On Humbert's writings concerning the legation of 1054 see H. Hoesch (1970) pp. 11–16, 27–31.
41 Humbert, De sancta Romana ecclesia (fragment A) in P. E. Schramm (1929) 2, 128–9. The phrase 'by human means' was an allusion to the Donation of Constantine, as also the reference to 'the earthly ... empire of the royal priesthood' (n. 39).
42 Leo IX, JL 4302, MPL 143, col. 751B.

the holy Scriptures and patristic writings.' Hence the pope 'makes almost the whole world run after God with delight and enthusiasm'.[43] This dynamic image appropriately conveys the unprecedentedly ener-getic activity of Leo IX, especially his ceaseless journeys and papal councils.

In this doctrine of the papal primacy the influence of the Donation of Constantine is apparent and that famous forgery also reinforced Leo's conception of the papal rights in southern Italy. The mid-eleventh century was a moment of rapid political change in that region, since the major power in southern Italy, the Byzantine empire, was clearly losing control of its territories of Apulia and Calabria. The ancient papal claim to rights of jurisdiction and property in southern Italy was given a new relevance when in 1050 the city of Benevento placed itself under the pope's protection. Henceforward Leo became increas-ingly preoccupied with the defence of Benevento against the threat presented by 'the most evil nation of the Normans'.[44] The Normans, who had appeared in southern Italy at the beginning of the century as mercenary soldiers, were by mid-century transforming themselves into princes, the dynasty of Aversa in the principality of Capua and that of Hauteville in the province of Apulia. After the failure of nego-tiations with Henry III for a German expedition against the Normans, Leo sought to cooperate with the representative of the Byzantine government, Argyros, 'prince of Bari and duke of Italy'.[45] The papal strategy failed: the force raised by Leo was defeated by the Normans at Civitate (18 June 1053). The pope was held captive by the Normans in Benevento for almost a year and he died soon after his return to Rome (19 April 1054).

As we shall see, Leo IX's biographers responded in different ways to the expedition against the Normans. The anonymous Lotharingian biographer hastily passed over the events. ('It is not our intention to dwell in lacrimose language on what happened on that expedition.')[46] A quarter of a century later Bonizo of Sutri applauded the papal expedition. 'God showed by signs and miracles that [the defeated papal army] had greatly pleased Him ... when He deigned to number them

---

43 Humbert, De sancta Romana ecclesia (fragment A) p. 128.

44 Life of Pope Leo IX II.21, below p. 150. See E. Steindorff (1881) pp. 240–3; W. Kölmel (1935) pp. 104–9; P. Partner (1972) pp. 113–14; H. Taviani-Carozzi (1996) pp. 184–6.

45 See below p. 150 n. 319.

46 Life of Pope Leo IX II.20, below p. 149.

among the saints.'[47] A decade later, however, Bruno of Segni wrote of Leo's own involvement: 'would that he had not gone there in person, but had only sent an army there to defend righteousness!'[48] Nevertheless all the papal biographers agreed that those members of the papal army who fell at Civitate were numbered 'among Christ's martyrs' and that 'it was through [Leo] that [they] attained this great glory'.[49] This belief clearly foreshadowed the theology of the First Crusade, as did Leo IX's own claim that the expedition of 1053 was undertaken with 'the intention of liberating Christendom'.[50]

Despite the failure of imperial aid in 1053 Leo IX's relations with Henry III were generally good. During his pontificate Leo spent almost as much time in the German kingdom as in Rome[51] and he remained devoted to Toul, to Lotharingia and to Germany. 'Leo had a burning desire to strengthen the commonwealth'[52] and gave loyal support to the emperor in times of crisis, excommunicating the rebels Godfrey, duke of Upper Lotharingia and Count Baldwin V of Flanders and mediating in the conflict with the kingdom of Hungary (1052).[53] The German popes of 1046–57 desired the patronage and protection of the emperor, knowing that their hold on Rome was insecure and that the great Roman families would seek the earliest opportunity to regain control of the papacy. During the first decade of the papal reform movement Henry III was an indispensable ally. When that movement came to maturity, however, in the pontificate of Gregory VII (1073–85), Henry IV became its bitter opponent. How had the situation of 1046–57 become so radically transformed twenty years after the death of Henry III? The answer is that Henry III died prematurely, too soon to establish a permanent German papacy. The regency government ruling in the name of his young son, Henry IV, was powerless to intervene in Rome. The vulnerable reforming party was,

47 Bonizo of Sutri, *Book to a Friend* V, below p. 193.

48 Bruno of Segni, *Sermon concerning Simoniacs* c. 5, below p. 383.

49 *Ibid.*, c. 6, below p. 385.

50 Leo IX, *JL* 4333, *MPL* 143, col. 779B: below p. 150. See C. Erdmann (1935) p. 110.

51 Cf. the emphasis on his German visits (June-December 1049, September 1050 – February 1051, August 1052 – February 1053) in the *Life of Pope Leo IX* II.11, 12, 15, 17, below pp. 137, 139–40, 142, 144.

52 *Ibid.*, II.17, below p. 144.

53 P. Kehr (1930) p. 56. Kehr concluded that Leo's 'personal sense of belonging to his homeland and to the emperor and the memory of his earlier connection with the German Church acted as a sufficient counterweight to his restless activity on behalf of the universal authority of the papacy and the reform of the Church, to avert serious conflict' (p. 57).

therefore, obliged to seek new allies to protect them from the Roman nobility. In April 1058 the rival families of the Crescentii and Tuscu-lani joined forces to restore the aristocratic papacy of the pre-reform era and enthroned Pope Benedict X.[54] In October 1061 the Roman families formed a coalition with other enemies of the reform papacy, the Lombard episcopate, and enthroned the antipope 'Honorius II' (Bishop Cadalus of Parma).[55] On both occasions the Roman reforming party, led by the cardinal bishops, needed allies powerful enough to defeat these formidable opponents.

The first of these was the new dynasty of Canossa-Lotharingia, formed when Godfrey 'the Bearded', deposed duke of Upper Lothar-ingia, married Beatrice, widow of Boniface II of Canossa, margrave of Tuscany, and assumed the office of margrave. It was surely not coincidental that Stephen IX (1057–8), the first pope elected by the Roman reform party after Henry III's death, was the brother of Godfrey 'the Bearded'.[56] Stephen IX's successors were both Tuscan bishops – Gerard of Florence, subsequently Pope Nicholas II (1058–61) and Anselm I of Lucca, subsequently Pope Alexander II (1061–73) – who, as popes, retained their sees in Tuscany and their close con-nection with Margrave Godfrey.[57] The alliance between the reform papacy and the house of Canossa-Lotharingia survived the death of Margrave Godfrey (1069) and became even stronger when the office of margrave was exercised by Beatrice of Tuscany and her daughter Matilda, both of whom were devoted supporters of Gregory VII.[58] The second of the new alliances of the reform papacy was with the Normans of southern Italy against whom Leo IX had campaigned in 1053. In August 1059 the Norman princes Robert Guiscard and Richard of Aversa were invested by Pope Nicholas II with the digni-ties respectively of duke of Apulia and Calabria and prince of Capua and they promised in return fealty and service. The purpose of this alliance was succinctly described by Bonizo of Sutri: 'with [the Normans'] aid [the pope] very rapidly freed the city of Rome from the tyranny' of the Roman families.'[59]

The period of the 'Tuscan papacy' of 1057–73[60] has been represented

54 See below p. 201.
55 See below p. 207.
56 See below p. 191.
57 W. Goez (1973) pp. 206–8; E. Goez (1995) pp. 155, 158.
58 H. E. J. Cowdrey (1998) pp. 297–303.
59 Bonizo, *Book to a Friend* VI, below p. 203.

as witnessing the liberation of the papacy from the control of the imperial government.[61] It is important to note that initially the Roman reform party did not desire this 'liberation'. They sought to maintain their links with the imperial court even as they formed their new alliances. They were anxious, for example, to obtain the approval of the imperial court for the election of Stephen IX and Nicholas II.[62] The most important reforming legislation of these years, the Papal Election Decree of 1059 – with its emphasis on the unique role of the cardinal bishops in nominating the pope – has been interpreted as 'the first stage towards the emancipation of the papacy'.[63] It is evident, however, from Cardinal Peter Damian's description of the decree in 1062 that the reformers who formulated it were not aiming to exclude the imperial court from the electoral procedure. 'That election must be made primarily through the judgement of the cardinal bishops; in the second place the clergy rightly gives its consent; thirdly, the favour of the people is to express approval; and then the whole matter must be suspended until the authority of the royal majesty is consulted.'[64] A study of Bonizo of Sutri's narrative will show how differently the reforming party would interpret the Papal Election Decree a quarter of a century after its promulgation.[65]

Meanwhile the desire of the Roman reformers for friendship with the imperial court survived a quarrel between Nicholas II and the German episcopate and regency government in 1061.[66] It even survived 'the schism of Cadalus', in which the imperial court supported the papal candidate of the Roman aristocracy and the Lombard bishops, Cadalus of Parma, and rejected the reformers' candidate, Alexander II (October 1061).[67] After the imperial government finally acknowledged

60 W. Goez (1973) pp. 206–7.

61 E.g. A. Fliche (1924) p. 325: 'The alliance sealed by Henry III between Germany and the holy see had been broken; the struggle of the priesthood and the empire was beginning.'

62 *Annales Altahenses* 1057, 1058, p. 54. See H.-G. Krause (1960) pp. 59–69; T. Schmidt (1977) pp. 62–3, 72–80.

63 A. Fliche (1924) pp. 323–4. For a summary of the scholarly debate on the significance of the Papal Election Decree see D. Jasper (1986) pp. 1–9.

64 Peter Damian, *Letter* 88 (*Briefe* 2, 526). Peter Damian added that this consultation had not been possible in the election of 1061 because 'danger … forced the procedure to be hastened as much as possible'. Cf. Peter Damian, *Letter* 89 (*Briefe* 2, 548–9).

65 Bonizo, *Book to a Friend* VI, IX, below pp. 206, 210, 252–3.

66 The cause of this quarrel is not known. Cf. Benzo of Alba, *To Emperor Henry IV* VII.2, below p. 373. See H.-G. Krause (1960) pp. 126–41; I. S. Robinson (1999) pp. 40–1.

67 See below pp. 206–8, 210, 373–4.

Alexander as pope at the synod of Mantua (May 1064), Peter Damian continued to remind the young King Henry IV that he was the divinely ordained defender of the papacy. 'The royal and the priestly dignity ... are bound together in the Christian people by a reciprocal treaty. Each must make use of the other.' The king is 'armed to resist the enemies of the Church'; the prayers of the priesthood 'make God well-disposed towards king and people'.[68] Henry IV echoed this language in his first letter to Gregory VII: 'the kingship and the priesthood ... always need each other's help'.[69] The pope responded (December 1074) with a vision of Henry IV as a reformer on the model of his father: 'learn that you rightfully hold the royal power if you incline your high authority to Christ, the King of kings, for the purposes of the restoration and defence of His churches'.[70] It was the disappointment of such hopes that precipitated the conflict of empire and papacy.

The 'Gregorian reform' – that is, the measures taken by Gregory VII to protect the Church from 'the tyrannical persecution' of Henry IV[71] – marked an important change of direction in the history of the papal reform. Gregory VII's version of the doctrine of the papal primacy that he inherited from the 1050s was succinctly expressed by his biographer, Paul of Bernried. The Roman church was 'the head and mistress of all religion, ... whose prerogative it is to correct all the powerful of the world before all others'.[72] The pope's claim to *political* supremacy became, in the context of the struggle with the German king, the most important aspect of the papal primacy. This Gregorian claim was influenced by the examples of the Old Testament prophets who rebuked kings and announced that they had been rejected by God. Gregory VII saw an analogy between himself and the prophet Samuel, while Henry IV, like King Saul, lost his throne because he had disobeyed God's commands.[73] Gregory's biographer, Paul of

---

68 Peter Damian, *Letter* 120 (*Briefe* 3, 389).

69 Henry IV, *Letter* 5, p. 8. This was the 'suppliant letter' by means of which Henry sought reconciliation with the papacy after the papal excommunication of five of his advisers for practising simony (Lent 1073): see below p. 306. See H. E. J. Cowdrey (1998) pp. 89, 95–6; I. S. Robinson (1999) pp. 125, 130.

70 Gregory VII, *Registrum* II.30, p. 164.

71 *Ibid.*, VIII.9, p. 527.

72 Paul of Bernried, *Life of Pope Gregory VII* c. 61, below p. 304.

73 Gregory VII, *Registrum* III.10, p. 267. This was the ultimatum of 8 December 1075, which provoked Henry IV into summoning the council of Worms: see below p. 309. The biblical allusion was to I Samuel 15:1–35.

Bernried emphasised the pope's resemblance to the prophet Elijah.[74] Gregory believed that the pope had the authority to depose a king for his misdeeds or 'because he was not useful enough to hold such great power'.[75] He likewise had the authority to ensure the appointment of 'a suitable king for the honour of holy Church', who would be 'obedient, humbly devoted and useful to holy Church'.[76]

The political dimension that Gregory VII gave to the papal primacy was extremely controversial. Already in 1076 it was condemned in Henry IV's propaganda as a dangerous innovation. Gregory had 'usurped to himself the kingship and the priesthood. In so doing he showed contempt for the pious ordination of God, which wished these to exist not as one but as two [powers]'.[77] The polemical writings of the Lotharingian monk Sigebert of Gembloux contain a careful analysis of Gregorian innovations. 'All [the popes] from Gregory I onwards were content to use only the spiritual sword, until the last Gregory, that is Hildebrand, who first girded himself – and by his example, other popes – with the sword of war against the emperor.'[78] In discarding the king and usurping the royal power for himself, Gregory had deprived himself of the means of reforming the Church. 'Who can separate the cause of the kingship from the cause of the priesthood? Unless the peace of God … joins kingship and priesthood in the one cornerstone of harmony, the building of the Church will totter on the foundation of faith.'[79] Without the support of the king to enforce papal reforming decrees, Gregory VII had been compelled to rely on random acts of violence by the laity against simoniacal and married clergy. In his efforts to impose purity on the priesthood Gregory 'brought down the swords of laymen on the necks of the clergy'.[80]

This hostile interpretation of Gregorian reforming measures was perhaps inspired by a widely disseminated papal letter of January 1075, in which Gregory announced his 'new counsels' for the reform of the Church.[81] The experience of the first two years of his pontificate

---

74 Paul of Bernried, *Life of Pope Gregory VII* c. 2–4, 6, 110–11, below pp. 263, 354.

75 Gregory VII, *Registrum* VIII.21, p. 554.

76 *Ibid.*, IX.3, p. 575.

77 Henry IV, *Letter* 13, p. 19.

78 Sigebert of Gembloux, *Epistola Leodicensium* c. 10, p. 462.

79 *Ibid.*, c. 11, p. 462.

80 *Ibid.*, c. 2, p. 453.

81 Gregory VII, *Registrum* II.45, pp. 182–5: see below pp. 287–9. On the dissemination of this letter see I. S. Robinson (1978b) pp. 76, 78.

persuaded Gregory that kings and bishops, the traditional rulers of Christian society, were incapable of assisting him in reforming the Church. 'When in my mind's eye I look over the western lands, whether to north or south,' he wrote in January 1075, 'I find hardly any bishops who conform to the law either in their appointment or in their way of life and who rule the Christian people in the love of Christ and not for worldly ambition. Among all the secular princes I know of none who place the honour of God before their own and righteousness before gain ... Since there is no prince who troubles himself about such things, *we* must protect the lives of religious men.'[82] Dereliction of duty on the part of bishops and kings compelled the pope to devise a new reforming strategy, as he explained to his allies, the south German dukes (11 January 1075). 'It seems to us much better to rebuild God's justice by means of new counsels than to let the souls of men perish together with the laws that they have neglected.' The pope's allies were commanded, 'whatever bishops may say or may not say about it', that they should not receive the offices of simoniac or married priests and that they must publicise this papal prohibition 'in the king's court and elsewhere in the assemblies of the kingdom'. Furthermore 'to the utmost of your power you are to prevent such men from administering the sacred mysteries, even, if necessary, by violence'.[83]

Gregory VII's 'new counsels' – the lay boycott of the masses of simoniacs and married priests and their removal from the altars 'if necessary, by violence' – were not a complete innovation. These measures were developed in the period 1057–75 by the reforming party in Milan, the Pataria. The preaching of the founders of the Pataria, Ariald and Landulf, against simony and clerical marriage in the Milanese church (1057–66) had provoked a bitter conflict between, on the one hand, the reformers and their allies among the populace, and, on the other hand, the archbishop of Milan, the senior clergy and the greater nobility (the 'captains').[84] The reform papacy became involved in this conflict, initially as a mediator but subsequently as an ally of the Pataria. The papacy shared the Patarine aim of eradicating simony and nicholaitism, but no less important was the opportunity presented by the Milanese conflict of humbling a proudly independent

82 Gregory VII, *Registrum* II.49, p. 189.

83 *Ibid.*, II.45, p. 184. See below p. 289.

84 For Bonizo of Sutri's history of the Pataria see below pp. 197–9, 211–12. See also H. E. J. Cowdrey (1968) pp. 25–48.

archbishopric that resisted the doctrine of the papal primacy. The imperial polemicist Benzo of Alba claimed that Pope Alexander II, a member of a noble Milanese family, 'originally invented the Pataria'.[85] Gregory VII's enemies in northern Italy called him 'the pope of the Patarini'.[86] Gregory's friendship with the Milanese knight Herlembald, leader of the Pataria in the years 1067–75, dated from the period when, as Archdeacon Hildebrand, he had been the foremost supporter of the Patarini at the papal court. As pope, he applauded Herlembald's 'pious solicitude in defence of the faith and for the restoration of sacred religion'[87] and regarded him as a 'most energetic knight of Christ', engaged in a holy war against the enemies of the Church.[88]

The papacy's support for the Milanese reformers set it on a collision course with the imperial court, which supported the anti-Patarine party in Milan. The Salian monarchs regarded the archbishop of Milan as their principal representative in the Italian kingdom. The attempt of the Patarini to elect their own candidate as archbishop in consultation with the pope but without consulting Henry IV (6 January 1072) seemed, therefore, to be a serious challenge to royal authority.[89] When the Patarini were decisively defeated by their Milanese enemies and Herlembald was murdered (18 June 1075), Henry IV sought to regain control by investing his chaplain Tedald with the archbishopric of Milan, ignoring the claim of the Patarine and papal candidate Atto.[90] Henry's action contributed significantly to the conflict between pope and king that broke out at the beginning of 1076. Gregory warned Henry in December 1075 that if he did not do penance for this and other 'offences' – notably his continued association with five royal advisers excommunicated by the pope for their involvement in simony – he faced excommunication and deposition from the kingship.[91] Henry IV was stung by this rebuke into his attempt at the council of Worms (24 January 1076) to force the pope's

---

85 Benzo, *To Emperor Henry IV* VII.2, below p. 374.

86 Petrus Crassus, *Defensio Heinrici IV regis* c. 3, pp. 437, 438. Cf. Benzo of Alba, *Ad Heinricum imperatorem* V.1, VI.2, pp. 444, 524.

87 Gregory VII, *Registrum* I.26, p. 44.

88 *Ibid.*, I.27, p. 45. See also Bonizo of Sutri's portrayal of Herlembald: below pp. 215, 229–30. See C. Erdmann (1935) pp. 129, 167–8.

89 See below p. 216.

90 See below p. 232.

91 Gregory VII, *Epistolae Vagantes* 14, p. 38: see below p. 321. This oral message was given to Henry by the bearers of the papal letter *Registrum* III.10, pp. 263–7. See H. E. J. Cowdrey (1998) pp. 132–4; I. S. Robinson (1999) pp. 140–2.

abdication. Gregory VII responded in the Lenten synod of 1076 with
the threatened sentence of excommunication and deposition.[92]

The unprecedented papal use of the power of binding and loosing to
deprive a king of his kingdom and of the fealty of his vassals was to
dominate the ensuing Investiture Contest. Already in summer 1076
Gregory perceived the need to persuade wavering supporters of the
legality of his proceedings.[93] The need to justify his innovatory claims
is apparent in the two biographies of Gregory VII contained in this
volume. In their accounts of the conflict – the council of Worms and
the Lenten synod of 1076, the reconciliation at Canossa in January
1077, the years of negotiations and the series of papal legations to
Germany in 1077–80, the second papal excommunication of Henry IV
in March 1080 and the papal recognition of the anti-king Rudolf,
elected by Henry's enemies in Germany – the biographers Bonizo of
Sutri and Paul of Bernried portrayed Henry IV as the aggressor and
Gregory VII as victim and martyr.[94] This interpretation of Gregory's
pontificate was already present in the last words attributed to the
pope on his deathbed (25 May 1085), in which he portrayed himself as
a martyr persecuted for righteousness' sake: 'I have loved righteousness and hated iniquity, therefore I die in exile.'[95] The anti-Gregorian
polemics prompted by the pope's excommunication of Henry IV
depicted Gregory as 'the standard-bearer of schism' and 'the enemy of
peace'. 'Nothing is too impious and criminal for him to take charge of,
while he arms some men against the king and spurs others to the war
that he is waging against everybody.'[96] 'What Christian ever caused
so many wars and killed so many men?'[97] It was as a refutation of such
polemics that Gregory's biographers presented him primarily as a
saint, a miracle-worker and a martyr for the catholic faith.

This book is a collection of biographies and other narrative sources
concerned principally with the lives of Leo IX and Gregory VII.
These works were composed by intellectuals with markedly different
ideas of reform, writing in different centres of learning. The anonymous author of the *Life of Leo IX* wrote in Lotharingia, perhaps in the

92 See below pp. 234–5, 310–18.

93 Gregory VII, *Registrum* IV.2, pp. 293–7.

94 See below pp. 239–46, 327–51.

95 See below p. 353.

96 Egilbert of Trier, *Letter* in: *Codex Udalrici* 159, p. 128.

97 Wido of Ferrara, *De scismate Hildebrandi* I.15, p. 545.

abbey of St-Evre in the diocese of Toul, completing his work before
1061. Bishop Bonizo of Sutri wrote his polemical history of the
Church, *The Book to a Friend*, in exile in Tuscany soon after the death
of Gregory VII in 1085 and that pope is the central figure in the
work. Paul of Bernried wrote his biography of Gregory VII in 1128,
perhaps in Regensburg, drawing on a large collection of late eleventh-
century Gregorian materials. Bishop Benzo of Alba completed his
polemic addressed to Henry IV in 1085 in Lombardy. The extract
translated here is his hostile account of the elections of the reforming
popes, intended to prove their illegality. Finally Bishop Bruno of
Segni composed his *Sermon concerning Simoniacs* probably in the later
1090s, when he was an active member of the papal curia. The first
nine chapters, containing a biography of Leo IX, are presented
here.

The Life of Pope Leo IX

The *Life of Pope Leo IX* is the most extensive of the eleventh-century
biographies of Pope Leo IX (1048–54), formerly Bishop Bruno of
Toul (1026–51).[98] It is attributed in the first printed edition (1615) to
'the contemporary author archdeacon Wibert'.[99] Subsequent editions
of the *Life*, developing this attribution, identified the author as Wibert,
archdeacon of Toul. The claim of the author to have associated with
Leo IX 'continually on the most familiar terms'[100] suggested that
Wibert had been archdeacon in Toul during Bruno-Leo's episcopate.[101]
P.-P. Brucker was the first to object to this identification (1889), on
the grounds that no archdeacon of Toul named Wibert can be identified in the period when the *Life* was composed.[102] Brucker found a

98 The *Bibliotheca hagiographica Latina antiquae et mediae aetatis* ed. Socii Bollandini
(1898/1901) lists twelve hagiographical works on Leo IX (nos. 4818–4829). The
Life translated here (which survives in twenty-two manuscripts) is *BHL* 4818.

99 *Vita S. Leonis IX Papae, Leucorum antea Episcopi. Wiberto Archidiacono coaetaneo
auctore* (Paris, 1615), edited by the Jesuit scholar J. Sirmond (✝1651). See H. Tritz
(1952) p. 215. The same attribution is found in the seventeenth-century codex
Oxford, Jesus College 79. See H. Tritz (1952) pp. 203–4; H.-G. Krause (1976) p. 49
n. 3.

100 *Life of Leo IX*, prologue, below p. 98.

101 Gottfried Henskens in *Acta Sanctorum Aprilis* 2 (Antwerp, 1675), 648C; J. Mabillon
in *Acta Sanctorum Ordinis Sancti Benedicti* 6/2 (Paris, 1701), 49, reprinted in *MPL*
143, col. 457D and J. M. Watterich, *Pontificum Romanorum Vitae* 1 (Leipzig, 1862),
LXXXV n. 1.

102 P.-P. Brucker (1889) 1, 367–71.

different attribution in the codex Bern, Stadt- und Hochschulbibliothek 24, the eleventh-century manuscript offering the most reliable
text of the *Life*. The title contains the phrase 'composed in Rome by
Archbishop Humbert'.[103] The biographer is thus identified as the
reformer Humbert, monk of Moyenmoutier (diocese of Toul), whom
Leo IX appointed archbishop of Sicily (1050) and cardinal bishop of
Silva Candida (1051).[104] A link between the *Life* and Humbert is also
suggested by the eleventh-century manuscript Bern, Stadt- und Hochschulbibliothek 292, copied in the monastery of St Arnulf in Metz.
The codex contains the *Life*, preceded by a collection of documents
concerning the schism of 1054 between Rome and Constantinople, the
so-called 'Letter-book of Cardinal Humbert'.[105] It was with materials
from this collection that Leo IX's biographer composed the two
chapters of the *Life* recording papal negotiations with the Byzantine
church (1053–4) and the expedition against the Normans (1053).[106]

The question of Humbert's authorship has long dominated the study
of the *Life*. P.-P. Brucker, who first noticed the attribution in Bern
MS 24, rejected the arguments in favour of his authorship.[107] H. Tritz
(1952) detected in the *Life* the characteristic style of Humbert.[108] H.
Hoffmann (1963), however, argued that the *Life* is too full of stylistic
infelicities and grammatical errors to be the work of 'such an
excellent stylist as Humbert'.[109] Returning to the question in 1970, H.
Hoesch suggested that the *Life* was not the work of a single author.
Humbert wrote only the first part of the biography (perhaps as far as
Book II, chapter 3; certainly not as far as chapter 9). The rest was the
work of an unknown continuator, possibly 'a monk in Metz or

103 The codex contains a collection of saints' lives, probably compiled in the archdiocese of Trier: see H. Tritz (1952) pp. 195–6. A similar attribution appeared in
an exemplar of the *Life* once possessed by the monastery of St-Hubert-en-
Ardennes: see H. Tritz (1952) pp. 201, 232.

104 R. Hüls (1977) pp. 131–4. H. Tritz (1952) p. 235 argued that the attribution to
'Archdeacon Wibert' in the manuscript used by Sirmond was the result of a scribal
misreading of 'Archbishop Humbert'.

105 H. Tritz (1952) pp. 196–7. On the 'Letter book' of Humbert see A. Michel (1940)
pp. 46–64; H. Hoesch (1970) pp. 11–16.

106 *Life of Leo IX* II.19, 20, below pp. 146–50.

107 P.-P. Brucker (1889) 1, 367–71; P. Schmid (1926) pp. 204–7 assumed that the
author was Wibert, but supposed him to have been influenced by Humbert's
reforming ideas.

108 H. Tritz (1952) pp. 229–72, applying the method of stylistic analysis used by A.
Michel to ascribe a series of other works to Humbert.

109 H. Hoffmann (1963) pp. 203–6.

Toul'.[110] In the most recent study of the *Life* H.-G. Krause rejected the thesis of the dual authorship and of Humbert's authorship of any part of the *Life*.[111]

The cumulative effect of the various arguments against Humbert's authorship is overwhelming. Firstly, there are obvious contradictions between some attitudes in the *Life* and those expressed in other works attributed to Humbert. Most of these appear in Book I, dealing with the early life of Bruno-Leo and his episcopate in Toul. First, the biographer wrote of Bishop Berthold of Toul (996–1019), who was responsible for Bruno's education, that he 'outdid his predecessors in his striving for genuine virtue' and 'adorned [Toul] with very many buildings, filled her with men of letters and restored the discipline of the monasteries within and without'.[112] This assessment differs sharply from the view of Berthold in the history of the abbots of Moyenmoutier, attributed to Humbert. In this account, Berthold, 'particularly attentive to the honour of the world, ... was a shrewd oppressor of the people and the monasteries with unaccustomed law, who is known to have inflicted an irreparable calamity on the monastery of Moyenmoutier'.[113] Even if Humbert was not the author of this work, as a monk of Moyenmoutier he probably shared this view of the bishop who had deprived his abbey of the village of Bergheim.[114] Second, the *Life* presents an approving portrait of a young Bruno devoted to the service of his kinsman, Emperor Conrad II. In 1026 Bruno, canon of Toul, on behalf of the ailing Bishop Herman (1019–26), commanded the Toul contingent of knights on Conrad II's first Italian expedition. 'In the direction of this secular warfare he immediately showed himself wise and circumspect, as if he had hitherto been engaged solely in affairs of this kind'. He chose camp-sites, assigned military duties, organised provisions. According to his biographer, Bruno

---

110 H. Hoesch (1970) pp. 243–53. The suggestion of dual authorship was based on an analysis of the visions and miracles in the *Life*, according to which visions abound in the earlier half of the biography, while the latter half is full of miracles. Hoesch claimed (on the basis of hagiographical works ascribed to Humbert) that visions had a special significance for Humbert, while he showed 'a critical reserve' towards miracle stories (pp. 243–9). This analysis was refuted by H.-G. Krause (see n. 111).

111 H.-G. Krause (1976) pp. 51–67.

112 *Life of Leo IX* I.2, below p. 101.

113 *Liber de sancti Hidulfi successoribus* c. 12, p. 92. This work was attributed to Humbert by A. Michel (1952–1953) pp. 225–59.

114 J. Choux (1957) pp. 204–11; H. Hoffmann (1963) p. 207; N. Bulst (1973) p. 103.

deserved his ecclesiastical honours 'because he served faithfully and
wisely in worldly affairs'.[115] As bishop of Toul, he continued to be in
demand as an adviser at the imperial court, since 'to those who were
shrewd in the affairs of this world he seemed shrewder than all other
men'. 'Through his wise intercession as an envoy and a counsellor' the
emperor was able to annex the kingdom of Burgundy and he also
conducted a successful peace legation to the French kingdom.[116] This
portrait of a churchman unusually competent in secular affairs and a
dutiful servant of the emperor is clearly at odds with the conduct
demanded in Humbert's *Three Books against the Simoniacs*, where he
wrote that 'laymen are to order and manage only their own concerns,
that is secular affars, while clerks order and manage only theirs, that
is ecclesiastical business.' He warned of 'the undisciplined ambition of
the clergy of our times', who 'magnify beyond measure the secular
power, especially the royal and imperial power, and diminish the
ecclesiastical dignity' and denounced the immersion of bishops in
secular affairs.[117]

The *Life* emphasises Bruno's close personal relationship with Conrad
II. He was 'loved by the emperor and the empress [Gisela] with such
a unique parental affection that he was admitted willingly to their
most secret counsels'.[118] Conrad II is invariably mentioned in lauda-
tory terms: 'the glorious Emperor Conrad', 'the celebrated emperor',
'the victorious King Conrad', 'Emperor Conrad of divine memory'.[119]
A significant passage in which Bruno-Leo is described as a reformer
refers to his partnership with the emperor and assumes that the saint
would reform both Church and empire. 'Every day [Conrad] grew to
love him more and more, foreseeing in him the future instrument that
would reform the discipline of holy religion and would strengthen the
Roman commonwealth, that was currently in decline'.[120] The account
of Bruno's appointment as bishop represents Conrad as accepting the
decision of the clergy and people of Toul to elect Bruno and giving up
his own plans for the advancement of his kinsman. Conrad congratu-
lates Bruno on an appointment 'without recourse to any venality':
'you will not seek the favour of my wife or any other mortal, lest you

115 *Life* I.7, below p. 108. See H. Bresslau (1879) p. 119.

116 *Ibid.*, I.15, 17, below pp. 121, 124.

117 Humbert, *Adversus simoniacos* III.9, 20, 21, pp. 208, 223, 225.

118 *Life* I.6, below p. 107.

119 *Ibid.*, I.6, I.10, I.12, I.13, below pp. 106, 113, 118, 119.

120 *Ibid.*, I.13, below p. 118.

should be the means by which the blemish of simoniacal heresy should spread among all the sheep entrusted to you.'[121] Here Conrad II is portrayed as an opponent of simony and a champion of canonical election. The biographer did not, however, have the same enthusiasm for his successor, Henry III. The account of Leo IX's mediation in the conflict between the empire and Hungary (1052) contains a negative judgement: 'because of the machinations of certain courtiers who envied the holy man's successes, the emperor refused to hear the prayers of the lord pope and, as a result, the Roman commonwealth lost the obedience of the kingdom of Hungary'.[122] In commending Conrad II as the enemy of simony and criticising Henry III's lack of judgement, the biographer's attitude was the opposite of that of Humbert. In *Against the Simoniacs* Humbert recalled how 'the madness of simoniacal transactions spread through Germany, Gaul and the whole of Italy from the times of the Ottos until Emperor Henry of august and divine memory, the son of Conrad. In his days he removed some part of so great a sacrilege from the ecclesiastical persons of the empire entrusted to him ... and wished to remove it all.'[123] According to Humbert, Henry III was the first emperor to oppose simony and Conrad II was included in the censure of the regime of the Ottonians.

A consistent theme of the *Life* is the loyalty of Bruno-Leo, as bishop and pope, to the empire and his respect for the rights of the emperor. The pope 'had a burning desire to strengthen the commonwealth' and 'laboured anxiously for the peace of the kingdom'.[124] Particularly significant was the biographer's account of the election of Bruno-Leo's successor as bishop of Toul. After his election to the papacy, Leo retained his former bishopric until 1051. His successor was Udo, provost of the cathedral of Toul, whom Leo had appointed chancellor of the Roman church in 1050. The *Life* emphasises that Udo was Leo's preferred successor and explains how the pope ensured his succession. He 'sent his own envoy to the imperial majesty to ensure

---

121 *Ibid.*, I.10, below p. 114. On Conrad II and simony see K.J. Benz (1977) pp. 190–217.

122 *Ibid.*, II.17, below p. 144. On only one occasion (the election of Leo at the council of Worms) Henry III is called 'the glorious Henry, emperor of the Romans' (II.4, below p. 130).

123 Humbert, *Adversus simoniacos* III.7, p. 206. See H. Hoffmann (1963) pp. 208–9.

124 *Life* II.17, below p. 144.

125 *Ibid.*, II.16, below p. 143. See E. Steindorff (1881) p. 139; H.-G. Krause (1976) pp. 73–4. On the retention of their bishoprics by the German popes see above p. 6.

that Udo was put in his place'.[125] The *Life* says nothing of the election
of Udo by the clergy and people of Toul, which is recorded in the *Deeds
of the Bishops of Toul* and which was prescribed by Leo's own reforming legislation.[126] Instead the biographer referred only to the act of
investiture with pastoral staff and ring by Henry III. It was precisely
this custom that Humbert denounced in his polemic *Against the
Simoniacs*: 'this very sinful practice has grown so widespread that it
alone is believed to be canonical and no one knows or pays heed to the
ecclesiastical rule'.[127] Equally incompatible with Humbert's authorship
is the insistence with which the author of the *Life* distanced himself
from 'the Romans'. The biographer concluded his final chapter: 'It
remains to describe the very many miracles that divine piety performed at his tomb; but this task we leave to the Romans, among whom
they are revealed every day.' In delegating the task of recording Leo IX's
miracles to 'the Romans', the biographer indicated that he had no access
to the information that was readily available to those who lived near
the pope's tomb.[128] Unlike Cardinal Humbert, he lived far from Rome.[129]

What the text of the *Life of Leo IX* reveals about its author is, first,
that he regarded Lotharingia as his homeland. The biographer described Duke Gozilo I of Lower Lotharingia (1023–44) and of Upper
Lotharingia (1033–44) as 'the warlike Duke Gozilo, our compatriot'.[130] He similarly revealed his local patriotism when he recorded
that Bruno-Leo was 'born in the territory of sweet Alsace'.[131] Second,
with his reference in Book I to Bishop Bruno of Toul as 'our father',[132]

---

126 *Gesta episcoporum Tullensium* c. 41, p. 645. Cf. Council of Rheims (1049) c. 1 in
   Anselm of St-Remi, *Historia dedicationis ecclesiae S. Remigii* c. 16, col. 1437A. See P.
   Schmid (1926) pp. 83–7.

127 Humbert, *Adversus simoniacos* III.11, p. 211. This contrast was emphasised by H.-
   G. Krause (1976) p. 74.

128 *Life* II.27, below p. 157. This was first noted by P.-P. Brucker (1889) 1, 370–1. Cf.
   the objection of H. Tritz (1952) p. 250 ('as a foreigner, Humbert ... could very
   probably speak of the Romans without including himself in their number'), which
   was answered by H.-G. Krause (1976) p. 77.

129 H.-G. Krause (1976) noted a further passage in which the biographer implicitly
   distanced himself from Rome: the miracle by which Leo's broken goblet was made
   whole (at a banquet during the Roman synod of 29 April 1050: cf. Anselm,
   Historia dedicationis c. 7, 18, col. 1421B, 1439A-1440A). The biographer based his
   account on the testimony of Archbishop Hugh I of Besançon; but, as H.-G. Krause
   pointed out, Cardinal Humbert was present on this occasion and, had he been the
   author of the *Life*, he would have written as an eyewitness of the miracle.

130 *Life* I.17, below p. 124.

131 *Ibid.*, I.1, below p. 99.

132 *Ibid.*, I.13, below p. 119.

the biographer placed himself in the diocese of Toul. He underlined his connection with the diocese when in Book II he mentioned Bishop Udo of Toul (1051–69). '[Leo] hoped that ... [Udo] could complete whatever he had left unfinished in the advancement of his original bishopric. This is now, with Christ's aid, in great measure being achieved and, we truly believe, Udo's holy devotion towards God increases daily.'[133] The biographer clearly had detailed knowledge of the interior of the cathedral of St Stephen in Toul, which figures in a vision of Heilwig, Bruno's mother, and in the miraculous healing of Bruno by St Blasius.[134] The biographer was also acquainted with prominent members of the clergy of Toul. He knew the identity of the two canons of Toul whom the clergy and people of Toul sent as envoys to the imperial court in 1026 to secure Bruno's appointment as their bishop.[135] He knew of Bruno's 'former intimate friend, Archdeacon Bezelin', who had died while accompanying him on a pilgrimage to Rome.[136] The *Life* also mentions, as informants about one of Bruno's visions, 'Walter, dean of the chapter of Toul, and his intimate confidant Warneher'.[137] Further evidence of the biographer's identification with the church of Toul is his interest in the local saint Bishop Gerard of Toul (962–94), whose cult Leo IX did much to promote.[138] The biographer reported Leo IX's canonisation of Gerard (2 May 1050) and translation of his relics (22 October 1050), 'as is fully and clearly set down in his Life and Miracles'.[139] This was the biography of St Gerard that Bruno of Toul had commissioned from Widrich, abbot of St-Evre, St-Mansuy and Moyenmoutier.[140]

Widrich, 'that man of pious life and conversation' appears in the chapters of the *Life* describing Bruno's solicitude for the monasteries of his diocese.[141] Widrich (who died soon after 1050) was the pupil of

133 *Ibid.*, II.16, below pp. 143–4.

134 *Ibid.*, I.4, 17, below pp. 103, 125.

135 *Ibid.*, I.9, below p. 111.

136 *Ibid.*, II.2, below p. 128.

137 *Ibid.*, II.3, below p. 129.

138 *Ibid.*, I.4, below p. 103. Heilwig, Leo's mother, experienced a vision of Gerard, signifying that her son was Gerard's chosen successor. See C. H. Brakel (1972) pp. 244, 274.

139 *Life* II.15, below p. 142.

140 Widrich, *Vita et miracula sancti Gerardi episcopi Tullensis* pp. 485–509. For the dedication to Bruno of Toul see *prefatio* p. 490.

141 *Life* I.14, below p. 120. See K. Hallinger (1950) pp. 82–3; N. Bulst (1973) pp. 95–8, 100–1, 105, 111–14.

the monastic reformer William 'of Volpiano', abbot of St-Bénigne, Dijon (990–1031), whom the biographer similarly revered.[142] Widrich was first provost and later abbot of St-Evre (in succession to William of St-Bénigne) and he was also appointed to govern the abbeys of St-Mansuy and Moyenmoutier after Bruno deposed their abbots for neglecting their duties (1026).[143] Widrich was the central figure in Bruno's reform of the monasteries of his diocese: 'through [his] foresight and steadfast intelligence the monastic life was revived again in those places, as is apparent today'.[144] Significantly this monastic reform is the only aspect of Bruno's diocesan activity mentioned in the *Life*. The biographer underlined Bruno-Leo's devotion to St Benedict. After a dangerous childhood illness 'Bruno was restored to health by St Benedict rather than by any other saint' because he was predestined to 'burn with the zeal of pious love for the establishment and the reform of the monastic life'.[145] His preoccupation with 'Benedict, the most blessed father of the monks', together with the echoes of the *Rule* of St Benedict in the *Life* suggest that the biographer himself was a monk.[146]

The biographer's loyalty to the abbey of St-Evre is unmistakable. He emphasised Bruno-Leo's 'great devotion towards the holy and glorious Aper', the bishop of Toul (*circa* 500) to whom the abbey of St-Evre was dedicated.[147] Among the saints' relics that Bruno always carried with him on journeys were 'the bones of St Aper, to whom he was particularly devoted'.[148] At Bruno's accession 'monastic religion ... had for a long time, alas! been in decline throughout his diocese' – 'except for the monastery of the holy confessor of Christ, Aper'. The abbey of St-Evre had already been reformed by Bishop Berthold, who had placed it under the direction of William of St-Bénigne, Dijon.[149] (In the *Life* Berthold escapes the harsh criticism of the Moyenmoutier

142 *Life* I.14, below p. 120.

143 *Ibid.*, I.12, 14, below pp. 117–18, 120. See N. Bulst (1973) pp. 100, 105.

144 *Life* I.12, below p. 118.

145 *Ibid.*, I.5, below p. 105. See P.-P. Brucker (1889) 1, 56–8; C. H. Brakel (1972) pp. 244, 250, 278.

146 *Life* I.9, 13, II.26, below pp. 113, 155. H. Tritz (1952) p. 253 noted that in II.19, p. 147, the biographer described Humbert, a former monk of Moyenmoutier, as 'brother Humbert', 'brother' being the term used in the *Rule* to designate a monk.

147 *Life* I.14, below p. 120. See C. H. Brakel (1972) p. 274.

148 *Life*. II.1, below p. 128.

149 *Ibid.*, I.12, below p. 117. See K. Hallinger (1950) p. 62; N. Bulst (1973) pp. 91–5.

chronicler and appears as a bishop who 'restored the discipline of the monasteries'.) Bishop Herman (1019–26) is censured for his treatment of the monks of St-Evre, 'against whom the mind of the bishop was greatly incited by the very insolent tongues of flatterers and envious persons'. They found in Bruno, however, 'a wall in their defence'.[150] Prosperity returned with Bruno's accession as bishop and the appointment of Widrich as abbot.[151]

The earliest reference to the *Life of Leo IX* links it with the abbey of St-Evre. In the *Deeds of the Bishops of Toul* the reader is referred to 'the book of his life and virtues, which is kept in the church of the blessed Aper'.[152] This seems to be a reference to the original manuscript of the *Life* and an indication that the *Life* was written in St-Evre.[153] Bruno's close relations with St-Evre[154] might well permit a monk of that abbey 'to associate with him on the most familiar terms', as the biographer claimed. This association enabled him 'to transcribe … not so much what I have heard, but what I have seen of this great bishop' but he did not feel competent to record Bruno's later career. 'It will be the duty of the wise and particularly of the Romans gratefully to transmit to the catholic Church a faithful account of what he achieved as Roman pope.'[155] Evidently the author remained in the diocese of Toul after Bruno's departure for Rome.

In Book II he altered his plan and decided to give an account of Leo IX's pontificate. His account, however, lacks detailed information, except for chapter 19, concerning papal relations with Constantinople in 1053–4, and chapter 20, concerning the campaign of 1053 against the Normans. For these two chapters he used identifiable sources associated with the papal curia: for chapter 19 materials from the so-called 'letter book of Cardinal Humbert'; for chapter 20 the letter of Leo IX to the Byzantine emperor Constantine IX, also found in the

---

150 *Life* I.6, p. 106.

151 *Ibid.*, I.14, p. 120.

152 *Gesta episcoporum Tullensium*, p. 644.

153 First suggested by P.-P. Brucker (1889) 1, 370. Cf. P. Schmid (1926) p. 79 n. 243; H.-G. Krause (1976) p. 51 n. 9. Brucker identified two clergy of Toul named Herbert (or Heribert), respectively primicerius and archdeacon, both associated with St-Evre and contemporary with the composition of the *Life*. Since the name Herbertus (Heribertus) might easily become through a scribal error 'Wibertus' (or 'Humbertus') Brucker argued that one of them might have written the *Life* in St-Evre.

154 Cf. Bruno, privilege for St-Evre, *Notitia de instauratione sancti Apri*, MPL 143, col. 581C-584B.

155 *Life* I, prologue, below p. 98.

'letter book'.[156] Elsewhere in Book II the only precise information relates to Germany: the assembly of Worms in December 1048; Leo IX's three visits to Germany (June–December 1049, September 1050 – February 1051, August 1052–February 1053); Udo's succession to the bishopric of Toul (1051).[157] All except one of the named persons who appear in Book II (except for chapters 19 and 20) came from north of the Alps. Most were German churchmen: the Lotharingian archbishops of Cologne and Trier, the bishops of Metz, Verdun, Toul (suffragans of Trier), Speyer and Freising, the Lotharingian abbots of St Arnulf in Metz and Gorze, canons of Toul.[158] One was a Burgundian (the archbishop of Besançon); two were French (the bishop of Langres and the abbot of St-Remi in Rheims).[159] The only Italian mentioned by name was Bishop Hugh of Assisi, who was known to the biographer because he spent Christmas 1048 in Toul as Bruno's guest. The *Life* also refers to 'the bishop of Sutri' and 'the archbishop of Ravenna', two enemies of Leo IX whose names were unknown to the biographer.[160] This is clearly a *Life* written from the perspective of a Lotharingian monk, whose awareness of his limitations had prompted his original intention of leaving the narrative of the papal career to 'the Romans'. He changed that intention perhaps as a result of obtaining the materials in 'the letter-book of Cardinal Humbert', together with information brought to Toul by important witnesses like Archbishop Hugh I of Besançon, who visited Toul in October 1050.[161] Nevertheless on the all-important question of the miracles at Leo IX's tomb the biographer still felt his limitations: 'this task we leave to the Romans, among whom they are revealed every day'.[162]

The dates of the different stages of composition of the *Life* were convincingly reconstructed by H. Tritz.[163] The Prologue to Book I was written after Leo's accession to the papacy and during his lifetime.[164]

---

156 *Ibid.*, II.19, below p. 146; II.20, p. 149. Cf. Leo IX, *JL* 4333, *MPL* 143, col. 777B–781A.

157 *Life* II.4, 11, 12, 15–17, below pp. 130, 137–40, 142–4.

158 *Ibid.*, II.2, 3, 4, 7, 11, 12, 15, 16, below pp. 128–9, 131, 133, 137, 139, 142–3.

159 *Ibid.*, II.11, 13, below pp. 138, 140.

160 *Ibid.*, II.4, 10, 15, below pp. 131, 137, 142.

161 Widrich, *Vita et miracula sancti Gerardi episcopi Tullensis*, c. 9, p. 509. See H.-G. Krause (1976) p. 76.

162 *Life* II.27, below p. 157.

163 H. Tritz (1952) pp. 219–29, responding to the arguments of P. Schmid (1926) pp. 204–7. See also H.-G. Krause (1976) p. 52 n. 12.

164 *Life* I, prologue, below pp. 97, 98.

Since the Prologue emphasises that Bruno-Leo 'now appears as the last in the list of the episcopal succession' of Toul, Leo cannot yet have secured the succession of his protégé Udo. The author began his work, therefore, after the council of Worms in December 1048 and before 18 August 1051 (the date of Udo's consecration).[165] Leo IX was still living when the biographer composed chapter 5 of Book I, describing the miraculous healing of young Bruno: 'even today in [Leo's] edifying conversations it is his custom to tell his closest friends how he perceived this clear instance of God's compassion towards him'.[166] Book I chapter 16, however, is a significant turning-point. 'Certain princes of [Bruno's] homeland ... incited Odo [II, count of Blois and Champagne] ... against the blessed bishop'. This description of Bruno-Leo as 'blessed' *(beatus)* for the first time has prompted the conclusion that the pope was dead when the biographer wrote this chapter.[167] It is equally likely that the preceding chapter was written after the pope's death (19 April 1054). Chapter 15 is a eulogy written in the past tense: 'There was in Bruno a remarkable and noble elegance of character ... He was so full of charity that he indiscriminately gave away almost all his possessions ... He was renowned for his immense knowledge of the divine and human arts ...'[168] In his prologue the biographer had pointedly refused to praise Leo, citing the proverb, 'Do not praise a man during his lifetime'.[169] Perhaps, therefore, it was the arrival in Toul of the news of Leo's death that inspired the eulogy of Book I chapter 15.

Tritz suggested that the final chapters of Book I and the whole of Book II were written at a single stretch.[170] These pages reveal that the *Life* was completed in the lifetime of Archbishop Hugh I of Besançon, who died on 27 July 1066, and of Bishop Udo of Toul, who died on 14 July 1069.[171] The clearest indication of the date of completion appears in

165 *Ibid.*, II.16, below p. 143.

166 *Ibid.*, I.5, below p. 105.

167 *Ibid.*, I.16, below p. 123. See J. M. Watterich, *Pontificum Romanorum Vitae* 1, lxxxv n. 7; M. Manitius (1923) p. 382; H. Tritz (1952) p. 222. Cf. *Life* I.17, p. 124: 'all honoured him with supreme veneration like a saint'.

168 *Life* I.15, below p. 121.

169 *Ibid.*, I, prologue, below p. 98. Cf. I.18, p. 126 and II.16, p. 144 (where he declined to praise Bishop Udo of Toul 'lest we incur the reputation of a flatterer, because it is safest to sing a man's praises only at the end').

170 H. Tritz (1952) p. 226.

171 *Life* II.13, below p. 140: 'There is a reliable witness of this incident in the person of the venerable Archbsihop Hugh of Besançon'; cf. II.11, p. 138. *Ibid.*, II.16, below p. 144: 'Udo's holy devotion towards God increases daily'.

the vision seen by Bruno on the eve of his election to the papacy, a detailed interpretation of which is given in the final chapter. In the vision Bruno found himself in the presence of St Peter and 'an infinite crowd of men dressed in white'. 'St Peter brought to him five golden chalices, but to another of his followers he gave three and to a third, only one chalice.' 'The five chalices offered to him by the blessed Peter signified the five years of his life [as pope]; the three chalices signified the three years of his successor, Victor [II]; the following single chalice, the one year of Stephen [IX] of blessed memory in the papacy.'[172] Both the account in Book II chapter 2 and the interpretation in chapter 27 must have been composed after the death of Pope Stephen IX on 29 March 1058. It seems fair to assume that had the biographer known the length of the pontificate of Stephen's successor, Nicholas II, he would have included this information in his prophetic vision. The biographer wrote his final chapter, therefore, before the death of Nicholas II on 19 or 20 July 1061.

The purpose of the *Life* was to 'transmit to posterity' 'for the edification of many' 'the divine virtues imprinted in' Bruno-Leo and the 'very many things about him that ought to be imitated'.[173] The biographer was perhaps paraphrasing Widrich of St-Evre in the preface to his *Life of St Gerard of Toul*, a work well known to him.[174] A major component of such a work of edification was meticulously detailed accounts of visions and miracles. Sixteen visions and twenty miracles are recorded in the *Life*. Miracles are numerous in Book II but almost absent from Book I. While visions are fairly evenly distributed throughout the biography (six in Book I, ten in Book II), only two miracles are recorded in the first book. This distribution reflects the fact that the biographer wrote Book II when the deceased Leo IX was beginning to be revered as a saint. What had begun as the biography of a distinguished bishop was transformed into a work of hagiography.[175]

Nine of the visions have a prophetic character, foretelling Bruno's election to the episcopate and to the papacy, the length of his pontificate,

---

172 *Ibid.*, II.2, 27, below pp. 129, 156.

173 *Ibid.*, I, prologue, below p. 98.

174 *Ibid.*, II.15, below p. 142. Cf. Widrich, *Vita sancti Gerardi episcopi Tullensis* c. 1, pp. 491–2: 'It is useful for the merits and virtues of the saints to be read to us, if through the imitation of their example we are prompted anew to holy conversation.' Widrich's work offered 'a beneficial example to posterity', 'useful edification to readers, eternal salvation to those who imitate [Gerard]'.

175 P. Schmid (1926) p. 206; H. Tritz (1952) pp. 228–9; H. Hoesch (1970) pp. 243–8; H.-G. Krause (1976) pp. 65–7.

his work as a reformer, his trials and suffering and his future blessedness.[176] Two of the visions and one of the miracles show Bruno enjoying 'the protection of heaven', being healed from lethal sickness and evading capture by enemies.[177] Five of the miracles in Book II are demonstrations of the sanctity of the pope, including the most widely disseminated of the miracles of Leo IX. In 1050 in Rome 'the grace of heaven made his miraculous merits known to all' when the pieces of his broken goblet spontaneously stuck together.[178] Book II also contains six miracles of healing performed 'by the merits of the saints and through [Leo's] intercession', including the healing of three demoniacs.[179] The visions and miracles recorded by the biographer in Book II chapter 21 were intended to justify the pope's conduct towards the Normans of southern Italy. The members of the papal army who had fallen at the battle of Civitate (18 June 1053) 'appeared in various ways to the faithful of Christ, saying that they ought not to be thought of as men to be mourned with funeral rites, but rather as united in heavenly glory with the holy martyrs'. Their burial place witnessed 'extraordinary miracles'.[180] The assurance that the fallen at Civitate had attained the glory of martyrdom is common to all the eleventh-century biographies of Leo IX and reflects the anxiety that the papal campaign and subsequent defeat had generated in reforming circles.[181] Finally, five of the miracles in Book II were divine punishments inflicted on erring prelates. Bishop Sibicho of Speyer was punished with paralysis for an unnamed crime; Bishop Nizo (Nitker) of Freising and his ally Archbishop Hunfrid of Ravenna were punished with death for their disobedience to the pope.[182] Two of the miraculous punishments occurred in cases of simony. In the Roman council of April 1049 the guilty bishop of Sutri was struck dead before he could take an oath to clear himself of the charge of simony.[183] In the council of Rheims (October 1049) the worthy Archbishop Hugh of

---

176 *Life* I.2, 4, 16, 18, II.2, 3, 5, 17, below pp. 100, 103, 123, 126, 129, 131, 144.

177 *Ibid.*, I.5, 17, below pp. 104, 125. (Cf. Widrich, *Vita sancti Gerardi episcopi* c. 22, p. 503). *Life* I.11, below p. 116.

178 *Ibid.*, II.5, 9, below pp. 132, 135. The broken goblet: *ibid.*, II.13, below p. 140. (See above p. 22 n. 129.) For the four other versions of this miracle see below pp. 140, 383.

179 *Ibid.*, II.1, 7, 14, 22, below pp. 128, 133, 141, 152. The healing of demoniacs: II.12, 16, 23, pp. 140, 143, 153. See C. H. Brakel (1972) p. 281.

180 *Life* II.21, below p. 151.

181 See above p. 8 and below pp. 52–3, 94.

182 *Life* II.12, 15, below pp. 139, 142–3.

183 *Ibid.*, II.10, below p. 137.

Besançon was struck dumb when he attempted to defend Bishop Hugh
of Langres against accusations of simony.[184]

The biographer's references to simony are the clearest indication of
his sympathy for Leo IX's reforming programme. His long account of
Bruno's election to the bishopric of Toul in 1026 emphasises the need
for bishops to avoid 'any venality', 'lest the blemish of simoniacal
heresy should spread among all the sheep entrusted to [them]'.[185] In
his first Roman council (April 1049) Leo 'condemned the heresy of
simony' and 'deposed certain bishops whom that heresy had marked
with the stain of its iniquity'.[186] Likewise in his council of Rheims
(October 1049) Leo 'deposed certain men infected with the heresy of
simony from the offices that they had received unjustly' and in his
council of Siponto (April 1050) he 'deposed from the office of archbishop
two men who had acquired the holy ministry in return for payment'.[187]
The biographer cited the *sententia* of Pope Gregory I concerning simony,
widely disseminated by the eleventh-century papal reform movement.
Bruno 'had learned from the words of the blessed Gregory [that
simony] has a threefold origin: by gift, by service, by favour'.[188] Of
Leo IX's preoccupation with the eradication of clerical marriage the
biographer said nothing. The reforming initiatives which he emphasised
in his account of Leo's first Roman council were that the pope
'restored to the churches the payment of tithes by all Christians' and
forbade marriages within the prohibited degrees of consanguinity. He
'put asunder the incestuous marriages that had been indiscreetly contracted among kindred in many regions of the world'.[189] The importance of these issues to Leo IX himself is apparent from the Roman
accounts of the sermon delivered by the pope on his deathbed.[190]

184 *Ibid.*, II.11, below p. 138.

185 *Ibid.*, I.10, below p. 114.

186 *Ibid.*, II.10, below p. 136. For the term 'simoniacal heresy' see J. Leclercq (1947)
pp. 523–30; J. Gilchrist (1965) pp. 209–35.

187 *Life* II.11, 14, below pp. 138, 141.

188 *Ibid.*, I.9, below p. 113. The source is Gregory I, *Homiliae in evangelio Iohannis*
I.4.4, *MPL* 76, col. 1091C–1092A, best known in the eleventh century from John
the Deacon, *Vita sancti Gregorii Magni* III.6, *MPL* 75, col. 132D–133A and from
the abbreviated version in Burchard of Worms, *Decretum* I.113, col. 583B. Cf. *Life*
I.6, below p. 107; Peter Damian, *Letters* 48, 69, pp. 58, 299; *Collectio in LXXIV
titulos* 133, pp. 89–90. See also H. Tritz (1952) p. 228; H. Hoesch (1970) p. 251.

189 *Life* II.10, below p. 137.

190 Libuin, *De obitu sancti Leonis papae IX* c. 3, col. 527D–528A; Bonus of Cervia, *Vita
et miracula Leonis IX* II.3, p. 290; Bruno of Segni, *Sermon concerning Simoniacs* c. 6,
below p. 386. The prohibition also appears among the decrees of Leo IX's council
of Rheims: see Anselm, *Historia dedicationis* c. 16, col. 1437B.

The biographer's conception of Leo IX as a reformer is made clear in his interpretation of a prophetic vision seen by Bruno-Leo on the eve of his papal election. The interpretation was that 'the beauty of the Church, indeed the Christian religion, throughout the various regions of the world had faded to a fearful extent and through Bruno it was, with Christ's help, brought back to its former dignity'.[191] Leo was to restore the discipline of the early Church. His first Roman council (1049) was devoted to 'preserving the catholic laws'. 'He restated the decisions of the four principal synods [Nicaea, Constantinople, Ephesus and Chalcedon] and confirmed that the decrees of all the preceding popes were to be respected'.[192] Of Leo's burial next to the altar of Pope Gregory I, the biographer commented: 'It is fitting that he is joined in this honourable burial with him whom he faithfully imitated in divine piety and in the restoration of holy Church.'[193] The language of restoration, renewal and reparation was characteristic of the writings of the contemporary ecclesiastical reform movement.[194] Another characteristic theme of the reforming literature of the 1050s is, however, entirely absent from the *Life of Leo IX:* namely the jurisdictional primacy of the papacy.[195] The theme of the Roman primacy permeates the dossier of materials on the relations of Rome and Constantinople in 1053–4, 'the letter-book of Cardinal Humbert'. The author of the *Life,* as we have seen, excerpted passages from this dossier (Book II chapters 19 and 20), but he showed no interest in 'the earthly and heavenly empire of the royal priesthood of the holy Roman see'.[196]

The biographer's reverence towards St Peter appears in his account of Bishop Bruno's pilgrimages to Rome. 'It was his most pious custom to visit almost every year the supreme pastor, the keeper of the keys of heaven and to beseech his help for the flock entrusted to him by God.'[197] The biographer emphasised that Bruno-Leo was chosen by St Peter as his successor, 'his fellow-worker' and 'companion'. St Peter revealed to him in prophetic visions the length of his pontificate and

---

191 *Life* II.3, below p. 130.

192 *Ibid.,* II.10, below p. 136.

193 *Ibid.,* II.27, below p. 156.

194 See above p. 1 and also P. E. Schramm (1929) pp. 238042; C. Miccoli (1966a) pp. 225–99.

195 See above pp. 7–8.

196 Leo IX, *JL* 4202, the first item in the 'Letter-book'. See above p. 7.

197 *Life* II.1, below p. 127

the place of his death.[198] The biographer's conception of the relationship of St Peter and his vicar, the pope, was not that expressed by
Gregory VII, who assimilated pope and saint – they were 'blessed
Peter the apostle and his vicar Pope Gregory who now lives in the
flesh' – in order to lay claim to the *principatus* of the prince of the
apostles.[199] There is no hint of this *principatus* in the *Life*, where the
conception of the papal office remains pre-Gregorian: the pope is essen-
tially 'the high-priest of the Roman pilgrimage, the dispenser of bene-
dictions and of privileges and of anathemas'.[200] It was in these terms
that the biographer evoked the authority of Leo IX. The multitude of
pilgrims who visited 'the residence of the supreme prince of the apostles'
'were refreshed by his encouragement and strengthened by his
blessing'. Others 'sent him their presents in the confidence that they
would receive from him the gift of the papal blessing'.[201] When the
biographer described the papal office, it was not in terms of *principatus*
but of pastoral care. The papacy was a 'cure of souls' and Leo was
moved always by 'anxiety for the sheep entrusted to him by God'.[202]

There are only two passages in the *Life* that have the character of
reforming polemic: the account of Bruno's accession to the see of Toul
and that of his election to the papacy. The biographer emphasised that
both these elections were conducted 'according to the authority of the
canons'.[203] While the biographer's report of the appointment of Bishop
Udo of Toul referred only to his investiture by the emperor,[204] his
account of the two elections of Bruno-Leo carefully distanced the
imperial power from the appointment procedures. On both occasions
Bruno-Leo was unanimously elected by the clergy and people against
his will: the involvement of the canonical electors, their unanimity
and the candidate's reluctance were all equally essential to the legality
of the election.[205] In the case of Toul, 'the clergy and people ...
gathered together by a unanimous wish, agreeing in their opinion,

198 *Ibid.*, II.2, 26, below pp. 129, 155.
199 Gregory VII, *Registrum* IX.3, p. 576. See A. Fliche (1926) p. 194 ('Gregory
    identified himself with the apostle, who spoke, legislated, judged and condemned
    through his mouth').
200 L. Duchesne (1908) p. 271. Cf. Y. M.-J. Congar (1968) pp. 146–51.
201 *Life* II.9, below p. 135.
202 *Ibid.*, II.5, 20, below pp. 131, 149.
203 *Ibid.*, I.8, II.6, below pp. 110, 132.
204 *Ibid.*, II.16, below p. 143. See above pp. 21–2.
205 P. Schmid (1926) pp. 14–57; H.-G. Krause (1960) pp. 28–34.

and asked harmoniously and continually for Bruno'. Conrad II, desiring
to promote his kinsman to 'a more exalted dignity' than the church of
Toul, attempted to hinder the election. Bruno, however, 'believed that
his only safe course was to accept the people's election, which drew
him into a life of humility and adversity, and to resist the promptings
of the emperor, which urged him on to greatness and prosperity.' His
accession, therefore, was the result of 'God's favour, which alone is
believed to have appointed [him] to the government of that church
without recourse to any venality'.[206]

The same themes recur in the account of Bruno's election to the papacy.
At the imperial assembly of Worms in December 1048 'suddenly,
without his suspecting anything [Bruno] was unanimously chosen to
undertake the burden of the papal office'. After 'a delay of three days
for reflection' he 'attempted to reverse their unanimous election' by
emphasising his unsuitability for the office; but the assembly was all
the more eager to elect him. 'He was compelled in the presence of the
envoys of the Romans to accept the office that was laid on him, on condition that he received the general consent of all the Roman clergy and
people without any disagreement.'[207] Bruno then departed for Rome,
not in the manner of a pope-elect but in 'the garment of a pilgrim,
contrary to the custom of all the popes'. To the Roman clergy and
people 'he said that the election of clergy and people should prevail
against the dispositions of others according to the authority of the
canons; he declared that he would gladly return to his homeland if his
election did not receive the approval of them all; he showed that it was
under compulsion that he had come to take up so heavy a burden.' In
reply the Roman clergy and people 'all unanimously acclaimed him'.[208]

These accounts of the elections have seemed to some historians to be
'in general ... an actual picture of proceedings', while to others they
have appeared inauthentic and coloured by the author's knowledge of
later reforming legislation.[209] Of the election to the bishopric of Toul
in 1026 no other account survives. A recent survey of episcopal elections
in Upper Lotharingia in the period of Bruno's episcopate concluded

206 *Life* I.8,9,10, below pp. 109, 112, 113, 114.

207 *Ibid.*, II.4, below pp. 130, 131.

208 *Ibid.*, II.5,6, below pp. 131, 132–3.

209 H. Tritz (1952) p. 256 (episcopal election), p. 258 (papal election). The account of
the 1026 election was accepted by K. J. Benz (1977) pp. 196–9. That Leo IX insisted
on a canonical election in Rome in 1049 was argued by H. Hoffmann (1963) p. 188
and J. Laudage (1984) p. 160 n. 179. For a contrary view see P. Schmid (1926) pp.
70–83; M. Parisse (1996) pp. 77–95.

that bishops were 'for the most part chosen and confirmed by royal authority'.[210] The best informed near-contemporary accounts of ecclesiastical appointments in the reign of Conrad II suggest a similar conclusion.[211] The more abundant information about the ecclesiastical appointments of Henry III indicates the dominant role played by the secular ruler,[212] offering a strong contrast to the account of Bruno's election in the *Life*. In its emphasis on 'the general consent of all the Roman clergy and people', the account of the papal election in the *Life* resembles those of the Gregorian polemicists Bonizo of Sutri and Bruno of Segni. According to Bonizo, Leo was reluctantly 'given to the Romans as their pope' by Henry III. During his journey to Rome, however, he encountered the young Hildebrand, who persuaded him not 'to take possession of the papacy at the command of the emperor'. Leo 'laid down the papal insignia' and travelled as a pilgrim. On his arrival in Rome 'the bishops and cardinals' elected him pope and 'the people followed their example'.[213] According to Bruno of Segni, Leo's reply to the election of Henry III and the council of Worms was: 'if the clergy and people [of Rome] willingly elect me as their pontiff, I shall do what you ask; otherwise, however, I shall not accept the election.' In Rome 'Bruno was elected to the papacy by the clergy and people according to Roman custom'.[214] This version of events is, however, contradicted by the contemporary accounts of the monks Herman of Reichenau and Anselm of St-Remi, Rheims, which emphasise the role of imperial authority and say nothing of a second election in Rome.[215]

---

210 M. Parisse (1996) pp. 88–92.

211 Wipo, *Gesta Chuonradi II imperatoris* c. 8, p. 30 ('How King Conrad appointed a bishop in Basel'). See K. J. Benz (1977) pp. 195–6. *Annales Altahenses maiores* [Niederaltaich Annals] 1038, p. 22 ('the emperor … reached Monte Cassino … and he himself placed an abbot there'). K. J. Benz (1977) pp. 203–7 preferred the tendentious late account of the *Chronicon monasterii Casinensis* II.63, pp. 288–93 to the earlier, well-informed account of the annalist of Niederaltaich, where the new abbot of Monte Cassino, Richer, had been a monk.

212 E.g. Herman of Reichenau, *Chronicon* 1047, p. 126 ('At that time the emperor appointed some prelates'). Cf. *Annales Altahenses maiores* 1048, p. 45 ('[The emperor] gave the bishopric of Bamberg to the chancellor Hartwig and … the abbey of Fulda to Ebbo').

213 Bonizo, *Book to a Friend* V, below p. 190.

214 Bruno, *Sermon concerning Simoniacs* c. 2, below p. 379. Bruno incorporated Bonizo's story of the admonition of Hildebrand, but in Bruno's version Hildebrand preaches to the converted. Cf. Bonus of Cervia, *Vita et miracula Leonis IX* I.2, p. 277 (Bruno 'unwillingly arrived in the city of Rome…').

215 Herman, *Chronicon* 1049, p. 128: 'Bishop Bruno of Toul was elected by the emperor and sent to Rome; he was received with the greatest honour and consecrated…'.

There are, therefore, two distinct versions of the election of Leo IX, that of the *Life* and of the Gregorian authors being the later version. The Gregorian writings are unmistakably polemical in character. In Bonizo of Sutri's work, composed in 1085, Leo IX's election is one of numerous examples intended to prove a central argument of the work: 'No emperor ... was permitted to involve himself in the election of any Roman pontiff.' The polemicist's purpose was to demonstrate that the election of King Henry IV's antipope Wibert of Ravenna ('Clement III') in 1080 was invalid.[216] The account composed by Bruno of Segni during the 1090s was similarly intended to support a central contention of his writings: 'all the secular powers and all laymen, however religious they may be, are barred from the ordering and administration of churches'.[217] It is likely that the account of the papal election in the *Life of Leo IX*, completed in the years 1058–61, was similarly shaped by polemical considerations. The biographer caused Bruno's episcopal and papal elections to conform to Leo IX's reforming decree of 1049, 'that no one is to be promoted to the government of a church without the election of clergy and people'.[218] Only in these chapters has the *Life* the character of a reforming polemic. Elsewhere, as we have seen, it was the evidence of Bruno-Leo's sanctity rather than his reforming activities that mainly preoccupied the biographer.

Numerous editions of the *Life (Vita Leonis IX papae)* are available. *Acta Sanctorum*, Aprilis 2 (Antwerp, 1675), 648–665 contains the edition of Gottfried Henskens. The edition of Jean Mabillon, *Acta Sanctorum Ordinis sancti Benedicti* 6/2 (Paris, 1701), 49–80, was reprinted by L. A. Muratori, *Rerum Italicarum scriptores* 3 (Milan, 1723), 282–99, by J. P. Migne, *Patrologia Latina* 143, col. 465–504 and by J. M. Watterich, *Pontificum Romanorum Vitae* 1, 127–70.[219] The recent edition by

Cf. *ibid.*, 1046, p. 126; 1048, p. 128. Anselm, *Historia dedicationis* c. 7, col. 1420CD: 'The Romans ... requested that, since the church had been bereaved of her pastor, [the emperor] should put another in his place'; cf. col. 1421BC. Cf. Lampert of Hersfeld, *Annales* 1049, p. 62.

216 Bonizo, *Book to a Friend* V, below p. 187. See also below p. 57.

217 Bruno, Letter to the cardinals, ed. G. Fransen (1972) p. 529. See below p. 379.

218 Council of Rheims (1049) c. 1: in Anselm, *Historia dedicationis* c. 16, col. 1437A. See also U.-R. Blumenthal (1976) p. 36. The biographer reinforced his message by including two 'authorities' cited by contemporary reformers in support of canonical election: Celestine I, *JK* 369 (*Epistola* 4.5, *MPL* 50, col. 434B–435A) and Leo I, *JK* 411 (*Epistola* 14.5, *MPL* 54, col. 673A). See below p. 110.

219 For the printing history of the *Vita* see H. Tritz (1952) pp. 214–19.

Michel Parisse is based on the two eleventh-century codices, Bern, Stadt- und Hochschulbibliothek 24 and 292.[220] An edition is currently being prepared for the *Monumenta Germaniae Historica* by Hans-Georg Krause.

The Book of Bishop Bonizo of Sutri which is entitled 'To a Friend'

Bonizo, bishop of Sutri, canonist, theologian, historian and polemicist, was one of the most prolific authors of the later eleventh century. His *Book which is entitled 'To a Friend'* is perhaps the best known of the polemics of the Investiture Contest. A fourteenth-century reader and an eighteenth-century editor called the work a 'History of the persecution of the Church'.[221] More recently it has been identified as a crucial contribution to the eleventh-century debate about holy war.[222] The work also contains the earliest biography of Pope Gregory VII, concluding with a refutation of the accusations of his detractors.

A series of studies has established the outline of Bonizo's career.[223] He was probably born *c.* 1045,[224] and, it is conjectured, he was not of noble origin.[225] That he was a Lombard is indicated by his keen interest in the archdiocese of Milan, the cult of St Ambrose and the

220 *La vie du pape Léon IX (Brunon, évêque de Toul)* (Les Classiques de l'histoire de France au moyen âge 38: Paris, 1997), with a French translation by Monique Goullet.

221 This title was added in a fourteenth-century hand in the unique manuscript, Munich, Bayerische Staatsbibliothek codex latinus 618. On this codex see P. Jaffé, edition of the *Liber ad amicum* pp. 583 n. 1, 602; E. Dümmler, edition p. 571; I. S. Robinson (1978c) pp. 303–5. The title was used by the first editor of the work, A. F. von Oefele, *Rerum Boicarum Scriptores* 2 (Augsburg, 1763), 781 and by J.M. Watterich, *Vitae pontificum Romanorum* 1, 256–70, 308–49.

222 C. Erdmann (1935) pp. 229–33.

223 H. Saur (1868) pp. 395–464; H. Lehmgrübner (1887) pp. 129–51; E. Dümmler, edition pp. 568–70; P. Fournier (1915) pp. 265–98; E. Perels, edition of Bonizo, *Liber de vita christiana* pp. XII-XIX; L. Gatto (1968) pp. 89–121; G. Miccoli (1970) pp. 246–59; W. Berschin (1972) pp. 3–21.

224 H. Saur (1886) pp. 419–20 derived this date from an analysis of the *Book* intended to establish the moment when Bonizo began to write as a contemporary (allegedly in 1059); W. Berschin (1972) p. 3 n. 3 from the probable date of his consecration as bishop. See also H. Lehmgrübner (1887) pp. 136–7; E. Perels, *Liber de vita christiana* p. XII ('very uncertain suggestions that oscillate between 1030 and 1045').

225 Bonizo, *Book to a Friend* VI, below p. 198: 'the poor, whom God chose to shame the strong'. See H. Saur (1868) p. 411; H. Lehmgrübner (1887) p. 129; G. Schwartz (1913) p. 192; E. Perels, *Liber de vita christiana* p. XII; W. Berschin (1972) p. 5 n. 7.

Milanese reform movement of the Pataria.[226] It is possible that before
his promotion to the bishopric of Sutri, Bonizo was a member of the
clergy of Piacenza. A letter of Gregory VII (27 November 1074) to
Bishop Denis of Piacenza identified 'the subdeacon Bonizo' as Denis's
opponent. The subdeacon was allied with the abbot of S. Sepolcro and
'the people of Piacenza' in a protracted dispute with the bishop.[227]
Denis of Piacenza, the acknowledged leader of the Lombard episcopate
in their opposition to the reform papacy, was deposed from his office
in the papal synod of Lent 1075.[228] Perhaps, therefore, Bonizo of Sutri
first came to Gregory VII's attention as one of the leaders of resistance to a formidable enemy of the papal reform movement.[229]

In the *Book to a Friend* Bonizo attributed the disturbances in Piacenza
to the influence of the Milanese Patarini. In 1067 that movement spread
to both Cremona and Piacenza. The Cremonese 'expelled the simoniacs
and the unchaste from their church. The men of Piacenza ..., submitting themselves without delay to the obedience of Rome, cast out
their bishop, Denis ... and all confirmed the Pataria on oath.'[230]
Bonizo also reported the destruction of the Patarine movement in
Piacenza during the Italian mission of Henry IV's envoy, Count
Eberhard 'the Bearded', who 'proclaimed the Patarini public enemies
of the king' in summer 1075. The Cremonese escaped the fate of the
Piacenzans because 'they were full of faith and fortified with
virtues'.[231] The author's admiration for the Cremonese is evident here
and in his account of the origins of the Cremonese reform movement
in 1067. The *Book to a Friend* alone identifies the movement's leader,
Christopher, abbot of SS. Peter and Paul in Cremona, and records the
violence suffered by Bishop Arnulf of Cremona in the agitation of

226 H. Saur (1868) p. 411; H. Lehmgrübner (1887) p. 130; E. Perels, *Liber de vita christiana* p. XII. See also below p. 51. The name Bonizo (Bonitho) occurs frequently in
eleventh-century sources from Lombardy and notably from Piacenza: W. von
Giesebrecht in *MGH Libelli* 1, 629; W. Berschin (1972) p. 3 n. 2.

227 Gregory VII, *Registrum* II.26, pp. 158–9. For the abbey of S. Sepolcro see *Italia
Pontificia* 5, 504.

228 Gregory VII, *Registrum* I.77, II.52a, 54, pp. 110, 197, 199. See G. Schwartz (1913)
p. 191.

229 The identification of 'the subdeacon Bonizo' with the polemicist was doubted by P.
Jaffé, edition p. 577 (because of the frequency with which the name 'Bonizo' occurs
in Lombard sources). Cf. W. Berschin (1972) p. 7 n. 20 ('it seems possible'). The
identification was accepted by H. Saur (1868) pp. 417–18; H. Lehmgrübner (1887)
p. 138; E. Perels, *Liber de vita christiana* p. XII; G. Miccoli (1970) p. 246.

230 Bonizo, *Book to a Friend* VI, below pp. 213–14.

231 *Ibid.*, VII, below p. 232. See G. Meyer von Knonau (1894) p. 571; I. S. Robinson
(1999) p. 139.

1067.[232] It is from the *Book to a Friend* that we learn of accusations made against the Cremonese reformers in the papal synod of March 1074 during 'a discussion of the business of the Piacenzans and the Cremonese'.[233] Bonizo's link with the Cremonese reform movement is apparent in an inscription from Cremona that provides the earliest reference to him as bishop of Sutri. On 3 October 1078 the church of the newly built abbey of St Thomas in Cremona 'was consecrated by the lord Bonizo, bishop of Sutri and papal legate'.[234] Bonizo was acting during the vacancy in the bishopric caused by the papal deposition of Bishop Arnulf, the enemy of the Cremonese reformers.[235] Bonizo's legation bears witness both to the trust placed in him by Gregory VII and to his acknowledged expertise in Lombard affairs.

Bonizo's appointment to Sutri – a diocese of strategic importance, one day's journey to the north of Rome – is evidence of that alliance between the Patarini and the papacy that is an important theme of the *Book to a Friend*. Bonizo had already visited Rome during the pontificate of Alexander II. He mentioned in his treatise on marriage his having seen Alexander 'with [his] own eyes in a synod held in the Lateran consistorium'.[236] This was perhaps the synod of Lent 1073, the only synod of Alexander II reported in the *Book to a Friend*.[237] Apart from the legation to Cremona in October 1078 we know of only two events in Bonizo's career as bishop of Sutri. First, he was present during the discussion of the eucharistic doctrine of Berengar of Tours that preceded the Roman synod of November 1078.[238] Second, during

---

232 Bonizo, *Book to a Friend* VI, below p. 212. *Ibid.*, VI, p. 213 alone preserves the letter Alexander II, *JL* 4637 commending 'the religious clergy and faithful laymen of Cremona' for their reforming zeal (see *Regesta pontificum Romanorum* 1, 581).

233 Bonizo, *Book to a Friend* VII, below p. 224.

234 The inscription survives in a seventeenth-century copy: see W. Berschin (1972) p. 9 n. 28. See also G. Schwartz (1913) p. 264; G. Miccoli (1970) p. 246.

235 Gregory VII, *Registrum* V.14a, c. 2, p. 369.

236 Bonizo, *De arbore parentele* ed. G. Miccoli (1966b) p. 394; see also W. Berschin (1972) p. 84. The term *consistorium* meant at this date a place of counsel: it did not yet signify a solemn assembly of the cardinals presided over by the pope: see I. S. Robinson (1990) p. 99.

237 Bonizo, *Book to a Friend* VI, below p. 218. See G. Miccoli (1966b) p. 382. W. Berschin (1972) p. 8 n. 22 argued in favour of the synod of 1072. Whether Bonizo attended as bishop or as envoy of the Piacenzan reformers is impossible to decide. His predecessor Mainard of Sutri is known only from his attendance at the Roman synod of 15 May 1070: see G. Schwartz (1913) p. 264; G. Miccoli (1970) p. 247.

238 According to the *Relatio* of Berengar of Tours: *Sacra Concilia* 19, 761; R.B.C. Huygens (1965) pp. 388–93. Bonizo appears here in the company of the cardinals and canonists Deusdedit and Atto (whose career as archbishop-elect of Milan he

King Henry IV's siege of Rome in 1082 'the venerable bishop of Sutri and some others were taken captive'.[239] The Swabian chronicler to whom we owe this information, subsequently described Bonizo as having been 'expelled from [Sutri] because of his fidelity towards St Peter'. Bonizo was never to recover control of his diocese, which became a stronghold of Henry IV's antipope 'Clement III' (Wibert of Ravenna).[240]

Bonizo's captivity had ended at least by March 1086, when he was present at the funeral of Bishop Anselm II of Lucca (†18 March 1086) in Mantua, in the jurisdiction of Matilda, margravine of Tuscany.[241] Anselm of Lucca, nephew of Pope Alexander II, was the faithful disciple of Gregory VII and his permanent legate in Lombardy and also the spiritual adviser of Matilda, the papacy's most reliable secular ally.[242] Anselm was about to be buried, according to his wish, in the abbey of S. Benedetto di Polirone, but the funeral was interrupted by the arrival of Bonizo. He declared 'that it was fitting for a bishop to be buried in an episcopal church. "So great a light," he said, "ought not to be hidden ... We, who know that he was most holy, ought to exalt him, as a truly worthy man."' The Mantuans responded to Bonizo's speech by seizing the body from the monks and burying Anselm in the cathedral church of St Peter, Mantua.[243] The reverence for Anselm here attributed to Bonizo in the saint's anonymous biography is echoed in Bonizo's own writings, where Anselm is acknowledged to be a saint.[244]

recorded in the *Book to a Friend*). See H. Lehmgrübner (1887) p. 140; E. Perels, *Liber de vita christiana* p. XIII n. 2; W. Berschin (1972) p. 9; H. E. J. Cowdrey (1998) pp. 497–8.

239 Bernold of St Blasien, *Chronicon* 1082, p. 437. Cf. Benzo of Alba, *Ad Heinricum IV* VI.4, p. 548 ('many rebels in chains'). For Bonizo's account of this siege see *Book IX*, below p. 249. See G. Meyer von Knonau (1900) p. 446; W. Berschin (1972) p. 10; H. E. J. Cowdrey (1998) p. 220.

240 Bernold, *Chronicon* 1089, p. 449. Cf. Rangerius of Lucca, *Vita metrica Anselmi episcopi Lucensis* p. 1299. See E. Perels, edition p. XIII; W. Berschin (1972) p. 10. The antipope appointed his nephew Otto as 'count of Sutri': see G. Meyer von Knonau (1903) p. 269.

241 *Vita Anselmi episcopi Lucensis* c. 42, p. 25.

242 On Anselm II of Lucca see Paul of Bernried, *Life of Gregory VII* c. 111, below p. 354. See also C. Violante (1961) pp. 399–407; K. G. Cushing (1998) pp. 43–63.

243 *Vita Anselmi* c. 42, p. 25. In the later version of Rangerius, *Vita metrica* p. 1299, Bonizo is represented as settling a dispute about the burial place of Anselm. See W. Berschin (1987) p. 281.

244 Bonizo, *Liber de vita christiana* II.30, p. 48: 'St Anselm, bishop of Lucca, whom God glorified after his death by many and various and great miracles'. Cf. *ibid.*, V.77, p. 204.

As we shall see, Anselm's influence is clearly present in the *Book to a Friend*, where Matilda of Tuscany also plays a significant role. Matilda's entourage 'was like a safe haven for catholics; for those bishops, monks and clergy, Italians and Germans, whom the king condemned, expelled and deposed, all hastened to the living fountain, namely to that kind lady'.[245] In 1086, at the time of Anselm's funeral, Bonizo was one of those members of the papal party who sought refuge at Matilda's court. A charter issued by the margravine in this year recorded that Bonizo was 'held in great honour by [Matilda] because of the excellent qualities of his mind'.[246]

In the final phase of his career Bonizo is found again in Piacenza, in the archdiocese of Wibert of Ravenna, the imperial antipope, the principal target of the *Book to a Friend*. Here between March 1086 and early summer 1088 Bonizo was elected bishop by a pro-papal faction. This episode is reported, firstly, in a characteristically obscure passage in the pro-imperial polemic of Bishop Benzo of Alba. Benzo called on Henry IV to punish the 'devils' in northern Italy, who, 'bringing everything into confusion, usurp ecclesiastical offices'. One of these was 'Bonizellus', that is, the exiled bishop of Sutri. 'It is impossible to describe the great deceptions that Bonizellus practised in the city of Piacenza and among the inhabitants of the surrounding countryside, pursuing his diabolical preaching and unlawfully consecrating churches'.[247] The Swabian chronicler Bernold gave a Gregorian version of events. Following the expulsion from Sutri, 'at length after many injuries, tribulations and exiles [Bonizo] was received by the catholics of Piacenza as their bishop'.[248] Three papal letters of April–June 1088 reveal the attitude of the new pope, Urban II, to the election in Piacenza. To his legate Cardinal Herman Urban II wrote that 'the bishop of Sutri' had not been elected 'by the whole of the church [of Piacenza] nor by the better clergy or laity', that is, the cathedral clergy and the nobility. He should 'remain in the bishopric of Piacenza' if he could do so 'canonically and in peace'. The correspondent 'M' – perhaps the archbishop of Milan – was instructed to enthrone Bonizo as bishop, if unanimous support for him was attainable in Piacenza. The pope described Bonizo as 'the bishop of Sutri, who is said to have laboured much in the Church', an assessment that

245 Donizo of Canossa, *Vita Mathildis comitissae* II, p. 385.
246 A. Overmann (1895) p. 153.
247 Benzo, *Ad Heinricum IV* I.21, p. 160.
248 Bernold, *Chronicon* 1089, p. 449.

is, as Ernst Perels wrote, 'somewhat cool'.[249] Urban's letter to Bonizo himself shows 'extreme reservations' about his cause. 'We have heard ... that very many, both clerks and laymen, disagree with your election to the bishopric of Piacenza and conspired against you.'[250]

The culmination of the conflict between Bonizo's adherents and opponents in Piacenza is reported in Bernold's annal for 1089. Bonizo 'was deprived of his eyes and maimed in almost all his limbs by the schismatics of that place and was crowned with martyrdom'.[251] Bernold believed that Bonizo had died as a result of this attack, but there is evidence, however, that Bernold's information was inaccurate. First, a fifteenth-century chronicle of the bishops of Piacenza, in its garbled account of Bonizo's career, records that 'he was blinded by the people of Piacenza; ... he was shamefully expelled and went to Cremona, where he died on 14 July and was buried in the church of S. Lorenzo'.[252] Second, the metrical biography of Anselm II of Lucca composed in the mid-1090s by his successor, Rangerius, seems to contain evidence of Bonizo's survival after the attack of 1089. Recording his presence at the funeral of Anselm in March 1086, the author described his past and future injuries: 'already suffering many things, expelled from the city of Sutri and wretched from his long exile for the sake of the faith, but not yet with a mutilated tongue, not yet without his sight and not yet lacking his nostrils and his two ears'.[253] This passage, more precise in its details of Bonizo's injuries than Bernold's account, envisages a maimed survivor of the attack of 1089, a living martyr whom Rangerius had himself seen.[254]

Third, a number of passages in Bonizo's canonical collection *Liber de vita christiana* have been interpreted as referring to his experiences in

249 Urban II, *JL* 5355–6, ed. P. Ewald, *Neues Archiv* 5 (1880), 353–4. Cf. *Italia Pontificia* 5, 448. See E. Perels, edition p. XIII n. 7.

250 Urban II, *JL* 5354, ed. P. Ewald, *Neues Archiv* 5 (1880), 353. See P. Fournier (1915) p. 292; so also W. Berschin (1972) p. 12.

251 Bernold, *Chronicon* 1089, p. 449.

252 Fabricius de Marliano, *Chronica*, ed. L. A. Muratori, *Rerum Italicarum Scriptores* 16, 630–1. See W. Berschin (1972) p. 13.

253 Rangerius, *Vita metrica* p. 1299.

254 P. Fournier (1915) p. 272; E. Perels, edition p. XIV; G. Miccoli (1970) pp. 248–9; W. Berschin (1972) p. 13 n. 45. His enemies in Piacenza treated Bonizo as the Milanese had treated the Patarine priest Liutprand in 1075 (Bonizo, *Book to a Friend* VII, p. 230). In this case the victim survived until 1113 (Landulf, *Historia Mediolanensis* c. 3, 35, 36, pp. 21–2, 35).

1089.[255] He wrote of the exemption from fasting of 'the crippled and weak, among whom I am numbered'. He wrote of the bishop's duty to his flock: 'Shall we not fight for the sheep entrusted to us even to the point of chains and prisons, to ridicule and scorn and, if necessary, even to the maiming of limbs and death?'[256] The most significant of his personal references in the *Liber de vita christiana* is to his polemic, no longer extant, against Hugh Candidus, cardinal priest of S. Clemente, who had rebelled against Gregory VII and joined the party of the antipope. 'Whoever wishes to know of the deeds of Pope Urban and his victory, should read the book that I wrote against the schismatic Hugh and he will find there what he wants fully and clearly explained.'[257] The 'victory' of Urban II reported in this lost polemic cannot be identified with certainty. Perhaps Bonizo referred to Urban's triumphant entry into Rome on 3 July 1089.[258] By 1091, however, Wibert was again master of Rome. If Bonizo's reference was to Urban II's decisive victory in the schism, it is necessary to relate it to an event like Urban's taking up residence in the Lateran palace in March 1094.[259] Even if the earlier date of 1089 is adopted for the 'victory' of Urban II, it is clear that Bonizo must have survived the mutilation in Piacenza by at least one or two years: long enough, that is, to compose the polemic against Hugh and then to compile the *Liber de vita christiana* with its reference to that polemic. The year of Bonizo's death may indeed have been as late as 1094.[260]

The only reference to Bonizo as an author in the century after his death occurs in the work of a south German bibliographer *c.* 1170, who

---

255 P. Fournier (1915) p. 274; E. Perels, edition p. XV; W. Berschin (1972) p. 14.

256 Bonizo, *Liber de vita christiana* V.80, p. 206; III.110, pp. 108–9. Cf. II.37, p. 50, on the subject of 'support for a fellow bishop expelled from his see for the sake of the catholic faith'.

257 *Ibid.*, IV.45, p. 133. Cf. Bonizo, *Libellus de sacramentis* ed. W. Berschin (1972) p. 151: 'the book that I wrote against the schismatic Hugh'. See F. Lerner (1931) pp. 4–6, 7, 12–14, 16–18, 34–7, 39, 42–3, 49–51, 59, 62–3; R. Hüls (1977) pp. 111, 158–60. Hugh was also a polemical target of the *Book to a Friend* see below p. 55.

258 Bernold, *Chronicon* 1089, pp. 449–50. See G. Meyer von Knonau (1903) pp. 269–70; A. Becker (1964) p. 102; J. Ziese (1982) p. 181.

259 G. Meyer von Knonau (1903) pp. 421–2.

260 W. Berschin (1972) p. 18 n. 68 argued for 1094 on the basis of the history of the bishops of Piacenza produced by Fabricius de Marliano in 1476 (see above n. 252). P. Fournier (1915) p. 270 made 1095 the *terminus ad quem* for Bonizo's death on the grounds that none of his writings shows knowledge of Urban II's councils of 1095, which ruled on a number of issues of particular interest to Bonizo. See also G. Miccoli (1970) p. 249.

remembered him as a Gregorian canonist. 'Bonizo of Sutri wrote excerpts from the canons in the time of Gregory VII'.[261] Our knowledge of Bonizo's writings is based on a narrow range of twelfth-century manuscripts, mainly Italian in origin. The *Liber de vita christiana* was the most widely disseminated of his writings, surviving in five twelfth-century Italian codices.[262] The treatise on marriage survives only in the Mantua codex of the canonical collection.[263] The treatise on the sacraments is found in three twelfth-century codices also containing the canonical collection and additionally in two fifteenth-century codices from Milan.[264] Bonizo's theological work, *Paradisus*, survives in a twelfth-century codex from northern Italy and in a fifteenth-century copy of this codex.[265] Three short pieces survive each in a single twelfth-century codex.[266] Bonizo's most famous work, the *Book to a Friend*, is found only in one mid-twelfth-century codex, probably south German in origin. The work was, however, known to at least four twelfth-century authors.[267]

The Book that is entitled 'to a Friend' was certainly written before the *Liber de vita christiana*, since the latter contains a detailed synopsis of the contents of the last five books of the *Book to a Friend*. 'If anyone wishes to know about the Tusculan Theophylact [Benedict IX], how the priest John sold the papacy and how at one and the same time Theophylact, Gregory [VI] and Silvester [III] did not so much govern as lay waste the Roman papacy and how King Henry [III], son of Conrad [II], freed the Roman church from such plagues, let

---

261 Anonymus Mellicensis [Wolfger of Prüfening?], *De scriptoribus ecclesiasticis* c. 112, p. 95 (an allusion to *Liber de vita christiana*).

262 E. Perels, introduction pp. XLV–LX; G. Miccoli (1966b) pp. 371–98; W. Berschin (1972) pp. 57–9; I. S. Robinson (1973b) pp. 135–9.

263 *De arbore parentele*, edited G. Miccoli (1966b). pp. 390–8. See also W. Berschin (1972) pp. 81–5; W. Berschin (1987) pp. 281–9.

264 *Libellus de sacramentis*, edited W. Berschin (1972), pp. 147–60. See also *ibid.*, pp. 78–81; G. Miccoli (1966b) p. 378; I. S. Robinson (1973b) pp. 135–6.

265 A collection of more than 300 sentences from Augustine's works, derived from the sixth-century compilation of Eugippius: see W. Berschin (1972) pp. 34–8, 119–46.

266 A sermon on penitence: W. Berschin (1972) pp. 91–3, 161–5. A letter about a fugitive monk: H. Haskins (1929) p. 77; W. Berschin (1972) p. 94. A *sententia* on lay investiture: H. Weisweiler (1938) pp. 251–2; W. Berschin (1972) p. 76.

267 On the codex see I. S. Robinson (1978c) p. 303. Rangerius of Lucca used Bonizo's work in his *Vita metrica* (see *MGH SS* 30/2, 1154 and n. 18), as did Donizo of Canossa in his *Vita Mathildis comitissae* (see below n. 300) and Paul of Bernried in his *Life of Gregory VII* (see below p. 75). On the use of the work by Boso, cardinal deacon of SS. Cosma e Damiano in his papal biographies see W. Berschin (1972) pp. 97–9.

him read the book that I composed, which is entitled *To a Friend*, and there he will find these matters set down in an orderly manner. He will also find there explained most clearly, however, how Pope Clement [II] was elected and how King Henry was consecrated emperor by him; and how many days his successor Damasus [II] survived in the papal office; and what the famous Leo [IX] did in the papal office and how he ended his life; and what his successor Victor [II] did or what novelty happened in his time; and how in the time of Stephen [IX], the brother of Duke Godfrey, the Pataria originated in Milan; and the conflict of Pope Nicholas [II] with the intruder Benedict [X] and what he did in the papal office; and the conflict of Pope Alexander [II] with Cadalus of Parma and his victory and what he did in the papal office and his death; and the election of Gregory VII and his life and character and how at the Lord's Nativity he was captured at the altar of St Mary by the cruel man Cencius and by God's grace freed on the same day; and the attack that he suffered from Emperor Henry [IV] and the quarrel that he had with Wibert [of Ravenna] and the assaults that he suffered; and the siege of the city and how he was freed by Robert, duke of the Normans and how he had a blessed and peaceful end.'[268] The death of Gregory VII on 25 May 1085 is the latest event recorded in the *Book to a Friend* that can be precisely dated. Bonizo added, however, that 'God continues to perform many thousands of miracles at [Gregory's] tomb to the present day', a report, cannot have been written immediately after Gregory's death. The work was, therefore, probably composed late in 1085 or in the first half of 1086.[269] Bonizo's *Book to a Friend* was part of the flurry of polemical activity in 1085–6 that centred on the character and actions of the deceased pope.[270]

Bonizo's purpose was to answer two questions put to him by the unnamed 'friend' of the title, who is addressed directly in the opening paragraph and again in the peroration of the work. 'Why in this time of calamity [is] mother Church … oppressed and is not set free? Why do the sons of obedience and peace lie prostrate, while the sons of Belial rejoice with their king… ?' Why is it that in 1085 the supporters of Gregory VII have been defeated, while Henry IV and his adherents are victorious? 'There is also a second question …: whether

268 Bonizo, *Liber de vita christiana* IV.45, pp. 132–3.

269 Bonizo, *Book to a Friend* IX, below p. 252. See E. Dümmler in *MGH Libelli* 1, 569 and n. 3; E. Perels, edition p. XVII; G. Miccoli (1970) pp. 247, 249.

270 C. Mirbt (1894) p. 82; I. S. Robinson (1978a) pp. 10–11.

it was and is lawful for a Christian to engage in an armed struggle for the sake of the faith.'[271] These were questions of particular relevance in the ambience in which this work was composed, the court of Margravine Matilda of Tuscany. This 'safe haven for catholics' sheltered other intellectuals who wrote about the conflict of the Gregorians and the Henricians in terms reminiscent of the *Book to a Friend*. Matilda's protégé Heribert, bishop of Reggio in Emilia, wrote about the crisis: 'What was Nero, what was Diocletian, what finally is [Henry] who at this time persecutes the Church: surely they are all the gates of hell?'[272] John of Mantua, in a work dedicated to Matilda, defended the legality of the 'armed struggle for the sake of the faith'. He urged the margravine to 'exercise vengeance with the material sword on the heresy that is springing up and subverting the greater part of the world'.[273] Bonizo's polemic similarly commends Matilda for her determination 'to oppose the heresy that now rages in the Church in every way, as far as her strength permits'.[274]

The most influential of the intellectuals at Matilda's court was Bishop Anselm II of Lucca, her spiritual adviser and Bonizo's admired colleague. Like Bonizo, Anselm was both the compiler of a canonical collection and a polemicist in the Gregorian cause, his unrelenting hostility towards Henry IV and his antipope appearing even in his commentary on the Psalms.[275] As Gregory VII's permanent legate in Lombardy, Anselm was also one of the leaders of the military resistance to the emperor and the antipope. This is how he is portrayed in the metrical biography by his successor, Rangerius of Lucca, another of the intellectuals in Matilda's circle. Anselm urged the margravine's knights to emulate Judas Maccabeus in their campaigns against the emperor. During the battle of Sorbara (2 July 1084) he raised the morale of her army through his prayers and exhortations.[276] Anselm's letter to King William I of England (*circa* 1085) shows him seeking military support for the beleaguered Gregory VII, requesting him 'to come to [the Roman church] so that you may speedily rescue her

271 Bonizo, *Book to a Friend* I, below p. 158. Cf. IX, p. 257.

272 Heribert, *Expositio in VII psalmos poenitentiales*, MPL 79, col. 626D. For the attribution see A. Mercati (1914) pp. 250–7. Heribert owed his bishopric to Matilda's intervention: Bernold, *Chronicon* 1085, p. 443. See G. Schwartz (1913) p. 198.

273 John of Mantua, *In Cantica Canticorum* p. 52. See B. Bischoff (1948) pp. 24–48.

274 Bonizo, *Book to a Friend* IX, below p. 261.

275 Anselm, *Tractatus psalmorum*, extant only in excerpts in Paul of Bernried, *Life of Gregory VII* c. 112, below pp. 355–6.

276 Rangerius, *Vita metrica* pp. 1234, 1292, 1293. See C. Erdmann (1935) p. 224.

from the hands of strangers'.[277] Books XII and XIII of Anselm's *Collectio canonum* and his polemic against the imperial antipope provided the theoretical justification for this warfare in defence of the Gregorian papacy. As Carl Erdmann observed, Anselm was 'the first canonist to give detailed consideration to the problem of ecclesiastical coercion and of war'.[278] Bonizo's *Book to a Friend* cites some of the canonical 'authorities' that Anselm used to defend the right of the Church to make war on her enemies.[279]

Anselm's *Book against Wibert* was intended to refute the arguments presented by the antipope Wibert of Ravenna in a letter to Anselm, no longer extant. Wibert's arguments can be partially reconstructed from Anselm's refutation and from the writings of Wibert's circle, which deny the legality of the war waged by Gregory VII's allies against the emperor. The antipope's supporter Bishop Wido of Ferrara emphasised the war guilt of Gregory VII: 'what Christian ever caused so many wars and killed so many men?' According to Wido, 'the role of Christian men is to teach, not to wage wars, to suffer with equanimity the injuries inflicted by others, not to avenge them. We do not read that Jesus or any of the saints did such a thing.'[280] In similar vein the antipope himself in his encyclical of 1091/2 brooded on 'how great [was] the shedding of human blood in the Italian and German kingdoms occasioned by [the Gregorians'] preaching'. Wibert promised to resort only 'to the arms that the Fathers used in defence of the Christian faith', namely synodal decrees.[281] In the lost letter to Anselm Wibert evidently accused him of indoctrinating Matilda of Tuscany with the Gregorians' false teaching concerning Christian warfare. 'You beseech me in Jesus's name,' rejoined Anselm, 'no longer to deceive, delude and dupe the most noble of women; but I call on God as my witness that ... she does not, as you claim, waste her possessions in vain, but rather lays up for herself an unfailing

277 Anselm, letter, in: *MGH Briefe der deutschen Kaiserzeit* 5, 17.

278 C. Erdmann (1935) p. 225. See also I. S. Robinson (1973a) pp. 186–8; K. G. Cushing (1995) pp. 353–71; K. G. Cushing (1998) pp. 122–41.

279 Bonizo seems not to have drawn his 'authorities' directly from Anselm's writings: the two canonists probably used a common source. See E. Perels, edition p. XXX; W. Berschin (1972) pp. 43–4, 53–7, 73–4.

280 Wido of Ferrara, *De scismate Hildebrandi* I.15, p. 545. Cf. II, pp. 554–6. On Wido's polemic as evidence of the views of Wibert's circle see C. Erdmann (1935) pp. 240–1; K. Jordan (1954) pp. 159–64.

281 Wibert, *Decretum Clementis papae* pp. 625, 622. For the date of this encyclical (*JL* 5329–30) see J. Ziese (1982) pp. 191–2.

treasure in heaven.' She was 'prepared not only to sacrifice all earthly considerations for the sake of defending righteousness but also to struggle even to the shedding of her own blood to bring about your confusion and for the sake of reverence for the glory and exaltation of holy Church, until the Lord delivers His enemy into the hands of a woman'.[282] This eulogy of Matilda seems to be echoed in Bonizo's *Book to a Friend*, where 'the knights of God' are exhorted to 'struggle for righteousness', following the example of 'the most excellent Countess Matilda'. She, 'neglecting all worldly considerations, is prepared to die rather than to break the law of God and to oppose the heresy that now rages in the Church in every way, as far as her strength permits. For we believe that it is into her hands that Sisera is sold.'[283]

In Henrician circles Matilda of Tuscany was portrayed as the most notorious exponent of the Gregorian concept of Christian warfare. 'Matilda, the protectress of Pope Hildebrand was inured by his secret conversations so that she is now impossible to restrain, animated by female passions so that she prefers war to peace'.[284] The polemicist Sigebert of Gembloux in 1103 denounced the Gregorian doctrine of Christian warfare, tracing its beginnings to the relations of Gregory VII and Matilda of Tuscany. 'It was Pope Hildebrand alone who originally laid his hands upon the sacred canons. Of him we read that he commanded Margravine Matilda for the remission of her sins to make war on Emperor Henry.'[285] Sigebert's claim is corroborated by the two anonymous biographies of Anselm II of Lucca. According to the earlier *Life of Anselm*, 'it was granted to [Matilda] in remission that, like another Deborah, she should judge the people, practise warfare and resist the heretics and schismatics'. The later *Life of Anselm* revised this passage: 'Matilda surrendered herself totally to [Gregory VII's] direction, receiving from him this command in remission of her sins: that like another Deborah, she should judge the people, practise warfare and resist the heretics and schismatics'.[286] Although no record is found in Gregory VII's letters of such a command to Matilda, the

---

282 Anselm, *Liber contra Wibertum* p. 527. The biblical allusion is to Judith 16:7.

283 Bonizo, *Book to a Friend* IX, below p. 261. The Canaanite general Sisera (Judges 4:9) here represents Henry IV.

284 Anonymous polemicist of Hersfeld, *Liber de unitate ecclesiae conservanda* II.36, p. 263 (1093). See Z. Zafarana (1966a) p. 648; J. Ziese (1982) p. 201.

285 Sigebert, *Epistola Leodicensium* c. 13, p. 464. See C. Erdmann (1935) p. 245.

286 *Vita Anselmi episcopi Lucensis* c. 11, p. 16. The biblical allusion is to Judges 4:4. *Anselmi episcopi Lucensis Vitae primariae fragmenta*, MGH SS 20, 694.

pope certainly wrote in similar language about potential allies of Matilda among the German princes. Gregory wrote to German correspondents (March 1081) of Duke Welf IV of Bavaria: 'we desire to place him wholly in the bosom of St Peter and to summon him especially to his service. If you know that there is such an inclination in him or in other powerful men, led by the love of St Peter, for the absolution of their sins, exert yourselves so that they perform this.' Gregory VII sought to raise an army of 'knights of St Peter', offering his recruits 'remission of sins', anticipating the spiritual rewards of the crusaders.[287]

When Wibert of Ravenna, anxious to persuade Matilda of the errors of the Gregorians, attacked the idea of 'the knighthood of St Peter', his polemic was perhaps the more formidable because he was Matilda's kinsman.[288] His polemic may have been provoked by Matilda's victory at Sorbara (2 July 1084) over an army of Lombards recruited by Wibert himself for Henry IV.[289] Wibert's letter evidently contained canonical 'authorities' supporting the view that it is not lawful for Christians to take up arms in defence of the faith. 'You have not understood the sayings of the holy Fathers that you placed in your letter,' replied Anselm of Lucca, citing 'authorities' especially from the writings of Augustine justifying the use of coercion against heretics.[290] Anselm's purpose was to ensure Matilda's continued loyalty to his party by convincing her that the Gregorian doctrine of Christian warfare conformed to Christian tradition. Bonizo's *Book to a Friend* was similarly composed to stifle any doubts raised by Wibert's letter in Matilda's entourage. Bonizo intended to prove from Scripture, from canon law, patristic writings and especially from Christian history that 'if it was ever lawful for a Christian to make war for any cause, it is lawful to make war by every means on the Wibertines'.[291]

Matilda and her dynasty play a central role in the narrative of the *Book to a Friend*. Book IV introduces Matilda's ancestor Count Adalbert Atto II of Canossa and her paternal grandfather Tedald, margrave of Canossa, to whom Bonizo attributed the successes in Italy respectively

287 Gregory VII, *Registrum* IX.3, p. 574. See C. Erdmann (1935) pp. 185–202.

288 J. Ziese (1982) pp. 4, 13–14.

289 G. Meyer von Knonau (1900) pp. 565–6; T. Struve (1995) p. 65.

290 Anselm, *Liber contra Wibertum* p. 525. C. Erdmann (1935) pp. 228–9; E. Pasztor (1987) pp. 375–421; K. G. Cushing (1998) pp. 223–4.

291 Bonizo, *Book to a Friend* IX, below p. 257.

of Otto I and Henry II.[292] In Book V appears 'the excellent duke
Boniface', 'the glorious duke and margrave', Matilda's father Boniface
of Canossa, margrave of Tuscany.[293] Matilda's mother 'the excellent
duchess Beatrice', 'the most blessed Beatrice' is portrayed in Book VI
as the heroine of the schism of the antipope Cadalus of Parma.[294]
Matilda's stepfather Godfrey 'the Bearded' of Verdun, margrave of
Tuscany is accorded special prominence as the assiduous defender of
the papacy and brother of 'the blessed Pope Stephen [IX]'.[295] Matilda's
role in the *Book to a Friend* is first apparent in Bonizo's account of the
defence of the Campagna against the prince of Capua (1067). 'The most
excellent Countess Matilda' participated in the successful expedition
of her stepfather, whom Archdeacon Hildebrand had 'summoned to
the aid of St Peter'. Bonizo used this opportunity to emphasise the
importance of Matilda to the Gregorian papacy. 'This was the first
service that the most excellent daughter of Boniface offered to the
blessed prince of the apostles. Not long afterwards as a result of many
services pleasing to God she deserved to be called the daughter of St
Peter.'[296] (This was the title with which Gregory VII addressed Matilda
and her mother Beatrice in his letters of 1073–4).[297] Matilda also
appears in the final exhortation of the work: 'Let the most glorious
knights of God ... endeavour to equal in goodness the most excellent
Countess Matilda, the daughter of St Peter.'[298]

It is not surprising, therefore, that two thirteenth-century historians
described the *Book to a Friend* as 'the book of Bonizo ... that he sent
to Countess Matilda' and 'the book that [Bonizo] wrote to Countess
Matilda'.[299] The former description perhaps suggests that this reader
had seen a copy of the *Book to a Friend* that once belonged to Matilda
of Tuscany. The presence of the work in Matilda's circle is also

292 *Ibid.*, IV, pp. 177, 180.

293 *Ibid.*, V, pp. 189, 194.

294 *Ibid.*, VII, pp. 221, 232; *Ibid.*, VI, p. 207.

295 *Ibid.*, V, p. 194; VI, p. 215; VII, p. 221.

296 *Ibid.*, VI, p. 216. No other eleventh-century account of this expedition mentions
Matilda's participation: see G. Meyer von Knonau (1890) pp. 543–7.

297 Gregory VII, *Registrum* I.11, 47, II.9, pp. 18, 73, 139. The title was also used by
Bernold, *Chronicon* 1093, 1097, pp. 455, 463, together with the title 'knight of St
Peter' (1085, 1093, pp. 443, 456).

298 Bonizo, *Book to a Friend* IX, below p. 261.

299 Jacobus de Voragine, *Legenda Aurea* and *Sermo III de sancta Trinitate*; Ricobald of
Ferrara, *Historia imperatorum*, cited by P. Jaffé in his edition p. 584, E. Dümmler in
his edition p. 570 and W. Berschin (1972) pp. 96–7.

indicated by the use made of it by her biographer Donizo, monk of S. Apollonio di Canossa.[300] Was Bonizo's work, therefore, composed specifically for Matilda? P. Jaffé (1865) concluded: 'The "friend" [in Bonizo's title] is a mere artifice, since it is abundantly clear that the book was written only for the sake of Countess Matilda.'[301] Jaffé's conclusion has generally been rejected, although there is perhaps some support for it in the only manuscript of the *Book to a Friend*.[302] Bonizo said no more of his 'friend' than that he was 'the sole protection from the trouble that has encompassed me'. This description suggests that the 'friend' was a layman who had supported or sheltered him at some moment of adversity before 1085/6.[303] W. von Giesebrecht looked for the 'friend' among the vassals of Matilda of Tuscany.[304] Perhaps the occasion for the composition of Bonizo's work was dissension among Matilda's vassals or the doubts of a prominent vassal about the legality of Matilda's rebellion against the emperor. Bonizo described two instances of such dissension, in 1075 and 1080.[305] It is possible that fears of another desertion in the months following Gregory VII's death prompted Bonizo to write the work ending with an appeal to 'the most glorious knights of God' to imitate Matilda in fighting against the enemies of the Gregorian party.

'When you previously asked me, dearest friend,' wrote Bonizo, 'whether it is lawful for a Christian to fight with weapons for the truth, you were requesting a history.'[306] Bonizo summarised the sources of his *hystoria* as 'the documents of the holy Fathers' and 'examples of those who fought for the truth'.[307] These were the basic materials of an

300 On the *Book* as a source of Donizo's work see A. Pannenborg (1872) pp. 19–22.

301 P. Jaffé, edition p. 584.

302 H. Saur (1868) p. 426; A. Pannenborg (1872) p. 19; E. Dümmler, edition pp. 569–70; W. Berschin (1972) p. 11 n. 35. But see also H. Lehmgrübner (1887) p. 143. The text in the codex Munich lat. 618 is followed by an anonymous polemic, composed between 1080 and 1100 for an unnamed 'most illustrious man' and his 'most noble consort'. Perhaps these persons were Matilda and her second husband Welf V of Bavaria: see I. S. Robinson (1978c) pp. 311–16.

303 Bonizo, *Book to a Friend* I, below p. 158. (The allusion is to Psalm 31:7.) Cf. H. Lehmgrübner (1887) p. 143.

304 W. von Giesebrecht in *MGH Libelli* 1, 630. H. Saur (1868) p. 426 n. 5 identified the 'friend' as 'Dodo, a young man of excellent character and a citizen of Cremona' mentioned by Bonizo, *Book to a Friend* VII, p. 224. Cf. W. Berschin (1972) p. 10: 'the friend' 'is to be sought among the knights of Cremona'.

305 Bonizo, *Book to a Friend* VII, IX, below pp. 227, 246. In 1083 many of Matilda's vassals again deserted her: see A. Overmann (1895) p. 150.

306 Bonizo, *Book to a Friend* IX, below p. 257.

307 *Ibid.*, p. 260.

eleventh-century polemical work: 'authorities' *(auctoritates)* and 'examples' *(exempla)*. 'Authorities' were passages quoted from canon law or patristic writings; 'examples' were case-studies from ancient and modern history.[308] Bonizo's 'examples of those who fought for the truth' included, from the earlier history of the Church, the citizens of Constantinople who defended their patriarch and Jovian and Valentinian, who resisted the pagan policies of Emperor Julian.[309] To these Bonizo added 'examples' from 'our own times': 'the men who fought against the Normans under the leadership of Pope Leo [IX]' and died at Civitate (June 1053) and two of Gregory VII's allies, the Milanese Patarine leader Herlembald, killed by his political opponents, and the Roman prefect Cencius, murdered by a personal enemy in Rome.[310] Bonizo regarded them as Christian martyrs: God 'crowned them with glory and honour and proved by signs and wonders that they had pleased Him'.[311] Bonizo undoubtedly reflected the opinion of Gregory VII, who in 1078 announced to the Roman synod of Lent the miracles at the tombs of Herlembald and the prefect Cencius and thus canonised these Gregorian allies.[312]

Bonizo's 'examples of those who fought for the truth' also served to answer that other question from his friend that had inspired the *Book to a Friend*. 'Why do the sons of obedience and peace lie prostrate, while the sons of Belial rejoice with their king, especially since [God] who orders all things is also He who judges in equity?'[313] Why did God permit Gregory VII to die in exile, while allowing Henry IV to capture Rome and set up Wibert of Ravenna as his antipope? This, the Henrician party claimed, was a divine judgement on the Gregorian papacy. Eleventh-century authors were accustomed to interpret success and failure as the consequence of divine intervention and in particular to regard battles as large-scale trials by combat in which divine judgement determined the outcome.[314] Henry IV's propaganda exploited this theme. Of his capture of Rome (March 1084) he wrote:

308 On the Gregorian conception of 'authorities': H. Fuhrmann (1973) pp. 175–203. On *exempla*: H. Liebeschütz (1950) pp. 67–8; H.-W. Goetz (1987) pp. 31–69.

309 Bonizo, *Book to a Friend* II, below pp. 164–5.

310 *Ibid.*, V, IX, pp. 193, 260; VII, IX, pp. 230, 261; VIII, IX, pp. 243, 261.

311 *Ibid.*, IX, pp. 260–1.

312 Berthold, *Annales* 1077, p. 305. See C. Erdmann (1935) pp. 130, 155, 197–8; H. E. J. Cowdrey (1985) p. 48; H. E. J. Cowdrey (1998) pp. 284, 328, 651.

313 Bonizo, *Book to a Friend* I, p. 158.

314 Cf. K.-G. Cram (1955) pp. 5–19.

'If our predecessors had achieved with ten thousand men what the
Lord has performed for us in Rome with, so to speak, only ten men, it
would have been regarded as a miracle.'[315] The death of his rival, the
anti-king Rudolf, was similarly interpreted as a divine judgement:
'The Lord has destroyed our vassal, the oath-breaker whom [Hilde-
brand] set up as king over us.'[316] The extent to which intellectuals
accepted this interpretation of events is apparent from the reaction of
Archbishop Lanfranc of Canterbury to Henry IV's success in Rome. 'I
believe that the glorious emperor did not attempt so great an enterprise without a good reason and that he could not have gained so
great a victory without great assistance from God.'[317]

This conventional interpretation of military victory can also be found
in the *Book to a Friend*. Bonizo wrote of Henry IV's victory over the
Saxons at Homburg (9 June 1075) that 'God [was] the author of his
success'. Henry, however, had not recognised the divine source of his
victory: 'he did not ... offer God thanks for the victory that He had
conferred, but his heart was lifted up and his eyes were raised too
high.' Arrogantly trusting in his own power, he chose to attack the
pope.[318] Bonizo's portrait of Henry IV, like that of Gregory VII, was
coloured by the Old Testament 'example' of King Saul (I Samuel
15:1–35). When after his victory over the Amalekites Saul failed to
obey the divine command, he was rejected by God and His prophet
Samuel. Victory undoubtedly came from God but, Bonizo explained,
God did not invariably grant victory to the righteous side. Hence
Bonizo's account of the defeat of Leo IX at Civitate (June 1053):
'Because God's purposes are like the great deep (Psalm 35:7), it
happened that by the ineffable providence of God, when battle was
joined, the Normans were victorious.'[319] For Bonizo the case-study of
this defeat, which so perturbed eleventh-century commentators,[320]
was of particular relevance to the question asked by his 'friend': 'why
... is [mother Church] oppressed and is not set free?' The answer

---

315 Henry IV, *Letter* 18, p. 27.

316 *Ibid.*, 17, p. 25.

317 Lanfranc, *Letter* 52, pp. 164–5.

318 Bonizo, *Book to a Friend* VII, p. 233.

319 Bonizo, *Book to a Friend* V, below p. 193. On the significance of Psalm 35:7 see K.-
U. Cram (1955) p. 5.

320 Cf. especially Peter Damian, *Letter* 87, p. 514; Herman of Reichenau, *Chronicon*
1053, p. 132. See C. Erdmann (1935) pp. 112, 131; I. S. Robinson (1978a) pp. 98–
9 and above pp. 8–9 and below pp. 94, 383–4.

was that 'the ineffable providence of God' had determined that 'sometimes [the Church] flourishes and sometimes she is diminished'.[321] In the case of Leo IX's defeat, all that the 'friend' needed to know was that 'God showed by signs and miracles that those who had fallen in battle fighting for righteousness had greatly pleased Him, giving great assurance to those who fought for righteousness thereafter, when He deigned to number them among the saints'.[322]

The 'examples' of the Patarine leader Herlembald and the Roman prefect Cencius were intended to convey the same message. Both were Gregorian heroes whose careers were violently cut short by enemies of the papal reform movement. The murder of Herlembald, 'the mighty soldier of God' (April 1075), meant the end of the Milanese reform movement of which he was the leader; but 'at his tomb God performs great miracles even to this day'.[323] Cencius, 'that most Christian man', was the most important ally of the reform papacy in Rome, whose murder was 'an irreparable loss' for the Gregorians. Bonizo, however, insisted that his was a success story: 'God performed many miracles through him'.[324] Another heroic failure among Gregory VII's allies was the anti-king Rudolf, elected king by the German enemies of Henry IV. Describing his death at the battle of Hohenmölsen (15 October 1080), Bonizo used the same scriptural text, Psalm 35:7, that he had applied to Leo IX's defeat. 'Because the Lord's purposes are like the great deep, by the ineffable providence of God Henry did not receive the scourges of the Lord according to his deserts, but as success, which added pride to his iniquity.' Like Saul, blind to his real situation, Henry IV rushed to his doom: 'not recognising the stratagems of Satan, he believed that his sin had pleased God.' His successes were illusory, for 'although he was not deposed in human eyes, he was nevertheless deposed before the eyes of God'.[325] By the same token Gregory VII was not truly defeated. Like his faithful supporters Herlembald and Cencius, he had won the crown of martyrdom and 'reigns with Peter in heaven'.[326]

---

321 Bonizo, *Book to a Friend* I, p. 158.

322 *Ibid.*, V, p. 193. Bruno, *Sermon concerning Simoniacs* c. 5, below p. 384 made Bonizo's message more explicit.

323 Bonizo, *Book to a Friend* VI, VII, below pp. 215, 229–30.

324 *Ibid.*, VIII, p. 243.

325 *Ibid.*, VIII, pp. 247–8; IX, p. 256.

326 *Ibid.*, IX, p. 252.

Bonizo placed the conflict between Gregory VII and Henry IV in the framework of a universal history, which he presented as a continuous struggle between 'the sons of obedience and peace' and 'the sons of Belial'. He concluded that it is only in heaven that the Church is permanently free 'and is not in slavery with her children' (Galatians 4:25). On earth the Church 'sometimes enjoys the greatest freedom and sometimes is oppressed; sometimes she flourishes and sometimes she is diminished'.[327] Bonizo's universal history begins with Genesis, interpreted according to the allegorical sense of Scripture.[328] From the contrasting figures of the two sons of Abraham, Isaac, son of a free woman, and Ishmael, son of a slave, Bonizo concluded that throughout history there are 'two peoples, one of the catholics, the other of the heretics', the latter incessantly persecuting the former. From the contrasting 'examples' of the expulsion of Ishmael's mother Hagar by Isaac's mother Sarah (Genesis 21:10), and the unjust treatment of Isaac by 'foreigners' (Genesis 26:20–1), Bonizo deduced that there were two types of persecution. 'Persecution that is inflicted on us by those who are outside [the Church] must be overcome by patient endurance, while persecution inflicted by those who are within ... must be fought with all our strength and weapons.' This distinction between the two types of persecution was Bonizo's answer to the complaint of Wibert of Ravenna, in his letter to Anselm II of Lucca, that the Gregorian doctrine of 'Christian warfare' ran counter to the authentic Christian teaching concerning violence. Christians must patiently suffer the 'persecution inflicted by those who are outside', in the manner of the martyrs of the early Church in the reigns of the pagan Roman emperors. The 'persecution' inflicted by 'those who are within' – that is, by Christian heretics and schismatics, like Henry IV and Wibert himself – could legitimately be met with force.[329]

That 'persecution from within' had culminated in the council of Brixen (June 1080), where Wibert was elected as Henry IV's antipope, to be enthroned four years later when Henry captured Rome. The council of Brixen casts a long shadow over the Book to a Friend. Bonizo inserted in his account of the central event in his history, the election of Gregory VII as pope (22 April 1073) a contrast between

327 *Ibid.*, I, p. 158.

328 On the allegorical sense of the Bible see B. Smalley (1952) pp. 1–26.

329 Bonizo, *Book to a Friend* I, p. 159. Bonizo forgot this distinction when in II, p. 164, he commended those Christians who 'openly resisted the insanity' of Emperor Julian the Apostate.

this lawful papal election and the illicit election of Wibert seven years later. Gregory was 'enthroned unwillingly in St Peter ad Vincula – not in Brixen'.[330] Bonizo reserved his fiercest vituperation for the two churchmen most prominent at Brixen: the antipope himself and Hugh Candidus, cardinal priest of S. Clemente, the only member of the Roman clergy to subscribe the conciliar decree of Brixen. Bonizo wrote that Hugh's 'actions were like his eyes: he was cross-eyed and his deeds were of the same twisted nature'.[331] Wibert was 'the pernicious man', 'the three-bodied chimera', 'the beast' (of Revelation 13:1– 8).[332] An accusation in the Brixen decree that preoccupied Bonizo was that Gregory VII's accession in 1073 had violated the decree of Pope Nicholas II according to which, 'whoever presumes to become pope without the consent of the Roman prince should be regarded by all not as a pope but as an apostate'.[333] This was a reference to the Papal Election Decree, although the text used by the council of Brixen was not that of 1059 but a falsified version drawn up perhaps in 1076.[334] The Papal Election Decree consequently receives careful attention in the *Book to a Friend*, Bonizo's response being complicated by the fact that the version of the decree that he knew did not contain the 'royal paragraph', which referred to 'the honour and reverence due' to Henry IV. Bonizo assumed that the decree excluded all lay participation in the election of the pope.[335]

In the *Book to a Friend* the freedom of the papal election is taken as an important index of the relative freedom or oppression of the universal Church at different periods in its history. The devout emperors like Valentinian I (364–75) and Louis the Pious (813–40) legislated to free papal elections from secular interference.[336] This principle was violated

---

330 Bonizo, *Book to a Friend* VII, p. 220. Cf. IX, p. 247: 'So diabolical a deed was unheard of from the day on which the nations first began to exist until the present day.'

331 Bonizo, *Book to a Friend* VI, p. 205. Cf. pp. 191, 214, 253. Brixen decree: *Die Briefe Heinrichs IV.*, p. 72. Hugh supplied the council with its accusations against Gregory VII. See G. Meyer von Knonau (1900) p. 290; J. Vogel (1983) p. 218; I. S. Robinson (1999) p. 198.

332 Bonizo, *Book to a Friend* IX, pp. 249–51. Cf. pp. 227, 247, 256.

333 Brixen decree: *Die Briefe Heinrichs IV*, p. 71.

334 D. Jasper (1986) pp. 69–88. This version, unlike that of 1059, gave the king a role in the nomination of the candidate.

335 Bonizo, *Book to a Friend* VI, pp. 204, 210; IX, pp. 252–3. The version known to Bonizo appears in full in his *Liber de vita christiana* IV.87, p. 156. See also above p. 11 and H.-G. Krause (1956) pp. 188–98; W. Berschin (1972) pp. 49–50; R. Schieffer (1981) p. 75; D. Jasper (1986) pp. 64 n. 255, 76–8.

336 Bonizo, *Book to a Friend* II, III, pp. 169, 171.

in 998 by Emperor Otto III, whose intervention in the affairs of the papacy merited spectacular and exemplary divine punishment. The mutilation of the papal intruder John XVI 'so displeased God and St Peter, the blessed prince of the apostles, that [Otto III] hateful to God died within two months without receiving the last rites before he could receive consecration as emperor … and was interred in hell'. Otto III, who had already been crowned emperor two years before the mutilation of John XVI, in fact died almost four years after the incident.[337] The ferocity of Bonizo's polemic against Otto III, with its grim fiction of immediate divine revenge, is to be explained by the close parallels between that emperor's relations with the papacy and those of Henry IV. These parallels were strikingly obvious to the contemporary Henrician polemicist Benzo of Alba. He reminded Henry IV that 'Otto III, whose great deeds are proclaimed throughout the whole world, punished the criminal presumption of a certain false pope' and urged him to do the same to Gregory VII.[338] Bonizo intended the fate of Otto III to reassure his readers that Henry IV's current prosperity would not last long.

When imperial power in Rome declined, the Roman noble clans seized the opportunity to oppress the papacy, assigning to themselves 'the empty title of patrician'.[339] With this allusion to 'the empty title of patrician' Bonizo reached the heart of his attack on the council of Brixen; for the legal basis of the council's proceedings had been Henry IV's office of 'patrician of the Romans'. The title of patrician – originally the title of the Byzantine emperor's representative in Rome, from the mid-eighth-century the title conferred by the popes on their protectors the Frankish kings – was usurped at the end of the tenth century by the most powerful Roman families.[340] During the early eleventh century the Roman family of Tusculani controlled the city and the papacy 'under the empty title of the patriciate, so that they seemed to possess the papacy by hereditary right'.[341] In December 1046 King Henry III 'freed the city from the tyranny of the patricians'. Here was an imperial intervention which, unlike that of Otto III, was beneficial. In Bonizo's fictionalised version Henry III came to

337 *Ibid.*, IV, pp. 179–80. See T.E. Moehs (1972) pp. 58–65.

338 Benzo, *To Emperor Henry IV* VII.2, below p. 367.

339 Bonizo, *Book to a Friend* III, p. 174.

340 Cf. P.E. Schramm (1929) pp. 59–63, 229–36; K.-J. Herrmann (1973) pp. 1–24; H. Vollrath (1974) pp. 11–44; G. Martin (1994) pp. 257–95.

341 Bonizo, *Book to a Friend* V, p. 182; cf. III, p. 175.

Rome not on his own initiative but at the earnest invitation of the
Roman clergy. Nevertheless the conduct even of this 'most wise and
thoroughly Christian man' had a serious flaw, for 'he seized the
tyranny of the patriciate' since 'he believed that by means of the
patriciate he could appoint the Roman pontiff'.[342] Divine punishment
soon demonstrated that 'no emperor ... was permitted to involve himself in the election of any Roman pontiff. For when in 1047 he elected
Pope Damasus II, 'by means of the tyranny of the patriciate', his candidate 'was dead in body and soul before twice ten days had elapsed'.[343]

The election of his successor Leo IX restored freedom to the Roman
church. Bonizo gave a version of the story also found in the biography
of Leo IX: that Leo IX insisted on a free election by the Roman clergy
before accepting the papacy. In Bonizo's version, however, the principal figure is 'Hildebrand, beloved of God', the future Gregory VII,
who, encountering the pope-elect on his journey to Rome, convinced
him 'that he who strove to take possession of the papacy at the command of the emperor was not an apostle but an apostate'. Leo therefore laid down the papal insignia' and submitted himself to election in
Rome by 'the bishops and cardinals'.[344] During the minority of Henry
IV, however, there was a renewed attempt to oppress the Roman
church, initiated by the most stubborn opponents of the reform
papacy, the Lombard bishops, who in 1061 sought the election of one
of their number, Cadalus of Parma, as pope. 'They said that their lord
[Henry IV], as the heir to the kingdom, was likewise heir to the
patriciate.'[345] The election of Cadalus ('Honorius II') was, like that of
Wibert of Ravenna in 1080, legitimised by the office of patrician,
which Henry IV claimed to have inherited from Henry III. Bonizo
used the same language to describe both these elections of antipopes:
'an act of wickedness such as never has been since the day in which
the nations began to be' (Daniel 12:1), 'a papal election in which none
of the Roman clergy or laity was present'. In this crisis, however, the
papacy found a champion in Hildebrand, who informed the imperial
representative 'that according to the decrees of the holy Fathers, no

342 *Ibid.*, V, pp. 184, 187.

343 *Ibid.*, p. 189. Damasus II was elected in December 1047 and died in August 1048.

344 Bonizo, *Book to a Friend* V, p. 190. (Bonizo also ascribed a role to Hildebrand in
    the election of Victor II (1054): *ibid.*, p. 194.) Cf. *Life of Leo IX* II.4–5, below pp.
    130–2.

345 Bonizo, *Book to a Friend* VI, p. 206. The leader of the Lombard bishops was
    Bonizo's old enemy, Denis of Piacenza. See G. Meyer von Knonau (1890) pp. 216–
    17, 223–9; T. Schmidt (1977) pp. 104–14, 125–31; I. S. Robinson (1999) pp. 41–2.

role was granted to kings in the election of Roman pontiffs'.[346]

Bonizo's polemic against Henry IV's office of patrician is framed by a history of papal-imperial relations from a Gregorian viewpoint. The alternating phases of freedom and oppression in papal history are linked with the conduct of the contemporary emperors, as Bonizo explained in Book II. 'Whosoever of the princes of the Roman empire ruled according to the fear of God and the advice of the bishops and who above all obeyed the Roman pontiff …, as long as they lived, governed the commonwealth in profound peace and exchanged death for eternal life. Those who were disobedient, however, came to a bad end.'[347] Bonizo's subsequent narrative contrasted the good Carolingians, Charlemagne and Louis the Pious – who 'governed the kingdoms … through the prudence of the priesthood' – with their descendant, 'the pernicious Lothar'. King Lothar II was excommunicated and deposed because of his opposition to Pope Nicholas I. For Bonizo, as for other Gregorian polemicists, the punishment of Lothar II (whose conflict with Nicholas I was presented in a greatly distorted form) offered a clear precedent for the excommunication and deposition of Henry IV.[348] Among subsequent rulers, King Henry I and his son Emperor Otto I each resembled the model Christian emperor Constantine I in being 'a very great builder of God's churches and disseminator of the Christian religion'. Otto I and Otto II were punctilious in respecting the rights of the Roman church. Emperor Henry II 'granted many privileges and donated the most splendid gifts to the Roman church' and 'made the apostles his heirs'.[349]

The subordination of the emperors and all secular powers to the Roman church was, in Bonizo's historical perspective, the necessary precondition for the peace and freedom of the Church. That Bonizo was thoroughly acquainted with the Gregorian conception of the Roman primacy is evident from his canonical collection, *Liber de vita christiana*. Book IV, a treatise on 'the excellence of the Roman church' noted 'that the Roman church is the head of all the churches', 'that the Roman church has never erred from the path of truth' and 'may be judged by no one', 'that he who tries to diminish the dignity of the Roman church is proved to be a heretic'. Bonizo's work here reflected the themes of Gregory VII's memorandum on papal authority, the

---

346 Bonizo, *Book to a Friend* VI, p. 209. See H.-G. Krause (1960) p. 195; G. Jenal (1974) pp. 255–6.

347 Bonizo, *Book to a Friend* II, p. 166.

348 *Ibid.*, III, pp. 170–3. On Lothar II in Gregorian polemic see H.-W. Goetz (1987) p. 39.

Dictatus papae, and of the other canon law collections inspired by Gregory VII.[350] The same themes appear in the *Book to a Friend.* From the earliest days of Christianity 'the Roman [see] was the foremost bishopric among Christians'.[351] Emperor Constantine I decreed 'that all bishops should have the Roman pontiff as their head, just as all secular officials obey the king'.[352] In the context of Milanese resistance to the doctrine of Roman supremacy Bonizo quoted the *sententia*: 'He who has withdrawn himself in any respect from the jurisdiction of the Roman church, is a heretic.'[353] Bonizo included in his narrative a defence of the authority of papal legates, which he placed in the context of a dispute between a papal legation and a metropolitan who defied their claims to jurisdiction in his homeland.[354] The concerns of the papal reform movement are also reflected in Bonizo's polemics against simony and nicholaitism, echoing the language of Gregory VII's reform legislation of 1074–5.[355] The leaders of the Milanese Patarini 'divulged to the people the errors of simoniacal corruption and proved more clearly than day how very wicked it was that priests and deacons living in concubinage should celebrate the sacraments'.[356] The antipope Cadalus of Parma 'was elected by his fellow fornicators and simoniacs'; Wibert of Ravenna made friends with 'the sons and kinsmen of priests living with concubines'; the Patarine leader Herlembald was martyred by 'the sellers of churches' in Milan.[357] Hildebrand as a papal legate 'hunted down simoniacal heresy and the detestable unchastity of the clergy as far as the Pyrenees and the British Sea'.[358] While Bonizo also emphasised that episcopal elections should be free of secular interference, there is no trace in the *Book to a Friend* (nor indeed in his later

349 Bonizo, *Book to a Friend* IV, pp. 176–9, 180–1.

350 Bonizo, *Liber de vita christiana* IV.1, 54, 58, 68, 82, pp. 136, 137, 141, 146. See P. Fournier (1920) pp. 271–396; H. Fuhrmann (1977) pp. 263–87; I. S. Robinson (1978a) pp. 39–49.

351 Bonizo, *Book to a Friend* I, p. 161.

352 *Ibid.,* II, p. 163. A reference to the Donation of Constantine and the legends of Pope Silvester I: see H. E. J. Cowdrey (1997) pp. 74–84.

353 Bonizo, *Book to a Friend* VI, p. 197. This *sententia* appears in Gregory VII, *Dictatus papae* 26 (*Registrum* II.55a, p. 207). See H. Fuhrmann (1977) pp. 263–87.

354 Bonizo, *Book to a Friend* VII, p. 222: the dispute between the legates, the cardinal bishops of Ostia and Palestrina, and Archbishop Liemar of Bremen (1074).

355 Gregory VII, *Epistolae Vagantes* 6–11, pp. 14–26. See H. E. J. Cowdrey (1998) pp. 543–6, 550–3.

356 Bonizo, *Book to a Friend* VI, pp. 198.

357 *Ibid.,* p. 206; VII, pp. 226, 229.

358 *Ibid.,* p. 199.

canonical collection) of Gregory VII's decrees against lay investiture.[359]

The principal subject-matter of the *Book to a Friend* is an account of the career of Hildebrand-Gregory VII, intended to defend his reputation from the accusations made in the council of Brixen (June 1080). Books V and VI demonstrate how 'ever since the days of the lord Pope Leo [IX] it [was] Hildebrand who exalted the holy Roman church and liberated [Rome]'.[360] Books VII–IX show how, as Pope Gregory VII, he 'ruled the universal Church in peace' until the 'diabolical deed' of the council of Brixen.[361] Hildebrand first appears in this narrative as the chaplain of Pope Gregory VI. Wishing 'to show reverence towards his lord', he accompanied him into exile in Germany in 1047. This close connection between Hildebrand and Gregory VI prompted the version of events at Sutri presented by Bonizo (in common with other Gregorian authors).[362] In this version Gregory VI, who was condemned for simony at Sutri, is rehabilitated as the champion of canonical elections. He had purchased the papacy from his predecessor Benedict IX because 'he could think of nothing better to do with [his] money than to restore to the clergy and people the right of election that had been unjustly removed by tyranny'. Realising during the synodal proceedings that he was guilty of simony, he resigned his office and was therefore not deposed by the synod.[363]

The most debated passage of the *Book to a Friend* follows the death of Gregory VI. 'The venerable Hildebrand travelled to Cluny [and] became a monk there'. Bonizo was the only eleventh-century author to claim Hildebrand as a monk of Cluny and it is much more likely that he was, as Bruno of Segni and Paul of Bernried claimed, a 'Roman monk'.[364] Bonizo's claim was perhaps inspired by his knowledge of Hildebrand-Gregory's friendship with Abbot Hugh I of Cluny or was a confused

359 R. Schieffer (1981) pp. 186, 197.

360 Bonizo, *Book to a Friend* VII, p. 220.

361 *Ibid.*, IX, p. 247.

362 Desiderius of Monte Cassino, *Dialogi* III, p. 1143; Bernold, *Chronicon* 1046, p. 425. This version of events was accepted by F.-J. Schmale (1979a) pp. 55–103; but see also E. Steindorff (1874) pp. 313–14; R.L. Poole (1934) pp. 185–222; H. E. J. Cowdrey (1998) p. 23.

363 Bonizo, *Book to a Friend* V, pp. 185–6.

364 *Ibid.*, p. 188. In the mid-twelfth century Otto of Freising, *Chronica* VI.33, p. 484, identified him as the prior of Cluny. Cf. Bruno of Segni, *Sermon concerning Simoniacs* c. 2, below p. 379; Paul of Bernried, *Life of Pope Gregory VII* c. 9, below p. 266. See G. B. Borino (1946) pp. 218–62; G. B. Borino (1952b) pp. 441–6; I. Schuster (1950) pp. 52–7; I. Schuster (1952) pp. 305–7; H. Hoffmann (1963) pp. 165–209; H. Fichtenau (1986) pp. 59–68.

memory of a visit to Cluny during Hildebrand's legatine journeys in
the 1050s. The story of the monastic profession was included in the
Book to a Friend in order to answer the charge in the conciliar decree
of Brixen that Hildebrand was a 'false monk' who 'seemed by his habit
to be a monk but in his profession was no monk, being subject to no
ecclesiastical discipline and to no master'.[365] The allegation that Hildebrand had broken his monastic vow of 'stability' – a 'runaway from St
Benedict [who wished] to be bound by no rule' – frequently occurred
in Henrician polemic.[366] Bonizo responded with an account of Hildebrand's monastic career that proved that he was no 'false monk'.
When Pope Leo IX wished to recruit Hildebrand to his entourage, he
'begged him from his abbot with many prayers and with great
difficulty' and appointed him subdeacon of the Roman church.
Hildebrand was compelled by his superiors to leave the monastic life
and there was, therefore, nothing illicit in his conduct.[367]

Bonizo's account of Hildebrand's election as pope (22 April 1073) was
linked with this rebuttal of the charge that he was a 'false monk'.
Henrician polemic claimed that Hildebrand's monastic profession
disqualified him from election to the papacy.[368] Bonizo's response was
to model his account of Hildebrand's election on that of Pope Gregory
I, the saint dragged from his monastery in Rome and compelled to
accept the papal office (590). Gregory VII, like Gregory I, was 'seized
by the people and dragged away and enthroned unwillingly' as
pope.[369] Bonizo's account of the papal election of April 1073 was
intended also as a rebuttal of another accusation of the council of
Brixen: that, driven by insatiable ambition, Hildebrand usurped the
papacy by violence.[370] (Eleventh-century prelates were expected to
show great reluctance in accepting high office: ambition to hold office
automatically disqualified the candidate.)[371] Bonizo's reply to this

365 Brixen decree: *Die Briefe Heinrichs IV.*, p. 70.
366 Benzo, *To Emperor Henry IV* VII.2, below p. 370. See I. S. Robinson (1978a) pp. 33–4.
367 Bonizo, *Book to a Friend* V, p. 191.
368 E.g. Henry IV, *Letter* 12, p. 16; Petrus Crassus, *Defensio Heinrici IV* c. 5, pp. 441–2.
369 Bonizo, *Book to a Friend* VII, p. 220. Cf. John the Deacon, *Vita sancti Gregorii Magni* I.44, *MPL* 75, col. 81B. The same device of modelling Gregory VII's election on that of Gregory I was used by Berthold of Reichenau, *Annales* 1073, p. 276; Bernold, *Chronicon* 1073, p. 430; Manegold of Lautenbach, *Liber ad Gebehardum* c. 14, pp. 336–7. See I. S. Robinson (1978a) pp. 31–9.
370 Brixen decree: *Die Briefe Heinrichs IV.* p. 71.
371 E.g. Gregory I, *Regula pastoralis* I.6, 10, *MPL* 77, col. 19D-20A; John the Deacon, *Vita sancti Gregorii Magni* I.44, *MPL* 75, col. 81B. See I. S. Robinson (1978a) p. 35.

accusation was that on two occasions Hildebrand had declined election to the papacy, in 1054[372] and in 1073. On the latter occasion, after he had been enthroned as pope against his will, Hildebrand sent a letter to Henry IV, threatening that if he remained pope, 'he would never bear patiently with [the king's] iniquity' and trusting that Henry would intervene to veto his election. 'Events, however, fell out quite differently from what he hoped.' In this passage Bonizo ascribed to the German king that right of veto in a papal election that he consistently denied him elsewhere in the *Book to a Friend*.[373] Once more Bonizo was rewriting the history of the election of Gregory VII in terms of that of Gregory I, who had 'secretly sent a letter to Emperor Maurice', begging him not to consent to his election as pope.[374]

Pope Gregory VII 'ruled the universal Church in peace', according to Bonizo, but he was persecuted by the enemies of reform. The 'pernicious Roman' Cencius, son of the prefect Stephen, sought to defraud the Roman church and, being detected in his crime, abducted the pope (25 December 1075) and held him prisoner.[375] Hugh Candidus, cardinal priest of S. Clemente and Wibert of Ravenna conspired against Gregory VII throughout his pontificate and Henry IV twice renounced his obedience to the pope. The emphasis on Gregory VII as the guardian of the peace of the Church against these adversaries was Bonizo's response to the accusation of the council of Brixen that Gregory VII had 'overturned ecclesiastical order, disturbed the government of the Christian empire [and] threatened the catholic and peace-loving king with the death of body and soul'.[376] A frequent theme of Henrician polemic was that Gregory VII was 'the enemy of peace' and 'the standard-bearer of schism'.[377] Bonizo's account of the pontificate of Gregory VII demonstrated that Henry IV and his accomplices were the aggressors, Gregory VII the victim.

---

372 Bonizo, *Book to a Friend* V, p. 193.

373 *Ibid.*, VII, p. 221. Bonizo was led into this inconsistency by his anxiety to contradict the Brixen decree, which accused Gregory VII of contravening 'the decree of Pope Nicholas' (Papal Election Decree) 'that whosoever presumes to become pope without the consent of the Roman prince was to be regarded by all not as a pope but as an apostate'. See G. B. Borino (1956b) pp. 313–43; C. Schneider (1972) pp. 41–7; H. E. J. Cowdrey (1998) p. 92.

374 John the Deacon, *Vita sancti Gregorii Magni* I.40, col. 79BC.

375 Bonizo, *Book to a Friend* VII, pp. 227–8, 231, 232–3.

376 Brixen decree p. 71.

377 Petrus Crassus, *Defensio Heinrici IV* c. 6, p. 445; *Codex Udalrici* 159, p. 130. See I. S. Robinson (1978a) pp. 95–8 and above p. 16.

From the beginning of his pontificate Gregory's purpose was 'to admonish the king that he should not sell bishoprics and that he should recognise that he was subject to the holy Roman church'.[378] Henry IV, however, despite his promises of cooperation, connived at the destruction of the Milanese reform movement and, emboldened by his victory over the Saxons (June 1075), dared to attack the pope in January 1076. 'The venerable Gregory, who was prepared to die for his sheep, did not suffer the offence against the holy Roman church to go unavenged' and excommunicated and deposed the king.[379] After the reconciliation at Canossa (January 1077) 'the king appeared superficially devout and obedient to the pope', but in reality he was insolent and disobedient.[380] In March 1080 'the venerable pope, who was prepared to die for the truth ... excommunicated the king who had addressed him so insolently.'[381] His courageous defence of righteousness and the cause of the Roman church ultimately brought persecution and death in exile. The Gregory VII of the *Book to a Friend* was a martyr for the catholic faith. Bonizo's readers were left in no doubt that Gregory VII's career had won divine approval: 'God continues to perform many thousands of miracles at his tomb to the present day.'[382] Of the gallery of martyrs assembled in the *Book to a Friend* for the consolation of his 'friend', Gregory VII was the most illustrious, his career demonstrating divine approval for the cause of the reform papacy.

First printed in 1763 by Felix Andreas Oefele in his *Rerum Boicarum Scriptores 2* (Augsburg), Bonizo's work is most readily accessible in three nineteenth-century editions. J. M. Watterich included Books V–IX of the *Liber ad amicum* in his *Pontificum Romanorum Vitae* 1, 75–9, 100–5, 184–7, 196–201, 207–13, 256–70, 308–49. Philipp Jaffé edited the work as *Bonithonis episcopi Sutrini Liber ad amicum* in his *Monumenta Gregoriana* (*Bibliotheca rerum germanicarum* 2: Berlin, 1865) pp. 603–89. The most recent edition is that of Ernst Dümmler, *Bonizonis episcopi Sutrini Liber ad amicum* in *Monumenta Germaniae Historica, Libelli de lite* 1, 568–620.

378 Bonizo, *Book to a Friend* VII, p. 221.
379 *Ibid.*, pp. 224, 233–5.
380 *Ibid.*, VIII, p. 241.
381 *Ibid.*, IX, p. 246.
382 *Ibid.*, p. 252.

Paul of Bernried, Life of Pope Gregory VII

Paul of Bernried's biography of Pope Gregory VII, written more than forty years after the pope's death, is one of the most important historical works of the early twelfth century. Polemical in character, it is nevertheless the product of unusually detailed and conscientious research. It is also a valuable record of the attitudes of a south German friendship circle devoted to reform, and evidence of the continuing interest in the personality and career of Gregory VII and his closest associates in the years following the settlement of the conflict of empire and papacy in the Concordat of Worms of 1122.

The only available information about the career of Paul is to be found in his biographies of his friend, the visionary and ascetic Herluca of Epfach, and of Gregory VII, and in his letters to correspondents in Milan.[383] There is a hint in the *Life of Gregory VII* that Paul's origins were in the diocese of Passau. Among the German adherents of the Gregorian party Paul expressed the greatest admiration for Bishop Udalric of Passau, whom Paul identified as 'the most reverend ordainer of this humble author'. During his episcopate (1092–1121), therefore, Udalric had ordained Paul to the priesthood.[384] It is clear from the evidence of his biography of Herluca that Paul spent many years in Regensburg.[385] The chronology of these years is provided by chapter 43 of the biography, describing Paul's third visit to Herluca in her retreat of Epfach (in the diocese of Augsburg). During this visit Herluca advised Paul to alter his decision to leave Regensburg. When, fourteen years later, Paul was actually compelled by political circumstances to leave the city, he at last learned from Herluca that the advice given on the former occasion had been revealed to her in a vision by her patron, St Laurence.[386] If, as is generally accepted, the year of Paul's expulsion from Regensburg was 1121,[387] it follows that the date of Paul's third visit to Herluca was 1107. Chapter 43 of the

383 The letters were edited by M. Magistretti (1897) pp. 494–504. See W. Wache (1936) pp. 261–333; H. Fuhrmann (1984) pp. 342–6, 353; F. Fuchs (1986) pp. 220–1.

384 Paul, *Life of Gregory VII* c. 121, below p. 362.

385 H. Fuhrmann (1989) p. 111 n. 1 referred to the dissertation of F. Fuchs, *Die mittelalterliche Bibliothek des Augustinerchorherrenstiftes St. Mang in Stadtamhof/ Regensburg* (Regensburg, 1987), demonstrating that Paul was never a canon of Regensburg cathedral, as suggested by M. Maier (1963) p. 331 and W. Wattenbach, R. Holtzmann and F.-J. Schmale (1976) pp. 244–5.

386 Paul, *Vita beatae Herlucae* c. 43, p. 556.

387 See below p. 66.

biography contains the further information that Paul was accompanied on this visit by Gebhard, 'my pupil, who for five years had
been my faithful companion at home and abroad'. Gebhard had,
therefore, become Paul's pupil in Regensburg in 1102, the earliest
known date in Paul's career.[388]

Herluca's concern to detain Paul in Regensburg suggests that she
regarded him as the leader of the Gregorian party there. For an
adherent of the Gregorian reform, Regensburg cannot have been a
congenial place in these years. Emperor Henry IV visited the city five
times during the last nine years of his reign and the bishop and
citizens remained loyal to him despite the 'very large sum of money
that he took from the men of Regensburg' to fund his war-effort.[389]
Bishop Gebhard IV of Regensburg (1089–1105) was regarded by the
Gregorian party as a simoniac. He 'had occupied the place of pastor
for sixteen years' when he was murdered by one of his own vassals
'whom he had insulted intolerably' and died without having been
consecrated bishop.[390] His successor Hartwig (1105–26) was a loyal
adherent of Emperor Henry V, active in his military expeditions and
an important figure at the imperial court in the earlier years of the
reign.[391] It is not surprising that Paul identified with the reformer
Udalric of Passau, who ordained him, rather than with the worldly
prelates of Regensburg. Paul explained to Herluca, when he sought
her advice in 1107, that he planned to leave the city because of 'the
hostility of the clergy of Regensburg': 'they hated me as the cause of
their uneasiness by virtue of my irreproachable life and my willing-
ness to speak the truth'.[392] It was presumably Paul's voicing of the
reforming ideas that appeared two decades later in his *Life of Gregory
VII* that earned him the resentment of clergy still hostile to papal
reforming legislation.

Fourteen years after he had become the object of the hostility of the

388 J. May (1887) p. 336 and n. 1; M. Maier (1963) p. 329 and n. 124; R. Schieffer
    (1988) col. 359.

389 *Annalium Ratisbonensium maiorum fragmentum, MGH SS rer. germ.* [4] (1891) p. 88.
    See G. Meyer von Knonau (1904) pp. 2, 60, 181, 194–6, 236–7; R. Kottje (1978)
    pp. 145–7; I. S. Robinson (1999) pp. 296, 306, 321–3.

390 Frutolf of Michelsberg, *Chronica* 1089, p. 104; Herrand of Halberstadt, *Epistola* p.
    289; *Anonymi Chronica imperatorum* 1105, p. 232. See G. Meyer von Knonau (1903)
    p. 262; E. Boshof (1991) pp. 141–2; I. S. Robinson (1999) p. 277.

391 G. Meyer von Knonau (1907) pp. 71, 84, 178–9, 285–6, 295, 330; E. Boshof (1991)
    pp. 148–50.

392 Paul, *Vita Herlucae* c. 43, p. 556.

66 THE PAPAL REFORM OF THE ELEVENTH CENTURY

clergy, Paul at last left Regensburg. According to his own account, he and his pupil Gebhard 'were expelled by the persecution of Henry V'.[393] The emperor was in Regensburg on 25 March 1121, during a visit to Bavaria and Swabia, and this was probably the occasion of Paul and Gebhard's expulsion.[394] Nothing is said in any other source of any 'persecution' of the Gregorian party during this visit. Perhaps the excommunication pronounced on Henry V by the new pope Calixtus II made adherents of the pope intolerable to the emperor.[395] Paul and Gebhard went to Bernried (in the diocese of Augsburg) on the western shore of the Starnbergersee, their arrival coinciding with that of their friend Herluca. She had been forced to leave Epfach after a residence of thirty-six years 'by the madness of wicked peasants' and was never able to return.[396] The friends found refuge in the house of regular canons that was being founded in Bernried about the time of their arrival. The first provost of Bernried was Sigeboto, formerly 'a priest in Epfach' and a member of the friendship circle of Herluca commemorated by Paul in his *Life of Herluca*.[397] It is possible that Paul participated in the foundation of Bernried. He certainly dedicated his biography of Herluca to the congregation of Bernried.[398] There is no evidence, however, that Paul himself became a regular canon of Bernried. The name 'Paul of Bernried', which has been given to the author since Jakob Gretser published his edition of Paul's works in 1610, is, therefore, a misleading one.[399]

Three passages in Paul's writings refer to a visit to Rome. The final chapter of the *Life of Herluca*, composed in 1130/1, mentions an encounter with another scholar 'when I was in Rome a few years ago'.[400]

393 *Ibid.*, c. 44, p. 556.

394 J. May (1887) pp. 339–40; W. Wattenbach, R. Holtzmann and F.-J. Schmale (1976) p. 244. According to M. Herrmann (1889) p. 565; J. Greving (1893) p. 7 and R. Schieffer (1988) col. 359: '*circa* 1120'. See also G. Meyer von Knonau (1909) p. 168.

395 At the end of the Council of Rheims, 30 October 1119, after the failure of negotiations about lay investiture: G. Meyer von Knonau (1909) pp. 135–6.

396 Paul, *Vita Herlucae* c. 44, p. 556. J. May (1887) p. 340 suggested that these peasants had been incensed against Herluca by the supporters of the married priests against whom she had spoken: see Paul, *Life* c. 114–15, 122, pp. 358–9, 362–3.

397 Paul, *Vita Herlucae* c. 40, p. 556. The date of the foundation is uncertain: see M. Herrmann (1889) p. 567 n. 1. On Bernried see O. Hartig (1935) pp. 183–8; J. Mois (1953) pp. 207–10; P. Classen (1960) p. 25; M. Maier (1963) p. 328 and n. 117.

398 Paul, *Vita Herlucae* prologue, p. 552 (identifying himself as 'Paul, a priest').

399 J. Gretser, *Commentarius Pauli Bernriedensis, antiqui scriptoris, de vita Gregorii VII pontificis maximi* (Ingolstadt, 1610). See W. Wattenbach, R. Holtzmann and F.-J. Schmale (1976) p. 244; H. Fuhrmann (1984) p. 342; R. Schieffer (1988) col. 359.

400 Paul, *Vita Herlucae* p. 555. On the date of composition see below p. 71.

Of the two references in the *Life of Gregory VII* one suggests a more precise date. Introducing his version of the widely disseminated miracle story of Hildebrand detecting a simoniac bishop, Paul claimed to be reporting 'as Pope Calixtus used to tell the story'.[401] If these references relate to the same visit, they indicate a stay in Rome during the pontificate of Calixtus II (1119–24). This visit was presumably connected with the privilege of Calixtus II, dated 12 November 1122 for 'the brethren professing the regular life in the church of St Martin ... in the place called Bernried'. The privilege received the congregation 'into the guardianship and protection of St Peter and the Roman church' and granted the canons the right of free election of their provost.[402] It is likely that Paul was commissioned by Sigeboto, provost of Bernried to travel to Rome to obtain this privilege for the new foundation.[403] The two passages from the *Life of Gregory VII* show that Paul used this visit to collect material for this biography. The final chapter of the *Life of Herluca* records his chance encounter with another scholar carrying out research in Rome, to whom Paul promised an account of the miracles experienced by Herluca.[404]

Before the summer of 1123 Paul had left Rome.[405] He celebrated Whitsun (3 June) 1123 in Milan, as is recalled in a letter sent in the names of Paul and his pupil Gebhard to their principal Milanese correspondent three years later.[406] The friendships formed during this visit to Milan were maintained in the correspondence that continued intermittently for more than twenty years. There survives a collection of eleven letters, one written by Paul alone, nine jointly by Paul and Gebhard and one by their principal correspondent, the Milanese canon Martinus Corvus, treasurer and later provost of S. Ambrogio. One of the letters of Paul and Gebhard was addressed to Archbishop

---

401 Paul, *Life* c. 17, p. 269; cf. c. 117, p. 359.

402 Calixtus II, *JL* 6993, *MPL* 163, col. 1257D-1258C. See M. Herrmann (1889) p. 570.

403 That Paul was accompanied by Gebhard was argued by M. Herrmann (1889) p. 570, on the basis of their joint correspondence with the Milanese clergy, which suggests that both Paul and Gebhard had made these acquaintances in Milan on the return journey from Rome.

404 Paul, *Vita Herlucae* c. 35, p. 555.

405 Paul, *Life* c. 33, p. 281: summer was 'a season which in Rome is very dangerous for the human body'. On the German perception of the danger of the Roman summer see also below pp. 127, 379.

406 M. Magistretti (1897) no. 11. See J. May (1887) p. 343; M. Herrmann (1889) p. 571.

Anselm V of Milan, another to Archbishop Obert of Milan. A principal theme of this exchange of letters between 'the Germans', as Paul and Gebhard called themselves, and the Milanese was scholarly research. The Milanese sought information about rare works of Ambrose of Milan. 'The Germans' sought liturgical manuscripts, the Ambrosian sacramentary and antiphonary, a list of the archbishops of Milan and information about the history of the archdiocese.[407]

These letters also contain biographical information about Paul and Gebhard. The letter written only in Paul's name (c. 1130) states that Gebhard was absent 'on a certain legation of the lord pope'. He had been ordained to the priesthood 'by apostolic authority' and therefore, like Paul himself, had been received 'into the protection and the special sonship of the Roman church'.[408] Paul considered himself to be a special son of the Roman church because he had been ordained by Bishop Udalric of Passau, who was a 'legate of the apostolic see'.[409] Gebhard must therefore have been ordained by someone of similar status. An obvious candidate is Archbishop Walter of Ravenna, the legate who at the beginning of the papal schism of 1130 came to Germany to win over King Lothar III and the German bishops to the cause of Pope Innocent II. He was present at the council of Würzburg (October 1130) where Innocent was unanimously acknowledged as pope.[410] Before his appointment to the archsee of Ravenna the reformer Walter had been a member of Paul's friendship circle in Regensburg.[411] Paul described him as 'a holy man, adorned with miracles' and as one of the two principal spiritual influences on him, the other being Herluca.[412] Perhaps Walter of Ravenna ordained the pupil of his old friend in 1130 and employed him in the work of his legation.

407 The correspondence was summarised by J. May (1887) pp. 341–4, 347–50; M. Herrmann (1889) pp. 571–81.

408 M. Magistretti (1897) no. VII. See J. May (1887) p. 350; M. Herrmann (1897) pp. 577–8.

409 Paul, *Life* c. 121, below p. 362. O. Schumann (1912) p. 74 n. 1 rejected Paul's claim that Udalric was a legate, but it was accepted by E. Boshof (1991) pp. 144–5. The decisive evidence is Paschal II's letter, *JL* 5970 (*Acta pontificum Romanorum inedita* 1, 78, no. 87), linking together Udalric and the papal legate Bishop Gebhard III of Constance as 'vicars of God and of the apostles'.

410 *Annalista Saxo* 1130, p. 767. See A. Hauck (1952) pp. 146–7.

411 H. Fuhrmann (1989) p. 111 n. 1 referred to the dissertation of F. Fuchs (see above p. 64 n. 385), demonstrating that Walter of Ravenna was never a canon of Regensburg, as claimed by G. Schwartz (1913) p. 160 and M. Maier (1963) p. 331.

412 Paul, *Vita Herlucae* prologue, p. 552.

Only in one of the later letters do Paul and Gebhard offer a clue to their whereabouts. They were replying to a question of Martinus Corvus about a saint named Udalric whose feast was celebrated on 14 July. They identified him as Udalric of Zell (✝1093). He 'formerly possessed, but abandoned for Christ's sake, this pleasant court (*curia*) in which we now live and preserve both his memory and that of St Magnus'.[413] Udalric of Zell had been born in Regensburg but left the city to become a monk of Cluny and later prior of Zell (in the Black Forest). According to his first biographer, he wished to found a monastery dedicated to his patron St Magnus in the vicinity of Regensburg on land that had belonged to his parents, but his plan was opposed by the bishop of Regensburg. Now, however, his object had been achieved: Paul and Gebhard lived in a religious house dedicated to St Magnus, where Udalric had once resided.[414] In 1138 the house of regular canons of St Mang (Magnus) was founded in Stadtamhof near Regensburg through the efforts of Gebhard, canon of Regensburg, who became the first provost. The evidence of the letter to Martinus Corvus makes it likely that this Gebhard was the pupil and companion of Paul. Moreover the community of St Mang adopted both the 'customs' of the regular canons of S. Maria in Portu, Ravenna, and the Ambrosian liturgy, echoes respectively of the friendship of Paul and Walter of Ravenna and the correspondence of Paul and Gebhard with Milanese clergy.[415] St Mang was 'the pleasant court' where Paul and Gebhard now preserved the memory of St Udalric and his patron, St Magnus.

From 1138 until his death (at an unknown date) Paul may have lived in St Mang, but during the fifteen years following his travels in Italy he perhaps returned to Regensburg.[416] The spiritual and intellectual climate of the city had been transformed since the days when Paul had experienced 'the hostility of the clergy of Regensburg'. The harbinger of change had been the abbey of Prüfening, founded by Bishop Otto of Bamberg near Regensburg in 1109 and settled with monks from Hirsau. Prüfening adopted not the traditional monasticism of its neighbour St

413 M. Magistretti (1897) no. XII. See J. May (1887) pp. 341–2; M. Herrmann (1889) p. 580; H. Fuhrmann (1988) p. 372.

414 *Vita prior sancti Udalrici prioris Cellensis* p. 253. See M. Herrmann (1889) p. 581; H. Fuhrmann (1988) pp. 372, 374. On Udalric of Zell see H. E. J. Cowdrey (1970) pp. 193–6.

415 M. Herrmann (1889) pp. 581–6; B. Sepp (1894) pp. 265–98; W. Wattenbach, R. Holtzmann and F.-J. Schmale (1976) p. 245; R. Schieffer (1988) col. 359–60.

416 C. Märtl (1986) pp. 158–60.

Emmeram of Regensburg but the reformed monasticism developed by Abbot William of Hirsau, one of the heroes of Paul's *Life of Gregory VII*.[417] Prüfening's importance as a centre of learning is apparent from the catalogue of ecclesiastical authors completed *c.* 1130 by the Prüfening bibliographer known as 'Anonymus Mellicensis' (who was perhaps Wolfger of Prüfening). What is striking about this catalogue is the prevalence of Gregorian writers. The bibliographer shared Paul's reverence for Bishop Anselm II of Lucca as saint and author.[418] He identified Bonizo of Sutri as a canonist 'in the times of Gregory VII'.[419] He knew of the works of Bruno of Segni, the chronicle of Berthold of Reichenau and the writings of Bernold of St Blasien.[420] He listed the works of Abbot William of Hirsau[421] and applauded the polemicist Manegold of Lautenbach as 'the master of modern masters'.[422] In the same period in which Prüfening became a centre where Gregorian ideas were preserved, Honorius Augustodunensis, encyclopaedist and populariser of Gregorian doctrine, resided for a time in Regensburg.[423]

The key figure in the reform movement in early twelfth-century Regensburg was Bishop Cuno I (1126–32), who was unexpectedly elected in the faction-fighting that followed the death of Bishop Hartwig. Born in Regensburg, Cuno had left the city in his youth to make his profession in the reformed monastery of Siegburg, where he became abbot (1105–26) and transformed the monastery into a major centre of reform.[424] (His career offers a parallel with other inhabitants of Regensburg who sought reformed institutions elsewhere: William, who left St Emmeram to become abbot of Hirsau; Udalric, who left to become a monk of Cluny;[425] and the friends Paul and Gebhard.) Cuno was a tireless reformer, energetic in preaching to the people of Regensburg and determined to introduce the monastic reform of Siegburg in

---

417 Paul, *Life* c. 113, below p. 357. See H.-G. Schmitz (1975) on the spiritual and cultural significance of Prüfening.

418 Anonymus Mellicensis [Wolfger of Prüfening?], *De scriptoribus ecclesiasticis* c. 100, p. 89. On this work see F. Fuchs (1986) pp. 213–26.

419 *De scriptoribus* c. 112, p. 95.

420 *Ibid.*, c. 83, 92, 101, pp. 82, 85, 89–90.

421 *Ibid.*, c. 108, p. 93.

422 *Ibid.*, c. 105, p. 91.

423 V. I. J. Flint (1972) pp. 215–42; C. Märtl (1986) p. 159.

424 J. Semmler (1959) pp. 46–8.

425 William of Hirsau: H. Jakobs (1961) pp. 7–8. Udalric of Zell: see above n. 414.

his diocese, influencing even the conservative monks of St Emmeram. He also sought to establish the regular canonical life in his cathedral chapter and elsewhere.[426] He recruited Gerhoch, provost of Reichersberg to assist him in his reforming activity and so introduced into Regensburg another scholar who 'deliberately preserved the memory of Gregory [VII]'.[427] Cuno's importance in early twelfth-century intellectual history lay in his ability to stimulate the creativity of the authors in his ambience. As abbot of Siegburg he had influenced the writings of the theologian Rupert of Deutz while the latter was a monk of Siegburg.[428] As bishop of Regensburg he encouraged Gerhoch of Reichersberg to compose his first work and introduced him to the writings of Rupert of Deutz, which influenced Gerhoch's later works.[429] It seems likely that Cuno exercised a similar influence on Paul of Bernried.

Recent research suggests that Paul's literary career began two decades earlier than previously supposed and that his earliest work was written in collaboration with his pupil Gebhard. This was the earlier *Life* of Udalric of Zell, composed before 1107.[430] This biography is further evidence of the devotion of Paul and Gebhard to the *memoria* of Udalric, which culminated in the foundation of St Mang. Udalric also appears in the *Life of Gregory VII*, celebrated as one of the 'four principal directors' of German religious life: he introduced the 'customs' of Cluny into Germany.[431] Paul's *Life of Herluca* shows that combination of hagiographical themes and reforming polemic that characterise the biographies of Udalric and Gregory VII. Paul drew much of his information from conversations with Herluca in Epfach and in Bernried, where she spent her last years. Composed in the third year after Herluca's death, which occurred perhaps in 1127, the *Life* was dedicated to 'the very small congregation of the monastery of

426 Gerhoch of Reichersberg, *De aedificio domus Dei* p. 137. See J. Semmler (1959) pp. 84–7, 96–102.

427 P. Classen (1960) p. 55.

428 J. Semmler (1959) pp. 48, 372–83.

429 Gerhoch, *De aedificio domus Dei* pp. 137, 139. See P. Classen (1960) p. 34.

430 *Vita prior sancti Udalrici prioris Cellensis* pp. 251–3. The attribution was made in the dissertation of W. Stratmann, *Forschungen zur Biographie Ulrichs von Zell* (Regensburg, 1984). The evidence includes 'an epistolary preface' to the *Vita* found in a manuscript of 1627, now edited by H. Fuhrmann (1988) pp. 375–7. F. Fuchs (1986) p. 220 n. 26 identified in a seventeenth-century library catalogue of St Mang what appears to be another work of Paul (now lost): 'Three dialogues'.

431 Paul, *Life* c. 118, p. 360. See Udalric of Zell, *Antiquiores consuetudines monasterii Cluniacensis*, *MPL* 149, col. 635A-778B.

Bernried', where Herluca was buried.[432] Herluca (born *c.* 1060) was influenced by the preaching of monks of Hirsau to desire the religious life, but her means were too limited to allow her to enter a convent. On the advice of William of Hirsau she remained in Epfach, devoting herself to prayer and charitable works. She lived in a circle of pious women, caring for orphan children, and suffered severe illness, while winning a great reputation and influence from her visions.[433] 'The virgin dedicated to God saw heavenly visions and received insights that did much to encourage Gregorian obedience.'[434] Herluca's visions offered divine confirmation of the validity of Gregorian reforming decrees, showing 'how the grace or the wrath of God promoted the decrees of our Gregory' against simony and clerical marriage.[435]

Unlike the biography of Herluca, that of Gregory VII lacks a preface and the name of the author. That the *Life of Gregory VII* was, however, written by Herluca's biographer appears from a passage in the *Life of Herluca*. The author writes of an unchaste priest whose offence was disclosed to Herluca in a vision: 'This is he of whom we also made mention in the *Life of Gregory*.'[436] The date of composition is incidentally disclosed in the chapter recording the death of Bishop Udalric of Passau. 'Seven years ago, after many struggles in defence of Gregorian doctrine ..., he fell asleep in the Lord, in the one-hundred-and-fifth year of his life.' Udalric died on 6 August 1121 and consequently the *Life of Gregory VII* was completed in 1128.[437] The author may have felt, as his work neared completion, that his account of the conflict of Gregory VII and Henry IV had a peculiarly topical relevance. On 18 December 1127 Conrad of Staufen 'tyrannically assumed the royal title'.[438] The election of Conrad, brother of Duke Frederick II of

---

432 Paul, *Vita Herlucae* prologue, p. 552. See M. Herrmann (1889) pp. 573–4; J. Mois (1953) p. 210; M. Maier (1963) p. 330. The only certain information is that Herluca was dead at the time of the composition of Paul's *Life* (c. 114, p. 358), that is, in 1128, and that in Paul's prologue to the *Vita Herlucae* p. 552, he recorded that their friendship (begun in 1102) lasted 'more than twenty years'.

433 A. Schnitzer (1969) pp. 5–15; R. Schnitzer, *Die Vita beatae Herlucae Pauls von Bernried. Eine Quelle zur gregorianische Reform in Süddeutschland* (dissertation: Munich, 1967).

434 Paul, *Life* c. 122, p. 362.

435 *Ibid.*, c. 113, p. 356. See, for example, Paul, *Vita Herlucae* c. 22, p. 554 (also in *Life* c. 114, p. 358); *Vita Herlucae* c. 24, p. 554 (also in *Life* c. 115, p. 358); *Vita Herlucae* c. 25, p. 554.

436 Paul, *Vita Herlucae* c. 22, p. 544. Cf. Paul, *Life* c. 114, p. 358.

437 Paul, *Life* c. 121, p. 362. See G. Meyer von Knonau (1909) p. 179.

438 *Annales Magdeburgenses* 1127, p. 183. See W. Bernhardi (1879) p. 139. This anti-king Conrad was the future King Conrad III (1138–52).

Swabia, as anti-king in opposition to King Lothar III, may have seemed to Paul and the reformers in Regensburg to be a sinister echo of the conflict of empire and papacy only recently settled by the concordat of Worms (1122). The Staufen princes were the grandsons of Henry IV, the insane tyrant of Paul's *Life of Gregory VII*. They were the heirs of Henry V, from whose persecution Paul had been forced to flee six years before. Lothar III was the former enemy of the Salian emperors (since his youthful rebellion against Henry IV in 1088) and the ally of Archbishop Adalbert of Mainz, the leading figure of the German Gregorian party. The German episcopate at once rallied to Lothar III and excommunicated the anti-king, Pope Honorius II following their example (19 April 1128).[439] When Conrad was crowned king of Italy by Archbishop Anselm V of Milan (29 June 1128), a papal legate excommunicated the archbishop at a legatine synod in Pavia.[440]

This crisis seems to have left an echo in Paul's *Life of Gregory VII*. Describing Henry IV's conduct in Italy in January 1077, Paul wrote: 'He sent envoys and humbly begged the pope to permit him to be crowned in a ceremony at St John's in Monza by the bishops of Pavia and Milan according to the custom of earlier kings'.[441] Paul's account is contradicted by the contemporary chronicler Berthold of Reichenau: 'Since [Henry] wished to be crowned in Pavia according to the custom of the king of the Lombards, he sent mediators to the pope so as to be given permission for this'.[442] Paul certainly knew Berthold's chronicle, using it elsewhere in his account of the events of 1077. Berthold was right about 'the custom of the king of the Lombards'. 'The only royal coronation in Monza for which there is definite evidence' was that of the anti-king Conrad of Staufen in 1128.[443] Paul seems deliberately to have amended Berthold's account in the light of that later ceremony. A second echo of the events of 1127–8 can perhaps be found in Paul's account of the first excommunication of Henry IV in the papal synod of Lent 1076. That papal sentence was intended to 'provide future

439 A. Hauck (1952) pp. 116–21; R. Somerville (1972c) pp. 341–6; H. Stoob (1974) pp. 438–61; I. S. Robinson (1990) pp. 441–2.
440 W. Bernhardi (1879) pp. 202, 207. For the negative impact of this Milanese support for the anti-king on the correspondence of Paul and Gebhard with Milan see J. May (1887) p. 347; M. Herrmann (1889) p. 572. The correspondence was resumed after Conrad left Milan in 1129.
441 Paul, *Life* c. 86, p. 329.
442 Berthold, *Annales* 1077, p. 290. See G. Meyer von Knonau (1894) pp. 769–71; J. Vogel (1983) pp. 29–32.

ages with a warning against transgression'.[444] When he wrote this, Paul may have been thinking of the sentence of 1076 as a precedent for the excommunication pronounced by Honorius II on the anti-king Conrad in 1128.

Five years before these events of 1127–8 Paul was already collecting materials for a biography during his visit to Rome. The inspiration for his work was presumably the reverence for Gregory VII that Paul encountered in his friendship-circle, the tradition of Gregory's sanctity that had been preserved by his mentor, Bishop Udalric of Passau and by Herluca's mentor, Abbot William of Hirsau. The reforming enthusiasm of Bishop Cuno I of Regensburg may have given a further stimulus to Paul's work. Another contributing factor may have been the First Lateran Council of March 1123, which ratified the concordat of Worms between emperor and pope and consolidated the legislation that the reform papacy had issued in the previous half-century. F.-J. Schmale suggested that Paul was present at the First Lateran Council.[445] Paul arrived in Rome in 1122 and is recorded in Milan on 3 June 1123; so that it is certainly possible for him to have attended the council. Paul's friend, Archbishop Walter of Ravenna played an active role in the council[446] and this may have been an incentive for Paul's own attendance. The council of 1123, the last papal council to be dominated by the characteristic Gregorian reform programme, may, therefore, have developed and clarified Paul's conception of Gregory VII's ideas of reform. The conciliar legislation placed particular emphasis on simony (canon 1), avoidance of contact with excommunicates (canon 2), the canonical election of bishops (canon 3) and clerical celibacy (canon 7), all of which issues, and especially the first and last, are of central importance to the *Life of Gregory VII*.[447]

---

443 C. Brühl (1968) p. 500. J. Greving (1893) pp. 80–2 remarked also on the coronation of King Conrad (in rebellion against his father, Emperor Henry IV) in 1093, which Landulf, *Historia Mediolanensis* c. 3, p. 21, placed in Monza. Other chroniclers placed it in Milan: see G. Meyer von Knonau (1903) p. 395 n. 6.

444 Paul, *Life* c. 75, p. 317.

445 W. Wattenbach, R. Holtzmann and F.J. Schmale (1976) pp. 244–5.

446 He was commissioned by the pope to judge a dispute between the archbishops of Pisa and Genoa: *Cafari Annales Ianuenses, MGH SS* 18, 16. See I. S. Robinson (1990) p. 134.

447 *Concilium Lateranense I, Conciliorum Oecumenicorum Decreta* pp. 190–3. See I. S. Robinson (1990) pp. 134–5. A major preoccupation of the council is missing from the *Life*: the renunciation of the investiture of bishops with ring and staff (canon 8). The *Life* contains no reference to Gregory VII's decrees against lay investiture.

The central theme of the First Lateran Council, as of all the papal councils of the later eleventh and twelfth centuries, was the primacy of the pope in the universal Church.[448] *The Life of Gregory VII* is permeated with reminders of the supreme authority of the pope. Gregory VII is represented as the 'most holy father, whom the divine clemency provided to rule the world in our time'.[449] St Peter is represented as 'our master and the prince of the Church', his authority underlined by quoting the Petrine texts from the Gospels (Matthew 16:18 and Luke 22:32).[450] The doctrine of the primacy is expressed in terms that are peculiarly Gregorian: that is, accentuating the pope's authority over the secular as well as the spiritual sphere. 'The Roman church ... is the head and mistress of all religion and [her] prerogative is to correct all the powerful of the world before all others ...'[451] The spectacle of the 'general council' of 1123 might have influenced these statements of the papal primacy, but they could equally have been inspired by Paul's reading of the Gregorian materials, highly polemical in character, that he had collected for his biography.

Paul's *Life of Gregory VII* draws on a variety of sources, papal letters and synodal protocols quoted verbatim and chronicles freely paraphrased, and the authors of many of these sources – Bonizo of Sutri, Berthold of Reichenau, Bernold of St Blasien and Donizo of Canossa – had an obviously polemical intention. From Bonizo's *Book to a Friend* Paul borrowed, for example, his account of the career of Gregory VII's Roman enemy Cencius Stephani, of Henry IV's conduct in 1075 and of 'the law of the Germans' concerning excommunicates (they lose their office if they remain excommunicate for a year).[452] His description of the virtuous character of the Roman prefect Cencius and his account of the abduction of Gregory VII on Christmas day 1075 combined the reports of Bonizo, Berthold of Reichenau and Bernold of St Blasien.[453] Paul's account of the miracle of Hildebrand, as papal legate, detecting a simoniac prelate, quotes Bonizo's account verbatim but refers to a different source: 'as Pope Calixtus used to tell the story'.[454] The Swabian chronicle of Berthold of Reichenau, staunchly Gregorian

448 I. S. Robinson (1990) pp. 131–3.
449 Paul, *Life* c. 75, p. 317.
450 *Ibid.*, c. 74, 61, pp. 316. 305.
451 *Ibid.*, c. 61, p. 304.
452 *Ibid.*, c. 47, 48, 64, 85, pp. 294–5, 308–9, 328.
453 *Ibid.*, c. 47, 49–51, pp. 294, 295–8.
454 *Ibid.*, c. 17, p. 269.

and bitterly anti-Henrician in tone, was the narrative source most used by Paul, notably for recounting the relations of Gregory VII and Henry IV and the election of Rudolf of Rheinfelden as anti-king.[455] Paul also made use of a second Swabian chronicle, that of Bernold of St Blasien, on two occasions quoting the chronicle verbatim. Paul also borrowed verbatim from Bernold's polemic against clerical unchastity the anecdote of the miraculous punishment of a guilty bishop.[456] The metrical biography of Matilda of Tuscany by Donizo, monk of Canossa (1115) provided Paul with some easily identifiable details for the account of the relations of Gregory VII and Henry IV.[457] In an appendix at the end of the biography Paul identified the pope's most distinguished disciples, beginning with Bishop Anselm II of Lucca. Paul quoted here an extract from Anselm's commentary on the Psalms, which survives only in this fragment.[458] Another document that survives only in the *Life of Gregory VII* is the 'Statement of King Rudolf and the princes of the empire' to the papal synod of March 1080, which, according to Paul, prompted the second excommunication of Henry IV.[459]

Students of the *Life* have speculated on the possible source of Paul's elaborate account of the accession of Rudolf in March 1077, more detailed than any contemporary account. W. von Giesebrecht's suggestion that Paul used 'a kind of official document that was intended to justify Rudolf's election' was developed by later authors, producing two different theories.[460] Either the source was a report of the election addressed to the pope by his legates at Forchheim, Cardinal deacon Bernard and Abbot Bernard of St Victor in Marseilles; or it was a lost polemic by Bernold of St Blasien in defence of the legality of the election.[461] No less noteworthy than the account of Rudolf's accession is the following chapter (97), defending his breach of the oath of fealty formerly sworn to Henry IV. Paul's argument and materials here

455 *Ibid.*, c. 58, 80, 82, 84, 86, 90, 92, 93, 95, 96, pp. 303, 324, 325, 327, 329, 332, 334, 335, 336, 337.
456 *Ibid.*, c. 84 (Canossa) 96 (Rudolf's coronation), pp. 327, 337. Cf. c. 8, p. 265 ('as we read in the chronicles of venerable men'); c. 82, 86, 92, 94, 95, 96, 98, pp. 325, 330, 334, 336, 337, 340; c. 81, p. 324 (Bishop Henry of Speyer).
457 *Ibid.*, c. 59, 60, 61, 64, 65, 66, 67, 69, 70, 75, pp. 304–5, 309–11, 312–13, 317.
458 *Ibid.*, c. 112, pp. 355–6.
459 *Ibid.*, c. 106, p. 347.
460 W. von Giesebrecht (1890) p. 1154 n. 1. Cf. G. Meyer von Knonau (1894) p. 781 n. 59.
461 J. Greving (1893) pp. 101–2; F. Rörig (1948) p. 28 n. 6.

closely resemble passages in polemical writings of Bernold.[462] Paul concluded with the theory that a king is bound by a contract (*pactum*) with his subjects. This political theory is best known from the formulation by the polemicist Manegold of Lautenbach (*c.* 1085).[463] Chapter 97 of the *Life* is evidently a paraphrase or a direct quotation from a German polemical work: perhaps the same work from which the account of Rudolf's accession was drawn.

Paul was, therefore, an assiduous collector of Gregorian materials, both German and Italian, who was perhaps mainly responsible for the availability of such material in the vicinity of Regensburg (notably the works of Anselm II of Lucca and Bonizo of Sutri).[464] The most important category of materials in his collection was that of papal letters, synodal protocols and other official documents. The *Life* contains fifteen documents found in Gregory VII's *Register* and ten 'wandering letters' (*epistolae vagantes*), which have survived outside the *Register*. A first group of three documents record Gregory VII's accession. A second group of six letters illustrate the papal reform programme of 1074–5. The remaining letters underpin Paul's narrative of the relations of Gregory VII and Henry IV.[465] The older historical scholarship assumed that Paul during his visit to Rome in 1122 transcribed directly from Gregory's *Register* (codex Registrum Vaticanum 2) the fifteen documents cited in the *Life* that are found also in the papal register. This view was refuted by H. Fuhrmann, who concluded that Paul obtained these documents from the collections of Gregory's letters that are known to have circulated in Germany in the last quarter of the eleventh century.[466] It was from such letter collections that eleventh-century German chroniclers, notably Hugh of Flavigny, obtained the letters of Gregory VII that they quoted in their chronicles. The group of six letters that Paul used as evidence of the reform programme of 1074–5 appears also in a letter collection made by Bernold of St

---

462 Paul, *Life* c. 97, below pp. 338–9.

463 *Ibid.*, p. 339.

464 Perhaps Paul's research accounts for the survival of the unique codex of Bonizo's *Book to a Friend*: see above p. 43. See W. Wattenbach, R. Holtzmann and F.-J. Schmale (1976) p. 246 n. 37; C. Märtl (1985) pp. 192–202; C. Märtl (1986) pp. 179–80; F. Fuchs (1986) pp. 223–4.

465 Paul, *Life* c. 27–9, pp. 275–9; c. 36–41, pp. 283–90; c. 76–8, below pp. 317–23; c. 83–4, pp. 326–8; c. 93, p. 334; c. 99–107, pp. 341–51.

466 H. Fuhrmann (1956) pp. 299–312, with a review of earlier literature. Paul referred to 'the register of the lord Pope Alexander' (c. 58, p. 302; cf. c. 61, p. 305), but quoted no letters of Alexander II. On the late eleventh-century letter collections see C. Erdmann (1936) pp. 1–46.

Blasien and circulated as an appendix to his polemic of 1075, *Apologeticus*.[467] Five more of Paul's letters occur also in three other letter collections and sixteen of Paul's letters are also found in Hugh of Flavigny's chronicle.[468] Of the papal documents cited by Paul, only five occur in no known letter collection or chronicle and these five show sufficient variation from the text in Gregory's *Register* to permit the conclusion that they were not directly copied from it.[469]

One final type of source material collected by Paul for the *Life* was miracle stories. The material that Paul specifically mentioned collecting in Rome in 1122 was of this character: Hildebrand's miraculous detection of a simoniac, derived from the conversation of Pope Calixtus II and another miracle derived 'from the report of the Romans'.[470] It was presumably also in Rome that Paul collected a third miracle, originally told by Alexander II's chamberlain, John.[471] Three of Paul's miracle stories of Hildebrand as archdeacon closely resemble anecdotes in the collection *Dicta Anselmi*, derived from the conversation of Archbishop Anselm of Canterbury by his companion, Alexander of Canterbury.[472] Two other Hildebrandine miracles in the *Life* that do not appear in the *Dicta Anselmi* nevertheless resemble the stories in that collection, in that they are set in Cluny and feature the archdeacon's miraculous detection of secret sins.[473] Perhaps all the miracles with a Cluniac setting in the *Dicta Anselmi* and in Paul's *Life* derive from a common source, a miracle collection of Cluniac origin. Another group of three miracles illustrates Hildebrand-Gregory's devotion to the Virgin Mary.[474] It is significant that Regensburg, and in particular the

467 Paul, *Life* c. 36–41, pp. 283–90. See I. S. Robinson (1978b) pp. 65–82.

468 Paul, *Life* c. 83, 84, 107, pp. 326–8, 347–51 (letter collections); c. 28, 37, 38, 41, 77, 78, 83, 84, 93, 100, 101, 102, 103, 105, 107, pp. 276–7, 284–7, 290, 318–23, 326–8, 334, 342–5, 346, 347–51 (Hugh of Flavigny).

469 H. Fuhrmann (1956) pp. 299–312.

470 Paul, *Life* c. 17, 117, pp. 269, 359.

471 *Ibid.*, c. 22, below p. 272. Cf. c. 26, 30–1, 34, pp. 275, 279–80, 282, perhaps also collected in Rome.

472 *Ibid.*, c. 18, 20, 119, pp. 270, 271, 360. A version of the miracle in c. 17, pp. 269–70 is also found in the *Dicta Anselmi*.

473 Paul, *Life* c. 19, 119, pp. 271, 361.

474 *Ibid.*, c. 23–4, pp. 273–4; c. 32–3, pp. 280–2. This group of miracles is also found, almost verbatim, in the collection of miracles of the Virgin Mary found in two early thirteenth-century codices, Graz, Universitätsbibliothek 713 and Basel, Universitätsbibliothek B.VIII.2. H. Fuhrmann (1989) pp. 111–19, concluded that the compilers of this collection were indebted to Paul, rather than that Paul was indebted to an earlier collection of Marian miracles.

monastery of Prüfening, became an important centre for the collection
of Marian miracles in the twelfth century.[475] Paul may have played a
role in this activity, perhaps contributing material collected in Rome.
Paul's preoccupation with miracles is evident also in his borrowings
from narrative sources, notably those of Bonizo of Sutri and Bernold.

Miracles and visions were central to Paul's purpose in the *Life of
Gregory VII*, which was to show 'how great a saint he was'.[476] In an
age in which literature placed too much emphasis on secular values,
wrote Paul, the memory of Gregory VII was vital for the spiritual
health of Christendom. 'This man's example' was 'a prop for holy
Church and an ornament of Christ's faithful and brings defeat for
impious heresies'.[477] Paul urged the reader to be in no doubt of the
divine authority with which this saint was invested. Reminding them
of 'the divine vengeance' that struck down his critics, Paul concluded:
'we exhort and beseech every man who reads this work to avoid the
tongues of the detractors if he prefers to enjoy the company of
Gregory at the resurrection rather than to suffer torments with the
detractors'.[478] Paul's intention to demonstrate the sanctity of Gregory
VII explains the structure of the biography. The *Life* begins with a
series of 'miracles involving fire', illustrating the prophetic character
of Hildebrand's name, meaning 'burning up of earthly desire', and
demonstrating the resemblance between Gregory's career and that of
the prophet Elijah (chapters 1–8). In his account of Hildebrand's early
life, Paul included visions of St Peter and St Paul directing Hildebrand to the service of the Roman church (chapters 11, 13–14) and a
group of miracles revealing Hildebrand's detection of misconduct,
foreseeing danger and healing the sick (chapters 17–20, 22). Gregory
VII's election to the papacy (chapters 27–9) is preceded by visions
predicting his accession (chapters 25–6) and followed by a vision of
the Holy Spirit at his consecration (chapters 30–1) and three miraculous healings performed by the new pope (chapters 34–5). The theme
of chapters 36–43 is Gregory VII's campaign against simony and
nicholaitism. The career of Gregory's principal enemy in Rome,
Cencius Stephani, culminating in his abduction of the pope on 25
December 1075, fills thirteen chapters (45–57).

---

475 E.g. the collection of Arnold and Botho, monks of Prüfening: see H.-G. Schmitz
(1975) pp. 240–325. See also H. Fuhrmann (1989) p. 119.

476 Paul, *Life* c. 112, p. 356.

477 *Ibid.*, c. 44, p. 292.

478 *Ibid.*, c. 80, p. 324.

The succeeding fifty chapters present a narrative of the relations of Gregory VII and Henry IV, intended to refute contemporary critics of the pope.[479] Paul's account revealed the 'youthful imperfections' of Henry IV, which no papal reproofs could correct (chapters 60–5). Stung by Gregory's rebuke, Henry commanded the pope 'to vacate his throne and to relinquish his church' (chapters 66–7). In response the papal synod of 1076 deposed the king and excommunicated him and his followers (chapters 69–75). The legal justification of the pope's proceedings and the remaining events of 1076, the conspiracy of the princes against Henry IV and the subsequent absolution of Henry at Canossa (January 1077) are presented through interpolated papal letters (chapters 76–8, 82–4). Chapters 88–98 contain an account, more detailed than any other section of the *Life*, of the conference of Henry IV's enemies in Forchheim and their decision to elect Rudolf of Rheinfelden as their king. Rudolf is here portrayed in the most positive terms as an ideal Christian king. After Rudolf's coronation the narrative of events from 1077 to 1080 consists solely of extracts from synodal protocols and papal letters (chapters 99–107).

The *Life* contains no information about events between June 1080 (the council of Brixen) and Gregory VII's death on 25 May 1085. The various setbacks of the Gregorian party – the death of the anti-king Rudolf, Henry IV's expedition to Italy, his eventual capture of Rome and his imperial coronation, Gregory's exile from Rome – are expressed only in the sentence: 'A most grievous persecution was accordingly launched against the man of God and he withdrew to Salerno'.[480] The narrative concludes with the deathbed of Gregory VII, his designation of Abbot Desiderius of Monte Cassino as his successor and his last words. The last fourteen chapters record the continuing influence of Gregory VII through his principal disciples and through miracles confirming the validity of his reforming decrees. Paul celebrated the fidelity of the 'most powerful advocates of Gregorian doctrine': Bishop Anselm II of Lucca (chapters 111–12), Herluca (chapters 114–15, 122–3), the 'four principal directors' of the religious life, Bishop Altman of Passau, Udalric of Zell, William of Hirsau and Abbot Siegfried of Schaffhausen (chapters 113, 118), the Gregorian martyrs Bishop Burchard II of Halberstadt and Archbishop Thiemo of Salzburg (chapters 120–1) and Bishop Udalric of Passau (chapter 121).

479 *Ibid.*, c. 58, p. 302.
480 *Ibid.*, c. 108, p. 351.

Paul's portrait of Gregory is principally concerned with his status as a saint, a focus of miraculous activity and a martyr. Paul compared Gregory to the prophet Elijah because of his 'divine fervour'.[481] Nevertheless the pope is not consistently cast in the mould of an aggressive Old Testament prophet rebuking the powerful – as Gregory VII had thought of himself[482] – but is mainly portrayed as a 'disciple of mercy [who] had no wish to be satiated with the punishment of offenders'.[483] He was an 'athlete of God', the traditional epithet of a Christian martyr. The *Life* would show 'how the most courageous athlete of God overcame the deceptions of enemies, temptations, dangers, slanders, mockery, capture and imprisonment for the Lord's name and finally with the Lord's help and support ... he overcame kings, tyrants, dukes, princes' and 'the servants of Antichrist' among the episcopate.[484] Gregory overcame these enemies by suffering a martyr's death. He suffered at the hands of the Roman nobleman Cencius Stephani, who abducted him and held him prisoner.[485] He suffered likewise at the hands of 'the insane Henry [IV]', 'the modern Nero', the 'protector of the nicholaites', 'that most wicked king', 'the precursor of Antichrist', 'the enemy of God and the Church', 'the blasphemous usurper, the tyrant, the renegade', 'the new Nebuchadnezzar'.[486] The final image of Gregory VII in Paul's portrayal is of martyrdom. He 'who had instructed the whole world and its princes concerning sin and righteousness and judgement' was overwhelmed by 'a most grievous persecution'. Finally in Salerno 'he was most powerfully purified ... and was found worthy to receive the sweet promise of heavenly consolation'.[487]

The *Life* was first edited by Jakob Gretser, *Commentarius Pauli Bernriedensis, antiqui scriptoris, de vita Gregorii VII. Pontificis Maximi* (Ingolstadt, 1610) pp. 19–254. This is the edition that is reprinted in *Patrologia Latina* 148, cols. 39A-104A and forms the basis of the text printed by J. M. Watterich, *Pontificum Romanorum Vitae* 1, 474–546. A new edition is being prepared for the *Monumenta Germaniae Historica* by Professor Horst Fuhrmann. Professor Fuhrmann kindly permitted

481 *Ibid.*, c. 2, 3, 4, 6, 110, pp. 263, 264, 354. Cf. c. 111, p. 354, where Anselm II of Lucca is cast as Elisha, Elijah's heir.
482 C. Schneider (1972) pp. 24–30, 33–5, 96–7, 120–3; H. E. J. Cowdrey (1998) pp. 567–8.
483 Paul, *Life* c. 79, below p. 323.
484 *Ibid.*, c. 44, p. 292.
485 *Ibid.*, c. 57, p. 301.
486 *Ibid.*, c. 2, 6, 26, 59, 70, 74, 75, 108, pp. 263, 265, 275, 303, 313, 316, 317, 351.
487 *Ibid.*, c. 108, 110, p. 351, 354.

me to see his collation of the manuscripts of the *Magnum Legendarium Austriacum* (Admont, Stiftsbibliothek 24; Heiligenkreuz, Stiftsbibliothek 12; Melk, Stiftsbibliothek 675; Vienna, Österreichische Nationalbibliothek 336). The *Life* is found only in this collection of saints' lives, compiled perhaps at the end of the twelfth century in Regensburg.

Appendix I: Benzo of Alba, To Emperor Henry IV, Book VII, 1–2

A short passage from Benzo of Alba's long polemical work addressed to Henry IV is found in Appendix I. The extract is included for the purposes of comparison with the interpretation of papal-imperial relations presented by Bonizo of Sutri in his *Book to a Friend* and as an illustration of the accusations against Gregory VII that Bonizo's work was intended to refute.

The author presented himself in his work as 'brother Benzo' and 'Bishop Benzo of Alba'.[488] Our knowledge of his career derives almost entirely from his writings.[489] The only independent evidence relates to his attendance at the papal synod of Lent 1059 in Rome.[490] A date of birth of *c.* 1010 seems to be suggested by Benzo's enthusiasm for the memory of Bishop Leo of Vercelli (998–1026), who presided over 'a golden age'. 'Benzo must have known Leo in his youth and received this strong impression then.'[491] Benzo's frequent use of Greek vocabulary and his hatred of the Norman princes of southern Italy ('dung of the world', 'sons of filth', 'robbers and tyrants') prompted the theory that he was of southern Italian origin.[492] Benzo's most recent biographer, however, argued, firstly, that Benzo's use of Greek suggests not a Greek-speaking native of southern Italy but a scholar affecting a recondite vocabulary; and secondly, that Benzo's hatred of the Normans is to be explained by their alliance with the reform papacy. Benzo is more likely to have come from northern Italy (as his

---

488 Benzo, *Ad Heinricum*, dedicatio, I.1, I.4, II.16, VII prologus, pp. 88, 90, 116, 244, 580.

489 See the following biographical studies: H. Lehmgrübner (1887) pp. 3–8; P.E. Schramm (1929) pp. 258–66; M. Manitius (1931) pp. 454–7; A. Fliche (1937) pp. 215–49; H. Seyffert, introduction, edition of Benzo, *Ad Heinricum* pp. 1–14.

490 See below p. 83.

491 P. E. Schramm (1929) p. 263. Cf. H. Lehmgrübner (1887) p. 5. See Benzo, *Ad Heinricum* IV.1[30], p. 362; IV.4[33], p. 380; IV.6[35], p. 404.

492 *Ibid.*, III.1, 2, 15[16]; II.2; III.16[17], pp. 268, 270, 274, 316; 196; 318. See H. Lehmgrübner (1887) pp. 3–4 (placing Benzo in Amalfi); A. Fliche (1937) p. 216 n. 1.

youthful acquaintance with Leo of Vercelli would suggest).[493] A few
indications in his writings suggest that Benzo's career began in the
imperial chapel.[494] Certainly the personnel of the chapel and the
chancery were well known to him.[495] When Benzo recommended his
book to 'royal chaplains heaving deep sighs for the reward of a
[bishop's] ring', he may have been reflecting on his own promotion to
the bishopric of Alba as a reward for long service in the imperial
chapel.[496] He perhaps owed his appointment to Emperor Henry III,
whom he revered as 'my lord of divine memory', 'the true emperor'.[497]

Benzo is first recorded as bishop of Alba in Lent 1059, when, together
with his metropolitan Archbishop Wido of Milan and the other
suffragans of his archdiocese, he attended Pope Nicholas II's Roman
synod. Bonizo of Sutri identified him among 'those stubborn bulls, the
Lombard bishops', noting their reluctance to attend and their subsequent concealment of the reforming decrees of the synod.[498] It was
at this synod that Benzo witnessed with horror the newfangled
ceremony in which Archdeacon Hildebrand crowned the pope 'with a
royal crown'.[499] Here also Benzo subscribed the Papal Election Decree
of 1059.[500] This subscription and Bonizo's reference to his presence at
the synod are the only evidence of Benzo's existence outside the
polemic that he addressed to Henry IV. Books II and III of that work
claim that in the years 1062–4 Benzo played a major role in upholding
the claims to the papacy of Bishop Cadalus of Parma ('Honorius II'),
the candidate promoted by the imperial government at the council of
Basel (28 October 1061). Benzo was commissioned by the young King
Henry IV and his mother, the empress regent Agnes, to ensure that
Cadalus was established safely in Rome. Benzo won over the Roman

---

493 H. Seyffert, introduction pp. 2–3, 26.

494 P. E. Schramm (1929) p. 258; J. Fleckenstein (1966) p. 258; H. Seyffert, introduction pp. 5–6.

495 Wibert of Ravenna and Bishop Bernard of Luni (I.10[28], p. 178); Gregory of
Vercelli (III.26[27], p. 342); Bishop Burchard of Lausanne (IV.13[42], pp. 432–
6); the archchancellors of Italy, Archbishops Pilgrim and Herman II of Cologne
(III.2, p. 274 and below p. 370). He urged Henry IV to 'meditate' on his book 'day
and night with [his] bishops and chaplains' (Dedicatio p. 88).

496 Benzo, *Ad Heinricum* I, p. 102.

497 *Ibid.*, III.3, 19[20], pp. 278. 322.

498 Bonizo, *Book to a Friend* VI, below p. 204. See G. Meyer von Knonau (1890) p.
134; G. Schwartz (1913) p. 91.

499 See below p. 372.

500 D. Jasper (1986) pp. 50, 118.

nobility and people, escorted Cadalus to Rome and was present in a skirmish with the Norman troops raised by Hildebrand to bar Cadalus's entry to the city. After a withdrawal to Parma, Benzo led a second expedition to Rome and continued to promote the cause of Cadalus until the imperial government abandoned him at the synod of Mantua (1064). No other source mentions Benzo's involvement in the 'schism of Cadalus', but Benzo's account contains details that suggest that he must have been an eyewitness of these events.[501] Likewise uncorroborated is Benzo's report of his mission to the imperial court to urge the young king to lead an expedition to Italy against the Normans.[502]

In Book VII of his polemic, written in 1084, the author described himself as infirm and an exile from his bishopric.[503] Already in 1080, he was threatened by opponents whom he called 'the new Buziani', who 'declare that there is neither king nor priesthood unless it is made by the witchcraft of Hyrcanus', that is, Hildebrand. 'They condemn masses; they teach their followers to sit in idleness': that is, they obeyed the decrees of Gregory VII to boycott the masses of simoniac and unchaste priests.[504] A passage in similar vein (c. 1085) declares that 'the plague of the Pataria has infected very many, if not all, of the clerical order ... I have nowhere to lay my head.'[505] Evidently Benzo was driven from Alba by a reforming faction, obedient to Gregory VII and perhaps linked with the Patarine reform movement originating in Milan.[506] Benzo's work is full of condemnations of the Patarini and of Pope Alexander II, who 'originally invented the Pataria'.[507] Benzo was prevented by the pain in his feet and by failing eyesight from attending the council of Brixen (June 1080).[508] He nevertheless tried to serve the king by persuading Henry's mother-in-law, Margravine Adelaide

501 G. Meyer von Knonau (1890) pp. 216–17, 223–9; F. Herberhold (1934) pp. 84–104; F. Herberhold (1947) pp. 477–503; T. Schmidt (1977) pp. 104–14, 125–31; J. Ziese (1982) pp. 21–3; H. Seyffert, introduction pp. 7–8.

502 Benzo, *Ad Heinricum* III.13–21[22], pp. 306–28.

503 *Ibid.*, VII.1, below p. 365. For the date see H. Seyffert, introduction p. 18.

504 Benzo, *Ad Heinricum* IV.13[42], p. 432. On the Gregorian boycott see above p. 14, below p. 289.

505 *Ibid.*, I.22, p. 162. (The biblical allusion is to Matthew 8:20.)

506 H. Lehmgrübner (1887) pp. 7, 55–6 suggested that Benzo was expelled in 1077. Cf. A. Fliche (1937) pp. 220, 221.

507 Benzo, *Ad Heinricum* IV.3[32], 5[34], V.1, pp. 376, 400, 442. Cf. also VII.2, below p. 374.

508 *Ibid.*, IV.11[40], p. 422, requesting his friend, Bishop Denis of Piacenza to 'be present in the judgement on my behalf'.

of Turin, to support him.⁵⁰⁹ On Henry's arrival in Italy, Benzo was sufficiently restored to health to join the royal army. He celebrated Whitsun (23 May) 1081 with the king outside the walls of Rome.⁵¹⁰ It was through his ingenuity, Benzo claimed, that in spring 1082 the royal army was able to cross the River Nerra in safety and save a march of three or four days.⁵¹¹ In March 1084 he witnessed Henry IV's entry into Rome, Wibert of Ravenna's consecration as Pope Clement III and the imperial coronation.⁵¹² Benzo had played, according to his own account, a notable part in the emperor's victory, but he had received no reward, evidently remaining 'a bishop without a bishopric' until his death.

The polemical work *To Emperor Henry IV*, which appeared in its present form *c.* 1085, is a collection of disparate pieces of verse and prose, composed perhaps over two decades and addressed to various dignitaries (Henry IV, Adelaide of Turin, Archbishops Adalbert of Bremen and Tedald of Milan, Bishops Burchard of Lausanne, Denis of Piacenza, Cunibert of Turin, Oger of Ivrea, William of Pavia). Of its seven books, II and III contain the earliest material, dealing with the events of the 'schism of Cadalus'. Book IV has the form of a series of letters to Benzo's fellow bishops, in which they are reminded of the 'golden age' of the Ottonians and of their duty of restoring that happy time. Book V looks forward to Henry IV's imperial coronation and contains the evidence of Benzo's efforts to convert Adelaide of Turin to her son-in-law's allegiance. Book VI describes Henry's Italian expedition including Henry's triumphant entry into Rome. Book VII deals with the illegality of Gregory VII's claim to the papacy. Book I, the last to be composed, contains an account of the imperial coronation and reflects on the rights and duties of emperors and on service and rewards. At many points, therefore, Benzo's composite work reflects on his own situation in 1085, a deserving imperial servant who has yet to receive his just reward.⁵¹³

---

509 *Ibid.*, IV.13[42], p. 434; V.9–11, pp. 480–90. Benzo believed that his diplomacy had been successful: *ibid.*, V.9, p. 480; VI narratio [4], p. 544.

510 *Ibid.*, VI praefatio, pp. 504–12.

511 *Ibid.*, pp. 516–20.

512 *Ibid.*, VI.6, pp. 562–4; I.9–12, pp. 124–34.

513 On the structure and content of Benzo's polemic see H. Lehmgrübner (1887) pp. 23–91; G. Meyer von Knonau (1903) pp. 88–97; A. Fliche (1937) pp. 223–49; W. Ullmann (1970) pp. 387–93; G. Koch (1972) pp. 42–3, 115–18; H. Seyffert, introduction pp. 15–48.

In the earlier historical literature Benzo's polemic was often entitled
'Panegyric of Henry IV' and this is the feature of the work that first
strikes the reader.[514] Henry IV is addressed as 'the divine Henry, august
emperor of the Romans, one hundred times a conqueror under the
King of kings' and 'the most Christian emperor', the Lord's anointed',
'the protector and friend of the holy Roman church', 'crowned by
God', 'the friend of divine law', 'most valiant Caesar'.[515] Benzo's work
was also a panegyric of the emperorship, ancient and modern.[516]
Benzo was keenly aware of the continuity of the imperial office. He
observed that at his imperial coronation Henry IV held 'in his right
hand the sceptre of the empire in the manner of Julius [Caesar],
Octavian [Augustus] and Tiberius'.[517] Henry IV was the heir to the
virtues as well as the power of his predecessors. 'Behold a new
Constantine [I] gives joy to the world!' 'Where the venerable Charles
[Charlemagne] and the great Ottos and the elder Henry [III] laboured
hard, they left the perfection of their work to their successors.'[518]

Above all Benzo desired Henry IV to share the virtues and the
authority of Emperor Otto III, the 'emperor of emperors, whose
nobility of spirit will be remembered forever and ever'.[519] 'To the
divine Henry, most serene king', runs the salutation of one of the earlier
letters, 'Benzo of Alba wishes ... the spirit of Otto III – would to
heaven that he receives the spirit of Otto III!'[520] Otto III's importance
was, in Benzo's view, that, more than any other emperor, he had
exploited to the full his authority over Church and papacy. 'Otto III,
whose great deeds are proclaimed throughout the whole world,
punished the criminal presumption of a certain false pope by mutilating his ears, tongue and nose and gouging out his eyes.'[521] Otto's
conduct towards the antipope John XVI was offered as a model to
Henry IV, who was confronted with the false pope Gregory VII.
Benzo reminded Henry to 'use special care in the appointment of

514 P. E. Schramm (1929) pp. 258–9.

515 Benzo, *Ad Heinricum* I.4, 17[18], III.23[24], 28[29], V.13[14], VI praefatio,
VI.5, 6, pp. 116, 118, 318, 330, 352, 496, 500, 550, 566.

516 P. E. Schramm (1929) pp. 259–66.

517 Benzo, *Ad Heinricum* I.9, p. 126; VI praefatio, p. 502.

518 *Ibid.*, VI.6, p. 566 (the antipope Wibert was 'another Silvester [I]'; I.13, p. 136
(this work was the subjugation of Apulia and Calabria).

519 *Ibid.*, VII.2, below p. 367. See P. E. Schramm (1929) pp. 262–3.

520 Benzo, *Ad Heinricum*, III.6, p. 284.

521 *Ibid.*, VII.2, below p. 367. Cf. the case of John XVI as presented by Bonizo, *Book to
a Friend* IV, below p. 179.

bishops, since he must consider that God Himself conceded to him, as His deputy, the power to advance men to higher rank'.[522] Benzo similarly reminded his fellow bishops that they were 'planted in the house of the Lord by the hands of the king', not by the hands of the pope, and that they 'cannot serve two lords'. They 'must be subject, therefore, to their planter, not to the supplanter', Hildebrand.[523] The crime that made Gregory VII the principal target of Benzo's polemic was his denial of the king's supreme authority over the Church and the emperor's supremacy over the papacy.

Gregory's name is invariably accompanied in Benzo's work with a stream of ingenious abuse, making play with the name of Hildebrand and offering variations on the theme of Hildebrand as a false monk. He was 'a devil in a cowl', 'the cowled Prandellus, servant of the devil', 'the extremely seditious little monk', 'the very false and diabolical little monk'.[524] Benzo echoed the charges made at the council of Brixen (June 1080) that Gregory VII was a heretic, a necromancer and murderer of his predecessors, who had obtained his promotion in the Church by payment.[525] The extract of Benzo's work translated here contains the core of his polemic against Gregory VII. It is an account of the role of the emperor in the appointment of popes, beginning with the reign of Constantine I, intended to demonstrate that, according to the most ancient tradition, 'no one was to presume to receive consecration until he obtained the imperial consent'. That was how Pope Gregory I (on whom Gregory VII claimed to model himself) obtained his office in 590 and how all legitimate popes were appointed from the fourth to the eleventh century. Gregory VII's election did not follow this tradition but was achieved by simony. Consequently 'Prandellus was not a pope', nor were those predecessors, Nicholas II and Alexander II, whom he had raised to the papacy.[526]

The edition of Karl Pertz in *Monumenta Germaniae Historica, Scriptores* 11 (1854), 590–681, has now been superseded by that of Hans Seyffert, *Benzo von Alba, Ad Heinricum IV. imperatorem libri VII* in *Monumenta Germaniae Historica, Scriptores rerum germanicarum in usum scholarum separatim editi* 65 (Hanover, 1996). The new edition contains a German

522 Benzo, *Ad Heinricum* I.8[26], p. 172.
523 *Ibid.*, IV prologus, p. 356.
524 Benzo, *Ad Heinricum* V.13[14], p. 496; VI.[4], p. 536; VI praefatio, p. 500; II.8, p. 214. See also below p. 370.
525 *Ibid.*, II.2, p. 198; II.4, p. 204; III.10, p. 298; VI.6, p. 566.
526 *Ibid.*, VII.2, below p. 376.

translation of Benzo's text, which is invaluable for understanding this most obscure of authors.

Appendix II: Bruno of Segni, The Sermon of the venerable Bishop Bruno concerning Simoniacs, chapters 1–9

The extract from the polemic of Bruno of Segni on simoniacs found in Appendix II consists of the short biography of Pope Leo IX that fills the first nine of the sixteen chapters of this work. It is included here for the purposes of comparison with the Lotharingian *Life of Leo IX* and Bonizo's account of Leo IX's pontificate and also as an illustration of the attitude of the papal curia at the end of the eleventh century towards the great reforming pope.

We are far better informed about the career of Bishop Bruno of Segni than that of the other authors included in this volume. Bruno's canonisation by Pope Lucius III in 1183 was the occasion for the composition of a biography, written by an anonymous author at the request of Bishop Peter of Segni (1179–1206).[527] There survives also an account of Bruno's career composed perhaps forty years earlier than the anonymous biography, originating in the abbey of Monte Cassino, where Bruno had been abbot from 1107 to 1111. The *Chronicle of Monte Cassino* records the abbatiate of Bruno in Book IV chapters 31–42.[528] In addition Peter the Deacon, monk and librarian of Monte Cassino, included in chapter 34 of his catalogue of *The illustrious men of the monastery of Monte Cassino* a detailed list of the writings of this 'most eminent and most brilliant defender and doctor of the Church'.[529]

Bruno was born between 1045 and 1050 in Solero near Asti.[530] The first firm evidence of Bruno's career is his own statement that he was a canon of the cathedral of Siena during the episcopate of Bishop Rudolf (1073–83).[531] Bruno owed his promotion to the episcopate to Gregory VII. He may first have come to the notice of the pope when

---

527 *Vita sancti Brunonis, Acta Sanctorum Julii* 4, 478–84. See R. Grégoire (1965) pp. 13, 58.

528 *Chronica monasterii Casinensis* IV.31–42, pp. 496–511.

529 Petrus Diaconus, *De viris illustribus Casinensis coenobii* c. 34, cols. 1040D-1042B.

530 According to *Chronica monasterii Casinensis* IV.31, p. 496 ('of an illustrious family'); *Vita sancti Brunonis* c. 3, p. 479 (of humble parentage). See R. Grégoire (1965) pp. 16–18 and also 23–4 (date of birth).

531 Bruno, *Expositio in Apocalypsim*, praefatio, *MPL* 165, col. 605AB. See B. Gigalski (1898) p. 30.

he attended the Roman synod of Lent 1079.[532] According to the anonymous biographer, after the synod Bruno was escorted to Segni by Cardinal bishop Peter of Albano at the suggestion of the pope. There he preached 'an excellent sermon' before the canons. The see of Segni being then vacant, the canons elected Bruno as their bishop on the advice of Peter of Albano and Bruno was prevailed on by Gregory VII to accept election.[533] He remained bishop of Segni until his death on 18 July 1123.[534] That Bruno was a protégé of Gregory VII is corroborated by his *Sermon concerning Simoniacs,* which records examples of the pope's familiar conversation. On one occasion Gregory rebuked his entourage, 'and me in particular, as it seemed to me, since he kept his eyes fixed on me', for not recording his 'many stories' about Leo IX.[535] Bruno seems to have contemplated writing a biography of Gregory VII 'in another work at another time', but no such work survives.[536]

Throughout the period of his episcopate Bruno enjoyed the dignity of a cardinal bishop. This status has been doubted, on the grounds that Segni was not one of the seven traditional cardinal bishoprics, but the evidence is incontrovertible.[537] He is first identified as a cardinal in a document recording an assembly of cardinals on 4 May 1082.[538] He is specifically described as 'cardinal bishop' in a letter of Pope Urban II reporting his election to the papacy (12 March 1088).[539] Bruno is also found with the title of cardinal in documents from outside the papal

---

532 *Vita sancti Brunonis* c. 6, p. 479. It was at this synod that Berengar of Tours was obliged to renounce his teachings on the eucharist. There is a claim (uncorroborated) in the anonymous biography that Bruno disputed with Berengar in the synod. See B. Gigalski (1898) pp. 32–3; R. Grégoire (1965) pp. 25–7.

533 *Vita sancti Brunonis* c. 8–12, pp. 479–80. According to *Chronica monasterii Casinensis* IV.31, p. 496, the pope who intervened on Bruno's behalf was Urban II (1088–99). The earliest charter of Bruno's episcopate is, however, dated 4 May 1082: see G. Schwartz (1913) p. 271. See also B. Gigalski (1898) pp. 34–5; R. Grégoire (1965) pp. 27–9; R. Hüls (1977) p. 129.

534 B. Gigalski (1898) p. 108; G. Schwartz (1913) p. 271; R. Grégoire (1965) p. 58. R. Hüls (1977) p. 129, gave the date 23 July 1123.

535 Bruno, *Sermon concerning Simoniacs* c. 3, below p. 381. Cf. c. 4, p. 382. For this miracle see also below p. 200.

536 Bruno, *Sermon* c. 2, p. 380.

537 B. Gigalski (1898) p. 43 n. 1; R. Grégoire (1965) p. 33 n. 86. But see H.-W. Klewitz (1957) pp. 37–44.

538 Z. Zafarana (1966b) pp. 399–403. See also H.-W. Klewitz (1957) p. 38; H. E. J. Cowdrey (1983) pp. 152–3; H. E. J. Cowdrey (1998) pp. 220–1.

539 Urban II, *JL* 5349, *MPL* 151, col. 284C-285D. See H.-W. Klewitz (1957) p. 39; A. Becker (1964) pp. 91–6.

curia.[540] The explanation is that during Bruno's episcopate the cardinal bishopric of Silva Candida was impossible to reclaim for the Gregorian obedience and it was therefore decided to include Segni among the cardinal bishoprics so that they would continue to be seven in number. It was a clear indication of the high regard in which Bruno was held in the papal curia from the beginning of his episcopate. For three decades he was a conspicuous figure in the curia. He formed a close friendship with the Gregorian hero Cardinal bishop Peter of Albano and with Cardinal deacon Damian, nephew of the great reformer Peter Damian and his successor at the abbey of Fonte Avellana (later created cardinal and abbot of Nonantola by Gregory VII).[541] A letter from the pontificate of Victor III (1086–7) identifies Bruno as 'librarian of the Roman church'. At this date the office of librarian included the duties of chancellor, so that during the four months of the pontificate Bruno directed the activity of the papal chancery.[542] During the years 1089–96 Bruno regularly subscribed papal letters, in which he was identified as an adviser of Urban II.[543] Bruno was a member of Urban's entourage when he made his momentous journey to France (1095–6). When Urban visited the abbey of Cluny and consecrated the high altar (25 October 1095), Bruno preached a sermon, which paid tribute to the wisdom of Abbot Hugh I.[544]

In the opening two years of the pontificate of Paschal II (1099–1118) Bruno's subscription again appears in papal letters.[545] The sudden change in direction in Bruno's career in 1102, when he entered the monastic life, is related in quite different ways in the two biographical sources. According to the Monte Cassino chronicle, Bruno arrived at the abbey of Monte Cassino and, to the astonishment and dismay of

540 In the anti-papal polemic of Garcia of Toledo, *De Albino et Rufino* c. 7, *MGH Libelli* 2, 433–5 and the chronicle of Herman of Tournai, *MGH SS* 14, 287.

541 *Vita sancti Brunonis* c. 6–10, pp. 479–80. See G. Miccoli (1960) pp. 49–50, 75–6. On Peter of Albano see also below p. 244. Bruno composed his *Commentarium in Isaiam* at the request of Damian: *Prologus in Isaiam* ed. A. Amelli (1903) p. 9. Cf. Bruno, *Expositio in Apocalypsim*, *MPL* 165, col. 605B.

542 L. Santifaller (1940) pp. 207, 435–6. See R. Grégoire (1965) pp. 32–3; H. E. J. Cowdrey (1983) pp. 208, 219.

543 Urban II, *JL* 5403, 5411, 5479, 5505–6, 5519, 5620, 5633–4, 5642, 5658–9, 5663: see R. Grégoire (1965) pp. 34–41; R. Hüls (1977) pp. 129–30.

544 *Sermo post consecrationem ecclesiae Cluniacensis*, *MPL* 151, col. 561–4. Cf. the digression on Hugh of Cluny in Bruno, *Sermon* c. 3, below p. 382.

545 *Italia Pontificia* 8, 290–1 (no. 6); Paschal II, *JL* 5837, 5843, 5864: see R. Grégoire (1965) pp. 42–3. Bruno was not, however, present at Paschal's election or consecration: see C. Servatius (1979) pp. 34, 42.

his entourage, 'he became a monk'. 'The people of Segni ... asked Pope Paschal II to compel [Bruno] to carry out the duties of his episcopal office rather than to have regard only to himself and to desire only to take his ease in the monastery of Monte Cassino, peaceful and far from the storms of the world.' Neither the pope nor the people of Segni could deflect Bruno from his purpose and at last Abbot Oderisius I of Monte Cassino (1087–1105) obtained permission for him to enter his abbey.[546] The version of the anonymous biographer, generally preferred by historians, is that Bruno fell ill in Apulia, while he was in the papal entourage. When he confided to Paschal II his wish to enter a monastery, the pope authorised his profession at Monte Cassino.[547] Both accounts agree that Bruno remained bishop of Segni after making his monastic profession and the Monte Cassino chronicle states that 'in obedience to the pope ... he was to spend forty days in the service of the Roman church' every year. As a consequence of this obligation Bruno undertook a legation to France in 1106.[548] On the death of Abbot Otto of Monte Cassino (1105–7) Bruno was elected abbot. 'When the pope subsequently came to this place,' wrote the Monte Cassino chronicler, 'he declared in an assembly of the brethren that not only was he worthy of being abbot, he would also be a worthy successor to himself in the apostolic see.'[549] Initially the new abbot's relations with Paschal were friendly. Bruno was present at the papal synod in Benevento in October 1108, where Paschal renewed the Gregorian decree against lay investiture.[550] When on 4 June 1109 Paschal canonised Bruno's old friend, Bishop Peter of Anagni, in Segni, the papal letter announcing the canonisation noted that Bruno had written a biography of the saint.[551]

The breakdown in Bruno's relations with the pope was part of the crisis in the Gregorian party precipitated in 1111 by 'the evil privilege extorted from Pope Paschal II by the violence of King Henry [V]'.[552] In February 1111 negotiations took place in Rome between Henry V

---

546 *Chronica monasterii Casinensis* IV.31, p. 497.

547 *Vita sancti Brunonis* c. 19–21, p. 482.

548 T. Schieffer (1935) pp. 175–8. He accompanied Prince Bohemund I of Antioch, who was seeking support for his eastern schemes.

549 *Chronica monasterii Casinensis* IV.31, p. 498. See R. Grégoire (1965) p. 50.

550 *Chronica monasterii Casinensis* IV.33, p. 499. See U.-R. Blumenthal (1978) p. 19; C. Servatius (1979) p. 211; S. Beulertz (1991) pp. 19, 140.

551 Paschal II, *JL* 6239, *MPL* 165, col. 1139A. See R. Grégoire (1965) pp. 51, 112–14.

552 Lateran synod of 1112, *MGH Constitutiones* 1, 571.

and Paschal II to settle the longstanding dispute concerning lay investiture. The failure of these negotiations prompted Henry V to take the pope prisoner and force on him the treaty of Ponte Mammolo (11 April 1111). Paschal regained his freedom by means of a papal privilege granting the emperor the right to lay investiture.[553] Among the prominent reformers who denounced this betrayal of the Gregorian stand against investiture was Bruno of Segni. He wrote to the pope reminding him of his earlier legislation on the subject and urging him to repudiate his concession to the emperor: 'with your apostolic authority condemn this heresy, which you yourself have often called heresy'.[554] To other correspondents he wrote: 'The lord pope loves neither me nor my advice ... I say what I have said before and I remain most firmly of the opinion of Gregory and Urban.'[555]

Paschal II's response to Bruno's intransigent Gregorian views was to command the monks of Monte Cassino to elect a new abbot and to require Bruno's resignation from his office, on the grounds that 'a bishop ought not simultaneously to be an abbot'.[556] Bruno withdrew to his diocese of Segni and played no further role in the activity of the papal curia. He was, however, present to hear the condemnation of 'the evil privilege' of 1111 in the papal synods of 1112 and 1116. A report of the latter synod offers a last glimpse of Bruno. When the pope condemned his 'evil privilege' and the whole synod shouted its agreement, 'Bishop Bruno of Segni cried out louder still: "We give thanks to Almighty God that we have heard the lord Pope Paschal ... with his own mouth condemning that privilege, which contains wickedness and heresy!"' He was at once rebuked by Paschal's closest adviser, the chancellor John of Gaeta (soon to be Pope Gelasius II): 'Do you call the Roman pontiff a heretic in this council and in our hearing?'[557] Bruno stubbornly repeated the word 'heresy', which he had used in his letter of 1111 to the pope and which had probably ensured his dismissal from Monte Cassino. His intransigent Gregorian stance now made him an uncomfortable presence in the papal curia where he had once been so prominent.

553 G. Meyer von Knonau (1907) pp. 141–72; C. Servatius (1979) pp. 219–52; I. S. Robinson (1990) pp. 424–9.

554 Bruno of Segni, *Epistola* 2, p. 564.

555 Bruno, *Epistola* 3, p. 565.

556 *Chronica monasterii Casinensis* IV.42, p. 511. See R. Grégoire (1965) pp. 54–5; C. Servatius (1979) pp. 300–2.

557 Ekkehard of Aura, *Chronica* III, 1116, p. 320.

'It is not to be thought that this man lived in idleness,' wrote the
Monte Cassino chronicler of the disgraced abbot. He was referring to
Bruno's literary works, which now fill two volumes of the *Patrologia
Latina* (164, 165). These works include 146 homilies on biblical subjects, six books of sermons, theological treatises and a polemic against
the Greek Church on the subject of the eucharist. The bulk of Bruno's
works, however, consists of commentaries on the Bible (the Pentateuch, Job, the Psalms, the Song of Songs, Isaiah, the Gospels and
Revelation).[558] Bruno's biblical commentaries carefully imitated the
scriptural exegesis of the Church Fathers in discarding the literal
meaning of the text for the 'spiritual senses', the allegorization of the
text.[559] The conviction that the pages of the Bible contained prophecies
of future events waiting to be deciphered by means of the allegorical
method led Bruno to conclude that some of the prophetic messages
related to his own times. Like the biblical commentaries of the circle
of Matilda of Tuscany, Bruno found in the words of Scripture explicit
confirmation of the reforming measures of the Gregorian papacy and
condemnation of the Henrician party.[560]

The same Gregorian attitudes inform the *Sermon concerning Simoniacs*,
which is partly a Gregorian polemic, partly a work of hagiography.
The work was perhaps composed in the late 1090s.[561] Bruno presented
Pope Leo IX above all as the saintly enemy of simony. Beginning
with a picture of the unreformed Church before *c.* 1050, when 'Simon
Magus possessed the Church, … [and] priests were not ashamed to
take wives',[562] the *Sermon* presents the life and miracles of the pope
who inaugurated the reform of the Church. The second half of the
work is a defence of the validity of the orders of clergy ordained by
simoniacs (albeit without simony): a contribution to a debate that had
preoccupied the reform movement since the middle of the eleventh

---

558 R. Grégoire (1965) pp. 67–129.

559 B. Smalley (1952) pp. 1–26.

560 I. S. Robinson (1983) pp. 69–98. See above p. 54.

561 The work is difficult to date: see E. Sackur, introduction to his edition p. 545 ('in
the time of Urban II'); B. Gigalski (1898) pp. 156–9 (probably 1094, but cannot
exclude the possibility of 1097–1101); H. Tritz (1952) pp. 298–9 (between 1085
and 1100); R. Grégoire (1965) pp. 109–111 (between 1085 and 1102). The *terminus
a quo* is the death of Gregory VII (below p. 381); the *terminus ad quem* is provided
by the information that Abbot Hugh I of Cluny, who died in 1109, was, when
Bruno wrote, 'an old man and full of days' (p. 382).

562 Bruno of Segni, *Sermon* c. 1, below p. 377.

563 For the significance of Bruno's work in this debate see L. Saltet (1907) pp. 223–4,
251–4; A. Schebler (1936) pp. 259–64.

century.[563] The *Sermon* consists, therefore, of two quite disparate sections. The first of these, which is translated here, is a saint's *Life* intended to be read on the saint's feast day, 19 April, the anniversary of Leo IX's death.[564] There follows a celebration of Leo's virtues – 'whatever qualifications are necessary to the episcopal order all joined together in him'[565] – and his miracles. One of the miracles is recounted on the authority of Gregory VII, another on that of Cardinal bishop John III of Porto.[566] The account of Leo's death and the ensuing miracles is taken, often verbatim, from the narrative of Libuin, subdeacon of the Roman church, composed soon after Leo's death.[567] Of particular interest is the report of Leo's expedition against the Normans and his defeat at the battle of Civitate (June 1053). While confident of the legitimacy of the pope's cause, Bruno had strong reservations about the wisdom of his military enterprise. 'Would that he had not gone there in person, but had only sent an army there to defend righteousness!'[568]

There is no evidence that Bruno knew the *Life of Leo IX* with which this collection begins.[569] Bruno's inspiration for his work was the memory of Gregory VII's conversations about Leo IX. The immediate stimulus was the vision experienced by Cardinal bishop John of Tusculum: 'the blessed Leo in pontifical vestments appeared to [John] in a dream' with a message for Bruno that the latter interpreted as 'a command' to write his biography.[570] John of Tusculum's vision and Bruno's response to it reveal the strength of the *memoria* of Leo IX in the papal curia half a century after his death. In its source materials and its inspiration Bruno's *Sermon* was as much a Roman work as the *Life of Leo IX*, with which this collection begins, was a Lotharingian work.

The text in *Patrologia Latina* 165, 1109–1122 and the incomplete text

---

564 Bruno, *Sermon* c. 1, p. 377. B. Gigalski (1898) pp. 159–60 considered the first part of the work to be a sermon on the occasion of the introduction of the feast of Leo IX in the church of Segni.

565 Bruno, *Sermon* c. 2, p. 378.

566 *Ibid.*, c. 4, 8, pp. 383, 388.

567 *Ibid.*, c. 6–7, pp. 385–8. For Libuin see H. Tritz (1952) pp. 321–46. See also R. Grégoire (1965) pp. 108–9.

568 Bruno, *Sermon* c. 5, p. 383. See C. Erdmann (1935) p. 112.

569 He may have known Bonizo's account of Leo IX in the *Book to a Friend* V, since Bonizo's version of the election of Leo, giving Hildebrand a prominent role (below p. 190) seems to have influenced Bruno's account (p. 379).

570 Bruno, *Sermon* c. 9, p. 389.

in J. M. Watterich, *Pontificum Romanorum Vitae* 1, 95–100 derive from the original edition of Maur Marchesi, *S. Brunonis Astensis, Signiensium episcopi Opera* 2 (Venice, 1651), 146–53. The modern edition is that of Ernst Sackur, *Brunonis episcopi Signini Libellus de symoniacis, Monumenta Germaniae Historica, Libelli de lite* 2 (Hanover, 1892), 543–62.

The Life of Pope Leo IX

Prologue

When, therefore, Bishop Herman[1] had gone the way of all flesh,[2] he
was succeeded by the venerable Bruno,[3] who had been miraculously
endowed by the Lord with preeminence of birth and distinction of
character.[4] Although he now appears as the last in the list of the
episcopal succession, he has nevertheless shone forth as the first by
virtue of the privilege of becoming the supreme pontiff.[5] Like the
morning star, which is the last to take up its position in the sky but
which approaches the sun more closely than the rest,[6] he, after a long
series of predecessors, conferred renown on the city of Toul, indeed on
the whole Christian world, by his priesthood and, putting to flight the
darkness of error by the force of his brightness, he has displayed the
true sun, his neighbour. He, who was chosen by heaven ages ago to
appear at his predestined time, incurs no disadvantage from the tardi-
ness of his birth. For the unchangeable Godhead, for whom things past
and things yet to come remain simultaneously present, has so arranged
the succession of mutable things that nothing seems to Him late or
out of season in the sequence of events. Indeed, to say nothing of other
matters, it is acknowledged that the redemption supremely necessary to
the human race was manifested at the end of time; and Paul, who
laboured more than all, was summoned from heaven after all the
apostles: hence he is found to have named himself 'one untimely born'.[7]

1 Herman, bishop of Toul (1019–26).

2 Cf. Joshua 23:14; I Kings 2:2.

3 Bruno, bishop of Toul (1026–51); Pope Leo IX (1048/9–1054).

4 The opening words ('When ... Bruno') reappear in the Toul chronicle *Gesta episcoporum
Tullensium* c. 38, p. 644, citing 'the book of his life and virtues, which is in the church
of St-Evre'. P. Schmid (1926) p. 206 suggested that the biography was a continuation of an existing work on the bishops of Toul; but see H. Tritz (1952) p. 225 n. 68.

5 H. Hoesch (1970) p. 246 detected a stylistic resemblance to the biography of
Deodatus of Nevers, attributed to Humbert of Moyenmoutier (c. 1.1, *MPL* 151,
col. 611C; cf. c. 3.21, col. 629B). H.-G. Krause (1976) p. 67 n. 78 argued that such
phrases are the commonplaces of hagiography.

6 Cf. Gregory I, *Moralia in Iob* X.18.34, *MPL* 75, col. 940B: 'It is right to compare
the life of the just with the morning-star'. See M. Parisse and M. Goullet, edition
of *Vita Leonis IX* p. 129.

7 I Corinthians 15:8.

Pursuing this subject no further, however, I shall devote my pen to the task that I have undertaken: to transcribe for the edification of many not so much what I have heard, but what I have seen of this great bishop.[8] His benevolence indeed, deigning to admit me, poor as I am, to associate with him continually on the most familiar terms,[9] made it possible for me, without any effort on his part, to discover very many things about him that ought to be imitated, together with information recounted by truthful and venerable persons. Some of his deeds I shall touch upon only superficially, others I shall deliberately pass over lest my account should be too long or I should be branded with the label of sycophant or – because he is still alive – I should be assailed with that proverb of Solomon: 'Do not praise a man during his lifetime.'[10] But since we have the purpose of praising in him the gifts of God, which ought to be praised even in a pagan, we do not praise the man, but Him by whom and through whom *every man coming into this world* is *enlightened*,[11] so that he thinks, says or does what is good. Do we claim that in this wretched existence, which assuredly is all temptation, so great a prelate ever lived or still lives without sin, which cannot happen even in the case of a one-day-old infant? But those whose care it is to publish for the use of others the divine virtues imprinted in any man, will not shame him by laying bare the man's sins that have already been covered up by God. Hence the Israelites at God's command carried away from Egypt the gold and silver that was formed into vessels, but left behind that that was fashioned into idols.[12]

With this preface our discourse begins. We shall believe ourselves to have been most successful in this, even if we transmit to posterity, albeit partially and in an undistinguished style, only his praiseworthy deeds as bishop of Toul. It will be the duty of the wise and particularly of the Romans,[13] however, gratefully to transmit to the catholic Church a faithful account of what he achieved as Roman pope.

---

8 Cf. Isidore of Seville, *Etymologiae* I.14.1: 'For among the ancients no one wrote history except him who was present and saw those things that were to be recorded.'

9 See above p. 25 and H. Tritz (1952) p. 247; H. Hoffmann (1963) p. 207; M. Parisse and M. Goullet, edition of *Vita* p. xxvi.

10 Cf. Ecclesiasticus 11:30.

11 John 1:9.

12 Cf. Exodus 12: 35–6.

13 Cf. II.27, below p. 157. See above p. 25 and H. Tritz (1952) p. 248; H. Hoffmann (1963) p. 208; H. Hoesch (1970) p. 248 n. 21; H.-G. Krause (1976) pp. 76–7.

The First Book

1 The venerable Bruno, therefore, derived from both his parents a lineage so noble that among his great-great-great-grandfathers and more distant ancestors, all those of whom we could obtain information either themselves governed a kingdom or an empire or held office next to kings and emperors.[14] He was born, however, in the territory of sweet Alsace;[15] his father was Hugh,[16] his mother Heilwig[17] and their piety caused many to praise God. His father was German by birth,[18] the cousin of Emperor Conrad,[19] most eloquent in his mother tongue and in French;[20] his mother was French and equally skilled in both languages. Their fathers and grandfathers from their earliest youth with unbounded courage fiercely suppressed those who resisted them with their weapons and their minds, defending themselves and their parties. In old age, casting aside all the pride of their kindred and the luxury of the world, they clothed themselves in the humility and poverty of Christ, giving their patrimonies to the churches, building monasteries on their properties with their own revenues. Thus, as perfect followers of Christ, at last they renounced even themselves: utterly rejecting the foolish wisdom of the world and with complete contrition, substituting the wise foolishness of God[21] and the monastic habit, they died a most praiseworthy death. Among the very many possessions that they distributed here and there to the holy

---

14 Cf. Desiderius of Monte Cassino, *Dialogi* III, prologus, p. 1143; *Chronica monasterii Casinensis* II.79, p. 324. Carolingian ancestry of Leo's father: E. Hlawitschka (1969) pp. 115–16; alleged royal ancestry of his mother: *ibid.*, p. 105 n. 114.

15 M. Parisse and M. Goullet, *Vita* p. xxvi saw here a reference to the author's *patria*.

16 Hugh [IV], count of Egisheim-Dagsburg. See H. Jakobs (1968) pp. 197–201; E. Hlawitschka (1969) pp. 103–37.

17 Heilwig (daughter of Count Ludwig). See H. Jakobs (1968) pp. 198–201; E. Hlawitschka (1969) pp. 103–6.

18 Cf. *Chronica monasterii Casinensis* II.79, p. 324; *Annales Romani* p. 470. See H. Taviani-Carozzi (1996) p. 205.

19 Conrad II, king of the Germans (1024–39), emperor (1027). (Cf. I.6, 8, 10, below pp. 106, 110, 114) Cf. *Annalista Saxo* 1048, p. 687 ('cousin'); Wipo, *Gesta Chuonradi imperatoris* c. 19, p. 39 ('kinsman'); Anselm of St-Remi, *Historia dedicationis ecclesiae S. Remigii* c. 7, col. 1420D. The precise relationship: H. Jakobs (1968) p. 199; E. Hlawitschka (1969) pp. 135–7; H. Zielinski (1984) p. 41.

20 M. Parisse and M. Goullet, *Vita* p. 129 n. 6 suggested 'the romance or French language', demonstrating 'the bilingualism of a family whose patrimony straddled the linguistic frontier'.

21 Cf. I Corinthians 1:20.

churches, they established two monasteries from their own property, namely that in Hesse in honour of the blessed Bishop Martin[22] and that of Altdorf[23] dedicated to the holy martyr Cyriacus.[24] They also greatly enlarged the monastery of Lure[25] with their own patrimonies. Imitating their piety, the excellent Count Hugh and his most devout wife, the parents of the lord Bruno, built the monastery of Woffenheim,[26] most suitable for the life of seclusion, endowed with the tithes of their estates, within their noble castle of Egisheim. In this monastery there now lives a congregation of nuns, dedicated to the veneration and glory of the salvific and most victorious Cross.

2 This couple displayed to all a way of life so distinguished and honourable that even churchmen and men in various ranks from bishops to laymen perceived in them something that they might imitate. For to hint only at the many aspects of their vigilance towards God, they used the ordeal of cold water to investigate whether the tithes of their property were being paid in full.[27] When the Almighty had decided to send a prelate to His Church through them, He deigned to foretell to the pregnant mother the greatness of the child whom she was carrying in her womb. For one night a man in a religious habit appeared to her in a vision and informed her that she had conceived a male offspring who would be great before God[28] and commanded that he should be named Bruno.[29]

---

22 See C. H. Brakel (1972) pp. 260, 275, 279–80. For Leo IX and the cult of Martin, bishop of Tours (✝397) see II.22, below p. 153.

23 Cf. Leo IX, privilege for Altdorf (28 November 1049), *JL* 4206: see E. Hlawitschka (1969) pp. 111, 113, 149 n. 262; C. H. Brakel (1972) pp. 259–61.

24 Leo and the cult of the Roman deacon and martyr Cyriacus (a victim of the persecution of Diocletian): I.15, below p. 121 (Leo composed a responsory in honour of Cyriacus). See C. H. Brakel (1972) pp. 259–64, 269, 281.

25 Merovingian foundation dedicated to Deicolus (the Irish hermit Dichil ✝ *c.* 625) in the Vosges. See E. Hlawitschka (1969) pp. 107–8, 149 n. 262; C. H. Brakel (1972) p. 276 n. 227.

26 The convent of the Holy Cross, Woffenheim. Cf. Leo IX's privilege, *JL* 4201, *MPL* 143, 635A–637B: see E. Hlawitschka pp. 103–4. Hugh and Heilwig were buried there (according to the charter of Countess Matilda of Mousson-Mömpelgard for Woffenheim, *c.* 1090, *ibid.*, p. 104 n. 109). See R. Bloch (1930) pp. 190, 195, 198–202, 221–2; B. Szabó-Bechstein (1985) p. 98.

27 Ordeal of cold water: R. Bartlett (1986) pp. 10–12, 23–5, 50–2. Leo IX and the payment of tithes: II.10, below p. 137. See G. Constable (1964) pp. 85–6, 95, 165–6, 215.

28 Cf. Luke 1:15.

29 Bruno (like Heilwig) was a name characteristic of the Ottonian dynasty: see E. Hlawitschka (1969) p. 105 n. 114. C. H. Brakel (1972) p. 243 suggested that the child was named after the Ottonian Archbishop Bruno of Cologne (953–65), who was perhaps a kinsman.

When he came into this world, on 21 June in the year 1002 since the Word of God was incarnated, in the fifteenth indiction – wonderful to relate! – the whole of his small body was found to be marked with little crosses.[30] His mother was deeply moved by the strangeness of this phenomenon and, convinced by the promise in her previous vision, contrary to her usual practice she allowed him to be fed with milk by no one except herself. After she had weaned him at the appropriate time, she entrusted him at five years old to Berthold, bishop of the holy church of Toul,[31] to be educated in the liberal arts and initiated in the study of literature.[32] This Berthold outdid his predecessors in his striving for genuine virtue. He enobled the city of Toul by attracting the sons of noblemen there; he greatly increased its wealth and glory in various ways: he adorned it with very many buildings, filled it with men of letters and restored the discipline of the monasteries inside and outside.[33]

3 Such was the suitable man who joyfully received the little child and caused him to be instructed in literature and all the virtues appropriate to noble boys. While his body grew in stature from day to day, the outstanding quality of his mind developed, finding favour with everyone, more than all his fellows. For as the most learned Father Jerome bears witness: 'Wax that was soft and easy to work was, through a certain natural flexibility, shaped by heaven, even though the workman's hands had ceased to fashion it.'[34] Being surrounded, therefore, by heavenly grace, he attracted to himself the good will of all men, because they perceived in him none of that pride that arises from the preeminence of royal lineage, riches, beauty and genius, to which the worldly are accustomed to respond at first with elation and

30 The biographer understood this as a prophecy of Leo's veneration for the Cross (cf. II.3, below p. 129): C. H. Brakel (1972) pp. 243–4, 276. The intensification of the cult of the Cross in Leo's lifetime: G. Schreiber (1948) p. 88; C. H. Brakel (1972) pp. 251, 258, 264, 265.

31 Berthold, bishop of Toul (996–1019). See E. Martin (1900) pp. 180–93.

32 Cf. Desiderius, *Dialogi* III prologus, p. 1143. The cathedral school of Toul: E. Lesne (1940) pp. 345–6. A. Michel (1948) p. 299 claimed that Bruno was educated in the monastery of St Evre, 'which probably accommodated the episcopal school'.

33 Berthold's reforms: see K. Hallinger (1950) p. 62; N. Bulst (1973) pp. 91–5. Cf. the view of Berthold found in the Moyenmoutier history, *Liber de sancti Hidulfi successoribus* c. 12, p. 92: 'Berthold ... was a shrewd oppressor of the people and the monasteries with unaccustomed laws, who is known to have inflicted an irreparable calamity on the monastery of Moyenmoutier'. He had taken the village of Bergheim, granted to Moyenmoutier by Henry II: see H. Tritz (1952) pp. 253–4; H. Hoffmann (1963) p. 207; N. Bulst (1973) p. 103.

34 Jerome, *Epistolae* LIII.3, *CSEL* 54, 446 (paraphrased).

soon afterwards with disgust. He was indeed kind to all men, even the most humble, cheerful in appearance and disposition and most obedient not only towards his superiors and equals but also towards his inferiors.

His contemporaries, although somewhat older than he, were two Adalberos, his kinsmen. The former, son of Duke Theoderic,[35] was snatched away from this world prematurely; the other, brother of Duke Hezilo and son of the distinguished prince Frederick,[36] was appointed the schoolmaster of his young kinsman Bruno, under the direction of the master of the schools, because he was already regarded as learned at that time. When subsequently he was received in the bishopric of Metz by the will of the clergy and people rather than by his own desire, this man enlightened our age especially by his preaching. Desirous from his youth to please God alone, he strove beyond the limitations of his age and strength to crucify his flesh together with his vices and lusts, burning so fiercely with the divine fire that even in the earliest period of his Christian noviciate he was thought to be more perfect than the most perfect.[37] Finally, to say nothing here of his supreme celibacy, his dovelike innocence, his serpentlike wisdom,[38] his keen perception and the mature dignity of his youthful genius, he inflicted such fasts and vigils upon himself that he could literally say with the blessed Job: 'My bone cleaves to my skin, to my wasted flesh.'[39]

4 The admirable boy Bruno, therefore, pursued his literary studies, indivisibly joined by brotherly affection to this colleague: they rejoiced together in their learning. Although they were surrounded by crowds of noble boys, these two nevertheless surpassed all their fellows both in their capacity for study and in the excellence of their moral characters. Indeed, as soon as it was appropriate for them as

---

35 Adalbero, bishop elect of Metz (✝1005), son of Duke Theoderic I of Upper Lotharingia (978–1026/7). See E. Hlawitschka (1969) pp. 109–10.

36 Adalbero III, bishop of Metz (1047–72), son of Count Frederick of the Moselgau (✝1019), brother of Henry [Hezilo] II, count of Luxemburg (1026–47), duke of Bavaria (1042–7): see E. Hlawitschka (1969) pp. 110–111; H. Zielinski (1984) p. 82; M. Twellenkamp (1991) pp. 414, 486, 495.

37 Cf. *Gesta episcoporum Mettensium* c. 49, p. 543 ('Adalbero, venerable for sanctity and religion, … a lover of peace and restorer of monasteries'); Sigebert of Gembloux, *Chronica* 1046, p. 358; Rudolf of St Trond, *Gesta abbatum Trudonensium* I.10, 12, pp. 233–4, 235. See E. Steindorff (1881) pp. 9–10.

38 Cf. Matthew 10:16.

39 Job 19:20.

beginners to go through the arts of the trivium,[40] not only were they famous for their prose and their verse, but they also understood and developed disputed questions with keen and agile minds or carefully resolved them.[41] They also acquainted themselves with the quadrivium,[42] investigating it with their natural talents, and were no less proficient in it, as will be apparent from what follows.

While these children were being educated together in that place, the mother of lord Bruno was informed of the future promotion of her son in the following dream. She saw herself entering the venerable basilica of the most blessed Stephen, the first martyr for Christ,[43] from the side of the bishop's chamber; and she saw herself meeting Bishop Gerard of holy memory[44] (who was glorified by heaven with miracles both in his lifetime and after his death) and saw him taking from his neck the *orarium* (which is commonly called a stole) and placing it on her sleeve. This vision predicted (as far as can be conjectured) that her son was destined by heaven to be the successor not only to his see but also to his zeal for good. For although the venerable Bruno is reckoned as the fifth bishop from lord Gerard,[45] it seems as though he was chosen by the latter alone and by none of his successors, since with God's approval it was Gerard whom he imitated before the others.

Because the pious dispensation of the Almighty is, however, accustomed to mingle scourges and temptations with His gifts, as we know to have happened to the blessed Job and the apostle Paul and nearly all the elect, it seems necessary to describe how Bruno ran into danger in his early youth and how he was immediately saved by the application of a heavenly remedy.

40 The first group of disciplines in the curriculum of the seven liberal arts, consisting of grammar, dialectic and rhetoric: see G. Paré, A. Brunet and P. Tremblay (1933) pp. 99–100; H. I. Marrou (1950) pp. 245, 524; J. Jolivet (1969) pp. 14–22.

41 I.e. they practised the art of dialectic (logic): see R.W. Southern (1953) pp. 174–5; J. Jolivet (1969) pp. 16–62.

42 The second group of disciplines of the seven liberal arts, consisting of arithmetic, geometry, astronomy and music. For Leo's interest in music see I.15, below p. 121.

43 The cathedral church of Toul, dedicated to St Stephen: see A. Haverkamp (1991) p. 175.

44 Gerard I, bishop of Toul (963–94). For Leo IX's canonisation of Gerard see II.15, below p. 141. As bishop of Toul Bruno commissioned a biography of Gerard: Widrich, *Vita sancti Gerardi* prefatio, p. 490. See A. Michel (1948) p. 316 and n. 45; H. Tritz (1952) p. 225 and n. 69; C. H. Brakel (1972) pp. 244, 274.

45 The bishops were Gerard I, Stephen (994–6), Berthold, Herman, Bruno: see A. Hauck (1952) p. 1000. If the biographer meant that Bruno was the fifth bishop *after* Gerard I, he perhaps alluded to the tradition that placed Robert, abbot of Mettlach between Stephen and Berthold: see E. Martin (1900) pp. 180–2.

5 Whenever he was free for a longer period than usual from the yoke
of school, he often visited the residence of his parents, delighting not
only in their genuine affection but also in their life of piety and the
most liberal management of their household and their treatment of
the knights and the servants. One summer, when according to his
custom he was staying with them at their noble castle of Egisheim,[46]
at nightfall on Saturday he was sleeping in a very pleasant bedroom.
A poisonous frog of the type called a toad or a natterjack[47] climbed on
to the right side of his face and fastening one of his front legs on his
cheek and the other under his lip and one back leg behind his ear and
the other under his chin, began cruelly to wound and to suck him.
Woken by the pain, Bruno felt the baleful weight of the horrible
animal lying on his face. Thunderstruck by so great and unexpected a
danger, he quickly leaped from the bed and, unable to endure the
excessive torment, he cast that venomous creature on to his bed with
a blow behind the ear using the open palm of his hand; since he feared
that if he had attempted to remove it with his fingers, it would have
gripped him more fiercely. As it was thrown on the bed, the evil beast
uttered a sound, but despite the fall it did not give up climbing up the
pillow, as Bruno saw in the moonlight that lit up the whole bedroom.
At once a crowd of servants came running in, alarmed by the sudden
cry of their beloved lord; they brought a lamp with them; but when
they approached, that noxious animal was nowhere to be seen. The
servants searched everywhere with the utmost care, but although all
the bedclothes were turned over and examined, nothing was found.
Whether it was real or imaginary, however, it certainly left behind
real injuries and pain. Bruno's entire face, throat and chest were
swollen; he became so ill that for some time there seemed to be no
hope of his recovery. His parents and all his kindred were prostrated
by grief for two whole months: believing that the only outcome would
be his death, they awaited that mournful ceremony of his funeral with
sighs and tears.

But beneficent Jesus, who is accustomed to bring succour when hope
is gone, quickly cheered the parents with the assurance of his full

---

46 Cf. *Annalista Saxo*, p. 687. Egisheim was the principal residence of Hugh's family:
see M. Parisse and M. Goullet, *Vita* p. x.

47 The biographer used the term *rubeta*, a venomous toad (Pliny the Elder, *Historia
Naturalis* VIII.31.48.110, XXXII.5.18.48). Cf. Isidore of Seville, *Etymologiae*
XII.6.58; Rabanus Maurus, *De universo* VIII.2, *MPL* 111, col. 228B (frogs as
demons); Hildegard of Bingen, *Liber subtilitatum* VIII.4, *MPL* 197, col. 1341AB
(the dangers of toads).

recovery and was mindful of His Church, which was to be comforted by this man, according to His plan. For after two months during which he could not rise from the bed unaided and after a week in which because of the growing severity of the illness, he remained speechless, finally, one day, as he was lying on his back with eyes wide open and watchful countenance he saw what seemed to be a ladder of light rising from his bed, passing through the window at his feet and reaching up to heaven.[48] An old man of splendid appearance, with venerable white hair, clad in a monastic habit, was climbing down the ladder, carrying in his right hand a remarkable cross on a long pole. When he reached the invalid, he held on to the ladder with his left hand; with his right hand he placed that cross firstly on his mouth, then made a sign with it on the patient's swellings and drew behind his ear the putridity caused by all the poison. Immediately returning by the way that he had come, he left the invalid feeling better. Bruno was at last able to speak to his kinsman, the clerk Adalbero, who was then sitting by his bed, and without delay charged him to spread the welcome news, relieving all his father's household from their long mourning. Some days later the skin behind his right ear broke and all the poison in his abcess burst out and he escaped safe and sound, to the great wonder and joy of all.

Even today in his edifying conversations it is his custom to tell his closest friends how he perceived this clear instance of God's compassion towards him and he declares that in that vision he immediately recognised as clear as day, by the appearance of his face and his habit, Benedict, the most blessed father of the monks.[49] He recalls even now how he recognised the external appearance of his figure as if he still has it before his eyes. Those who read what follows will certainly cease to wonder that Bruno was restored to health by St Benedict rather than by any other saint. As my discourse proceeds, readers will be able to understand how he burned with the zeal of pious love for the establishment and the reform of the monastic life.

6 After the death of his mentor, the lord Berthold,[50] Bruno was ready to show equal obedience to his successor Herman, as if he kept

---

48 Cf. Genesis 28:12.

49 Benedict of Nursia (✝543/8), author of the monastic *Rule*. For Leo and the cult of Benedict see P.-P. Brucker (1889) 1, 56–8; A. Michel (1948) p. 299; H. Tritz (1952) p. 252; C. H. Brakel (1972) pp. 244, 250, 278; J. Wollasch (1985) p. 42. On the phrase 'even today in his edifying conversations': H. Tritz (1952) p. 220.

50 24/25 August 1019: A. Hauck (1952) p. 1000.

perpetually in his mind that saying of the blessed Gregory: *He who has not learned to be a subject, should not dare to be in command; he who does not know how to show obedience to superiors, should not demand obedience from subjects.*[51] He had compassion indeed on those who were suffering adversity at that time, especially the reverend monks of the venerable St Aper,[52] against whom the mind of the bishop was greatly incited by the very insolent tongues of flatterers and envious persons.[53] Sometimes he stationed himself, as far as he was able, as a wall in their defence;[54] at other times, when he could do no more, he *wept with those who wept.*[55] Through his authority and diligence, during Herman's episcopate the institution and the prebends of the canons in the cathedral of the most blessed deacon and protomartyr Stephen were preserved undiminished in the condition in which they had been granted by the worthy bishops, his predecessors.

Since, however, *for everything there is a season,*[56] according to the dispensation of the Creator of time, who is outside time, who leads back His own along foreign roads to what is godly, it happened that the excellent youth was placed by his parents and relatives in the charge of the glorious Emperor Conrad,[57] his kinsman, to be educated in his court and to serve in his chapel.[58] There, before many days had passed, he won for himself the goodwill of all the courtiers, as one who was shown to be worthy of favour by his way of life, his wisdom, his birth and his beauty. Although, therefore, there were several men in the court named Bruno, he alone deserved to be called Bruno the Good. Every day he increasingly justified his claim to this title without

51 Gregory I, *Dialogi* I.1, *MPL* 77, col. 156C.

52 The monastery of St-Evre (diocese of Toul), dedicated to St Aper, bishop of Toul (*c.* 507). See N. Bulst (1973) pp. 32–3, 90–100.

53 Cf. Ralph Glaber, *Vita domni Willelmi abbatis* c. 11, p. 284: 'Herman ... began to detest the monks and their customs so much that he even laid hands on the most worthy brother named Widrich [see below I.12, p. 117] ... to beat him with his staff.' See K. Hallinger (1950) p. 82; N. Bulst (1973) p. 95 n. 88. The episcopate of Herman: E. Martin (1900) pp. 191–3.

54 He entered the fraternity of prayer of the monks of St-Evre: see Bruno of Toul, privilege for St-Evre, *MPL* 143, col. 582 ('in which [St-Evre] I enjoyed fellowship before our episcopacy'). See A. Michel (1948) p. 299; H. Hoffmann (1963) pp. 184–5; N. Bulst (1973) p. 96.

55 Romans 12:15.

56 Ecclesiastes 3:1.

57 Elected king on 8 September 1024. On the biographer's view of Conrad (cf. I.8, 9, 13. below pp. 110–13, 118) see H. Hoffmann (1963) p. 208; K.J. Benz (1977) p. 197.

58 J. Fleckenstein (1966) pp. 192, 204, 225.

incurring the jealousy of his colleagues: he accommodated himself to the lesser men with reasonable condescension and sympathised with the magnates, showing a noble dignity. He was moreover loved by the emperor and the empress[59] with such a unique parental affection that he was admitted willingly to their most secret counsels; his opinion was awaited with reverence and delight and, once stated, was accepted without hesitation. Although they daily resolved and incessantly strove to raise him to the highest honour and, if I may speak openly, to give him a bishopric exceedingly rich in temporal possessions, he himself, forewarned by the unimpeachable and golden pen of the lord Gregory, began to distrust this plan, fearing that heaven would accuse him of obtaining office as *a reward for service*,[60] a practice from which no bodily fatigue and no loss of family property could deter some of his colleagues in their hope of gaining even the smallest promotion.[61] Because he was not allowed to leave the emperor's side, therefore, and because it was not agreeable to him to serve at court, he resolved in his own mind, with God alone as his confidant and witness, that if it pleased God that he should be summoned to rule some poor church, he would undertake it more eagerly than if the royal majesty, prompted by personal affection, pushed him into an office of supreme power and wealth. Such a resolution must indeed be regarded as all the more admirable at a time of youthful immaturity, because it is so rarely found even in grave old age.

Now, however, it seems necessary for me to say how this man, who desired to humiliate himself before God, was exalted by Him little by little in a miraculous manner, as the prophet declares in the Book of Kings: *'I shall honour* him *who honours me; but those who despise me will be slightly esteemed.'*[62]

7 In his twenty-third year, therefore, when he had entered the latter phase of his adolescence, and in the year 1025 from the incarnation of the Word of God, the noble Bruno, invested with the office of deacon, set out, in place of his bishop Herman, on the expedition of Emperor

---

59 Gisela (✝1043), whose sister Matilda married Bruno's kinsman, Duke Frederick II of Upper Lotharingia: D. Mertens (1991) pp. 226–7, 230, 232, 234, 239–44, 248.

60 Gregory I, *Homiliae in evangelio Iohannis* I.4.4, *MPL* 76, col. 1091C–1092A, disseminated in John the Deacon, *Vita sancti Gregorii Magni* III.6, *MPL* 75, col. 132D–133A. See also I.9, below p. 113 and n. 90.

61 Cf. the denunciations of Humbert of Silva Candida, *Adversus simoniacos* III.20–1, pp. 223–6; Peter Damian, *Letter* 69, pp. 298–309.

62 I Samuel 2:30.

Conrad to Lombardy[63] and notably to Milan, which was then in rebellion.[64] For since his bishop was burdened with age and disease, on the orders both of the bishop himself and of the emperor, Bruno was charged with the command and organisation of the forces of knights bringing aid to the emperor from Toul,[65] nevertheless in all things saving his order.[66] In the direction of this secular warfare he immediately showed himself wise and circumspect, as if he had hitherto been engaged solely in affairs of this kind. He chose the site for his men's camp; he organised their posts and their guard-duties; he took charge of expenditure and wages at the appropriate times and places; he distributed to each of his men his rations in reasonable quantity. He took care to assign to each man a suitable task and so regulated their service that everyone, whether nobleman or commoner, need be concerned only with his own duties. His solicitude indeed ensured the protection of his men and the defeat of the enemy and brought him well deserved praise. Thus directing them by his advice and urging them on by his commands, he successfully achieved through them an outcome that was advantageous both to them and to the expedition in general. So it happened that in *rendering to Caesar what is Caesar's and to God what* belongs to *God,*[67] who commands through His apostle that *every soul should be subject to the higher powers, since there is no power except from* Him,[68] he attained his own goal the more rapidly by following an alien route. Because he served faithfully and wisely in worldly affairs, he was rewarded in full in spiritual matters so that, being *set over much,*[69] he both was raised up nearer to his Creator and felt a deeper compassion for his neighbour.

63 Conrad II's first Italian expedition, February 1026–May 1027, during which he was crowned king in Milan and emperor in Rome: see H. Bresslau (1879) pp. 119–88, 456–9.

64 The biographer confused Conrad's first Italian expedition with the second expedition (1036–8), when the Milanese rebellion occurred: H. Bresslau (1879) p. 119 n. 7.

65 According to the list of military obligations *(indiculus)* of 982, the church of Toul was to send twenty fully equipped warriors to the royal host: *MGH Constitutiones* 1, 633 (no. 436). See K. F. Werner (1968) pp. 823–32; M. Parisse (1996) p. 78 and n. 6. On the military obligations of the churches see F. Prinz (1971) pp. 147–200.

66 I.e. the canon law prohibition on the bearing of arms by the clergy. Cf. Burchard of Worms, *Decretum* II.211, 212, col. 661BC. See C. Erdmann (1935) pp. 11–13; F. Prinz (1971) pp. 1–35.

67 Matthew 22:21. See C. Erdmann (1935) p. 107; C. H. Brakel (1972) p. 282.

68 Romans 13:1. On the significance of this passage in medieval political thought see W. Affeldt (1969).

69 Matthew 25:21.

8 Finally at the beginning of the year 1026 from the incarnation of the Son of God, Herman, bishop of Toul was snatched away from this fleshly existence during Lent, while he was residing in Cologne on one of his estates.[70] Immediately the clergy and people,[71] bereaved of their ruler, gathered together by a unanimous wish, agreeing in their opinion, and asked harmoniously and continually for Bruno, whom they had long desired and always loved. Then, impatient of any delay, they sent the emperor a letter of prayer and entreaty about their unanimous election.[72] The substance of the letter may be told briefly, as follows.[73] After prefacing their letter with expressions of respect and appropriate greeting, they recounted the tragedy that had so severely afflicted them, saying that they were attacked and harassed on all sides with almost daily plundering and strife, since they were situated on the borders of three kingdoms, namely on the frontier of his empire.[74] In this situation their danger from their enemies was all the greater because of the huge distance that separated them from the emperor's presence.[75] Moreover their city was continually claimed by the kings of the French with many and various stratagems.[76] If the emperor would deign to prevent the ruin of the commonwealth and the persecution of his subjects, he would send them a pastor who was noble and of the greatest wisdom, through whose energy and diligence he would be able to ward off their enemies' rage against them. To find such a man would certainly not require great labour, since the unanimous choice of the clergy and people was in the entourage of the

---

70 1 April 1026. He was a native of Cologne: H. Bresslau (1879) p. 190.

71 The biographer emphasises that Bruno's appointment conformed to the canonical principle of election 'by clergy and people': see P. Schmid (1926) p. 16. According to H. Tritz (1952) p. 256, this account 'offers an actual picture of proceedings'; cf. K. J. Benz (1977) pp. 196–9. P. Schmid (1926) pp. 78–83 and M. Parisse (1996) pp. 77–95 argued that this is an inauthentic account, coloured by the biographer's knowledge of Leo's subsequent reforming legislation. See also above p. 32.

72 The importance of unanimity in legitimating an election: P. Schmid (1926) pp. 43–4.

73 M. Parisse (1996) p. 93: 'it is scarcely credible that [the two letters cited here] existed in the form given by the Life'.

74 The River Meuse, the effective frontier of the German and French kingdoms, bisected the diocese of Toul, leaving the western part of the diocese under the jurisdiction of the count of Champagne. The south-western neighbour of Toul was the kingdom of Burgundy: see M. Parisse (1996) pp. 79–82.

75 Cf. Adalbold of Utrecht, *Vita Heinrici II* c. 19, *MGH SS* 4, 688, on Henry II's reason for visiting Upper Lotharingia (1003): 'the land that the king was not in the habit of visiting most often abounds in the cries and the groans of the poor'. See H. J. Rieckenberg (1942) p. 104; H. Hoffmann (1963) pp. 181–2.

76 M. Parisse (1996) p. 81.

imperial majesty, his kinsman Bruno, beloved of God and of all good men. He was very well known to them, since he was their own foster-son and had been instructed among them and by them in the knowledge of the liberal arts, a man *blameless in his conduct*,[77] who had been promoted according to canon law through the individual ecclesiastical ranks to the order of deacon. It was not only the citizens of Toul, together with the inhabitants of the suburbs, who sought him, but also the people of the surrounding neighbourhood and the bishops of the province. Let the emperor, therefore, confer on them, with the approval of God and of the elect himself, either this man or no one: for they had in their minds that decree of the blessed Pope Celestine: *Everyone is to receive the reward of his service in the church in which he has spent his life in all the offices. He is not to seize another man's office nor should he dare to claim for himself the salary owed to another. Clerks are to possess the power of opposition if they see that they are oppressed and they are not to be afraid to resist whatever they know to have been imposed on them unlawfully. If they do not receive their due recompense, they must at least have freedom of judgement concerning him who is to rule them.*[78] They knew also that decree of the lord Leo, the celebrated doctor. *No one is to be set over subjects who are unwilling and who did not ask for him, lest the city should either despise or hate the bishop whom it has not chosen and lest the city that is not permitted to have whom it wants, should become less pious than is fitting.*[79] Even if a secular power could violate so evident and so canonical an authority, it nevertheless would never succeed in taking away the electors' approval of their elect. Finally, therefore, his imperial highness should be influenced by their unanimous and heartfelt prayer: in this instance he should pay heed to the interests of the Church rather than to family affection, which according to the way of the world, would prompt him to promote Bruno to a more exalted office.

Meanwhile a special letter was sent to the lord Bruno, which strove to express the desire and the concern of all the clergy, the abbots and all the religious communities and all the people of the diocese of Toul, as follows. Since, on being bereaved of their pastor, they had unanimously elected none other than him and demanded him from the

77 Philippians 3:6.

78 Celestine I, *JK* 369: *Epistola* 4.5, *MPL* 50, col. 435A (disseminated in Burchard, *Decretum* I.7, col. 551CD). This text was central to the reformers' conception of canonical election: e.g. Humbert, *Adversus simoniacos* III.5, p. 204; Peter Damian, *Letters* 88, 89, pp. 518, 525, 543. See P. Schmid (1926) p. 22.

79 Leo I, *JK* 411: *Epistola* 14.5, *MPL* 54, col. 673A.

emperor, he should by no means oppose them, for the love and the fear of the Almighty. Lest he should feel repelled by their poverty, of which he had always been well aware, they adjured him by Him who, although He was rich, made Himself poor for our sakes,[80] that he should not (showing an arrogance that they had hitherto not suspected him to possess) regard it as an insult that such base and mean people should choose a person of such great fame and nobility and deny him to greater cities, more suited to his merits; this they asked for the sake of Him who *humbled Himself* for us *even to death*.[81] They wished to be allowed to enjoy the fruit of their labour and to be sustained in their turn by him to whom they had given sustenance, because according to the Apostle, *it is the hard-working farmer who ought to have the first share of the fruits*.[82] For it was logical that the church that had deserved to educate such a man, on suffering bereavement deserved to have such a man as its pastor, who could say those special words of the good and supreme Shepherd (according to the measure granted by heaven to mortals): *I know my own and my own know me*.[83] They were indeed not unaware that the piety of the secular prince was determined to promote him to a higher office because of their kinship and because his company was pleasing to him. If, therefore, he considered that he ought to listen to their call, they for their part would pray continually to the heavenly Emperor to heap heavenly and earthly honour on Bruno. If, however, he believed that their call must be rejected, because in a worldly manner he longed for a more exalted office, divine justice would intervene to take revenge for his contempt for them, so that he would never attain the honour that he sought, nor any other office.

9 These letters were carried by the lord Norbert, then a monk of praiseworthy life but formerly a canon of St Stephen the first martyr,[84] and Lietard, still a canon,[85] who, more eager and active than their travelling companions, had been appointed by the clergy and people as the executors of such an important task. The letters afflicted both

---

80 Cf. II Corinthians 8:9.

81 Philippians 2:8.

82 II Timothy 2:6.

83 John 10:14.

84 Norbert, canon of Toul, subsequently monk (perhaps of St-Evre) and abbot of Moyenmoutier: see H. Tritz (1952) p. 273; N. Bulst (1973) p. 105.

85 According to the version of the *Life* found in the Austrian Legendary, Lietard was 'afterwards made a monk': see H. Tritz (1952) p. 273.

men, the emperor and the lord Bruno, who was most dear to him, with a flood of many and various cares. Although the emperor indeed rejoiced that the pure and fraternal love that he bore the venerable Bruno, both because of their kinship and because of his zeal, was commended and approved by the praises and the testimony of many, he was nevertheless greatly saddened because he felt that his own desire to strive on his behalf for a more exalted dignity in the world had been obstructed. He feared to offend God if he rejected the unanimous prayer of His church; but he was grieved at not rewarding so great a man according to his deserts.[86] Why do I linger on these details? Caught in this state of hesitation, he attempted with all his ingenuity, by means of envoys sent from his own entourage, to deflect the lord Bruno from his purpose. Now he recalled the very frequent conflicts and the pillaging that that church had suffered; now he exaggerated its poverty; now he said that that city, situated on the furthermost frontier of his empire, was very rarely or never regarded as a worthy residence for emperors;[87] now he said that he could not bear with equanimity the idea of his kinsman, dearer to him than anything else, being separated from him by so great a distance. Let Bruno, therefore, spare himself and consider both his own interests and tranquillity and the wishes and the distress of the emperor, who loved him from the depths of his heart. Let him be deaf to the appeals of those who thought more of their own needs and their own comfort than of his safety and honour, especially since the emperor was earnestly looking out for an office worthy of his birth and merit.

Since, however, *there are many* counsels *in a man's heart, but the will of the Lord will* be done, as Solomon says,[88] the letter sent to him by the people of the church influenced the mind of the venerable Bruno, devoted to God, in a totally different fashion. He perceived in their unanimous and humble invitation a summons to humble himself from the Master of humility himself, who shrank from becoming a king among men and came even to the Cross. He did not forget that previous resolution of his, according to which he chose rather to serve Christ in perpetuity, *content with all* humility, *poverty and self-*

---

86 On the biographer's portrayal of Conrad II see K.J. Benz (1977) pp. 196–202 ('a ruler who is entirely obedient to the prescriptions of ecclesiastical law'). Humbert, *Adversus simoniacos* III.7, p. 206 branded Conrad as a simoniac. Conrad's biographer Wipo (c. 8, p. 30) recorded a case of simony in 1025.

87 Cf. H. J. Rieckenberg (1942) p. 104: in the early eleventh century 'none of the routes through Upper Lotharingia had great significance for the itinerary of the ruler'.

88 Proverbs 19:21.

abnegation,[89] than to achieve greatness in this world by corrupting the
integrity of his conscience, that is, by some form of venality, which, as
he had learned from the words of the blessed Gregory, has a threefold
origin: *by gift, by service, by favour.*[90] Understanding that without doubt
ecclesiastical offices were plunged into confusion and ruin by these
three lackeys of venality and ambition and that it was not easy to find
any man who was free of them, he believed that his only safe course
was to accept the people's election, which drew him into a life of
humility and adversity, and to resist the promptings of the emperor,
which urged him on to greatness and prosperity. It is praiseworthy
indeed for someone to shun prosperity for God's sake, but it is much
more praiseworthy to offer oneself willingly to adversity. Hence it
was that when Moses was summoned by heaven to leadership, he
made excuses, set himself aside and requested another, saying, *I beseech
you, Lord, send whom You will send,*[91] and Isaiah, although not designated by name, threw himself into the ignominy of nakedness and
manifold suffering,[92] declaring, *Here am I; send me.*[93] Inspired by these
and other incentives to virtue and full of the oil of divine grace, the
more strongly he was buffeted by the winds of carnal affections, the
more eagerly he kindled the flame of right intention. So it came about
that the contrary wind sent by the emperor and his court increased
and fostered, rather than diminishing and extinguishing, the fire of
divine sacrifice on the altar of his pious spirit.

10 Gratefully embracing, therefore, that sentence of blessed Peter,
*Humble yourselves under the mighty hand of God, that in due time he may
exalt you,*[94] and avoiding any delay, Bruno presented to the emperor,
who was still opposing him, the letter sent to him by the clergy and
people; although as he did so, his face was suffused with an ingenuous
and (so to speak) virginal blush. When the celebrated emperor had
been apprised of the contents of the letter, he was moved to tears and
his outward demeanour made clear, with his copious lamentations,

89 Cf. *Regula Benedicti* VII.49, *CSEL* 75, 53.

90 Gregory I, *Homiliae in evangelio Iohannis* I.4.4, *MPL* 76, col. 1091C-1092A (in John
    the Deacon, *Vita Gregorii* III.6, *MPL* 75, col. 132D-133A and abbreviated in
    Burchard, *Decretum* I.113, col. 583B). Cf. I.6, above p. 107. This was a key text of
    the reformers: e.g. Peter Damian, *Letters* 48, 69, pp. 58, 299. See H. Hoesch (1970)
    p. 251.

91 Exodus 4: 13.

92 Isaiah 20:2–3.

93 Isaiah 6:8.

94 I Peter 5:6.

how deep were his inner feelings for Bruno. Finally, after an interval of silence he uttered this speech. 'I see, my most dear kinsman, that my plan for your promotion, the product of long deliberation, has been opposed, or rather overcome, by the plan of heaven, to which I am compelled to surrender and which I support, as I must; for to resist any longer would bring about the ruin of both of us and of many others. May the compassion of the Almighty, who knows best what is good for us, be with you now in this office. I am now reconciled to that outcome that I cannot avoid. You will be content with God's favour, which alone is believed to have appointed you to the government of that church without recourse to any venality, and you will not seek the favour of my wife[95] or any other mortal, lest you should be the means by which the blemish of simoniacal heresy should spread among all the sheep entrusted to you.[96] For there is no doubt that He who has begun *a noble task*[97] in you, will complete it as quickly as possible. Fix your thoughts on His love, freely given, and He will nourish you according to the truthful promise of His divine judgement. As for the consolation of our counsel and aid, whatever value it might have, you should be in no doubt that I shall always be anxious for your prosperity, more than that of all the others of your order; for both your tireless and faithful service and the mutual affection of the bonds of kinship recommend you to us. Concern yourself solely with the faithful service of the Almighty and strive to increase those natural qualities of goodness for which you have been praised from the cradle.' Strengthened by these and other words of the gentle emperor, the venerable Bruno willingly submitted himself to the burdensome task, trusting only in God, since he knew that he had been called not to experience the joys of prosperity but to endure danger and severe hardship.

11 When he received the gift of the office of bishop, he left his colleagues in the imperial court in the deepest sorrow, because they used to rely on his wholesome advice and he was an active mediator, who assiduously defended their interests. Although they congratulated him on the conferring of the high honour, they nevertheless

---

95 Cf. Wipo, *Gesta Chuonradi* c. 8, p. 31 describing Gisela's involvement in the simoniacal appointment of Udalric of Basel (1025). According to Wipo (c. 4, p. 24), she 'was in higher esteem than all [Conrad's advisers] for her prudence and counsel'. See H. Bresslau (1879) p. 192 n. 3; R. Schetter (1935) pp. 18–20, 52–3.

96 The biographer portrays Conrad 'as an opponent of simony': H. Hoffmann (1963) p. 208. See above p. 20.

97 I Timothy 3:1.

grieved at the loss of the delightful solace of his comradeship and
conversation. He received leave to depart from the imperial majesty,
but at the very moment of his departure the bad news was brought to
him that, unless he took precautions, he would be ambushed by the
Lombards, who in their arrogance were at that time rebelling against
the emperor. For it happened that in those days the royal army was
besieging the Milanese fortress of Orba,[98] because the traitors who
had broken faith and refused to submit to the emperor were hiding
there. Bruno was therefore warned by his friends to avoid their
ambush by changing his route: they added that it would be more
advantageous to seek out another route, even if it was rather longer,
than carelessly to fall into the enemy's hands for the sake of taking a
shortcut. He, however, knew no fear, like that saying of Solomon, *The
righteous man, as bold as a lion, will be without fear.*[99] defended by *the
shield of faith*, furnished with *the breastplate of righteousness* and *the
helmet* and hope *of salvation*,[100] he spoke as follows to those who were
dissuading him from the straight road. 'Let us commit all the care of
our safety to the hands of the Almighty, because no one can harm him
whom heaven wishes to protect. If, however, He has decided to purify
me from the dross of my sins by means of the fire of tribulation, I do
not refuse to surrender myself to be shaped according to the will of
the good Artificer, since *the object that is moulded* must not *say* in
protest *to its moulder, Why have you made me thus?*[101] Let us *go by the
king's highway*[102] without a diversion and suffer gladly whatever the
supreme Judge has provided for us.' Spurring on his companions with
these wise words of encouragement, he set off on the route that he
had chosen, certain of the help of heaven.

He was, however, a vessel of humility dedicated to God and was afraid
that he would be branded with the reputation of arrogance if he
entirely rejected the advice of his friends: he therefore partly followed
their wishes, in that he separated from the main body of his entourage
and set off with a small number of companions one day in advance of

98 Capriata d'Orba or Castelletto d'Orba (diocese of Acqui), probably the possession
   of the Aledramid dynasty, whose head, Margrave William III of Montferrat, was
   a leader of the rebellion. The biographer's assumption that this was a Milanese
   fortress derives from his error above p. 108 and n. 64. Cf. Wipo, *Gesta* c. 12, p. 33.
   Orba was captured in April or May 1026. See H. Bresslau (1879) p. 125.
99 Proverbs 28:1.
100 Ephesians 6:14, 17.
101 Romans 9:20.
102 Numbers 21:22.

the rest. Meanwhile ambushes were laid in nearly all the remote Lombàrd settlements where Bruno hoped to spend the night in order to recover his strength: such ambushes were prepared especially in the city of Ivrea.[103] He entered the city, however, when the sun was burning at the highest point of the heavens, accompanied (as I have said) by few companions, no more than five; and by God's grace he passed through the throngs of people in the city and no one interrupted his journey by speaking to him, nor did the need arise for him to speak to anyone. But when the sun was illuminating the ocean waves, the travelling companions whom he had left behind him entered the city. They were immediately attacked by men emerging from all their hiding-places, who seized on their long desired prey with the violence of dogs. They looked in all their faces, seeking only Bruno; but Bruno, rescued by the strength of Christ, was the only one of them not to be found. All night long the Lombards asked questions about him, whether he had already departed or was yet to arrive, but they did not guess his true actions. The suspicion arose that he had already passed through the city and rapid couriers were sent to pursue him. But the beloved bishop had already reached the frontier of Italy and had entered the place called Carema,[104] where the protection of heaven through its miraculous wisdom set him free. For his few companions, tired by their long journey, had decided to stay there to rest. But he, having a presentiment, taking only one man with him, passed through the gates of Carema, intending to wait until his companions had refreshed themselves with a short rest. When he had departed from them within the space of two arrow-shots, the pursuers suddenly arrived at a breathless pace. They found his companions already lying down exhausted, took them prisoner and rapidly brought them back to Ivrea, hoping that they had found the long sought prey; but God wished by means of a happy miracle to make sport of them. By this means the divine power disappointed the wicked of their hope and delivered the faithful man from their fury. Heaven also soon restored to him in full all his property undamaged, through the intervention of his kinswoman,[105] the niece of Rudolf,

---

103 Conrad II celebrated Christmas 1026 in Ivrea (Wipo, *Gesta* c. 15, p. 35; Herman, *Chronicon* 1027, p. 120).

104 *Ad Cameram.* According to M. Parisse and M. Goullet, *Vita* p. 130, this was La Chambre in the valley of Maurienne; according to H. Bresslau (1879) p. 192 n. 4 it was the modern Carema. Bruno chose the route over the Great St Bernard pass.

105 Berta (granddaughter of King Conrad of Burgundy, mother of Count Gerold of Geneva): see E. Hlawitschka (1991) pp. 190–1, 209, 211.

king of Burgundy,[106] and wife of Bruno's brother Gerard,[107] a very active and distinguished knight.

12 Bruno's journey was completed under favourable auspices; he was received with applause by all the cities through which he passed, while he was eagerly awaited by his own citizens, who were frantic with the desire to see him. Finally, on Ascension day, 20 May,[108] he was welcomed by them all with immeasurable joy, elected and acclaimed in the presence of all the magnates of Gallia Belgica and enthroned as bishop by his kinsman, the lord Theoderic, bishop of Metz.[109]

Knowing that in the house of God he must be *a lamp* that was *not* hidden *under a bushel* but placed *on a* glittering *lampstand*,[110] he immediately strove with vigilant care to stir up the fire of divine religion, which he had always kept glowing within himself, and by his words and example he fervently kindled in his subjects a zeal for heavenly virtue. As the worldly expression goes, *the more the fire is covered, the more it flares up:*[111] so the heat of heavenly love, long enclosed within him, began to burn, as one whose nature from his infancy was accustomed to glow with the inspiration of Christ. He therefore directed his sagacious energy above all to increase monastic religion, which, except for the monastery of the holy confessor of Christ, Aper,[112] had for a long time, alas! been in decline throughout his diocese. Soon after his election he deposed the abbots of the monasteries of Moyenmoutier[113] and Saint-Mansuy,[114] who, neglecting the care of the souls committed to him, supposed that they had been appointed solely to exercise power over external affairs. He commended these houses to the venerable lord Widrich, then provost of the monastery of St

106 Rudolf III, king of Burgundy (993–1032).

107 Gerard, who died in the 1030s, is named in Leo IX, *JL*4201 (privilege for Woffenheim): see E. Hlawitschka (1969) pp. 104, 111.

108 In 1026 Ascension day fell on 19 May.

109 Theoderic II, bishop of Metz (1006–47), brother of Count Frederick of Moselgau, uncle of Adalbero III of Metz (above p. 102).

110 Matthew 5:15.

111 Ovid, *Metamorphoses* I.4.64: see H.-G. Krause (1976) p. 71.

112 St-Evre: see above p. 106. On Bruno's accession he was granted his request to be remembered in the prayers of the brethren of St Evre 'all the days of my life' (*MPL* 143, col. 582D-583A).

113 Hardulf, abbot of Moyenmoutier (1011–16, 1018–26; 1016–18: master of the school in St-Evre). See K. Hallinger (1950) pp. 82, 444; N. Bulst (1973) pp. 104–5.

114 Abbot's name unknown. See K. Hallinger (1950) pp. 63, 444; N. Bulst (1973) pp. 99–100; M. Schaeffer (1982) pp. 55–63.

Evre,[115] through whose foresight and steadfast intelligence the monastic life was revived again in those places, as is apparent today.

13 The victorious King Conrad heard rumours of Bruno's most praiseworthy deeds and every day he grew to love him more and more, foreseeing in him the future faithful instrument that would reform the discipline of holy religion and would strengthen the Roman commonwealth, that was currently in decline.[116] Since he had for pressing reasons deferred until the following Easter[117] the imperial consecration that he was to receive from the lord pope[118] in Rome, he felt compelled by the ties of perfect affection to order Bruno likewise to defer his episcopal ordination, so that together they might both receive consecration in their predestined offices at the same time in the basilica from the same vicar of the keeper of the keys of heaven. But Bruno, beloved of God, the guardian of true humility and observer of the precepts of divine authority, learned that some men were eaten up by jealousy because of this earthly honour conferred on him by the emperor. Since moreover the archbishop of Trier,[119] citing a certain privilege of his, desired to oppose the royal will, our bishop immediately went to the king with the resolute prayer that he should distance himself from such a quarrel, saying that he would rather be deprived of the honour of this consecration than remain in conflict with anyone in the future. It was a task of supreme difficulty to persuade the lord emperor to change his mind.

Bruno then took an affectionate leave of him and, returning to Gallia Belgica, he humbly requested episcopal consecration from the lord Archbishop Poppo of Trier and they decided on the time that this holy ordination should take place. Bruno, therefore, came to Trier and

---

115 Widrich († soon after 1050), pupil of Abbot William of St-Bénigne, Dijon; abbot of St-Evre, St-Mansuy and Moyenmoutier (see below p. 120). See K. Hallinger (1950) pp. 82–3; N. Bulst (1973) pp. 100, 105.

116 Cf. Sigebert of Gembloux, *Vita Deoderici episcopi Mettensis* c. 7, *MGH SS* 4, 467: 'the commonwealth was reformed, the peace of the churches was restored and the integrity of religion was renewed' (on the regime of Emperor Otto I). On this language of reform and renewal in the eleventh century see P. E. Schramm (1929) pp. 188–305; G. B. Ladner (1982) pp. 1–33.

117 26 March 1027.

118 Pope John XIX (1024–33).

119 Poppo, archbishop of Trier (1015–47). On the rights of archbishops and metropolitans see Humbert, *Adversus simoniacos* I.5, p. 108; III.5, p. 204. The bishops of a province could not be appointed without the metropolitan's consent and he must consecrate them or give permission for another prelate to perform the consecration. See R. Foreville (1974) pp. 272–81.

inquired into the customary order of consecration; but there a com-
plication arose that delayed the holding of the ceremony for so long
that the dear father returned home disappointed, having failed to
achieve his purpose. For that archbishop issued a privilege, which
included this unnecessary regulation, impossible for anyone to keep:
that before any of his suffragans could receive ordination, he must
promise, with heaven as his witness, that he would seek the archbishop's advice before performing any action and, without exception,
would not presume to do anything except according to the archbishop's command or will, as if he were his slave.[120] The faithful Bruno,
remembering the divine scripture, that *a faithless and foolish promise is
displeasing* to God,[121] absolutely refused to make this unreasonable
promise, lest he should be rendered guilty of hypocrisy through his
inability to keep the promise. Both sides persisted in their argument
for a long time and the outcome was that our father had to leave Trier
having achieved nothing.

When he learned this, Emperor Conrad of divine memory[122] summoned both men to his palace in Worms[123] and at their meeting,
through the exercise of imperial authority, the archbishop was at last
convinced by the demonstration of right reason. He ceased to insist
on the unnecessary promise that he had unjustly demanded: he
requested only that he should receive the promise that in the conduct
of ecclesiastical business Bruno would rely on the authority of his
counsel. When this promise had been accepted, the sacred ordination
took place on 9 September[124] amidst general rejoicing. From this time
forward they both continued to be bound together in perfect

120 On the oath of obedience see H. Bresslau (1879) p. 224 n. 4: 'I promise that ... I
will be faithful and obedient to the [metropolitan] church ... and to you ... and
your successors according to my order, saving my fidelity to Emperor Conrad.'
See also T. Gottlob (1936) pp. 154–5. Poppo had been enthroned as archbishop
only after a long conflict in which the archbishop elect Adalbero, brother of
Empress Cunigunde, had claimed the archbishopric. M. Parisse (1996) pp. 87–8
related Poppo's attitude in 1027 to this earlier struggle: fearing Bruno as a royal
kinsman, he determined to exercise a strict control over him. The consecration
would usually have taken place in Toul and involved the bishops of Metz and
Verdun.

121 Ecclesiastes 5:3.

122 On the biographer's view of Conrad: H. Hoffmann (1963) p. 208 and above p. 20.

123 Early September 1027: perhaps the occasion mentioned by Wipo, *Gesta Chuonradi*
c. 21, p. 41.

124 9 September 1027 was a Saturday. Since episcopal consecrations must take place
on Sundays (*Decretales Pseudoisidorianae* p. 75), the biographer probably meant 10
September.

friendship.[125] We have recounted these events so precisely, in order to make known the humility of this man and to show how careful he was to avoid the blemish of falsehood, as far as was humanly possible.

14 Returning, therefore, to his own see, he was welcomed with universal joy and at once – so great was his devotion towards the holy and glorious Aper[126] – he appointed the lord Widrich, that man of pious life and conversation, over the monastery of St-Evre with the title of abbot, according to the will and at the request of the lord William, at that time the venerable father of that place,[127] whose holy reputation is remembered in all the lands on this side of the sea.[128] With the bishop's support Father Widrich exerted himself greatly in increasing the beauty of his monastery. It was now almost falling into ruins and he began to rebuild it from its foundations, for which purpose the bishop supplied him with thirty pounds from his own resources.[129] Bruno also gave the abbot the charge of the abbeys of Moyenmoutier and Saint-Mansuy,[130] to which he granted several churches, so as to strengthen the condition of holy religion within them. He established a devout congregation of nuns in the monastery of Poussay,[131] which had been begun by his predecessor[132] using the episcopal revenues, but was finished to perfection by Bruno's exertions, complete with buildings and revenues. As the mother of this congregation he appointed a woman of noble birth and praiseworthy life named Berenna,[133] through whose earnest solicitude the passion

125 E.g. in 1030 Bruno attended the provincial synod held by Poppo: H. Beyer (1860) p. 355 (no. 302). Cf. the privileges of Leo IX for Trier, including the primacy over Gallia Belgica (*JL* 4158, 4160–1, April 1049): H. Beyer (1860) pp. 383–5 (nos. 329–31). See E. Boshof (1978) pp. 37–41.

126 Cf. Bruno of Toul, charter for St-Evre, 1044, *MPL* 143, 587C–592A.

127 William ('of Volpiano'), abbot of St-Bénigne, Dijon (990–1031), abbot of St-Evre for more than two decades. See K. Hallinger (1950) p. 838; N. Bulst (1973) pp. 96–7.

128 Cf. Ralph Glaber, *Vita domni Willelmi* c. 14, p. 296: 'kings regarded [William] as a father, bishops regarded him as a master, abbots and monks as an archangel, all men in common as a friend of God and a teacher of their salvation'.

129 Cf. Bruno of Toul, *Notitia de instauratione coenobii sancti Apri*, *MPL* 143, col. 581C–584B (*c.* 1030).

130 Widrich previously ruled these monasteries with the title of provost: see N. Bulst (1973) pp. 100, 105.

131 R. Bloch (1930) pp. 192, 209; C. H. Brakel (1972) p. 245; M. Parisse (1983) pp. 103–18.

132 Berthold: see R. Bloch (1930) pp. 192, 211.

133 Cf. Leo IX, *JL* 4175, *MPL* 143, 615A, privilege for Abbess Berenna confirming her convent's possessions. See R. Bloch (1930) pp. 192, 209, 211.

for divine service has grown and flourished there and, with the help of
God's grace, will continue to flourish and grow for long generations
to come.

15 There was also in Bruno a remarkable and noble elegance of
character, together with a magnificent physical beauty, which the
liberality of the Almighty had conferred on him beyond all the other
men of his age, so that whatever he did pleased everyone and
whatever he said delighted the hearts of all with the deepest feelings
of love. He possessed the innocence of the dove, together with the
wisdom of the serpent,[134] in such abundance that to those who were
shrewd in the affairs of this world he seemed shrewder than all other
men and those who were wise in heavenly things greatly revered him
for his innocence and purity of mind. He was so full of charity that he
indiscriminately gave away almost all his possessions and it often
happened that he lived in poverty in the midst of the wealth of others.
He devoted himself before all things and above all things to the work
of almsgiving and, unimpeded by secular business, he allowed no day
to pass without spending the morning in the service of crowds of poor
men. Following the Lord's example, he washed their feet[135] and he
gave them adequate food. He was filled with the devotion of a contrite
heart and the tearful lamentations of remorse to such a miraculous
degree that he never turned to the face of the Almighty in private
prayer[136] or in the performance of the divine office without bathing his
face and chest with a continuous flood of tears. In this way he
constantly offered himself as a sacrifice before the countenance of the
divine majesty, knowing for certain that *the sacrifice acceptable to God is
a broken spirit.*[137]

He was renowned for his immense knowledge of the divine and
human arts and especially for his delightful skill in the art of music,
in which he could not only equal the ancient authors but also was
superior to some of them in the sweetness of melody. For he
composed responsories venerating the glorious martyr Cyriacus[138]
and the holy Hildulf, archbishop of Trier,[139] the blessed virgin

134 Cf. Matthew 10:16.
135 Cf. John 13:5.
136 H. Tritz (1952) p. 252: an allusion to the *Rule* of Benedict 52.4, *CSEL* 75, 135.
137 Psalm 50:19.
138 Cf. C. H. Brakel (1972) pp. 259–64, 269, 281.
139 Hildulf, bishop of Trier, missionary, founder of Moyenmoutier (✝707). On Leo IX
    and his cult: C. H. Brakel (1972) pp. 246, 247, 269, 275.

Odilia[140] and the venerable doctor Gregory, the apostle of the English;[141] and he elaborated the hymns of the divine services with wonderful ornamentation.[142] He was moreover so eminently endowed with the gift of humility and patience that if he chanced to rebuke one of his subjects for an offence that he had committed and the latter, as often happened, was moved by impatience and ill temper to retort with many improprieties and insults upon the bishop who censured him, Bruno repaid the insulting words not with blows[143] but with tears of condolence.[144]

16 Observing that Bruno had gained a reputation from these and other good actions, the enemy of the human race[145] strove by all means to oppose his piety and, although he could never turn him from the right path, nevertheless through his agents he strove to deter him from his holy resolution, using the arrows of temptation and adversity. For certain princes of his homeland, who saw that he was conspicuous for his wisdom, envied the way in which he prevailed over all other men in the counsels of the imperial majesty. While they could not lay their toils for him among the courtiers, all of whom were bound to him by too deep an affection, they pursued their cunning

---

140 Odilia, first abbess of Hohenburg (✝ c. 720), daughter of Duke Eticho of Alsace, patron saint of Alsace. On Leo's alleged descent from the dynasty of the Etichones: F. Vollmer (1957) p. 178. Leo and the cult of Odilia: C. H. Brakel (1972) pp. 246, 247, 269, 275.

141 Pope Gregory I (590–604). Leo and the cult of Gregory: C. H. Brakel (1972) pp. 246, 259–60, 279.

142 An eleventh-century obituary of Leo IX called him 'an eminent musician': E. Dümmler (1876) p. 176. Cf. Sigebert of Gembloux, *Catalogus de viris illustribus* c. 150, pp. 94–5; Anonymus Mellicensis [Wolfger of Prüfening?], *De scriptoribus ecclesiasticis* c. 85, p. 83; *Annalista Saxo* 1048, p. 687. But see Richerus of Senones (✝1267), *Gesta Senoniensis ecclesiae* II.18, *MGH SS* 15, 280: 'Humbert, abbot [*sic*] of Moyenmoutier … composed hymns, which are called responsories, of the saints Cyriacus the martyr, Columbanus, Odilia the virgin, Pope Gregory, the bishops Hildulf and Deodatus … and gave them to Bishop Bruno of Toul to be set to music.' Concerning which see A. Michel (1948) p. 317 and H. Hoesch (1970) pp. 24–5. For independent evidence of Leo as poet as well as composer: P. Paulin (1950) pp. 123–32; H.-G. Krause (1976) p. 58 n. 37; M. Bernard (1980) pp. 89–100.

143 Cf. Anonymus Haserensis, *De episcopis Eichstetensibus* c. 37, pp. 264–5 (Leo refused to 'impose fasts or blows on anyone'). For instances of bishops inflicting corporal punishment on their subjects see the case of Bruno's predecessor, Herman, above p. 106 n. 53, and Archbishop Adalbert of Bremen: Adam of Bremen, *Gesta Hammaburgensis ecclesiae pontificum* III.38, p. 180. See S. Weinfurter (1992) p. 65.

144 The version of the *Life* in the Austrian Legendary adds here a passage describing Bruno's intercessions at times of natural disaster. See H. Tritz (1952) p. 354.

145 I.e. Satan. (The name in Hebrew means 'enemy'.)

machinations against him among strangers. They therefore incited
Odo, count of the neighbouring march of the French,[146] against the
blessed[147] bishop and laboured, using manifold hostile devices, to dis-
possess him of the emperor's confidence. You might then see in Bruno
loyalty struggling manfully against the deceptions of many men,
enduring with equanimity and remarkable patience the darts of all his
enemies, lamenting with heartfelt compassion the losses inflicted on
his subjects, easily pardoning even his greatest enemies with affectionate charity. It is not necessary, however, to recount the warlike
attacks, the destruction, the plundering and the conflagrations
suffered by the church which had been committed to him, until the
grace of the Almighty deigned to bring to a rapid end those hostilities
against him, rooted as they were in iniquity, and chose to bring pious
consolation to His faithful servant by means of a vision.

One night, while he was still hardpressed by hostile attacks,[148] overcome by the fatigue of manifold anxieties, reflecting on the wretched
condition of the people subject to him and tearfully ascribing the
responsibility for it to himself, he fell asleep and saw in a dream a
person with an angelic countenance, who presented to him a sphere
more brilliant than the sun, which seemed to contain within it a model
of the whole world. He saw there in particular two human beings of
outstanding beauty and when he desired to learn their names, this
sentence resounded in his ears: 'Know that these are Mary Magdalene[149] and Bishop Galienus, whose company you will have the happiness to share in the future.' Just as he joyfully received the sphere in
his hands, intending to place it in his bosom, he awoke from the
prophetic dream. It is no wonder that it was predicted that he would
be the equal of the blessed Mary, since he shared her merits both in
the degree of his love of God and in his continuous flow of tears, like

146 Odo II, count of Blois and Champagne (+1037), nephew of King Rudolf III of
   Burgundy and Conrad II's rival for the Burgundian succession: see H. Bresslau
   (1884) pp. 13–17; M. Bur (1977) pp. 171–4.
147 Cf. H. Tritz (1952) p. 222: 'Bruno ... is called [here] "blessed" for the first time ...
   From the use of this term we may deduce that the pope had died when the author
   wrote this.' I.e. the biographer wrote this chapter after 19 April 1054.
148 Cf. Sigebert of Gembloux, *Chronica* 1036, p. 357: 'Odo, making war on the
   emperor, invaded Lotharingia, laid siege to ... Toul and would in no way moderate his rage'; Ralph Glaber, *Historiae* III.38, p. 160. Odo made two separate
   incursions against Lotharingia in 1037, while Conrad II was campaigning in
   Lombardy: see H. Bresslau (1884) pp. 254–6, 267–8.
149 Leo IX's role in the spread of the cult of Mary Magdalene: C. H. Brakel (1972) pp.
   247, 253, 254–6, 269, 277 n. 238, 278.

the waters of a fountain.[150] Although we still do not know who this Galienus was,[151] there is no doubt that he was of great merit, since the voice of God declared him the equal of so praiseworthy a man.

17 This vision was followed by a powerful demonstration of the consolation of divine grace: Count Odo met a shameful death[152] at the hands of the warlike Duke Gozilo,[153] our compatriot,[154] and peace was restored by this blessed bishop, with Christ's consent, not only in the kingdom of Lotharingia but also in the adjacent provinces. Through his wise intervention as an envoy and a counsellor, the kingdom of Austrasia,[155] which was originally held by King Rudolf of Burgundy, was annexed to and incorporated in the Roman empire. The bishop was also sent as an envoy to make peace between Conrad, emperor of the Romans, and Robert, king of France.[156] France is the witness of how creditably he performed that legation. France indeed still describes as a novelty how resplendent he was in the greatness of his wisdom, his humility, his practical ability in all that he undertook, how noble he was in mind and body, how fitting was the delivery of the message of his legation. All received him with exceeding affection like a father; all honoured him with supreme veneration like a saint. He established a peace and harmony between the two kingdoms so durable that as long as those princes lived, and as long as their sons and successors (both called Henry)[157] lived, no one was able, whatever

---

150 Cf. Luke 7:38. The *Rhythmus sancti Leonis IX papae* attributed to Leo describes the penitent Mary Magdalene: C. H. Brakel (1972) p. 278.

151 Modern scholarship has similarly failed to identify Galienus.

152 At the battle of Bar, 15 November 1037. See H. Bresslau (1884) pp. 270–3.

153 Gozilo I, duke of Lower Lotharingia (1023–44), duke of Upper Lotharingia (1033–44). See E. Boshof (1978a) pp. 119–20; M. Werner (1991) p. 378.

154 See above p. 22.

155 I.e. Burgundy. Rudolf III recognised Conrad II as his successor in summer 1027. Conrad was crowned king in Burgundy on 2 February 1033 and the annexation was completed on 1 August 1034 with the submission of his opponents: see H. Bresslau (1879) pp. 221–2; H. Bresslau (1884) pp. 69–72, 107–17.

156 Robert II, king of the French (996–1031). H. Bresslau (1884) pp. 74 n. 2, 76–7 suggested that these negotiations took place not in the reign of Robert II but in 1033 (Conrad's meeting with King Henry I of France in Deville on the Meuse). Alternatively the biographer may have had a confused recollection of the agreement between Emperor Henry III and King Henry I of France in Ivois in October 1048. Bruno of Toul was identified as the negotiator on the German side in 1048 by Anselm of St-Remi, *Historia dedicationis* c. 7, col. 1421A. See E. Boshof (1978a) pp. 96–7.

157 Henry III, king of the Germans (1039–56), emperor (1046); Henry I, king of the French (1031–60).

arts of deception he used, to sow discord between the two kingdoms.

But the envious enemy of the human race, reflecting that he could not divert the devout Bruno from the righteous path by means of his agents, made a personal attack on him, heaven permitting him to do so, and oppressed him with extreme bodily weakness, which lasted for a whole year. He was attended by the whole multitude of the people, griefstricken and despairing of his recovery; he was also attended by a company of doctors, whose own expressions of despair added to the general grief; the faces of all were bathed in tears; he himself had now lost hope of survival. Then he was inspired by heaven to order himself to be carried by night to the altar of St Blasius,[158] trusting that he would very rapidly be freed from his present danger by the merits of that saint. There he was caught up in an ecstasy (I do not mean a dream, since sleep entirely deserted him) and seemed to see St Blasius leave the altar, look at him and ask him compassionately about the nature of his illness. It seemed to Bruno that he saw all his feeble entrails opened up, that the saint washed them with a merciful hand and that, restoring them with medicine, he put them all back in their place and returned whence he had come. Recovering from his ecstasy, Bruno rose from his bed fit and well and, summoning those who were standing by, he cheerfully related the vision that he had seen. As the martyr had commanded, he sang the responsory, *What god is great like our God?*[159] in a joyful voice with those who were present and after he had performed the night offices, he quickly returned to his house on his own two feet.[160]

18 Since, however, my pen hastens to write down more important matters,[161] it seems fitting to record briefly this memorable story concerning his mother.[162] It is not easy to express in words how great was the sincerity of her devotion, how great was her generosity in almsgiving, even to her last farthing, how incessantly she persevered in divine prayers, vigils and fasts, how patiently she endured bodily

158 Blasius, bishop of Sebaste, martyr (✝316). The miracle echoed the healing of Bishop Gerard of Toul by St Blasius: Widrich, *Vita sancti Gerardi* c. 22, p. 503. On Leo and the cult of St Blasius: C. H. Brakel (1972) pp. 248, 264, 268, 269, 274, 279.

159 Psalm 76:14.

160 The version of the *Life* in the Austrian Legendary adds a chapter describing how Bruno 'unceasingly and strenuously ruled the church of Toul for twenty years'. See H. Tritz (1952) pp. 274–5, 278–86; edition: pp. 354–8.

161 H. Tritz (1952) p. 226 and H.-G. Krause (1976) p. 69 n. 83 pointed out that these words refer to the account of Leo's papacy, the subject of Book II.

162 Heilwig: see above p. 99 and n. 17.

torments; but all was made clear in her death, the occasion when praises can safely be sung.[163] Because of an excess of fluid her body swelled to such a state of corpulence that she could hardly be conveyed in a carriage when occasion demanded. Since this weight seemed to her intolerable, she frequently implored the grace of Christ, shedding copious tears, that just as the womb of one mother had brought her into the world, so the arms of one woman might be able to commit her to an earthly tomb. Her voice was heard by *the dayspring from on high*.[164] For long illness at last so weakened and diminished her that almost all the fluid in her flesh dried up and only her bones clung together, held in place by the skin and the sinews. As she approached the end of her life, she gave away for the use of the poor everything that she had accumulated, not from her husband's revenues but from savings from her daily expenditure. After being strengthened by the holy unction and by sharing in the lifegiving communion, she lay for a long time motionless and without the breath of life, amidst the lamentations of her whole household, together with crowds of the poor, widows and orphans. Suddenly recovering her breath, she ordered that the confused clamour of wailing should be silenced, commanded that they should all be turned out of the house and kept with her only Regelindis, abbess of the monastery of the Holy Cross,[165] and her own husband. When, wondering and tearful, they asked what she wished for herself, she said, 'Do not mourn for me, as for one about to die, since just now the most pious mother of God, Mary,[166] was with me, consoling me with most sweet courtesy, and she promised that I should be with her forever and should live happily in heavenly glory. I have only one request to make of you, most beloved husband: that you will not be annoyed by my humble petition.' When he, unaware of what was to come, joyfully promised that he would readily perform whatever she commanded, she said, 'I pray that, just as I proceeded naked from my mother's womb, so the womb of the earth should receive me naked in my tomb and that you should faithfully spend on the poor whatever jewelry you have prepared to bury with me.' Her husband agreed to her request, although unwillingly, and after she with the greatest eagerness had laid aside her human existence, he caused her to be buried in the manner in which she had appointed.[167]

163 Cf. Ecclesiasticus 11:30.

164 Luke 1:78.

165 Woffenheim: see above p. 100 n. 26.

166 Cf. C. H. Brakel (1972) pp. 276–7.

167 Cf. the obsequies of Monica, mother of Augustine (*Confessiones* IX.11.27, *CC* 27, 149).

I have recounted this with such care so that it may be clear to readers both present and future how great was the faith and the piety of this woman and how fervent she was in almsgiving. It seems appropriate, however, to drop our ship's anchor here and after drawing breath a little and repairing our sails, we may be able successfully to cross the ocean.[168]

The Second Book

1 Since through Christ's favour we are about to proceed with the work that we have undertaken and to tell how the blessed man came to the office of pope and what happened to him while in that office, or rather, what the Lord wished to accomplish through him during his lifetime, it seems fitting to show the circumstances preceding this event and to make known how heavenly grace revealed to him what was to happen.

It was his most pious custom to visit almost every year the supreme pastor, the keeper of the keys of heaven,[169] and to beseech his help for the flock entrusted to him by God.[170] On one occasion when he undertook the customary journey in the company of more than five hundred clergy and laymen, who were drawn by the worthiness of his merits, his courtesy and his sanctity to follow him as his inseparable entourage, they were all overtaken by a deadly pestilence, caused by the injurious Italian climate,[171] such that no one who was infected with the sickness had any hope of postponing his death even for a day. Greatly saddened by the affliction of his companions, the man of the Lord was led by divine grace to find a rapid remedy. For with his own hand he soaked in wine the relics of the saints that he carried with

---

168 For the representation of a literary work as a sea voyage, see, for example, Jerome, *Epistolae* I.2, *CSEL* 54, 1–2.

169 Cf. Peter Damian, *Letter* 40, p. 497 (Leo IX was 'he who, in the place of Peter, holds the keys of the Church'). St Peter as 'the keeper of the keys' (Matthew 16:19) and the pope as 'vicar of St Peter': Y.M.-J. Congar (1968) pp. 146–63; M. Maccarrone (1974) pp. 21–122.

170 Orderic Vitalis, *Historia ecclesiastica* I.24, p. 158 (a visit to Rome in 1047). Records of episcopal visits motivated by reverence for St Peter and the papacy (*ad limina* visits) became frequent from Leo's pontificate but had been rare before 1048. Widrich, *Vita sancti Gerardi* c. 7, p. 496 recorded that Bruno's admired predecessor, Gerard of Toul frequently visited Rome to show his reverence for St Peter.

171 Cf. below pp. 281, 379.

him, especially the bones of St Aper, to whom he was particularly devoted.[172] Whoever took the slightest drop of this, immediately recovered, however weak he had become, if he could only taste the flavour of the liquid. Throughout the journey Bruno offered the sacrifice of the divine sacrament almost every day and during the celebration of mass he reminded those present to correct their morals and to repent: thus he both encouraged them all by his pious exhortations to fix their minds on heaven and he freed them all by his holy prayers from the threat of death. Throughout the night, therefore, a crowd of his fellow travellers and of local inhabitants, driven by necessity, maintained a vigil with lanterns at his lodgings and in the morning they went away restored to health by the merits of the saints and through his intercession. After news of these circumstances spread very rapidly through all parts of the Roman world, the man of the Lord was held in the highest veneration and love for him was deeply in the hearts of all. When he perceived this, he was not exalted among men but he incessantly preached the greatness of Christ.

2 It was his constant custom, when he surrendered himself to his nightly rest, to commend himself most fervently to the relics of the saints, so that, freed from worldly cares, he might deliver his mind up to holy contemplation and receive in this meditation the sleep necessary for his body. One night, when he fell asleep with this pious purpose, he had a vision in which he was brought to the cathedral of the city of Worms,[173] where he saw an infinite crowd of men dressed in white, the greater part of whom seemed to be priests. Among them he recognised a former intimate friend, Archdeacon Bezelin,[174] who had died while accompanying him on the journey to Rome. When he asked him what this great crowd was, he learned that these were all men who had ended their earthly lives in the service of the prince of the apostles. As he gazed in amazement, the blessed Peter, keeper of the keys of heaven, arrived and said that that multitude would receive holy communion from Bruno's hands. Clad in pontifical vestments, Bruno was led by blessed Peter, together with the first martyr Stephen,[175] to

172 Leo's devotion to Aper, bishop of Toul and the cult in Toul: C. H. Brakel (1972) p. 274. Cf. Widrich, *Vita sancti Gerardi episcopi* c. 18, pp. 500–1.

173 The vision is set in Worms because it was there that Bruno was to be elected to the papacy: C. H. Brakel (1972) p. 248; H.-G. Krause (1976) p. 68 n. 80.

174 On the significance of this reference to the archdeacon and subsequently to other clergy of Toul: H. Tritz (1952) p. 253.

175 Stephen (Acts 7: 55–9) was the patron saint of Toul. Leo IX and the cult of Stephen: *JL* 4249, *MPL* 143, 668B. See C. H. Brakel (1972) pp. 248–9, 267, 281.

the altar of the church to the sound of an indescribably melodious chant and after he had performed the holy office, they all received the life-giving gift from his hands. It also seemed to him that after the holy communion St Peter brought to him five golden chalices, but to another of his followers he gave three and to a third, only one chalice. When he told this to the members of his household, he wondered what it might portend; but the meaning will be explained later in its proper place.[176]

3 On another occasion it seemed to him during his quiet repose that an ugly old woman addressed him importunately and requested his friendship in familiar but sincere speech. Her face was so frightening, her clothes so ragged and her shaggy hair stood up so hideously that she was scarcely recognisable as human. Daunted by the horror of her ugliness, he very much wished to avoid her, but she strove all the more to cling to him. The man of the Lord was driven by her unmannerly conduct to mark her face with the sign of the cross. She fell to the ground like a dead woman but rose up again, her appearance now one of wonderful beauty. Awakened by the terror of the vision, he rose for the night vigils, then once again surrendered his body to sleep, still amazed by what he had seen. It seemed to him that while he slept, the venerable Abbot Odilo[177] stood by his side and he asked him what this vision portended for him. Odilo most joyfully replied with this prophecy: 'Blessed are you and you have freed his soul from death.' That this was not a fiction is proved by the worthy evidence of venerable men, namely the lord Walter, dean of the chapter of Toul, and his intimate confidant Warneher,[178] who declared that he had heard him telling such a story with tears in his eyes and wondering much about its meaning. It is not extraordinary that such things were revealed to him by the supreme Godhead, since his constant sighs in bed at night, his frequent beating of his breast and his bedclothes often found, according to the reliable evidence of his chamberlains, to

---

176 The explanation appears in II.27, below p. 156. The recipients of the chalices were the future popes, Leo IX, Victor II and Stephen IX, the number of chalices signifying the length of their pontificates. The vision also appears in the *Gesta episcoporum Tullensium* c. 40, p. 645. Cf. Anonymus Haserensis, *De episcopis Eichstetensibus* c. 37, p. 265: a version in which Peter gave five chalices to Leo, after which a youth brought three chalices, signifying Victor II's pontificate. Another version appears in the anonymous Beneventan *Life of Leo IX*: see the partial edition of J. M. Watterich (1862) p. 148 n. 1. See H. Tritz (1952) pp. 220–1; C. H. Brakel (1972) p. 248; H.-G. Krause (1976) p. 68.

177 Odilo, abbot of Cluny (996–1049).

178 On the biographer's knowledge of the clergy of Toul: H. Tritz (1952) p. 253.

have been watered by his tears,[179] all show that he was worthy of a divine vision. No one can be in any doubt about the meaning of that vision of the woman, however, if he has read of the almost identical dream of Constantine the Great concerning the restoration of the city of Byzantium.[180] For it is certain that the beauty of the Church, indeed the Christian religion, throughout the various regions of the world had faded to a fearful extent and through Bruno it was, with Christ's help, brought back to its former dignity.[181]

4 Meanwhile a great council of bishops and other princes was held in the city of Worms[182] in the presence of the glorious Henry II, emperor of the Romans.[183] Among those who were summoned was this bishop worthy of Christ; for nothing of importance was decided at the imperial court without his advice;[184] and suddenly, without his suspecting anything, he was unanimously chosen to undertake the burden of the papal office. For a long time he was inclined by his humility to avoid the office, but being urged more and more to accept it, he requested a delay of three days for reflection, which he spent in fasting and prayer, taking almost no food and drink. When he was once more pressed to obey their will, he spontaneously pronounced his confession before them all, attempting to reverse their unanimous election by revealing the enormity of his offences. Who can describe the flood of tears that he shed in his public confession, his immoderate weeping, arousing everyone's sympathy? The mouths of all men unanimously resounded with the pious saying: *God does not wish a son of so many tears to perish.*[185] Seeing, therefore, that there was no way in which he could escape the emperor's command[186] and the unanimous

---

179 On Leo's tears of repentance (also the theme of the *Rhythmus sancti Leonis IX papae*): C. H. Brakel (1972) pp. 278–9. Cf. Gregory VII's 'gift of remorse': Paul of Bernried, *Life of Gregory VII* c. 32, below p. 281.

180 Emperor Constantine I's vision was recorded by Aldhelm, *De virginitate* c. 25, *MGH Auctores antiquissimi* 15, 258–9. See J. Stevenson (1998) pp. 189–206. I owe this reference to Dr Mark Humphries.

181 On the eleventh-century language of reform see above p. 1.

182 Henry III was in Worms on 1 December 1048 (*Diploma Heinrici III* 226).

183 King Henry III of Germany is called here Emperor Henry II (as often in his imperial diplomas) because the first German king of this name, Henry I (911–36), did not receive the imperial title. See below p. 365 n.1.

184 P. Kehr (1930) p. 28 noted, on the evidence of Henry III's diplomas, that this claim was greatly exaggerated.

185 Augustine, *Confessiones* III.12.21, *CC* 27, 39.

186 Cf. Anselm, *Historia dedicationis* c. 7, col. 1420D (the will of the emperor was the dominant factor in the election).

desire of all, he was compelled in the presence of the envoys of the
Romans to accept the office that was laid on him, on condition that he
received the general consent of all the Roman clergy and people
without any disagreement.[187] He then returned to his own see of Toul,
where he celebrated the Lord's Nativity[188] with supreme devotion, in
the company of four bishops, namely Hugh of the city of Assisi,[189] the
envoy of the Romans, Archbishop Eberhard of Trier,[190] Adalbero of
Metz and Bishop Theoderic of Verdun.[191]

5 From there Bruno set off on the journey to Rome[192] and, guided by
humility, he put on the garment of a pilgrim, contrary to the custom
of all the popes. He devoted himself tirelessly to prayer and divine
contemplation, full of anxiety, not so much because of the duties
committed to him but because of the cure of souls that he was to
undertake. Engaged in these meditations, while resting in the city of
Aosta,[193] he received consolation from heaven, when through divine
revelation he heard a harmonious melody resounding from angel
voices, singing most sweetly: *The Lord says, I think thoughts of peace
and not of evil; you will call upon me and I shall hearken to you; I shall
bring you back from captivity from all places.*[194] Encouraged by this pious
consolation and now rendered more certain of divine help, he set off
to complete his journey and, as was appropriate for a personage of
such great merit, he was surrounded by innumerable crowds coming
from all sides. Among those who joined him was a handmaid of God
of religious life, who was commanded by heaven to admonish him in
these terms: 'As soon as you set foot inside the doors of the church of

187 This 'condition' was also recorded by Bruno of Segni, *Sermon* c. 2, below p. 379. A
different explanation of Leo's second election in Rome is given by Bonizo, *Book to
a Friend* V, below p. 190. See E. Steindorff (1881) pp. 54–5; P. Schmid (1926) pp.
57–94; P. Kehr (1930) p. 607; H. Tritz (1952) p. 257; H. Hoffmann (1963) pp. 203–
4; J. Laudage (1984) p. 160.

188 25 December 1048.

189 Hugh, bishop of Assisi (1028–59) subscribed a charter of Bishop Bruno in
December 1048. See E. Steindorff (1881) p. 55 n. 1; G. Schwartz (1913) p. 228.

190 Eberhard, archbishop of Trier (1047–66).

191 Theoderic, bishop of Verdun (1046–89).

192 On 27 December 1048: Anselm, *Historia dedicationis* c. 7, col. 1421B.

193 *Augusta*. According to E. Steindorff (1881) p. 70, Aosta (assuming that Leo entered
Italy by the Great St Bernard pass); according to M. Parisse and M. Goullet, *Vita*
p. 75 n. 57, Augst (diocese of Basel).

194 Jeremiah 29:10–12, 14. The same vision was recorded by Sigebert, *Chronica* 1048,
p. 359. Orderic Vitalis, *Historia ecclesiastica* I.24, p. 158, dated this vision on
Bruno's visit to Rome, 1047.

the prince of the apostles, do not forget to use these divine words, *Peace be on this house* and on all those who dwell in it.'[195] He humbly received and devoutly carried out this command of the Lord.

He came with that great entourage to the River Taro, which was in flood and had overflowed its banks so much that everyone was compelled to remain there for seven days. The man of the Lord, however, saddened by the distress of the people waiting for such a long time in his entourage, summoned the aid of heaven and began the consecration of the church of St John,[196] which had been built in the vicinity. Before he had completed the divine office of consecration, the river had become calm and the waters had receded, so as to offer a safe crossing to every traveller. The whole multitude who were present declared that this had happened because of the merits of this blessed man.

6 Thus strengthened by the consolation of the Almighty, he approached Rome and the whole city prepared to meet him with hymn-singing. He, however, undertook the long journey barefoot and inclined his mind to devotion and shedding tears rather than to the pleasure of praise. Who can describe the love felt by his contrite heart for devout prayer, his sighs and groans, his tears that constantly flowed like streams, when it is beyond the reach of any one's understanding, much less capable of being expressed in words? After a long period during which, like Christ, he offered himself on the altar of his heart, *a living sacrifice, holy, acceptable to God,*[197] he began in the presence of the clergy and people to make known the heavenly exhortation with which he was filled. He explained briefly that the emperor had chosen him for such a difficult office; he requested them to express their will concerning him, whatever it might be; he said that the election of clergy and people should prevail against the dispositions of others according to the authority of the canons;[198] he declared that he would gladly return to his homeland if his election did not receive the approval of them all; he showed that it was under

195 Cf. Matthew 10:12–13.

196 John the Baptist was revered in the eleventh century particularly as a protector against water. Before departing for Italy Leo had dedicated a church to him outside the gates of Moyenmoutier. Leo's devotion to his cult: Leo IX, *JL* 4317, *MPL* 143, 743B. See C. H. Brakel (1972) pp. 249, 277.

197 Romans 12:1.

198 H. Hoesch (1970) p. 252 n. 31: here 'the reforming tendency of the *Life* becomes revolutionary ... The criticism of Henry III is inescapable'. The authenticity of this account was defended by H. Tritz (1952) p. 258, H. Hoffmann (1963) p. 188 and J. Laudage (1984) p. 160 n. 179. For the contrary view see P. Schmid (1926) pp. 70–83.

compulsion that he had come to take up so heavy a burden. When he saw that they all unanimously acclaimed him,[199] he renewed his exhortation, bidding them reform their lives, and humbly asked for their prayers and for absolution. Then by the favour of divine grace and to universal applause, he was consecrated and on the first Sunday of Lent, 12 February, he was enthroned in the apostolic see.[200] Who can attempt to describe with brevity the extent of the devout fervour to serve the Almighty that sprang up in him, the energy and skill that he brought to the conduct of ecclesiastical affairs, when almost the whole world is insufficient to express these things?

7 I think that I ought not to conceal the great indulgence shown by the divine mercy to his brother Hugh[201] as a result of Bruno's worthy prayers. Hugh had died long before Bruno was elected to the papacy. When this blessed man was travelling to Rome for the sake of this ordination and had reached Popolonia, his brother appeared in a vision to a certain clerk, a reliable witness, and humbly requested him to intercede with the lord pope on his behalf. It seemed to that clerk that Hugh was in a place filled with indescribable beauty, surrounded by many who rejoiced with him, seated on a throne but without a footstool, so that his feet were hanging down without support. When the clerk questioned him about his present condition, he replied that all was well with him, except for the fact that his feet were unsupported and hung down in a troublesome manner. He asked the clerk to intercede with his blessed brother when he came to receive papal consecration, so that Bruno would remember him when he passed through the doors of the church of the prince of the apostles, saying that divine piety would grant him this indulgence in response to Bruno's prayers. The clerk described this vision to the holy pontiff and encouraged him to appeal to the grace of Christ for the salvation of his brother. The latter subsequently appeared to the lord pope in a vision and joyfully rendered countless thanks, since through the pope's merits the divine mercy had freed him from all his troubles.

8 This man, most devoted to God, imitated the character and life of Leo the Great,[202] whose name he bore, or rather, he followed with all

199 There was a party in Rome that desired the election of Archbishop Halinard of Lyons: *Chronicon sancti Benigni Divionensis* p. 237.

200 12 February 1049: see E. Steindorff (1881) p. 71 n. 3.

201 Mentioned in Leo IX's privilege for Woffenheim, *JL* 4201, *MPL* 143, col. 635B: see E. Hlawitschka (1969) pp. 103–4, 111.

202 Pope Leo I (440–61). See C. H. Brakel (1972) p. 249.

his might the *Lion of the tribe of Judah*[203] and became an example of
virtuous living for all men. He glittered and shone as *a lamp*[204] placed
not under a bushel but on a lamp-stand[205] and as the true *salt of the earth,*
[206] he poured the seasoning of heavenly wisdom into the minds of all
men. Although the diadem of Christ adorned him with the jewels of
all the virtues, however, these virtues shone in him with particular
splendour: mercy and patience, quick to pardon offenders; wonderful
compassion, that wept with those who confessed their crimes; a
generosity in almsgiving that gave away everything, even to the point
of impoverishing himself.

But since the goad of adversity usually falls on those who are in the
service of heaven, as a divine trial, which demonstrates the fervour of
an individual's love for God, this venerable father was afflicted by
trouble and sadness at the beginning of his residence in Rome. When
he arrived there, he found that there were no papal revenues and
everything that he had brought with him had already been consumed
by domestic needs or distributed in alms. The full purses that his
companions had brought with them were empty; there was no hope of
sustenance, unless they sold their own clothes for whatever they
could get for them and then flee, bringing back the excellent father to
his homeland by some secret means. The blessed man rejected their
advice and wisely admonished them to trust in the consolation of
heaven; but nevertheless in his mercy and compassion he deeply
sympathised with their distress. As the day approached that all his
companions had designated for their clandestine departure, behold!
envoys arrived from the nobility of the province of Benevento,
bringing gifts appropriate to the papal dignity and earnestly and
humbly seeking to obtain his blessing and consolation.[207] The prelate
worthy of God received them in a manner befitting his honour and
strengthened them with the holy blessing, not so much rejoicing at
the offering of gifts as giving thanks to God for the devotion of the
faithful. Then, turning to those whose excessive anxiety had recently
driven them to despair, he charitably rebuked them and exhorted
them never again to forget God's mercy.

203 Revelation 5:5. *Leo* (Latin) means 'lion': cf. Bruno of Segni, *Sermon* c. 2, below p.
  380.

204 John 5:35.

205 Matthew 5:15.

206 Matthew 5:13.

207 Leo's relations with Benevento: O. Vehse (1930–1) pp. 93–6; W. Kölmel (1935) pp.
  151–4; J. Deér (1972) pp. 88–9; P. Partner (1972) pp. 111–13.

9 Thereafter the fame of the blessed man spread among the people; his renown became known through all the nations to the ends of the earth; everywhere the glory of Christ was proclaimed in the person of his admirable servant; the name of Pope Leo resounded harmoniously in every mouth throughout the world. It is scarcely remarkable that rational creatures sang his praises, when even irrational animals (wonderful to relate!) articulated human words to proclaim his name. For it is alleged by truthful reporters that in Benevento a cock[208] frequently repeated his name and instead of uttering its natural sound, loudly cried, 'Pope Leo!' to the amazement of all. It is also said that in those days there was in the territory of Apulia a dog,[209] which when barking used to produce the human words 'my God'. It is not incredible, however, that a brute beast should somehow have called upon God's mercy in that region, where it is certain that the Christian religion had almost entirely perished and where the inhabitants of the country had been subjected to a foreign power,[210] to such an extent that only the voice of an irrational animal might inspire them to invoke the aid of heaven.

The widespread rumour of his extraordinary renown prompted unusually large numbers of people to visit the residence of the supreme prince of the apostles and all were refreshed by his encouragement and strengthened by his blessing. Certain persons who did not have the opportunity of an audience with him sent him their presents in the confidence that they would receive from him the gift of the papal blessing. Together with other good actions, it was his practice not to spend on himself or on his entourage the offerings that were placed at his feet according to the papal custom:[211] instead he used them all for the needs of the poor. Among the many who strove to visit his presence, the king of Denmark[212] sent him a parrot as a gift, in which divine grace appeared through an admirable virtue. Certain birds can indeed be mastered by hunger and taught to pronounce human

---

208 Cf. *De bestiis et aliis rebus* I.36, *MPL* 177, col. 33B–34C, citing Gregory I, *Moralia* XXX.3.9, *MPL* 76, col. 527D–528A.

209 Cf. *De bestiis* II.17, col. 65C–66B; III.11, col. 86B–88A. See P. Boglioni (1985) p. 955.

210 I.e. the Normans: cf. II.20, below p. 149.

211 These voluntary gifts by pilgrims were later known as *benedictiones*: K. Jordan (1933–34) pp. 80–3; I. S. Robinson (1990) pp. 262–5.

212 Swein Estrithson, king of Denmark (1047–74). He requested permission from Leo to establish a metropolitan see in his kingdom and was reminded of Denmark's obligation to pay 'Peter's pence' to the papacy: see K. Jordan (1933–34) pp. 66, 78.

words;[213] but it is said that this bird without compulsion throughout the journey on which he was brought to the lord pontiff continued to say, 'I am going to the pope.' Immediately on being presented to him, without being taught, the bird exclaimed in a sweet voice, 'Pope Leo!' Whenever this venerable pastor, fatigued by the conduct of business, retired to his private room or when some sadness chanced to oppress his mind, afflicted by excessive cares, this bird often alleviated his distress and, by sweetly and succinctly repeating 'Pope Leo', he restored his mental vigour. No one should blame this righteous man for finding consolation in the singing of this bird, since we read that the blessed Augustine, when weeping unconsolably for the death of his mother, turned to music to alleviate his grief[214] and that St Anthony[215] permitted a little pleasure at certain times to those observing the rigour of the monastic life.

10 He demonstrated how great was the wisdom that he devoted to preserving the catholic laws in the first Roman council that he held,[216] in the company of many bishops, where in his discourse he restated the decisions of the four principal synods[217] and confirmed that the decrees of all the preceding popes were to be respected. He also condemned the heresy of simony,[218] which had already invaded some regions of the world[219] and in the same council he deposed certain bishops whom that heresy had marked with the stain of its iniquity. It would be improper to pass over in silence the events of that council, in which Christ deigned to strengthen with His grace the authority of

---

213 Cf. *De bestiis* III.28, *MPL* 177, col. 94D–95A. See P. Boglioni (1985) p. 955.

214 Cf. Augustine, *Confessiones* IX.12.31, *CC* 27, 151.

215 Anthony 'the Great', monk (†356). Cf. Athanasius, *Vita sancti Antonii* c. 13, *MPG* 26, 863B.

216 Cf. Herman, *Chronicon* 1049, p. 128 ('in the week after Easter week', i.e. 2–8 April). Cf. Bonizo, *Book to a Friend* V, below p. 191. The *acta* of the Roman synod of 1049 have not survived. See *Sacra Concilia* 19, col. 721–6; E. Steindorff (1881) pp. 78–80; O. Capitani (1966) p. 144; E. Petrucci (1977) pp. 31–2.

217 Nicea (325), Constantinople (381), Ephesus (431) and Chalcedon (451), whose authority, according to Gregory I, *Registrum* I.25, *MGH Epistolae* 1, 36, was equivalent to that of the four Gospels.

218 Cf. Peter Damian, *Letter* 40, pp. 498–9: Leo 'annulled all the ordinations of simoniacs with the authority of synodal vigour'. J.J. Ryan (1956) p. 50 related this passage to the 1049 Roman synod. Cf. O. Capitani (1966) pp. 132–5. On the term 'heresy of simony' see J. Leclercq (1947) pp. 523–30; J. Gilchrist (1965) pp. 209–35.

219 Cf. Humbert, *Adversus simoniacos* III.7, p. 206: simony 'raged throughout Germany and Gaul and the whole of Italy from the times of the Ottonians until Emperor Henry [III]'.

the pope. For the bishop of Sutri,[220] on being accused of the offence of simony, wished to exculpate himself unjustly and produced false witnesses; but as he was about to take the oath, he was suddenly struck down; he was carried outside and not long afterwards he ended his life. All who heard of it were so terrified that no one thereafter attempted to escape ignominy by taking a false oath in the presence of the pope.

He restored to the churches the payment of tithes by all Christians,[221] a practice previously unknown in Apulia and in certain other regions of the world; he forbade the sale of altars on pain of anathema;[222] he decreed that the part of the tithes belonging to the bishop should be held by the prelate himself or by anyone to whom he wished to give it, but he freely granted the part belonging to the altar to the pastor of that church. He put asunder the incestuous marriages that had been indiscreetly contracted among kindred in many regions of the world and separated very many nobles who were joined together in such vile unions.[223] He also strove to restate very many other chapters of the canons, which we shall avoid enumerating, lest the reader should find it tedious.

11 While he laboured in these holy endeavours, he revisited his homeland and was received in Cologne[224] by Archbishop Herman,[225] the most noble and most venerable man of his whole nation. At his request the lord pope granted this privilege to the cathedral church of

220 Either Dominicus II of Sutri (known from a single appearance at the Roman synod of 1027) or an unidentified successor: see G. Schwartz (1913) p. 264. Cf. Bonizo, *Book to a Friend* V, below p. 191.

221 Cf. Bishop Airard of Nantes, charter (*c.* 1050), cited by G. Constable (1964) pp. 85–6: Leo IX 'issued a decree that all laymen must under pain of excommunication give up the revenues of churches to their ministers and allow the tithes of altars to be paid to those who serve them'.

222 Cf. Leo IX, Council of Rheims, c. 2 in: Anselm, *Historia dedicationis* c. 16, col. 1437A. The sale of altars as simony: N.-N. Hughebaert (1947) p. 426.

223 For a similar canon in the council of Rheims, c. 11: Anselm, *Historia* c. 16, col. 1437B. See also Leo's last words in the version of Bruno of Segni, *Sermon* c. 7, below p. 386. This theme recurred in the legislation of the reform papacy: Nicholas II, *JL* 4405–6, ed. R. Schieffer (1981) pp. 222–3. Cf. Peter Damian, *Letters* 19 [1046], 36 [*c.* 1050], pp. 179–99, 339–45.

224 He had arrived in Cologne by 29 June 1049 (feast of SS. Peter and Paul: Anselm, *Historia* c. 8, col. 1422A) and was still there on 5 July (*Diploma Heinrici III* 238). See E. Steindorff (1881) p. 83; R. Schieffer (1991) p. 7.

225 Herman II, archbishop of Cologne (1036–56). See P. Kehr (1930) p. 25 ('the most influential personality among the German metropolitans'); H. Zielinski (1984) pp. 229–30; R. Schieffer (1991) pp. 5–9.

Cologne: that every day seven cardinal priests, clad in sandals, should celebrate the divine office before the altar of St Peter. The pope also gave him and his successors the office of chancellor of the holy Roman see, conferring on him the church of St John at the Latin Gate.[226]

Then he was invited by Herimar, abbot of the venerable monastery of St Remigius, bishop of Rheims,[227] to consecrate the church rebuilt in his honour.[228] It is not easy to describe how great a multitude came from the ends of the earth to be in his presence, Spanish, Bretons, Scots and Englishmen. In this assembly there was a large group of bishops, including Hugh, the venerable archbishop of Besançon,[229] beloved of God and men, whose delightful eloquence and courtesy were outstanding; with whom none of his predecessors or successors can compare in the work of restoring the property of his church; in whom the admirable power of Christ then appeared. For when the council of bishops was held there,[230] the glorious pope deposed certain men infected with the heresy of simony from the offices that they had received unjustly. Among them was Hugh, bishop of Langres,[231] the subject of many horrible accusations, who was summoned to give an account of himself; and he desired the archbishop of Besançon, as a most eloquent man, to be his advocate and spokesman. The latter was compelled by the lord pope to present his case, but when he began to speak, he was suddenly struck dumb in the presence of the whole assembly; so that it was clearly evident that God would not allow the tongue of so great a prelate to be defiled by false excuses for un-doubted crimes. Hugh of Langres was so terrified by this miracle that he fled by night from the judgement of the council. Meanwhile every-one deplored and bewailed the misfortune of the archbishop; but the lord pope turned to Christ with heartfelt contrition and loosened the

226 Leo IX, *JL* 4271 ed. E. Boshof and H. Wolter (1976) pp. 113–14. See D. Lück (1970b) pp. 1–50; E. Boshof (1978b) pp. 41–2.

227 Herimar, abbot of St-Remi, Rheims (1048–71).

228 2 October 1049. Cf. Herimar's invitation in Anselm, *Historia* c. 7, col. 1421B; Leo IX, letter to the faithful in France, *JL* 4185, *MPL* 143, col. 616C, exhorting them to observe Remigius's feast-day on 1 October. See C. H. Brakel (1972) pp. 252–4, 275; J. Hourlier (1981) pp. 181–261.

229 Hugh of Salins, archbishop of Besançon (1031–66), arch-chancellor of the Burgun-dian kingdom. See P. Kehr (1930) pp. 42–7.

230 Council of Rheims, 3–5 October 1049. See *Sacra Concilia* 19, col. 727–46; E. Steindorff (1881) pp. 87–92; J. Hourlier (1946–1955) pp. 55–9; O. Capitani (1966) pp. 149–81; U.-R. Blumenthal (1976) pp. 23–48.

231 Hugh of Breteuil, bishop of Langres (1031–52). For the accusations: Anselm, *Historia* c. 14, col. 1432BC.

archbishop's shackled tongue by means of his holy prayers. Subsequently that bishop of Langres was inspired by heaven to repent. He returned to the lord pope, confessed his offences publicly in floods of tears and freely undertook his penance: going to Rome barefoot, he deserved to receive absolution from our pious pastor.[232] During his return journey he was overcome by his excessive fasting and by the weakness of his body and departed this life, still persevering in good deeds.[233]

12 The pope returned by way of the city of Metz, where he was petitioned by the venerable Abbot Guarinus[234] to consecrate the basilica of the holy Bishop Arnulf in that city.[235] There he was prevailed on by the lord Siegfried, abbot of Gorze[236] to compose a sweet-sounding melody in honour of the glorious martyr Gorgonius[237] as a responsory for the night office. He then held a general council in Mainz,[238] in which Bishop Sibicho of Speyer[239] was accused of a crime and wished to exculpate himself with a fearful oath on the body of the Lord.[240] It is said, however, that his jaw was seized by paralysis and so it remained as long as he lived. I wished briefly to refer to this here, so that those who heard of it would know how horrible it is to submit to a judgement of this kind, even with a sound conscience; for as holy Scripture says, *It is a fearful thing to fall into the hands of the living God.*[241]

Finally the excellent lord pope dedicated a church in honour of the living Cross at Reichenau[242] and there God marvellously demonstrated

232 1051. Cf. *Chronicon sancti Benigni Divionensis* p. 237.

233 In 1052. Cf. *Chronicon s. Benigni* pp. 237–8. See E. Steindorff (1881) pp. 163 n. 3, 219–20.

234 Guarinus, abbot of St Arnulf, Metz (✝ c. 1050). See N. Bulst (1973) pp. 84–5, 87, 219.

235 Cf. *Gesta episcoporum Mettensium* c. 48, p. 543. See R. Bloch (1930) pp. 210, 229.

236 Siegfried, abbot of Gorze (c. 1030–1055).

237 Gorgonius of Nicomedia (✝303), martyr, patron saint of the abbey of Gorze. See P. Paulin (1950) pp. 129–30; C. H. Brakel (1972) pp. 257, 260; M. Bernard (1980) pp. 89–100. See also I.15, above p. 121.

238 Council of Mainz, 19–26 October 1049. See *MGH Constitutiones* 1, 97 (no. 51); E. Steindorff (1881) pp. 93–9.

239 Sibicho (Sigebod), bishop of Speyer (1039–54).

240 'Accused of the offence of adultery, [he] was purged by the ordeal of the holy wafer' (Adam of Bremen, *Gesta* III.30, p. 172). Sibicho's evil reputation: Herman, *Chronicon* 1039, 1052, pp. 123, 131. See A. U. Friedmann (1994) pp. 113–20.

241 Hebrews 10:31.

242 He was on the island of Reichenau from 23 to 26 November 1049: Herman, *Chronicon* 1049, p. 129. See R. Bloch (1930) p. 195; C. H. Brakel (1972) pp. 264–5.

his grace through the medium of His own servant. For during the celebration of the holy mass a man possessed by a demon was brought there. He was bound with chains and could hardly be controlled by the crowd; he was a prey to insane violence, uttering terrible shrieks, shouts and roars, drowning the harmonious hymn-singing of all the clergy with his fearsome cries. The servant of Christ was about to begin the canon of the mass and he could not endure noise of this kind when he was on the point of devoting his mind wholly to God. He therefore made the sign of the cross from afar and gestured for silence and, in less time than it takes to relate, the demon was struck dumb and the man, released from his chains and restored to health, returned to his home amidst universal wonder.[243]

13 He returned to Rome[244] and cheered the people, saddened by his long absence, and there also the grace of heaven made his miraculous merits known to all. Herimar, abbot of the monastery of St Remigius, bishop of Rheims (whom we have already mentioned), had offered him a goblet made from precious maplewood as a remembrance of him, which the holy man had decided, because of his love of the giver, to keep for his own use. On one occasion, however, a servant who was about to serve him a drink, found the goblet broken into many pieces. The Lord's elect ordered all the fragments to be brought to him and, little suspecting what was to happen, he playfully fitted them all together and cheerfully said to those who were present, 'The majesty of the Almighty has the power to restore these fragments to their original whole condition.' As soon as he said this, all the pieces immediately coalesced, so that the mark of a fracture like a very fine hair apparent all the way round the goblet was the sole reminder of the event; but what was more remarkable, no liquid that was poured into it ever leaked out of it.[245] There is a reliable witness of this incident in the person of the venerable Archbishop Hugh of Besançon,[246] who

---

243 On Leo's healing of demoniacs (cf. II.16, 23, below pp. 143, 153) see C. H. Brakel (1972) p. 281.

244 After celebrating Christmas 1049 in Verona: E. Steindorff (1881) p. 103.

245 Other versions of the miracle: Anselm, *Historia dedicationis* c. 7, 18, col. 1421B, 1439A–1440A, (dating it at a banquet during the synod of April 1050 in Rome); Desiderius of Monte Cassino, *Dialogi* III.1, pp. 1143–4; Amatus, *L'Ystoire de li Normant* III.21, pp. 134–5; Bruno of Segni, *Sermon* c. 4, below p. 382. As Desiderius noted (p. 1144), it resembled a miracle of St Benedict recorded by Gregory I, *Dialogi* II.1, *MPL* 66, 128AB. See H.-G. Krause (1976) pp. 74–6.

246 In October 1050 Hugh was in Toul, at the elevation of the relics of St Gerard (Widrich, *Vita et miracula Gerardi episcopi* c. 9, p. 509). This was presumably the occasion when the biographer learned this story: see H.-G. Krause (1976) p. 76.

testified in tears that he was present and rejoiced that he had stolen that vessel from the holy man in a pious theft.[247]

14 Always mindful of the office committed to him by God, like *the faithful and wise* servant *distributing their measure of wheat at the proper time*,[248] he set out for the territory of Apulia in order to restore the Christian religion, which seemed almost to have perished in that land. He was concerned above all to establish harmony between the natives of the region and the Normans, whom the princes of the kingdom had originally welcomed to aid them against the foreign peoples, but whom they would not willingly endure when they became very savage tyrants and ravagers of their homeland.[249] Seriously intent on this holy work, he came to Benevento,[250] where he stayed for some time and, led by divine grace, offered his assistance to a female invalid. Weakened by continuous illness for almost fifteen years, she could not leave her own bed unless she was carried and hence all her limbs were shrivelled by the sickness of palsy. It was revealed to her that she would recover her health without delay after she had drunk from the water in which the blessed pastor had washed his sacred hands after the celebration of mass. She obtained this water and drank it with faith and hope; and next day she went, restored to health, to the holy ceremony of mass to give thanks to God and to the holy pontiff. Burning with zeal for holy religion, the venerable prelate held a council in Siponto[251] and deposed from the office of archbishop two men who had acquired the holy ministry in return for payment, each of them striving to outdo the other through the vice of pride.[252]

15 Resuming his travels, the pope returned to Rome.[253] There, urged by a revelation from heaven, he decided to number among the saints the blessed Gerard, formerly the bishop of his own see, that is of Toul.[254]

247 On the 'pious theft' of relics see P. Geary (1978).

248 Luke 12:42.

249 For a similar contemporary German view of the Normans: Herman, *Chronicon* 1053, p. 132. See H. Hoffmann (1969) pp. 95–144.

250 Before 15 April 1050: *Annales Beneventani* [codex 3] 1050, p. 179 . See W. Kölmel (1935) pp. 94–5, 152–3.

251 15 April (Easter day) 1050. See *Sacra Concilia* 19, col. 793–4.

252 Cf. Amatus, *L'Ystoire de li Normant* III.16, p. 131. See W. Kölmel (1935) p. 153.

253 He had returned by 29 April 1050, when he held a synod in Rome (*Sacra Concilia* 19, col. 759–72).

254 On 2 May 1050 during the synod: Leo IX, *JL* 4219, *MPL* 143, 644D-647D. The authenticity of this letter and the fact of the canonisation were questioned by J. Choux (1963) pp. 75–9, 91–2 and defended by H.-G. Krause (1976) pp. 77–85. The

That same year he returned to his homeland and with high solemnity he translated Gerard's holy relics,[255] as is fully and clearly set down in his Life and Miracles.[256]

The pope was involved in much strife against invaders of the property of the holy Roman see, and especially against the bishop of Ravenna,[257] who was filled with the spirit of obstinacy and rebellion and who was supported by some of the officials in the palace,[258] who envied the glory of the lord pope. The leader in fomenting the dissension was Nizo, bishop of Freising,[259] on whom the divine power saw fit to visit a terrible vengeance, in this manner. He was sent to Italy to deliver the emperor's instructions and, arriving in Ravenna, he promoted the cause of the Ravennese bishop by making slanderous speeches against this blessed man. Putting his finger on his throat, he uttered this blasphemy: 'May this throat be cut by the sword if I do not bring about his deposition from the papal office!' At the very moment that he said this, he was afflicted by an unbearable pain in his throat and he died impenitent on the third day after this.[260] Because of his incorrigible presumption the archbishop of Ravenna was anathematised by the holy pope[261] and for that reason he was summoned to Augsburg by the emperor's command.[262] After he had restored what he had unlawfully usurped, as justice demanded, he was compelled to seek absolution. He prostrated himself at the feet of the holy man, although in his heart he remained obstinate, and all the assembled bishops begged for his absolution. The blessed man said, 'May the almighty Lord grant him absolution from all his crimes according to

importance of this case in the history of papal canonisations: E. W. Kemp (1948) pp. 63–4; R. Klauser (1954) p. 98.

255 On 22 October 1050: Widrich, *Translatio beati Gerardi* p. 509.

256 Widrich, *Vita et miracula sancti Gerardi episcopi* pp. 485–509.

257 Hunfrid, archbishop of Ravenna (1046–51): see G. Schwartz (1913) pp. 156–7.

258 Hunfrid (kinsman of the counts of Achalm) had served at the imperial court as chancellor for the Italian kingdom (1045–6): see P. Kehr (1930) pp. 37, 40.

259 Nitker (Nizo), bishop of Freising (1039–52). Cf. the hostile account of Herman, *Chronicon* 1052, p. 131. See P. Kehr (1930) p. 29.

260 6 April 1052 or 1053: see A. Hauck (1952) p. 1003. Cf. Herman, *Chronicon* 1052, p. 131 (summoned 'to Ravenna at the emperor's command, he perished there by a sudden death'); *Chronicon Benedictoburanum* p. 221. See E. Steindorff (1881) pp. 170–1.

261 At a synod in Vercelli, September 1050: Herman, *Chronicon* 1050, p. 129. See G. Schwartz (1913) p. 157.

262 2 February 1051: Herman, *Chronicon* 1051, p. 129. See E. Steindorff (1881) p. 138.

the degree of his piety.' When, however, the archbishop rose with a mocking smile, still swollen with pride, the venerable father burst into tears and said privately to the bystanders, 'Alas! this wretched man is dead.' He was indeed immediately overcome by faintness and he had scarcely been brought back to his homeland before he was rapidly deprived of life and of the office of which he was so proud.[263]

16 The magnificent pastor returned to Rome and during the Easter solemnities,[264] as he was about to celebrate the offering of the divine sacrament at the church of St Laurence, in the holy ceremony of the mass they brought to him a woman who was filled by a demon and had lost her sanity. Seeing that she was raving ceaselessly and unable to bear the noise of the bystanders who were dragging the woman along in chains, he turned towards them and, making the sign of the cross, he ordered them to remain at a distance. Immediately the unclean invader left the woman and she returned to her home, sane and healed.

Now established in Rome, he was anxious about the spiritual health of those souls who had first been committed to his special care[265] and he elected the venerable provost Udo as his successor in the holy see of Toul[266] and sent his own envoy to the imperial majesty to ensure that Udo was put in his place.[267] Because of the probity of his character, his fervour for holy religion and his pious intentions, Leo judged him worthy of this office and, embracing him with fatherly affection, called him his own son. He hoped that, thanks to the wisdom in divine and human affairs that Udo possessed in great abundance, he could complete whatever he had left unfinished in the advancement of his original bishopric. This is now, with Christ's aid, in great measure

---

263 He died on 23 or 24 August 1051 ('suddenly of poison', according to Herman, *Chronicon* 1051, p. 130). See G. Schwartz (1913) p. 157.

264 31 March 1051.

265 Like his predecessors, Clement II and Damasus II, Leo had retained his former bishopric as pope: see W. Goez (1970) pp. 27–59; G. Frech (1991) pp. 324–32.

266 Udo, bishop of Toul (1051–69). Since the beginning of the pontificate he had served as chancellor of the Roman church. See P. Kehr (1930) p. 55; H. Zielinski (1984) pp. 48, 154 n. 536.

267 Cf. *Gesta episcoporum Tullensium* c. 41, p. 645: Leo 'decided, after an election by clergy and people had first occurred, to put him in his own place ... and, having sent envoys to Henry III, ruler of the Roman empire, to substitute him as his successor.' H.-G. Krause (1976) pp. 73–4 noted that the biographer said nothing of this election by the clergy and people, emphasising instead Leo's designation and Udo's investiture by the emperor (a procedure castigated by Humbert, *Adversus simoniacos* III.11, p. 211). See H. Hoffmann (1963) p. 192; R. Schieffer (1981) p. 34.

being achieved and, we truly believe, Udo's holy devotion towards God increases daily.[268] We think, however, that we ought to desist from praising him, lest we incur the reputation of a flatterer, because it is safest to sing a man's praises only at the end.[269]

17 Leo had a burning desire to strengthen the commonwealth. When, therefore, the princes of Hungary were recently at odds with the Roman empire,[270] he sent numerous legates,[271] so that they would not refuse to pay the ancient tributes to the emperor with their customary obedience.[272] They agreed to do so, if pardon was granted to them for their past actions. The pope was consequently compelled by his holy piety to visit his old homeland for a third time[273] and address his persuasive prayers to the emperor for mercy for those accused of planning a war against the empire.[274] Because of the machinations of certain courtiers who envied the holy man's successes, the emperor refused to hear the prayers of the lord pope and as a result the Roman commonwealth lost the obedience of the kingdom of Hungary and the frontier of our homeland is still suffering devastation, plunder and conflagrations.[275]

While he remained there for a time, labouring anxiously for the peace of the kingdom, divine providence wished to reveal to him in dreams what the future held for him. He seemed to be standing on a lofty peak and the members of his household were seeking refuge with him from some danger. He sheltered them under his pluvial (which is

268 On the significance of this passage in dating the *Life* (Udo died 14 July 1069): H. Tritz (1952) p. 221.

269 Cf. Ecclesiasticus 11:30.

270 Henry III's expeditions of 1051–2 against King Andreas I of Hungary: see E. Steindorff (1880) pp. 155–60, 179–82; E. Boshof (1986) p. 184.

271 Abbot Hugh I of Cluny served as legate: Gilo, *Vita sancti Hugonis abbatis* I.6, p. 55; Hildebert of Le Mans, *Vita sancti Hugonis abbatis* c. 7. col. 864. H. Diener (1959) p. 358 and A. Kohnle (1993) pp. 75–6, 292 dated this legation in '1051 or summer 1052'.

272 Cf. Herman, *Chronicon* 1047, 1053, pp. 127, 133 ('annual tribute and devoted service').

273 August 1052–February 1053: see E. Steindorff (1880) pp. 181–2, 233.

274 According to Herman, *Chronicon* 1052, p. 131: 'Leo at Andreas's invitation had intervened to make peace … Finding [Henry] in agreement with him in all things but discovering that Andreas on the contrary was less obedient to his advice, he was angry and threatened him with excommunication, as one who had deceived the apostolic see'. Cf. *Annales Altahenses* 1052, p. 48. See E. Boshof (1986) p. 184.

275 I.e. the sporadic warfare that continued throughout Henry IV's minority until the German victory of September 1063: see G. Meyer von Knonau (1890) pp. 92–3, 95–6, 192–8, 342–8; E. Boshof (1986) pp. 185–6; I. S. Robinson (1999) pp. 34–6, 53.

customarily called a cape) and observed that the garment was stained
with the blood of those who were under it. This vision made him
certain that grief was at hand for him and his followers and, like
wheat that must be stored on the Lord's threshing-floor,[276] he prepared himself to bear the trial. Returning to Italy, therefore, he
decided to hold a council in Mantua,[277] but it was thrown into disorder
by a faction of bishops who feared the severity of his just judgement.
The men of their households, fomenters of crime, provoked a sudden
tumult against the household of the lord pope, as they stood quietly in
front of the basilica in which the public council was being held, so that
the holy man was compelled to rise in the middle of the session and
go out of doors to stop the noise. Those men hateful to God showed
no reverence for his presence but became more and more obstinate in
their wickedness. They tried before his eyes to strike down his servants, who were disarmed and fleeing to him for refuge and to drive
them back from the doors of the church, to prevent them from finding
safety there, so that a storm of arrows and stones flew about the head
of the holy man and wounded some men who desired to defend him
with their garments. Because of this tumult, which was quelled with
extreme difficulty, the council did not proceed with the same rigour
with which it had begun.[278] On the following day all the instigators of
this sedition were condemned after a strict investigation, but they
were absolved with merciful indulgence by the most pious father, lest
the harshness of his judgement against them should seem to be
prompted by vengeance.

18 It seems unworthy to allow to sink into oblivion a memorable
event, which is said to have happened in Leo's time in Narni, to the
glory of heaven, and which is recorded to have been witnessed by all
the inhabitants of that city, from the least to the greatest. For two
years before this venerable pope celebrated the Lord's Nativity in that
place,[279] it happened that one day in summer a crowd without number
passed before the city walls. Struck by astonishment and terror at their
appearance, all the inhabitants climbed on the walls, as if to defend the
city from capture. The crowd covered an infinite area of ground
extending as far as human sight could reach, and it was moving at a

276 Cf. Matthew 3:12; Luke 3:17.

277 21 February 1053: *Sacra Concilia* 19, col. 799–800.

278 Cf. Herman, *Chronicon* 1053, p. 132: Leo 'celebrated Quinquagesima [21 Febru-
    ary] in Mantua and some of his household were killed in a tumult there'.

279 25 December 1051: see E. Steindorff (1881) p. 165.

very rapid pace towards the east. Their clothes and their faces all appeared to be of remarkable splendour, with venerable white hair and all characterised by virtually the same beauty. All who watched from the walls of the city were dumbfounded by this miracle and the crowd did not cease to hasten by from early morning until the ninth hour. At sunset, however, that wonderful crowd gradually began to thin out and one of the watchers on the wall, bolder than the rest, dared to go outside and, trembling, approached more closely to see if he could recognise any of them. Then among the last of the crowd he saw a former acquaintance, a citizen of that very city, a trustworthy and pious man, who had departed this life not long before. Calling him by name, he adjured him by heaven to approach him and requested him to explain what this great crowd was. He replied, 'Although you are unworthy to understand the divine mysteries, you may know that we are sinful souls, who do not yet deserve to possess the joys of the heavenly kingdom. As a penance we continually travel around the holy places and we are now coming from the monastery of St Martin in Marmoutier[280] and are on our way to the monastery of Mary, the blessed mother of God in Farfa.'[281] So saying, he disappeared and left his interlocutor consumed with terror. He fell ill and was confined to his bed for a whole year; and it was from his mouth that the lord pope learned these things.

19 At that time there arose the heresy of the *fermentacei*,[282] which poured scorn on *the*[283] *holy Roman see, or rather the whole Latin and western Church*, for offering a living sacrifice to God in unleavened bread. *The bishops Michael of Constantinople*[284] *and Leo of Ochrida*[285] set down this *slander* in written form, *wilfully breathing out pestilential*

---

280 The abbey of Marmoutier (diocese of Tours).

281 The abbey of Farfa in Sabina.

282 This term, intended to denigrate Byzantine theologians criticising the use of unleavened bread (azymes) by the western Church, is not found elsewhere in the polemical literature of 1053–4: see H. Hoesch (1970) p. 251. On the schism of 1054 between the Greek and Latin churches see R. Mayne (1954) pp. 133–48; S. Runciman (1955) pp. 38–54; J. M. Hussey (1966) pp. 459–63; E. Petrucci (1973) pp. 733–831.

283 /283 A quotation from the so-called 'Letter book of Cardinal Humbert' (the eleventh-century manuscript Bern, latinus 292), namely the summary preceding the Latin translation of the letter to John of Trani: *MPL* 143, col. 929A; A. Michel (1940) p. 56; H. Tritz (1952) p. 261; H. Hoesch (1970) p. 13.

284 Michael Cerullarius, patriarch of Constantinople (1043–58).

285 Leo, archbishop of Ochrida. On the letter to John of Trani see E. Petrucci (1973) pp. 751–69.

vapours against the holy and apostolic faith. *This slander, composed in Greek, was sent to Bishop John of Trani,*[286] *as an affront to all the Latins. In Trani it was shown to brother Humbert, bishop of the holy church of Silva Candida,*[287] *through whose efforts it was translated into Latin and brought to the lord Pope Leo IX.*[283] The renowned pope then composed a very lucid *little*[288] *book*[289] *to counter their presumptuous charges and excessive vanities.*[288] He attempted to lead them back to the way of truth, but as they subsequently did not accept correction, he condemned them with ecclesiastical anathema.[290] *Brother*[291] *Humbert also composed a reply* to their rotten writings *in the form of a dialogue between a citizen of Constantinople and a citizen of Rome,*[292] *which he wrote in Latin at the time of his legation to Constantinople*[293] *and which was translated into Greek by the command of the religious and orthodox Emperor Constantine Monomachus*[294] *in the year 1054.*[291] Lord Frederick, then chancellor and later elected by God to the Roman and apostolic see,[295] also wrote a polemical reply[296] to certain objections published by *Nicetas,*[297] *monk* of Constantinople, *also known as Pectoratus,*[298] *against the Latin Church,* in *a book* that he *entitled 'Concerning unleavened bread, the sabbath and the*

286 John, bishop of Trani, in Apulia (✝1059?).

287 Humbert, cardinal bishop of Silva Candida (1050–61): see R. Hüls (1977) pp. 131–4.

288 /288 Another quotation from the 'Letter book of Humbert', the summary introducing 'Letter I to Michael Cerullarius' (see n. 289): see *MPL* 143, col. 744B; A. Michel (1940) p. 60; H. Tritz (1952) p. 261; H. Hoesch (1970) p. 12.

289 'Letter I to Michael Cerullarius', ed. C. Will, *Acta et scripta* pp. 65–85, attributed by A. Michel (1924) pp. 44–54 and H. Hoesch (1970) p. 27 to Humbert. See also E. Petrucci (1977) pp. 103–26.

290 The excommunication was pronounced by Leo IX's legates on 16 July 1054: see A. Michel (1940) pp. 46–50; E. Petrucci (1973) pp. 824–31.

291 Another quotation from the 'Letter book of Humbert', the summary introducing Humbert's *Dialogus* (see n. 292): *MPL* 143, col. 931C; A. Michel (1940) p. 58; H. Tritz (1952) p. 261; H. Hoesch (1970) p. 13.

292 Humbert, *Dialogus inter Constantinopolitanum et Romanum* ed. C. Will, *Acta et scripta* pp. 93–126.

293 June–July 1054: see R. Hüls (1977) p. 131.

294 Constantine IX Monomachus (1042–55).

295 Frederick, cardinal priest of S. Grisogono, abbot of Monte Cassino; Pope Stephen IX (1057–8).

296 *Contradictio adversus Nicetam* ed. C. Will, *Acta et scripta* pp. 136–50, attributed to Humbert by A. Michel (1930) pp. 153–208; H. Hoesch (1970) pp. 29, 250.

297 /297 A quotation from Humbert, *Brevis commemoratio* I, ed. C. Will, *Acta et scripta* p. 151. See A. Michel (1940) pp. 55–6; H. Tritz (1952) p. 262.

298 Nicetas Sthetatos (or Pectoratus, meaning 'lion-hearted'), monk of Studion (*c.* 1000–*c.* 1080), polemicist and mystic.

marriages of priests'.[299] This polemic was *translated into Greek* and read out in public in the presence of the emperor and Nicetas was compelled to condemn and burn his writings after a disputation[300] held in *the monastery of Studion in the city of Constantinople.*[297]

The renowned pope had indeed sent to Constantinople *legates*[301] *of the holy Roman see: namely,* the aforesaid *Humbert, Archbishop Peter of Amalfi*[302] *and Frederick,* at that time *deacon and chancellor.*[301] *Nicetas*[303] *received from them a complete answer to his propositions; once again of his own accord he anathematised all that he had said and done or attempted to do against the primary and apostolic see; he was received by them into communion and became their intimate friend.*[303] *Since*[304] *Michael,* bishop of Constantinople, however, *avoided their presence and would hold no talks with them, persevering in his folly, the envoys* of the lord pope *went to the church of S. Sophia and complained of his obstinacy. When the clergy had prepared for mass in the customary manner, on Saturday*[305] *at the third hour, they placed a document of excommunication on the main altar before the eyes of the clergy and people. They departed immediately, shaking the dust from their feet as a testimony against them, according to the words of the Gospel,*[306] *and declared, 'God look upon you and judge.'*[307] *They then put in order the churches of the Latins in Constantinople and pronounced an anathema on all who thereafter received communion from the hands of a Greek who disparaged the Roman rite. With the leave of the orthodox emperor,* from whom they received *the kiss of peace, they gladly returned,* bringing *the gifts that the emperor had conferred on St Peter and on themselves. The emperor was furious* with *Michael* for having refused to come *to a council* held in his *presence* and that of *the envoys* of the lord pope and indeed for having *incited the people to rise up* against him. *He deprived* Michael's *friends and*

---

299 The Latin text of Nicetas's work: ed. C. Will, *Acta et scripta* pp. 127–36. See A. Michel (1935) pp. 308–36.

300 On 24 June 1054: see A. Michel (1930) pp. 180, 202; E. Petrucci (1977) pp. 90–2. Nicetas later composed another work against the Latins on the procession of the Holy Spirit.

301 /301 Humbert, *Brevis commemoratio* ed. C. Will, *Acta et scripta* pp. 150–1. See H. Tritz (1952) p. 263.

302 Peter, archbishop of Amalfi (1048–63).

303 /303 Humbert, *Brevis commemoratio* II.1, p. 151. See H. Tritz (1952) p. 263.

304 /304 Humbert, *Brevis commemoratio* III, p. 151. See H. Tritz (1952) pp. 263–5.

305 16 July 1054. See A. Michel (1940) pp. 46–50; A. Michel (1954) pp. 351–440; E. Petrucci (1977) pp. 92–6.

306 Luke 9:5.

307 Exodus 5:21.

associates of their honours, turned them out of the palace and never[308] *abated the severity of his anger against him.*[304]

20 Meanwhile the most pious pastor, in his anxiety for the sheep entrusted to him by God, was moved by a generous compassion for the unheard-of afflictions of the people of Apulia. He therefore gathered a considerable retinue and once again made for Benevento, attempting by all possible means to check the extreme savagery and fury of the Normans.[309] It is not our intention to dwell in lacrimose language on what happened on that expedition, since the pope himself made it all known in a short letter to the emperor of Constantinople. For he said, among other things: *Seeing*[310] *with that solicitude with which I must watch over all the churches, how the undisciplined and hostile nation* of the Normans *rose up against the churches of God with unheard-of fury and with an ungodliness worse than that of the pagans, how they slaughtered Christians everywhere and afflicted some of them with new and horrible tortures even unto death, how without any human feeling they spared neither child nor old man nor did they spare the weakness of woman; how they made no distinction between sacred and profane,*[311] *how they plundered and burned the basilicas of the saints and tore them to the ground, I very often rebuked their perversity,* reminding, *beseeching, preaching, urging in season and out of season,*[312] *and I threatened them with the terror of divine and human punishment.*[313] *But because,* as *the wise man says, 'No one can make straight what God has made crooked'*[314] *and 'The fool is not corrected by words',*[315] *their malice has become so hardened and obstinate that with every day it has added bad deeds to worse. Consequently, choosing not only to use the property of others but also to exhaust my own resources in liberating Christ's sheep, I considered it necessary to raise a defensive force from wherever men could be recruited*[316] *to bear witness to their iniquity and,*

308 Humbert's text is: 'even now has not abated the severity of his anger against him'. The biographer's emendation was made after Constantine IX's death (11 January 1055).

309 May–June 1053: see E. Steindorff (1881) pp. 240–3; W. Kölmel (1935) pp. 104–9; P. Partner (1972) pp. 113–14; H. Taviani-Carozzi (1996) pp. 184–6.

310 /310 Leo IX, *JL* 4333, *MPL* 143, col. 778C-779B; ed. C. Will, *Acta et scripta* p. 87, attributed to Humbert by A. Michel (1924) pp. 59, 74; H. Hoesch (1970) p. 29.

311 Ezechiel 22:26.

312 Cf. II Timothy 4:2.

313 Cf. Bonizo, *Book to a Friend* V, below p. 193.

314 Ecclesiastes 7:14.

315 Cf. Ecclesiastes 1:15.

316 After Henry III's promise of an army was withdrawn, Leo recruited troops in Germany on his own account (Herman, *Chronicon* 1053, p. 132). His force was

if it was expedient, to curb their arrogance; for I have learned from the Apostle that princes do not bear the sword in vain but are servants of God, executing His wrath on every evildoer[317] *and that princes are not a terror to good conduct but to bad, and kings and dukes are sent by God to punish malefactors.*[318] *Supported, therefore, by such forces as the limited time and the present emergency permitted, I decided to seek conference and counsel of your most faithful man, the glorious duke and commander Argyros;*[319] *not that I desired the destruction or planned the death of any of the Normans or of any men, but that those who do not dread the judgements of heaven might at least come to their senses through the fear of men. Meanwhile, while we were trying to break down their obstinacy with our salutary warnings and while they were responding with false promises of total subjection,*[320] *they launched a sudden attack against our forces; but now they are grieving rather than rejoicing over their victory.*[321] *For, as Your Piety has taken pains to write for our consolation, as a result of their presumption they may expect an even greater wrath to overtake them in the future after those losses that they have already suffered in their ranks. We ourselves, trusting that divine aid will be with us and that human help will not fail us, shall not give up our intention of liberating Christendom nor shall we give any rest in our time,*[322] *until holy Church, now so much in danger, is at rest.'*[310] These are the words of the lord pope.

21 The most evil nation of the Normans, after slaughtering the household of the very gentle pope, but not without great loss to themselves,[323] attacked the fortress known as Civitate. There the blessed man, unaware of what had happened, awaited his troops, supposing them to have been delayed. When he saw the advancing enemy and

---

augmented by those of Italian princes, including the duke of Gaeta and the counts of Aquino, Teano and Teate: see E. Steindorff (1881) pp. 216, 240–1.

317 Romans 13:3–4.

318 I Peter 2:14.

319 Argyros, 'prince of Bari and duke of Italy', patrician, the Byzantine emperor's representative in southern Italy, 1045–58. See V. von Falkenhausen (1967) pp. 58–61, 93–4, 187–90; H. Bloch (1986) pp. 34–6.

320 Cf. Herman, *Chronicon* 1053, p. 132 ('they promised subjection and service and said that they wished to hold [their conquests] by his good will and grace'); Amatus of Monte Cassino, *L'Ystoire de li Normant* III.39, p. 153. See J. Deér (1972) p. 100.

321 The battle of Civitate (18 June 1053), in which the papal army was defeated by the Normans. See E. Steindorff (1881) pp. 245–50; H. Taviani-Carozzi (1996) pp. 181–211.

322 Cf. Psalm 131:5.

323 Cf. *Annales Romani* p. 470.

understood what had happened to his own men, he resumed his journey towards Benevento[324] with the throng of clergy who had remained with him and, to the astonishment of all his enemies, he passed through their ranks *like a lion, bold and fearless.*[325] After contemplating his admirable self-confidence, their minds were changed and they were converted to obedience and, kissing his footprints, they earnestly requested the pardon that they so little deserved.[326] The holy man said to them the few words that were appropriate to the circumstances and strove to obtain an honourable burial for those who had been slain in his service, interring them in a neighbouring church that had long been in ruins. Since they had been willing to suffer a pious death for the Christian faith and for the liberation of an oppressed people, divine grace demonstrated by means of manifold revelations that they rejoiced forever in the kingdom of heaven. For they appeared in various ways to the faithful of Christ, saying that they ought not to be thought of as men to be mourned with funeral rites, but rather as united in heavenly glory with the holy martyrs.[327] A basilica of elegant workmanship was built over them by those who had brought about their deaths and to this was added a community of the servants of God,[328] through whom the almighty power of God performed extraordinary miracles. The most savage nation of the Normans was filled with terror by these events: they laid aside their cruelty, thereafter showing friendship towards the people among whom they lived and treating them as fellow countrymen and, as long as he lived, they served the pope faithfully and with all due submission.

22 The distinguished pastor arrived in Benevento, the Normans having obediently escorted him throughout the whole journey, without

---

324 For other accounts that represent Leo's journey to Benevento as voluntary see Bruno of Segni, *Sermon* c. 6, below p. 384 and the sources listed in E. Steindorff (1881) p. 252 n. 3. But see Herman, *Chronicon* 1053, pp. 132–3; Bonizo, *Book to a Friend* V, below p. 193 (Leo was 'a captive').

325 Proverbs 28:1.

326 Cf. the Escorial *Life of Leo IX* c. 7, ed. H. Tritz (1952) p. 362; *Chronica monasterii Casinensis* II.84, p. 333; *Annales Romani* p. 470.

327 The other biographies of Leo record that the fallen knights appeared to the pope on his deathbed and that he recognised them as martyrs: Libuin, *De obitu sancti Leonis papae* c. 1.2, col. 527AB; Bonus of Cervia, *Vita et miracula Leonis IX* pp. 289–90; Bruno of Segni, *Sermon* c. 6, below p. 385. On the miracles associated with the fallen: Bonizo, *Book to a Friend* V, IX, pp. 193, 260. On this campaign as the first papal 'crusade': C. Erdmann (1935) pp. 110–14; H. E. J. Cowdrey (1985) p. 48.

328 C. Erdmann (1935) p. 114 ('We shall give no credence to [this] report'), referring to Otto of Freising, *Chronica* VI.33, p. 301.

needing to be ordered to do so.[329] He remained there for a year,[330] occupying himself with the holy virtues, patience, fasting, vigils and prayers. He shunned the comfort of a bed; instead, wearing a hair-shirt next to his skin, lying down on a mat placed on the ground, with his head on a stone, he spent a very little of the night hours in sleep, but devoted the rest of the night to reciting the psalter in its entirety and performing innumerable genuflexions. He repeated the whole of the psalter every day and when he offered the divine sacrifice of the mass, he tirelessly completed the manifold cycle of prayers.[331] Another admirable characteristic of his conduct was the fact that, although he was now more than fifty years old, he was so zealous that he learned to read the Holy Scriptures in Greek. Since his heart overflowed with piety and mercy to an incredible degree, an innumerable crowd of poor people incessantly came to benefit from his generosity and he provided for their needs without any discrimination.

While he was devoting himself to these pious deeds, late one night, when all the members of his household had retired to sleep, the pope was walking through the empty spaces of his palace, preceded by a lantern-bearer and accompanied by a servant-boy. He saw, lying in a corner, a leper covered with sores, clad in rags, wasting away in his ghastly rottenness: overwhelmed by extreme sickness, he could not move a step and could hardly produce a word from his worn-out body. The venerable father spoke to him on his knees for a long time in a friendly manner, then, wrapping him up in his own garments, he carried him on his shoulders to the bed which had been prepared for him in the manner befitting a pope: he fastened the inner door while his servant lay asleep and devoted himself to his customary reciting of psalms in a neighbouring oratory. When long afterwards he returned to sleep on the ground according to his custom, he could not find the leper whom he had placed on his high bed, covered with his clothes, and, waking the servant-boy, he asked him where the poor man had gone. The astonished servant looked in all the corners of the house and carefully tried all the doors, but finding them all bolted, he returned in utter amazement. The lord pope, dumbfounded by this event, yielded

---

329 He arrived on 23 June 1053 (*Chronica monasterii Casinensis* II.84, p. 333). Cf. *Annales Beneventani* (codex 3) 1053, p. 180. Cf. Herman, *Chronicon* 1053, p. 133 (Leo 'was not permitted to depart'); *Annales Altahenses* 1053, p. 49 ('detained ... unwillingly').

330 Until 12 March 1054: *Chronica monasterii Casinensis* II.84, p. 333.

331 Cf. Desiderius, *Dialogi* III, prologus, p. 1143 (an apparent reference to the papal stay in Benevento).

up his tired limbs to restful sleep. I do not know what heavenly revelation he saw in his dreams, but in the morning he ordered the servant-boy with a fearful adjuration never, as long as he lived, to reveal to anyone what had happened. I believe that Christ appeared to him in a dream, clad in his garments, just as He had appeared to the blessed Bishop Martin,[332] or that, like the monk Martirius,[333] he saw the leper leaping from his arms and ascending into heaven, but because of his humility he wished to conceal this miracle, lest through the praise of his fellow men he might be infected by the poison of pride. He would not at any rate have ordered the matter to be concealed in this way, issuing so formidable a prohibition, without a good reason.

23 On another day, when he was alone in that same place, pre-occupied with reciting the holy psalms with only a single clerk, behold! a peasant arrived, bringing with him his insane daughter. He declared, sighing deeply, that she was often tormented by a very evil demon and with tears and groans begged for her to be freed by the pope's merits. The pious father tried for a long time to oppose his entreaties and ordered him to direct his humble prayers to the saints whose innumerable relics were kept in that place and to gain their help. But the peasant, persistent in his purpose, or rather, streng-thened in his steadfast faith, said that he would not go away from there until he had obtained divine help through his blessing. Overcome by his rude insistence, the holy man found a grain of salt nearby, blessed it and put it in the girl's mouth, invoking the name of God; and immediately the demon was expelled, together with some corrupt blood, and the joyful father returned home with his daughter restored to health.[334] Very many admirable stories could be told of this blessed man, but I must make allowances for the fastidious reader or the incredulous hearer and, after briefly recalling his passing, I shall bring an end to this work.

24 After *finishing the good fight and the race,*[335] every day he burned with a greater desire for heavenly blessedness and as he might say with Paul, *The world has been crucified to me, and I to the world,* [336] so he

---

332 Martin, bishop of Tours (316/17–397[401]). Cf. Sulpicius Severus, *Vita sancti Martini* c. 3, *CSEL* 1, 113. See C. H. Brakel (1972) pp. 279–80.

333 Cf. Gregory I, *Homiliae in evangelio* XXXIX.10, *MPL* 76, col. 1300BD: Martirius wrapped a leper in his cloak and carried him to his monastery, where the leper proved to be Christ. Cf. Sigebert of Gembloux, *Chronica* 1048, p. 359.

334 Leo's healing of demoniacs: C. H. Brakel (1972) p. 281.

335 Cf. II Timothy 4:7.

336 Galatians 6:14.

was anxious entirely to renounce the cares of this life, to such an extent that, although he was still in the body, he seemed to enjoy the blessed purity of the life of the angels.[337] He spent his nights more often than had been his custom in celebrating the sacraments for the repose of the souls of those who had died in innocence. Although this work had seemed to him of supreme importance throughout his time on earth, nevertheless as the day of his death approached, he devoted himself to this glorious work with more fervent zeal and with a greater number of vows. Since divine providence works for the salvation of its servants sometimes by rewarding and sometimes by punishing them, when Leo had reached the pinnacle of virtue, he was so chastised by salutary sufferings that he lost all his desire for food and he was compelled by the pain of advancing disease to continue the fasts that he had formerly practised voluntarily, offering his exhausted body only a cup of water for its sustenance.

25 Meanwhile the anniversary of the day of his ordination came round,[338] which every year he was accustomed to devote to praying to Christ with more than his usual fervour. Although the increasing pain of his illness was now weakening the vital organs of a body already exhausted by labouring for God, he was nevertheless strengthened by the Holy Spirit, which had directed the whole course of his life; so that he celebrated the solemnities of the mass on that day with the honour belonging to the apostolic dignity and the Beneventans, among whom he was then living, were delighted by his courtesy and kindness. This was his last celebration of the divine sacraments, as if he was bidding farewell to the living mysteries, of which he had always shown himself worthy. Certain that his vocation was at an end, he caused himself to be carried to Rome in a litter.[339] During this journey heaven reunited him not only with his own men but also with those who had recently been his enemies, so that a numerous troop of Normans (who, as we described above, had long been at odds with this man) rode before him, serving as his escort and most sincerely devoted to him.[340] It was undoubtedly fitting that this most courageous defender

---

337 Cf. J. Wollasch (1985) p. 42: 'Leo IX's ... manner of life is characterised in his biography in monastic language.'

338 12 February 1054.

339 Cf. *Annales Romani* p. 470: 'his litter was placed on horses and he returned to Rome with those of his knights who had escaped [the battle of Civitate]'.

340 Count Humphrey of Apulia conducted him as far as Capua: *Chronica monasterii Casinensis* II.84, p. 333.

of the Christian religion, as he approached the palace of Christ, his
King, should be conducted in a noble and victorious triumph, preceded
by a tamed multitude of the enemies whom he had now subdued. He
remained for a little time in the Lateran palace, waiting to learn what
most merciful decision had been made about him by the Judge who
sees the inner man.

26 Blessed Peter did not forget the long labour that his fellow-
worker, this memorable man, had devoted to ruling the sheepfold of
the Church and he resolved to secure him as a companion, since he
himself would share in the sublime honour and glory that Leo, led by
the grace of the supreme Shepherd, conferred on the Roman church.
Leo was informed by divine revelation, therefore, that his release from
this life would take place only in the neighbourhood of the oratory of
the blessed Peter. Giving thanks for such a vision and realising that
he had been visited by divine compassion, he was immediately conveyed again in a litter and so entered the oratory of the blessed Peter.
There, his tears flowing from the depths of his heart, raising to God
not only his hands but also his pure mind, he invoked the mercy of the
Lord in his secret prayers.[341] He was then carried into the nearby
episcopal residence,[342] where he was visited by a throng of the faithful,
who flocked to him to express their love. Since they considered that
he would not be detained for much longer in the prison of the body
and as great crowds of bishops, abbots and other faithful men had
flocked there, they decided that he should be anointed with holy oil in
their presence.[343] This filled him with joy and, greatly fortified by the
communion of the Lord's body and blood, he spoke to God in the
following prayer in the German language,[344] as those who were present
bore witness: 'Lord of compassion, the unique salvation of all who
have found redemption, if your all-seeing majesty judges that I should
continue to serve the general interests of your people, I beg that I
may be granted relief from the pain of my present sickness by the
swift medicine of your presence. If your providence decides otherwise,
I pray, Lord, that I may be permitted to leave the habitation of the
body as soon as possible.' When he had finished his prayers, he turned
his attention to those who were standing by and thanked each of them
for the service that he had given him. Composing his tired limbs for

341 Cf. *Rule* of Benedict c. 52.4, *CSEL* 75, 135.
342 Sunday, 17 April 1054: Libuin, *De obitu sancti Leonis papae* c. 1.2, col. 527AB.
343 Cf. Libuin, *De obitu* c. 1.7, col. 534A.
344 Cf. above c. 1, p. 99. See H. Taviani-Carozzi (1996) pp. 205–6.

rest, he said that his pain was more bearable than usual. The crowd of faithful bystanders believed that he would soon slough off his earthly body and, sobbing and sighing, they performed the appropriate final rites for his departing soul. The blessed man silenced them and said, 'Defer what you are doing until tomorrow at the third hour and wait for the Lord's omnipotence to do with me what pleases Him.' On the following day at the third hour,[345] therefore, a numerous throng of the faithful assembled, vigilant and affectionate, and about the ninth hour his spirit left his body and went to heaven, accompanied by their most devout prayers.

27 The whole population of Rome flocked to his funeral, which was performed with supreme reverence; and, as he himself had determined, he was buried next to the altar of the blessed Pope Gregory before the doors of the church.[346] It is fitting that he is joined in this honourable burial with him whom he faithfully imitated in divine piety and in the restoration of holy Church.[347] His life and sanctity are briefly described in this distich:

Rome, victorious and widowed, mourns for Leo IX.
Among her many future rulers, she will hardly have such a father.[348]

This eminent man was released from the labours of this life at the age of fifty, in the year of the Lord's Incarnation 1055,[349] in the twenty-eighth year of his episcopate in Toul and the sixth year of his papacy. He reigned in Rome indeed for five years, with the addition of two months and nine days, fulfilling the vision that we recounted above, in the prophecy of the chalices.[350] For the five chalices offered to him by the blessed Peter signified the five years of his life; the three chalices signified the three years of his successor, Victor;[351] the following single chalice, the one year of Stephen of blessed memory[352] in the papacy.

---

345 19 April 1054. See E. Steindorff (1881) p. 267.

346 Cf. Herman, *Chronicon* 1054, p. 133.

347 Leo and the cult of Gregory I: C. H. Brakel (1972) pp. 246, 259–60 and above I.15, p. 122.

348 In the version of this biography in the Austrian Legendary this distich reads 'she will hardly have his equal': see H. Tritz (1952) p. 275

349 1054.

350 See above II.2, p. 129.

351 Victor II (1054–7).

352 Stephen IX (1057–8). This passage must have been written after Stephen's death on 29 March 1058.

It remains, however, to describe the very many miracles that divine piety performed at his tomb;[353] but this task we leave to the Romans, among whom they are revealed every day.[354] Our task is with devout prayers to invoke his merits, so that, now that he is placed in heavenly glory, he may deign to open for us his heart of piety and mercy, with which he overflowed in his earthly life. Then with his most holy aid we may break the bonds of our sins and deserve to share in the glory of heaven, according to the will of Him who performs miracles through His saints, who sing His praises and give thanks forever and ever. Amen.

353 For the miracle collections of the Roman subdeacon Libuin, Bishop Bonus of Cervia and the anonymous compilations see H. Tritz (1952) pp. 310–11, 321–53. Contemporary references to Leo's miracles outside Rome: Herman, *Chronicon* 1054, p. 133; *Annales Altahenses* 1054, pp. 49–50; Anonymus Haserensis, *De episcopis Eichstetensibus* c. 38, p. 265; Desiderius, *Dialogi* III.3, pp. 1145–6. See also Bonizo, *Book to a Friend* V, below p. 193; Bruno of Segni, *Sermon* c. 7, below pp. 387–8.

354 See above p. 22.

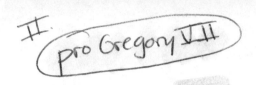

The Book of Bishop Bonizo of Sutri which is entitled 'To a Friend'

Book I

You, the sole protection *from the trouble that has encompassed me,*[1] ask me why in this time of calamity does mother Church lie groaning on the earth, why does she cry out to God and her prayers are not heard, why is she oppressed and is not set free? Why do the sons of obedience and peace lie prostrate, while *the sons of Belial*[2] *rejoice* with *their king,*[3] especially since He who orders all things is also He who *judges with equity*?[4] There is also a second question prompting you to seek from me the authority of ancient examples from the holy Fathers: whether it was and is lawful for a Christian to engage in an armed struggle for the sake of the faith? It will be easy to reply to your vacillating thoughts – if you bring to these matters an attentive ear and a sound intellect – both because we have an answer ready and because it seems to me extremely necessary to write it down at this time. Trusting, therefore, in the mercy of God, who *makes the tongues of babes speak clearly*[5] we embark on our discourse.

Our mother the Church, *who is above* and who *is* not *in slavery with her children*[6] sometimes enjoys the greatest freedom and sometimes is oppressed; sometimes she flourishes and sometimes she is diminished.[7] For no one will deserve to be the fellow citizen of Abel in the heavenly kingdom unless he has been cleansed of all impurity by the malicious persecution of Cain in this world. Thus when Enoch was found to be worthy, he was taken up lest his heart become altered by malice.[8]

---

1 Psalm 31:7.

2 Deuteronomy 13:13.

3 Psalm 149:2. An allusion to Henry IV, king of the Germans (1056–1106), emperor (1084).

4 Psalm 97:9.

5 Wisdom of Solomon 10:21.

6 Galatians 4:26, 25.

7 W. Berschin (1972) p. 40 suggested as a source Pope Leo I, *Sermo* 82, *MPL* 54, 426A.

8 Cf. Hebrews 11:4–5.

Thus Noah, the restorer of the human race, after nearly six hundred years during which he suffered much at the hands of those who had dishonoured themselves by unlawful intermarriage,[9] escaped with his household when the world perished under the avenging flood.[10] Even though the children of Jerusalem were once held captive, they were not in servitude.[11] Even though they *sat down by the waters*, they *wept* and did not delight in the rivers. They *hung up* their *lyres on the willows* and did not *sing* their *song in a foreign land*, but sighed for Jerusalem. For that reason, *wretched daughter of Babylon*, *blessed* are they who *dash your little ones against the rock*.[12] Thus that Hebrew[13] who would not be detained in Ur of the Chaldeans, did not submit himself to the pride of Babylon. Instead he travelled to Jerusalem, beheld Melchizedek and was blessed by him[14] and he was called by the Almighty *the father of a multitude of nations*.[15] What is written? *He had two sons*, one by a slave woman and one by a free woman, but the son of the slave woman was a son according to the flesh, while that of the free woman was a son *according to the promise*.[16] They are the two peoples, one of the catholics, the other of the heretics.[17] *Just as in those days the son according to the flesh persecuted the son according to the spirit, so it is likewise happening now. But what does Scripture say? 'Cast out the slave woman with her son; for the son of the slave woman shall not be heir with the son of the free woman.'*[18] After Sarah complained to Abraham, therefore, and after the angel intervened, Ishmael was disinherited and persecuted, but Isaac was endowed with his inheritance.[19]

There is, however, another type of persecution, which Isaac himself

9 Cf. Genesis 7:6, 6:2–4.

10 Cf. Hebrews 11:7.

11 Perhaps an allusion to Bonizo's captivity in 1082: see above p. 39.

12 Psalm 136:1–2, 4, 8–9.

13 Abraham: cf. Genesis 11:31.

14 Cf. Genesis 14:18–20.

15 Genesis 17:4–5; Romans 4:17. Cf. Isidore of Seville, *De ortu et obitu patrum* c. 5, 6, *MPL* 83, 152B–153A.

16 Galatians 4:22–3. I.e. Ishmael, son of the slave Hagar (Genesis 16:15) and Isaac, son of Sarah (Genesis 21:3).

17 Bonizo's allegorical interpretation of Ishmael's treatment as the righteous persecution of heretics by the Church derived from Augustine, *Epistola* 185 c. 9, *CSEL* 57, 8–9, cited in Bonizo, *Liber de vita christiana* VII.17, p. 243 (under the title 'That the Church can practise persecution').

18 Galatians 4:29–30.

19 Genesis 21:10–14, 17–18.

suffered patiently. He *dug the wells of water* which *his father had dug* before and he *found water* and foreigners *quarrelled over* it.[20] He did not resist them but bore it patiently until he *found Abundance* and from Abundance he came to Beersheba,[21] which is interpreted 'the seventh well':[22] that is, rest. This demonstrates more clearly than day that persecution that is inflicted on us by those who are outside must be overcome by patient endurance, while persecution inflicted by those who are inside, must first be cut down with the scythe of the Gospel[23] and afterwards must be fought with all our strength and weapons. We shall demonstrate this better by means of examples.

Why do we confine ourselves to allegory?[24] Let us come now to Gospel truth; let us come to *the light that enlightens every man entering the world;*[25] let us come to the words that are more durable than heaven and earth and let us find that we have no friendship and nothing in common with the world. We must not lament, therefore, when we are oppressed, but must rather rejoice. For thus says the Saviour: *Do not wonder that the world hates you,*[26] *know that it has hated me before it hated you,*[27] and again: *My peace I give to you, peace I leave with you; not as* this *world gives do I give to you.*[28] How great an honour it is to share the feeling of God's Son that the world is our enemy, so that we can have the *Father who* is *in heaven*[29] as our friend! He subsequently called on us to suffer, saying: *Do not fear those who kill the body but cannot kill the soul,*[30] and a little later: *If any man comes after me, let him deny himself and take up his cross and follow me.*[31] For if we are members of the supreme head,[32] we must by imitating Him and clinging to Him reach that place where we know for certain that He

20 Genesis 26:18, 21.

21 Cf. Genesis 26:32–3.

22 Cf. Jerome, *Liber interpretationis hebraicorum nominum, CC* 72, 62.

23 I.e. excommunication: see W. Berschin (1972) p. 41.

24 Cf. Galatians 4:24. For Bonizo's use of the allegorical sense of scripture see W. Berschin (1972) pp. 40–1.

25 John 1:9.

26 I John 3:13.

27 John 15:18.

28 John 14:27.

29 Matthew 6:9.

30 Matthew 10:28.

31 Matthew 16:24.

32 Cf. I Corinthians 6:15.

has gone. Through dishonour and scourging and mockery and the most shameful death of the cross He attained to the glory of the Resurrection and *being made perfect*,[33] He was crowned with glory and honour and is seated at the right hand of God, the Father almighty. Thus if we are children of the supreme Father, we also through worldly sufferings must abide with Him, so that we may rise again and reign together with Him.

Those first founders of our mother *without spot or wrinkle*[34] taught this in their writings and demonstrated it by their example. For what did the principal shepherd[35] and the *chosen instrument*[36] and the *sons of thunder*[37] and the brothers of the Lord and the other leaders of the Lord's flock teach us if not to abandon the world with its pomps and to *set* our *minds on things that are above, not on things that are on earth?*[38] They also demonstrated this by their example, when *they left the presence of the council, rejoicing that they were counted worthy to suffer dishonour for the name of Jesus.*[39] Afterwards, therefore, *their sound went out to all the earth*,[40] they were *made perfect*[41] and were appointed princes over all the earth. They were followed by the army of martyrs clad in white, who met death through various tortures, some decapitated, some flayed alive, some burned, some drowned in rivers, some pierced by spikes, some buried alive, some deprived of their eyes, some maimed in their limbs, some *sawn in two*, some *stoned*, some *suffered scourging and even chains and imprisonment, they went about in skins of sheep and goats.*[42] It was the episcopate that led them to achieve such distinction and glory. Although what the episcopate preached in words and demonstrated by example was now diffused almost throughout the whole world, nevertheless the Roman bishopric was the foremost bishopric among Christians. Beginning with the blessed prince of the apostles,[43] for nearly two hundred years, until the time of

33 Hebrews 5:9.
34 Ephesians 5:27. I.e. the Church.
35 Peter. Cf. John 21:15–17.
36 Paul: cf. Acts 5:41.
37 James and John, the sons of Zebedee: cf. Mark 3:17.
38 Colossians 3:2.
39 Acts 5:41.
40 Romans 10:18.
41 Hebrews 5:9.
42 Cf. Hebrews 11:36–7.
43 P. Jaffé's edition adds here 'Peter'.

the pious Constantine,[44] the papacy contended with the ancient enemy day and night with continuous success in battle and triumphed thirty-three times[45] over that ancient serpent.[46] It did not cease to struggle by suffering, subduing *principalities and powers*,[47] until the leader of the Roman empire himself[48] submitted to the Christian religion.

Book II

When Constantine was baptised by Silvester,[1] bishop of the holy Roman church, and crowned by him with the imperial diadem, the temples were closed and the churches opened; the portrait of the Saviour began to be painted on the walls and the statues of Jupiter were publicly pulled down; altars began to be set up and images to be cast down;[2] peace was restored to the churches throughout the world, although it was not to last long.

For in the time of that pious prince Arius appeared, the greatest of the destroyers of the Church, from whom the Arian heresy originated[3] and a myriad of heretical innovations and there is no doubt that every Christian *must fight* against these *for the sake of his office*.[4] For the ancient serpent lamented the fact that the imperial power, by means of which he used to persecute the Christian religion, had been taken from him and he gave himself up entirely to his rage. Using men like

44 Constantine I ('the Great'), emperor (306–37).

45 Cf. Bonizo, *Liber de vita christiana* III.110, p. 109: 'we are admonished [to martyrdom] ... especially by the examples of the Roman pontiffs, who from St Peter up to the time of the pious Constantine, succeeding each other on thirty-three occasions, did not fear to die, until they subjected the Roman prince himself to the Christian religion'. Bonizo supposed Silvester I, in whose pontificate the persecution of Christianity ended, to be the thirty-third pope (*ibid.*, IV.33, p. 123).

46 Satan: cf. Revelation 12:9; 20:2.

47 Ephesians 6:12.

48 Constantine I.

1 Pope Silvester I (314–35).

2 Cf. Bonizo, *Liber de vita christiana* IV.98, p. 164; Bonizo, *Libellus de sacramentis* ed. W. Berschin (1972) p. 159.

3 Arius, priest of Alexandria (*c.* 250–*c.* 336) taught that Christ was a creature, not of the same nature as God. His teaching was condemned by the Council of Nicea (325).

4 Gregory I, *Registrum* XII.9, *MGH Epistolae* 1, 357 (quoted in John the Deacon, *Vita Gregorii I* III.4, *MPL* 75, col. 131D).

himself, intoxicated with a false idea of righteousness, he did not cease to stain the purity of the Church; he does not cease to do so, nor will he cease until the time of him *who exalts himself against every so-called god or object of worship.*[5]

Since, however, we have begun to speak of Constantine, let us proceed with the praises of Constantine. It was Constantine who brought the law into harmony with the teaching of the Gospel, so that all bishops should have the Roman pontiff as their head, just as all secular officials obey the king.[6] He was the finder of the Lord's cross, the greatest propagator of the name of Christ, the founder of the bountiful new Rome,[7] the foremost builder of basilicas.[8] It was he who assembled for us the holy synod of Nicea,[9] in which he prepared the presidential seat for all the bishops, while he himself sat on a footstool,[10] judging it unfitting that the seat of the emperor should be placed among the thrones of those who will *sit in judgement on the twelve tribes of Israel.*[11] When one day petitions containing accusations were presented to him by the bishops, he is reputed to have said, 'God forbid that I should judge gods. For it is said of you, *I have said that you are gods.*[12] Nor is it right that the greater should be judged by the lesser.'[13] It was he of whom we read that he said, 'If I found anyone wearing a religious habit doing evil, I should cover him with my cloak, lest the dignity of so great a name should be brought into disrepute.'[14] He left sons who were heirs at least to his kingdom, but not to his religion.

5 II Thessalonians 2:4 (i.e. the Antichrist).

6 A partial quotation from *Actus Silvestri*: see W. Berschin (1972) p. 44. Cf. Bonizo, *Liber de vita christiana* IV.33, p. 124. See H. E. J. Cowdrey (1997b) pp. 83–4.

7 Constantinople.

8 Cassiodorus-Epiphanius, *Historia ecclesiastica tripartita* I.7, *CSEL* 71, 26; Rufinus, *Historia ecclesiastica* I.7–8, *MPL* 21, col. 475–478. Cf. Bonizo, *Liber de vita christiana* IV.98, p. 164. See H. E. J. Cowdrey (1997b) p. 84.

9 First Council of Nicea, 325.

10 Cf. Cassiodorus-Epiphanius, II.5, *CSEL* 71, 90.

11 Matthew 19:28.

12 Psalm 81:6. Bonizo probably derived this text (Rufinus of Aquileia, *Historia ecclesiastica* I.2, *MPL* 21, col. 468B) from Nicholas I, *Epistola* 88, *MGH Epistolae* 6, 456. This anecdote was used by Gregory VII, *Registrum* IV.2, VIII.21, pp. 296, 553; Urban II, *JL* 5367, *MPL* 151, col. 290B; Deusdedit, *Libellus contra invasores et symoniacos* V.10, pp. 350–1; Placidus, *Liber de honore ecclesiae* 90, p. 613. See W. Berschin (1972) p. 44; H. E. J. Cowdrey (1997b) pp. 65–6, 81, 84.

13 Perhaps an allusion to Rufinus, *Historia* I.2, *MPL* 21, col. 468B; Cassiodorus-Epiphanius, II.2, *CSEL* 71, 86. See W. Berschin (1972) pp. 44–5.

14 Cf. Cassiodorus-Epiphanius, II.24, pp. 124–5.

For his son Constantius,[15] who on the death of his brothers succeeded to the monarchy after him, devastated the Church to an astonishing degree in his zeal for the Arian heresy. For he sent some bishops into exile[16] and put others to the sword. When he attempted to expel Bishop Paul of Constantinople by means of the prefect Hermogenes, the Catholic people, armed with zeal for the divine law, fought for the truth so vigorously that they burned the prefect with all his house and household. This deed was not condemned, but rather praised by the wise.[17] What shall I say of the Alexandrians and of their great sufferings for the sake of St Athanasius[18] and their mighty and praiseworthy battles against the Arians in their zeal for the orthodox faith?[19] What of the Milanese? When Constantius wished to take prisoner bishops who were hiding in a church, they took up arms to resist him and seized the prisoners from his bloody hands.[20] Since Constantius was not the equal of his father, but instead like the pagans he persecuted the bishops *with zeal for God but without knowledge*,[21] in his time the state was greatly troubled. For the Persians crossed the Roman frontiers[22] and the powerful race of the Franks invaded the banks of the Rhine and up to this day has been subject to Christian, although not to Roman dominion.

On the death of Constantius, Julian[23] succeeded to his kingdom, an apostate and a man hateful to God. For three years, during which he did not so much govern the Roman empire as lay it waste, it is not easy to say how many priests he slaughtered and how many Christians he afflicted with various tortures. There were at that time, however, men not only of the priestly but also of the military order, who openly resisted his insanity: like Jovian,[24] who succeeded to his power. He

---

15 Constantius II (337–61).

16 Cf. Cassiodorus-Epiphanius, V.17, p. 241. See Bonizo, *Liber de vita christiana* IV.36, p. 125.

17 According to Bonizo's source, Cassiodorus-Epiphanius, IV.13, pp. 168–9, 'the furious populace resisted [Hermogenes] in an irrational manner'. See C. Erdmann (1935) p. 230.

18 Athanasius, patriarch of Alexandria (*c.* 296–373).

19 Cf. Cassiodorus-Epiphanius, IV.17, pp. 171–2.

20 Perhaps a confused allusion to *ibid.*, V.15, pp. 234–5. See C. Erdmann (1935) p. 230. Bonizo saw here a precedent for the activities of the Milanese Patarini.

21 Romans 10:2.

22 Cf. Cassiodorus-Epiphanius, IV.34, p. 206.

23 Julian (361–3).

24 Jovian (363–4).

had been the commander of a thousand men, but he gave up his office rather than renounce his faith.[25] Nor should I omit to mention the fervour of divine love shown by Valentinian.[26] When one day in the course of his duties, for he was the leader of a cohort of the legions, he was preceding the king as he entered the temple of Fortune and as the priest was sprinkling those who entered with water, as the custom was, it happened that this most Christian man noticed a drop on his cloak. Ah! inflamed with zeal for the name of Christ, in the presence of the most cruel emperor and at the entrance of the temple he at once laid the priest low with a blow of his fist, exclaiming that as a Christian he was stained rather than purified by that sprinkling. This deed was so pleasing to God that, before a year had passed,[27] He gave him the government of the whole Roman empire. For Julian met a dishonourable death among the Persians and Jovian succeeded to the empire but was laid to rest before a year had passed. On his death, Valentinian, a cultivated and most Christian man, succeeded to his kingdom.[28] At the beginning of his reign he made his brother, named Valens,[29] his colleague in the empire, alas! giving him jurisdiction over all the east, while he himself governed the western regions.

He made Milan his imperial residence. After the death of the heretic Auxentius and after the holy Dionysius had been peacefully laid to rest,[30] it happened that the bishops of Italy assembled there so that they might together elect a bishop. To achieve this, they particularly desired the presence of the king. When the latter heard of this, he utterly refused to comply and made a law in accordance with the Gospel, that no secular prince or magnate should dare to involve himself in the election of a patriarch, metropolitan or bishop, and that if this occurred, such an election would be invalid,[31] adding, 'Elect according to the decrees of the canons such a man as can heal our

25 Cf. Cassiodorus-Epiphanius, VII.1, p. 376.

26 Valentinian I (364–75).

27 Cf. Cassiodorus-Epiphanius, VI.35, pp. 357–8: 'when a year and a few months had passed'.

28 Cf. *ibid.*, VII.7, p. 393.

29 Valens (364–78).

30 The Arian Auxentius (✝374) was installed as bishop after Bishop Dionysius of Milan was exiled (355) for resisting the attempts of Constantius II to impose religious harmony: see M. Humphries (1999) pp. 49–50, 116–17, 147–8.

31 A fuller version of this text was cited by Bonizo, *Liber de vita christiana* II.17, p. 42. The actual source was the Fourth Council of Constantinople (869–70) c. 22, *MPL* 129, col. 160AB. See W. Berschin (1972) p. 45.

wounds.'[32] Mindful of the humility of this most pious prince, God on high answered his prayer and gave to him and to the church Ambrose[33] as bishop. As long as he lived, he showed himself most devoted to the priests of God and governed the Roman empire in peace.

From the reign of the pious Constantine until the cruel regime of the Lombards, whosoever of the princes of the Roman empire ruled according to the fear of God and the advice of the bishops and above all obeyed the Roman pontiff, protecting the churches, esteeming the clergy and honouring the priests, as long as they lived, they governed the state in profound peace and exchanged death for eternal life. Those who were disobedient, however, came to a bad end, like Valens, the brother of Valentinian. On the death of Valentinian, when his son Valentinian[34] had succeeded him, together with his mother Justina,[35] who was a heretic, Valens seized power and, being a thorough Arian, he laid waste the eastern churches and sent the bishops into exile. In his time the Goths and Massagetae crossed Istria, seized Illyria and invaded Epirus and afterwards, coming to Chalcedon, they killed the wicked man and laid siege to Constantinople.[36] Wonderful to relate, however, his widow Dominica did what her husband had been unable to do and liberated the city from the barbarians.[37]

There were other pernicious men too, like Zeno[38] and Constantine[39] and Anastasius,[40] who was destroyed by a thunderbolt from heaven after he spoke evil of the pope;[41] and Valentinian, who was expelled from his kingdom, together with his mother, Justina, but was restored

---

32 Cf. Cassiodorus-Epiphanius, VII.8, p. 394. See W. Berschin (1972) p. 45.

33 Ambrose, bishop of Milan (373–97).

34 Valentinian II (375–92).

35 Justina (✝390). On her support for the Arians see Cassiodorus-Epiphanius, IX.20, p. 527.

36 Cf. ibid., VIII.7, 15, pp. 478, 489–90. The Visigoths defeated Valens at the battle of Adrianople (378).

37 Cf. Cassiodorus-Epiphanius, IX.1, p. 493.

38 Zeno (474–91).

39 Presumably Constantius II, who is mentioned in the passage in Nicholas I, Epistola 88, MGH Epistolae 6, 458 (Bonizo, Liber de vita christiana IV.86a, p. 154) on which this sentence is based.

40 Anastasius I (491–518). Cf. Bede, De temporum ratione c. 66, CC 123B, 520.

41 Hormisdas (514–23).

by the pious prince Theodosius;[42] and Basil[43] and Leo[44] and Maurice,[45] who, together with his wife and children, was condemned to death by Phocas.[46] There were also very many others who dishonoured the priests of God and tried to take away the privileges of the Roman church and they had no peace during their lives and they fell into eternal perdition. In their days a Persian army invaded Mesopotamia and the most evil race of the Saracens withdrew the whole of Africa, Marmarica, Lybia, Egypt, Arabia, Judea and Phoenicia from Roman control. From the north the savagery of the Huns, the storm of the Goths and the hurricane of the Vandals devastated the whole of the west, while *the tenth horn of the beast*,[47] that is, the fury of the Lombards, drawn from the sheath of the Lord's wrath, invaded the Italian regions. It is better to remain silent than to say little about this persecution.[48]

There were besides very religious emperors like Theodosius and Honorius[49] and the other Theodosius[50] and the pious pair Martian[51] and Valentinian[52] and Constantine[53] and Irene[54] and Leo[55] and Justinian[56] and certain others. They, as we said before above, both governed the state in profound peace and exchanged death for eternal life. In the reign of the first Theodosius Ambrose and Augustine[57] and Jerome[58] passed their earthly lives, they who have left us many salutary rules of conduct. Ambrose was protected by the weapons of the people when

---

42 Theodosius I (379–95). The restoration occurred in 388.

43 Basil I (867–86).

44 Perhaps Leo III (717–41), the iconoclast emperor.

45 Maurice (582–602).

46 Phocas (602–10).

47 Cf. Revelation 17:12, 16.

48 Cf. Bonizo, *Liber de vita christiana* VII.29, pp. 249–50.

49 Honorius (395–423). This sentence imitates a passage in Nicholas I, *Epistola* 88, p. 458 (above n. 39).

50 Theodosius II (408–50).

51 Martian (450–7).

52 Valentinian III (424–55).

53 Constantine VI (780–97).

54 Irene (797–802), mother of Constantine VI.

55 Leo I (457–74).

56 Justinian I (527–65).

57 Augustine, bishop of Hippo (395–430).

58 Jerome (c. 342–419).

Valentinian and Justina ordered him to be expelled from the church and the priest of God did not censure, but rather praised the divine fervour of the people.[59] At that same period the venerable Augustine exhorted the prince Boniface to plunder and destroy the Donatists and Circumcelliones.[60]

Since I have mentioned the religious princes, however, I have thought it necessary to include in this work something about their lives and the laws that they promulgated. Let us now begin with Theodosius himself. After he assumed the government of the kingdom, he miraculously defeated and subdued the barbarians and expelled the Arians from the churches, which he gave to orthodox men. He compelled the Persians to remain within their own frontiers and drove the tyrant Maximus from his kingdom.[61] Meanwhile, once the kingdom had been pacified, he came to Thessalonica and, with the licence characteristic of a king, not seeking any advice, he commanded that the people should be killed. When he then came to Milan, he was forbidden by the blessed Ambrose to enter the doors of the church. Acknowledging his sin, he wept publicly outside the church for as long as was necessary to obtain pardon and he issued a law that the judgements of princes must be open to inspection for forty days before being considered valid.[62]

The laws promulgated by his sons, Archadius[63] and Honorius, bear witness to the great reverence they felt for the priests of God. For example: *The august emperors Archadius and Honorius to the chief prefect Theodorus. Whoever commits a sacrilege of this kind, forcing his way into a catholic church and causing any injury to the priests and ministers or to the religious ceremonies or to the place itself, the outrage is to be punished by the rulers of the province. The governor of the province should be aware that an injury to the priests and ministers of the catholic church, to the place itself or*

---

59 Ambrose, *Epistolae* I.22, *MPL* 16, col. 1022B. But see Peter Damian, *Letter* 87, p. 514 ('Surely Ambrose did not make war on the Arians who cruelly attacked him and his church?'). See C. Erdmann (1935) p. 231.

60 See below p. 258.

61 Cf. Cassiodorus-Epiphanius, IX.4, 19, 21, 23, pp. 501–2, 526–7, 530, 531–2.

62 Cf. *ibid.*, IX.30, pp. 541–6. See also below p. 259. This example was used by Gregory VII, *Registrum* IV.2, VIII.21, pp. 294, 554, as a precedent for excommunicating Henry IV and later figured in polemic: Bernard of Hildesheim, *Liber canonum* c. 25, p. 497; Wido of Ferrara, *De scismate Hildebrandi* I.6, p. 539; Placidus of Nonantola, *Liber de honore ecclesiae* c. 60, p. 594. See R. Schieffer (1972b) pp. 334–9, 359–70; H.-W. Goetz (1987) pp. 38–41.

63 Archadius (395–408).

to divine worship must be avenged by a capital sentence on those who confess or who are convicted. And subsequently: All men should consider it praiseworthy that the savage injuries inflicted on priests are censured as public crimes and that such offences are requited with vengeance et cetera.[64]

Let us hear what the pious pair Martian and Valentinian wrote to the blessed Pope Leo[65]. We believe it just to address your holiness first of all with a holy letter, since you possess the primacy in the faith among the bishops, summoning and requesting your holiness to pray to the eternal Godhead for the stability and the continuance of our empire.[66] Observe how Constantine – not Constantine I but the other pious emperor of that name[67] – wrote to the Pope Donus.[68] Through the grace of Almighty God there is in us no favouritism of any kind, but we shall observe equality towards both parties. We shall in no way exercise coercion in any particular against those who enjoy your favour, but shall regard them as worthy of every suitable honour and reward and recognition. If there is agreement between the two parties, well and good, but if they do not agree, we shall bring them with all humanity into conformity with you. And subsequently: For we can summon and solicit all Christians to complete amendment and unity, but we have no wish to exercise coercion.[69] Consider what another Emperor Constantine[70] and Irene wrote to Pope Hadrian.[71] We beg you, blessed father, or rather the Lord God, who desires all men to be saved and to come to the knowledge of the truth,[72] begs that you present yourself and make no delay and come here.[73] Hear what Justinian wrote to the holy Pope John[74] in the laws that he promulgated. We beg you, beloved father, to send us a letter in which you make known to us that your holiness supports all who rightly confess the aforesaid truths and condemns the [treachery] of those who, in the Jewish manner, dare to deny the true faith.[75]

64 Codex Iustinianus I.3.10, derived from Gregory I, Registrum XIII.50, MGH Epistolae 2, 145. See W. Berschin (1972) p. 45.

65 Leo I (440–61).

66 Derived from Nicholas I, Epistola 88, MGH Epistolae 6, 458. (Cf. Bonizo, Liber de vita christiana IV.86a, pp. 148–56.) See W. Berschin (1972) p. 45.

67 Constantine IV (668–85).

68 Donus (676–8).

69 Again from Nicholas I, Epistola 88, p. 458 (above n. 66).

70 Constantine VI.

71 Hadrian I (772–95).

72 I Timothy 2:4.

73 Again from Nicholas I, Epistola 88, p. 458 (above n. 66).

74 John II (532–5).

75 Again from Nicholas I, Epistola 88, p. 458 (above n. 66).

After the Lombard fury invaded the Italian regions (as we described above), it is not easy to say how many kinds of punishments and what sad and most cruel deaths they inflicted on the Christians during the three years in which they remained pagans. After they were baptised into the Arian heresy, their cruelty was hardly less and so for one hundred and forty years in which they not so much governed Italy as laid it waste, they practised a most cruel tyranny.[76] Anyone who wishes to learn about these calamities, may read the book of the *Dialogues*[77] and the deeds of the holy popes,[78] where he will find disaster upon disaster and misery upon misery.

Book III

When, in the time of the supreme pontiff Hadrian, the pope saw himself overwhelmed by many misfortunes, *he*[1] *sent his apostolic letters by sea to Charles, the most excellent king of the Franks,*[2] *beseeching him, like his father of holy memory, Pippin,* [3] *to aid the holy Church of God* against the arrogance and tyranny of Desiderius, king of the Lombards.[4] *Then King Charles, protected by God, assembling the whole multitude of the army of his kingdom, for six months* besieged Desiderius in the city of Pavia. *As the festival of Easter drew near, he was impelled by a strong desire to hasten to the threshold of the apostles. The pontiff sent the venerable crosses, that is, the banners, to meet him, together with all the divisions of knights and boys bearing branches of olives or palms. The moment that the most excellent king saw those most holy crosses and banners, he immediately dismounted from his horse and proceeded on foot to St Peter with his men. On the Saturday before Easter day*[5] *the venerable pontiff awaited him on the steps of the apostle's church with the Roman clergy and people. The king*

---

76 The Lombards invaded Italy in 568. Their kingdom was conquered by Charlemagne in 774, as described in Book III.

77 I.e. Gregory I, *Dialogi, MPL* 77, 149–432.

78 I.e. the *Liber pontificalis*. See H. Leclercq (1930) col. 354–466.

1 /1 Extracts, partly abbreviated, from the *Life of Hadrian I, Liber pontificalis* 1, 493–9. Anselm of Lucca, *Collectio canonum* I.81 and Deusdedit, *Collectio canonum* IV.160 cited similar extracts to illustrate Charlemagne's reverence for the papacy.

2 Charles (Charlemagne), king of the Franks (768–814), emperor (800).

3 Pippin III, king of the Franks (751–68).

4 Desiderius, king of the Lombards (756–74).

5 2 April 774.

*advanced, kissing all the steps of St Peter's, and approached the pontiff. After
they had embraced, the most Christian king held the pontiff's hand and so,
hastening with all his men to the confession of blessed Peter, he threw himself
on the earth and fulfilled his vows to God and His holy apostle. The king
then earnestly begged the pontiff to give him permission to enter Rome in
order to pray in the various churches. They went down together to the body
of blessed Peter with the judges of the Romans and the Franks and,
strengthening themselves by mutual oaths, they entered Rome without delay.
After celebrating the festival of Easter, on Wednesday[6] he offered rich gifts to
blessed Peter and returned to the siege of Pavia. With the help of God* and
of that apostle *he banished King Desiderius of the Lombards together with
his wife and made his kingdom subject to himself.*[1]

On his death his son Louis[7] succeeded him, a most gentle man, who
was the first of all the Frankish kings to be raised to the dignity of
emperor.[8] He made many offerings to St Peter, restored the privileges
of ancient times and ratified the following law for the future. *In the
case of the election of the Roman pontiffs no man, neither slave nor free, is to
presume to place any hindrance in the way of those of the Romans whom
ancient custom admits to this election through the ordinance of the holy
Fathers. If anyone presumes to contravene this ordinance of ours, he is to be
exiled. Moreover we forbid any of our envoys to devise any impediment to the
aforesaid election.*[9] After his death the empire was most honourably
governed for many years until the time of his descendant, the pernicious Lothar.[10] If anyone is anxious to learn more, let him read the
laws that they promulgated and let him see the tombs of the martyrs
that they beautified with gold and jewels and their basilicas adorned
with astonishing beauty and also the monasteries that they con-
structed for both sexes and the common dwelling places for clergy

---

6 6 April 774.

7 Louis 'the Pious', emperor (813–40).

8 'Bonizo actually knew no better than to say that Louis the Pious [rather than
Charlemagne] was the first emperor of the Frankish race': E. Perels (1931) pp.
363–79. His misconception was shared by other authors: e.g. Rangerius of Lucca
(*Vita metrica Anselmi Lucensis* p. 1154); Gerhoch of Reichersberg (*De investigatione
Antichristi* I.69, p. 389). See W. Berschin (1972) pp. 42–3; H. Vollrath (1974) pp.
24–5.

9 Part of the *Constitutio Romana* of Emperor Lothar I of 824 c. 3, in the expanded
version found in the *Ottonianum*, the privilege of Otto I for the Roman church, c.
16 (*MGH Constitutiones* 1, 26, no. 12). Cf. Anselm of Lucca, *Collectio canonum* VI.31.
See E. Perels (1931) pp. 369–70; W. Berschin (1972) pp. 46–7.

10 King Lothar II (855–69).

following the regular life that they first inaugurated.[11] From the relics
that survive in our own time the reader can perceive that they were
most Christian and most pleasing to God. These, however, are the
laws that they promulgated.

From the edicts of the Emperors Charles and Louis. *Mindful of the holy
canons, so that in God's name holy Church may enjoy her honour more freely,
we give our consent to the ecclesiastical order that [bishops] are to be elected
by the choice of the clergy and people of their own diocese according to the
decrees of the canons, free from personal influence and bribes, on account of
their meritorious lives and their intellectual gifts, so that by their word and
example they may prove beneficial to their subjects everywhere.*[12] Secondly, a
decree of Emperor Charles. *We will and command that all men subject,
with God's help, to our jurisdiction – both Romans and Franks, Alamans,
Bavarians, Thuringians, Frisians, Gauls, Burgundians, Bretons, Lombards,
Gascons, Beneventans, Goths, Spanish and all other men subject to us, by
whatever legal bond or customary usage they are bound – all are to keep as
perpetual law this sentence from the sixteenth book of the Emperor Theodosius, chapter eleven, in the examination of Duke Ablavius, which we have
sent them in writing and which we have placed in our capitulary, on the
advice of all our faithful men, to be regarded as law. Anyone involved in a
lawsuit, whether as [possessor or] claimant, whether at the beginning of the
litigation or after some time, whether during the trial or when sentence is
being pronounced, if he chooses to refer the case to the judgement of a bishop
of holy church, instantly without any hesitation, even if the other party
contests the decision, the dispute of the litigants is to be referred to the
judgement of the bishops. For the authority of holy religion investigates and
brings to light many things which are prevented by sophistical quibbles from
being disclosed in a trial. Therefore all cases, involving either military or
civil law, in which sentence is pronounced by bishops, are to be confirmed as
lawful in perpetuity and a case that has been settled by the judgements of the
bishops is not allowed to be protracted any further. Moreover all judges are
to accept without hesitation the evidence of even a single bishop and if the
evidence of a bishop is contested by any party, the latter is not to be heard. By
means of this salutary edict we confirm and we resolve that whatever is*

11 Cf. Bonizo, *Liber de vita christiana* V.77, p. 204: 'In the time of Emperor Louis [the
   Pious] the canonical life was first found among the Franks and the Germans.' For
   Bonizo on the 'common life' or 'canonical life' of the clergy: below p. 208 and n. 89.

12 Louis the Pious, *Capitulare ecclesiasticum* of 818/819, c. 2 (*MGH Capitularia* 1, 276),
   collected in Ansegis, *Capitularium* I.78 (*ibid.*, p. 405). W. Berschin (1972) p. 47
   noted that Bonizo's text shows the same variants as Anselm of Lucca, *Collectio*
   IV.42 and Deusdedit, *Collectio* IV.280.

affirmed by the authority of truth, whatever pronouncement is made according to justice by a holy man of unblemished conscience is to be respected as perpetual law.[13] These are laws worthy of Christian emperors, who governed their kingdom not, as is the custom of the Greek emperors, by the agency of subtle eunuchs but through the prudence of the priesthood. For that reason they were blessed so that, however long they lived in this world, they enjoyed profound peace and they will reign perpetually with Christ in the world to come.

The aforementioned Lothar, however, was often admonished by Pope Nicholas[14] to repudiate his concubine, Waldrada, and when he refused to do so, he deserved the sentence of excommunication.[15] The wretched man failed to come to his senses but, *adding sin to sin,*[16] he dared to defame the lord pope of the elder see of Rome. Hence he was not only excommunicated but also deposed from the office of emperor and from all power over the Franks. The histories of the Franks and the fact that their kingdom is divided even to this day bear witness to the great harm that he inflicted on the Romans, to the fact that he insulted the lord pope and poured scorn on him when he offered a defence of his conduct and to the fact that he took possession of the church of St Peter with an army[17] and they bear witness also to his most shameful death.

While the kingdom of the Franks was being destroyed by pride, the Italian kingdom suffered a variety of disasters. For it was not so much governed as laid waste, sometimes by the tyranny of the Lombards, at other times by the violence of the Burgundians, but mainly by the

13 Benedictus Levita, *Capitularium* II.366, *MGH Leges* 2b, 91 (altered and abbreviated). Bonizo's text resembles that of Anselm of Lucca, *Collectio* III.105. See W. Berschin (1972) p. 47.

14 Nicholas I (858–67).

15 Nicholas quashed the proceedings of the Frankish synods that had recognised Lothar II's marriage to Waldrada. Lothar submitted to the papal judgement. Cf. Bonizo, *Liber de vita christiana* IV.44, p. 131: 'Nicholas ... excommunicated ... the western emperor *(sic)* named Lothar for associating with Waldrada, his concubine'. Bonizo's polemical distortion (cf. below, p. 238) resembles that of other Gregorian authors using it as a precedent for Henry IV's deposition: Manegold, *Ad Gebehardum* c. 29, pp. 362–3; Bernard, *Liber canonum* c. 25, pp. 496–7; Bernold, *Apologeticae rationes* p. 97 and *De solutione iuramentorum* p. 148; Deusdedit, *Libellus contra invasores* c. 3, p. 346. See H.-W. Goetz (1987) p. 39.

16 Ecclesiasticus 5:5.

17 Bonizo confused King Lothar II with his brother, Emperor Louis II, who entered Rome (864) in an unsuccessful attempt to force Nicholas to recognise Lothar's marriage with Waldrada.

(Saraens)

arrogance of the Salians.[18] At that time the Roman church was subject
to the most dangerous vicissitudes. For since the Roman emperors[19]
were prevented by the repeated attacks of barbarian nations[20] from
bringing help and since the Franks (as we mentioned above) were
divided and alienated from the Church, the captains of the city of
Rome assigned to themselves the empty title of patrician and most
vigorously laid waste to the Roman church. That title is indeed so
meaningless that it is never found in the registers of the Roman
magistrates either in pagan or in Christian times.[21] For if there had
been such an office, records of the periods of administration of the
patricians or of the laws promulgated by them or of inscriptions with
their names would be found; but such evidence is nowhere found in
the Roman laws. Supposing, however, that such an office could perhaps participate in the appointment of an emperor, it would be totally
unfit to be involved in the appointment of the supreme pontiff. I shall
briefly explain, if I can, how this imposture originated. When Rome
was hardpressed by the rage of the Goths, the swords of the Vandals
and the fury of the Lombards, the Romans could not withstand the
attacks of the barbarians and entreated the emperors for military
protection, which, as circumstances permitted, they most willingly
provided. For they sent from their own entourage certain eunuchs,
excellent men like Narses[22] and Belisarius[23] and several others, whom
they created military commanders. They came to Italy and very often
put the barbarians to flight, although sometimes they confined

18 J. M. Watterich (1862) suggested the reading 'Saracens'.

19 I.e. the Byzantine emperors.

20 The manuscript reads 'senators'. P. Jaffé (1865) corrected this to 'Saracens', E.
Dümmler (1891) to 'nations'.

21 This polemic against the patriciate is resumed below pp. 179, 182. Before the mid-
eighth century the Byzantine emperor's representative in Rome had the title of
'patrician', the highest dignity that the emperor could bestow. The popes of the
second half of the eighth century gave the same title to the Frankish kings, to
underline their duty of defending the papacy. In the early eleventh century the
title was used by the greatest Roman noble families to signify their control over
the city of Rome and the papacy. Emperor Henry III assumed the title when he
intervened in Rome in 1046 and as 'patrician' elected four German popes (below
pp. 187–8). Henry IV claimed to have inherited the title from his father. It was the
fact that Henry IV (*Letter* 11, p. 15) based his proceedings against Gregory VII on
this office that provoked Bonizo's polemic against 'the empty title'. See P. E.
Schramm (1929) pp. 59–63, 229–36; K.-J. Herrmann (1973) pp. 1–24; H. Vollrath
(1974) pp. 11–44; G. Martin (1994) pp. 257–95.

22 Narses (*c.* 472–568), general of Justinian I.

23 Belisarius (✝565), general of Justinian I.

themselves to defending the city walls. The Roman people in their simplicity called them 'patricians', meaning 'fathers of the city', just as even today they call the great men of the city of Rome their protectors. But let us follow events in their correct sequence.

The captains of the city, whom we mentioned above, obtained a tyrannical power and did whatever they wished. For not only did they defile the office of cardinal, abbot and bishop with the most foul practice of sale and purchase, but they even gave away the office of pontiff of the Roman church, with no regard for moral worth or for the prerogatives of so great a church but solely according to their liking and according to the amount of money that was offered to them. They conferred it not only on clergy but even on laymen, so that it often happened that on one and the same day a candidate was both layman and pontiff.[24] While the head languished in this manner, the other limbs were so enfeebled that not only the ministers of the altar of secondary rank, the priests and deacons, but also the bishops themselves were everywhere reputed to be keeping concubines, so that this custom now shrugged off the shame that had been attached to it and the most foul custom of sale and purchase seemed almost to escape the imputation of a criminal offence. This development occurred moreover not merely in the region of the Roman church but throughout the western world. When *the shepherd* is silent or even *takes to flight*, when indeed *the wolf* is appointed guardian, who will stand up for *the sheep?*[25] While this was happening, the most vile nation of the Saracens plundered the coastline of Italy and then seized part of Calabria and the whole of Sicily.[26] From the north the powerful nation of the Hungarians crossed Istria, laid waste all the neighbouring regions and in addition plundered the whole of Germany and Gaul as far as the English Channel. Finally they came by way of the kingdoms of the Burgundians to Italy and plundered it to such an extent that almost [all] the peasants were led away captive and the land was made a wilderness.

---

24 Cf. Bonizo, *Liber de vita christiana* IV.44, pp. 131, 132, citing Benedict [V?] and John XIX.

25 Cf. John 10:12.

26 Cf. Bonizo, *Liber de vita christiana* IV.44, pp. 130, 131.

Book IV

While the Hungarians were raging in their savage frenzy, there appeared a certain king of the Saxons and Franks named Otto.[1] He twice defeated them in battle and after a third battle in which they were almost annihilated,[2] he forced them to dwell within their own frontiers. Since I have mentioned this great king, it seems to me worthwhile to write about his ancestry and how he attained the dignity of the Roman kingship.

A Saxon by birth, he was the son of Henry, the great king of the Saxons and the Franks.[3] The latter was originally duke of the Saxons but after the death of Conrad, king of the Franks,[4] he received the insignia of the kingship from Eberhard,[5] Conrad's brother. After receiving the royal insignia, Henry very rapidly pacified the Frankish territory and fought a battle to free Saxony from the dominion of the Hungarians.[6] He then expelled King Arnulf[7] and subjected Bavaria to his authority, afterwards conferring the duchy on his son Henry.[8] He received the surrender of Burchard, duke of the Swabians.[9] He next brought western Francia[10] under his authority through the agency of his son-in-law Cunibert.[11] He also gave another daughter[12] in marriage to Louis, king of the Latins and Franks.[13] After all these affairs had been settled and he had designated his son Otto as king in his place, this very great builder of God's churches and disseminator of the Christian religion was blessed with a peaceful end.

His son Otto, a magnificent and most Christian man, succeeded him. It was he (as we said before) who first conquered the Hungarians and

1 Otto I, king of the Germans (936–73), emperor (962).

2 Battle of the Lech (10 August 955).

3 Henry I, king of the Germans (919–36).

4 Conrad I, king of the Germans (911–19).

5 Eberhard, duke of Franconia (918–39).

6 At *Riade* (15 March 933).

7 Arnulf, duke of Bavaria (907–37), elected king by the Bavarians in 919.

8 Henry I, duke of Bavaria (947–55), invested with the duchy by his brother, Otto I.

9 Burchard II, duke of Swabia (917–26) submitted in 919.

10 I.e. Lotharingia, which submitted in 925.

11 Giselbert, duke of Lotharingia (915–39).

12 Gerberga (✝984), the daughter previously married to Giselbert of Lotharingia before she married Louis in 939.

13 Louis IV ('d'Outremer'), king of the French (936–54).

freed not only his own kingdom but also the whole of the west from their dominion. When his kinsman Louis[14] was driven from his father's throne by the tyranny of Hugh,[15] Otto restored him to his kingdom. For he entered Francia with his army, besieged and captured the city of Rheims, entered Paris and pursued Hugh, the perpetrator of the tyranny, as far as the English Channel.[16] From there he came to Aachen and commanded that the eagle, the standard of the Romans which many times stood firm with outstretched wings against the Germans, should hover over the French, as it does to this day.[17] From here he came to Mainz and, when King Rudolf of the Burgundians[18] waged war on him, he deprived him of both life and kingdom. His lance, the symbol of his authority, is borne before our emperors up to this day.[19] After these achievements this great king, who had lost his first wife,[20] heard of the fame of the most noble and wise Adelaide,[21] widow of the late King Lothar of the Lombards.[22] The tyrant Berengar[23] had for many years besieged her, together with Count Atto,[24] in Canossa. Moved to pity by the misfortunes of so great a queen and full of admiration for the fidelity of so great a count, Otto determined to bring help. He very quickly assembled a great army and, after Berengar had been killed[25] and his sons[26] expelled from the kingdom, on the advice of Count Atto he took to himself both a kingdom and a wife in complete tranquillity.

Next, again on Atto's advice, desiring to see Rome, he took an oath of security to John, pope of the city of Rome[27] in these terms. *I, King*

14 His brother-in-law Louis IV of France.

15 Hugh the Great, duke of the Franks (923–56).

16 September-October 946.

17 On Bonizo's attitude to Otto: W. Berschin (1972) p. 114 n. 511.

18 Rudolf II, king of Burgundy (912–37).

19 Rudolf II lost neither life nor kingdom to Otto. He had sold the holy lance to Henry I: see P. E. Schramm (1955) pp. 534–7.

20 Edgitha of England (†946).

21 Adelaide of Burgundy (†999).

22 Lothar, king of Italy (948–50).

23 Berengar II, margrave of Ivrea, king of Italy (950–63).

24 Count Adalbert Atto II of Canossa, ancestor of Matilda, margravine of Tuscany: see Donizo, *Vita Mathildis* I.1, p. 357.

25 Berengar was taken prisoner in 963. He died in 966 in Bamberg.

26 Adalbert of Ivrea, king of Italy († 975), Margrave Wido of Ivrea († 965) and Conrad.

27 John XII (955–63).

Otto, promise and swear to you, the lord Pope John, by the Father and the Son and the Holy Spirit and by the wood of the living Cross and by these saints' relics, that, if God permits me to come to Rome, I shall exalt the holy Roman church and you, her ruler, according to my ability. You will never lose your life or limbs or your honour by my will or consent or by my advice or at my request. I shall hold no court of law nor make any appointment in Rome concerning all the affairs pertaining to you or to the Romans except on your advice. If any part of the land of St Peter comes into our power, I shall restore it to you. I shall ensure that the man to whom I commit the Italian kingdom takes an oath to be your helper in defending the land of St Peter according to his ability.[28] He next went to Rome and was given an honourable reception by the Romans and received the imperial consecration from the lord pope and he was the first of all the German kings to be called emperor.[29] Once Italy was peaceful, he returned to Saxony with his wife. She bore him a son and successor to his name and his kingdom,[30] to whom he gave a wife of Roman blood, namely the daughter of the emperor of Constantinople.[31] After Otto had built a church of extraordinary beauty in Magdeburg and after he had brought many of the heathen peoples to the way of truth, he was overcome by weariness and his life came to an end.[32] His body was buried in the church of Magdeburg with fitting honour.

When his son succeeded to the empire, he proved himself the equal of his father in all respects and began to be most zealous in his care for the churches and most devoted to the Christian religion. When he had put the affairs of his kingdom in good order, he hastened to Rome and received consecration as emperor.[33] He next made for Apulia, where he waged war on the ruler of Constantinople.[34] Defeated twice on the same day, he emerged from a third encounter victorious.[35] Returning

---

28 Otto I, oath of security to John XII, *MGH Constitutiones* 1, 21 (no. 10). E. Perels (1931) p. 371 concluded that the text given by Bonizo and that of Anselm of Lucca, *Collectio* I.86 and Deusdedit, *Collectio* IV.420 derived from a common source. See H. Fuhrmann (1966) pp. 124–5, 145–6; W. Berschin (1972) pp. 47–8.

29 2 February 962.

30 Otto II, king of the Germans, emperor (973–83).

31 Theophano, niece of John I Tzimisces (✝991).

32 7 May 973.

33 Otto II was crowned co-emperor with his father on 25 December 967.

34 Basil II (976–1025) and Constantine VIII (976–1028).

35 After initial success against the Byzantine power in southern Italy, his army was annihilated at Cap Colonne by Abul Kassim, emir of Palermo (13 July 982).

to Rome, he was seized by fever and died[36] at the threshold of the
apostles and there he was buried and rests in peace.[37] He was truly
blessed, indeed infinitely blessed, since among that great number of
emperors and kings he alone was rewarded with burial in the company of the popes, together with the prince of the apostles. He left a
son to be the heir at least to his kingdom and his name:[38] would that
he had also been heir to his piety! He began to reign when he was still
a boy and, on reaching adulthood, he was persuaded by his mother[39]
to send a certain Bishop John of Piacenza,[40] a Greek by birth, on an
embassy overseas to obtain for him a wife of Roman blood.

At that time a certain captain of the city of Rome named Crescentius,[41] who had claimed for himself the meaningless title of patrician,
set up a tyranny and expelled from the papacy the lord pope[42] who
had crowned Otto II, that is, the father of this youth. When the king
crossed the Alps, Crescentius was struck by fear at his approach and
the news that the pope was already awaiting the king in Ravenna
filled him with dread. He thought that he could pacify the anger of the
king and queen in this way: namely, by appointing to the papacy that
Bishop John whom we mentioned above, who was the close friend of
the king and the bedfellow of the queen.[43] But *no* knowledge, *no
counsel can avail against the Lord.*[44] For when the king came to Rome,
he subjected Crescentius to a long siege, captured and beheaded him.
As for the intruder in the papacy, he deprived him of his sight and
mutilated him in all his limbs,[45] showing zeal for justice but more
anger than befitted a just man. This deed so displeased God and Peter,
the blessed prince of the apostles, that this man, hateful to God, died
without receiving the last rites, before he could receive consecration

36 7 December 983.

37 In the basilica of St Peter.

38 Otto III, king of the Germans (983–1002), emperor (996).

39 This embassy took place in 995, four years after the death of Theophano.

40 John Philagathos, bishop of Piacenza (988–97), antipope John XVI (997–8).

41 Crescentius II Nomentanus, count of Terracina (†998).

42 Gregory V (996–9) was exiled from Rome by Crescentius II Nomentanus. The
pope who had crowned Otto II was John XIII. Cf. Bonizo, *Liber de vita christiana*
IV.44, pp. 131–2.

43 John Philagathos had been the favourite of Theophano and Otto III's tutor. Cf.
Bonizo, *Liber de vita christiana* IV.44, p. 132.

44 Proverbs 21:30.

45 Cf. Bonizo, *Liber de vita christiana* IV.44, p. 132: 'he ordered the pope to be led
through the streets of the Leonine city, deprived of his eyes and crippled in his
limbs, to the dishonour and shame of the order of the priesthood.'

as emperor[46] and *precisely* before *Cinthia concealed the world for a* third *time.*[47] Although he died in the suburbs[48] not thirty miles away from the city, all the Romans by general agreement refused him burial. His body was cut up with knives, joined together by the physicians' art and conveyed to Saxony in a bier.[49] After he died and was interred in hell, all the Saxon, Frankish, Bavarian and Swabian princes met together and elected as their king Henry,[50] a most Christian man of the same family and of worthy character.

Meanwhile the Lombards, finding this a suitable moment, met in Pavia and elected as their king Arduin,[51] a man who was strong in military terms but ill advised and lacking in foresight. The duke and margrave Tedald,[52] however, withdrew from this conspiracy and commended himself and his property to the German king. It was with his advice and aid that, after the many and various dangers of war, King Henry gained control of Italy. He came to Rome and was enriched with the office of emperor by the lord Pope Benedict.[53] What more is there to tell? He gained possession of the principality of Apulia by peaceful means.[54] He granted many privileges and donated the most splendid gifts to the Roman church. Afterwards he came to Pavia and, although the city did not at that time oppose him, he captured it by means of guile rather than weapons and caused it to be burned[55] before he crossed the mountains. He founded the bishopric of Bamberg, using his own property since he had no sons and he gave it to St Peter in a charter of dedication.[56] There he built a magnificently decorated church to the blessed princes of the apostles. It was in his time that King Stephen of the Hungarians[57] received the sacrament of

46 He had been crowned emperor by Gregory V on 21 May 996.
47 I.e. within two months (paraphrasing Lucan, *Pharsalia* II.577). Cf. *Liber de vita christiana* IV.44, p. 132: 'before thirty days were over'. In fact Otto III died nearly four years after the mutilation of John XVI.
48 24 January 1002 in the castle of Paterno near Mount Soracte.
49 He was buried in Aachen (5 April 1002).
50 Henry II, king of the Germans (1002–24), emperor (1014).
51 Arduin, margrave of Ivrea, king of Italy (1002–15).
52 Tedald, margrave of Canossa (982–c.1015), grandfather of Matilda: see Donizo, *Vita Mathildis* I.3, p.361.
53 Benedict VIII (1012–24) crowned Henry II emperor on 14 February 1014.
54 An allusion to his third Italian expedition, 1021–2.
55 The burning of Pavia occurred during the first Italian expedition, 1004.
56 Council of Frankfurt, 1 November 1007 (*MGH Constitutiones* 1, 59–61, no. 29).
57 Stephen I, king of Hungary (997–1038).

baptism and caused all his subjects to be baptised. Since Henry had no sons, he made the apostles his heirs and when his life drew to a close, he was blessed with a peaceful end.[58] His body was most becomingly buried in the church of the blessed apostles, which he himself dedicated.

Book V

Conrad,[1] a Franconian by birth and a most warlike man, succeeded to the kingship. After the death of Emperor Henry, he defeated the Bohemians in battle, returned with the regalia which they had brought with them and very rapidly quelled a rebellion in Germany.[2] When a certain Cuno, duke of the Bavarians, claimed for himself a part of the dignity of the kingship, he drove him out of his duchy, stripped him of his patrimony and forced him to flee into Hungary.[3] He then entered Saxony and, when he had settled all the affairs of the kingdom according to his will, attacked the Liutizi and defeated them in battle, forcing them to flee as far as *Bellagrast*.[4] When he had done this, he sent worthy envoys, as was fitting, to the lord pope and begged that a banner might be sent to him from St Peter, so that, fortified with this, he would be able to subject the Hungarian throne to his lordship. When the pope heard this, he willingly granted the request and sent noble men from his side, namely, the bishop of Porto[5] and the most noble Roman Belinzo de Marmorato,[6] giving them this command: that, if it did not displease the king, they themselves should carry the banners in the front line of battle, but that if this displeased the king, they should inform him, 'We have promised you victory. See that you do not ascribe this victory to yourself but to the apostles.' This was done. When battle was joined, the Hungarians fled; the lance of the

58 13 July 1024.

1 The Salian Conrad II, king of the Germans, 1024–39; emperor, 1027.

2 Perhaps a confused reminiscence of Conrad's campaigns of 1029, 1031 and 1032 against the Polish king Mieszko and of the peace concluded in Merseburg (July 1033), according to which Mieszko renounced the use of the royal insignia.

3 It was Conrad's son, Henry III, who deposed Duke Conrad (Cuno) of Bavaria (April 1053).

4 Conrad's successful campaign against the Slav confederation of the Liutizi (1035): Wipo, *Gesta Chuonradi* c. 33, pp. 52–3. The place name *Bellagrast* is unidentifiable.

5 Bishop John I of Porto, legate of Benedict IX, 1044: see W. Kölmel (1935) p. 84 n.74; R. Hüls (1977) p. 118 n. 8.

6 See K.-J. Herrmann (1973) pp. 44–5. On the banner: C. Erdmann (1935) pp. 43–4.

Hungarian king was captured and was brought to Rome by those same envoys and it appears to this day before the confession of St Peter the apostle as a token of victory.[7]

Meanwhile, having obtained victory in Hungary, Conrad entered Italy and took prisoner Archbishop Aribert of Milan; but the latter escaped and fled.[8] Coming thence to Rome, he received consecration as emperor.[9] He returned to Milan, but when he had laid waste certain of the suburbs, he was driven off by the city and so he crossed the Alps without achieving his objective. He was seized by a fever and died[10] and his body was buried with fitting honours in Speyer.

His son Henry[11] succeeded him, a most wise and thoroughly Christian man. At the beginning of his reign, he defeated and very rapidly pacified the rebellious Hungarians.[12] When he had duly settled all the affairs of the kingdom and was deciding to advance into Italy, messengers came from the city of Rome, delaying him and causing him extreme anxiety. For, as we have mentioned above,[13] the captains of the city of Rome, and especially the Tusculani, were laying waste the Roman church under the empty title of the patriciate, so that they seemed to possess the papacy by hereditary right. Indeed on the death of John[14] – who was the brother of Pope Benedict and who on one and the same day was both prefect and pope – when Theophylact,[15] who was the son of Alberic,[16] had succeeded him, his brother Gregory[17]

---

7 It was Henry III who won this victory (Menfö, 5 July 1044). Cf. Gregory VII, *Registrum* II.13, p. 145: 'Emperor Henry ... having achieved the victory, ... sent the lance and the crown to the body of St Peter ...' See E. Steindorff (1874) p. 234 n. 2.

8 Archbishop Aribert of Milan (1018–44): see G. Schwartz (1913) pp. 78–9. On his conflict with Conrad II (1037): H. E. J. Cowdrey (1966) pp. 1–15.

9 Bonizo placed Conrad's imperial coronation (26 March 1027) in the context of his second Italian expedition, 1037.

10 4 June 1039.

11 Henry III, king of the Germans, 1039–56; emperor, 1046.

12 His Hungarian campaigns of 1042–4 culminated in the battle of Menfö (see n. 7).

13 See above pp. 174–5.

14 John XIX (1024–32, †?6 November), brother of Benedict VIII (1012–24). Cf. Bonizo, *Liber de vita christiana* IV.44, p. 132.

15 Benedict IX (1032–46). His reputation among reformers: Peter Damian, *Letter* 72, pp. 337–8; Desiderius of Monte Cassino, *Dialogi* III, prologue, p. 1141. See R.L. Poole (1934) pp. 199–200, 202–6.

16 Alberic III, 'consul and duke' († c. 1044), brother of John XIX and Benedict VIII. See W. Kölmel (1935) pp. 68–9; K.-J. Herrmann (1973) pp. 18–20.

17 Gregory II, count of Tusculum († before 1064).

claimed for himself the title of the patriciate.

At this time Theophylact, who changed his name to Benedict and who feared neither God nor man, after committing many squalid adulteries and murders with his own hands, finally – since he wished to marry his cousin, namely the daughter of Gerard de Saxo,[18] and since the latter declared that he would never give her to him unless he gave up the papacy – he went to a certain priest named John,[19] who was then thought to be of great merit. On his advice he condemned himself and renounced the papacy.[20] This advice would have been extremely praiseworthy, if only the most foul sin had not followed. For this same priest, led astray by unlawful ambition and disbursing huge sums of money,[21] seized this opportunity to force all the Roman people to swear an oath to him and thus he rose to the dignity of pope. Changing his name, they called him Gregory. After this happened, *Gregory VI* Gerard de Saxo,[22] together with other captains, chose for themselves a certain bishop of Sabina as pope, whose name they changed to Silvester.[23] When they heard of this, the brothers Gregory the patrician and Peter[24] once more raised to the papal office Theophylact, who had been disappointed in his hope of a wife.

What remedy could we find for such great calamities, except in that voice in the Gospel which comforted the apostle, saying, *I have prayed for you, Peter, that your faith may not fail?*[25] Certainly and truly the faith of Peter has not failed, nor will the faith of the Roman church fail

---

18 Perhaps a kinsman of the counts of Galeria or the related family of Cita Castellana: W. Kölmel (1935) p. 160; K.-J. Herrmann (1973) p. 153. The story of the pope's marriage is also found in *Annales Altahenses* 1046, p. 42.

19 John Gratian, archpriest of St John at the Latin Gate; Pope Gregory VI (1045–6). See G. B. Borino (1916) pp. 141–252, 295–410; R. L. Poole (1934) pp. 206–13; H. E. J. Cowdrey (1998) pp. 22–6.

20 1 May 1045: *Annales Romani* p. 468.

21 2,000 pounds (Codex Vaticanus latinus 1340, ed. L. Duchesne, 1892, p. 270); 1,500 pounds (Cardinal Beno, *Gesta Romanae ecclesiae* II.7, p. 378). Cf. the treatise *De ordinando pontifice* (1047/8): Gregory 'did not give the money, but he consented to his friends and kinsmen giving it': H. H. Anton (1982) pp. 36–7, 78.

22 Gerard supported Benedict IX when the Romans rebelled against him (7 January 1045): *Annales Romani* p. 468.

23 John, cardinal bishop of Sabina; Silvester III (elected 10 January; consecrated 13 or 20 January; deposed 10 March 1045): R. Hüls (1977) p. 125. Bonizo placed Silvester's and Gregory's elections in the wrong order. See R. L. Poole (1934) pp. 150–1, 197–8.

24 Gregory II and Peter of Tusculum, brothers of Benedict IX, whom they restored to the papacy, 10 March 1045.

25 Luke 22:32.

through all eternity. For in this great and mighty tempest God raised up the spirit of a certain Peter, the Roman archdeacon,[26] who called together the bishops, cardinals, clerks and monks and men and women whom the fear of God had in some measure affected. He withdrew himself from the communion of the aforesaid intruders and, led by zeal for God, like Onias, that Hebrew priest of old, he crossed the Alps, approached the king – *not* for the sake of *making accusations but for the general welfare*[27] of the Church – and falling at his feet, besought him with tears to succour his desolate mother with all speed. When all the bishops who were then present had been called together,[28] he commanded them to go to Rome with the king and to assemble a synod and this was done without delay. That pretender Gregory, who seemed to be the ruler of the Roman church, was requested by the king to meet him and, being conscious of no wrongdoing on his part, as the event subsequently made clear, he came as far as Piacenza and found the king there. He was received honourably by the latter, as befitted a pope.[29] For the bishops who were then present did not think that it was compatible with religion to condemn any bishop without judicial proceedings, much less one who seemed to be the bishop of so great a see. Thus travelling together, they came to Sutri.

When they had arrived there, the king asked the pope, as he seemed to be, to assemble a synod.[30] This he granted and confirmed by a decree, for he was an inexperienced man of remarkable simplicity. When the synod had been assembled, therefore, he who held the office of Roman pontiff took part in it and by his command the patriarchs, metropolitans and bishops participated according to their sees,[31] among whom was, as it happened, Poppo, patriarch of Aquileia,[32] a very eloquent

26 Peter 'who is also called Mancius' appears in a privilege of Benedict IX (April 1044) as deacon and a letter of Victor II (13 May 1057) as archdeacon: G. B. Borino (1948) p. 481; R. Hüls (1977) p. 251; D. Jasper (1986) pp. 39–40. Bonizo alone reported Peter's mission to Germany, but cf. Beno, *Gesta Romanae ecclesiae* II.8, p. 378: Henry III was 'urged by the prayers of the religious cardinals'.

27 II Maccabees 4:4.

28 A reminiscence either of the synod of Aachen, summer 1046, or the synod of Pavia, October 1046: see E. Steindorff (1874) pp. 294–7, 307–10, 497–500; F.-J. Schmale (1979a) pp. 60–2.

29 Cf. Herman of Reichenau, *Chronicon* 1046, p. 126.

30 According to Desiderius, *Dialogi* III, p. 1141 and *Annales Romani* p. 469, Henry himself convoked the synod, to which he invited Gregory. H. Zimmermann (1968) p. 126 disputed the accuracy of Bonizo's statement; but see F.-J. Schmale (1979a) p. 89.

31 20 December 1046.

32 Poppo, patriarch of Aquileia (1019–42): G. Schwartz (1913) p. 32. His successor, Eberhard, may have been present at Sutri.

man, and Bishop Bruno of Augsburg[33] and Archbishop Raimbald of
Arles[34] and several others. When the question of the intruder Silvester
arose, it was the judgement of all that he should be deprived of both
the episcopal and the priestly office and that he should be delivered up
to a monastery for the rest of his life.[35] In the case of Theophylact
they judged that he should lose his office, especially since, as Roman
pontiff, he himself had judged that he should be deposed.[36] But what
were they to do, where should they turn in the case of the third
claimant, since they were *not permitted to bring accusations and to bear
witness*[37] against the judge?

When the bishops begged him to explain the circumstances of his
election, as he was a simple man, he disclosed the entire innocence of
his election. He said that by God's mercy he had been a priest of good
character and reputation and from his boyhood he had always lived
chastely.[38] At that time this seemed to the Romans not only praiseworthy but almost angelic. He said that for this reason he had acquired
large sums of money which he saved in order to repair church roofs or
perform some new and great work in the city of Rome. When, however, his thoughts turned very frequently to the tyranny of the
patricians and how they appointed bishops without any election by
the clergy and people, he could think of nothing better to do with this
money than to restore to the clergy and people the right of election
that had been unjustly removed by tyranny. When the religious men
heard this, they began with the greatest reverence to point out to him
the cunning devices of the ancient enemy and said that nothing venal
was holy. Under the influence of these and other admonitions he
immediately began to receive the Holy Spirit into his mind and,

33 Bruno, bishop of Augsburg (1006–29). Bonizo's inclusion of Bruno and Poppo has
been used as grounds for describing the account as a fabrication: E. Steindorff
(1874) p. 458. But see F.-J. Schmale (1979a) pp. 89–90.

34 Raimbald, archbishop of Arles (1031–65).

35 Henry compelled him 'to return to his own see': Beno, *Gesta Romanae ecclesiae* II.8,
p. 378. He remained bishop of Sabina until 1062: R. Hüls (1977) p. 125.

36 The synod judged that Benedict's resignation made proceedings against him
unnecessary: F.-J. Schmale (1979a) p. 99.

37 Anacletus I, *Decreta* c.3, *Decretales Pseudoisidorianae* p. 68 (Bonizo, *Liber de vita
christiana* III.42, p. 85). The canonical principle that no pope can be judged by an
earthly tribunal: H. Zimmermann (1968) pp. 158–204.

38 Cf. Desiderius, *Dialogi* III, p. 1142. E. Steindorff (1874) pp. 459–60 noted the
inconsistency in this characterisation of Gregory VI. Bonizo previously described
him as 'led astray by unlawful ambition' and forcing the Romans to swear fidelity
to him.

realising that he had had *zeal for God but it was not enlightened*,[39] he
addressed the bishops in these words. 'I call on God to witness in my
soul, brethren, that I believed that from this deed I should earn
remission of sins and the grace of God. But because I now recognise
the wiles of the ancient enemy, take counsel together in public about
what is to be done with me.' They replied to him: '*Reflect*[40] *on your case
in your own bosom; judge yourself out of your own mouth*. For it is better
for you to live here as a poor man with St Peter, for whose love
you have done this, so that you may be rich throughout eternity, than
for the present to glitter with riches like Simon Magus, who has
deceived you, and to perish throughout eternity.' When he had *heard*
this, he passed sentence *on himself* in this manner, saying: 'I, Gregory,
bishop, servant of the servants of God, *judge myself*[40] worthy to be
removed from the office of bishop of Rome, because of the most
wicked venality of simoniacal heresy which, through the cunning of
the ancient enemy, has crept into my election.' And he added: 'Does
this please you?' They replied: 'What pleases you, we confirm.'[41]
When the synod had been celebrated in a lawful manner, the king,
together with the bishops, came [to Rome] in great distress, both
because they had no pope who might confer the imperial power upon
the king and because, although the clergy had the right to elect
another pope, the people had no right to approve a successor. For
John had bound [the people] by an oath never to approve another
pope in his lifetime.

Nevertheless, since they had no one in their own diocese – for, as we
recorded above,[42] when the head languishes, the other limbs are so
weak that in so great a church scarcely one man could be found who
was not illiterate or simoniac or living in concubinage[43] – in this emer-

39 Romans 10:2.

40 /40 This formula also appears in Bonizo's account of the abdication of Pope
    Marcellinus (304) in his *Liber de vita christiana* IV.29, p. 122. The source is a
    version of the *Liber pontificalis* (cf. L. Duchesne's introduction, *Liber pontificalis* 2,
    XXVB). On the significance of this borrowing see W. Berschin (1972) pp. 71–2;
    F.-J. Schmale (1979a) p. 90 n. 128.

41 This 'Gregorian' version is also found in Desiderius, *Dialogi* III, p. 1143 and
    Bernold of St. Blasien, *Chronicon* 1046, p. 425 (*c.* 1075). That Gregory VI was in
    fact deposed is apparent from three contemporary references: Peter Damian, *Letter*
    72, p. 363; *De ordinando pontifice, MGH Libelli* 1, 80, 83; Herman of Reichenau,
    Chronicon 1046, p. 126. See R. L. Poole (1934) pp. 195–9; F.-J. Schmale (1979a) pp.
    86–91, 99–103.

42 See above p. 175.

43 Cf. Desiderius, *Dialogi* III, p. 1143.

(Clement II)

gency they elected Bishop Suidger of Bamberg,[44] even though the canons forbid anyone to ascend to the office of Roman pontiff who has not been ordained priest or deacon in that church.[45] Few laymen, other than those who had not sworn an oath to John, consented to his election. He, the first of all the long series of Roman pontiffs since the blessed prince of the apostles to have been consecrated elsewhere, was called pope. According to the decrees of the blessed Pope Innocent, however, *What necessity finds for a remedy ought certainly to cease as soon as the emergency is over; for the legitimate order is one thing and a usurpation enforced by a temporary emergency is quite another.*[46]

After the king had been adorned with the imperial dignity,[47] he took pity on the misfortunes of the state and freed the city from the tyranny of the patricians. This would have been extremely praiseworthy, if only he had not immediately afterwards dishonoured the undertaking. For, misled by rumours among the people, to which no very great credence ought to be given, he seized the tyranny of the patriciate – as though any dignity established in the order of the laity possessed a greater prerogative than that of imperial majesty. What could be more bitter or more cruel than this misfortune: that he who shortly before had punished the Tusculani for their tyranny should wish to resemble those whom he had condemned? For what attracted the mind of so great a man to such an offence, except that he believed that by means of the patriciate he could appoint the Roman pontiff?[48] Alas! where was the prudence of so many bishops, where was the knowledge of so many men skilled in the law, that they should believe that what was not permitted to lords should be permitted to servants? No emperor exercising the supreme office was ever permitted to involve himself in the election of any Roman pontiff: will this then be permitted

44 Suidger, bishop of Bamberg (1040–7); Pope Clement II (1046–7), elected 24 December.

45 Lateran synod of 769, *MGH Concilia* 2, 86. See H.-G. Krause (1960) pp. 34–5; H. Zimmermann (1968) pp. 24, 132 n. 41.

46 Innocent I, *Decreta* c. 55 (*JK* 303) in Dionysius Exiguus, *Collectio decretorum*, *MPL* 67, 260 and *Decretales Pseudoisidorianae* p. 550 (cited by Bonizo, *Liber de vita christiana* I.44, II.63, pp. 33, 68). Cf. *Chronica monasterii Casinensis* II.77, p. 322: Clement II's election was 'necessary rather than canonical'. On *necessitas* see P. Schmid (1926) p. 12 and n. 28.

47 25 December 1046.

48 Cf. *Annales Romani* p. 469 (Henry 'placed on his head the circlet with which the Romans since ancient times crowned their patricians … and they granted him the appointing of popes'); Benzo of Alba, *To Henry IV* VII.2, below p. 369. See H. Vollrath (1974) pp. 14–25; D. M. Whitton (1980) pp. 33–7; G. Martin (1994) pp. 257–95. On the patriciate see also above pp. 56–7, 174–5, 182.

to *a man set under authority*?[49] But some may say: 'We have read that Charlemagne was also designated with the title of the patriciate.' If they have read that, why have they not understood it? For in the time of Charlemagne, Constantine and Irene[50] were governing the Roman empire. What more, therefore, could be conferred on the most excellent king of the Franks at this time than that he should be called father or protector of the city of Rome? For this is what we read: *Charles, king of the Franks and of the Lombards and patrician of the Romans.* We have never read that he was honoured with the imperial power.[51] After his death, however, his son Louis[52] was the first of all the kings not possessing Roman blood to receive consecration as emperor and, since he had the highest authority, he did not seek the lowest. But now let us return to the narrative.

When the affairs of Italy had been put into good order, Emperor Henry returned to his homeland, bringing with him the venerable John, whom we mentioned above.[53] The latter was followed by Hildebrand, beloved of God, who wished to show reverence towards his lord. For he had previously been his chaplain.[54] Not long afterwards, when the aforesaid John had reached the banks of the Rhine, he succumbed to a mortal disease.[55] When he had died and had been laid to rest, the venerable Hildebrand travelled to Cluny, became a monk there and devoted himself entirely to the pursuit of wisdom among religious men.[56]

49 Luke 7:8.

50 The Byzantine emperor Constantine VI and his mother Empress Irene.

51 Cf. Bonizo, *Liber de vita christiana* IV.44, p. 130. The claim that Charlemagne was never emperor: above p. 171 n. 8.

52 Emperor Louis 'the Pious'. See above p. 171.

53 May 1047: see E. Steindorff (1881) p. 7.

54 Hildebrand, subdeacon, later archdeacon of the Roman church, Pope Gregory VII (1073–85). As Gregory VI's chaplain: S. Haider (1979) pp. 38–70; H. E. J. Cowdrey (1998) p. 29. Gregory VII, *Registrum* VII.14a, p. 483 recalled that he 'went unwillingly beyond the mountains with the lord Pope Gregory' . Cf. Beno, *Gesta Romanae ecclesiae* II.8, p. 378: the Roman church 'condemned Gregory VI, together with his disciple Hildebrand, to banishment in Germany'; 'Hildebrand was the heir both of [Gregory's] treachery and of his money'.

55 October or November 1047: G. B. Borino (1916) p. 390; H. H. Anton (1982) p. 46.

56 G. B. Borino (1946) pp. 218–62 and (1952b) pp. 441–6 accepted Bonizo's account of this monastic profession in Cluny. See also H. Fichtenau (1986) pp. 59–68. For an opposite view see I. Schuster (1950) pp. 52–7 and (1952) pp. 305–7. In the necrology of Marcigny-sur-Loire, the closest approximation to the lost necrologies of Cluny, Gregory VII's name does not appear among the popes listed as 'monks of our congregation': J. Wollasch (1971) p. 61. Gregory VII's only precise reference to his exile (*Registrum* I.79, p. 113), refers to 'the discipline in which we were

Meanwhile, on the death of Pope Clement,[57] the Romans approached
the emperor, asking to be given a pope, to which he agreed. By means
of the tyranny of the patriciate he gave them a certain bishop from his
own side,[58] a man brimful of pride, and ordered the excellent Duke Boniface[59] to bring him to Rome and to enthrone him on his behalf. This
was done and they called the man by the new name of Damasus. After
he intruded himself into the see of Peter, he was dead in body and soul
before twice ten days had elapsed.[60] When they heard of so sudden a
death, the bishops beyond the mountains feared to go to Rome any more.

Meanwhile, although they were terrified by the swiftness of the pope's
death, the Romans, because they could no longer be without a pope,
ventured north, crossed the Alps, reached Saxony, found the king there
and begged to be given a pope.[61] This, however, could not easily be
done at that moment, since the bishops refused to go to Rome.[62] He
resolved, therefore, to visit the Rhineland, believing that he could find
a bishop in the kingdom of the Lotharingians whom he might give to
the Romans as their pope; and this was done. For after many prayers
and at the request of the Romans, the most noble Bruno, bishop of
Toul,[63] adorned with an honourable character, was with difficulty
persuaded ...[64]

---

nourished in the church of Cologne in the time of [Archbishop Herman II, 1036–
56]'. This suggested to E. Sackur (1894) pp. 139–40 an 'exile in the Lower
Rhineland': see also A. Fliche (1924a) pp. 113–28, 375–9; H. Hoffmann (1963) pp.
165–209; H. E. J. Cowdrey (1998) pp. 29–30. Bonizo's claim was perhaps based on
Gregory VII's close relationship with Abbot Hugh I of Cluny: see F. S. Schmitt
(1956) 1–18. For Paul of Bernried's version of Hildebrand's monastic career see
below pp. 266 and the version of Bruno of Segni, *Sermon* c. 2, below p. 379.

57 9 October 1047.

58 Poppo, bishop of Brixen (?1039–48); Pope Damasus II (1047–8). The Romans'
embassy to the emperor: *Annales Romani*, p. 469.

59 Boniface of Canossa, margrave of Tuscany (1027–52), father of Matilda of
Tuscany. In fact Boniface assisted Benedict IX's attempt to regain control of the
papacy and defied the emperor's command to conduct Damasus to Rome. He gave
way only when the emperor threatened to come to Italy. See H. H. Anton (1972)
pp. 552–3; K.-J. Herrmann (1973) p. 162; E. Goez (1995) p. 139.

60 Damasus II, elected December 1047, consecrated 17 July 1048, died 9 August.
According to Beno, *Gesta Romanae ecclesiae* II.8, p. 378, he was poisoned.

61 Late September or early October 1048 in Pöhlde: E. Steindorff (1881) pp. 40, 53.
Cf. Beno, *Gesta* II.8, p. 378.

62 *Chronicon Sancti Benigni Divionensis* p. 237: the Romans, with imperial approval,
offered the papacy to Archbishop Halinard of Lyons, who declined the honour.

63 Bruno, bishop of Toul (1026–51); Pope Leo IX (1048–54). He was elected at an
assembly in Worms, December 1048: see above p. 130.

64 This sentence is incomplete in the codex.

When he came to Besançon, the venerable abbot of Cluny[65] set out to meet him, bringing in his entourage the venerable Hildebrand, whom we mentioned above. When the latter had heard from someone the reasons for the journey, he began to request the abbot not to go thither, saying that he who strove to take possession of the papacy at the command of the emperor was not an apostle but an apostate. When the venerable father heard this, he remained silent, but when he arrived in Besançon, he took the earliest opportunity of making it known to the venerable bishop, telling him also of the moral probity and the blameless life [of Hildebrand]. What more is there to tell? The bishop asked for a talk with him.[66] This was done and *when the three were gathered in the Lord's name*, according to the word of the Gospel, God was *in the midst of them*.[67] For [Bruno] accepted [Hildebrand's] advice, laid down the papal insignia that he wore and, putting on a mantle,[68] he hastened to the threshold of the apostles. Entering the church of the prince of the apostles, he addressed the Roman clergy and people thus. 'Brethren, I have listened to your legation, which I ought not to oppose and I have come hither to you, firstly to fulfil a vow of prayer and then because I wished to obey your commands.' The bishops and cardinals replied, 'The reason for our summoning you was that we might elect you as our pope'; whereupon the archdeacon cried out in the customary manner, 'St Peter has elected the lord Leo as pope !' The people followed their example and repeatedly shouted this out and the cardinals and bishops, as is the custom, enthroned [him] in the seat of the prince of the blessed apostles.[69] After he had obtained the papal dignity, he promoted to the

65 Bonizo seems to have dated this incident at the only moment in the eleventh century when there was a vacancy in the abbatiate of Cluny. Odilo of Cluny died 1 January 1049; Hugh I was elected 20 February 1049: H. Diener (1959) p. 357. Leo IX set off for Rome 27 December 1048 and was consecrated 12 February 1049: *Life of Leo IX* II.4,6 above pp. 131, 133. Bonizo's version of this encounter in Besançon is nowhere corroborated. See the version of this anecdote in Bruno of Segni, *Sermon* c. 2, below p. 379.

66 Cf. Gregory VII, *Registrum* VII.14a, p. 483 (his return to Rome 'with my lord Pope Leo'); Beno, *Gesta* II.9, p. 379: 'Hildebrand was permitted, through the emperor's excessive indulgence, to return in [Leo's] entourage.... He imposed himself on Bruno, talking constantly during the journey. As he approached Rome he obtained from him the office of one of the custodians of the altar of blessed Peter').

67 Matthew 18:20.

68 Cf. *Life of Leo IX* II.5 above p. 131.

69 12 February 1049. On this second election see above pp. 33–5, 57. Cf. Bruno of Segni, *Sermon* c.2, below p. 379. See also H. Tritz (1952) p. 257; H. Hoffmann (1963) pp. 203–4; D. M. Whitton (1980) p. 38; J. Laudage (1984) p. 160.

office of subdeacon the venerable Hildebrand,[70] the giver of such sound advice, whom he begged from his abbot with many prayers and with great difficulty, and he made him steward of the holy Roman church.[71] On the latter's advice he then assembled a synod in which the bishops of various regions met together and in which it was forbidden under pain of anathema for any bishop to sell archdeaconries, provostships, abbacies or the benefices of churches, prebends or the commendations of churches or altars and forbidden for priests, deacons and subdeacons to take wives.[72] This proceeding moved the ancient serpent[73] to great anger. When the bishops first heard of this, they were silent, not having the strength to resist the truth, but afterwards, at the persuasion of the enemy of the human race, they disobediently concealed it.

Meanwhile in Rome bishops, cardinals and abbots who had been ordained through simoniacal heresy were deposed[74] and others from various provinces were ordained in their place: for example, from the region of Lyons, Bishop Humbert of Silva Candida;[75] from Burgundian stock, Stephen, abbot and cardinal[76]; from Remiremont, Hugh Candidus,[77] who afterwards apostasised; Frederick, the brother of Duke Godfrey;[78] from Compiègne, a certain Azelinus, bishop of Sutri;[79] from the region

---

70 Cf. Desiderius, *Dialogi* III.1, p. 1143.

71 Cf. Otto of Freising, *Chronica* VI.33, p. 484. The description of Hildebrand as 'steward' (*economus*) may be a confused allusion to his being given the charge of the monastery of S. Paolo fuori le Mura (May–November 1050): see T. Schmidt (1977) pp. 197–201; H. E. J. Cowdrey (1998) p. 31. Alternatively it may be a wrongly dated reference to his duties as archdeacon (1059–73).

72 Roman council of April 1049: Peter Damian, *Letter* 40, pp. 498–500; *Life of Leo IX* II.10, above pp. 136–7.

73 Satan (Revelation 12:9).

74 E.g. the bishop of Sutri mentioned in *Life of Leo IX* II.10, above p. 137.

75 Humbert, cardinal bishop of Silva Candida (1050–61). Cf. Benzo, *To Henry IV* VII.2, below p. 370 ('a monk from Burgundy'). See R. Hüls (1977) pp. 131–3.

76 Stephen, cardinal priest of S. Grisogono (1057–69), abbot of S. Gregorio in Clivo Scauro, Rome. See R. Somerville (1977) pp. 157–66.

77 Hugh Candidus, clerk in the abbey of Remiremont, cardinal priest of S. Clemente (?1049–85), cardinal bishop of Palestrina (1085–?1099). See F. Lerner (1931) pp. 7–10; R. Hüls (1977) pp. 111, 158–60. For Bonizo's lost polemic 'against Hugh the schismatic' see above p. 42.

78 Frederick of Lotharingia (brother of Godfrey 'the Bearded'), archdeacon of St Lambert, Liège, cardinal deacon, papal chancellor, abbot of Monte Cassino, cardinal priest of S. Grisogono, Pope Stephen IX (1057–8). See R. Hüls (1977) pp. 168–9, 248.

79 Azelinus (Kilinus), bishop of Sutri. See G. Schwartz (1913) p. 264.

of Ravenna, Peter Damian,[80] a most eloquent man; and very many others. Then the *strong man, fully armed*, who had *guarded his palace in complete peace*,[81] felt himself in bondage.

In the following year the pope assembled a synod in which all men, both clerks and laymen, were commanded by the authority of St Peter and the Roman church to abstain from the communion of priests and deacons who committed fornication.[82] This synod plunged a sword into the bowels of the enemy.[83] For unchaste priests and deacons were excluded from the office of the altar, not only in Rome but also throughout the neighbouring regions and through the whole of Tuscany, with the aid of monks, religious men, zealous in their preaching.[84]

This blessed pope also sent his legates to Constantinople, having questions on certain topics with which to challenge the Greek bishops. Among their number was the aforementioned Frederick, brother of the great Duke Godfrey.[85] They came to Constantinople and were honourably received by the Emperor Monomachus.[86] After they had very rapidly settled the business of the bishops, which was the reason for their coming, they returned to their own land endowed with the most magnificent gifts and bearing immense offerings to St Peter.

Meanwhile the very powerful nation of the Normans, who had removed Apulia and Calabria from the dominion of the kingdom of the Greeks, made an attack on the Beneventans. The Beneventans were compelled by this calamity to come to Rome and beg for help from the lord pope, surrendering Benevento to St Peter by a charter of donation.[87] Thereupon, provoked not only by the attack on the lands of the holy Roman church but also by the very severe torments that they were inflicting on Christians, [the pope] struck them first with the

80 Peter Damian, prior of Fonte Avellana, cardinal bishop of Ostia (1057–72). See R. Hüls (1977) pp. 99–100.

81 Luke 11:21, applied to Satan in the *Glossa Ordinaria*: 'the devil, a *strong man fully armed* to do harm … *guards his palace*, that is, the world'.

82 Roman council of 12 April 1050. See E. Steindorff (1881) pp. 119–20.

83 I.e. Satan.

84 Probably a reference to the reforming activity of John Gualbert, abbot of Vallombrosa (1036–73). His friendship with Leo IX: Andreas of Strumi, *Vita Johannis Gualberti* c. 22, p. 1087. See W. Goez (1973) pp. 229–32.

85 Humbert, Archbishop Peter of Amalfi and the chancellor Frederick were sent to Constantinople at the beginning of 1054 with the papal response to Leo of Ochrida's criticisms of the Latin rite. See above pp. 146–9.

86 Constantine IX Monomachus, Byzantine emperor (1043–58).

87 August 1050. See O. Vehse (1930–1) pp. 93–4; W. Kölmel (1935) pp. 98–100.

sword of excommunication and then judged that they must be punished with the material sword. Because, however, God's purposes are *like the great deep*,[88] it happened that by the ineffable providence of God, when battle was joined, the Normans were victorious.[89] They brought the pope through the midst of the carnage to Benevento, a captive but honourably treated, as was his due.[90] What more is there to tell? God showed by signs and miracles that those who had fallen in battle fighting for righteousness had greatly pleased Him. He gave great confidence to those who fought for righteousness thereafter, when He deigned to number them among the saints.[91] After these events the most blessed pope returned to Rome.[92] When he had reached the church of the prince of the apostles, he was seized by weakness and was carried before the confession of that apostle. In the presence of all the clergy and people of Rome he handed over the care of that church to Hildebrand, beloved of God,[93] and gave up his spirit to heaven.[94] His body was buried in that church with great honour. The sick come to his tomb and are healed and up to [this day] the infirm are freed from diverse ailments.[95]

When the venerable Hildebrand realised that the Roman clergy and people had agreed to his election, with many tears and supplications he eventually persuaded them to follow his counsel in the election of a pope. Immediately he crossed the Alps[96] in the company of religious

88 Psalm 35:7. On the significance of this verse: K.-U. Cram (1955) p. 5.

89 The Norman princes Count Humphrey of Apulia, his brother Robert Guiscard and Richard, count of Aversa defeated the papal army at Civitate on 18 June 1053. See above pp. 8–9.

90 23 June 1053 (*Chronica monasterii Casinensis* II.84, p. 333). Cf. *Life of Leo IX* II.20, above p. 151.

91 See below p. 260. Cf. *Life of Leo IX* II.20, above p. 151; Bruno of Segni, *Sermon* c.5, 6, below pp. 383–4; Libuin, *De obitu Leonis papae*, col. 527AB; Bonus of Cervia, *Vita et miracula* ed. A. Poncelet (1906) pp. 287, 289–90. See C. Erdmann (1935) pp. 111–2, 231.

92 24 or 25 March 1054: see E. Steindorff (1881) p. 266.

93 Hildebrand was not in Rome at the time of Leo IX's death. Cf. Berengar of Tours, *Rescriptum contra Lanfrannum* pp. 52–4: Hildebrand was at the legatine council of Tours when 'he was given the news that Pope Leo had departed this life'. See T. Schieffer (1934) pp. 50–3; J. de Montclos (1971) pp. 149–62.

94 19 April 1054.

95 Cf. *Life of Leo IX* II.27, above p. 157; Desiderius, *Dialogi* III.3, p. 1145. See E. Steindorff (1881) p. 268 n.2.

96 Bonizo alone claimed that Hildebrand was a papal candidate in 1054. Hildebrand as the Roman envoy to the imperial court: *Chronica monasterii Casinensis* II.86, p. 335; Beno, *Gesta Romanae ecclesiae* II.10, p. 379 ('Hildebrand ... ran to and fro from

men and approached the emperor. He became bound to him in such friendship that he demonstrated to him in their frequent conversations how great a sin he had committed in making appointments to the papacy.[97] The emperor, agreeing with his sound advice, laid down the tyranny of the patriciate and granted to the Roman clergy and people the election of the supreme pontiff according to their ancient privileges.[98] Forthwith they brought back with them to Rome, against his will and against that of the emperor himself, the steward of the emperor, the bishop of Eichstätt.[99] When, according to ancient custom, the clergy had elected and the people acclaimed him in the church of St Peter, the cardinals immediately, as their custom is, enthroned him and called him by a different name, that of Victor.

It was during the pontificate of this pope that the glorious duke and margrave Boniface died, leaving infants as his heirs.[100] Not long afterwards, however, Duke Godfrey, a magnificent man, most active in military affairs, came to Italy and took his widow to wife.[101] When the emperor heard of this, he came to Italy but did not find him in the Lombard kingdom.[102] On his arrival in Lombardy, therefore, the king first took the daughter of Otto and Adelaide, who was still an infant,

Rome to the emperor, from the emperor to Rome, without consulting the Roman church'). See H. E. J. Cowdrey (1998) pp. 33–5 and n. 31.

97 Cf. Gregory VII, *Registrum* I.19, p. 32 ('Emperor Henry of praiseworthy memory treated me, among all the Italians in his court, with special honour'); Synod of Worms, 24 January 1076 (Henry IV, *Letters* p. 67) ('In the time of the late good Emperor Henry you bound yourself by an oath never to accept the papacy yourself in the lifetime of the emperor or of his son'). See T. Schmidt (1973) pp. 374–86; H. E. J. Cowdrey (1998) pp. 33–4.

98 Except for *Chronica monasterii Casinensis* II.86, p. 335, which attributes to Hildebrand a leading role in the election, the other accounts suggest that it resembled the previous elections of German popes, Henry III nominating his own candidate. See E. Steindorff (1881) pp. 285, 292–3, 477–82; D. M. Whitton (1980) p. 39.

99 Gebhard, bishop of Eichstätt (1042–57); Pope Victor II (1055–7). Gebhard declined the papacy at an assembly in Mainz (September 1054) but was prevailed on to accept it at an assembly in Regensburg (March 1055). In describing him as the emperor's 'steward', Bonizo meant that he was at this time Henry III's principal adviser: cf. *Anonymus Haserensis de episcopis Eichstetensibus* c.35, p. 264.

100 Boniface II of Canossa, margrave of Tuscany †6 May 1052. His children: Frederick, Beatrice (below n. 107) and Matilda, future margravine of Tuscany (†1115). See E. Goez (1995) pp. 10, 20, 201.

101 Beatrice (†1076), daughter of Duke Frederick II of Upper Lotharingia, widow of Boniface married Godfrey 'the Bearded' (deposed duke of Upper Lotharingia, later duke of Lower Lotharingia †1069), in 1054 without imperial permission. See E. Goez (1995) pp. 22, 202.

102 He reached Verona by 7 April 1054 and celebrated Easter (16 April) in Mantua: E. Steindorff (1881) pp. 298–9.

as a bride for his son.[103] Then, when all the affairs of the Lombard kingdom had been settled, he was invited by the pope to be present at a synod in Florence. In that synod, on the advice of the venerable Hildebrand, the heresy of simony and the most foul practice of fornication of priests were struck down by the divine sword.[104] For in that same synod many bishops were deposed for the offence of simoniacal [heresy] and several for that of fornication, among whom the bishop of that very city was deposed.[105] Why do I delay longer? When the council had been solemnly celebrated, the emperor, strengthened by the pope's blessing, returned to Lombardy. On his arrival there he cunningly took prisoner both Beatrice and the only daughter of Boniface, named Matilda[106] (for a short while before his son and elder daughter had died, through whose malice I know not)[107] and took them with him beyond the mountains. He sought to gain the inheritance of Boniface and little knew that his last hour would soon be upon him. For, shaken by fever, immediately on reaching Lotharingia he summoned to him the magnificent Duke Godfrey and restored to him his wife, together with the daughter of Boniface and all her possessions.[108] Begging him repeatedly to show fidelity to his son, who had already been designated king,[109] he died a few days later.[110] His body was buried with that of his father in Speyer and his son, together with the latter's mother,[111] took up the reins of government. A few days afterwards,

---

103 Bertha of Turin (†1087), daughter of Otto, count of Savoy and Adelaide, margravine of Turin, betrothed to the five-year-old Henry IV in Zürich, 25 December 1055. See E. Steindorff (1881) p. 324; G. Meyer von Knonau (1890) pp. 9–10.

104 Council of Florence, Whitsun (4 June) 1055: see E. Steindorff (1881) p. 306 n.3.

105 Gerard, bishop of Florence (below p. 202 n. 38) was not deposed at this council. Bonizo confused him with his successor, Peter Mezzabarba, deposed as a simoniac, 30 March 1068. See G. Schwartz (1913) pp. 209–10.

106 Beatrice submitted in Florence during the emperor's visit (27 May–9 June 1055). See E. Goez (1995) pp. 24, 30, 141, 203–4.

107 Their deaths must have occurred soon after 17 December 1053: see E. Goez (1995) pp. 21, 203–4. Cf. Landulf Senior, *Historia Mediolanensis* III.31, p. 97 ('two brothers [sic]' of Matilda, 'whom she believed to have been killed through the cunning of Emperor Henry IV [sic]').

108 P. F. Kehr (1930) pp. 22–3 suggested that Godfrey submitted to Henry III in June 1056 in Lotharingia. See also E. Boshof (1978a) pp. 116–7; E. Goez (1995) pp. 142–3.

109 Henry IV, designated king 25 December 1050 in Pöhlde, elected by the princes November 1053 in Tribur, crowned 17 July 1054 in Aachen.

110 5 October 1056 in Bodfeld.

111 Agnes of Poitou, queen (1043), empress (†1077).

however, the pope also died.[112] After his death the clergy of the Roman church met together and with the acclamation of the people they elected Frederick, abbot of the monastery of Monte Cassino (whom we mentioned above), and they changed his name to Stephen.[113] According to ancient custom they consecrated him Roman pontiff at the altar of St Peter. He promoted the venerable Hildebrand to the order of deacons and ordained him archdeacon of the holy Roman church.[114]

Book VI

It was at that time that the church of Milan, which for almost two hundred years had withdrawn itself in scornful pride from the jurisdiction of the Roman church,[1] first recognised that it was subject, together with the other churches. I have decided to include in this work how this came about, since I believe that it is necessary for posterity [to know] about it.

The city of Milan, the metropolis of the whole of Lombardy, was in the days of the Roman emperors an imperial city, in which many religious bishops flourished, among whom was the blessed Ambrose, the jewel of the priesthood, the flowers of whose eloquence still diffuse their sweetness in the Church today.[2] He was the first to follow the eastern practice and cause the antiphon to be chanted in church. Long afterwards, however, the blessed Gregory gave westerners the duty of chanting. He recognised that the kingdom of God lies not only in the unity of the chant but rather in obedience and peace and he permitted the Milanese church to chant according to its ancient custom, that church being united to the holy Roman church in all the sacraments. This he did out of reverence for the blessed doctor

---

112 28 July 1057.

113 Stephen IX, elected 2 August 1057, consecrated 3 August. See G. Meyer von Knonau (1890) pp. 29–31; E. Goez (1995) p. 152.

114 Hildebrand's earliest appearance as archdeacon is in a diploma of 14 October 1059: L. Santifaller (1940) p. 164; G. B. Borino (1948) pp. 463–516; R. Hüls (1977) p. 250. D. Jasper (1986) pp. 34–46 argued that Hildebrand became archdeacon in summer 1058. See also H. E. J. Cowdrey (1998) pp. 37–9 and n. 46.

1 Cf. Bonizo, *Liber de vita christiana* IV.1, p. 113 '(The Milanese ... swelling with scornful pride, say that their church was founded not by Peter or by his successors, but by Barnabas'). Cf. Arnulf of Milan, *Liber gestorum recentium* III.13, 15, pp. 184–5, 189–90. See H. E. J. Cowdrey (1968) p. 27.

2 Ambrose, bishop of Milan (✝397), patron saint of Milan. Cf. Bonizo, *Liber de vita christiana* I.43, p. 31.

Ambrose, whom he himself followed, mingling the latter's antiphons in his own chants.[3] A long time afterwards, when the aforesaid church had delivered itself up completely to the slavery of simoniacal heresy, its bishops, fearing the judgement of Rome, disseminated this proverb among the people, 'Let the Ambrosian church keep its own status',[4] attempting to refute as a falsehood the fact that Ambrose very often declared in his writings that he who has withdrawn himself in any respect from the jurisdiction of the Roman church, is a heretic.[5]

In the time of the aforesaid Roman pontiff,[6] Wido,[7] an illiterate man, living in concubinage and a simoniac without any shame, was laying waste the Milanese church. In the time of this Wido there were in that city two clerks, one of whom was named Landulf,[8] a cultivated and most eloquent man, sprung from a noble family, and the other named Ariald,[9] a man extremely learned in liberal studies,[10] originating from

3 Bonizo, *Libellus de sacramentis* ed. W. Berschin (1972) p. 156; Bonizo, *Liber de vita christiana* IV.41, p. 127. For Ambrose and the antiphon: Augustine, *Confessiones* IX.7.15, CC 27, 141–2. For Pope Gregory I (590–604) and the chant: John the Deacon, *Vita Gregorii Magni* II.6–10, *MPL* 75, col. 90C-92A. See D. Hiley (1993) pp. 140, 490, 503–13.

4 Peter Damian, *Letter* 65, p. 231 ('the murmuring' of the Milanese people 'that the Ambrosian church must not be subject to Roman laws'); Arnulf, *Liber gestorum recentium* III.15, 20, IV.10, pp. 188–90, 215 ('the honour [integrity] of St. Ambrose' as the rallying cry of the Milanese anti-reform party). The cult of the patron saint in Milan: H. C. Peyer (1955) pp. 25–45; H. E. J. Cowdrey (1968) pp. 26–7.

5 W. Berschin (1972) p. 48 suggested as likely sources Ambrose, *Epistola* 11.4, *MPL* 16, col. 946A and *De excessu fratris sui Satyri* I.47, *CSEL* 73, 235. Other versions of this saying: Peter Damian, *Letter* 88, p. 521; Arnulf, *Liber* V.7, p. 226; Gregory VII, *Registrum* VII.24, pp. 504–5. Best known from Gregory VII, *Dictatus papae*, *Registrum* II.55a, p. 207 ('That he who does not agree with the Roman church is held not to be a catholic'). See K. Hofmann (1933) p. 65; J.J. Ryan (1956) pp. 78–80; H. Fuhrmann (1977) pp. 263–87; O. Hageneder (1978) pp. 36–7.

6 Stephen IX.

7 Wido, archbishop of Milan (1045–71). Cf. Arnulf, *Liber* III.1, p. 167 ('an uneducated man who came from the country'); Landulf Senior, *Historia Mediolanensis* III.3, p. 74 . See G. Schwartz (1913) pp. 79–80.

8 Landulf Cotta (✝ c. 1061), 'one of the notaries' of the Milanese church (Landulf Senior, *Historia* III.5, p. 76); 'of senatorial descent' (Peter Damian, *Letter* 70, p. 311). See C. Violante (1955) pp. 177–8; G. Miccoli (1966a) pp. 114, 125, 145–9; H. Keller (1973) pp. 338–9; H. Keller (1977) pp. 184–6; H. Gritsch (1980) pp. 17–18; P. Golinelli (1984) pp. 38–9.

9 Ariald (✝1066), deacon of the Milanese church. See C.D. Fonseca (1962) pp. 135–9; G. Miccoli (1966a) pp. 101–60; C. Violante (1968) pp. 599–600; P. Golinelli (1984) p. 35. C. Violante (1968) p. 601 and H. Keller (1979) p. 166 concluded that he came (as Bonizo claimed) of a valvassor family.

10 Cf. Andreas of Strumi, *Vita sancti Arialdi* c.4, p. 1051 ('he had an excellent knowledge of both liberal and divine literature'). The seven liberal arts were divided into

a family of knightly status, who was afterwards crowned with martyr-dom.[11] They very frequently studied sacred books and especially those of the blessed Ambrose and discovered how great an offence it is to *hide the talent*[12] entrusted to them. Committing themselves, therefore, to God and to the blessed prince of the apostles, one day with the help of divine grace they preached a sermon to the people,[13] in which they divulged to the people the errors of simoniacal corruption and proved more clearly than day how very wicked it was that priests and deacons living in concubinage should celebrate the sacraments.[14] They declared, on the evidence of the blessed Ambrose, that it was heretical not to obey the Roman church.[15] When they heard this, those who were predestined to life, freely accepted it, especially the poor, whom *God chose to shame the strong.*[16] The multitude of the clergy, however, which in that church was as innumerable *as the sands of the sea,*[17] stirred up the captains and the lesser vassals, the sellers of churches and their kindred and the kinsmen of their concubines and, when discord arose, they attempted to silence them, but they were disap-pointed in their hope. For as the number of the faithful grew daily, the wonderful athletes of God laboured the more ardently with their preaching. When their iniquity was made public, the enemies of God were daily *driven back and defeated,*[18] to the point that the aforesaid bishop himself was one day driven from his church.[19]

When the simoniacs saw this, being unable to resist the truth and so great a multitude, they were confounded and, reproaching them with

the *trivium* (grammar, dialectic, rhetoric) and *quadrivium* (arithmetic, geometry, astronomy, music). See H. I. Marrou (1950) pp. 245, 524; J. Jolivet (1969) pp. 13–22.

11 27 June 1066. See below p. 211.

12 Matthew 25:25.

13 Cf. Arnulf, *Liber* III.9, pp. 176–8; Andreas, *Vita Arialdi* c.4, p. 1051–2. See G. Miccoli (1966a) pp. 103–5; H. E. J. Cowdrey (1968) pp. 29–30; C. Violante (1968) p. 604; H. Keller (1973) p. 337; P. Golinelli (1984) p. 26.

14 The version of Ariald's sermon in Andreas, *Vita Arialdi* c.10, p. 1055 cites Pseudo-Ambrose, *De dignitate sacerdotali* c.5, *MPL* 17, col. 575B-576B. See G. Miccoli (1966a) pp. 117–23.

15 See above n. 5.

16 I Corinthians 1:27.

17 I Kings 4:20.

18 II Maccabees 13:19.

19 Perhaps an allusion to the tumult on 10 May 1057, described by Landulf Senior, *Historia* III.8, p. 79. The violence accompanying the beginning of the Milanese reform movement: C. Violante (1955) pp. 181, 188; C. Violante (1968) pp. 621, 627.

their poverty, called them 'Patarini', that is, 'ragged men'.[20] The former, since they *said 'raca' to their brother* (for the Greek *raca* means 'ragged' in Latin), were *liable to judgement*,[21] while the latter were blessed and *worthy to suffer dishonour for the name of Jesus*.[22] What more is there to tell? Every day the glorious race of the Patarini grew, to such an extent that they decided to send worthy men to Rome, who asked the blessed Pope Stephen to send back with them religious bishops who would rebuild their church from the foundations.[23] For in all that crowd of clergy, too numerous to count, scarcely five could be found in a thousand who were not stained by simoniacal heresy. When the pope heard this, he rejoiced and immediately sent from his side certain bishops, accompanied by the archdeacon Hildebrand, beloved of God.[24] When they arrived in Milan, they did not find the archbishop there, for, accused by his conscience, he fled their presence;[25] but they were received most honourably by the people, as was fitting. They remained for some days, strengthening the people with their preaching.

After this had been accomplished, Hildebrand, beloved of God, travelled all the way to the province of Lyons and there he celebrated a great council and hunted down simoniacal heresy and the detestable offence of clerical unchastity as far as the Pyrenees and the English

---

20 Cf. the interpretation of Arnulf, *Liber* IV.11, pp. 217–8: 'the Greek "pathos" means in Latin "disturbance"'; hence the Patarini were disturbers of the peace. The name 'Patarini' was used exclusively by the movement's enemies: the reformers used Bonizo's term 'the faithful'. The significance of the name: E. Werner (1956) pp. 138–44; H. E. J. Cowdrey (1968) p. 32n.2; G. Cracco (1974) pp. 357–87. The role of the poor in the Milanese reform: E. Werner (1956) pp. 111–64; C. Violante (1968) pp. 597–687: H. Keller (1970) pp. 34–64.

21 Matthew 5:22 (an obscure Greek term of abuse left untranslated by the Vulgate).

22 Acts 5:41.

23 According to Arnulf, *Liber* III.10–11, p. 181, it was the Milanese clergy who first sought the help of Stephen IX against the Patarini. The pope 'commanded the archbishop to assemble a synod', which met in Fontaneto (near Novara) in autumn 1057. Ariald and Landulf, refusing to attend, were excommunicated. Subsequently 'Ariald set out for Rome, bearing an exculpatory letter' denouncing the Milanese clergy as 'nicholaites and simoniacs and utterly disobedient to the Roman church'. Chronology of these events: C. Violante (1955) pp. 197–8; G. Lucchesi (1972) 1, 139.

24 Hildebrand (still subdeacon) was accompanied by Bishop Anselm I of Lucca (of Milanese birth: below p. 206 n. 64). See C. Violante (1955) pp. 206–7; T. Schmidt (1977) pp. 61–2; H. Gritsch (1980) p. 15; H. E. J. Cowdrey (1998) p. 35.

25 Wido was in Germany in August and October 1057. He was at the imperial court in Pöhlde, 27 December 1057, with the legates Hildebrand and Anselm: Gundechar, *Liber pontificalis Eichstetensis* p. 246. See C. Violante (1955) pp. 193, 205.

Channel. In that council God performed a great and obvious miracle through that archdeacon.[26] There happened to be present in that synod the archbishop of Embrun,[27] an exceedingly eloquent man. He was accused by certain men of simoniacal heresy, but during the following night he turned all his accusers into friends by means of bribes and when morning came, he taunted the judge with the words, *'Where are they who accused* me? *No one has condemned*[28] me.' When the archdeacon heard this, he said to the bishop, 'Do you believe, bishop, that the Holy Spirit is of one substance and deity with the Father and the Son?' When the latter replied, 'I believe it', he said, 'Say, *Glory be to the Father and to the Son and to the Holy Spirit.'* The bishop confidently began this versicle and said, *Glory be to the Father and to the Son,* but he was unable to pronounce the name of the Holy Spirit. After often beginning afresh and being unable to go any further, he threw himself at the archdeacon's feet and freely acknowledged himself a simoniac. As soon as he had been deposed from his bishopric, he confessed in a clear voice, *Glory be to the Father and to the Son and to the Holy Spirit.* This deed instilled so great a terror in the simoniacs that on that very day eighteen bishops acknowledged themselves to be simoniacs and gave up their episcopal sees.[29] When this most holy synod had been celebrated and ecclesiastical affairs lawfully settled, he returned with all speed to the supreme pontiff.

The blessed Pope Stephen is said to have had the spirit of prophecy. For a few days later, before he died, he called the bishops, cardinals and deacons and addressed them in these words. 'I know, brethren,

26 This, the most widely disseminated Hildebrand anecdote, is found in six other near-contemporary versions: (1) Peter Damian, *Letter* 72, pp. 344–5, December 1059/ July 1061 (placing the synod in Victor II's pontificate in 'Gaul'); (2) Desiderius of Monte Cassino, *Dialogi* III.5, p. 1148, *c.* 1073 (in Victor II's pontificate in 'Gaul'); (3) Paul of Bernried, *Life of Gregory VII* c. 17, below p. 269, 1128 (in Leo IX's pontificate in Lyons); (4) Alexander of Canterbury, *Dicta Anselmi. Miracula* c. 28, *Memorials of St. Anselm* pp. 215–6, 1115 / 1120) (in a 'general council' in France, over which Alexander II presided); (5) William of Malmesbury, *Gesta regum Anglorum* p. 324, *c.* 1120; (6) Bruno of Segni, *Sermon* c. 3, below p. 381, 1090s, on the authority of Gregory VII represented it as a miracle of Leo IX, as did Alexander of Canterbury in an earlier version of his work: F. S. Schmitt (1956) pp. 17–18. T. Schieffer (1935) pp. 55–7 and H. Diener (1959) pp. 359, 379 placed this synod in February 1056 in Chalon-sur-Saône (province of Lyons). See also A. Stacpoole (1967) pp. 341–63; W. Berschin (1972) p. 96 n.434; I. S. Robinson (1978d) pp. 6–7; R. Schieffer (1981) p. 69; H. E. J. Cowdrey (1998) pp. 32–3.

27 Hugh, archbishop of Embrun. See T. Schieffer (1935) p. 56.

28 John 8:10.

29 Hildebrand 'deposed six bishops entangled in various offences': Peter Damian, *Letter* 72, p. 345.

that after my death there shall rise up among you men, loving themselves, who will seize this see not according to the decrees of the holy Fathers but through the assistance of lay persons.' When they heard this, they all denied it with equal vehemence and mutually bound themselves by an oath taken with their hands in that of the pope that they would never ascend the papal throne nor consent to others ascending it otherwise than as the decrees of the holy Fathers demand.[30] A few days later the pope arrived in the region of Tuscany and, overcome by weakness, he gave up his spirit to heaven.[31] After his death, it happened that in Rome the captains and especially Gregory of Tusculum,[32] who had formerly claimed for himself the empty office of patrician, set up a tyranny and raised to the papacy a certain cardinal bishop of Velletri,[33] contrary to the oath which he had already sworn in the hand of the late pope. Changing his name, they called him Benedict.

While these events were taking place, the wife of Emperor Henry with her infant son exercised the government of the kingdom, as we recounted above.[34] With feminine temerity she did much that was against the law.[35] At the beginning of her reign she committed all the affairs of the Italian kingdom to a certain Wibert of Parma, a man of noble birth, and appointed him chancellor.[36] Meanwhile Hildebrand, beloved of God, met the cardinal bishops, deacons and priests in

30 According to Peter Damian, *Letter* 58, pp. 193–4 (1058), Stephen commanded that the Roman clergy and people 'should elect no pope ... until [Hildebrand's] return' from his legation to the imperial court. Cf. *Chronica monasterii Casinensis* II.98, p. 356. See H. E. J. Cowdrey (1998) p. 36.

31 29 March 1058 in Florence.

32 Count Gregory II of Tusculum: above p. 182 and n. 17. Other accounts of this papal election, 5 April 1058: Peter Damian, *Letter* 58, pp. 191–3; *Chronica monasterii Casinensis* II.99, pp. 356–7; *Annales Romani* pp. 470–1. See G. Meyer von Knonau (1890) pp. 85–6; H.-G. Krause (1960) pp. 62–3; T. Schmidt (1977) pp. 72–5.

33 John II Mincius, cardinal bishop of Velletri; Pope Benedict X (1058–9). See G. Schwartz (1913) p. 275; O. Capitani (1966) pp. 366–70; R. Hüls (1977) p. 144; T. Schmidt (1977) pp. 78–80.

34 Empress Agnes and King Henry IV (born 11 November 1050).

35 Cf. below p. 206 and Bonizo, *Liber de vita christiana* VII.29, pp. 249–50 ('It is ordained in the Roman laws concerning women that they are neither to wield authority nor to exercise secular government ... Nowhere do we read that women have governed without remarkable damage to their subjects.')

36 Wibert of Parma, archbishop of Ravenna (1072–1100); antipope 'Clement III' (1084–1100). His kinship with the house of Canossa: J. Ziese (1982) pp. 4–7. He was probably appointed chancellor in June 1058: M. L. Bulst-Thiele (1933) p. 44; J. Ziese (1982) pp. 14–15.

Siena[37] and they elected Gerard, bishop of the city of Florence, whom they called by the new name of Nicholas.[38] He summoned Wibert, chancellor of the Italian kingdom to a synod,[39] in the name of St Peter and according to true obedience, together with the magnificent man Godfrey[40] and the bishops not only of Tuscany but also of Lombardy. They were to come to Sutri and decide on a plan concerning the perjurer and intruder.[41] When Benedict heard that they were approaching Sutri, conscience stricken, he abandoned the see that he had usurped and returned to his own home. This news was subsequently reported in Sutri and the venerable Nicholas entered Rome victorious without having to fight a single battle.[42] He was honourably received by all the clergy and people and he was enthroned by the cardinals in the see of St Peter.[43] Not long afterwards Benedict (whose other name was Mincius) came and prostrated himself at the pope's feet, declaring that he had been the victim of coercion but nevertheless not denying his perjury and the offence of usurpation. On the basis of his own confession he was deposed from the rank of bishop and from the priesthood.[44]

After this had been done, the magnificent Duke Godfrey, together with the chancellor and the bishops, returned home. The venerable pope, protected by God, however, entered Apulia and absolved the Normans

37 6 December 1058. Bonizo omitted the preliminary negotiations of the Roman reform party with the German court, June 1058: *Annales Altahenses* 1058, p. 54; Lampert of Hersfeld, *Annales* 1059 [1058], p. 74. Hildebrand's role in the election: Benzo of Alba, *To Henry IV* VII.2, below p. 372; *Chronica monasterii Casinensis* III.12, p. 373; *Annales Romani* p. 471. See G. B. Borino (1948) pp. 491–501; H.-G. Krause (1960) pp. 63–9; J. Wollasch (1968) pp. 205–20; D. Hägermann (1970a) pp. 352–61; D. Hägermann (1970b) pp. 169–70; D. Jasper (1986) p. 42 n.160; E. Goez (1995) pp. 154–5; H. E. J. Cowdrey (1998) pp. 43–4.

38 Gerard, bishop of Florence (1045–61); Pope Nicholas II (1058–61). See G. Schwartz (1913) pp. 209–10.

39 Wibert was presumably the envoy sent by the German court to give approval for Gerard's designation: G. Meyer von Knonau (1890) pp. 118, 677; H.-G. Krause (1960) p. 69; J. Ziese (1982) p. 19–20.

40 Godfrey 'the Bearded' of Lotharingia, margrave of Tuscany (above p. 194 n. 101). See W. Mohr (1976) p. 32; E. Goez (1995) p. 154.

41 Synod of Sutri, January 1059. See H. Zimmermann (1968) pp. 142–3; T. Schmidt (1977) pp. 77–8; J. Ziese (1982) p. 20.

42 Mid-January 1059. But see *Annales Romani* p. 471: 'every day there were battles and killings in the city'.

43 24 January 1059. See G. Meyer von Knonau (1890) p. 120.

44 He was deprived of the papal, episcopal and priestly offices and placed in the church of S. Agnese in Rome, where he was still living in Gregory VII's pontificate. G. Schwartz (1913) p. 275; W. Kölmel (1935) p. 134 n.191; R. Hüls (1977) p. 144 dated the deposition in March or April 1060.

from the bond of excommunication and invested them with the whole
of Apulia and Calabria. He received from them the surrender of the
lands of St Peter which they had previously invaded, with the exception
of Benevento, and compelled them to swear an oath to him.[45] With
their aid he very rapidly freed the city of Rome from the tyranny of
the captains. For not only did they trample on the pride of Tusculum,
Palestrina and Nomentana, but passing through Rome, they destroyed
Galeria and all the fortresses of Count Gerard as far as Sutri and this
feat freed the city of Rome from the domination of the captains.[46]

Once this had been achieved, the Normans returned to Apulia and
envoys from the Milanese requested the pope to have mercy on the
desolate condition of their church. The venerable pope, therefore,
without delay sent Peter Damian, bishop of Ostia, a man endowed
with every kind of knowledge, to visit the church of Milan.[47] On his
arrival he rebuilt with great discretion whatever he found there in a
state of ruin. For he selected priests and deacons, the most religious
whom he could find, of chaste life and good reputation, who had not
paid for their ordination, even though they had been ordained by a
simoniac, and he reconciled them and gave them the government of
the church. Of their number many devout men still survive in our
own time. This action seemed blameworthy to some men, but to the
wise it seemed most praiseworthy.[48] For what more laudable course

45 Nicholas II celebrated the synod of Melfi, 23 August 1059 in the presence of
Robert Guiscard, duke of Apulia and Calabria and Richard I, prince of Capua. The
excommunication, of which no record survives, had presumably been
incurred by attacks on Benevento. See P. F. Kehr (1934) pp. 15–24; J. Deér (1972)
pp. 63–76; H. Hoffmann (1978) pp. 137–80. On the significance of the term 'lands
of St Peter': J. Deér (1972) pp. 72–3.

46 Bonizo's account conflates two Norman expeditions carefully distinguished in the
Annales Romani p. 471: one following the Easter synod of 1059, the other 'in the
harvest season'. See G. Meyer von Knonau (1890) p. 150 n.57; G. B. Borino (1948)
pp. 509 n.136, 511; J. Deér (1972) p. 101; H. E. J. Cowdrey (1998) p. 61. D.
Whitton (1980) pp. 260–1 pointed out that Bonizo exaggerated the damage inflicted
in 1059 on 'the domination of the captains'.

47 He was accompanied by Bishop Anselm I of Lucca. See Peter Damian, *Letter* 65, pp.
228–47; Arnulf, *Liber* III.12, p. 182; Landulf Senior, *Historia* III.5, pp. 85–8. The
legation was dated between Nicholas's consecration (24 January 1059) and the
Lateran synod of 13 April 1059 by F. Dressler (1954) pp. 130 n. 221, 134; autumn
1059 or winter 1059–60 by G. Lucchesi (1972) 1, 136, 148; winter 1060–1 by G. B.
Borino (1948) pp. 479–80.

48 Cf. Peter Damian, *Letter* 65, pp. 236–46. Bonizo's account refers to the contemporary debate on the validity of simoniacal ordinations, which Peter Damian had
defended in *Letter* 40, pp. 384–509 (*Liber Gratissimus*) against the 'rigorist' views of
reformers such as Humbert of Silva Candida. Cf. Bonizo's own defence of the
validity of the orders of heretics, schismatics and excommunicates: *Liber de vita*

could be found at that time than to prevent such a church from perishing from the lack of a priesthood?

Not long afterwards, however, the pope assembled a synod in which Bishop Wido of Milan is known to have participated, whether he liked it or not, under compulsion from the Patarini.[49] He brought with him those stubborn bulls, the Lombard bishops: that is, Cunibert of Turin,[50] Giselmus of Asti,[51] Benzo of Alba,[52] Gregory of Vercelli,[53] Otto of Novara,[54] Opizo of Lodi[55] and Adelman of Brescia.[56] They were all commanded in that synod to exclude from the altar priests and deacons living in concubinage. They also decreed that *no mercy was to be shown towards simoniacs.*[57] In this synod by the common counsel of all the bishops this law was decreed concerning the election of the pope, which was subscribed by one hundred and thirteen bishops.[58] *Whoever is enthroned in the apostolic see without the harmonious canonical election of the cardinals and the rest of the religious clergy is held to be not apostolic but apostate. It is also lawful for the cardinals, together with other godfearing persons, both clergy and laymen, both to anathematize an intruder and to expel him from the apostolic see with human aid and effort and to place there one whom they judge to be worthy. If they cannot*

---

christiana I.43–4, pp. 31–3. See L. Saltet (1907) pp. 196–8, 220–1; A. Schebler (1936) pp. 252–4.

49 Lateran synod of April 1059. Cf. Arnulf, *Liber* III.15 ('Lo! your metropolitan is summoned to a Roman synod, contrary to custom'). For Wido's subscription see D. Jasper (1986) p. 111. See also G. Meyer von Knonau (1890) pp. 133–4; L. Gatto (1968) pp. 104–5; D. Jasper (1986) pp. 49–50.

50 Cunibert, bishop of Turin (1046–82): see G. Schwartz (1913) pp. 131–3; D. Jasper (1986) p. 118.

51 Girelmus, bishop of Asti (1054–65): see G. Schwartz (1913) p. 95; D. Jasper (1986) pp. 49–50, 119.

52 Benzo, bishop of Alba (1059–?1089), polemicist: see above pp. 82–3.

53 Gregory, bishop of Vercelli (1044–77): see G. Schwartz (1913) pp. 137–8; D. Jasper (1986) pp. 30–1, 119.

54 Otto, bishop of Novara (1053/4–78/9): see G. Schwartz (1913) pp. 124–5; D. Jasper (1986) p. 119.

55 Opizo, bishop of Lodi (?1059–?1083): see G. Schwartz (1913) p. 121.

56 Adelman, bishop of Brescia (1057–61): see G. Schwartz (1913) p. 107; R. W. Southern (1953) pp. 197–9.

57 Nicholas II, *Decretum contra simoniacos* (*JL* 4431a), *MGH Constitutiones* 1, 550.

58 The number 113 is given in Nicholas II's letters, *JL* 4404–6; by Lanfranc of Bec, *De corpore et sanguine Domini* c.1, *MPL* 150, col. 409B; ed. R.B.C. Huygens (1965) p. 371. The number of bishops subscribing the Papal Election Decree was 79: D. Jasper (1986) p. 31 n.108.

achieve this within the city, they may by apostolic authority perform the election in an assembly outside the city in a place which pleases them and to the elect is conceded authority to rule and dispose of property in the interests of the holy Roman church, according to the current circumstances, as if he was already enthroned.[59]

When the council had been lawfully celebrated, the Lombard bishops returned home. Since, however, they had received large sums of money from priests and deacons living in concubinage, they concealed the pope's decrees, with one exception, namely the bishop of Brescia. On arrival in Brescia, after publicly reading out the pope's decrees, he was beaten by the clergy and almost killed.[60] This event served in no small way to promote the growth of the Pataria. For not only in Brescia but also in Cremona and Piacenza and in all the other provinces many people abstained from the communion of priests who lived in concubinage.[61]

It was also in the time of this pope that the Roman cardinal Hugh Candidus (whom we described above as having been ordained by the blessed Pope Leo) withdrew from the fellowship of the Roman church.[62] Of the perversity of his character it is better to say nothing at all than to say a little. Yet to record everything as briefly as possible, his actions were like his eyes: he was cross-eyed and his deeds were of the same twisted nature. Meanwhile the number of the faithful increased not only throughout Italy but also throughout the whole of Gaul. Every day the simoniacs became more notorious and priests living in concubinage were rejected.

When the venerable Pope Nicholas had been in the papal office only a few years, he died a blessed death.[63] After his death the Roman clergy

1059

59 A quotation not from the Papal Election Decree of April 1059, but from two later texts summarising its contents: Nicholas II, *Synodica generalis* (*JL* 4405), ed. R. Schieffer (1981) p. 214; Nicholas II, *Decretum contra simoniacos* (*JL* 4431a), *MGH Constitutiones* 1, 551. This quotation appears also in Bonizo, *Liber de vita christiana* IV.87, p. 156; Anselm of Lucca, *Collectio canonum* IV.13, pp. 272–3; Deusdedit, *Collectio canonum* I.69, p. 107 (with slight variations). See H.-G. Krause (1956) pp. 192–3; W. Berschin (1972) pp. 49–50; R. Schieffer (1981) p. 75; D. Jasper (1986) pp. 64 n. 255, 76–8. See also below pp. 210, 252–3.

60 Adelman. See G. Meyer von Knonau (1890) p. 142.

61 See below pp. 212–13, 230, 231–2.

62 Cardinal Hugh Candidus (above p. 191 and n. 77). Cf. *Vita Anselmi Lucensis* p. 19: 'white of countenance, very black of mind'. See F. Lerner (1931) pp. 12–13; R. Hüls (1977) p. 159.

63 19 or 20 July 1061: see T. Schmidt (1977) p. 81.

and people elected Bishop Anselm of Lucca[64] according to the decrees of the Fathers.[65] Milanese by birth, sprung from noble stock, a man skilled in both fields of learning,[66] he was called by the new name of Alexander. Meanwhile the Lombard bishops, finding this a suitable moment, met together under the leadership of Wibert (whom we mentioned above as the chancellor)[67] and held *a council of evildoers.*[68] Here they resolved that they would have a pope from nowhere except the paradise of Italy and such a one who would understand how to have compassion on their weaknesses. Next they went over the mountains and won over the all too feminine mind of the empress, inventing fictions which sounded like truth. For they said that their lord, as the heir to the kingdom, was likewise heir to the patriciate[69] and that the blessed Nicholas had declared in his decree that no one should henceforward be numbered among the popes, who was not elected with the consent of the king.[70] The empress was deceived by these and other such artifices and with feminine presumption[71] gave her consent to an act of wickedness *such as never has been since* the day *in which the nations began to be.*[72] There, in a papal election in which none of the Roman clergy or laity was present, a pontiff was elected by his fellow fornicators and simoniacs.[73] Receiving the cross and the papal insignia from the hands of the king and queen, he came to Rome

---

64 Anselm da Baggio, bishop of Lucca (1056–73); Pope Alexander II (1061–73). See C. Violante (1961) pp. 399–407; T. Schmidt (1977) pp. 1–10; K. G. Cushing (1998) pp. 43–63.

65 During the night of 30 September–1 October 1061. See G. Meyer von Knonau (1890) pp. 220–2; H.-G. Krause (1960) pp. 149–51; T. Schmidt (1977) pp. 80–8.

66 I.e. both the seven liberal arts and theology. Cf. Alexander II, *JL* 4669, *MPL* 146, 1353 (to Lanfranc of Bec). On his education: T. Schmidt (1977) pp. 10–25.

67 Bishops Denis of Piacenza and Gregory of Vercelli were the ringleaders: Peter Damian, *Letter* 88, p. 524. On Wibert's role: J. Ziese (1982) p. 21.

68 Psalm 21:17.

69 The envoys were Count Gerard of Galeria and the abbot of S. Gregorio Magno. See G. Meyer von Knonau (1890) pp. 217, 224–5; H.-G. Krause (1960) pp. 107, 149; H. Vollrath (1974) pp. 26–31; T. Schmidt (1977) pp. 104–11.

70 A reference to the 'royal paragraph' of the Papal Election Decree, 1059: 'let [the cardinal bishops] elect [a pope] ... saving the honour and reverence due to our beloved son Henry'. See D. Jasper (1986) pp. 104–5 (edition) and pp. 5 n. 16, 101 n.13 (bibliography). Bonizo did not know this paragraph and treated his opponents' references to it as unauthentic: see also below pp. 252–3. See H.-G. Krause (1960) p. 196; R. Schieffer (1981) p. 75.

71 Cf. above p. 201 n. 35.

72 Daniel 12:1.

73 At an assembly of princes in Basel on 28 October 1061: see T. Schmidt (1977) pp. 108–10, 126–7.

out of the north, whence, according to Jeremiah, *evil shall break forth upon* all *the inhabitants of the land.*[74] They elected Cadalus of Parma,[75] a man well provided with riches, destitute of virtues. He entered Lombardy surrounded by many knights, having in his train the obstinate bishops of Lombardy, who did not know how to bear *the easy yoke*[76] of the Lord. Then the simoniacs rejoiced, the priests living in concubinage danced for joy. What more is there to tell? According to the word of the Gospel, all their rejoicing was humbled to the earth by the opposition of one woman[77] and the power of the proud, great as it was, vanished like smoke when Beatrice[78] alone opposed it. Not long afterwards, however, Cadalus secretly came to Bologna, where he waited for his knights. Once he had gathered them together, he came to Rome, bringing with him a huge mass of gold and silver.[79] There was at that time in Rome no lack of pestilential fellows, selfish, greedy and covetous, who joined with him. Among them were the Roman captains,[80] who wished to oppress the city of Rome and to bring it back under their power, as in ancient times.

Meanwhile the man *hateful to God* [81] set up camp in the field of Nero and when battle was joined, by the secret judgement of God he appeared to be the victor.[82] Nevertheless – O unutterable providence of God, wonderful mercy of God! – before a month had passed by, on the arrival of Duke Godfrey in Rome, this victor was begging with difficulty to depart as if he was the vanquished, showering the duke with many prayers and magnificent gifts.[83] Cadalus came to Parma,

74 Jeremiah 1:14.

75 Cadalus, bishop of Parma (1046–?1071); antipope 'Honorius II'. See G. Schwartz (1913) pp. 186–7; F. Herberhold (1934) pp. 84–104.

76 Matthew 11:30.

77 Cf. Genesis 3:15; Revelation 12:13.

78 Beatrice of Tuscany (above p. 194 n. 101) barred Cadalus's way to Rome through the lands of the house of Canossa, winter 1061–2. See E. Goez (1995) pp. 158–9, 206.

79 Cadalus's army reached Sutri on 25 March 1062: see Benzo, *Ad Heinricum IV* II.9, p. 216.

80 The most prominent were Count Gerard of Galeria and Cencius Stephani. See F. Herberhold (1947) pp. 485–6; T. Schmidt (1977) pp. 111–14.

81 Romans 1:30.

82 The battle on the Field of Nero (on the right bank of the Tiber, north of the Leonine city), 14 April 1062. The forces recruited by Hildebrand were routed with great loss and Cadalus seized the Leonine city. See G. Meyer von Knonau (1890) pp. 254–6.

83 Godfrey 'the Bearded' intervened in mid-May 1062: *Annales Altahenses* 1062, pp. 60–1. See G. Meyer von Knonau (1890) pp. 262–3; F. Herberhold (1947) pp. 491–2; H.-G. Krause (1960) pp. 151–2; H. Zimmermann (1968) p. 150; T. Schmidt (1977) pp. 117–18.

the workshop of iniquity; he collected money and, after a year had passed by, he entered Romagna like a thief. There he gathered a great number of knights by giving away a great sum of money and with the aid of the captains and certain pernicious Romans he entered the Leonine city by night and seized the church of St Peter. When morning came, however, the knights who had accompanied him were invaded by a terror from heaven so great that they all took flight, even though no one forced them to go, and he was left alone in the church.[84] On the advice of Cencius,[85] a certain pernicious Roman, he entered the castle of Sant'Angelo[86] and defended himself there. He was besieged in that fortress for two years[87] and suffered many and various calamities there, until he was given leave to depart, although not before he obtained his release from Cencius with three hundred pounds of silver. Left with a single retainer, with the assistance of a single mule, travelling among pilgrims, with difficulty he reached Berceto.[88]

While this was happening, the canonical life originated in Milan, a development which provoked envy among enemies.[89] A few days after these events Landulf, the clerk of Milan whom we mentioned above, died and was laid to rest in peace.[90]

Meanwhile the archbishops, bishops, abbots, dukes and counts of Germany held an assembly in which they decided that the empress

84 May or June 1063. He secured control of the Leonine city and the Giovannipoli, the fortifications near S. Paolo fuori le Mura, but was expelled by Godfrey 'the Bearded' with a Norman army. See G. Meyer von Knonau (1890) pp. 312–7; F. Herberhold (1947) pp. 496–500; T. Schmidt (1977) pp. 121–2.

85 Cencius Stephani (de Praefecto) (✝1077), son of the Roman prefect Stephen. See G. B. Borino (1952a) pp. 373–440; D. Whitton (1980) pp. 223–35: H. E. J. Cowdrey (1998) pp. 326–8.

86 On the importance of this fortress: C. Cecchelli (1947) pp. 103–23; C. Cecchelli (1951) pp. 27–67.

87 He was still in Rome early in 1064 , but had returned to northern Italy before the synod of Mantua, May 1064. See G. Meyer von Knonau (1890) pp. 377–8, 380; F. Herberhold (1947) p. 502.

88 In the diocese of Parma.

89 Cf. Bonizo, Liber de vita christiana V.77, p. 204: 'In our own times in Italy the clergy in Milan, at the command of Pope Alexander, began to live in common, having no possessions'. Cf. above p. 172; Andreas of Strumi, Vita Arialdi, p. 1058. In his study of the eleventh-century canonical reform C. Dereine (1946) p. 374 dated the Milanese initiative 'c. 1063'. See also C. Dereine (1948) p. 291; G. Miccoli (1966a) pp. 136–7, 274–5.

90 The Patarine leader Landulf (above pp. 197 n. 8). P. Golinelli (1984) p. 16 gave the date 'c. 1061'.

should henceforward live in retirement.[91] They judged it unfitting
that the kingdom should be subject to a female ruler, firstly because
she was a nun[92] and it was unbecoming for her to concern herself with
secular affairs and, secondly, because their lord seemed to have reached
maturity.[93] They determined by general agreement that the venerable
Archbishop Anno of Cologne[94] should exercise the government for
the king and the queen[95] and, deposing Wibert, they made Gregory of
Vercelli chancellor of the Italian kingdom.[96]

Anno considered that his best course of action was to unite the kingship with the priestly power. He came to Italy and, arriving in Rome,[97]
asked the pope why he dared to accept the office of Roman pontiff
without the king's command. Hildebrand beloved of God told him
that, according to the decrees of the holy Fathers, no role was granted
to kings in the election of Roman pontiffs, to which he replied that
this was permitted him by virtue of the office of patrician. The
venerable archdeacon immediately countered with these statements of
synodal law. From the synod of Symmachus, in which one hundred
and fifty bishops were present: *Bishop Laurentius of Milan said, 'It was
resolved that no layman is to hold any power in the Church. He is forced to
comply and does not possess the authority of command.' Bishop Eulalius of
the church of Syracuse said, 'It is written that no power of ordering*

91 Empress Agnes's regency ended not through the decision of an assembly of princes
but after the abduction of the boy king at Kaiserswerth on the Rhine, April 1062.
See G. Meyer von Knonau (1890) pp. 274–9, especially pp. 279 n. 77 and 286 n. 97
on Bonizo's account; T. Struve (1984) pp. 103–4 (no. 252); I. S. Robinson (1999) pp.
43–5.

92 It was after the abduction of her son that she withdrew from court and lived a
religious life on her own estates. See G. Meyer von Knonau (1890) pp. 231, 280–1;
M. L. Bulst-Thiele (1933) pp. 80–1; T. Struve (1984) pp. 95, 104.

93 Henry IV was declared of age, 29 March 1065: see G. Meyer von Knonau (1890)
pp. 400–6; T. Struve (1984) pp. 159–60; I. S. Robinson (1999) pp. 51–2.

94 Anno II, archbishop of Cologne (1056–75), leader of the conspiracy that abducted
Henry IV and the dominant politician at court, 1062–4: see G. Meyer von Knonau
(1890) pp. 274–9, 284–91, 333–5, 385–7; G. Jenal (1974) pp. 177–95, 276–81; I. S.
Robinson (1999) pp. 45–51.

95 The wedding of Henry IV and Queen Bertha took place in 1066: below p. 210.

96 Wibert's last appearance as chancellor was 24 June 1063. His successor, Bishop
Gregory of Vercelli (above n. 53) first appeared 27 September 1063. If Wibert was
deposed, as Bonizo claimed, in an assembly of princes, it must have been in
Allstedt, June 1063. See J. Ziese (1982) pp. 23–5.

97 Anno came to Italy to attend the synod of Mantua (31 May 1064). See G. Jenal
(1974) p. 263 n. 225. Bonizo's fictional dialogue between Anno and Hildebrand was
'a faithful reflection of the conflicts between Gregorians and anti-Gregorians in the
mid-1080s concerning the legitimacy of Gregory VII': H.-G. Krause (1960) p. 195.

ecclesiastical affairs has ever been ascribed to laymen, however devout they may be.'[98] When Anno contradicted with the decrees of Pope Nicholas, he was very quickly countered with the decree of the same Pope Nicholas which was subscribed by one hundred and thirteen bishops.[99] The archbishop then requested the lord pope that he might deign to assemble a synod and give an account of himself.[100] When the pope heard this, although it was inconsistent with the dignity of the Roman pontiffs, he nevertheless promised to do so, since necessity urged it. He immediately summoned a synod in Mantua, in which he could meet Cadalus and the bishops of the Lombards. The Lombard bishops, together with their metropolitan, all met there except, however, for Cadalus, whose conscience reproached him, so that he feared to come.[101] The venerable pope came to Mantua, gave an account of himself and very rapidly turned all his enemies into friends. For immediately all the Lombard bishops fell at his feet, confessed their guilt and sought and obtained pardon.[102] With kingship and priesthood thus united, the pope returned to Rome with honour, while every bishop went with all speed to his own see. Duke Godfrey[103] and Otto the Saxon, duke of the Bavarians[104] were present at this great council.

After these transactions the king took to wife Bertha, beloved of God, the daughter of Otto and Adelaide, whom his father had given him

---

98 Pope Symmachus, *Decretum synodale* (502) c.3, *MGH Auctores antiquissimi* 12, 447. Cf. Bonizo, *Liber de vita christiana* II.18–19, p. 42; Anselm of Lucca, *Collectio* V.9, 10; Deusdedit, *Collectio* IV.54. See W. Berschin (1972) p. 50.

99 H.-G. Krause (1960) p. 195: 'the decrees of Pope Nicholas' cited by Anno and 'the decree' cited by Hildebrand were in fact the same document, the Papal Election Decree of 1059. The confusion arose because Bonizo was unaware that the 'royal paragraph' was an authentic part of the decree. See above pp. 205, 206 nn. 59, 70 and below pp. 252–3.

100 The synod was convoked by the German court: H.-G. Krause (1960) p. 195 n. 131. Bonizo upheld the canonical principle that such a synod could lawfully be summoned only by the pope: cf. his account of the synod of Sutri, 1046, above p. 184.

101 Cadalus, in Acquanegra (north-west of Mantua), refused to attend the synod unless he presided over it. See G. Jenal (1974) pp. 247, 263–7.

102 Bonizo described the events only of the first day of the synod, omitting the tumultuous events of the second day, when Cadalus's supporters sought to reverse the previous day's decision. See G. Meyer von Knonau (1890) pp. 383–5.

103 The account of Benzo, *Ad Heinricum IV* III.26–28[29], pp. 342–54 assumes that Godfrey 'the Bearded', margrave of Tuscany was absent: hence the conclusion of E. Goez (1995) pp. 160–1. But G. Jenal (1974) p. 269 supposed that Godfrey escorted Anno to Mantua.

104 Otto, count of Northeim, duke of Bavaria (1061–70), †1083. See K.-H. Lange (1961) p. 21.

when they were both still infants.[105] When the marriage had been lawfully celebrated, he began to conduct the government of the kingdom
on his own account.[106] Soon afterwards, at the request of Archbishop
Wido of Milan, he gave the bishopric of Cremona to the latter's
nephew, Arnulf.[107] I shall not trouble to tell how Arnulf swore an oath
to the Cremonese before he was elected and how from the beginning
he appeared to be of a shallow character,[108] because I believe that it is
very well known to many readers.

The sellers of churches, that is, the Milanese captains and lesser vassals,
were griefstricken when they saw themselves deprived of money.
They therefore seized the opportunity of a certain sermon that the
venerable Ariald preached to the people, saying that it was not lawful
to fast in the days of Whitsuntide, to cause a riot among the people,
on the pretext that this was contrary to the liturgical practice of St
Ambrose.[109] They plundered the house of the clergy living the common life and, a few days later, drove Ariald himself out of the city.[110]
As he was setting off for another country, he was joined by a certain
man, a priest but in name only,[111] who delivered him up to the kinsmen of the archbishop.[112] They took him, maimed him in all his limbs
and drowned him in a lake.[113] His body was revealed after it had lain
underwater for ten months.[114] When Herlembald,[115] the brother of

105 Summer 1066: see G. Meyer von Knonau (1890) pp. 525–6.

106 After the enforced withdrawal of Archbishop Adalbert of Bremen from court (January
1066) Henry never again allowed a single adviser to dominate decision-making.

107 Arnulf, bishop of Cremona (?1066– c.1091), deposed by Gregory VII, 1078. See G.
Schwartz (1913) p. 112.

108 But see Peter Damian, *Letter* 65, p. 243 (1059): 'an honourable and prudent clerk'.

109 Ariald's sermon: Andreas, *Vita Arialdi* c.17, pp. 1061–2. See C. Violante (1968) p.
672 n. 291; A. Ambrosioni (1988) p. 205 n. 19.

110 The Whit Sunday riots in Milan, 4 June 1066. Cf. Arnulf, *Liber gestorum recentium*
III.18, p. 193; Andreas, *Vita Arialdi* c.20, p. 1065. See C.D. Fonseca (1962) p. 138;
H. Keller (1973) pp. 340–1.

111 Cf. Andreas, *Vita* c.21, p. 1067: 'a certain priest of the neighbourhood, recently
returned from Jerusalem'.

112 To the lady Oliva, niece of Archbishop Wido: Landulf Senior, *Historia Mediolanensis* III.30, p. 95.

113 Lago Maggiore, 27 June 1066: see G. Meyer von Knonau (1890) p. 541; C. D.
Fonseca (1962) p. 139.

114 3 May 1067: see Andreas, *Vita* c.23, p. 1070.

115 Herlembald Cotta, Patarine leader (✝1075). See C. Erdmann (1935) pp. 128–31;
H. E. J. Cowdrey (1968) pp. 31, 35; H. Keller (1977) pp. 184–6; P. Golinelli (1984)
p. 39; see also above n. 8. It is likely that Herlembald had been associated with the
Patarini since 1063/4: C. Violante (1968) p. 640 n. 170.

Landulf, heard of this, he gathered all the Patarini together and laid siege to the fortress of the archbishop's kinsmen, until they delivered up to him the body of the venerable Ariald.[116] The body was brought to Milan and buried with the greatest honour in the church of St Celsus.[117] There through his merits various infirmities are still healed today.[118]

Meanwhile in Cremona the word of God prospered miraculously. To be sure, I shall not trouble to tell how twelve men, led by the zeal of God, swore an oath on the advice of the lord Abbot Christopher;[119] how all the people of Cremona imitated them; how they turned out all the priests and deacons living in concubinage; how they flogged the bishop himself[120] when he attempted to arrest a priest of the Patarini on the very day of the Lord's Passion[121] and how after Easter day they sent worthy men as envoys to the pope. I have, however, decided to include in this work the defence which the venerable pope confided to the men of Cremona through these same envoys.

Alexander,[122] [bishop] servant of the servants of God, to the religious clergy and faithful laymen of the church of Cremona, greeting and apostolic blessing. We offer abundant thanks to God, the inspirer of all good things and the author of good will, who has armed you against the enemy of the human race with the weapons of His virtues and has fervently incited you to destroy simoniacal heresy and the filthiness of unchaste clergy. For He has raised [you] up, as I learn from your letter, against the cunning of the ancient enemy. He who, like a two-headed snake, wickedly vomited over you through his twin gullets the poison of his iniquity, is gasping for breath, transfixed by the javelin of your holy zeal and stabbed by the dagger of your virtue. It is obvious that He who in former times pronounced sentence of damnation on the serpent in paradise,[123] has roused you, as one man, against the present-day cunning of the secret dragon. In order, therefore, that the vigour of this holy apostolic see

---

116 At Rocca d'Arona: Landulf Senior, *Historia* III.30, p. 96; Andreas, *Vita* c. 23, pp. 1070–1.

117 Whit Sunday (27 May) 1067. See G. Meyer von Knonau (1890) p. 558; C. D. Fonseca (1962) p. 139.

118 The cult of Ariald: Andreas, *Vita* p. 1075. See C.D. Fonseca (1962) p. 139.

119 Christopher, abbot of SS. Peter and Paul, Cremona is identified in papal privileges of 24 March 1071 and 10 March 1078: *Acta pontificum Romanorum inedita* ed. J. Pflugk-Harttung 2, 115 (no. 150); 3, 14 (no. 15).

120 Arnulf (above n. 107).

121 8 April 1067. See W. Berschin (1972) p. 7.

122 Alexander II, *JL* 4637 (dated 1067 in *Regesta pontificum Romanorum* 1, 581), known only from its inclusion in Bonizo's work. See W. Berschin (1972) pp. 7, 24, 110 n. 502.

123 Genesis 3: 14–15.

may assist your holy endeavours, we decree that in all circumstances you must
observe the following command, which we have no doubt has been intended
by our holy predecessors and by almost all the makers of the holy canons:
namely, that subdeacons and deacons, but especially priests, who indulge in
carnal relations with women or are polluted with the filth of simony, shall
both lose their ecclesiastical benefices and be deprived of the office of dignity
which they have assumed. For it is intolerable that anyone who is deprived of
the honour of the order which he has received either through fleshly incontin-
ence or through trafficking in sacrilegious venality, should enjoy ecclesiastical
power any more. We command other clergy, however, those namely who
perform lesser offices, if they are bound to lawful wives, to remain in their
places and we do not deny [them] adequate benefices at the Church's expense.
But so that you may take counsel and receive answers from our authority on
other matters besides these that are indispensable for you, we exhort you that
prudent men from among you shall not disdain to come to the synod which,
under God's direction, we shall celebrate after next Easter,[124] *so that they*
may clearly explain to us, not through the medium of a letter but through a
verbal communication, whatever you require of us and what will be of use to
you. To this war that you have begun with the zeal of divine fervour the
Roman see hastens not slothfully, but with all the urgency of virtue; she
stretches forth her arm; she interposes the shield of defence and incites you to
attack the members of the devil with greater and greater vigour. Therefore
let each of you, girded with the sword of divine virtue, say, 'Who[125] *is on the*
Lord's side? Come to me' and, like Moses, let him rush from gate to gate
throughout the camp,[125] *a fiery warrior against the sacrilegious, so that he*
may close with slaughtered corpses the door of simoniacal venality and clerical
adultery, through which the devil has entered your church. May the Almighty,
O most beloved sons, bless you with His right hand and, through the offices
of His blessed apostle Peter, open to you the door of the kingdom of heaven.

Fired by these salubrious reminders, the men of Cremona immediately began to obey God's commands and expelled the simoniacs and
the unchaste from their church. The men of Piacenza imitated them,
submitting themselves without delay to the obedience of Rome. They
cast out their bishop, Denis,[126] who had been excommunicated by the

---

124 23 March 1068. Alexander 'according to his custom held a synod of bishops on the
Sunday after Easter' (*Annales Altahenses* 1068, p. 74), i.e. 30 March 1068. See
Regesta pontificum Romanorum 1, 583.

125 /125 Exodus 32: 26–7.

126 Denis, bishop of Piacenza (1048/9–?1082): see G. Schwartz (1913) p. 191; G.
Fornasari (1989) pp. 297–305. Bonizo's is the only reference to his excommunication in Alexander's pontificate.

pope, and all confirmed the Pataria on oath.

At this same time Hugh Candidus (whom we mentioned above), after suffering many and various afflictions under Cadalus, at length came to the venerable pope and sought and obtained pardon.[127] He was sent to Spain to perform the office of legate,[128] but whatever he built up, he destroyed again. For at first he persecuted the simoniacs very strenuously, but subsequently he accepted their money and reconciled them. When word of this reached Rome, they immediately recalled him from Spain and commanded him to live in Rome.[129] They showed him this humanity above all out of reverence for him who had ordained him, namely the blessed Pope Leo.[130]

Meanwhile Archbishop Wido came to Milan and was moved by penitence to lay down his pontifical insignia and to live in a private manner.[131] When the sellers of churches (whom we mentioned above) saw this, they very quickly turned his capricious mind to evil and gave him lethal advice: to sell the bishopric to a certain clerk named Godfrey[132] (who was sprung from noble parentage and was an extremely eloquent man, but ready for any crime) and to take refuge in his fortress. This was done without delay. On the advice of the simoniacs, the Milanese captains and the Lombard bishops, this Godfrey crossed the Alps, approached the king and found the king's youthful mind an easy prey.[133] For he promised that he would destroy the Pataria, capture Herlembald alive and send him over the mountains, if the king would invest him with the Milanese bishopric. In return for this promise and for a small sum of money he received the investiture which he asked for, but he did not obtain the bishopric.

127 He must have been reconciled as early as 1063, since in that year he held a legatine council in Avignon: J. Ramackers (1931–2) p. 32 n. 1.

128 His legation began before the death of King Ferdinand I of León-Castile (27 December 1065) and continued until November 1068: F. Lerner (1931) pp. 18–31; G. Säbekow (1931) pp. 13–14.

129 He was in Rome in 1069: Alexander II, *JL* 4651, cited by R. Hüls (1977) p. 159. Bonizo's allegations are not corroborated elsewhere: F. Lerner (1931) pp. 31, 35. Hugh undertook a second legation in 1071: below p. 217.

130 See above p. 191.

131 Cf. Arnulf, *Liber* III.20, pp. 196–7: he was 'now aged and had long been crippled by weakness in all his limbs'.

132 Godfrey, archbishop of Milan (1071–5): see G. Schwartz (1913) pp. 80–1. He belonged to the *capitanei* family of Castiglione Olona: H. Keller (1979) p. 67 n. 14.

133 In 1071, according to *Annales Altahenses* p. 82. See G. Meyer von Knonau (1894) pp. 101–2; H. E. J. Cowdrey (1968) p. 36; H. Keller (1973) p. 344.

For when he heard of his endeavour, Herlembald protected by God gathered a multitude of the army of God and withdrew from his control all the fortresses belonging to the jurisdiction of the bishop. He subsequently besieged him for many days in Castiglione, his hereditary castle.[134] While he was under siege and seemed about to be taken prisoner, the simoniac and unchaste clergy set fire to the middle of the city of Milan during the night, the author of this deed being a certain clerk, whose name I leave to the intelligent reader to find out, knowing for certain and affirming without hesitation that the author of so great a crime is unworthy of the priesthood.[135] What more is there to tell? The fire swept through buildings and destroyed the glorious basilicas of the blessed martyrs, until at last it consumed half the city. When news of this reached the Milanese who chanced to be absent at the siege, a very great terror seized them and they at once returned home, leaving Herlembald with a few godfearing men. The mighty soldier of God, however, stood, like Judas Maccabeus,[136] unperturbed; he strengthened the siege and celebrated the holy day of Easter[137] there. When the festival of Easter was over, Godfrey, having with him a multitude of cavalry and foot-soldiers, fought with Herlembald and took to flight. Thus by God's mercy the soldier of God obtained a bloodless victory and returned to Milan.[138]

It was at this same time that the Normans invaded the Campagna.[139] When Hildebrand beloved of God learned of this, he immediately summoned the magnificent Duke Godfrey[140] to the aid of St Peter. For that duke had chanced to come to Italy at this time, bringing with him the most excellent Countess Matilda, daughter of the famous Duke Boniface. He gathered the whole multitude of his army and came to

134 On this 'truly impregnable fortification' (Arnulf, *Liber* III.21, p. 199): see H. Keller (1979) p. 64.

135 12 March 1071, according to Arnulf, *Liber* III.22, p. 200; 3 March, according to *Notae sanctae Mariae Mediolanenses, MGH SS* 18, 385. The perpetrator has not been identified.

136 The Jewish commander Judas Maccabeus (✝160 B.C.), who resisted the persecution inflicted by the Syrian empire. See C. Erdmann (1935) p. 231.

137 24 April 1071.

138 'When the days of Easter were drawing nigh': Arnulf, *Liber* III.22, p. 200. Herlembald failed to take Castiglione.

139 Richard I, prince of Capua in 1066 captured Ceprano and plundered the Campagna as far as Rome. (Alexander II had entrusted responsibility for defending the Campagna to William of Montreuil, Richard's rebellious son-in-law.) See G. Meyer von Knonau (1890) pp. 543–7; F. Chalandon (1907) pp. 221–5.

140 Godfrey 'the Bearded' (above p. 194 n. 101).

Rome with his wife and the most noble Matilda; he expelled the Normans from the Campagna without a battle and restored it to Roman jurisdiction.[141] This was the first service that the most excellent daughter of Boniface offered to the blessed prince of the apostles. Not long afterwards, as a result of her many services pleasing to God, she deserved to be called the daughter of St Peter.[142]

After these events Herlembald protected by God, wishing to free the Milanese church from the slavery of simony and following the advice of the pope and of Hildebrand beloved of God, on the day of the holy Epiphany,[143] supported by the religious clergy not only of Milan but also of Cremona and Piacenza, resolved to have Otto[144] as bishop, by the election of the clergy according to the decrees of the holy Fathers. He was a clerk of that same church, noble indeed in his birth but nobler still in his conduct, elected by the religious clergy and approved by the catholic people. The ancient serpent beheld this with an unfavourable eye. He found certain men after his own heart and through them stirred up a riot among the people. Fully armed, they surrounded the palace where Herlembald protected by God was now residing with the archbishop elect; they seized the palace, plundering everything; they wounded the archbishop elect, dragged him to the altar of St Mary and forced him to swear never again to intervene in that bishopric.[145] They next delivered him up to a clerk of that church to be guarded until morning. When morning came, however, Herlembald protected by God arrived undaunted at the church. When the sellers of churches and the kinsmen of the unchaste priests saw him, they set up a cry and joined battle, but by God's mercy the soldier of God very rapidly gained the victory. For he forced the enemies of God to flee far from the city, restored twofold all the church property that had been stolen by the enemies of God and took

---

141 Godfrey's campaign forced the Normans back over the River Garigliano (mid-1067) but was less decisive than Bonizo claimed. No other source mentions the participation of his step-daughter, Matilda (above p. 194 n. 100). See G. Meyer von Knonau (1890) pp. 551–6; H. E. J. Cowdrey (1983) p. 120; E. Goez (1995) pp. 161, 209.

142 See C. Erdmann (1935) p. 232 and also above pp. 46–50.

143 6 January 1072. Cf. Arnulf, *Liber* III.23, pp. 203–4; Landulf Senior, *Historia* III.29, p. 95. See G. Meyer von Knonau (1894) pp. 175–6; H. E. J. Cowdrey (1968) p. 36; H. Keller (1973) p. 344.

144 Atto, archbishop of Milan (1072); cardinal priest of S. Marco (✝ before 1086): see G. Schwartz (1913) pp. 81–2; R. Abbondanza (1962) pp. 564–5; R. Hüls (1977) p. 185.

145 Cf. Arnulf, *Liber* III.23, p. 205; IV.2, p. 206; Landulf, *Historia* III.29, p. 95. See H. E. J. Cowdrey (1968) p. 36; H. Keller (1973) p. 345; A. Lucioni (1981) pp. 63–70.

possession of the church and the palace.[146] The Lord's elect could have
been enthroned that very day without any opposition, if only the bond
of the oath had not stood in the way. For this reason religious men
were sent to Rome, who explained matters to the pope.

When the venerable Alexander heard of it, he said that an oath taken
against ecclesiastical law must not be kept and he judged by a general
decree of the cardinal bishops, priests and deacons that [Otto] was
the rightful elect of Milan.[147] He next sent a letter to the king, in
which he admonished him as a son to cast out the hatred for the
servants of God that he had conceived in his mind and to allow the
Milanese church to have a bishop according to God.[148] On hearing
this, the king immediately sent his advisers[149] from his side. They came
to Lombardy and set up their court in Novara, where they assembled
a crowd of bishops and there confirmed on oath that it was the king's
will that Godfrey should be consecrated.[150] When the Lombard
bishops heard this, although they had been excommunicated from the
church, they gladly consecrated – or rather, execrated – him.[151] It
chanced that certain clergy of the Milanese church were present at
this execration and among them was Tedald,[152] who was to invade
that diocese in Godfrey's lifetime. Learning of this, the venerable Otto,
the elect of Milan, turned to the Roman see, where all ecclesiastical
cases are settled.[153]

Hugh Candidus, whom we mentioned above, sought from the lord pope
a legation in France.[154] There he laboured mightily against divine and

146 7 January 1072. But Arnulf, *Liber* III.23, p. 205 claimed that neither Milanese
faction was victorious.

147 Cf. Arnulf, *Liber* IV.2, p. 206: 'Archdeacon Hildebrand judged on his own
authority (since he was a cardinal) that the oath imposed on [Atto] by violence
was to be regarded as utterly invalid'. See H. E. J. Cowdrey (1998) p. 70.

148 This letter has not survived. Cf. Gregory VII, *Registrum* IV.1, p. 290; *JL* 4999:
Epistolae Vagantes 14, p. 34: when he was 'still in the office of deacon' Hildebrand
'often admonished [Henry] by letters and envoys to desist from his wickedness'.

149 Bonizo identified the principal envoy as Rapoto: see p. 232.

150 Arnulf, *Liber* IV.3, pp. 207–8 dated this assembly at the time of Alexander's death
(21 April 1073). F.-J. Schmale (1979b) p. 332 dated it before the Roman synod of
April 1072.

151 Cf. Gregory VII, *Registrum* I.11, p. 18.

152 Tedald, archbishop of Milan (1075–85): see G. Schwartz (1913) pp. 82–3. See p. 232.

153 Arnulf, *Liber* IV.4, pp. 208–9 dated Atto's withdrawal to Rome after Gregory
VII's accession, 22 April 1073.

154 He intervened in Toulouse on 15 August 1071: F. Lerner (1931) p. 35; T. Schieffer
(1934) p. 75.

human law, as will be told subsequently in its right place. At this same period Cadalus, bishop of Parma perished in body and soul.[155] Not long afterwards the bishop of Ravenna also died.[156] Meanwhile Wibert of Parma, whom we mentioned above, made remarkable efforts to obtain the bishopric of Parma.[157] For he approached the king and overwhelmed him with many prayers and gifts in order that the bishopric might be given to him. His petitions, however, were in vain, since he was resisted by all men, both kinsmen and strangers, great and small, clergy and laity; so he betook himself to the empress, who chanced to be present at that time, and through her intervention he received the bishopric of Ravenna.[158] That of Parma, however, was given to Eberhard, a clerk of Cologne.[159] Wibert came to Lombardy and entered Ravenna with a huge crowd and with a great show of power, as his custom was. Not many days afterwards, during the season of Lent,[160] he came for the sake of consecration to Rome, where a synod had already been celebrated. In that synod Hugh Candidus was publicly accused of simony by the monks of Cluny and by certain religious bishops.[161] There also at the instigation of the empress the pope publicly excommunicated certain counsellors of the king who wished to separate him from the unity of the Church.[162] But let us now

155 This is the only clue to the date of Cadalus's death, apparently late 1071: G. Schwartz (1913) pp. 186–7.

156 Henry, archbishop of Ravenna (1052–72) probably died 1 January 1072: G. Schwartz (1913) pp. 157–8.

157 J. Ziese (1982) pp. 26–7 discounted this story; but D. Lück (1970a) p. 32 saw in this appointment of a member of the clergy of Cologne the deliberate thwarting of Wibert's ambitions by Anno of Cologne.

158 Agnes was present at the German court in Worms on 25 July 1072: see G. Meyer von Knonau (1894) pp. 160–2; M.L. Bulst-Thiele (1933) pp. 92–3.

159 Eberhard, bishop of Parma (1072–85): see G. Schwartz (1913) p. 187.

160 Between 13 February and 24 March 1073. G. Miccoli (1966b) pp. 382, 394 argued that Bonizo was present at this synod.

161 Gregory VII, *Registrum* I.6, p. 9 (30 April 1073) instructed his legates in France to make peace between Hugh Candidus and Abbot Hugh and the congregation of Cluny. For Hugh's previous association with Hugh Candidus (1068): H. Diener (1959) pp. 362–3; H. E. J. Cowdrey (1970) pp. 223–4. See also F. Lerner (1931) pp. 36–8; G. Säbekow (1931) p. 17; T. Schieffer (1934) pp. 75–6; R. Hüls (1977) p. 159; H. E. J. Cowdrey (1998) p. 473.

162 Bonizo alone recorded this excommunication in the Lenten synod of 1073. The same royal advisers were excommunicated by Gregory VII in the Lenten synod of 1075 (*Registrum* II.52a, p. 196). Bonizo identified one of these advisers as Count Eberhard (p. 231). Lampert, *Annales* 1076, p. 282 identified two others as Udalric of Godesheim and Hartman. See G. Meyer von Knonau (1894) pp. 198–9; M. L. Bulst-Thiele (1933) pp. 97–8; R. Schieffer (1981) pp. 109–10.

return to the narrative.

Wibert came to Rome, accompanied by Bishop Denis of Piacenza, who had been deposed many years before by the same pope,[163] and, clothing himself in the feigned simplicity of a sheep, he deceived many, especially Hildebrand, beloved of God. Although the latter on many occasions asked the pope to give Wibert his blessing, the pope refused his consent[164] and he is said to have declared, full of the spirit of prophecy, '*I* indeed *am already at the point of being sacrificed and the time of my departure has come,*[165] but you will feel his hatred.' The event subsequently proved this to be true. What more is there to tell? After his consecration had been solemnly celebrated, Wibert bound himself by an oath to be faithful to Pope Alexander and his successors, provided that they were elected by the better cardinals and not appointed by emperor, king or patrician.[166] He kept this oath well. For when the venerable Alexander was dead and the venerable Hildebrand had been elected by the better cardinals, the pious archbishop performed the subjection due to him so well that, when he was summoned to the synod, he came and sat in that synod at the pope's right hand, according to the privilege of his church, and acknowledged in every way that he was the pope, spontaneously and not as the result of an extorted confession.[167] But let us return to the correct order of events. The festival of Easter was celebrated[168] and then Wibert obtained from the blessed pope and the venerable archdeacon permission to return to Ravenna. Before he had entered that city, the pope's death was announced to him. For on the day of the nativity of St George, the blessed Alexander rendered up his spirit to heaven.[169]

---

163 J. Ziese (1982) p. 29 suggested that Wibert brought this suffragan of Ravenna (above p. 213, n. 126) with him to Rome to effect a reconciliation with the pope.

164 Bonizo alone recorded this refusal, doubted by J. Ziese (1982) p. 32 n. 10, but accepted by T. Schmidt (1977) pp. 171–2; H. E. J. Cowdrey (1998) p. 63. Cf. Gregory VII, *Registrum* I.3, p. 6, concerning 'the charity that … [Wibert] promised to show to the Roman church and to me in particular'.

165 II Timothy 4:6.

166 Text of Wibert's oath: Deusdedit, *Collectio canonum* IV.423, p. 599. From the ninth century the popes demanded from the archbishops of Ravenna, on conferring the pallium, an oath confirming their conformity with the Roman church in faith and morals. See J. Ziese (1982) pp. 32–3.

167 March 1074: see p. 224. This privilege was conferred by Pope Clement II, 1047: see J. Ziese (1982) pp. 35–6.

168 31 March 1073.

169 23 April. According to Gregory VII, *Registrum* I.6, p. 9, he died on 21 April 1073. See G. Meyer von Knonau (1894) p. 202 n. 27.

Book VII

On the same day as the body of the pope was being buried in the church of the Holy Saviour[1] and while the venerable Hildebrand was preoccupied with his funeral, there was suddenly a gathering of clergy and of men and women shouting, 'Hildebrand for bishop!'[2] When he heard it, the venerable archdeacon was struck with terror and quickly ran to the pulpit, wishing to calm the people, but Hugh Candidus[3] forestalled him and addressed the people thus. 'Brethren, you know that ever since the days of the lord Pope Leo it has been Hildebrand who has exalted the holy Roman church and liberated this city. Therefore, because we cannot have a better, or even as good a man to elect to the Roman bishopric, let us elect him: a man ordained in our church, known to you and to us and excellent in all respects.' After the cardinal bishops, priests and deacons and the clergy next in rank had cried out, as is customary, 'St Peter elects Pope Gregory', he was immediately seized[4] by the people and dragged away and enthroned in St Peter ad Vincula[5] – not in Brixen[6] – unwillingly.

The next day, revolving in his mind the great danger that he had fallen

1 22 April 1073 in the Lateran church. If, as G. Miccoli (1966b) p. 382 argued, Bonizo was at the Lenten synod of 1073 (above p. 218 n. 160), perhaps he was still in Rome for the funeral and Gregory VII's election.

2 Cf. Gregory VII, *Registrum* I.3, p. 5. See G. Meyer von Knonau (1894) pp. 203–9; A. Fliche (1924b) pp. 71–90; P. Schmid (1926) pp. 151–71; H.-G. Krause (1960) pp. 159–69; H. E. J. Cowdrey (1998) pp. 72–4.

3 Cf. Gregory VII, *Registrum* I.6, p. 9: Hugh Candidus 'was present at both [deathbed and election]'. No other account ascribes the leading role to Hugh. A. Fliche (1924b) pp. 74–5 and (1926) p. 74 argued that Bonizo invented this role to discredit Hugh's allegations against the legality of the election in 1076 and 1080 (below pp. 234, 247). But see F. Lerner (1931) pp. 38–43; H. E. J. Cowdrey (1998) p. 73.

4 /4 Cf. John the Deacon, *Vita Gregorii Magni* I.44, *MPL* 75, col. 81B, describing the election of Gregory I (590): he was 'recognised, seized, dragged away and consecrated supreme pontiff'. Anti-Gregorian polemicists drew on the same passage to satirise Hildebrand's election. Benzo of Alba, *To Henry IV* VII.2, below p. 375; Wido of Ferrara, *De scismate Hildebrandi* II, p. 553: 'Hildebrand was captured, Hildebrand was torn to pieces, Hildebrand was dragged away, Hildebrand was elected.' Other Gregorian authors using John the Deacon's account: I. S. Robinson (1978a) pp. 31–9. See H. E. J. Cowdrey (1998) p. 73.

5 S. Pietro in Vincoli was, like St Peter's basilica, a traditional place for the papal enthronement, e.g. Alexander II, October 1061. See T. Schmidt (1977) p. 88.

6 Bonizo contrasted Gregory's lawful election with the intrusion of anti-pope Clement III (Wibert of Ravenna) at the council of Brixen (25 June 1080). See below p. 246 and above pp. 54–5, 61.

into, he began to vacillate and to be full of sadness. Nevertheless he summoned his reserves of faith and hope, which he did very effectively, and found that he could do no other than to notify his election to the king and through his means avoid the papal burden that had been thrust upon him, if he could. He immediately sent him a letter informing him of the death of the pope and announcing his own election and threatened that if the king *gave his consent*[7] to this election, he would never bear patiently with his iniquity. Events, however, fell out quite differently from what he hoped. For the king instantly sent Bishop Gregory of Vercelli, the chancellor of the Italian kingdom, to confirm his election and to be present at his consecration. This he did.[8] On the day of the fast of Whitsuntide[9] he was ordained a priest and on the Nativity of the Apostles[10] he was consecrated bishop at the altar of the apostles by the cardinals according to ancient custom. The empress[11] was present at his consecration, together with the excellent Duchess Beatrice, then a widow. For the magnificent Duke Godfrey had died a few days before.[12]

As soon as he undertook the administration of the holy Roman church, the venerable pontiff considered that his best course was at the outset to warn the king not to sell bishoprics and to recognise that he was subject to the holy Roman church. He at once appointed the glorious empress, the mother of the king, to be the agent of this holy legation, having with her in her entourage the venerable bishops

7 Cf. John the Deacon, *Vita Gregorii* I.40, *MPL* 75, col. 79BC. Bonizo's account is modelled on an incident in Gregory I's election: 'he secretly sent a letter to Emperor Maurice, adjuring him and demanding with many a prayer that he should never *give his consent* to the people'. Gregory VII could not have written such a letter to Henry IV since he regarded him as 'outside the communion' (*Registrum* I.85, p. 121), having failed to dismiss the counsellors excommunicated in the Lenten synod of 1073 (above p. 218 n. 162). Until he repented and was reconciled to the pope, Gregory could have no contact with him. Cf. *Registrum* I.21, p. 35. See G. B. Borino (1956a) pp. 361–74; G. B. Borino (1956b) pp. 313–43; C. Schneider (1972) pp. 41–7; H. E. J. Cowdrey (1998) p. 92.

8 No other source places Gregory of Vercelli at the consecration. According to Abbot Walo of St Arnulf, Metz's letter to Gregory VII, 'that devil of Vercelli, together with his accomplices, labours to prevent your being confirmed in the see' (ed. J. M. Watterich [1862] pp. 740–2). See H. E. J. Cowdrey (1998) p. 93.

9 22 May 1073, the Ember Wednesday after Pentecost and the earliest canonical opportunity for the ordination.

10 Saturday, 29 June 1073. In fact he was consecrated a day later: H. E. J. Cowdrey (1998) p. 74. Canon law required episcopal consecrations to be performed on Sunday.

11 Agnes had resided mainly in Italy since her son's coming of age (March 1065): see M. L. Bulst-Thiele (1933) p. 97.

12 Godfrey 'the Bearded', duke of Lower Lotharingia died on 24 December 1069.

Gerald of Ostia,[13] Hubert of Palestrina[14] and Rainald of Como.[15] She crossed the Alps and found her son in the region of Bavaria.[16] What more is there to tell? The Roman legates were received with honour by the king and after he had listened to their corrective advice every day for many days, he at last dismissed from his society five of his familiars whom Pope Alexander had previously excommunicated.[17] He was then requested to be present at a synod. He made a pretence of assembling the bishops, while inwardly determining that in no circumstances would a council be celebrated in his kingdom, as the event subsequently proved.[18] For the council was disrupted by the efforts of Archbishop Liemar of Bremen,[19] a most eloquent man, exceptionally learned in liberal studies.[20] For he said that, according to ancient privileges, the right of acting as the deputy of the Roman pontiff in the territory of Germany was granted to the bishop of Mainz and consequently it was not lawful for Roman legates to celebrate a synod within the area of his legation.[21] He thus failed to take into consideration that chapter of Leo I sent to the bishop of Thessaly, in which we read: 'For the pope commits his functions to all archbishops in such a way *that* they are *summoned to share in* his *responsibilities, but not in the fullness of power.*'[22]

13 Gerald, cardinal bishop of Ostia (1072/3–1077): see R. Hüls (1977) pp. 100–1. The legation began in March 1074: O. Schumann (1912) pp. 23, 26; H. E. J. Cowdrey (1998) p. 98.

14 Hubert, cardinal bishop of Palestrina (?1073–?1082): see R. Hüls (1977) p. 110.

15 Rainald, bishop of Como (1061–84): see G. Schwartz (1913) p. 49; W. Goez (1974) p. 490.

16 In 'Pforzheim in Swabia' (Berthold, *Annales* 1074, p. 276). The reconciliation of the king took place in Nuremberg, 27 April 1074: G. Meyer von Knonau (1894) pp. 377–8; I. S. Robinson (1999) pp. 132–3.

17 Bonizo alone reported the dismissal of these advisers (above p. 218 n. 162). According to Berthold, *Annales* 1074, p. 277, the advisers promised the legates 'that they would return all the property of the churches that they had unjustly acquired'. See H. E. J. Cowdrey (1998) p. 99.

18 There is no evidence that Henry supported the episcopate in their opposition to a reforming synod. Henry was not blamed in Rome for the failure of the synod: Gregory VII, *Registrum* II.30, pp. 163–5. See C. Erdmann (1938) pp. 242–55; C. Schneider (1972) pp. 84–5; H. E. J. Cowdrey (1998) p. 99.

19 Liemar, archbishop of Bremen (1072–1101).

20 Cf. below p. 254. Cf. Adam of Bremen, *Gesta Hammaburgensis ecclesiae pontificum* pp. 2, 281 (Liemar's 'worldly wisdom' and 'study of divine philosophy').

21 Liemar's explanation: letter to Bishop Hezilo of Hildesheim, *MGH Die Briefe der deutschen Kaiserzeit* 5, 15–35. See C. Erdmann (1938) pp. 238–9.

22 Pope Leo I, letter to his deputy, Bishop Anastasius of Thessalonica, JK 411 (*MPL* 67, 293). The most frequent canonical text in Bonizo's writings, appearing in *Liber*

What more need be said? Archbishop Liemar was for this reason suspended by the Roman legates from the office of a priest.[23] Then, as the council had been disrupted by his cunning and since the king had promised that he would freely perform all that the Roman legates demanded, the legates returned with honour to Rome, laden with great gifts and bearing with them a letter from the king, in which he promised the due subjection in all respects to the venerable Pope Gregory.[24] A few days later, however, a certain Herman, bishop of Bamberg,[25] came to Rome for the purpose of receiving the pallium. He had already been mentioned in the king's letter, which informed the pope that the king had been deceived by certain malign persons into conferring the bishopric on him in return for money. When enquiry was made and this was found to be so, Herman was deposed from the bishopric[26] and another[27] enthroned in his place by the command of the lord pope.[28] The latter was afterwards endowed with the dignity of the pallium by the same pope.[29] The same procedure was followed in the case of the bishop of Constance.[30]

While this was happening, the Milanese captains, the sellers of churches

---

de vita christiana III.30, III.108, IV.80, pp. 81, 108, 146. His reinterpretation of the text applied it to the powers of all archbishops vis-à-vis the pope. See R. L. Benson (1967) pp. 195–217, especially p. 210; W. Berschin (1972) pp. 50–1.

23 The legates ordered him to explain himself at the autumn synod, 30 November 1074 (above n. 21). When he failed to do so, the pope suspended him: Gregory VII, *Registrum* II.28, p. 161.

24 Not extant. Cf. Gregory VII, *Registrum* II.30, p. 163: Henry 'sent us by [the legates] a demonstration of appropriate greetings and devoted service'.

25 Herman, bishop of Bamberg (1065–75). See R. Schieffer (1972a) pp. 22–46; R. Schieffer (1975) pp. 55–76.

26 The Roman synod of 1075 suspended Herman (*Registrum* II.52a, p. 196). On 12 April the pope deposed Herman for simony (*Registrum* II.76, p. 239). Herman set out for Rome to recover his office and 'sending his envoys in advance with abundant gifts' he tried 'to corrupt the [pope's] innocence and [his] colleagues' integrity' (*Registrum* III.3, p. 247). See also below p. 254.

27 Rupert, bishop of Bamberg (1075–1102).

28 Henry IV invested Rupert with the bishopric on 30 November 1075. On papal and royal cooperation in this appointment: Gebhard of Salzburg, *Epistola ad Herimannum Mettensem* c.34, p. 279. See R. Schieffer (1981) p. 127.

29 Leo IX is known to have conferred the pallium on the bishop of Bamberg (*JL* 4287) and Bishop Gunther of Bamberg reported receiving the pallium in the early 1060s (letter in *Codex Udalrici* 203, p. 53). Gregory VII described Bamberg as 'the special daughter of the Roman church' (*Registrum* II.76, III.1, pp. 239, 243).

30 Bishop Charles (Carloman) of Constance (1070–1) was accused of simony at the council of Mainz and resigned his office (1071). His successor, Otto (1071–86) was accused of disobedience in 1075, excommunicated in 1076 and deposed in 1080.

whom we mentioned above, had a conference with the king and turned his mind to evil courses; for they promised him that they would destroy the Pataria and kill Herlembald. The king heard this gladly and willingly promised whatever they asked for.[31]

Meanwhile the venerable Gregory, suspecting no evil of the king, assembled a synod.[32] Bishop Wibert of Ravenna attended, together with an innumerable crowd of bishops gathered from various provinces. In the course of a discussion of the Piacenzans and the Cremonese, Wibert made extraordinary accusations against the Cremonese. It became perfectly obvious, however, through the intervention of Dodo, a young man of excellent character and a citizen of Cremona, that Wibert was lying. For in the presence of the whole synod Dodo both absolved the Cremonese from infamy and branded Wibert himself with infamy.[33] What more is there to tell? When these and other matters were settled, Robert[34] was excommunicated in that synod, together with the Normans. Present at that synod were the most excellent Countess Matilda,[35] Margrave Azzo[36] and Gisulf, prince of Salerno.[37] When the council had been lawfully celebrated and while the bishops returned to their own sees, Wibert remained with the pope in Rome.[38] He promised the pope that he would undertake a great expedition against the Normans and that he would participate in the pope's campaign against the counts of Bagnorea after Easter.[39] By

31 While Bonizo's report suggests that this meeting, not otherwise recorded, occurred before the papal synod of March 1074, a later reference to the meeting (p. 229) seems to place it a year later.

32 Lenten synod, 9–15 March 1074: Gregory VII, *Registrum* I.42–3, pp. 65, 66.

33 Wido of Ferrara, *De scismate Hildebrandi* I.10, p. 543 (writing in Wibert of Ravenna's entourage *c.*1086) recalled the unseemly treatment by the Cremonese of 'a certain priest taken in adultery'. If Wibert was Wido's source – see A. Fliche (1937) pp. 275–7 – this may have been the issue raised by Wibert at the synod. See J. Ziese (1982) pp. 36–7.

34 Robert Guiscard, duke of Apulia and Calabria (✝1085) was punished for his attack on Benevento early in 1074. Cf. Gregory VII, *Registrum* I.85a, p. 123.

35 Cf. Gregory VII, *Registrum* I.40, p. 63 (3 January 1074) to Matilda of Tuscany.

36 Margrave Albert Azzo II of Este (✝1097), father of Welf IV of Bavaria, accused of contracting an uncanonical third marriage: *Registrum* I.57, II.9, pp. 84, 139.

37 Gisulf II, prince of Salerno (1052–77 ✝ after 1088).

38 Cf. *Vita Anselmi episcopi Lucensis* p. 19. See J. Ziese (1982) p. 38.

39 After 20 April 1074. 'The counts of Bagnorea' cannot be identified: F. Schneider (1914) 111–12. See also P. Partner (1972) pp. 127–8. Wibert's involvement was recorded only by Bonizo, whose emphasis on his participation must be seen in the context of Wibert's later polemic against Gregory's military activities: C. Erdmann (1935) p. 232. See above p. 46.

means of these and other such crafty devices he deceived the mind of the pope, who suspected no evil.

Wibert's mind, however, harboured the anger of a savage monster and pondered very different objectives, as events were to demonstrate. For throughout almost the whole period of Lent,[40] while he lingered in Rome, going about the city under the pretext of a pilgrimage, he made friends with any pernicious men whom he could find and with those men who hated the pope *for righteousness' sake*[41] and gave them money and bound them by means of an oath. Among these men was Cencius, son of the prefect Stephen, whom we mentioned above as being associated with Cadalus in the time of Pope Alexander.[42] On the death of his father,[43] in Pope Alexander's time, he had wished to obtain the office of prefect but he had been rejected by all the Romans because of the ferocity of his temper and it was with universal agreement that the office of prefect was given to another Cencius, the son of a certain prefect John.[44] Although he bore the same name, the latter was utterly different in his character. The former Cencius hoped for all things evil; the latter for all good.[45] The former without any motive killed his godfather and utterly destroyed his house. He was the partner of brigands and the helper of robbers and, after many different adulteries that he himself committed or whose perpetrators he protected, he transformed Rome from a free woman into a slave. For he built a tower of remarkable size on the bridge of St Peter and forced all who crossed there to pay tribute.[46] Such was the pestilent

---

40 5 March – 19 April 1074.

41 Cf. Matthew 5:10.

42 See above p. 208 n. 85.

43 On the problem of 'the prefect Stephen' see D. Whitton (1980) pp. 223–5. No Roman prefect of this name is found after the death of the prefect Stephen in 1002, who cannot have been the father of Cencius Stephani, who died in 1077. There are, however, long periods in the eleventh century when the prefect's name is unknown: e.g. 1017–36 and 1051–9. See also G. B. Borino (1952a) pp. 411–12. The office of prefect: L. Halphen (1907) pp. 16–27, 147–56; P. Toubert (1973) p. 1353.

44 Cencius, Roman prefect (?1071–1077), son of the prefect John Tiniosus (✝ before March 1065). See C. Erdmann (1935) pp. 197–8, 231–2; G. B. Borino (1952a) pp. 412–13; C. Violante (1968) p. 683 n. 324.

45 The relations of the prefect Cencius with the Roman reform party: Peter Damian, *Letters* 135, 145, 155: 3, 456–62, 527–31; 4, 71–3; Berthold, *Annales* 1077, p. 304; Bernold, *Chronicon* 1077, p. 434; Paul of Bernried, *Life of Gregory VII* c.47, below p. 294.

46 He possessed a tower in the district of Parione, where he imprisoned Gregory VII, 25 December 1075 (see p. 232): *Life of Gregory VII: Liber pontificalis* 2, 262. See G. B. Borino (1952a) pp. 413, 431, 434. He also held the Castel S. Angelo in the time

man whom Wibert bound to himself and it was through his means that he armed himself against holy Church.

There were besides in Rome many pernicious men who loathed righteousness, such as the sons and kinsmen of priests living with concubines. From the beginning of his pontificate, however, the venerable pope gave all Roman clergy the option either of living canonically, possessing no private property, according to the rule of the saints, or of quitting the Church's property and living a separate existence in their own homes.[47] Many of these men preferred to live privately rather than to bear the *easy yoke*[48] of the Lord and they were extraordinarily hostile towards the pope, and not only they but their kinsmen also.

There was moreover in Rome an ancient and very evil custom that the blessed pope completely eradicated from that church in his time. For there were in the church of the blessed prince of the apostles more than sixty sextons, who were laymen with wives and several of them also with concubines, whose duty it was to guard that church day and night.[49] All the altars except the greatest were under their control and they sold them daily for prayers. They were all clean-shaven and wore mitres on their heads and claimed to be priests and cardinals and thus they deceived pilgrims who came to pray and especially the crowds of Lombard peasants, who believed them to be priests and trusted in their prayers. *In the dead of night, when all was quiet,*[50] they used the pretext of their guard-duties to perpetrate various robberies and foul debaucheries. With great difficulty the blessed pope drove these men out of the church of the prince of apostles and entrusted it to the guardianship of religious priests. Such were the friends that Wibert made for himself. The venerable Gregory, however, ordered the church of St Peter to be closed to pilgrims until

---

of the antipope Cadalus: above p. 208. The reference here is to another structure on the chief pilgrim route to the Leonine city and St Peter's: D. Whitton (1980) p. 234.

47 For the 'canonical life' of the clergy: above p. 208 n. 89. In the Lateran synod of 1059 Hildebrand had recommended the general adoption of 'the apostolic, that is the common life': A. Werminghoff (1902) pp. 669–75. Cf. Gregory VII, *Registrum* VI.11, pp. 412–13. See C. Dereine (1961) pp. 108–118; G. Picasso (1989) pp. 163–6. Gregory's attempt to enforce the canonical life in Rome: T. Schmidt (1972) pp. 219.

48 Matthew 11:30.

49 Bonizo's editor, E. Dümmler (1891) p. 603 n. 6, saw a parallel between these sextons and the 'custodians' of the cathedral of Arezzo in the 1070s (some laymen, some clergy, the majority married), described in the *Historia custodum Aretinorum*, *MGH SS* 30/2, 1468–82. See R. W. Southern (1953) pp. 128–30.

50 Cf. Virgil, *Georgica* 1, 247.

morning. For until guards were placed to watch throughout the night, many murders were committed there and there were opportunities for many thefts and adulteries.

There was in that church yet another very evil custom that the venerable pope completely eradicated. Every day before first light and very often before dawn had begun to appear, the cardinals in their greed for profit used to celebrate masses at the altar of the prince of the apostles. This the pope forbade them all to do, on St Peter's authority as well as his own, so that they were not permitted thereafter to celebrate mass at the altar of St Peter before the third hour of the day. This measure won him great unpopularity. What more is there to tell? Wibert, like Catiline,[51] made friends with all the evildoers whom he could find. Then, as the festival of Easter was drawing near,[52] he sought and obtained permission from the venerable pope to return to Ravenna, promising that after Easter he would lead an army against the counts of Bagnorea.

Meanwhile the venerable Gregory prepared to make an expedition against the Normans. Meeting Duchess Beatrice at the castle of St Fabian,[53] he summoned her to the expedition, together with her daughter.[54] Although they wished to obey the pope's command with a clear conscience, a disturbance among the lesser vassals in Lombardy prevented them. An insurrection suddenly occurred, which dispersed the expedition and thus the pope returned to Rome with the business unfinished and Beatrice returned to her own territory with her daughter.[55]

Not long afterwards in the suburbs of Rome the pope was suddenly attacked by faintness.[56] Cencius, whom we mentioned above, believing that the pope was already at the point of death, suddenly discharged the hatred that he had harboured in his mind. For in those days he was the executor of a certain Cencius, namely the son of Count

51 Cf. Sallust, *Catilina* 14. This account of Wibert's conspiracy in Lent 1074 is probably a fiction intended to discredit the later anti-pope: J. Ziese (1982) p. 38.

52 20 April 1074.

53 Cf. Gregory VII, *Registrum* I.85, p. 123 (15 June 1074): 'issued on campaign at St Fabian', i.e. Fiano, at the end of the Via Tiberina north of Rome.

54 Matilda: see above p. 194 n. 100. Cf. Amatus, *L'Ystoire de li Normant* VII.12, p. 305. See G. Meyer von Knonau (1894) pp. 416–17; E. Goez (1995) pp. 72, 228–9.

55 No other record survives of this disturbance: E. Goez (1995) p. 229. According to Amatus, *L'Ystoire* VII.13, p. 306, Beatrice's Pisan contingent refused to serve with their enemy, Gisulf II of Salerno.

56 Cf. Gregory VII, *Registrum* II.9, p. 138 (16 October 1074): 'beyond the hope of all those who were with us, we have escaped bodily infirmity'.

Gerard,[57] who had left an estate in his will to the blessed princes of the apostles. That man hateful to God, however, believing the pope to be already dead or near to death, committed the crimes both of sacrilege and perjury by falsifying the will and devoting the estate to his own use, giving only two hundred pounds to the princes of the apostles. When in the meantime the pope recovered, Cencius began to be agitated by this business. What more need I relate? He was convicted of having acted very wickedly and, having given guarantees, he restored the estate to the princes of the apostles according to the will of the dead man.

His fury, however, would not rest. For it was on the advice of this pernicious man that Hugh Candidus, whom we mentioned above,[58] was for a second time converted to an apostate. He journeyed to Apulia and vigorously stirred up Robert[59] and the Normans (who had previously been excommunicated by the pope) against the holy Roman church. For he said that they had been wrongly excommunicated and that the pope was not a pontiff according to the decrees of the holy Fathers, but rather an intruder in the holy Roman church, and he added that he and his supporters would confer the imperial crown on Robert if with his armed might he would expel the pope from the church. After he had murmured this proposal day in, day out, publicly and in private in the court of the duke, however, this was the reply that he obtained from that very prudent duke. 'Since you have need of it, receive from me, if you please, a gift of gold or silver or any other currency, or aid in the form of horses or mules, but you cannot persuade me to take arms against the Roman pontiff. For it is unlawful to believe that it is possible, in response to your or anyone else's hostility, to depose a pope who has been enthroned by the election of the clergy and the approval of the people when the papal throne was vacant, and who has been consecrated at the altar of St Peter by the cardinal bishops.'[60] After being thus shamed and rejected, he betook

57 The families of Cencius Stephani and Gerard of Galeria both originated in Arezzo: see D. Whitton (1980) pp. 224–7. Bonizo is the only source for these transactions.

58 On the implausible character of this report of an alliance between Hugh Candidus (above p. 191 n. 77) and Cencius Stephani: F. Lerner (1931) p. 49.

59 The excommunication of Robert Guiscard: above p. 224 and n. 34. This account of Hugh's relations with Guiscard is implausible: A. Fliche (1926) p. 67 n. 2; F. Lerner (1931) pp. 49–50.

60 Bonizo presumably ascribed this fictional defence of Gregory VII's election to the excommunicate Robert Guiscard because of the duke's subsequent role as defender of the pope in 1084–5: see p. 251.

himself to Wibert, his ally in iniquity.[61]

While these events were taking place, the Milanese captains and lesser vassals, the sellers of churches, returned from their conference with the king[62] and stirred up great strife in Milan by devising certain stratagems. For they attracted the support of the simple folk, who were disinclined to riot, by saying that their aim was to swear allegiance to the cause of the blessed Ambrose.[63] Herlembald, protected by God (of whom we have spoken above) saw how the machinations of the devil increased little by little and burned with anger. He realised that there was nothing more important for him to do than to take up arms like the mighty Judas[64] to defend himself and the people of God who wished to fight for righteousness. What more is there to tell? Every day the number of the unfaithful increased and from day to day the number of the Patarini diminished. It was also at that same time that the whole of the city of Milan was consumed by fire,[65] in which many wonderful churches and in particular the mother church[66] were utterly destroyed. This event gave additional fighting strength to the enemy of mankind. For all men, both friends and enemies, declared with a single voice that this was the fault of the Patarini.[67]

After Easter[68] they suddenly assembled an army and a host of conspirators and they attacked Herlembald, who was not suspecting any mischief. When he attempted to fight back, they murdered him in the open street[69] and pursued and plundered the others. For a whole day

61 J. Ziese (1982) p. 44 dated the cooperation between Hugh and Wibert of Ravenna in constructing 'an anti-Gregorian coalition' in northern Italy to autumn of 1075.

62 See above p. 224 n. 31.

63 For 'the honour [integrity] of St Ambrose' as the rallying-cry of the Milanese anti-Patarine party see above p. 197 n. 4 and H. Keller (1973) pp. 340–1.

64 Judas Maccabeus. See above p. 215 and n. 136.

65 30 March 1075, according to Arnulf, *Liber* IV.8, pp. 212–14 and an inscription in the Milanese church of S. Stefano (W. Wattenbach, *MGH SS* 8, 27 n 55),

66 S. Maria Maggiore, on the site of the present cathedral: see A. Ambrosioni (1988) pp. 208–9.

67 According to Arnulf, critic of the Patarini, the fire was a divine punishment inflicted on all the Milanese (*Liber* IV.8, p. 214).

68 After 5 April 1075. These disturbances were caused by Herlembald's attempt to impose the Roman Easter observances on Milan: Arnulf, *Liber* IV.10, pp. 215–16; Landulf Senior, *Historia* III.30, pp. 96–7. See also G. Meyer von Knonau (1894) pp. 474–6; H. E. J. Cowdrey (1968) pp. 38–9; H. Keller (1973) p. 346.

69 15 April: A. Lucioni (1981) pp. 233–4 n. 14. Herlembald's assassin was the noble Milanese Arnaldus, grandfather of Arnaldus de Raude, 'one of the consuls' of Milan in 1136: Landulf de sancto Paulo, *Historia Mediolanensis* c.66, p. 48.

they shamefully left him, naked and unburied, forgetting his birth and dignity, to the disgrace of all Christendom. At night, however, he received honourable burial by religious men at the church of St Dionysius.[70] At his tomb God performs great miracles even to this day.[71] On the following day, however, [the conspirators] mutilated the ears and nose of a certain priest named Liprand.[72] Those who did not join in the conspiracy were either killed or plundered of their property. Many of the latter came to Cremona[73] and there were most honourably received by the brethren. When they heard of the death of Herlembald, however, all catholics, not only in Rome but as far as the English Channel, were griefstricken, *saying* as they *mourned, How is the mighty fallen,* who fought the war of the Lord.[74]

Meanwhile Pope Gregory assembled a synod during Lent.[75] Wibert was summoned there and, when he refused to come, he was suspended from the office of bishop for the offence of perjury.[76] Hugh Candidus was removed from the church forever,[77] according to the command of the apostle, who said, *As for a man who is heretical, after admonishing him* a first *and second time, have nothing more to do with him.*[78]

---

70 An inscription printed by A. Rimoldi (1964) col. 5, refers to the translation of Herlembald in the monastery of San Dionigi in Milan, 1095. See C. Violante (1983) pp. 66–74.

71 In the papal synod of Lent 1078 Gregory VII proclaimed these miracles and thus canonised Herlembald: Berthold, *Annales* 1077, p. 305. See C. Erdmann (1935) pp. 129–30.

72 The Patarine priest Liutprand (✝1113) earned the enmity of the Milanese establishment by usurping the place of the cathedral clergy in the Easter observances organised by Herlembald in 1075. On his mutilation (cf. Ezechiel 23:25) see Arnulf, *Liber* IV.9, 10, pp. 214, 216; Landulf Senior, *Historia* III.30, p. 97; Landulf de S. Paulo, *Historia* c.3, p. 21; Gregory VII's letter of condolence to Liutprand, JL 4973 (Studi e testi 190, 1957, pp. 94–5). See G. B. Ladner (1956) pp. 222–3; H. E. J. Cowdrey (1968) p. 38; H. Keller (1979) pp. 210–11; J. Vogel (1983) p. 15.

73 See H. Gritsch (1980) p. 26 and n. 72.

74 I Maccabees 9:21.

75 24–28 March 1075.

76 There is no reference to Wibert of Ravenna in the synodal proceedings (Gregory VII, *Registrum* II.52a, pp. 196–7), which record that the synod deposed his suffragan, Denis of Piacenza. J. Ziese (1982) pp. 41–3 suggested that Wibert was present at the Lenten synod of 1075.

77 His deposition is not mentioned in the synodal proceedings (*Registrum* II.52a, pp. 196–7). According to Lampert, *Annales* 1076, p. 253, Hugh was deposed 'a few days before' the council of Worms, 24 January 1076. See also F. Lerner (1931) pp. 50–1; R.Hüls (1977) p. 159.

78 Titus 3:10.

It happened that at this time Cencius, that man hateful to God whom we mentioned above, was held in captivity by the prefect of the city of Rome.[79] He received a capital sentence according to Roman laws. He was undeservedly allowed to live and was set free, however, at the behest of the glorious Matilda,[80] who was present at that time, and of many Roman citizens, after he had surrendered hostages into the hands of the pope, together with the *tower* by means of which he strove to ascend *to heaven*.[81] This tower was utterly destroyed.[82] Meanwhile in Ravenna Wibert was cunningly arming against his lord, the pope.[83] He sent letters summoning together the stubborn Lombard bishops, in particular Archbishop Tedald of Milan,[84] and incited them against the pope. Since this Tedald has been mentioned, however, I shall explain briefly, if I can, how he came to the bishopric of Milan.

When, after the glorious Herlembald had been martyred for the name of Jesus, his death was announced to the king,[85] the latter remembered the promise that he had previously made to the Milanese captains and he at once sent to Italy Count Eberhard,[86] his adviser, whom Pope Alexander had previously excommunicated. Eberhard came to Lombardy and immediately summoned an assembly to Roncaglia, where he thanked the Milanese for the killing of Herlembald and invited them to cross the mountains, promising to give them, as their lord, a bishop whom they desired. He then proclaimed the Patarini public enemies of the king and he put to flight several of the men of Piacenza who were stationed in the neighbourhood and whom he found unprepared, owing to their feebleness of purpose. He received the surrender

79 Cencius, son of John Tiniosus: above p. 225 n. 44. Cf. Beno, *Gesta Romanae ecclesiae* I.8, p. 372 (Gregory 'long crucified [Cencius Stephani] with a thousand thousand deaths in a vessel covered everywhere with spikes'); Wido of Ferrara, *De scismate Hildebrandi* II, p. 557. See G. B. Borino (1952a) pp. 414–15.

80 Matilda of Tuscany's involvement is mentioned only in Bonizo's account. Cf. Paul of Bernried, *Life of Gregory VII* c. 47, below p. 294. See A. Overmann (1895) p. 135.

81 Genesis 11: 4 (a reference to the tower of Babel).

82 The tower mentioned above p. 225 n. 46.

83 Bonizo alone ascribed to Wibert the leadership of the Lombard opposition, 1075. J. Ziese (1982) p. 44 suggested that Tedald was more likely to have played this role.

84 See above p. 217 n. 152.

85 Cf. Arnulf, *Liber* V.1, p. 221.

86 Count Eberhard (✝1078), active in the service of Henry IV, 1069–78: see G. Tellenbach (1988) p. 359. His excommunication (1073): above p. 218 n. 162. His presence in Italy was recorded by Amatus, *L'Ystoire de li Normant* VII.27, p. 298. G. Meyer von Knonau (1894) p. 571 n. 160 dated the mission in early autumn, 1075.

of certain other Piacenzans, but they were freed on the advice of the most blessed Beatrice.[87] Eberhard heard that the men of Cremona were full of faith and fortified with virtues and he left them unmolested, not because he feared God but because he was powerless against them. What more is there to tell? The Milanese captains, the sellers of the churches, at the command of the king and on the worst advice, elected for themselves Tedald, a clerk of the Milanese church, who had previously sworn fealty to Godfrey.[88] He was a man of noble birth, rather stout in body but thin in virtues. Such was the man whom they brought with them to the king[89] and the king – forgetting the investiture that he had previously conferred on Godfrey and thinking little of the oath that Rapoto[90] had formerly sworn on his behalf to the bishops in Novara, that it was the king's will that Godfrey should be consecrated – invested this man in the lifetime of the other, contrary not only to the divine laws and the conduct of Christian kings, but even to the custom of tyrants. Such was the man who laid waste the Milanese church. Wibert sent to him Hugh Candidus,[91] so that by the latter's advice he might approach the king and pervert his mind to evil and this he did.

It was at that time that a heinous and unheard of offence was committed in Rome. For Cencius, hateful to God, hatched a conspiracy and in the very night of Christ's Nativity, while the pope was celebrating mass at the altar of Mary, the holy Mother of God, which is called *ad Presepe*,[92] seized him and violently dragged him, wounded, to the tower of extraordinary strength that he possessed in Rome.[93]

87 Beatrice of Tuscany's intervention is mentioned only by Bonizo. See E. Goez (1995) pp. 167, 230.

88 Archbishop Godfrey of Milan: above p. 217.

89 Cf. Arnulf, *Liber* V.5, pp. 222–3: 'When the Milanese approached the king ... , Tedald, a certain subdeacon of the Milanese church was serving in the royal chapel. The king ... at length conferred on him the Ambrosian archbishopric'. See G. Meyer von Knonau (1894) pp. 573–4; H. E. J. Cowdrey (1968) pp. 39–41; H. Keller (1979) p. 440.

90 See above p. 217. Rapoto was one of the 'three religious men, vassals' of Henry IV, mentioned in Gregory VII, *Registrum* III.10, p. 267. See G. Meyer von Knonau (1894) p. 580 n. 168.

91 See above pp. 229 n. 61, 231 n. 83.

92 The midnight mass of Christmas Eve 1075 in the basilica of S. Maria Maggiore. D. Whitton (1980) p. 233 suggested that Cencius inherited family lands near the basilica and that this determined his choice of location for the abduction. See G. B. Borino (1952a) pp. 431–6; D. Whitton (1980) pp. 247–8; H. E. J. Cowdrey (1998) pp. 326–8.

93 The biography of Gregory VII, *Liber pontificalis* 2, 262, identifies this as Cencius's tower in the district of Parione: above p. 225 n. 46.

What more can I say? The Romans immediately besieged the tower and in the morning they took it by force and would have killed the villain, had not the most blessed Gregory, the disciple of a good master, liberated him from death by his prayers and entreaties.[94] On the following day, after the pope had returned to the Lateran, the Romans expelled from the city the author of that great offence, together with all his supporters,[95] and destroyed his towers utterly.

While these events were happening, the Saxons rebelled.[96] We have omitted writing down the cause of their rebellion because it would take too long, but one thing we know: that they resorted to such extreme hostilities because of the heavy and unaccustomed burden of servitude that certain men attempted to impose on them.[97] Let us now follow the correct order of events. As soon as the Saxons rebelled, the king entered Saxony with a large and strong force, having with him the excellent Duke Rudolf,[98] Duke Welf,[99] the celebrated Duke Godfrey,[100] husband of the most noble Matilda, Duke Theoderic[101] and an innumerable host of margraves and counts. They made a sudden attack on the unprepared Saxons and obtained the victory, albeit a most cruel one.[102] For in that battle fifteen thousand men are said to have perished on the king's side[103] and after such a victory he returned to Franconia with his business still unsettled. He immediately assembled a multitude of bishops,[104] but he did not pray to God, the author of his success, nor did he offer Him thanks for the victory that He had conferred, but his *heart* was *lifted up* and his *eyes* were *raised too high*.

94 According to Beno, *Gesta* I.8, p. 372, Gregory 'afterwards faithlessly avenged himself'.

95 His brother Stephen was still in Rome in 1077: see p. 243.

96 This rebellion of the Saxons and Thuringians broke out in August 1073. The rebels finally surrendered in October 1075.

97 The Saxons' claim that they were defending their liberty against Henry IV's tyranny: Lampert, *Annales* 1073, pp. 140–1, 146–7, 151; Bruno, *Saxonicum bellum* c. 16, 25–6, pp. 22 1, 28 81.

98 Rudolf of Rheinfelden, duke of Swabia, anti-king (1077–80).

99 Welf IV, duke of Bavaria (✝1101).

100 Godfrey III 'the Hunchback' of Verdun, duke of Lower Lotharingia (✝1076).

101 Theoderic II of Châtenois, duke of Upper Lotharingia (✝1115).

102 Battle of Homburg, 9 June 1075: G. Meyer von Knonau (1894) pp. 496–506, 874–84; I. S. Robinson (1999) pp. 100–2.

103 Cf. Lampert, *Annales* 1075, p. 222 ('because of the loss of the most eminent men, the victors suffered greater damage than the defeated'); Bruno, *Saxonicum bellum* c. 46, p. 45.

104 Council of Worms, 24 January 1076.

He *set* his *mouth against the heavens*[105] and, taking the advice of Hugh Candidus,[106] he sent a letter, which he forced his bishops to subscribe,[107] renouncing the lord pope, who had governed the universal Church in peace for three years. He followed the example of the pernicious Lothar,[108] whom we mentioned above, paying no heed, alas! to that chapter of Leo III, which reads: 'Whoever separates himself from the community of the Roman church, cannot enter the gates of heaven nor be freed from the chains of sin.'[109]

Meanwhile the letter that destroyed the unity of the Church was brought to Rome by envoys,[110] for the king urgently commanded it. When they arrived in Piacenza, they assembled all the Lombard bishops, who were commanded on the king's behalf to confirm the king's action. Events, however, fell out quite differently from what they hoped. For under the leadership of Bishop Denis of Piacenza they all individually swore in public that they would never again show obedience to the pope.[111] They next appointed a certain clerk named Roland[112] from that workshop of iniquity, the city of Parma, to be the bearer of this legation. He chanced to arrive in Rome at the time when the pope was presiding over a synod.[113] Filled with the spirit of the devil, in the midst of the synod, acting on behalf of the king, that is to say of a layman, he forbade him to exercise the papal office and commanded him to descend from the see.[114] This would

105 Psalm 72:9.

106 Cf. Lampert, *Annales* 1076, p. 253: 'Hugh the White intervened, ... bringing with him something like a tragedy of the life and appointment of the pope with theatrical inventions'. See F. Lerner (1931) pp. 51–3.

107 The letter subscribed by two archbishops and 24 bishops, *Die Briefe Heinrichs IV.* pp. 65–8. See W. Goez (1968) pp. 117–44; C. Schneider (1972) pp. 146–53; H. Zimmermann (1970) pp. 121–31; I. S. Robinson (1999) pp. 143–6.

108 King Lothar II: see above p. 173.

109 This text is not found in the extant documents of Pope Leo III (795–816). W. Berschin (1972) p. 51 saw a resemblance to Cyprian, *De catholicae ecclesiae unitate* c. 6, *CSEL* 3/1, 214.

110 Bishops Huzman of Speyer and Burchard of Basel, escorted by Count Eberhard (above p. 231 and n. 86).

111 Council of Piacenza: G. Meyer von Knonau (1894) pp. 629–30; I. S. Robinson (1999) p. 147.

112 Roland of Parma, bishop of Treviso (c. 1076–c. 1090). See G. Schwartz (1913) p. 61.

113 Lenten synod, 14–20 February 1076 (*Registrum* III.10a, pp. 268–71). See G. Meyer von Knonau (1894) p. 632 n. 25; H. E. J. Cowdrey (1998) pp. 140–2.

114 Cf. Empress Agnes, letter to Bishop Altman of Passau (in Hugh of Flavigny, *Chronicon* II, p. 435): 'The envoys ... told the pope on behalf of my son to arise and give up the apostolic see. They were immediately taken prisoner by the Romans.'

have been culpable even if it had been said by the bishops themselves
to a priest of lesser rank without a trial. He next ordered the cardinals
to journey beyond the mountains and to choose a pope for themselves
there. The venerable Gregory, however, following the example of a
good master, first saved his reviler from death;[115] then, quietening the
tumult with difficulty, he joyfully celebrated the synod. The following
day letters were brought to the pope from the bishops beyond the
mountains, in which they confessed that they had sinned and erred
and begged his pardon, promising that they would henceforward
show him the obedience due to a father.[116] When the time was at hand,
however, at which the synod should have been dissolved, the venerable Gregory, who was prepared to die for his sheep, did not suffer
the offence against the holy Roman church to go unavenged. On the
advice of all the bishops, who numbered 110,[117] he excommunicated
the king, who did not recognise that he was one of the sheep of Christ,
as the chief of this unheard-of rebellion; and he condemned him to be
deprived of the kingship.[118]

This was indeed neither innovatory nor reprehensible, because it was
done as commanded by the rules of the holy Fathers. For in the
Council of Chalcedon, in which 600 bishops were present, we read
about Dioscorus of Alexandria. *Since the second transgression greatly surpassed his previous iniquity – for he presumed to pronounce excommunication
on the most holy Pope Leo – Bishop Anatolius of Constantinople said,
Dioscorus has not been condemned for aberration from the faith, but because
he excommunicated the lord Archbishop Leo.*[119] Do we read there of any
investigation whether Dioscorus pronounced that excommunication
justly or unjustly? Not at all: there is absolutely no doubt that they
punished him because he, although an inferior, attempted to attack

---

115 Cf. Bruno, *Saxonicum bellum* c. 68, p. 60: 'the envoy would have met a wretched
   death, torn limb from limb, if he had not found protection at the feet of the pope.'
116 *Ibid.,* c. 65, p. 57 (the bishops 'at the first opportunity sent the pope suppliant
   letters of confession and acknowledged their guilt to him'). The synod suspended
   all the bishops who subscribed the letter of 24 January, threatening deposition if
   they were not reconciled by 1 August 1076: *Registrum* III.10a, pp. 268–9.
117 Bonizo alone gave the number of participating bishops. The synodal protocol
   mentions only 'a crowd of bishops and abbots and clergy and laity of different
   orders'.
118 Gregory VII, *Registrum* III.10a, pp. 270–1.
119 Council of Chalcedon (451), cited from Nicholas I, *Epistola* 88, *MGH Epistolae* 6,
   467 with slight alterations. See E. Perels (1931) p. 370; W. Berschin (1972) p. 51.
   On Dioscorus, patriarch of Alexandria: Bonizo, *Liber de vita christiana* IV.40, p.
   126.

and to injure his superior. Notice what the holy fathers in the Eighth Synod decreed concerning this case. *Believing that the word of the Lord that Christ spoke to the holy apostles and His disciples – that 'he who receives you, receives me and he who rejects you, rejects me' – was also said to all who, after them and according to their model, were appointed to be supreme pontiffs and princes of pastors in the Catholic Church, we have decreed that none of the mighty of this world should attempt to dishonour or depose from their thrones any of those who preside over the patriarchal sees, but should judge them worthy of all honour and reverence, especially indeed the most holy pope of the elder see of Rome, next the patriarchs of Alexandria, Antioch and Jerusalem, thereafter the patriarch of Constantinople, and that no one should write anything against the most holy pope of the elder see of Rome with the motive of making libellous allegations, as Focius has recently done and as Dioscorus did long before. Whoever resorts to such bragging and audacity as to offer insults to the see of Peter, prince of the apostles, like Focius and Dioscorus, either in written or unwritten form, shall receive the same or an equivalent condemnation as they did. If indeed anyone exercising God's power attempts to drive out the aforesaid pope of the apostolic see or any of the other patriarchs, let him be anathema. Moreover if a universal synod is assembled and any uncertainty or dispute arises concerning the holy church of the Romans, the question ought to be examined and progress made towards achieving a solution with veneration and fitting reverence; but let no one presumptuously pronounce judgement against the supreme bishop of the elder see of Rome.*[120] Lo! you have heard that imitators of Focius and Dioscorus must be condemned simply for defaming the Roman pontiff and you have also heard that when the mighty attempt to drive the pope of the elder see of Rome from his see, they are anathematised. It is not reprehensible, therefore, to excommunicate a king who tried to expel the pope from his see without a trial, because this is confirmed by the rules of the holy Fathers. Nor is it unusual to do this, since we read that Roman pontiffs have not only excommunicated many [kings and emperors] for less important reasons, but also deposed them from the kingship. This will be made clearer by means of examples.

Pope Innocent excommunicated Emperor Archadius, son of Theodosius the Great, because he was present at the deposition of John Chrysostom, which was decreed by Theophilus of Alexandria and by the other eastern patriarchs with the agreement of other bishops but without the consent of the Roman pontiff. The pope also annulled their sentence of

---

120 Fourth Council of Constantinople (869/870) c.21, *MPL* 129, col. 159–60 (a more accurate version in Bonizo, *Liber de vita christiana* IV.95, pp. 159–60). See W. Berschin (1972) pp. 51–2. On Photius, patriarch of Constantinople: below p. 238 n. 127.

deposition.[121] As soon as that most dutiful emperor became aware of the fact, he did not rebel, but humbly sought and obtained pardon. Pope Constantine excommunicated Emperor Justin, son of Justinian, because he did not give a fitting reception to his legates. The emperor subsequently prostrated himself and his kingship at the pope's feet in a street of the city of Constantinople until he obtained the pardon which he sought.[122] Pope Anastasius excommunicated Emperor Athanasius and when the latter spoke about the pope in an impudent manner, he was struck by lightning in his own palace and died.[123] Pope Gregory III not only excommunicated Emperor Leo, but also deprived him of his kingdom.[124] Pope Stephen deposed Charles, brother of King Pippin, from the kingship and put Pippin in his place.[125] Moreover the doctor Gregory, the Roman pope, deprived of his office anyone who violated the terms of his privilege. For in a certain privilege of his subscribed *Gregory to Senator, priest and abbot of a hospital of the Franks* is found among other things: *We declare that everything contained in this text of our command and decree is to be observed in perpetuity both by you and by all who succeed to your rank and office and by those whom it can concern. If any king, priest, judge or secular person, knowing the text of our decree, attempts to contravene it, let him lose his office of power and honour and let him know that he is answerable to divine judgement for the iniquity that he has done.*[126] What shall I say of Nicholas,

---

121 Cf. the spurious letter of Innocent I (402–17), *JK* †290, cited by Gregory VII, *Registrum* VIII.21, p. 554 (15 March 1081) as a precedent for the excommunication of Henry IV and also by Gregorian polemicists: Bernard, *Liber canonum* c.25, p. 495; Bernold, *Apologeticae rationes* p. 97; Bernold, *De solutione iuramentorum* p. 148.

122 Cf. Bonizo, *Liber de vita christiana* IV.43, p. 129. Pope Constantine I (708–15) was not the contemporary of 'Justin, son of Justinian' (i.e. Justinian I's successor, Justin II, 565–78) but of the emperors Justinian II (705–11) and Philippicus (711–13). The Gregorian polemicists Bernard, *Liber canonum* c. 25, p. 496, and Bernold, *Chronicon* 711, p. 417, recorded an anecdote of Pope Constantine excommunicating Philippicus.

123 Cf. Bonizo, *Liber de vita christiana* IV.40, p. 126. No other author recorded this fictitious anecdote of Pope Anastasius II (496–8) and Emperor Anastasius I (491–518).

124 Cf. Bonizo, *Liber de vita christiana* IV.43, p. 129. No other author recorded this fictitious account of the relations of Gregory III (731–41) and Emperor Leo III (717–41).

125 Cf. Bonizo, *Liber de vita christiana* IV.43, p. 129. No other author mentioned this imaginary involvement of Stephen II (752–7) in the retirement of Carloman from the office of mayor of the palace (747).

126 Gregory I, *Registrum* XIII.11, pp. 376, 378. Gregory VII first used this anathema clause from a privilege of Gregory I as a precedent for his excommunication of Henry IV (*Registrum* VIII.21, p. 550). A version of this 'authority' was disseminated in the 'Swabian appendix' of the *Collection in 74 Titles* c. 330, p. 196.

who excommunicated two emperors at one and the same time: namely, the eastern emperor Michael, for expelling Ignatius, bishop of Constantinople from his see without the pope giving judgement, and the western emperor, named Lothar, for associating with Waldrada, his concubine.[127]

Why do I speak of the Roman pontiffs, when Ambrose, bishop of Milan, the lily of the Church,[128] excommunicated the tyrant Maximus[129] and also excommunicated Emperor Theodosius and expelled him from the church?[130] And who, unless he is weak in the head, does not know that the royal power is subject to bishops? Who believes that he is exempt from the authority of the Roman pontiff, except those who because of their sins do not deserve to be numbered among the sheep of Jesus?[131] But let us now follow the order of events.

Book VIII

Meanwhile, after the news of the ban imposed on the king resounded in the ears of the people, the whole of our Roman world trembled and the Italians and those beyond the mountains pronounced upon it in different ways. For the Italians summoned *a council of evildoers*[1] to Pavia after Easter,[2] in which all the Lombard bishops and abbots together, under the leadership of Wibert,[3] imitated Focius and Dioscorus[4]

---

127 Cf. Bonizo, *Liber de vita christiana* IV.44, p. 131. Pope Nicholas I (858–67) upheld the claim of Ignatius to be patriarch of Constantinople and excommunicated his successor, Photius. There is no record of his excommunicating Emperor Michael III (842–67). For the case of Lothar II see above p. 173 and n. 15.

128 Cf. Bonizo, *Liber de vita christiana* I.43, II.63, pp. 31, 69.

129 Cf. Paulinus of Milan, *Vita sancti Ambrosii* c. 19, *MPL* 14, col. 33C.

130 See above p. 168. This was one of the precedents used by Gregory VII, *Registrum* IV.2, VIII.21, pp. 294, 554 and by the Gregorian polemicists Bernard, *Liber canonum* c. 25, p. 496; Bernold, *Apologeticae rationes* p. 97; Placidus, *Liber de honore ecclesiae* c. 60, p. 594.

131 John 21:17. Cf. Gregory VII, *Registrum* VIII.21, p. 548.

1 Psalm 21:17.

2 27 March 1076.

3 J. Ziese (1982) pp. 45–6 doubted that Wibert of Ravenna was the ringleader and that their Lombard council excommunicated Gregory VII. According to the only other account, Arnulf, *Liber gestorum recentium* V.7, pp. 226–7, the Lombards simply rejected Gregory's sentence of excommunication.

4 See above pp. 235–6 n. 119, 120.

by excommunicating the lord pope of the elder see of Rome. It was unheard of from the beginning of the world that the enemy of the human race should at one and the same time arm so many lunatic bishops against the holy Roman church.

While these events were taking place in Italy at the devil's behest, the princes beyond the mountains met together[5] and held a council of the sane, in which they put both parties, so to speak, on trial, in order that it might become clear whether or not the pope could excommunicate the king and whether or not he had been justly excommunicated. For they did not wish to break their law, which prescribed that an excommunicate who was not absolved from his excommunication before a year and a day, should lose his office and all his authority.[6] After the council had considered the decrees of the holy Fathers and the precedents of their ancestors, therefore, the most prudent bishops of that kingdom, the abbots and the clergy decreed that the king could be excommunicated by the pope and that he was justly excommunicated for imitating Focius and Dioscorus. What more is there to tell? They considered that their best course at this time was to confirm this on oath and, led by Dukes Rudolf,[7] Welf[8] and Theoderic[9] (for Godfrey, the husband of the most excellent Matilda, had died a few days before),[10] by other princes and by the bishops of the kingdom, they declared that if the king would acquiesce in their advice, they would bring the pope beyond the mountains before the end of the year to absolve him from the bond of excommunication without any malign intention and they swore an oath that they would force the king to wait, as a private person, for the pope's judgement on him.[11] When this was done, they all again swore unanimously that if

---

5 Assembly of Tribur, 16 October – 1 November 1076. See G. Meyer von Knonau (1894) pp. 729–35, 885–93; C. Schneider (1972) pp. 171–87; H. Beumann (1973) pp. 33–44; E. Hlawitschka (1974) pp. 25–45; H. E. J. Cowdrey (1998) pp. 150–3; I. S. Robinson (1999) pp. 155–8.

6 Cf. Berthold, *Annales* 1076, p. 287: 'if [Henry's] offence continued beyond the anniversary of his excommunication, they would no longer regard him as king'; Lampert, *Annales* 1076, p. 281; Bruno, *Saxonicum bellum* c. 88, p. 83.

7 Duke Rudolf of Swabia.

8 Duke Welf IV of Bavaria.

9 Duke Theoderic of Upper Lotharingia.

10 Duke Godfrey III of Lower Lotharingia was murdered on 26 February 1076: G. Meyer von Knonau (1894) pp. 650–2.

11 Henry IV, 'Promise of Oppenheim' (*Die Briefe Heinrichs IV.* p. 69). The princes invited Gregory VII to judge their grievances against the king at an assembly in Augsburg, 2 February 1077.

the king was willing to observe the oath administered to him, they would accompany him on an expedition to Italy and, when he had received the imperial crown, they would attack the Normans and free Apulia and Calabria from their rule.[12] If, however, through his sinful conduct he rendered invalid the oath administered to him, they would never thereafter accept him as their lord or their king. In the meantime they sent the bishop of Trier[13] to Rome, to bring the pope beyond the mountains to Augsburg. How he was captured by guile in Piacenza and not freed until a letter for his release was brought from Speyer[14] to the bishop of Piacenza,[15] I omit to tell, lest the story prove too long.

Meanwhile the venerable Gregory set out on the difficult journey to Augsburg in the interests of peace.[16] A very hard winter was then setting in.[17] Suddenly, however, the king, caring little for his oath, entered Italy.[18] There are those who say that he wished to capture the pope unawares, which seems likely enough. For Bishop Gregory of Vercelli, his chancellor, who had been commanded by the princes to bring the pope over the mountains, heard, as soon as he had crossed the chain of the Apennines, that he had arrived secretly in the city of Vercelli.[19] When this news was announced to the pope, he immediately entered Canossa, the very secure fortress of the most excellent Matilda.[20]

---

12 Bonizo alone reported this improbable undertaking by the princes.

13 Udo, archbishop of Trier (1066–78). According to Berthold, *Annales* 1076, p. 287, Udo's mission was to deliver the text of the king's 'Promise', while the princes sent their own envoys to arrange the pope's journey to Augsburg.

14 After the assembly of Tribur, Henry IV withdrew to Speyer, where he lived as a penitent preparing for his absolution from excommunication: G. Meyer von Knonau (1894) p. 735.

15 Bonizo alone reported this intervention by his old enemy, Denis of Piacenza (above p. 37). According to Berthold, *Annales* 1076, p. 287, Udo arrived in Rome *after* the envoys of the princes, whose departure had been later than his own.

16 He was in Florence on 28 December 1076, intending to reach Mantua by 8 January 1077: see H. E. J. Cowdrey (1998) p. 154.

17 On the unusual harshness of the winter of 1076–7: Lampert, *Annales* 1076, p. 284. See G. Meyer von Knonau (1894) p. 750 n. 7.

18 Celebrating Christmas 1076 in Besançon, the king travelled to Italy by way of the Mont Cenis pass: see G. Meyer von Knonau (1894) pp. 748–52.

19 This is the only record of Gregory of Vercelli's involvement in escorting the pope to Augsburg. He was subsequently one of the king's oath-helpers at Canossa: see G. Meyer von Knonau (1894) pp. 754, 761.

20 The importance of Canossa to the family of Matilda of Tuscany: L. Tondelli (1952) pp. 365–71. Henry IV's absolution: G. Meyer von Knonau (1894) pp. 755–62, 894–903; K.F. Morrison (1962) pp. 121–48; T. Struve (1995) pp. 44–5; H. E. J. Cowdrey (1998) pp. 156–66; I. S. Robinson (1999) pp. 160–4.

Meanwhile, when the king saw that his devices were made public, he discarded all his ferocity, or so it seemed, and clad in dovelike simplicity, he came to Canossa and remained for some days barefoot amidst the snow and ice, deceiving all the less wise.[21] He obtained from the venerable Gregory (although the latter was not unaware of his cunning) the absolution that he sought, through the mediation of the Lord's sacrament during the celebration of mass in this manner.[22] He placed himself at the Lord's table as a participant with bishops, abbots and religious clergy and laymen standing by, on these terms: that if he had indeed humbled himself in mind and body and if he truly believed that he was the rightful pope and if he believed that he had been excommunicated for imitating the example of Focius and Dioscorus and if he believed that he could be absolved by the pope, then the sacrament would prove to him the means of salvation, as it was to the apostles. If, however, he thought otherwise, he would be like Judas: *after the morsel, Satan* would *enter into* him.[23] What more is there to relate? After mass had been celebrated, they shared a banquet. Then the king and all those who had been absolved from excommunication were commanded to beware of association with excommunicates. There are some, however, who say that he took an oath to the pope on his life, his limbs and his honour.[24] For my part, I do not assert what I do not know. Meanwhile, after he was absolved from the ban, the king appeared superficially devout and obedient to the pope. For in the daytime he separated himself from the company of all the bishops,[25] considering them to be excommunicate. During the night he acquiesced in their criminal counsels and pondered on that course of action that subsequently became manifest. This was the way in which he behaved

---

21 25–27 January 1077. Cf. Gregory VII, *Registrum* IV.12, p. 313. Like other Gregorian authors, Bonizo represented this absolution as a 'pretended reconciliation' (cf. Berthold, *Annales* 1077, pp. 289–90; Bernold, *Chronicon* 1077, p. 433; Bruno, *Saxonicum bellum* c. 90, p. 84). See I. S. Robinson (1979) pp. 724–5.

22 Gregory VII 'received [Henry] into the grace of communion': *Registrum* IV.12, p. 313; *Epistolae Vagantes* 19, p. 52. Lampert, *Annales* 1077, pp. 296–7 and Berthold, *Annales* 1077, p. 433 claimed that he avoided taking communion. See H. E. J. Cowdrey (1998) p. 158 n. 358.

23 John 13: 27. Lampert, *Annales* 1077, pp. 295–7 similarly claimed that the pope ascribed to the communion the character of an ordeal.

24 Cf. 'the oath of Henry, king of the Germans', in Gregory VII, *Registrum* IV.12a, pp. 314–15.

25 P. Jaffé (1865) p. 672 suggested the reading 'all the Lombard bishops'. Cf. Berthold, *Annales* 1077, p. 291: Henry was warned at Canossa to 'beware the anathema of the Lombards'.

during the whole time he remained in Piacenza,[26] being cowed in particular by the presence of his mother, the most religious empress,[27] who happened to be there.

It was at that time that Cencius, *hateful to God* (whom we mentioned above), came to him. During the day the king refused to see him, since he was excommunicate, but at night he surrendered completely to his pernicious counsels.[28] When he saw that he could not remove the pope from the fortress of Canossa, he made for Pavia. There Cencius, *hateful to God*, died a miserable death. Wibert and the other excommunicates celebrated his obsequies with remarkable pomp.[29]

While these events were taking place in Italy, the princes beyond the mountains met at Forchheim and set up as their king, Duke Rudolf, a man great in counsel and mighty in arms.[30] This event caused great consternation throughout the Roman world.[31] When he heard of the election of Rudolf, the king, who was still in Pavia, was remarkably shaken.[32] Since, however, he was a man of deep counsel and extraordinarily shrewd, feigning humility, he requested the pope through his envoys to excommunicate Rudolf. This the pope promised to do instantly, if on being summoned Rudolf could give no reasonable explanation for his actions. For it seemed uncanonical to excommunicate him before he had been summoned to his trial.[33] In wild and

26 He was there on 17 February 1077 in the company of the bishops of Vercelli, Pavia and Turin: G. Meyer von Knonau (1894) p. 766; J. Vogel (1983) p. 25.

27 Empress Agnes in Piacenza: M. Black-Veldtrup (1995) p. 99. She was expected at Canossa (Berthold, *Annales* 1077, p. 289).

28 Cencius Stephani: see above pp. 232–3. According to Berthold, *Annales* 1077, pp. 290–1, Henry continually deferred his meeting with Cencius, so that the latter died without seeing the king.

29 Cencius died of a tumour in his throat: Berthold, *Annales* 1077, p. 291. Wibert of Ravenna was present in the king's entourage in Pavia (Henry IV, *Diploma* 293, April 1077), but his participation in Cencius's funeral was probably a polemical invention of Bonizo intended to discredit him: J. Ziese (1982) p. 46.

30 The assembly of Forchheim began 13 March 1077; Rudolf of Swabia was elected 15 March: see Paul of Bernried, *Life of Gregory VII* c. 93–6, below pp. 334–7. See also G. Meyer von Knonau (1900) pp. 3–8, 627–38; W. Böhme (1970) pp. 65–75; W. Schlesinger (1973) pp. 61–85; W. Giese (1979) pp. 37–49; I. S. Robinson (1979) pp. 721–33; H. E. J. Cowdrey (1998) pp. 167–71; I. S. Robinson (1999) pp. 165–70.

31 Anti-Gregorian propaganda accused Gregory VII of complicity in the election of Rudolf. Cf. Gregory VII, *Registrum* VII.14a, c. 7, IX.29, pp. 484, 613. See I. S. Robinson (1979) pp. 730–1; H. E. J. Cowdrey (1998) p. 171; I. S. Robinson (1999) p. 169.

32 Cf. Arnulf, *Liber* V.10, pp. 231–2.

33 Cf. Gregory VII, *Registrum* VII.14a, c. 7, p. 485, 'Henry began to entreat me to help him against Rudolf. I replied that I would gladly do so, when I had heard the arguments on both sides and learned whom justice most favoured.'

ungovernable haste the king crossed the mountains and rapidly recovered control of Bavaria and Franconia.[34] What more is there to tell? With no less energy Rudolf invaded Franconia, a most grievous battle was joined and many thousands of men were slain on both sides.[35] Some say that Henry was the victor of this battle, but very many others ascribe the victory in this conflict to Rudolf.[36] Whoever was the victor, however, his was a most bloody victory.

Meanwhile in Rome a serious crime and an irreparable loss suddenly occurred. For the prefect Cencius,[37] that most Christian man, was killed through the treachery of Stephen, brother of the man *hateful to God*,[38] whom we mentioned above. When his body was brought to St Peter's in Rome, God performed many miracles through him.[39] The Romans, however, made common cause to seize the fortress in which the criminal had taken refuge. They severed his head and hands and gave his body to the flames, hanging his head and hands in the archway of St Peter's. Of the remaining instigators of this great crime they killed some and banished the rest from their homeland.

A few days after these events the venerable Pope Gregory returned with honour to Rome[40] and immediately assembled a synod, in which the envoys of both kings were present.[41] They were commanded by

34 Henry entered Bavaria and held court in Regensburg (1 May), Ulm (end of May) and Nuremberg (11–13 June): G. Meyer von Knonau (1900) pp. 17, 19–22, 36–7, 42.

35 Presumably the battle of Mellrichstadt, 7 August 1078: cf. below n. 44. See G. Meyer von Knonau (1900) pp. 135–46; K.-G. Cram (1955) pp. 140–3; H. E. J. Cowdrey (1998) p. 183; I. S. Robinson (1999) pp. 181–2.

36 Cf. Frutolf of Michelsberg, *Chronica* 1078, p. 90: 'it was uncertain whose was the victory, because both armies fled rapidly to their own lands'. Henry tried to represent Mellrichstadt as a Henrician victory in letters to the pope, the Romans and the Lombards (Berthold, *Annales* 1078, p. 313): see J. Vogel (1983) pp. 123–4.

37 The death of Cencius, son of John Tiniosus, occurred in summer 1077. See G. Meyer von Knonau (1900) pp. 81–2; H. E. J. Cowdrey (1998) p. 328.

38 Stephen, brother of Cencius Stephani: see G. B. Borino (1952) p. 440; D. Whitton (1980) p. 225.

39 In the Lent synod 1078 Gregory VII proclaimed these miracles and thus canonised Cencius: Berthold, *Annales* 1077, p. 305. Cf. also above p. 230 and n. 71. See C. Erdmann (1935) pp. 197–8, 231, 232; H. E. J. Cowdrey (1985) p. 48; H. E. J. Cowdrey (1998) p. 328.

40 He had returned from northern Italy by 16 September 1077: see G. Meyer von Knonau (1900) p. 81; H. E. J. Cowdrey (1998) p. 179.

41 In the Roman synod of 27 February–3 March 1078 Henry was represented by Bishops Benno II of Osnabrück and Theoderic of Verdun. Rudolf's envoys are not identified. See G. Meyer von Knonau (1900) pp. 103–7; J. Vogel (1983) pp. 104–8; H. E. J. Cowdrey (1998) p. 180; I. S. Robinson (1999) pp. 178–9.

the authority of St Peter that they should not fight, but should choose
a place in which the bishops of both parties could meet in safety, to
offer an explanation of their conduct before the legates of the holy
Roman church.[42] This useful council[43] was broken off, however, through
the instigation of the devil and there was another fierce battle, in which
many thousands of men were killed on both sides, especially Bohemians.[44] When news of this reached the pope the following Lent (for
this most grievous battle had been fought on the feast day of St
Agatha),[45] he assembled a synod, in which the envoys of both kings
were present. They were both prepared to swear that it was not
through the fault of their lord that the council had been broken off.[46]
Which of them perjured himself I refrain from saying, because the
evidence is not sufficiently clear. What more can I say? The venerable
pope decided to send religious bishops beyond the mountains, who
were to forbid the kings to make war on each other and to summon
the bishops to a council.[47] They were namely Peter, bishop of Albano,[48]
a most religious man (who before becoming a bishop, in the time of
Pope Alexander, passed unharmed through the flames at the command of his abbot in order to counter simoniacal heresy)[49] and Udalric,
bishop of Padua,[50] an extremely eloquent man and particularly loyal

42 Gregory VII, *Registrum* V.14a, c. 6, pp. 370–1: see Paul of Bernried, *Life of Gregory
VII* c. 99, below pp. 341–2.

43 Henry IV and an unidentified papal legate held negotiations with the Saxons at
Fritzlar in Hesse. See G. Meyer von Knonau (1900) pp. 123–6; O. Schumann (1912)
p. 45; W. Giese (1979) pp. 169–70; J. Vogel (1983) pp. 113–14; H. E. J. Cowdrey
(1998) pp. 182–3; I. S. Robinson (1999) pp. 179–80.

44 Bonizo's account duplicates the battle of Mellrichstadt (above n. 35). Henry's
Bohemian allies did not arrive in time to take part in the battle: see G. Meyer von
Knonau (1900) p. 141. Bonizo was probably thinking of the battle of Flarchheim
(below p. 245), in which many Bohemians were killed.

45 5 February. E. Dümmler (p. 611 n. 9) considered this a scribal error for 'St Afra' (7
August).

46 Roman synod, 19 November 1078 (Gregory VII, *Registrum* VI.5b, pp. 400–1). See
G. Meyer von Knonau (1900) pp. 163–4; J. Vogel (1983) pp. 126–7; H. E. J.
Cowdrey (1998) p. 184; I. S. Robinson (1999) pp. 182–3.

47 Legation sent to Germany after the papal synod of February 1079 (below p. 245).
See G. Meyer von Knonau (1900) pp. 182–3; O. Schumann (1912) pp. 46–52; J. Vogel
(1983) pp. 142–4; H. E. J. Cowdrey (1998) p. 188; I. S. Robinson (1999) p. 186.

48 Peter 'Igneus', cardinal bishop of Albano (?1072–1089): see R. Hüls (1977) p. 90.

49 Peter, a monk of Vallombrosa in the time of Abbot John Gualbert, underwent the
ordeal by fire on 13 February 1068 in order to convict Bishop Peter Mezzabarba of
Florence of simony. See G. Meyer von Knonau (1890) pp. 600–1; G. Miccoli (1960)
pp. 147–57; H. E. J. Cowdrey (1998) pp. 66–7.

50 Udalric, bishop of Padua (1064–80): see G. Schwartz (1913) pp. 57–8; G. B. Borino
(1958) pp. 63–79; G. Miccoli (1960) p. 68.

to King Henry, and also the patriarch of Aquileia.[51] They crossed the Alps and found the king in Bavaria.[52] They could not, however, prevail upon the king, not by pleading nor by prayers nor by any stratagem, to allow them to hold a synod in his kingdom, unless they were willing to excommunicate Rudolf without summoning him to judgement. Since they refused to do this, as the canons forbade them to do, they returned to Rome with their business unfinished.[53] Another savage battle was fought and many thousands of men were killed on both sides.[54]

Book IX

King Henry meanwhile took counsel and sent envoys to Rome, namely Archbishop Liemar of Bremen, whom we mentioned above,[1] and the bishop of Bamberg[2] and very many others.[3] They brought an insolent and unprecedented message: that if the pope was prepared to excommunicate Rudolf without a trial, the king would show him due obedience, but if not, he would acquire for himself a pope who would do his bidding.[4] The venerable pope, however, was ready to die for the truth. Not only did he not condemn [Rudolf], who offered an explanation of

51 Henry, patriarch of Aquileia (1077–84): see G. Schwartz (1913) p. 34.

52 In Regensburg 'around Whitsun' (12 May): Berthold, *Annales* 1079, p. 320.

53 Henry IV and the legates held a conference with the Saxon supporters of the anti-king Rudolf in Fritzlar (June) and in Würzburg (August). Henry demanded the excommunication of Rudolf, who failed to attend. The legates returned to Rome late in 1079. See G. Meyer von Knonau (1900) pp. 209–15, 224–5; O. Schumann (1912) pp. 46–52; J. Vogel (1983) pp. 160–6; H. E. J. Cowdrey (1998) pp. 189–90, 192–3; I. S. Robinson (1999) pp. 190–1.

54 Presumably the battle of Flarchheim, 27 January 1080: see G. Meyer von Knonau (1900) pp. 238–41, 639–43; J. Vogel (1983) pp. 185–6; H. E. J. Cowdrey (1998) p. 194; I. S. Robinson (1999) pp. 193–4.

1 See above p. 222. The envoys went to the papal synod of 7 March 1080: Gregory VII, *Registrum* VII.14a, pp. 479–87; Paul of Bernried, *Life of Gregory VII* c. 106–7, below p. 347. See also G. Meyer von Knonau (1900) pp. 246–56; J. Vogel (1983) pp. 186–97; H. E. J. Cowdrey (1998) pp. 194–9; I. S. Robinson (1999) pp. 194–6.

2 Rupert, bishop of Bamberg (1075–1102).

3 Including 'archdeacon Burchard' (Wenrich, *Epistola* c. 8, p. 297).

4 Bonizo alone reported this message. His account was accepted by J. Vogel (1983) pp. 187–8, who based on this report his explanation of Gregory VII's decision to excommunicate Henry IV in 1080. Gregory himself said nothing of a plan such as Bonizo mentioned (*Registrum* VII.14a, c. 7, p. 484: below p. 349). See H. E. J. Cowdrey (1998) p. 195; I. S. Robinson (1999) p. 195.

his conduct, but he also excommunicated the king who had addressed him so insolently.[5] This action caused a great disturbance among the Roman people. Meanwhile the envoys of the king arrived in Tuscany and attempted to withdraw the province from the jurisdiction of the most excellent Countess Matilda. Since *the common people*, always *desirous of novelties*,[6] were unfaithful to their former lords and because the common people are unfaithful by nature, the envoys were easily able to achieve what they wished.[7] Leaving Margrave Albert[8] and Count Boso[9] in the region of Tuscany, they next came to Lombardy and summoned all the princes of the Lombards to a conference in Brixen and, having divided the royal and the priestly authority, they returned to the king. The venerable pope meanwhile held a conference with Robert, duke of the Normans, beyond Aquino after Whitsun and absolved him from excommunication. The latter became his vassal and received from him the whole principality of Apulia and Calabria.[10]

While these events were taking place, the bishops and princes of the Lombards met in Brixen. The king hastened to join them there with his bishops and the princes from beyond the mountains.[11] After a very wicked consultation Wibert was elected Roman pontiff there by men just like himself, despite the fact that no Roman clerk or layman was present[12] and the fact that Pope Gregory was then presiding over the Roman

5 Gregory VII, *Registrum* VII.14a, c. 7, pp. 483–7; Paul of Bernried, *Life of Gregory VII* c. 107, below pp. 348–51.

6 Sallust, *Catilina* 28,4.

7 Gregory VII, *Registrum* IX.3, p. 574 (Matilda of Tuscany's vassals 'refused to resist' Henry); *Vita Anselmi episcopi Lucensis* c. 21, p. 20 ('very many of her men abandoned her'). See A. Overmann (1895) p. 148.

8 Presumably the 'Margrave Adalbert' of Henry IV, *Diplomas* 293, 338–9, 340, 345, 359 and listed among the enemies of Matilda by Bernold, *Chronicon* 1085, p. 443. See A. Overmann (1895) p. 148; G. Meyer von Knonau (1900) p. 261; A. Gawlik (1970) pp. 59–60, 66–9, 180; T. Struve (1995) pp. 55–6.

9 Presumably the 'Count Boso of Sabbioneta, vassal and standard-bearer of the bishop of Parma' of Henry IV, *Diploma* 341and Bernold, *Chronicon* 1085, p. 443. See A. Overmann (1895) p. 148; G. Meyer von Knonau (1900) p. 261; A. Gawlik (1970) p. 180; T. Struve (1995) p. 56.

10 Robert Guiscard, duke of Apulia and Calabria renewed his fealty to the pope at Ceprano on 29 June 1080, a month after Whitsun (31 May): Gregory VII, *Registrum* VIII.1a, pp. 514–15.

11 For the council of Brixen, 25 June 1080 and the elevation of Wibert of Ravenna (as 'Clement III') see G. Meyer von Knonau (1900) pp. 284–96; J. Ziese (1982) pp. 55–64; J. Vogel (1983) pp. 209–19; H. E. J. Cowdrey (1998) pp. 201–3; I. S. Robinson (1999) pp. 198–201.

12 For Bonizo on the canonical procedures for electing the pope (and the Papal Election Decree, 1059) see above pp. 54–8.

7

see and had now ruled the universal Church in peace for five years.[13] So diabolical a deed was unheard of *from the day on which the nations first began to exist until* [14] the present day. Because one sin often brings on another, he progressed from the root of pride to perjury, from perjury he fell into disobedience, from disobedience Wibert incurred excommunication, from excommunication he fell into idolatry. Such was the man, as we have described above, whom the king chose as his pope, although none of the Roman clergy or laity was present or gave consent, except Hugh Candidus, who for his sins had long been separated from the Church.[15] Such was the man to whom the king was persuaded by Bishop Denis of Piacenza to swear that he would receive the imperial crown from him.[16] What more is there to tell? They were all so blinded that they did not look upon the face of the earth nor see how far from the city of Rome they had pitched their camp. Alas for shame! all those who were present knelt down and adored the false prophet.[17] Those who adored him, however, were completely separated from the bosom of mother Church. It was in this fashion, therefore, that the king celebrated the feast of the princes of the apostles[18] and, strengthened by the blessing of so great a pope, he returned to his own land. Wibert, taking with him the papal vestments,[19] entered Italy with his supporters.

Because, however, the Lord's purposes are *like the great deep*,[20] by the ineffable providence of God Henry did not receive the scourges of the Lord, according to his deserts, but success, which added pride to his iniquity. For not long afterwards he entered Saxony with a strong and numerous force. Rudolf advanced against him, a very fierce battle

13 Actually seven years.

14 Daniel 12:1.

15 Hugh Candidus (see above p. 191 n. 77) subscribed the synodal decree of Brixen 'on behalf of all the Roman cardinals' (*Die Briefe Heinrichs IV.* p. 72). See F. Lerner (1931) p. 54.

16 Bonizo alone recorded this detail, which is credible, given Denis's leadership of the Lombard episcopate's opposition to the papacy (see above pp. 37, 234). See J. Ziese (1982) p. 61; I. S. Robinson (1999) p. 199.

17 A reference to the ceremony of 'adoratio' (*proskynesis*) by which the faithful acknowledged the pope: E. Eichmann (1951) pp. 36–40; N. Gussone (1978) p. 251. An allusion is probably also intended to Revelation 13:4 (see below n. 28).

18 29 June (feast of SS. Peter and Paul).

19 Wibert was clad in the papal insignia at Brixen, but subsequently made no claim to the title or insignia until 1084, when he was enthroned in Rome. See J. Ziese (1982) pp. 62–3.

20 Psalm 35:7.

ensued and Henry turned tail in cowardly fashion. In the course of
that battle Rudolf, although victorious, perished.[21] Rudolf did not die
as cowards are accustomed to die, cut down while fleeing or seeking a
hiding-place. Instead he was found by his men stricken and lying
amidst the slaughter of his foes, on the bodies of the dead.[22] The news
of his death reached Henry eight days later, when he was hiding in a
certain fortress, contemplating flight. At once he *lifted up* his *horn on
high* and *spoke iniquity against God*[23] and, not recognising the stratagems of Satan, he believed that his sin had pleased God. A few days
after these events occurred, his son[24] fought against the army of the
most excellent Matilda and obtained the victory.[25]

Elated with these successes, he suddenly entered Italy[26] and after
Easter[27] he made for Rome, bringing his beast[28] with him and on the
vigil of Pentecost[29] he pitched camp in the field of Nero. But, O God,
who could not but be astounded at men of such great sagacity displaying such insanity? For even if they had lost their intellectual
vision, they had not lost the eyes in their heads. Surely they saw when
they brought him, how honourably he was received by the Romans?
For instead of candles, lances were to be seen; instead of choirs of
clergy there were armed men; instead of praises there were reproaches;

21 Battle of Hohenmölsen ('battle on the Grune' or 'on the Elster'), 15 October 1080.
See G. Meyer von Knonau (1900) pp. 337–41, 644–52; H. E. J. Cowdrey (1998) pp.
206–7; I. S. Robinson (1999) pp. 202–4. Henry IV's cowardice was a common
theme of anti-Henrician chronicles: see I. S. Robinson (1999) pp. 348–9.

22 Rudolf died of his wounds either on the evening of the battle or on the following
day, 16 October: G. Meyer von Knonau (1900) p. 650. The anti-Henrician chroniclers emphasised the heroic manner of his death: Bernold, *Chronicon* 1080, p. 436;
Bruno, *Saxonicum bellum* c. 124, pp. 117–18.

23 Psalm 74:6. Henry IV's whereabouts after the battle: G. Meyer von Knonau (1900)
p. 339.

24 Identified by W. von Giesebrecht (1890) p. 504 as Henry IV's heir, Conrad (1074–
1101), since 1077 his father's representative in the Italian kingdom: E. Goez (1996)
pp. 7–8. G. Meyer von Knonau (1890) pp. 613 n. 14; (1900) pp. 296 n. 112, 316 and
n. 145; (1903) p. 377, believed that this was the illegitimate son (name unknown)
said to have died at the siege of Monteveglio in 1092: T. Struve (1995) p. 74.

25 Battle of Volta, south of Lake Garda, mid-October 1080: see A. Overmann (1895)
p. 147; T. Struve (1995) pp. 47–8; H. E. J. Cowdrey (1998) pp. 206, 210, 301.

26 By the Brenner Pass in March 1081: G. Meyer von Knonau (1900) pp. 377–80; H.
E. J. Cowdrey (1998) p. 213; I. S. Robinson (1999) p. 211.

27 4 April 1081.

28 The beast of Revelation 13:1–8.

29 22 May. See G. Meyer von Knonau (1900) p. 388.

instead of applause there was wailing.[30] What more can be said? Because of their refusal to accept the false pope, the Romans had to endure the devastation of their fields, numerous murders, various disasters and misfortunes,[31] until the king returned to Lombardy with that man, his business unfinished.[32] The following winter, however, he entered Romagna again, bringing the pernicious man[33] with him, plundering *Wibert* towns and tearing down castles, and finally he laid siege to Rome for the whole of Lent.[34] After Easter[35] his army overran all the cities and the neighbouring castles, while he himself returned to Lombardy,[36] leaving Wibert in Tivoli.[37] Wibert, like *Alcimus, strove to obtain the priesthood for himself.*[38] For throughout the summer season[39] he inflicted great depredations and various mutilations on the Roman citizens. He next set fire to the cornfields and pastures, wickedly planning to impoverish or to starve his sons.

The following winter the king once more returned to Rome.[40] Oaths were sworn to confirm that all the religious men, whatever their kingdom of origin, who wished to visit Rome, should have safe-conduct.[41] After he took prisoner the bishop of Ostia[42] and other religious monks

30 Henry IV, *Letter* 16, p. 23, complained that the Romans had not welcomed him with the traditional ceremonies for the emperor elect. He had evidently hoped to be crowned emperor on Whitsunday 1081: G. Meyer von Knonau (1900) p. 390.

31 Cf. *Chronica monasterii Casinensis* III.70, p. 452; *Vita Heinrici IV imperatoris* c. 6, p. 23. See G. Meyer von Knonau (1900) pp. 391–2.

32 He remained outside Rome until at least 23 June 1081; by 10 July he was in Siena: G. Meyer von Knonau (1900) pp. 392–3, 395–6, 401–2. The role of Wibert of Ravenna: J. Ziese (1982) pp. 74–8.

33 The presence of Wibert was also reported by Benzo, *Ad Heinricum IV* VI prefatio, p. 511 and Bernold, *Chronicon* 1082, p. 437. See J. Ziese (1982) p. 74.

34 9 March–23 April 1082.

35 24 April.

36 Bonizo was an eyewitness of Henry IV's withdrawal from Rome. Cf. Bernold, *Chronicon* 1082, p. 437, 'after capturing the venerable bishop of Sutri and some others, Henry ... returned to Lombardy'. See W. Berschin (1972) p. 10.

37 Tivoli as Wibert's headquarters during the siege of Rome: J. Ziese (1982) p. 76.

38 I Maccabees 7:21. Alcimus was unlawfully made high priest by the Syrian ruler Demetrius.

39 The codex reads 'festival' (*festivum tempus*). P. Jaffé (1865) amended this to 'summer' (*estivum tempus*).

40 Perhaps February 1083: see G. Meyer von Knonau (1900) p. 470 n. 2.

41 Cf. Gregory VII, *Epistolae Vagantes* 51, p. 124; Bernold, *Chronicon* 1083, p. 438. See H. E. J. Cowdrey (1998) p. 225.

42 Odo I, cardinal bishop of Ostia; Pope Urban II, 1088–99: see R. Hüls (1977) pp. 102–3. Odo had come to Henry's court as a papal legate and was subsequently detained there. See A. Becker (1964) pp. 60–1.

and clergy, the king saw that he was regarded as excommunicate by the abbot of Cluny[43] and by all the bishops, clergy and monks and he immediately resorted to artful subterfuges. For in order to win the people's favour, he said that he was willing to receive the imperial crown from the venerable Gregory.[44] When the Roman people heard this, not only the laymen but even those who were regarded as religious, both the bishops and the clergy, the abbots and monks, began with floods of tears to beseech the pope to have pity on their native land, which was almost ruined. The venerable pope, however, who was prepared to die for the truth, utterly refused to perform this, unless he first made public satisfaction for his excommunication.[45] This the king, conscience-stricken, would not do. For many days the Romans begged the venerable pope to receive the king and when he remained unmoved by all their prayers, the king gradually began to gain the goodwill of the people.

After he had won over almost all the Romans by bribery, terror and violence,[46] in sheer desperation because of the strength of mind of the venerable Gregory, he decided to place Wibert in the see of St Peter, to the shame and dishonour of the whole Church.[47] Since he had no cardinal bishops nor priests of the holy Roman church nor deacons nor co-provincial bishops, to whom it belongs by custom to enthrone the pope (for no one of that great number was with him, except for him who had exiled himself from the faith: for they had previously chosen rather to lose their own sees and if necessary to be maimed in all their limbs than to be party to such a defilement), he was enthroned in the see of St Peter by the bishop of Modena, the bishop of Bologna and the bishop of Cervia.[48] Such a monstrous act was un-

---

43 Abbot Hugh I of Cluny, Henry IV's godfather, may have attempted to reconcile king and pope in 1083: Rainald of Vézelay, *Vita Hugonis abbatis* IV.26, 903D–904A and H. E. J. Cowdrey (1978) p. 29 n. 42. See H. Diener (1959) pp. 368, 387; A. Kohnle (1993) pp. 114–16, 316; H. E. J. Cowdrey (1998) p. 224.

44 Henry IV concluded a secret treaty with the Romans in summer 1083 according to which he should be crowned emperor the following autumn by Gregory VII or another pope elected 'on [Henry's] advice': Oath of the Romans ed. H. E. J. Cowdrey (1983) p. 248.

45 Cf. Bernold, *Chronicon* 1084, p. 439.

46 On 3 June 1083 Henry had captured the Leonine city. On 21 March 1084 he was able to enter the old city. See G. Meyer von Knonau (1900) pp. 472–8, 526–8; H. E. J. Cowdrey (1998) pp. 222, 228; I. S. Robinson (1999) pp. 224, 227.

47 24 March 1084. See G. Meyer von Knonau (1900) pp. 529–30; J. Ziese (1982) pp. 89–94.

48 Heribert, bishop of Modena; Siegfried, bishop of Bologna; Hildebrand, bishop of Cervia (?): see G. Schwartz (1913) pp. 183–4, 164, 167. All were diocesans of the

[handwritten annotation: ⊅ wibert then consecrated Henry IV]

heard of from the beginning of time. It was from such a man that he then received consecration as emperor at Eastertide[49] and so he entered the city, bringing with him the three-bodied chimera,[50] and reached the Lateran palace. As soon as the venerable Gregory became aware of the agitation among the people, however, he established himself in the citadel of Sant'Angelo, whereupon the king armed all the Romans to lay siege to it.[51] Concealing his knowledge of the approach of the mighty Duke Robert, the king destroyed the residence on the Capitol and, coming to the church of St Peter with Wibert, he utterly destroyed the city of St Peter that Pope Leo IV had built.[52] With this *[handwritten: May]* farewell gesture to the Romans, he retreated, together with Wibert.[53]

Before he had reached Siena,[54] however, the mighty Duke Robert *[handwritten: 1084]* attacked Rome. His army captured the treacherous city, not like Henry after a period of three years, but on the day following his arrival.[55] He freed the pope from the siege and *by flame and sword*[56] he made himself master of all the quarters of the city of Rome. He next spent many days in the Lateran palace and sold many thousands of the Romans like Jews, but others he took captive to Calabria.[57] They deserved such

---

archdiocese of Ravenna. Their participation was unlawful because 'the privilege of this ordination was conceded by the holy Fathers only to the cardinal bishops of Ostia, Albano and Porto: Gebhard of Salzburg, letter (cited in Hugh of Flavigny, *Chronicon* II, pp. 459–60).

49 31 March 1084. See G. Meyer von Knonau (1900) p. 534; J. Ziese (1982) pp. 105–7; I. S. Robinson (1999) pp. 229–31.

50 Cf. Horace, *Carmina* 1.27, 23, 24.

51 Cf. Henry IV, *Letter* 18, p. 28; Bernold, *Chronicon* 1084, p. 440 (an unsuccessful attack by Henry's troops on the Castel S. Angelo in Easter week). See G. Meyer von Knonau (1900) pp. 540–5; H. E. J. Cowdrey (1998) p. 229; I. S. Robinson (1999) p. 232; R. Krautheimer (2000) p. 149.

52 I.e. the Leonine city (Rome on the right bank of the Tiber, including St Peter's), fortified by Leo IV (847–55). No other author records this destruction. Bonizo may have been thinking of the destruction (April or early May 1084) of the house of the Corsi on the Capitol and the fortress in the Septizonium. See G. Meyer von Knonau (1900) pp. 542–4, 549 n.33; H. E. J. Cowdrey (1998) pp. 228–9.

53 21 May 1084. See G. Meyer von Knonau (1900) p. 549.

54 June. Cf. Wido of Ferrara, *De scismate* I.20, p. 549. See G. Meyer von Knonau (1900) pp. 567–8; I. S. Robinson (1999) p. 233.

55 28 May. See G. Meyer von Knonau (1900) pp. 551–4; H. E. J. Cowdrey (1998) pp. 230–1.

56 Cf. Virgil, *Aeneid* 10.232.

57 The destruction in Rome: Wido of Ferrara, *De scismate* I.20, p. 549; Hugh of Flavigny, *Chronicon* II, p. 462. See G. Meyer von Knonau (1900) pp. 552–4; R. Krautheimer (2000) pp. 149–50.

a punishment for, like the Jews, they had betrayed their shepherd. What more is there to say? The venerable pope accompanied Robert to Salerno[58] and remained there for some days, offering the most salutary advice to the people.[59] Not long afterwards, however, his body was seized by sickness and he rendered up his spirit to heaven.[60] God continues to perform many thousands of miracles at his tomb to this present day.[61] He was truly thrice and four times blessed, since he deserved *to suffer dishonour for the name of Jesus.*[62] Indeed he reigns with Peter in heaven, while the other man is universally hated and regarded as pope by no living person, although some men call him pope to find favour with the king. Nevertheless there are some men who, for the king's sake, invent fictions, wishing to brand the lord Gregory with infamy, but to no avail.

For there are those who say that he was not lawfully pope, because of a certain decree of Nicholas II, according to which it was forbidden under pain of anathema that anyone should dare to aspire to the Roman papacy except with the consent of the king and his son.[63] Every consideration will proclaim this to be totally false, but even if it were true, it would be of no importance. For, although it is lawful for the Roman pontiffs to moderate the severity of the canons to suit the needs of the times, nevertheless they are not permitted to destroy them completely.[64] For what else is it than to destroy the law of Christ, if men break the decrees of the holy Roman pontiffs, who founded the Church with their blood, and render invalid the sacrosanct four

---

58 Travelling by way of Monte Cassino and Benevento: see G. Meyer von Knonau (1900) pp. 559–69; H. E. J. Cowdrey (1998) p. 231.

59 Cf. Paul of Bernried, *Life of Gregory VII* c. 124, below, pp. 363–4.

60 25 May 1085. See G. Meyer von Knonau (1903) pp. 59–60; H. E. J. Cowdrey (1998) p. 677.

61 In the cathedral of San Matteo, Salerno. See G. Meyer von Knonau (1903) pp. 61–2; H. E. J. Cowdrey (1998) p. 678.

62 Acts 5:41.

63 I.e. Papal Election Decree of 1059 (see above pp. 204, 206) Bonizo erroneously supposed the phrase in the 'royal paragraph' – showing 'the honour and reverence due to our beloved son Henry [IV] ... and his successors' – to refer to Henry III and Henry IV. The same error appears in the Henrician polemic of 1084/5 *Dicta cuiusdam* p. 459 (no one 'may intrude himself [in the apostolic see] without the election and consent of the emperors Henry, father and son'), which may, therefore, have been Bonizo's source. See H.-G. Krause (1960) p. 190.

64 Cf. Bonizo, *Liber de vita christiana* I.44, p. 33, paraphrasing Nicholas I, *Epistola* 88 (*JE* 2796), *MGH Epistolae* 6, 480 and Innocent I, *Decreta* c. 55 (*JK* 303). Cf. Bonizo above p. 187. See W. Berschin (1972) p. 52.

councils, which are to be venerated by men like the four Gospels.[65] Let
us, however, free the lord Nicholas of good memory from this dis-
graceful imputation and let us demonstrate by means of suitable witnesses that he did not issue such a document. Let Wibert, from whom
the emperor received the imperial crown, appear as a suitable witness
and let him convict them of speaking a falsehood. For if it is true,
according to the decrees of Nicholas, that no one is to be regarded as
a pope unless he has been elected Roman pontiff with the consent of
the king, since Alexander was enthroned in the Roman see without
his consent,[66] it follows that Alexander was not a pope but an excommunicate. If, however, he was an excommunicate and separated from
the church of God, how does this affect Wibert, whom he consecrated
bishop?[67] He could not confer a blessing if he did not possess it, but
instead conferred the curse that he possessed. If, therefore, he is
accursed, how is he now pope? All this, however, is false. For Wibert
lawfully received episcopal consecration and Pope Alexander, who
obtained the office of Roman pontiff against the will of the king, was
legally appointed pope, on the evidence of Wibert.

The same assumption can be made in the case of the emperor. For if
this decree was authentic, why did a man of such great prudence and
ingenuity give his obedience for so many years to Pope Alexander and
why did he receive the imperial crown from Wibert, the latter's
bishop? Let Hugh Candidus, the Roman cardinal, appear as a third
witness and prove that they lied. Why did he elect Gregory on the
very day of the pope's burial? For if the decree is authentic, then he is
excommunicate and if excommunicate, he is a man of evil repute. If he
is a man of evil repute, however, how could Hugh alone elect Wibert
as pope, against the will of the citizens of Rome, in Brixen? The decree,
however, is false and as foolish as children's games, although there is
no doubt that the venerable Gregory had the consent of the king for
his ordination. For Bishop Gregory of Vercelli was sent by the king
and was present at his consecration.[68] If the king had any objection to
him, it behoved him to say so at the beginning, before he had given an
honourable reception to his legates, before he had publicly received
from them absolution from his excommunication, before he had sent

65 Cf. Gregory I, *Registrum* I.25, *MGH Epistolae* 1, 36 (the councils of Nicea, Constantinople, Ephesus and Chalcedon).
66 See above p. 209.
67 See above p. 219.
68 See above p. 221.

Bishop Herman of Bamberg to him to be deposed in Rome, before he had placed another man in the latter's see at his command.[69]

If the king said that he had then been a young man, deceived by the cunning of his counsellors, what are we to say of Archbishop Liemar of Bremen, the wisest of men, most skilled in all the arts? Surely after he was suspended from his office by the legates of that pope, did he not abstain from performing the office of priest until he had come from Saxony to Rome,[70] bringing with him the philosophers of the kingdom, Widukind of Cologne, the provost Wezilo (who subsequently was the ruin of the church of Mainz)[71] and Meinhard of Bamberg,[72] and with them he fell at the feet of the pope and tearfully sought pardon, until he obtained it and recovered the priestly office? Indeed I might say, if he was not pope, why did the king receive from him absolution from excommunication at Canossa, unless there are those who would say that an extorted confession is not a confession. Those who say this have failed to understand the decrees of the blessed Alexander, the fifth Roman pontiff after blessed Peter.[73] For they say that there is no extorted confession unless a man is forced by torture or threats either to deny the truth or to sin by idolatry.[74] To acknowledge the truth unwillingly is characteristic of guilty men and this is not an extorted confession but an unwitting one, when a man is forced to acknowledge what he had malevolently resolved to deny, so disclosing the truth.

There are others who say that the venerable Gregory was lawfully pope, but that he spoke a sentence of condemnation against himself. For in the second week after Easter in St Peter's,[75] when he had

---

69 See above p. 223.

70 1075. See above p. 223. His journey to Rome: C. Erdmann (1938) pp. 266–7; C. Schneider (1972) p. 126; H. E. J. Cowdrey (1998) p. 124.

71 Wezilo, clerk of Halberstadt; archbishop of Mainz (1084–8): see G. Meyer von Knonau (1900) p. 578.

72 Meinhard, master of the cathedral school of Bamberg; imperial anti-bishop of Würzburg (1085–8). See C. Erdmann (1938) p. 20.

73 Cf. Bonizo, *Liber de vita christiana* IV.5, p. 115.

74 Cf. Pseudo-Alexander I, *Decreta, Decretales Pseudoisidorianae* p. 98.

75 13 April 1080. Cf. Beno, *Gesta Romanae ecclesiae* I.7, p. 371 ('By the next feast of St Peter King Henry will be dead or will be deposed from the kingship.... By no means retain me as pope ... if this prophecy has not come to pass by the time of that feast'); Sigebert of Gembloux, *Chronica* 1080, p. 364 ('he prophesied truly, but his conjecture about the false king deceived him, since he wished to interpret it as referring to King Henry'). H. E. J. Cowdrey (1998) p. 199 n. 550 suggested that this story may be based on the actual prophecy of *Epistolae Vagantes* 13, p. 30

excommunicated the king, he added, 'Let it be known to all of you that if he does not recover his senses by the feast of St Peter,[76] he will die or be deposed. If this does not happen, I ought no more to be believed.' Those who have no true understanding of these words, eagerly seize on them and each twists them in a false sense according to his will. These words, however, were not a sentence of condemnation pronounced against himself. For it is one thing to say, 'I ought not to be believed' and another to say, 'I judge that I must be deposed.' For it cannot be called a true sentence, if it is passed before the case is tried. Nor will a sentence have any validity if it is pronounced without proper reflection. Moreover, although simple folk interpret it in a sense other than the true one, everyone of sound mind has no doubt that he spoke the truth. For if, as it is written in the Law, whoever prophesies in the name of the Lord and the event that he foretold does not happen, let him be stoned, because he has taken the name of the Lord in vain,[77] how are we to interpret the case of Jonah? He prophesied the destruction of Nineveh,[78] but when Nineveh was not destroyed, he neither died nor was rejected. Surely this destruction is to be understood as a spiritual one, according to the text, *Overthrow the wicked and they are no more.*[79] Thus the voice of the Lord spoke to the first man, *In the day that you* taste, *you shall die*,[80] but there is proof that he lived for more than nine hundred years after eating what was forbidden,[81] because the death with which he was threatened was punishment, not the natural death by which the soul is released from the bonds of the body. For we learn from Scripture that there are three kinds of death. The first is spiritual, according to which the soul is dead to vices and lives in God, concerning which it is written, *Blessed are the dead, who die in the Lord.*[82] The second is natural, by which the soul is liberated from the bonds of the body. The third is punishment, of which is written, *The soul that sins, shall die.*[83] This is

---

(spring or summer 1076?) that 'the feast of St Peter will not pass by before it has become clear to all that [Henry] was most justly excommunicated'.

76 29 June 1080.

77 A garbled reminiscence of Jeremiah 14: 15; cf. Deuteronomy 18:20.

78 Jonah 3:4.

79 Proverbs 12:7.

80 Genesis 2:17.

81 Genesis 5:5.

82 Revelation 14:13.

83 Ezechiel 18:4.

undoubtedly the death by which he died, who knelt and *worshipped the beast*[84] in Brixen.

Some say, however, that he was not deposed from the kingship on that day, but they do not understand that 'or' is a disjunctive, not an affirmative conjunction:[85] although he was not deposed in human eyes, he was nevertheless deposed in the eyes of God. For who will deny that after Samuel said to Saul, 'God *will tear the kingdom* away from you this day *and will give it* to one better than you'[86] and that after David was anointed, Saul reigned in human eyes, full of the spirit of the devil, until the most cruel battle of Gilboa and his own destruction?[87] How much better it would have been for him if he had been deprived of the royal power on that day on which he was rejected by the Lord, rather than that, filled with lust for the kingship, he should have commanded Doeg the Edomite to slay the priests of the Lord and to kill *eighty men* clad *in the linen ephod.*[88] How much better if (as I said) on that same day on which he was rejected, he had *worshipped* the devil in the guise of Samuel[89] and had not heard his words, *You and your sons shall be with me tomorrow.*[90] What more is there to say? It is perfectly clear that he was dead and deposed on that day on which he knelt and worshipped Wibert.

There are again certain men who say that the venerable Gregory was truly the Roman pontiff, but that he excommunicated the king unjustly, according to the decree of Felix, pope and martyr, which reads: *'No one who has been despoiled of his property or expelled from his see can be* excommunicated or *judged* before *everything* has been restored to him' and so forth.[91] This text seems to apply specifically to

---

84 Revelation 13:4: i.e. the antipope Wibert.

85 Cf. Isidore of Seville, *Etymologiae* I.12.2, II.27.5. See W. Berschin (1972) p. 6 n. 12.

86 I Samuel 28:17.

87 *Ibid.,* 31: 1–6.

88 *Ibid.,* 22:18.

89 *Ibid.,* 28:14.

90 *Ibid.,* 28:19.

91 Pseudo-Isidore, *Praefatio* c. 6, *Decretales Pseudoisidorianae* p. 18 (cf. *Decreta Felicis [I]* c. 10; *Decreta Felicis [II]* c. 12, *ibid.,* pp. 201, 486). This argument (the *exceptio spolii*) had been cited in defence of Henry IV at the confrontation between representatives of the papal and imperial parties at Gerstungen-Berka (20–21 January 1085). The Gregorian synod of Quedlinburg, held by the legate, Cardinal bishop Odo of Ostia (20 April 1085), subsequently excommunicated 'the sect ... that declares that laymen despoiled of their goods are not subject to judgement' (Bernold, *Chronicon* 1085, p. 442). See G. Meyer von Knonau (1903) pp. 14–21;

bishops;[92] but even if that were not the case, it will be demonstrated very clearly both that it offers no support to their argument and that the king was justly excommunicated. For if there had been any dispute about the kingship and whether he exercised the government of the kingdom justly or unjustly, then I concede that he ought to be restored to his office before being excommunicated and judged.[93] But the dispute between the pope and the king arose solely from the fact that, like Focius and Dioscorus,[94] the king *set* his *mouth against the heavens*[95] and attempted to drive from his throne the lord pope of the elder see of Rome. The second excommunication, however, was pronounced because, although the king had been admonished once and twice and three times not to do battle and to provide an opportunity for holding a council in his kingdom, he refused to obey.[96] The pope imitated the teacher of the Gentiles when he said that he was *ready to punish every disobedience*[97] and he took measures to suppress the rebellion of his arrogant son, wishing not to destroy him but to summon him to penitence.

But when previously you asked me, dearest friend, whether it is lawful for a Christian to fight with weapons for the truth, you were requesting a history. This I have now composed – for although it is very well known to many readers, it will nevertheless benefit posterity – so that you will recognise that, if it was ever lawful for a Christian to make war for any cause, it is lawful to make war by every means on the Wibertines. For if the blessed Gregory commanded everyone to fight against the heresy of the simoniacs and neophytes *for the sake of their office*,[98] there is no doubt that they must fight even more against

---

A. Becker (1964) pp. 71–4; I. S. Robinson (1978a) pp. 105–9; J. Vogel (1982) pp. 179–84; H. E. J. Cowdrey (1998) pp. 238–9.

92 Cf. Odo of Ostia, encyclical (*Briefsammlungen der Zeit Heinrichs IV*, p. 378) denying that 'this [text], which refers specifically to bishops, was said of all men in general'.

93 Cf. Bernard, *Liber canonum* c.14, p. 487: Henry was not condemned 'on account of the kingdom of Saxony'.

94 Cf. above pp. 235–6, 238–9.

95 Psalm 72:9.

96 Cf. Gregory VII, *Registrum* VII.14a, c. 7, p. 486: ('not fearing the danger of disobedience ... by preventing the holding of a conference').

97 Cf. II Corinthians 10:6.

98 Cf. Gregory I, *Registrum* XII.9 (*JE* 1859), *MGH Epistolae* 2, 357 (cited from John the Deacon, *Vita Gregorii* III.4, *MPL* 75, 131D). Cf. Bonizo, *Liber de vita christiana* III.24, p. 79. See A. Michel (1943) p. 44; J.J. Ryan (1956) p. 45; J. Gilchrist (1965) p. 210 n. 3.

this, which is the mother of all heresies. Nor shall we judge knights to
be strangers to the kingdom of God, since the Baptist did not shun
knights, but commanded them to fight and to *be content with* their
wages.[99] Surely our Lord Jesus Christ preferred the faith of a centurion
to that of the children of Israel and did not refuse to cure his servant.[100] After His glorious ascension into the heavens the first of the
Gentiles to believe were knights and their alms and prayers were so
acceptable[101] that when Simon Peter entered the house of Cornelius,
the latter and those who were with him received the gifts of the Holy
Spirit before Peter laid his hands on them and cleansed them with the
water of baptism.[102] They returned to their duties after baptism and
fought under the command of Gentile leaders.[103] If it was lawful to
fight for an earthly king, will it not be lawful to fight for the King of
Heaven? If it was lawful to fight for the state, will it not be lawful to
fight for righteousness? If it was lawful to fight against barbarians,
will it not be lawful to fight against heretics?

Surely, as we read in the *History of the Franks*, St Hilary armed King
Clovis against the heretical Arians?[104] Moreover the blessed Augustine,
the eminent doctor, exhorted Bonifacius to plunder and persecute the
Circumcelliones and the Donatists and wrote to him, among other
things: *Augustine sends greetings to the admirable man Bonifacius. You
complain of the severity of the battle. I would not have you hesitate and I
shall give you and your men useful advice. Seize your weapons in your
hands, let the author's prayer ring in your ears because when the battle is
fought, God looks down with open eyes and He gives the palm and the
victory to that party that He considers to be just.*[105] *Do not think that it is
impossible to please God by making war. This is what the holy David did, to
whose greatness the Lord bore witness: I shall place the fruit of your womb
upon your throne. This is what the centurion did, of whom the Lord said,
Truly, I say to you, not even in Israel have I found such faith. This is what*

---

99 Luke 3:14.

100 Matthew 8:10.

101 Acts 10:4, 31.

102 Acts 10:44–7.

103 The sense of this sentence is incomplete, although there is no lacuna in the codex.

104 Gregory of Tours, *Historia Francorum* II.37, *MGH, Scriptores rerum Merovin-
gicarum* 1, 100.

105 Pseudo-Augustine, *Epistola* 13, *MPL* 33, col. 1098, also found in Anselm of Lucca,
Collectio XIII.5 and Anselm, *Liber contra Wibertum* p. 524. See W. Berschin (1972)
pp. 53–4.

Cornelius did, whose alms were acceptable to God. What shall I say?[106] *It is by necessity, not by will that the enemy is slain in battle.*[107] This same author, dealing with the sermon delivered by the Lord on the mount and reaching the passage in the Beatitudes, *Blessed are those who are persecuted for righteousness' sake,*[108] said that those who inflict persecution for righteousness' sake are equally as blessed as those who suffer persecution for righteousness' sake.[109]

Jerome remembered this in his treatise on the Pentateuch, saying: 'If the Hebrew is commanded not to spare his father or mother or the wife who sleeps in his bosom, if they wish to turn him away from the truth, how much more, O Christian, should you recognise that you must not spare the heretic who tears the garment of the Lord Jesus?'[110] The same author wrote to Rusticus of Narbonne: *Cruelty inflicted on God's behalf is not impiety.*[111] St Jerome in his treatise on Jeremiah wrote to Eusebius of Cremona: 'To destroy *murderers*, adulterers and wicked men condemned to death *is not* to commit homicide *but* to keep *the laws.*'[112] The venerable Ambrose, a jewel among priests,[113] boasted in one of his letters that he had been defended from the rage of Empress Justina by the weapons of the people.[114] The most holy Gregory, the star of gold, was censured by Emperor Maurice because he had granted to the soldiers defending the walls of the city of Rome more abundant allowance of food and weapons than they were accustomed to receive from the emperor. But let us hear what he wrote to Velox, captain of the military. *It now seems useful to despatch some soldiers there, whom*

106 Augustine, *Epistola* 189.4, *CSEL* 57, 133–4, also found in Anselm, *Collectio* XIII.4 and Anselm, *Liber contra Wibertum* p. 524. Bonizo's version contains a number of interpolations: W. Berschin (1972) pp. 53–4.

107 Augustine, *Epistola* 189.6, p. 135. Cf. Anselm, *Collectio* XIII.4. See W. Berschin (1972) p. 54.

108 Matthew 5:10.

109 Augustine, *Epistola* 185.11, pp. 9–10. The passage of which Bonizo gives a highly tendentious summary here appears in his *Liber de vita christiana* VII.17, p. 243. Cf. Anselm, *Collectio* XIII.14; Anselm, *Liber contra Wibertum* p. 523. See W. Berschin (1972) pp. 54–5.

110 Deuteronomy 13:6. This passage has not been identified in Jerome's works: see W. Berschin (1972) p. 55.

111 Jerome, *Epistola* 109 c. 3 (actually to the priest Riparius), *CSEL* 55, 354.

112 Jerome, *Commentarii in Ieremiam* IV.22, *MPL* 24, col. 811D. Bonizo gave a different version of this text in his *Liber de vita christiana* X.75, p. 332. See W. Berschin (1972) p. 55.

113 See above p. 196.

114 Cf. Ambrose, *Epistolae* I.22, *MPL* 16, 1022B. See above p. 168 and n. 59.

Your Honour should take care to admonish and exhort so that they are ready for their work. You should find an opportunity to speak with our most glorious sons Marcius and Vitalius and do whatever they command you to do with God's help for the sake of the state. If you learn that Ariulf has advanced as far as the region of Ravenna, appear at his back, as befits brave men.[115] He also wrote to Marcius and Vitalius among other things: *Glorious sons, be wary, because, as I have learned, the enemy has assembled a multitude and is said to be still in arms. If he wishes to incur God's wrath by despatching his forces here, you are, with the Lord's help, to lay waste his lands.*[116] The same author wrote in his *Moralia*: 'To kill a cruel man is not an act of cruelty.'[117]

You have heard these documents of the holy Fathers: take notice of the examples of those who fought for the truth. We have read that the prefect Hermogenes, who persecuted Bishop Paul of Constantinople out of zeal for the Arian heresy, was burned with all his household by the orthodox and we know that this deed won not reproaches but praise from all men.[118] What shall I say of the Alexandrians? Are they not praised throughout the whole world for the various battles and conflicts in which they engaged against the Arians?[119] Are not the Milanese deservedly exalted and glorified by Catholics for liberating the orthodox bishops who fled into their church from the power of Constantius?[120] Did not Bishop Cyril of Alexandria, who was praised in the Council of Ephesus,[121] place among the martyrs the monk Amonius, who struck the prefect Orestes with a rock, incited by *a zeal for God, but not fully enlightened*,[122] and was stoned for this on the order of Orestes?[123]

Let us now come to our own times and see what the Almighty conferred on the men who fought against the Normans under the leadership of Pope Leo. For He crowned them with glory and honour and proved

---

115 Gregory I, *Registrum* II.7, *MGH Epistolae* 1, 106. Cf. Anselm of Lucca, *Liber contra Wibertum* p. 525. See W. Berschin (1972) p. 55.

116 Gregory I, *Registrum* II.33, *MGH Epistolae* 1, 130. Cf. Anselm *Liber contra Wibertum* p. 525. See W. Berschin (1972) pp. 55–6.

117 This text is not found in Gregory I, *Moralia in Iob.*.

118 See above p. 164.

119 See above p. 164.

120 See above p. 164.

121 Council of Ephesus (431), *MPL* 84, col. 151B.

122 Romans 10:2.

123 Cassiodorus-Epiphanius, *Historia ecclesiastica tripartita* XI.11, *CSEL* 71, 643.

by signs and wonders that they had pleased Him.[124] What shall I say of the religious man Herlembald[125] and of that most Christian man, the Roman prefect Cencius,[126] at whose tombs God performs many miracles?

Let the most glorious knights of God fight for the truth, therefore, let them struggle for righteousness, let them fight with a true heart against the heresy that *exalts* itself *and opposes every so-called god or object of worship.*[127] Let them endeavour to equal in goodness the most excellent Countess Matilda, the daughter of St. Peter, who with a virile mind, neglecting all worldly considerations, is prepared to die rather than to break the law of God and to oppose the heresy that now rages in the Church in every way, as far as her strength permits. For we believe that it is *into* her *hand* that *Sisera is sold,*[128] and *like Jabin,* he will be *destroyed at the river of Kishon.*[129] Because he has *ravaged* God's *vine* and *fed on* it like the *wild boar,*[130] he has *become dung for the ground.*[131] We, however, according to the nature of our office, shall pray that he will be *burned with fire,* will be *cut down* and *may* very suddenly *perish at the rebuke of Thy countenance.*[132]

124 See above p. 193.
125 See above pp. 229–30.
126 See above p. 243.
127 II Thessalonians 2:4.
128 Judges 4:9. Donizo, *Vita Mathildis* II.749, p. 394, used the same biblical parallel to describe Matilda's rebellion against Henry IV: 'like Jael, she has now struck a great nail into the temple of Sisera' (Judges 4:21). See T. Struve (1995) p. 58.
129 Psalm 82:10.
130 Psalm 79:15.
131 Psalm 82:11.
132 Psalm 79:17.

Paul of Bernried, The Life of Pope Gregory VII

1 Gregory VII, therefore,[1] *on* whom *the spirit of* Gregory I[2] truly *rested,*[3] was a Tuscan by birth[4] and his father was named Bonicus[5]. He himself received in baptism *the name* Hildebrand, *which prophetically foreshadowed future events.*[6] For 'Hildebrand' in the German vernacular means 'burning up of earthly desire',[7] which the psalmist besought heaven to bestow on him: *Prove me, O Lord, and try me; test my reins and my heart.*[8] It was fitting that this name was given in baptism, as John the Baptist said, *I indeed baptise you with water for repentance, but He who is coming after me is mightier than I, whose sandals I am not worthy to carry; He will baptise you with the Holy Spirit and with fire.*[9] Of this fire the Saviour said, *I came to cast fire upon the earth and would that it were already kindled.*[10] Since this man would one day with *the fiery eloquence*[11] of the Lord ward off the fiery darts of the enemy from the house of the Lord, it was fitting that the fire of which he would give the most fervent proofs of charity and truth, should appear in his name.

2 We possess even more powerful prognostications of the divine fervour that was in him, because of which, when we chanced to read

---

1 The biography seems to have lost its introduction. The allusion to Gregory I suggests that the lost introduction drew a comparison between Gregory VII and Gregory I.

2 Pope Gregory I (590–604). On the parallels drawn between the two popes by Gregorian polemicists: I. S. Robinson (1978a) pp. 31–9.

3 Cf. II Kings 2:15.

4 Cf. Benzo of Alba, *To Henry IV* VII.2, below p. 370 (Hildebrand 'was from Tuscany'). The claim that he was born in Sovana (southern Tuscany) is found only in the biography by Boso, *Liber pontificalis* 2, 360.

5 R. L. Poole (1934) pp. 185–222 linked Hildebrand with the Pierleoni, G. Marchetti-Longhi (1947) pp. 287–333 with the Roman family of the Ildebrandini-Stefaneschi, H. E. J. Cowdrey (1998) p. 27 the Aldebrandini (southern Tuscany). See also R. Hüls (1977) pp. 268–9.

6 Cf. *Vita sancti Maioli* I.1, *MPL* 137, col. 746C. See J. Greving (1893) pp. 10–11.

7 Cf. J.M. Watterich p. 474 ('the conflagration of battle'); J. Greving (1893) p. 12.

8 Psalm 25:2.

9 Matthew 3:11.

10 Luke 12:49.

11 Cf. Psalm 118:140.

Isidore on the origins and the deaths of the patriarchs, we compared him to the prophet Elijah in days of old. For there, if my memory does not deceive me, it is said that the head of the newly born Elijah was lighted up by a ball of fire[12] to foreshadow that ardent striving for heaven which would later inflame him against the transgressions of wicked kings and the seductions of false prophets.[13] In a similar fashion, sparks of fire were seen to appear on the clothes of the infant Gregory or Hildebrand, doubtless to predict the fervour of holy zeal by which he himself was ignited against the oppressive arrogance of the insane Henry[14] and the insupportable licence of unchaste priests. This vision of the sparks was quite frequently witnessed and is said to have been first observed by St Majolus, the father of the monastery of Cluny,[15] who applied to him that saying about the blessed John the Baptist: this boy *will be great before the Lord.*[16]

3 Finally let us record without interruption all that we have learned of the visions of fire associated with him. A flame was once seen issuing from his head, making the resemblance to Elijah plainer, always bearing in mind the difference in their time of life. The former portent of future prophetic rebuke occurred in infancy, while the latter sign of future apostolic judgement happened at the age of maturity.

4 There was also some resemblance to Elijah[17] in the fact that a perverter of justice who showed contempt for Hildebrand was fearfully punished by fire from heaven. For when he was serving as the archdeacon of his predecessor, Alexander,[18] a certain poor man brought his tearful complaint to the Roman pontiff. He was the victim of an intolerable injustice, the theft of his inheritance by a very evil and formidably powerful man.[19] When the pope, dreading that he would come to harm from that irreverent and impudent character, was afraid to give a just judgement in support of the wretched man's case, *the*

12 Isidore of Seville, *De ortu et obitu Patrum* c. 64, *MPL* 83, 141A.

13 *Ibid.*, c. 61, 140C.

14 Henry IV, king of the Germans (1056–1106), emperor (1084).

15 Majolus, abbot of Cluny died 994; Hildebrand was born *c.* 1015: see H. E. J. Cowdrey (1998) p. 28. J. Greving (1893) p. 12 n. 4 suggested that Paul confused Majolus with his successor Odilo (994–1048), about whom he heard this story from the monks of St Mary on the Aventine.

16 Luke 1:15.

17 Cf. II Kings 1:9–12.

18 Alexander II (1061–73).

19 See J. Greving (1893) p. 13; H. E. J. Cowdrey (1998) p. 58.

righteous Hildebrand, *bold as a lion*,[20] tried at first to rouse up and strengthen the pope to inflict punishment. He was utterly unable, however, to free him *from* his *timidity of spirit*[21] and he requested that that office of mercy and truth should be entrusted to himself. Immediately on receiving this, he delivered a sentence of anathema against the robber. The latter either felt no fear or was ashamed to show fear of that grave judgement. Three days afterwards he was showing off his horsemanship among his comrades in a more boastful and insolent manner than usual, when he was suddenly struck down by a bolt of lightning and, like hardhearted Pharaoh,[22] he sank *in the lake that burns with fire.*[23]

5 Meanwhile he had that famous dream, a prophecy of papal excellence and power, that fire came out of his mouth that set the whole world on fire: doubtless indeed that *fire* that the Lord Jesus Christ *cast upon the earth* and eagerly *wished* to *be kindled*.[24] But the impious did not understand this and the wicked knew nothing of it. For because they blasphemed against the Holy Spirit and called Him, in the person of His servant (whom they *convicted of sin*),[25] 'hell brand', they became subject to the just punishment of God for their unpardonable offence and incurred the perpetual misery of an evil name and in a wonderful manner, which brought salvation to the pious, became lethal to the impious.[26]

6 Here follows the kind of miracle that is well known from the example not only of Elijah[27] but also of *innocent Abel*[28] and of the most wise Solomon[29] and of others among the Fathers: namely that the

20 Proverbs 28:1.

21 Psalm 54:9.

22 Cf. Exodus 14:28.

23 Revelation 21:8.

24 Luke 12:49.

25 John 8:46.

26 'Among the Germans Hildebrand was called, according to the etymology of his name *hell brand* (*Gesta episcoporum Halberstadensium, MGH SS* 23, 98). Cf. Wenrich of Trier, *Epistola* c. 2, p. 286 ('it was fitting that fire marked out ... the child, since ... it has now set alight the whole world'); Beno, *Gesta Romanae ecclesiae* II.6, p. 377 (Hildebrand 'struck his sleeves and fire leaped out in the form of sparks and by means of these miracles he deluded the eyes of the simple, who took it for a sign of sanctity').

27 Cf. I Kings 18:38.

28 Matthew 23:35; cf. Genesis 4:4.

29 I Kings 8:64.

Holy Spirit fell on their offerings under the semblance of fire. For after he was raised up by God to the watchtower of the apostles Peter and Paul and broadcast *their voice through all the earth* and spread *their words to the end of the world*,[30] he stirred up against himself the most grievous persecution of the modern Nero,[31] that is, King Henry IV, to whom in his shameful criminality all preaching of the truth, like a consuming fire, was intolerable. Of necessity, therefore, he was forced to *flee from town to town*[32] and sought for a while the protection of the most Christian Countess Matilda.[33]

7 It once happened that while he was her guest[34] and *his abode was established in peace and his dwelling place in Zion*, that is, in the watch-tower of heavenly contemplation,[35] the wheel of time revolved and the day was at hand that is usually known as the Lord's Supper,[36] which is particularly dedicated to the pontifical offices. In order to celebrate this festival he went to the abbey called Nonantola,[37] which had rejoiced in the patronage of his holy predecessors Silvester and Hadrian.[38] He was proceeding with the holy ministrations and had already completed the consecration of the chrism, when suddenly a bright light from heaven lit up the consecrated liquid like fire and he was glorified like the ancient Fathers by this sign of divine acceptance.

8 It seems appropriate now to end these miracles involving fire with the miraculous extinguishing of a fire which, as we read in the chron-icles of venerable men,[39] happened in this way. When the aforesaid

---

30 Psalm 18:5; Romans 10:18.

31 Gregorian polemicists equated Henry IV with Emperor Nero (54–68) as a persecutor of the Church: Gebhard of Salzburg, *Epistola* c. 32, p. 278; Manegold, *Liber ad Gebehardum* c. 43, p. 385; Bernard of Hildesheim, *Liber canonum* c. 43, p. 513; Deusdedit, *Libellus contra invasores* II.11, p. 329; II.12, p. 330.

32 Matthew 10:23; Matthew 23:34.

33 Matilda, margravine of Tuscany (✝1115).

34 In the months following Henry IV's absolution at Canossa, 1077 (below p. 327).

35 Psalm 75:3. Cf. *Glossa Ordinaria* on Psalm 75:3: '*in Zion*, that is his dwelling place will be in contemplation'.

36 Thursday in Holy Week, 13 April 1077.

37 There is no corroboration for this visit, but it is not improbable. A late tradition placing Gregory in Nonantola on Easter day: A. Overmann (1895) p. 141.

38 The abbey possessed relics of Pope Silvester I (314–35) and Pope Hadrian III (884–5). J. Greving (1893) p. 13 n. 4 suggested that Paul visited Nonantola on his Italian journey.

39 Bernold of St Blasien, *Chronicon* 1082, p. 437.

Henry was besieging the walls of the city of Rome with a hostile army, he set fire to a certain place so that the people would be drawn away from defending their ramparts by the need to avert the danger of a conflagration and he might burst into the city without meeting any resistance. Gregory, mighty in the faith of Christ, saw through this cunning device and made the sign of the cross and immediately he extinguished the blaze, just as if he had poured on it the Tiber in full flood, and commanded the populace to return to the defence of the ramparts.

9 We intend to return again to his boyhood, during which he was entrusted by his parents to his uncle, the abbot of the monastery of Mary, the holy mother of God, on the Aventine Hill,[40] to be educated in the liberal sciences and trained in moral discipline.[41] In a short time he demonstrated the admirable fruits of both branches of this instruction.

10 Now that he had entered adolescence, he departed for Francia in order to subdue the wantonness of the flesh there by means both of the irksomeness of foreign travel and of perseverance in scholarship.[42] When after some years he was about to return to Rome, through the secret foresight of God he stayed for a little time at the court of Henry III[43] so that the *progress* of the man who was to be raised up to the summit of the priesthood would be *made manifest to all men*[44] from

---

40 The abbey of St Mary on the Aventine had adopted the 'customs' of Cluny and the abbots of Cluny stayed there when visiting Rome. The abbot whom Paul's (uncorroborated) account claims as Hildebrand's uncle has not been identified: see G. Miccoli (1966c) p. 295; H. Fichtenau (1986) pp. 60–1; H. E. J. Cowdrey (1998) p. 28.

41 Paul evidently believed Hildebrand to have been an oblate, dedicated to the monastic life: see J. Greving (1893) p. 18. G. B. Borino (1946) pp. 240, 259–60 interpreted Paul's statement as meaning simply that Hildebrand received his education at the hands of his uncle, the abbot. But see I. Schuster (1950) pp. 52–7; I. Schuster (1952) pp. 305–7; H. Fichtenau (1986) pp. 59–68. Gregory VII was brought up in Rome since his 'infancy' (*Registrum* I.39, III.10a, pp. 62, 270) and 'educated in the bosom of this mother church from his boyhood' (*Registrum* I.1*, p. 2). Cf. Bruno of Segni, *Sermon* c. 2, below p. 379 ('a certain Roman monk').

42 Evidently a reference to the exile of 1047–8: above p. 60. The term *Francia* might signify Burgundy (the stay in Cluny claimed by Bonizo of Sutri) or Lotharingia, where Hildebrand spent at least part of his exile: above p. 188 n. 56. Cf. Bruno of Segni, *Sermon* c. 2, below p. 379. See H. E. J. Cowdrey (1998) p. 29.

43 Henry III, king of the Germans (1039–56), emperor (1046). Perhaps an allusion to Hildebrand's legation of 1054 to the imperial court: see Bonizo, *Book to a Friend* V, above p. 194 and Benzo of Alba, *To Henry IV* VII.2, below p. 370. Gregory VII's recollections of Henry III: above p. 194 n. 97.

44 I Timothy 4:15.

the supreme eminence of the kingship. Hence the emperor himself said that he had never heard a man preaching *the word of God with such great boldness.*[45] The most excellent of the bishops who took counsel for the commonwealth also *wondered at the gracious words which proceeded out of his mouth.*[46]

11 Afterwards he returned to Rome and, applying himself to the pursuit of perfection and striving to double *the talents* of intellect and practical ability that he had *received*[47] from God, he sensed that the idle *men of his own house* were *his enemies*[48] and proved that saying of the Truth, '*No prophet is* received *in his own country.*'[49] Wishing to show forbearance to the envious and to seek the greater fruits of charity, therefore, he decided to return to the territories of Germany and Gaul. When he reached Aquapendente,[50] the blessed Peter, who had already decided on his elevation to his own see, appeared to him in a vision and forbade him to go any further. Hildebrand, however, thought that this apparition was a delusion and he did not turn back from his planned journey. On the second night he again ignored a similar vision. Then on the third night he was utterly terrified by the apparition of the apostle threatening him with severe punishment if he did not return and thus he recalled him to the relief of the Roman church.

12 In those days, on the death of Damasus II,[51] Leo IX[52] succeeded, who cordially venerated and cherished the prudence and holiness of that praiseworthy man and began to make use of his advice in all matters.[53] Their harmonious cooperation tore up the thorns in the Lord's field[54] and bore much fruit.

13 Meanwhile he was ordained subdeacon by that same pope[55] and he

45 Acts 4:31.

46 Luke 4:22.

47 Cf. Matthew 25:16–24.

48 Cf. Micah 7:6; Matthew 10:36.

49 Luke 4:24.

50 In the papal patrimony, north of Orvieto. No other source records this miracle.

51 Damasus II (1047–8) †9 August.

52 Leo IX (1048/9–1054), elected December 1048, consecrated 12 February 1049.

53 Cf. Gregory VII, *Registrum* I.79, p. 113 (referring to his advice, 'which the blessed Leo took ill'); Bonizo, *Book to a Friend* V, above p. 191 and Bruno of Segni, *Sermon* c. 2, below p. 380. See H. E. J. Cowdrey (1998) p. 30.

54 Cf. Matthew 13:7; Mark 4:7; Luke 8:7.

55 Cf. Desiderius of Monte Cassino, *Dialogi* III.1, p. 1143; Bonizo, *Book to a Friend* V, above pp. 190–1.

was given authority over the monastery of St Paul, which was in a wretched and forsaken condition.[56] At the outset he was greatly strengthened by this vision. The blessed Paul appeared to him in his basilica, standing with a shovel in his hands, clearing cow dung from the pavement and throwing it outside. When the onlooker stood idly by, the apostle rebuked him, asking why he did not help him, and commanded him to take a shovel and cast out the dung as he himself was doing. For after the brigands of Campania had seized the income [of the monastery], the observance of the Rule and of a holy life had become so lax that cattle freely entered the house of prayer and polluted it and the women who performed the necessary duties in the refectory disgraced the reputation of the very few monks who remained. Hildebrand therefore removed all the filth and regained possession of adequate provisions and gathered a distinguished congregation of regular monks and because of their discipline and religion that place is still held in veneration today.

14 Finally he began to have such extraordinary confidence in the efficacy of their prayers that if ever he was not liberated by them from his misfortunes, he took it as a most certain sign that there was an impediment in the form of some transgression among them. After this was corrected by an investigation in his own presence, their prayers would hasten his liberation in the usual way. They were indeed a blessed father[57] and blessed sons, among whom there was no place for ignorance and no fault went unpunished but was made public following the example of Joshua[58] and chastised, according to the command of the apostle, *in the spirit of gentleness.*[59] Nevertheless any men, whatever their profession, who presumed to commit more serious offences in St Paul's, especially involving impurity or sacrilege, *were* immediately *destroyed by the Destroyer*[60] to avenge the dignity of the apostle. For just as we read that in the time of Gregory I the blessed

---

56 The abbey of St Paul-without-the-Walls. Cf. *Liber pontificalis* 2, 275: 'afterwards [Leo IX] gave him the church of the holy apostle Paul to rule'. After Airard became bishop of Nantes (1050), retaining the title of abbot of St Paul's (✝1060?), Hildebrand served for twenty years as the administrator of the abbey without the abbatial title. See I. Schuster (1934) p. 77; H. E. J. Cowdrey (1998) p. 31.

57 Paul seems to suppose that Hildebrand was abbot of St Paul's: see J. Greving (1893) pp. 22–4.

58 Cf. Josuah 7:16–25.

59 Galatians 6:1.

60 I Corinthians 10:10.

apostle Andrew was the avenger of his sanctuary,[61] so also in the days of Hildebrand, who was Gregory VII, the blessed apostle Paul appeared as the defender of his sanctuary, both apostles working alongside their servants.

15 Meanwhile the spiritual *vinedresser*, that is, the holy Pope Leo, inspected and greatly admired the *fruit* of his *vine branch* because *he abode in* Christ *and* Christ *in him*[62] and he enlarged Christ's *home* in *him* by ordaining him deacon and *in order that* he *might bear more fruit*,[63] he made him archdeacon of the Roman church.[64]

16 Afterwards he was sent to the territory of Gaul to exercise the office of vicar of the pope,[65] which had been entrusted to him, so that he could justly say with the apostle, *Thanks be to God, who in Christ always leads us in triumph and through us spreads the fragrance of the knowledge of Him everywhere. For we are the aroma of Christ to God among those who are being saved and among those who are perishing, to one a fragrance from death to death, to the other a fragrance from life to life.*[66]

17 Lyons, which is the foremost see of Gaul,[67] was the first to experience this fragrance when he held a synod. For, as Pope Calixtus[68] used to tell the story, on the first day of the council a certain false bishop[69] was accused of obtaining his bishopric by simony, but since the trial could not be completed, it was postponed until the following day. Meanwhile what was the accused man, aware of his guilt, to do, where was he to turn? He did not dare to try to bribe the judge, whose mind was more inflexible than adamant, since he had no doubt that this

---

61 Cf. John the Deacon, *Vita Gregorii I* IV.97, MPL 75, col. 239B-240B.

62 John 15:4–5.

63 John 15:2.

64 Hildebrand's earliest appearance as archdeacon was 14 October 1059: G. B. Borino (1948) pp. 463–516; D. Jasper (1986) pp. 34–46; H. E. J. Cowdrey (1998) pp. 37–9 and above p. 196.

65 Paul seems to refer to the second of Hildebrand's two known legations to France, that for Victor II, 1056. See T. Schieffer (1934) pp. 50–3, 55–8; H. E. J. Cowdrey (1998) pp. 32–3.

66 II Corinthians 2:14–15.

67 In 1079 Gregory VII recognised the primacy of Lyons over the ecclesiastical province of Gallia Lugdunensis (archdioceses of Lyons, Rouen, Tours and Sens), on the basis of Pseudo-Isidorean authority. See H. Fuhrmann (1954) pp. 61–84; R. Somerville (1972) pp. 11, 124; F. Villard (1991) pp. 421–34; H. E. J. Cowdrey (1998) pp. 389–94, 602–4.

68 Calixtus II (1119–24). See above, p. 67.

69 Bonizo, *Book to a Friend* VI, p. 200 identified him as Hugh of Embrun.

would provoke rather than placate that most passionate lover of truth. He therefore paid out money to *stop the mouths*[70] both of the accusers and of the witnesses and, puffed up with the violence of his newly acquired security, he *taunted*[71] the judge when the synod reassembled next day, saying, *Where are they who accused me? No one has condemned me.*[72] Hearing this, the zealous man of God sighed a deep sigh and, with a disdainful gesture that showed how his heart burned for those men who had been corrupted, he *said* to the corruptor, *'Do you believe, bishop, that the Holy Spirit is of one substance and deity with the Father and the Son?'* On receiving the reply, *'I believe it'*, he said, *'Say, Glory to the Father and to the Son and to the Holy Spirit.'* He confidently began *this versicle* which commends faith in the Holy Trinity (which the Fathers at Nicea caused to be sung and which the blessed Jerome recommended to Pope Damasus to be sung with individual psalms)[73] *and he said, 'Glory to the Father and to the Son', but he was unable to pronounce the name of the Holy Spirit.*[71] On being urged to make a second attempt, he broke down at the word 'Son' and on being allowed to start afresh for the third time, he fell silent on the word 'Father'. Then at last he threw himself at the feet of the envoy and he confessed openly that he was a simoniac. As soon as he had been deposed from his bishopric, he exclaimed in a clear voice, 'Glory to the Father and to the Son and to the Holy Spirit.' Several false bishops are said to have felt remorse at these tokens of divine knowledge, to have made a spontaneous confession of their bad consciences and rightfully to have laid down the offices that they had acquired wrongfully.

18 The venerable archdeacon held another synod, at which Abbot Hugh of Cluny[74] was present, during which he deposed a certain bishop according to judicial process. Leaving that place together, they reached a certain river, which they crossed, the archdeacon preceding the abbot. After crossing the river, he turned, looked back and said, 'Why do you think such things of me?' The abbot, however, replied, 'Are you God, that you assert your knowledge of men's thoughts?' 'I am not God,' he said, 'but nevertheless I heard what you were turning

---

70 Cf. Psalm 106:42.

71 /71 Paul here used Bonizo's account, above p. 200.

72 John 8:10.

73 Paul was mistaken about the origins of the doxology: J. Greving (1893) p. 28 n. 3.

74 Hugh I of Cluny (1049–1109) was at the legatine council of Chalon-sur-Saône, 13 February 1056: see H. Diener (1959) p. 359; A. Kohnle (1993) p. 293. According to T. Schieffer (1934) pp. 55–7; A. Kohnle (1993) pp. 77–8; H. E. J. Cowdrey (1998) p. 32, this council was the occasion of the miracle described in chapter 17.

over in your mind. For you said in your heart that I deposed that
bishop for the sake of vainglory rather than divine zeal.' The abbot's
conscience reproached him and he said, 'I beg you to explain to me
how you could perceive that.' 'Because I looked back at you as you
came across the river,' he replied, 'and I saw something like a thread
stretched from your mouth to my ears and from this I perceived the
thought.'[75]

19 On another day, when both the archdeacon and the abbot of Cluny
had entered a certain church, the abbot's chamberlain,[76] as he stood at
prayer, secretly produced some coins from his pouch and counted
them from hand to hand for the purpose of paying their expenses.
Interrupting his prayer, the archdeacon cried out, 'Depart, devil!' and
forced him to leave the church. Then the abbot said, 'You are acting
cruelly because you are not allowing us to finish our prayers.' 'Ask
your monk about his prayer,' he replied, 'and you can learn why I did
it.' The abbot, therefore, questioned him and found that he had been
counting coins. The archdeacon aptly concluded, 'And I saw a most
loathsome spirit in front of him, which imitated his actions.'[77]

20 On that same journey they came to a city severely afflicted by
plague, in which he saw an angel of God[78] brandishing *a sword* ready *to
slay.*[79] When they went to an oratory, according to custom, therefore,
he asked the abbot to abridge his prayers and to leave the city as
quickly as possible, otherwise they would all perish. The abbot obeyed
his command and rapidly returned to their lodging and lo! he found
that their two travelling companions had been overtaken by sudden
death. After they had very hastily abandoned the place of pestilence,
the abbot, once he was free to ask questions, inquired of the venerable
deacon what he had seen, to insist on so great a haste, and he heard
the account given above.[80]

75 Another version of this anecdote: Alexander of Canterbury, *Memorials of St Anselm*
   pp. 211–12; William of Malmesbury, *Gesta regum Anglorum* III, pp. 322–3. See R. W.
   Southern (1953) p. 139; A. Stacpoole (1967) pp. 351–3; A. Kohnle (1993) pp. 78–9.

76 One chamberlain from Hugh's abbatiate, Jarento, is identified in Gilo, *Vita Hugonis
   abbatis* c. 31, 43, pp. 76, 83. For the duties of the office of chamberlain in Cluny
   (second in importance only to the prior): Bernard of Cluny, *Ordo Cluniacensis* I.5,
   pp. 145–7; Udalrich of Zell, *Antiquiores consuetudines* III.11, col. 751.

77 This story is otherwise unknown: A. Stacpoole (1967) pp. 341–63.

78 Cf. I Chronicles 21:16.

79 Jeremiah 15:3.

80 Another version of this anecdote: Alexander of Canterbury, *Memorials of St Anselm*
   pp. 212–13; William of Malmesbury, *Gesta regum* III, pp. 323–4. See A. Stacpoole
   (1967) pp. 353–4.

21 Meanwhile he was making for Rome and, when he heard that Pope Stephen[81] had died and a certain Benedict[82] had been placed in the apostolic see by evil and violent men, contrary to canon law, he hastened his journey. Assembling a synod of bishops in Tuscany, he condemned Benedict according to the judgement of the Holy Spirit. He enthroned in the apostolic see Gerard, the venerable bishop of the city of Florence, who had been elected with the common consent of good men, and he named him Nicholas II.[83] When the latter died after two years,[84] Alexander II succeeded.[85]

22 The latter's chamberlain, John by name,[86] was accustomed to tell the story of a miracle of divine healing performed on him by the venerable Hildebrand when he was still archdeacon. For when this John was in Tusculum, tormented by the severe pain of a fever, he *sent* an envoy to *entreat* the blessed man with might and main *to come* to him *without delay.*[87] Nor was there any delay because, knowing him to be a man of great worth, he did not refuse to come. John was overjoyed at his coming; he made over all his possessions to him and also committed himself to his care, humbly imploring him to devote himself to praying to their Lord for him and to exhort religious men to do the same. Then the man of God, shaken to his innermost being by his personal piety, turned everyone out of the room and for a very long time devoted himself to prayer tearfully and without any sound of words. When he had completed his prayers, he summoned the countess with whom John was staying and encouraged her to have a meal of chicken prepared for the sick man. She opposed him, since she knew that his stomach was so weakened by his long infirmity that for some weeks past he had shrunk from taking food. But the man of God replied to her, 'Do not delay! For you must know that it will not be prepared as quickly as he will desire it.' And the event proved this to be

---

81 Stephen IX (1057–8) †29 March.

82 Benedict X (1058–9), elected 5 April.

83 Gerard of Florence (1045–61), elected Pope Nicholas II, 6 December 1058.

84 Nicholas II †27 July 1061.

85 Alexander II (1061–73), elected 30 September. This chapter is based on the accounts of Bonizo, *Book to a Friend* VI (above p. 202) and Bernold, *Chronicon* 1058, p. 427.

86 For the chamberlain John see P. E. Schramm (1930) p. 302. K. Jordan (1933–4) pp. 90–102 concluded that the first identifiable papal chamberlain was Peter in the pontificates of Urban II and Paschal II.

87 Acts 9:38.

so. For when he had eaten enough, he fell asleep and after his slumbers he immediately recovered fully from that most serious illness.

23 The[88] blessed man was again sent by the lord pope to set the churches in order and, among the many good works that he performed, led by the spirit of truth, he rescued a certain bishop, assailed by false accusations, from the malice of the wicked.[89] Returning to Rome, he entered the basilica of the blessed apostle Peter to pray and offer thanks. It was his habitual practice to go to the portrait of blessed Mary, the mother of God, which was inside that basilica, to fall before it in adoration and to pour out his heart in weeping. When he had approached, therefore, following this custom, he saw – wonderful to relate – that the image was bathed in tears and she seemed to be expressing her grief at some annoyance offered to her beloved. But he was *filled with wonder and amazement*[90] and, after being struck motionless with astonishment, he himself wept as abundantly as she did and, completing his prayers, returned to the Lateran palace to pay his respects to the lord pope. The latter immediately mentioned the accusation, conveyed to him by a false rumour, that he had exonerated the aforementioned bishop in return for gifts, which clearly explained what was meant by the appearance of suffering on the part of the holy picture. But when he had begun to give an account of himself, his face shining with wisdom, all his enemies who were present blushed with shame and, in the words of the blessed Jerome, *the false rumour* was *quickly suppressed*[91] and the biting tongue was slit, since that man's life was recommended both by his words and by his example. When he went from there to visit the picture again, according to his custom, he saw that it was miraculously changed and was similing on him, as on a conqueror.

24 Lest these miracles seem incredible – since, although they concern saints, they involve inanimate things – we wish to impart confidence by citing the more commendable writings of the orthodox Fathers, borrowing some examples that we do not consider ineffective against

---

88 /88 This passage appears in the collection of miracles of the Virgin Mary in Graz, University Library MS. 713 and Basel, University Library MS. B.VIII.2. The compilers took this material from Paul's *Life*: H. Fuhrmann (1989) pp. 111–19.

89 There is no other reference to this incident. The only legation performed by Hildebrand in Alexander II's pontificate was to Salerno: H. E. J. Cowdrey (1998) p. 58.

90 Acts 3:10.

91 Jerome, *Epistola* 54.13, *CSEL* 54, 480.

such incredulity. For thus we read in the proceedings of the seventh universal council, assembled on the authority of Pope Hadrian I.[92] *The priest Dionysius of the church of Ascalon told the story of the anchorite Abbot John, saying that he was a great man of the current generation, and he proclaimed this miracle, showing that his life was pleasing to God. The old man was living in a cave in the region of Sochus, an estate almost nine miles[93] distant from Jerusalem. The old man kept in the cave a picture of our holy and pure lady, the mother of God, Mary ever virgin, holding Christ our Lord in her arms. Whenever he wished to travel anywhere, whether to the far-off deserts or to Jerusalem to worship the holy cross and the holy places and even to pray on Mount Sinai or to the martyrs who were faraway from Jerusalem (for it was as if the old man was a friend of the martyrs: sometimes he travelled to St John of Ephesus, sometimes to St Theodore in Euchaita or to St Tecla in Seleucia or to St Sergius in Arapha), he prepared a candle and lit it, as his custom was, and standing to pray that his journey might be arranged for him, he said to the Lady, bending towards her picture: 'Holy Lady, mother of God, since I have a long way to walk, occupying many days, do you take care of your candle and keep it unextinguished according to my plan. For I shall walk with your aid as my companion.' After he had said this to the picture, he departed. When his proposed journeys were completed, he returned sometimes after sojourning for a month, sometimes two or three, at times five or six months, and he would find the candle trimmed and burning, as he had arranged it when about to depart on his journey and he never saw it extinguished of its own accord, neither when he rose from sleep nor when he returned to the cave from the desert.*[88] Again in those same proceedings from the life of St Theodore the archimandrite.[94] *When he was about twelve years old, there was bubonic plague on that estate and he himself was sick almost to death. They carried him for some distance into the oratory of St. John the Baptist, which was next to the estate, and stretched him out at the entrance to the altar. Above him in a niche stood a picture of the Saviour Jesus Christ. When he was afflicted by the pain of the buboes, suddenly drops of dew fell on him from the picture and immediately by God's grace he recovered from the pain and was made whole and he went to his home.* Since these examples are sufficient to strengthen faith, let us return to our narrative.

---

92 Second Council of Nicea (Seventh Ecumenical Council), 787, actio 5 (Latin version of Anastasius Bibliothecarius), *Sacra Concilia* 13, 194E-195C.

93 Error in the codices of Paul's *Life*: the conciliar *actio* reads 'twenty miles'.

94 Second Council of Nicea, actio 4, *Sacra Concilia* 13, 190E-191B.

25 The venerable Hildebrand, therefore, saw a vision predicting that
he would soon acquire the power of the papacy. Simon Magus[95] appeared
to him, capering and rejoicing on a ship, and he himself appeared to
fall on him, to wrestle with him, to subdue him under his feet and to
fetter him with indissoluble bonds. There are few who do not know
that a ship signifies the Church,[96] in which, before the pontificate of this
blessed man, Simon Magus in the persons of his followers had certainly
sported with sacrilegious venality, freely and shamelessly buying and
selling ecclesiastical offices. We shall describe in the appropriate place
how he was laid low and fettered by this champion of God.

26 During this time certain Pisans were spending the night in prayer
in the basilica of blessed Peter, when lo! they saw the prince of the
apostles himself in his own house walking up and down with this, his
predestined heir, and commanding him to collect the dung of various
beasts of burden that seemed to lie scattered here and there, to put it
into a sack that appeared to be close at hand and to carry it out on his
back. It is clear indeed that this animal dung signified the excesses
and foulness of various men, especially of the nicholaites[97] and their
protector, Henry IV; but how it was picked up and carried away we
shall, if God wills it, show in time. Now let us set down the lawful
proceedings of his election after the death of Pope Alexander,[98] just as
his electors themselves described it.

27 How Pope Gregory was elected. *In[99] the reign of our Lord Jesus
Christ, in the year 1073 of His most merciful incarnation, in the eleventh
indiction, on Monday, 22 April, the day of the burial of the lord Pope
Alexander II of good memory, in order that the apostolic see should not
mourn long after being deprived of its own pastor,[100] we, the cardinal clergy,
acolytes, subdeacons, deacons and priests of the holy Roman catholic and*

95 Simon Magus (Acts 8:9–24), regarded by reformers as the first heresiarch, founder
   of the heresy of simony. See H. E. J. Cowdrey (1993) pp. 77–90.
96 The various references in the Gospels to Christ on board ship were interpreted by
   biblical exegetes as allegories of the Church: see I. S. Robinson (1988) pp. 255–7.
97 On the term 'nicholaites' (cf. Revelation 2:6, 15): Peter Damian, *Letter* 65, p. 230:
   'Clergy who are joined to women against the rule of ecclesiastical chastity are
   called nicholaites.' See E. Amann (1931) col. 499–506; G. Fornasari (1981) p. 7 n.
   5; H. E. J. Cowdrey (1993) pp. 88–90; H. E. J. Cowdrey (1998) pp. 550–3.
98 21 April 1073.
99 /99 Protocol of Gregory VII's election, *Registrum* I.1*, pp. 1–2. See H.-G. Krause
   (1960) pp. 159–69; W. Goez (1968) pp. 117–44; H. E. J. Cowdrey (1998) pp. 72–
   3. On Paul's use of this text see H. Fuhrmann (1956) pp. 304, 305, 307, 308.
100 Cf. *Liber diurnus* formulae 60, 61, pp. 51, 55.

apostolic church, assembled in the basilica of the blessed Peter ad Vincula,[101]
*with the consent of the venerable bishops, abbots, clergy and monks who were
present and with the acclamation of very great crowds of people of both sexes
and various ranks, elected as our pastor and supreme pontiff a religious man,
proficient in the wisdom of both branches of knowledge, a most distinguished
lover of equity and justice, strong in adversity, moderate in prosperity and,
according to the saying of the apostle, adorned with a good character, pure,
sober, chaste, hospitable, ruling his own household well,*[102] *very nobly bred
and taught in the bosom of this mother church from his boyhood*[103] *and,
because of his meritorious life, raised to the office of archdeacon that he holds
to this day: namely, Archdeacon Hildebrand, whom from this time forward
to all eternity we approve and wish to be and to be called Pope Gregory.
'Does this please you?' – 'It pleases us.' – Do you want him?' – 'We want
him.' – 'Do you approve of him?' – 'We approve.'*[104] *Enacted in Rome on 22
April in the eleventh indiction.*[99]

28 Gregory himself also immediately despatched these letters concerning his election. The first letter of Gregory VII. *Gregory,*[105] *elected
Roman pontiff, to Desiderius, abbot of the monastery of St Benedict at Monte
Cassino,*[106] *greeting in Christ Jesus. Our lord Pope Alexander has died. His
death lies heavily upon me: it has shaken me to the core and thrown me into
confusion.*[107] *For on his death the Roman people, contrary to their custom,
remained so quiet and resigned the management of affairs into our hands so
that it was quite clear that this happened through the mercy of God. After
taking advice, we settled that after a three-day fast,*[108] *after the funeral
service and after general prayer supported by almsgiving we should come to
a decision, sustained by the aid of heaven, about what seemed best to do
concerning the election of the Roman pontiff. But suddenly, as our aforesaid*

101 See Bonizo, *Book to a Friend* VII, above p. 220.

102 Cf. I Timothy 3:2.

103 See above p. 266 n. 41.

104 On this formula of approbation (*laudatio*): H.-W. Klewitz (1960) pp. 161–2.

105 /105 Gregory VII, *Registrum* I.1, pp. 3–4 (23 April 1073). H. Fuhrmann (1956) pp.
307, 308 considered it 'doubtful' that Paul transcribed this letter directly from the
papal register.

106 Desiderius (Dauferius), abbot of Monte Cassino, cardinal priest of S. Cecilia; Pope
Victor III (1086–7).

107 Cf. Psalm 54:5; Jeremiah 31:20 (Lamentations 2:11). These biblical texts, together
with those below nn. 111–12, occur in the Holy Week liturgy, as Old Testament
prophecies of Christ's passion. See C. Schneider (1972) pp. 24–7.

108 The papal election must take place only after a delay of three days: *Liber diurnus*
formula 60, p. 51. See H. E. J. Cowdrey (1998) p. 72.

lord Pope Alexander was being brought for burial in the church of the Saviour,[109] there arose a great tumult[110] and noise among the people and they threw themselves upon me like madmen, so that I could say with the prophet, 'I have come into deep waters and the flood sweeps over me. I am weary with my crying; my throat is parched'[111] and 'fear and trembling come upon me and darkness overwhelms me'.[112] But because I am lying in bed, utterly fatigued and I cannot dictate this satisfactorily, I forbear to give an account of my distress. I ask you, therefore, for the sake of the Lord Almighty, to appeal to the brethren and sons whom you foster in Christ and as an act of true charity to call on them to pray to God for me so that prayer, which should have saved me from falling into danger, will at least protect me now that I am placed in danger. But you yourself are not to omit to come to us as soon as possible, knowing as you do how much the Roman church needs you and trusts in your prudence. Greet the lady Agnes[113] and Rainald, the venerable bishop of Como[114] on our behalf and faithfully entreat them on our behalf to show how great is the love they bear us. Given in Rome on 23 April in the eleventh indiction.[105]

29 Gregory,[115] elected Roman pontiff, to Duke Godfrey,[116] greetings in Christ. The happiness that, as we know from your letter,[117] you feel at our advancement is pleasing, not that it pleases us for our own sake but because we have no doubt that it derives from a fount of sincere love and from a faithful mind. For our advancement, which causes you and the other faithful to have a kind opinion of us and to rejoice, engenders in us the bitterness of inner pain and the distress of overwhelming anxiety. For we see what great disquiet surrounds us, we feel how heavily the weight of the burden we have taken up presses upon us and, therefore, whenever the sense of our own weakness troubles us, our soul desires the repose of death in Christ rather than life amidst such great dangers. The thought of the office entrusted to us agitates us so much that, if our trust in the prayers of devout men, next to

109 The Lateran basilica.

110 Cf. I Samuel 14:19.

111 Psalm 68:3–4 (quoted by Gregory I, describing his own election: *Registrum* I.5,7, pp. 6, 9). See I. S. Robinson (1978a) p. 31; H. E. J. Cowdrey (1998) p. 73.

112 Psalm 54:6.

113 Empress Agnes, consort of Henry III (✝1077).

114 Rainald, bishop of Como (1061–92).

115 /115 Gregory VII, *Registrum* I.9, pp. 13–15 (6 May 1073). H. Fuhrmann (1956) pp. 307–8 considered it 'doubtful' that Paul derived this letter directly from Gregory's register.

116 Godfrey III ('the Hunchback'), duke of Lower Lotharingia (✝1076).

117 Godfrey's letter of congratulations has not survived.

God, did not sustain us, our mind would sink under the sheer number of our concerns. For sinfulness is so prevalent that almost the whole world is bent on wickedness[118] and all men and especially those who exercise authority in the Church strive rather to throw the Church into confusion than to defend and liberate[119] her in faithful devotion and they pursue gain or the desire for glory in this world, arraying themselves like enemies against everything pertaining to religion and God's righteousness. We deplore this all the more because, having assumed the government of the universal Church in this time of trouble, we can neither perform our duties properly nor safely neglect them. Nevertheless, because we know that God has granted you the virtue of faith and steadfastness, possessing all the trust in you that is owing to a most beloved son of St Peter, we wish there to be no doubt whatsoever in your mind of our unchangeable love and our most prompt support of your official duties. Concerning the king,[120] you can clearly understand our opinion and our wishes. We believe that, as far as the Lord permits us to know,[121] there is no one who is more concerned or more ardently desirous of his present and future glory than ourselves. This is our will: that at the first opportunity that is offered to us, we shall, with paternal love and admonition, reach an agreement with him through our messengers concerning those matters that we regard as affecting the advancement of the Church and the honour of the office of king.[122] If he listens to us, we shall rejoice as much for his sake as for our own. He will most certainly be able himself to profit from maintaining righteousness, in accordance with our warnings and advice. But if, which we by no means desire, he does not follow our example, giving back hatred for love, showing contempt towards almighty God for the great office that He has conferred on him and neglecting His righteousness, then may God forfend that we should fall foul of those threatening words, 'Cursed is the man who keeps back his sword from bloodshed!'[123] For we are not free to disregard the law of God as a kindness to any person or to depart from the path of rectitude as a favour to any man, but we say with the apostle, 'If I wished to please men, I should not be a servant of God.'[124] Given in Rome on

---

118 I John 5:19.

119 The papal register reads 'celebrate'.

120 Henry IV of Germany.

121 Cf. Philippians 4:2.

122 This statement contradicts Bonizo's claim (above p. 221) that Gregory 'sent [Henry IV] a letter … announcing his own election'. See G. B. Borino (1956b) pp. 313–43; H. E. J. Cowdrey (1998) p. 92 n. 64; I. S. Robinson (1999) p. 129.

123 Jeremiah 48:10. On this text (quoted ten times in Gregory's register): see C. Schneider (1972) p. 35 n. 92; H. E. J. Cowdrey (1998) pp. 567–9.

124 Galatians 1:10.

6 May in the eleventh indiction.[115]

30 He was afterwards confirmed by being consecrated pope[125] and the heavenly Father showed how acceptable he was to Him according to the example of the Gospel, since He *revealed to babes* the mysteries that He *hid from the wise and understanding*.[126] For two peasants were drawn by a laudable curiosity, when they learned of the arrival of a new pope in the Lateran diocese,[127] and urged on by mutual encouragement to see him, they hastened to the church.[128] When they arrived there, they found him near the altar, celebrating the rite of the mass. They gazed at him inquisitively, making a careful observation of all the movements of his body and his gestures. But one of them was gripped by amazement when he saw a dove coming down from heaven, settling on Gregory's right shoulder and covering his head with its outstretched wings. When the service was over, the dove stretched out its neck and, as it seemed to him, dipped its beak into the chalice and, withdrawing it, immediately returned whence it had come. The peasant, stupefied by the new miracle, recovered after a while and returned to his own home.

31 The following night three men in fine clothes and with shining faces appeared to him. One of them both in his clothing and in his grey hair called to mind the figure of Peter, as he customarily appeared in pictures;[129] the second with his shining face and tall stature struck the onlooker both with amazement and with fear; he did not investigate so closely the appearance of the third man. For a long time he was undecided about which of the three would be the easiest to speak to and at last, addressing the grey-haired old man, inquired *which of them was the greatest*[130] and by what name he was known. He received the reply that he was called 'the Sun'[131] and in addition he was rebuked with these words: 'Why have you not made known to Gregory

---

125 Sunday, 30 June: see above p. 221 n. 10.

126 Matthew 11:25; Luke 10:21.

127 I.e. the diocese of Rome, which the Lateran church served as cathedral.

128 Cf. *Chronica monasterii Casinensis* III.54, pp. 435–6, recording a similar miracle in Monte Cassino, July 1084. This anecdote was perhaps inspired by John the Deacon, *Vita Gregorii* IV.69, 70, *MPL* 75, col. 222A, 222B.

129 Cf. Peter Damian, *Letter* 159, pp. 91–2. Representations of St Peter in the late eleventh and early twelfth centuries: H. Bloch (1986) pp. 140, 146, 149, 150, 154, 165–6, 489, 490, 511, 559, 560, 561, 563, 568, 569.

130 Mark 9:33; Luke 9:46.

131 'The sun of righteousness' (Malachi 4:2), according to *Chronica monasterii Casinensis* III.54, p. 436.

what you saw yesterday?' He, however, was thoroughly terrified and declared that he had seen nothing. 'Have you forgotten,' he said, 'that yesterday during the celebration of the mass you saw a dove rest on his shoulder?' And he repeated to him the whole vision as he had seen it. Then he commanded him to go to Gregory as soon as possible, because he was about to leave that place on that day, and to give him a full account of the vision. In the morning the peasant, uncertain what to do and telling himself that the vision was an illusion, went to a certain religious man in that same place and made known to him what he had seen. The advice that he received was that he should pray with all his strength to the Lord that if this vision had come from Him, He should deign to reveal it to him a second and a third time. This the peasant devoutly performed. On the second night he received another warning and he devoted himself all the more earnestly to his prayers. On the third night, however, the same men behaved even more threateningly than before and one of them commanded him that, if he wished to continue to live, he should not hesitate to inform the lord pope as he had been ordered and he added, 'As you failed to comply with our commands while he was close at hand, you must make the long journey after him.' He, however, desiring yet more reassurance from them, said, 'But I am a peasant, an ignorant man. What sign will be given to me, so that I may be believed by such a personage?' That one among them who was accustomed to speak for the rest said, 'Say this to Gregory and he will recognise the truth of it: that he has deserved to obtain from the Lord almighty what he was thinking of as he approached the altar on that day.' The peasant came to Gregory and, seeking a secret conversation with him, he faithfully informed him of the reason for his journey and his trouble. Smiling benevolently and recognising the sign, Gregory allowed the peasant, a messenger with so great an embassy, to depart for his home with the apostolic blessing.

32 On[132] another occasion, when he was in the grip of a very serious illness, one of his nieces came to visit him and asked him how she might practise chastity. Then, to soothe his niece's mind about his sickness, taking her necklace in his hand, he asked her whether she wished to marry. After he had recovered his health, when he turned his attention to his usual prayers, he could neither remember past evils nor express his hopes or desires for future good and, to conclude

132 / 132 This passage appears in the collection of Marian miracles in the Graz and Basel manuscripts (above n. 88).

briefly, he could not even squeeze out a single tear. For a long time he sadly reflected on what he had done, how he had transgressed and offended God: in fine, what fault he had committed to lose that gift of remorse[133] that had graciously been given to him. At last, moderating his sorrow, he was advised to request religious men to join him in beseeching the Lord with fasting and prayer to deign to reveal to him the offence for which the gift that he had previously possessed had been removed from him. This was performed with fitting piety. At the end of two weeks of nightly vigils and disciplining the flesh, the pious and ready Hearer bestowed on him his heart's desire. For the blessed mother of God appeared in a vision to a certain blameless and honest man[134] and commanded him: 'Go and say to Gregory that, although I have chosen him to be a member of my choir' – doubtless the choir of virgins – 'his behaviour has been the opposite of what it should have been.' Deeply moved by this strange utterance, Gregory became even more uncertain and began to pray more earnestly that God's mercy would show him more clearly what it was. The most holy Virgin Mary, mother of the Lord, appeared again in his sleep to the afore-mentioned man and said, 'You are to say this to Gregory. It was because he touched his niece's necklace in a way that offended the dignity of our order that he has lost the grace that he possessed. Now that he has performed penance for his sin, however, he will receive the gift of tears.' This reminds us of the saying, *It is well for a man not to touch a woman.*[135]

33 One summer, a season that in Rome is very dangerous for the human body, when that man of God lay burning with fever for a whole week, the blessed mother of God, Mary ever virgin appeared to him and, to show her displeasure, she turned and struck his stomach with her hand and went out. Then for another week he was so enfeebled that men expected him to die and could scarcely perceive him breathing. At the end of the week that blessed mother of God came to him again at about the sixth hour of the day and asked him how he fared and if he regarded himself as having suffered enough punishment. He replied to her, 'Whatever you will, most pious lady.' Then, seeming

133 See H. Fuhrmann (1989) p. 117 and n. 19.

134 John Gualbert, abbot of Vallombrosa, according to J. Greving (1893) p. 34 n. 3. Cf. Andreas of Strumi, *Vita Iohannis Gualberti* c. 85, p. 1102: whenever the gift of tears eluded Gregory while celebrating mass, he had only to remember John Gualbert to recover that gift. See H. Fuhrmann (1989) p. 117 n. 20; H. E. J. Cowdrey (1998) pp. 66–7.

135 I Corinthians 7:1.

with a gentle hand to anoint his body, she vanished from his sight. He immediately asked for his vestments, as if he was about to enter the church in procession. Those who were with him thought that extreme weakness had dulled his sanity. He declared, however, that there was nothing wrong with him and forced them to dress him in the vestments and bring him to the church. Once this was done, he recovered his health and strength so completely that on the following day he celebrated the holy rite of the mass publicly in the church of the Saviour.[132]

34 Meanwhile heaven showed to Herman, who was at that time a cardinal but subsequently became bishop of the church of Brescia,[136] how much obedience ought to be displayed to so great a man. For one day, when he was summoned by him to the table, he did not come and the following night a terrible figure appeared to him and violently rebuked him, saying, 'Why, wretched man, did you imitate the obstinacy of Dathan and Abiram, neglecting Gregory's invitation to a meal, just as they arrogantly rejected Moses's summons to a council?[137] Has it escaped your notice how many thousands of thousands have plunged into hell because of the disobedience of the first man? Hurry, therefore, to make amends, if you wish to avoid the condemnation due to rebels.'[138] As soon as an opportunity presented itself, therefore, he threw himself at the feet of the most merciful pope and by means of tearful supplication he obtained pardon without delay.

35 We should like now to include two miracles of healing performed by heaven through the agency of blessed Gregory, lest they should chance to escape our memory, once we have entered the more impenetrable parts of the forest of this history. On one occasion, when according to custom he was washing his sacred hands, the washing water became like milk and a certain sick man who consumed it in the hope of recovering his health was immediately free from sickness. On another occasion, when he was sheltering in the county of the glorious Matilda[139] to escape the fury of his persecutors (which we shall

136 Herman, cardinal priest of SS. Quattro Coronati, bishop of Brescia (1087–1116): see G. Schwartz (1913) pp. 108–9; R. Hüls (1977) p. 201.

137 Cf. Numbers 16:12–13 (frequently cited in Gregorian polemics as archetypal rebels).

138 On this monastic conception of rebellion see William of Hirsau, *Consuetudines Hirsaugienses* I.51, *MPL* 150, col. 982D: 'It is called rebellion when a certain matter is enjoined on a brother and, although he does not dare to oppose it in words, he nevertheless disdains to perform it.'

139 Tuscany (see above n. 34), January to June 1077.

describe more fully hereafter), one day the venerable Bishop Hubald of Mantua[140] mentioned to him that his cook was so oppressed by illness that he could not rise from his bed. Since there was no substitute to perform the requisite duties, Gregory, with the *faith comparable to a grain of mustardseed,*[141] *moved the mountain*[142] of sickness and aroused the sick man, bidding him provide for the guests. In the same hour that he heard the voice giving him this command, he arose and furnished all that was needed.

36 It is now time to set down some decretal letters of the blessed pope against simoniacs and nicholaites sent to Gaul and Germany[143] and to deduce from them, as we promised, some explanation of that sack full of dung that, as we said above, was seen by the Pisans.[144] It does not seem absurd to compare the announcement of a lawful judgement condemning and repressing the shameful conduct of those heretics and their supporters with a sack containing animal dung. In a sense the holy man held the sack when he sent these letters and for a long time patiently awaited the conversion of those whom he censured; but he carried the sack out of the church when they clung to their errors and he excommunicated them with the consent of a synod. The first of these letters to meet our eyes is that sent to Otto, bishop of Constance,[145] as follows.

Gregory,[146] *bishop, servant of the servants of God, to his beloved brother in Christ,* Otto, *bishop of* Constance, *greeting and apostolic blessing. The urgency of your messengers, who wished to return in haste, did not allow us to inform you fully, brother, of what was decided in the Roman synod.*[147] *We thought it necessary to write to you this at least: that in that synod, following*[148] *the*

---

140 Hubald,bishop of Mantua (*c.* 1086–*c.* 1098): see G. Schwartz (1913) pp. 54–5.

141 Cf. Matthew 17:19; Luke 17:6.

142 Cf. I Corinthians 13:2.

143 J. Greving (1893) p. 36 noted a similarity with Hugh of Flavigny, *Chronicon* II, p. 426.

144 See above p. 275.

145 Otto, bishop of Constance (1071–86).

146 /146 Gregory VII, *Epistolae Vagantes* 8, pp. 16–18 (*JL* 4933: February–March 1075?). On the role of Bernold of St Blasien, *Apologeticus* c. 1, pp. 60–1 in disseminating this letter: I. S. Robinson (1978b) pp. 65–82.

147 Synod of Lent 1074: G. B. Borino (1959–61) pp. 277–95; C. Schneider (1972) p. 118 n. 365. Synod of Lent 1075: C. Erdmann (1938) pp. 227 n. 3, 247 n. 3, 275, H. E. J. Cowdrey, *Epistolae Vagantes* pp. 160–1; I. S. Robinson (1978b) p. 71.

148 The rest of the letter is identical with Gregory's letters to the archbishops of Mainz and Magdeburg, *Epistolae Vagantes* 6, 7, pp. 14–16.

authority of the holy Fathers, we judged that those who have been promoted to any rank or office in holy orders by means of <u>simoniacal heresy</u>, that is, through the intervention of money, are no longer to have any opportunity of serving in holy Church. Those also who acquire churches by means of the gift of money are to lose them entirely and no one hereafter is allowed to sell or buy them. Moreover those who commit the crime of fornication must not celebrate mass nor serve at the altar in the lesser orders. We also decided that, if they show contempt for our decrees, or rather those of the holy Fathers, the people are by no means to accept their ministrations, so that those who are not corrected from the love of God and the dignity of their office, may be brought to their senses by the shame of the world and the rebuke of the people. Strive, therefore, brother, to show yourself to be our fellow worker in this enterprise and to tear up these offences by the roots from your churches with such zeal that you may deserve to obtain the reward of a good shepherd from God and that the Roman church must rejoice in you as a most dear brother and a zealous fellow worker.[146]

37 The following letter records how arrogantly the aforementioned bishop responded to, or rather scoffed at, the wholesome decrees.

Gregory,[149] *bishop, servant of the servants of God, to Otto, bishop of Constance, greeting and apostolic blessing. News has reached us about you, brother, which I was very unwilling and sad to hear and which, if it was brought to our attention about even the least member of the Christian people, would doubtless have to be punished by the most severe judgement and the most rigid discipline. For when, influenced by apostolic authority and by the truthful judgements of the holy Fathers, we were fired, as our office demands, to eliminate simoniacal heresy and to enjoin the chastity of the clergy, we placed this duty of obedience on our colleague, the venerable archbishop of Mainz,*[150] *whose suffragans are very many and scattered, that both on his own part and through his assistants he should most assiduously force the decree on all the clergy and declare that it should be kept inviolably. It pleased us also to prepare a special letter on this same subject,*[151] *sealed with our own seal to you, to whom belong the very numerous clergy of the diocese of Constance and its very widely dispersed people, so that, supported by the authority of this letter, you might the more securely and more courageously obey our commands and drive out of the Lord's sanctuary both simoniacal heresy and the*

---

149 /149 Gregory VII, *Epistolae Vagantes* 9, pp. 18–22 (*JL* 4970: late 1075?). See I. S. Robinson (1978b) pp. 69–82: Paul's source was the letter collection compiled by Bernold of St Blasien, surviving in Sélestat MS 13, fol. 41r-42v.

150 Siegfried, archbishop of Mainz (1060–84).

151 Gregory VII, *Epistolae Vagantes* 8: see above p. 283.

foul pollution of lecherous intercourse. For the greatest weight attaches to the apostolic authority of the blessed Paul, according to which, including fornicators and adulterers among the other wicked men, he added his definitive command and condemnation 'not even to eat with such a one'.[152] *The whole company of the catholic Church moreover are virgins or the chaste or the married. Whoever is found to be outside these three orders, therefore, is not included among the sons of the Church or within the boundaries of the Christian religion. If we have certain knowledge, therefore, that even the least important layman is living in concubinage, we rightly prevent him from receiving the sacraments of the altar, as a member cut off from the body of the Lord, until he repents. How then is one who can by no means be a sharer in the holy sacraments, to be a dispenser or minister of them? We are influenced by that pronouncement of the blessed Pope Leo, who absolutely removed from subdeacons permission to contract marriages.*[153] *Later pontiffs of the holy Roman church, especially the excellent doctor Gregory,*[154] *confirmed that decree of blessed Leo as law, so that subsequently the bonds of matrimony were entirely forbidden to these three ecclesiastical orders, priests, deacons and subdeacons. But when we communicated all these matters to you so that, with a bishop's care, you would see to it that they were respected, you set your heart not on things above but on things on earth below*[155] *and, as we learn, you have loosened the reins of lust to the aforesaid orders so that those who had joined themselves to women, might persist in their disgrace and those who had not married, were not afraid of your prohibitions.*[156] *What impudence, what extraordinary audacity, that a bishop should despise the decrees of the apostolic see, should overthrow the commands of the holy Fathers, nay, should force on his subjects from his superior position and his bishop's throne something contrary to those commands and repugnant to the Christian faith! For this reason, we order you by apostolic authority to present yourself at our next synod in the first week of Lent,*[157] *to answer according to canon law both for this disobedience and contempt towards the apostolic see and for all the accusations that have been made against you.*[149]

bishop writes back and counters...

152 Cf. I Corinthians 5:11.

153 Leo I, *Epistola* 14.4, *MPL* 54, 672B–673A.

154 Pope Gregory I. Perhaps an allusion to Gregory I, *Registrum* IX.110, *MGH Epistolae* 2, 115. Cf. Bernold, *Apologeticus* c. 11, p. 71.

155 Cf. Colossians 3:1–2.

156 Otto failed to prevent the rejection of the papal decree against clerical marriage by the clergy of his diocese: C. Erdmann (1938) p. 274 n. 3.

157 14–22 February 1076.

286 THE PAPAL REFORM OF THE ELEVENTH CENTURY

38 In addition he charged the clergy and people not to obey a disobedient bishop.[158]

Gregory,[159] bishop, servant of the servants of God, to the clergy and laymen, greater and lesser, dwelling in the bishopric of Constance who love the law of Christ, greeting and apostolic blessing. We sent to our brother, your bishop Otto, a letter of exhortation[160] in which, as our office necessitates, we enjoined on him by apostolic authority that he should drive out simoniacal heresy utterly from his church and uphold the chastity of the clergy by zealous preaching and to exercise episcopal vigilance in steadfastly maintaining it. For the words of the Gospels and of the apostles, the decrees of the authentic synods and the commands of the excellent doctors so strongly recommend this to us, that we cannot conceal and neglect it without great damage to our soul and to the Christian people. But your bishop was swayed neither by reverence for the command of blessed Peter nor by the duty attaching to his office and, as we have been informed, has not troubled to perform what we, like a father, urged him to do. Moreover, committing the offence not only of disobedience but also of rebellion, as we understand, he has openly permitted to his clergy things totally contrary to our command, or rather that of blessed Peter, so that those who already kept women, continued to keep them and those who did not, lawlessly and rashly entered into liaisons.[161] When we heard of this, we were aggrieved and wrote him a second letter,[162] making known to him our passionate indignation and repeating the same command more emphatically. Not only that, we summoned him to the Roman synod that will take place in the first week of next Lent, so that he may give an account of himself and explain the reasons for his disobedience – if he has any reasonable explanation – in the hearing of the whole assembly. We inform you of these things, dearest brothers,[163] in order to take care of the salvation of your souls. For if he shamelessly wishes to be hostile and insolent towards blessed Peter and the holy apostolic see, it is perfectly clear that one who does not honour his mother or father ought rightfully not to demand or request obedience from his own sons. For it is unbecoming that one who refuses to submit to his master, should himself demand a master's authority over pupils.

---

158 Cf. the rubric in Bernold's letter collection: 'The people are not to obey a bishop who despises the aforementioned decrees'.

159 /159 Gregory VII, *Epistolae Vagantes* 10, pp. 22–6 (*JL* 4971: late 1075?). See I. S. Robinson (1978b) p. 78: Paul found this letter in Bernold's collection.

160 *Epistolae Vagantes* 8: see above p. 283.

161 See above n. 156.

162 *Epistolae Vagantes* 9: see above p. 284.

163 The reading in all other copies is 'sons'.

Therefore, as we said before, we command by apostolic authority all the adherents of God and of blessed Peter, both the greater and the lesser, to show him none of the reverence of obedience, if he wishes to persist in his hardness of heart. And you are not to imagine that this is a danger to your souls. For if, as we have so often said before, he wishes to oppose papal commands, we absolve you by the authority of blessed Peter from every bond of subjection to him, so that even if anyone is bound to him by the obligation of an oath, he is still not liable to show fidelity to him, so long as he is a rebel against almighty God and the apostolic see. For no one owes obedience to any person against his Creator, who must be preferred before all men: rather we must resist anyone who shows contempt towards God, so that he may, through coercion if by no other means, learn to return to the road of righteousness. For how great a danger and how alien from the law of Christ it is not to show obedience, especially to the apostolic see, you can learn from the words of the blessed prophet Samuel, which the most holy Pope Gregory took pains to expound in the last book of the Morals.[164] *In order that you may have ready access to these words, we are sending you a copy of them, so that you may know beyond doubt that we are saying nothing new to you, but making known the ancient teaching of the holy Fathers. 'Hence Samuel says: "To obey is better than sacrifice and to hearken than the fat of rams. For rebellion is as the sin of divination and stubbornness is as iniquity and idolatry." Obedience is indeed rightly preferred to sacrifice, because sacrifice involves the killing of another's flesh, but obedience involves the death of our own will. The more someone controls his pride in his own will and sacrifices himself before God's eyes with the sword of His commandment, the more rapidly he pleases God. By contrast, disobedience is called the sin of witchcraft in order to demonstrate how great is the virtue of obedience. By considering the opposite, it becomes more apparent what is to be said in praise of obedience. For if "rebellion is as the sin of divination and stubbornness is as iniquity and idolatry", it is obedience alone that possesses the reward of faith and anyone without it is incontestably proved to be an infidel, even if he seems to be faithful.'*[159]

39 In addition, a letter *to laymen on the necessity of carrying out the above decrees.*[165]

Gregory,[166] *bishop, servant of the servants of God, to his beloved sons, the*

---

164 I Samuel 15:22–3; Gregory I, *Moralia* XXXV.28, *MPL* 76, col. 765BC.

165 Cf. the rubric in Bernold's collection: 'The same [author] to laymen on the necessity of carrying out the above decrees.'

166 /166 Gregory VII, *Registrum* II.45, pp. 182–5 (11 January 1075), lacking the final paragraph (addressed only to Rudolf) that appears in the papal register. This

dukes Berthold,[167] *Rudolf*[168] *and* Welf,[169] *greeting and apostolic blessing. We know, prudent men, that you are considering, in your clearsighted way, the wretched* dissolution[170] *of the Christian religion, which because of our sins is now in such an extremity that no living person has seen unhappier times nor is any record found since the time of our holy father Silvester.*[171] *But we who have been raised up to rule over the people and summoned and appointed to be bishops for the profit of their souls, are the principal cause of so great an evil. For the good or evil of subjects comes, as from first principles, from the government of those who undertake either worldly office or spiritual direction. If they pursue only their own glory and the pleasures of this world, they cannot live without bringing confusion on themselves and their people, since as a result of their evil deeds and their pursuit of wicked desires they both bind up their right to exercise authority through their fault and loosen the reins of sinning to others by their example.*[172] *For they do not transgress through ignorance or lack of forethought: instead, resisting the Holy Spirit presumptuously and obstinately, they cast aside divine laws of which they are well aware and despise the apostolic decrees. For the archbishops and bishops of your land know – what ought also to be known to all the faithful – that it is forbidden in the holy canons that those who have been promoted to any rank or office of holy orders by means of simoniacal heresy, that is, through the intervention of money, should any longer have any opportunity of serving in holy Church and that those who commit the crime of fornication should celebrate mass or serve at the altar in the lesser orders. Although the holy and apostolic mother Church since the time of Pope Leo*[173] *has often, in councils and through legates and letters, reminded, requested and, by the authority received through blessed Peter, commanded* bishops *to renew and observe, both in themselves and in the peoples committed to them, these rules, which were neglected by men of former times, nevertheless hitherto, with very few exceptions, they have been disobedient and have made no effort to put an end to such a cursed custom by their prohibition nor to*

---

letter appears in Bernold's letter collection, which was probably Paul's direct source: I. S. Robinson (1978b) pp. 76, 78.

167 Berthold I (of Zähringen), duke of Carinthia (✝1078).

168 Rudolf of Rheinfelden, duke of Swabia (1057–79), anti-king (1077–80).

169 Welf IV, duke of Bavaria (✝1101). Welf's name does not appear in the version of this letter in the papal register.

170 The papal register reads 'desolation'.

171 Pope Silvester I (314–35). I.e. 'since the Roman empire became a Christian institution'.

172 Cf. Gregory I, *Moralia* II.16, XII.50, *MPL* 75, 568C, 1012C.

173 Leo IX.

punish it with severity, paying no heed to what is written, that 'rebellion is the sin of divination and stubbornness is as the crime of idolatry'.[174] *Since, therefore, we understand that the divine* mysteries *are performed unworthily and that the people are led astray by men who despise the apostolic commands – or rather the commands of the Holy Spirit – and who encourage the wickedness of their subjects by their criminal forbearance, it is fitting that the one on whom above all rests the guardianship of the Lord's flock, should watch out for these evils using some other means. For it seems to us much better to rebuild God's justice by means of new counsels than to let the souls of men perish, together with the laws that they have neglected.*[175] *We therefore now turn to you and to all in whose fidelity and devotion we trust and* we *ask and admonish you by apostolic authority that – whatever bishops may say or may not say about it – you should in no way accept the offices of those whom you know to have been promoted and ordained through simony or who commit the crime of fornication. You are bound by your obedience to publish* or urge *this in the king's court and elsewhere in the assemblies of the kingdom and to the utmost of your power you are to prevent such men from administering the sacred mysteries, even if necessary by violence. But if any persons begin to babble against you that this is none of your business, tell them this: that they are to come to us to dispute with us about your salvation and that of the people and the obedience enjoined on you. Given in Rome on 11 January in the thirteenth indiction.*[166]

40 In addition, a letter to laymen in support of the same decrees.

Gregory,[176] *bishop, servant of the servants of God, to* his beloved son in Christ and most noble *Count Adalbert and his wife,*[177] *greeting and apostolic blessing. We give thanks to God that both laymen and women elevate their mind to God and gladly embrace the practice of religion and strive to uphold it. For those who are invited and appointed to be bishops in order to profit men's souls and who ought to teach their subjects the way of truth by their word and example, in these times, seduced by the devil, not only abandon the law of God but* also *do not cease to oppose and to overturn it with all their might. It is not to be wondered at if those whose ordinations were heretical or whose lives are buried in every kind of impurity and villainy – who, while they neither correct nor even pay heed to the crimes of*

---

174 I Samuel 15:23.

175 See I. S. Robinson (1978c) pp. 114–16; H. E. J. Cowdrey (1998) pp. 118–19.

176 /176 Gregory VII, *Registrum* II.11, pp. 142–3 (26 October 1074). Paul's version, unlike the papal register, includes the full address: H. Fuhrmann (1956) p. 303. I. S. Robinson (1978b) pp. 78–80: Paul found it in Bernold's letter collection.

177 Probably Adalbert II, count of Calw (†1099) and his wife Wiltrud (†1093).

*which they themselves are guilty, have also the offences of their subjects on
their own consciences, as a result either of neglect or fear – do not curb the
wrongdoing of the lesser orders. The prophet rightly said of them, 'Let their
eyes be darkened, so that they cannot see'* and so forth.[178] *Therefore, whatever they may babble against you, or rather against justice, and when, in order
to defend their own wickedness, they object that you are illiterate, remain
steadfast in the* virtue[179] *and constancy of your faith and firmly believe and
hold fast to what you are told by the apostolic see about bishops and priests
who are simoniacs or commit fornication.*[176]

41 That no one is to obey bishops who show contempt for or neglect
the aforesaid decrees.

Gregory,[180] *bishop, servant of the servants of God, to all the clergy and
laymen who are in the kingdom of the Germans, greeting and apostolic
blessing. We have heard that certain of the bishops who dwell among you
either consent to or overlook priests', deacons' and subdeacons' liaisons with
women. We command you by no means to obey them or consent to their
precepts, just as they themselves do not obey the precepts of the apostolic see
and do not agree with the authority of the holy Fathers, since divine
Scripture bears witness that an equal punishment falls on those who do the
deed and those who approve of it.*[181] *May almighty and merciful God, who
beyond our hope and our merit pities and consoles us in all our tribulation,
open your hearts to His law and confirm you in His commandments, so that
He may bring you, absolved from all your sins by the authority of blessed
Peter, to reign in His heavenly kingdom. Amen.*[180]

42 These letters were followed by a general synod[182] over which he
presided, in which, as his deeds show,[183] sentence of excommunication
was pronounced against all simoniacal and nicholaite heretics who,
hardened in the errors of their sect, knowingly disobedient towards
the synodal judgements of the holy Fathers and their decrees and
showing the recalcitrance and obstinacy of apostates towards them,
resisted with determination and wilfulness. Behold! the sack full of

---

178 Psalm 68:24.

179 The papal register reads 'purity'.

180 /180 Gregory VII, *Epistolae Vagantes* 11, p. 26 (*JL* 4902: late 1075?). I. S.
     Robinson (1978b) pp. 78–9: Paul found this letter in Bernold's letter collection.

181 Cf. Romans 1:32.

182 Probably the Roman synod of 24–28 February 1075.

183 J. Greving (1893) pp. 38–9 thought this expression 'his *gesta*' was a reference to
     Gregory VII's register. W.M. Peitz (1911) p. 245 thought it was a lost biography
     of Gregory. See also H. Fuhrmann (1956) p. 301 n. 7.

animal dung, which hitherto he had carried,[184] by *convincing, rebuking
and exhorting, unfailing in patience and in teaching,*[185] he would henceforward carry outside by the just punishment of divine zeal, according
to the procedure that the Lord made clear to His avengers through the
prophet Ezechiel, who said, *Begin at my sanctuary.*[186] For *the outcry against
Sodom and Gomorrah* had *become very great*[187] up to the time of his pontificate since the aforesaid heretics and their supporters, unruly and
with too much freedom to sin, *proclaimed their sin like Sodom and did
not hide it,*[188] so that *if the Lord of hosts had not left us the seed* of correction in him, *we should have been like Sodom and become like Gomorrah.*[189]

43 Inspired by reports of these synodal proceedings, the clergy of
Bamberg brought to his attention the simoniacal appointment of their
false bishop, named Herman.[190] He, however, had gathered together a
considerable sum of money and a store of precious metal and vestments and he hoped to be able to soften the pope's severity by means
of bribes.[191] As he drew near to Rome, he prevailed on the venerable
Herman, bishop of the church of Metz and legate of the apostolic see,
who then chanced to be his travelling companion,[192] to go in advance
to the lord pope and intercede for him. When he had attempted to do
this and had contrived to address him with humane and placatory
arguments, the *righteous* man, accustomed as he was to *shake his hands,
lest they hold a bribe,*[193] seated in his chamber, kindled by the Holy
Spirit, replied, 'If he wishes to remain in communion with the faithful,
make him return to his own land and do penance by submitting to the
heavy yoke of the monastic rule,[194] because – *God be gracious to me!*[195]

184 See above p. 275.

185 II Timothy 4:2.

186 Ezechiel 9:6.

187 Genesis 18:20.

188 Isaiah 3:9.

189 Isaiah 1:9.

190 Herman I, bishop of Bamberg (1065–75) †1084. The hostility of his cathedral
    chapter seems to have been caused by his favour towards the monastic at the
    expense of the canonical life. See R. Schieffer (1972a) pp. 22–46; R. Schieffer
    (1975) pp. 55–76; H. E. J. Cowdrey (1998) pp. 113–14, 124–6.

191 Cf. Gregory VII, *Registrum* III.3, p. 247. See above p. 223.

192 Herman, bishop of Metz (1072–90). He had interceded with the pope on behalf of
    Herman of Bamberg at Eastertide 1074: Gregory VII, *Registrum* I.84, p. 120.

193 Isaiah 33:15.

194 Herman eventually entered the abbey of Münsterschwarzach (diocese of Würz-
    burg): see G. Meyer von Knonau (1894) p. 544.

195 Cf. I Samuel 24:7, 26:11; II Samuel 23:17; I Kings 21:3.

– *though* he *were to give me* this *house full of gold and silver*,[196] I should never agree to his performing the office of bishop.' It was in this way, therefore, that this simoniac was removed from the priesthood.[197]

44 We consider it inappropriate to pass over in silence how the most courageous athlete of God overcame the deceptions of enemies, temptations, dangers, slanders, mockery, capture and imprisonment for the Lord's name and finally with the Lord's help and support and led on by the approval of the apostles he overcame kings, tyrants, dukes, princes as well as those who take captive men's souls, destroyers, together with wolves, that is, the servants of Antichrist, archbishops, bishops and other invaders of churches, so that the people of holy Church may learn how far our world had once declined in the time of so great a pastor. For it seems unseemly and improper to consign this father's work to oblivion, when instances of profane behaviour are remembered by laymen as models of valour. If indeed this man's example is stored in a retentive memory, it becomes a prop for holy Church and an ornament of Christ's faithful and brings defeat for impious heresies. For it was from this source that the principles of justice sprang up again, from this source that, in a manner of speaking, the victory of the Church and the inheritance of eternal happiness developed.

45 There was in the city a certain man,[198] *the son of perdition*,[199] the most wicked and most dangerous of all men, the recollection of whom indeed pollutes the very air; for whom perjury, deception, riotous living, treachery, murders, frauds, slanders, conspiracies, cheating, deceitfulness and secret meetings were a delight and who believed that anything that was virtuous was inimical to him; the father of thieves and the ally of perjurers, the shield of deception and the spear of adultery, the helmet of murderers and the buckler of treason, the armour of fraud, the guardian of slander, anxious to engage in conspiracy, a designer of deceit, smiling at trickery and a pit for the wicked to meet in. Every heretic and every wicked man hastened to seek refuge with him; scandals sought concealment under his wings; *Leviathan* himself, *the twisting serpent*,[200] rested sweetly and pleasantly

---

196 Cf. Numbers 22:18, 24:13.

197 Cf. Gregory VII, *Registrum* II.76, III.1, pp. 239, 243.

198 Cencius Stephani (Cencius de Praefecto) +1077. On Paul's refusal to name him: J. Greving (1893) p. 42 n. 3. See G. B. Borino (1952) pp. 373–440; D. Whitton (1980) pp. 223–35; H. E. J. Cowdrey (1998) pp. 326–8.

199 John 17:12; II Thessalonians 2:3.

200 Cf. Isaiah 27:1; Job 26:13.

under his shade. As the culmination of such fellowship he had built very many towers in the city[201] and, ignoring God's and men's hostility towards him, he set about accomplishing whatever the inciter of malice, that is, the devil set before the eyes of his evil mind. His words to him indeed were gentle and sweet, but ultimately they proved to be darts and wormwood. To complete his own perdition he killed a man who was his godfather, broke into his house before his deed was fully known and destroyed it.[202] Having committed this serious crime, he withdrew into the tower[203] that he had built in the lifetime of his father, Stephen, the prefect of the city.[204]

46 The man of God was inspired to punish his villainy and, together with Pope Alexander, who was then still alive, he bound him with the chains of his curse and anathema.[205] Plunging further to his own destruction, however, that man hastened to *the son of perdition*,[206] that is, King Henry,[207] together with certain men with whom he had joined forces, namely Nicholas[208] and Bertram.[209] After they had taken counsel together most irreligiously, he conducted the heretic Cadalus of Parma[210] to Rome and received him as his guest and assisted him by fighting many battles in the city.[211] All the simoniacal heretics offered him what comfort they could and they planned to throw holy Church into disorder by his means. When at last that heresiarch died, however, this man in his perplexity promised that he would come to an agreement with the lord pope and swear fealty to him; and this he did.[212] But how can there be fidelity, when it is not combined with

201 Cf. Bonizo, *Book to a Friend* VII, above p. 225.

202 Cf. *ibid.* VII, p. 225.

203 Presumably the tower in the district of Parione, where he held Gregory prisoner on 25 December 1075: below p. 298.

204 The date of Stephen's period of office is unknown: see above p. 225 n. 43.

205 Cadalus of Parma was elected 28 October 1061: see above p. 207.

206 John 17:12; II Thessalonians 2:3.

207 The eleven-year-old Henry IV. Paul ascribed to Cencius the role played by Count Gerard of Galeria and the abbot of S. Gregorio al Celio: above p. 206 n. 69.

208 Perhaps 'Nicholas, master of the sacred palace', identified by Benzo of Alba, *Ad Heinricum IV* II.4, p. 205. See F. Herberhold (1947) p. 485.

209 Perhaps Bertram, brother of Conte de Iohanne Guidone: see G. B. Borino (1952) p. 384.

210 Cadalus, bishop of Parma (1046–?1071); anti-pope 'Honorius II'. See G. Schwartz (1913) pp. 186–7.

211 Cf. Bonizo, *Book to a Friend* VI, above p. 208.

212 Cf. Beno, *Gesta Romanae ecclesiae* I.8, p. 372 ('Cencius ... formerly [Gregory VII's] vassal').

truth? Because of the power of the high priest, his position was like that of a captive robber, but the heir of hell ceaselessly and audaciously perpetrated whatever crimes he could. While the venerable Gregory exhorted him to give up such a career, every day he turned to worse offences. And so it came to pass that he stationed murderous men in that tower of remarkable size that he had built above St Peter's bridge, so that they might seize plunder from the property of those who entered and left the city.[213]

47 For this reason the prefect of the city, Cencius by name[214] – certainly a prudent man, worthy of all honour, dear to God and men, who was not like a layman but more like a faithful monk serving God[215] and who honoured justice in all things – one day took him prisoner and delivered up this great brigand, as he deserved, to a squalid prison.[216] At length, through the intervention of certain noble persons[217] and through the clemency of the lord pope he was released, after swearing oaths on the body of St Peter that his conduct would improve, after giving hostages and after surrendering the tower in which he trusted. Then *battering-rams and engines of war*[218] were brought and it was utterly destroyed with iron hammers[219] and thus the city was quiet for a while and the faction of the wicked was troubled with great fear and fell silent.

48 But what did the wretched man do? He approached, either personally or through his envoys, whatever wicked men he could, even those at a great distance. He himself wandered through Apulia and Lucania, visiting Guiscard[220] and other excommunicates and after conferring with them, he decided that the time was opportune to

---

213 See Bonizo *Book to a Friend* VII, above p. 225 and n. 46.

214 Cencius, Roman prefect (?1071–1077), son of the prefect John Tiniosus. See G. B. Borino (1952a) pp. 412–13; C. Violante (1968) p. 683 n. 324.

215 Cf. Berthold, *Annales* 1077, p. 304 ('he earnestly wished ... to enter the perfection of the monastic life but he was forbidden this on his obedience by the pope'); Bernold, *Chronicon* 1077, p. 434; Bonizo *Book to a Friend* VII, above p. 225 and n. 45. See C. Erdmann (1935) pp. 197–8, 231–2.

216 Cf. Bonizo *Book to a Friend* VII, above p. 231.

217 Matilda of Tuscany and 'many Roman citizens': Bonizo, above p. 231.

218 II Maccabees 12:15.

219 Cf. Bonizo, *Book to a Friend* VII, above p. 231. See D. Whitton (1980) p. 234.

220 Robert Guiscard, duke of Apulia and Calabria (✝1085), excommunicated 1074: Gregory VII, *Registrum* I.85a, p. 123. This was the mission that Bonizo *Book to a Friend* VII, above p. 228, ascribed to Cardinal Hugh Candidus on Cencius's advice.

capture and kill the lord pope. He sent his son[221] to Wibert, the heretic of Ravenna,[222] to obtain his agreement to this same pact. A letter about his intrigue was likewise sent to the king,[223] promising that the father himself would appear in the royal presence.[224] Having devised his destructive plans, he remained quiet for a time, doubtless waiting for *an opportunity* to capture him and *to betray him*[225] to wicked people who would kill him. But the Lord almighty – who through His own captivity freed the world and took the devil prisoner – amended the state of the Church through the captivity and bloodshed of that father and not only prevented *the son of iniquity* from *harming*[226] him, but also deprived him of his own property.

49 After nearly a year had gone by, the time of the servant of the devil arrived. For, as the feast of the Lord's nativity drew near,[227] he began to urge the fellow conspirators with whom he had laid his plans to gather together promptly and apply their minds to that most shameful act, promising them unutterable benefits, future freedom, unlimited advantages. He became in all respects the imitator of his master, the devil, who promised himself the possession of the whole world through the death of the Lord alone; but, as it is written, when he had captured others, he was himself taken prisoner; when he had begun to *despoil*, he was himself *despoiled*;[228] when he had striven for forbidden things that he did not yet possess, he lost the gains that he had made. If indeed that wretched man, his servant, had realised in his heart and mind that he would be plundered of so much property, perhaps in some way he might have drawn back his hand from perpetrating so great a crime, out of love for his property rather than love of God. Since, however, the malice that filled him, blinded him, he attempted to bring his plan into effect, not fearing – or rather,

---

221 His only recorded son was Tebaldus, an enemy of the papacy in the pontificate of Paschal II: see D. Whitton (1980) pp. 225–6.

222 Wibert, archbishop of Ravenna (1072–1100); anti-pope 'Clement III' (1084–1100). This was the mission that Bonizo *Book to a Friend* VII, above p. 229, ascribed to Hugh Candidus.

223 Henry IV was probably not involved in Cencius's conspiracy: G. B. Borino (1952a) p. 419; D. Whitton (1980) p. 247.

224 Cencius's visit to Henry IV's court, 1077: Bonizo *Book to a Friend* VIII, above p. 242 and n. 28.

225 Matthew 26:16.

226 Psalm 88:23.

227 Christmas Eve 1075. Cf. Bonizo *Book to a Friend* VII, above p. 232. Paul knew also the short account by Bernold, *Chronicon* 1076, pp. 431–2.

228 Isaiah 33:1.

ignoring – the danger to his soul, and like another Judas[229] he laid
hands on his lord and the Lord's anointed. On the day of the great
festival the pope hastened with a small number of clergy and laymen
to celebrate the office of the vigil, as the custom is, to the church of
blessed Mary, which is called 'the Greater'[230] because of the merits
obtained through so many prayers. For the custom of the city was
always, in a festival of such exceptional solemnity, for everyone to
flock to that church and spend the whole of that night in eager
vigilance and in hymns and praise. But, as the Lord ordained that the
blood of so great a father should be shed in order to reinvigorate the
Church, the populace was prevented from assembling at that time, so
that the servant of the devil, his mind eagerly bent on his destruction,
could carry out his evil intention. For on Christmas Eve the sky poured
forth so great a deluge of water that it seemed to everyone that the
primeval flood[231] was at hand. A man could hardly leave his home and
enter the house of his nextdoor neighbour if some emergency
demanded it, much less enter a church situated at so great a distance.
It was said that *the elemental spirits of the universe*[232] were somehow
predicting a future deed of shameful and unheard-of villainy.

50 What more is there to tell? The night was at hand in which the
son of darkness attacked the servant of the light. He sent out scouts,
who met with other spies. For they had recruited a group of the inhabitants of that quarter of the city near that church, who kept watch and
sent word to the wicked man of everything that they had found out.
Then he hastily assembled his troops clad in mail, ordering that, after
accomplishing the victory of the slaughter or the triumph of the
abduction of a single man, each of them had a horse that he could
mount, lest someone contemplated an attack on them. At length they
reached the church. The glorious pope, standing at the crib, was
reciting the first mass of the night, according to religious practice,
and both he and his clergy had received the Lord's body, while the
others who were present were still receiving that sacrament, when
suddenly a loud shouting and a great howling unexpectedly broke out
and filled the church. Then, ranging through the church with drawn

---

229 Judas Iscariot. Paul's scriptural parallels with the events of Holy Week: J.
Greving (1893) p. 48.

230 The midnight mass of Christmas Eve in the basilica of S. Maria Maggiore: see
Bonizo VII, above p. 232 and n. 92.

231 Genesis 7:4–24.

232 Galatians 4:3; Colossians 2:8, 2:20.

swords, striking at those whom they could reach, they converged on
the site of the crib, where the excellent pope was seated. There they
struck down a number of men and, breaking down those little doors
with their cruel hands, they entered the small corner where was the
crib of the eternal King and His mother. Then *they laid hands on him
and seized him.*[233] One of them drew his sword and would have cut off
his head, but God willed that he should be unable to do it.[234] Nevertheless he was struck on the forehead and seriously wounded. Striking
out as they went with violent hands, they dragged him from the
church, leaving the mass unfinished. But he, like *a gentle lamb,*[235] lifted
up his eyes to heaven and made no reply to them;[236] he did nor cry out
nor did he resist nor pray them to show some mercy. At length,
stripping him of his pallium and chasuble, of his dalmatic and tunicle,
they dragged him like a thief, clad only in his alb and his stole, and
mounted him behind a certain sacrilegious man. He who had struck
him on the forehead with a sword, however, was seized by a demon
before the entrance hall of that church. For a long time he rolled
about, foaming at the mouth and, his horse fleeing with him, he was
never found again.

51 Word of such an evil deed quickly threw the whole city into
turmoil. Who could ever describe such weeping and such sad wailing?
For, as the city was accustomed to celebrate our Lord's nativity more
solemnly than other cities, so it was now moved to proclaim the great
sadness that had befallen it. Heaven and earth were struck with terror
by this act and the hearts of all men were prepared to punish such
great villainy. The words of the prophet were fulfilled: the days of
your feasting are *turned* into lamentation and your joy *into mourning*[237]
and *she wept bitterly in the night, tears on her cheeks; she has none to comfort
her.*[238] Then the holy Church of God said, '*O that my head were waters
and my eyes a fountain of tears, that I might weep day and night'*[239]and
'Come, *all* the *peoples and behold my suffering.'*[240] Then *every* man *took up*

233 Mark 14:46; Matthew 26:50 (the arrest of Jesus).

234 Cf. Bernold, *Chronicon* 1076, pp. 431–2 ('one knight ... determined to kill him, but
    when the sword was brandished over his head, [the knight] was seized by extrene
    terror and fell to the ground').

235 Jeremiah 11:19.

236 Cf. Isaiah 53:7.

237 Amos 8:10.

238 Lamentations 1:2.

239 Jeremiah 9:1.

240 Lamentations 1:18.

the lament and she who was *sitting in the bridal chamber* was *mourning.*[241]
When *the shepherd* was *struck down*[242] and the clergy were running
hither and thither, the [brigands] stripped almost all the altars. Nowhere
was the divine office celebrated in the churches that day, with the
exception of the service already mentioned. The elements, which had
hitherto been disturbed, once more appeared tranquil so as not to
hinder the people in their zeal for the Lord.[243] The earth absorbed
almost all the water that had fallen on it in the excessive downpour
and revealed to them a dry road for the accomplishment of their
vengeance. All that night, therefore, war-trumpets were sounded and
knights scoured all the approaches to the city, lest by some stratagem
he might be carried out of the city; but nowhere was there any trace
of him. There was general uncertainty, no one knowing whether he
was alive or dead, until the people assembled in the Capitol were
informed that he was being held captive in a certain tower.[244] Then all
the peoples raised their voices to the heavens. But as soon as daylight
was restored to the earth, innumerable people, all urging each other
on, came to the house of Antichrist. They joined battle, therefore, but
at the first encounter the enemy took flight and the whole faction shut
themselves up in that tower. Then fire was laid to every part of the
ramparts; *battering-rams and engines of war*[245] were brought; the wall
was broken down and all the worldly goods contained there became
the spoil of the people of the Lord. No one shunned danger, but every
man, forgetful of himself, fought as hard as he could.

52 Afterwards a certain man, together with his wife, a noblewoman,
attended father Gregory and for some time they comforted him. For,
as he was suffering both from excessively harsh treatment and from
the cold of the winter's night, the husband brought furs to warm him
and placed his feet in the folds of his own garments. But the wife,
weeping bitterly, tended the wound of our father, raw from the
excessive flow of his rose-coloured blood, and applied a remedy of her
own and exclaimed against all those murderous and sacrilegious
enemies of God. She proved without doubt to be another Mary.[246] For

241 I Maccabees 1:28.

242 Cf. Zechariah 13:7; Matthew 26:31; Mark 14:27.

243 Cf. I Kings 19:10, 14; I Maccabees 2:54.

244 Cencius's tower in the district of Parione: G. B. Borino (1952a) p. 434; D. Whitton
(1980) p. 234.

245 II Maccabees 12:15.

246 These persons have not been identified. The noble Roman matron is here cast in
the role of Mary Magdalene: J. Greving (1893) p. 48.

just as the latter, bewailing her transgressions, bathed the Lord's feet with her tears, so this woman washed the great pastor with her tears, as she told of the crimes of all those men. Mary *kissed the feet* of the Lord and Saviour and afterwards she was able even to wash his head; but this woman – the servant of God, the servant of the Lord, at first purified by baptism, at last kindled by the ardour of her heart – kissed his head and breast and *wet* them *with her tears*.[247] O memorable heart, O praiseworthy liver[248] of a most devout woman, how great an ardour of charity hung about you, when before your very eyes you discerned the servant of the eternal King, ill treated and wounded by the hands of wicked men and you did not desist from pronouncing deserved reproaches and curses against the servants of Satan with your chaste mouth, now purified by the holy kisses that you had placed on the feet, the hands and the head of that great father. It is easy to believe that you would *lay down* your *life for the sake of*[249] your father's life and pass through incalculable torment rather than see your lord a captive and subject to such ill treatment. The noble-minded heroine fought with the hands of all and, a companion of all in a reward without measure, she heaped up for herself the profit of mercy.

53 But equally as great as her courage and faith were the treachery and loquacity of another woman. For just as long ago at the time of the Lord's passion *the maid who kept the door* frightened Peter,[250] so this woman disturbed his vicar with her sharp taunts. She was indeed the sister of that traitor and consequently was not afraid to curse so great a father. Another man, however, the servant and lackey of that traitor, holding a drawn sword, blasphemed and declared that on that very day he would cut off the great man's head. The very swift judgement of God did not delay in punishing his impiety; for a spear hurled from outside pierced his throat, the passage of his ill-omened voice, threw him, trembling and dying, to the ground and thus sent him to hell.

54 At this moment, however, the traitor saw that the tower would be captured and that the danger of death hung over him and he was

247 Luke 7:38, 44.

248 The liver was regarded as the seat of the affections. Cf. Isidore of Seville, *De differentiis verborum* II.67, *MPL* 83, col. 80B.

249 Cf. John 15:13.

250 John 18:17. Cencius's sister (otherwise unknown) is cast in the role of the maid-servant in the house of Annas who questioned Peter after Jesus's arrest. See J. Greving (1893) p. 48.

forced to fall at the feet of the blessed pope, saying, 'You have always taught mercy, father, and through your teaching you have achieved perfection; you have converted the erring and strengthened the converts. Receive an erring man who is turning aside from his iniquities; strengthen the convert, lest the depths of despair swallow me. I have sinned, I have erred, I have been treacherous, I have committed murder, I have been guilty of sacrilege; I have broken into the chamber of the mother of the eternal King and with violent hands I have violated the manger and the sacristy of God's Son and, like a perjured and sacrilegious parricide, with polluted hands I dragged you, my father and lord, from His bosom. Receive me, free me, protect me, grant mercy, give relief, advice and support, inflict punishment, impose penance, imprisonment, exile, flight from the fatherland and by pronouncing the Lord's judgement on me, placate the people, who are more than usually enraged. Take me in your holy hands, polluted as I am, and grant me as a penitent the interval of this day. I know in my heart that the gallows are rightly ready for me, I contemplate a fitting punishment and therefore with a prostrate body and a humble heart I surrender myself into your power.'

55 Then the most merciful pope, pious soul that he was, addressed the man who thus humbled himself: 'I see that you are a prey to poisonous bitterness and that the eyes of your mind are covered with filth and squalor and cannot see the splendour of the true light in which we have been working for so long. You yourself know how many religious men I urged to exhort you and how many paternal exhortations I myself addressed to you. Not only did you not assent to them but you even rushed headlong into worse conduct. Nevertheless the door of life still stands open to you, if only your heart is converted.' The other immediately sank to the ground and again confessed that he was guilty and wretched, promising to perform without hesitation everything that was enjoined on him. At last the most gentle man was moved by his innate piety to reply, 'Whatever injury you have inflicted on me, like a father I make allowance for; but I decree that your offence against God and His mother and the apostles and the whole Church must be expiated in this way: that first you make the journey to Jerusalem and afterwards, if you return from there alive, you place yourself in our hands and under our advice so that you may somehow succeed in restoring to yourself the grace of almighty God and, just as you have hitherto been a model of subversion to all the sons of the Church, so for the future you may become a model of conversion.' He therefore promised, most willingly, as it

seemed, to do everything that he was commanded and so he gained his freedom that day.[251]

56 At last the pious pope, standing at the window, signalled with outstretched hands to the raging crowd that they should be calm and that some of the chief men should ascend the tower. When some of them pondered what they ought to do, he exhorted them to begin. They launched an attack and broke into the tower and thus he was brought out, all the crowds weeping and shouting in their joy and piety. For they saw that he was totally bespattered with blood and, horrorstruck, they raised their voices to heaven. After this victory they all joyfully gathered, together with Pope Gregory, in the church of the mother of God from which he had been dragged away that night. Then the father of all at that very hour completed the celebration of the mass[252] that he had been prevented from finishing at night by the servants of the devil and he conferred the grace of the Lord's blessing on those returning from so great a victory.

57 Then, after they had eaten their fill, they met again to investigate more fully all the men who had allied themselves with the enemy of God. When they were found, all their property was given up to plunder and destruction and they were left with nothing at all except their own persons, which they saved by taking to flight. But while the people in the aforesaid church gave thanks to God for the liberation of their pastor, that wicked Judas fled with his wife and children and brothers and thus, abandoning his property, he escaped naked.[253] For afterwards the people arrived and seized whatever they could of what had formerly belonged to him. The towers and houses were pulled down, but the estates were held in common in the public treasury. The son of perdition and servant of Antichrist, however, damned before the foundation of the earth, after his escape not only failed to perform what he had promised, but also, in company with impious men like himself, did not shrink, as long as he lived, from giving evil counsel against his liberator.

58 Having dealt with these matters, let us come to his dealings with King Henry and declare the innocence of Pope Gregory and proclaim as best we can to the present and also to future generations the evil

---

251 Cf. Berthold, *Annales* 1076, p. 282 ('he confessed his sin and promised obedience and fitting penitence and satisfaction with, however, simulated piety').

252 Cf. Berthold, *Annales* 1076, p. 282.

253 Cf. Berthold, *Annales* 1076, p. 282 (he 'fled from the city by night'); Bonizo, *Book to a Friend* VII, above p. 233 (he was expelled 'on the following day').

that he received in return for good. For I believe that there are some men who, out of ignorance partly of the events and partly of the authorities of the holy Fathers or of the decretals, are not at all afraid to endanger their own salvation by censuring our common father, branding him wth infamy and – which is utterly evil in God's eyes – to redouble their unthinkable curses against him. If divine inspiration happened to move them to act from the desire to learn the truth rather than from an instinct of insolent pride, they would question truthful and religious men of proven worth and would believe them. For they have countless bishops, strong in the faith: to mention one of many, Gerald of Ostia,[254] who because of his meritorious life was chosen by the apostolic see from the region of Gaul[255] and obtained the seventh throne[256] among the cardinal bishops. He was sent by the apostolic see to investigate the case of that king and in his efforts to confirm the evidence that was given to him, he experienced very many hardships, dangers, fetters and imprisonment for the sake of the truth.[257] They also have the bishop of Palestrina,[258] who was sent from the city of Rome to suffer this same hardship.[259] There is besides Peter of Albano,[260] who, in order to bear witness to the truth against the simoniacs, walked barefoot over a huge pyre[261] and, as is found written in the register of the lord Pope Alexander II,[262] he emerged unharmed. There are also very many men from the lands beyond the mountains: Udo of Trier,[263] Herman of Metz, Altman of Passau,[264] Adalbero of Würzburg[265] and Hugh of Die,[266] at whose election so great

254 Gerald, cardinal bishop of Ostia (1072–7): see R. Hüls (1977) p. 100.

255 Formerly master of the cathedral school in Regensburg, grand prior of Cluny.

256 Actually 'the first throne': Ostia was the senior cardinal bishopric.

257 Papal legate in Germany, 1074: below p. 306. As legate in Lombardy, 1077, he was imprisoned by Bishop Denis of Piacenza: G. Meyer von Knonau (1894) p. 769.

258 Hubert, cardinal bishop of Palestrina (?1073–82): see R. Hüls (1977) pp. 110–11.

259 He accompanied Gerald on the 1074 legation (below p. 306) but Gerald's fellow prisoner in 1077 was Bishop Anselm II of Lucca.

260 Peter 'Igneus', cardinal bishop of Albano (1072–89): see R. Hüls (1977) pp. 90–1.

261 13 February 1068: see above p. 244 and n. 49.

262 Alexander II's papal register has not survived: H. Fuhrmann (1956) p. 301 n. 7.

263 Udo, archbishop of Trier (1066–78): see below pp. 343–4.

264 Altmann, bishop of Passau (1065–91), Gregory's permanent legate in Germany: see below p. 360.

265 Adalbero, bishop of Würzburg (1045–90): see below p. 352.

266 Hugh, bishop of Die (1074–82), archbishop of Lyons (1082–1106), Gregory's permanent legate in France: below p. 352.

a light is said to have come down from heaven that it was brighter than day and in the minds of all who were present there was no doubt that the Holy Spirit had arrived.[267] To satisfy the unbelievers, let men of other orders be assembled: namely, the abbot of Cluny, that king's father at his baptism[268] and Bernard of Marseilles,[269] who twice became a confessor because of the most fervent warmth of his faith, suffering exiles and chains for God's sake;[270] Rapoto, who indeed, it is claimed, was desired by the people as their king because of his noble blood and his honourable character;[271] Adalbert and Udalschalk,[272] to whom the negotiations were entrusted both by the king and also by the pope.

59 So that the other sex is not left out, let us also include the honourable woman, rich both in religion and in secular power, namely Queen Agnes, the mother of that most wicked king, a queen indeed who gave up her royal diadem, abandoned this world and adhered irremovably to the footsteps of God and His mother and His apostles Peter and Paul;[273] in addition Beatrice[274] and her most noble daughter Matilda, who, although they carried out the worldly duties of dukes and governed Italy, were made like Deborah, who, when she judged Israel, scattered Jabin with all his men in *the torrent Kishon;*[275] that is, they often confounded the wicked and ground them down. They indeed

267 Cf. Berthold, *Annales* 1078, pp. 306–7 ('made bishop not by human but by divine election'); Hugh of Flavigny, *Chronicon* II, p. 410.

268 On Abbot Hugh I as Henry IV's godfather: J. Lynch (1985) pp. 800–26.

269 Bernard, abbot of St Victor in Marseilles (✝1079).

270 During his 1077 legation to Germany (below p. 332) he was imprisoned by Count Udalric II of Lenzburg. After the battle of Mellrichstadt (1078) he was again taken prisoner. See G. Meyer von Knonau (1900) pp. 30, 143.

271 Evidently Rabbodi, one of the three envoys who delivered to Henry IV Gregory's ultimatum of 8 December 1075 (*Registrum* III.10, pp. 263–7) and perhaps also the papal envoy to the German princes whom Gregory called 'our son Rapoto' (*Epistolae Vagantes* 19, p. 52). Nothing is known of his being 'desired by the people as their king'. Perhaps he was a candidate in the election at Forchheim, March 1077 (below p. 334).

272 The royal envoys Adelpreth and Uodescalki, Rabbodi's colleagues in 1075.

273 After 1062 Agnes withdrew from court to live a religious life on her estates; in 1065 she left Germany for the abbey of Fruttuaria and then settled in Rome. See above p. 209 n. 92.

274 Beatrice, margravine of Tuscany (✝1076).

275 Judges 4:13; 5:21. The Old Testament parallel of Deborah was frequently applied to Matilda, margravine of Tuscany (✝1115) by Gregorian authors: *Vita Anselmi Lucensis* c. 11, p. 16; Rangerius, *Vita metrica Anselmi* p. 1232; Donizo, *Vita Mathildis* II.8, p. 394.

were mediators between the lord pope and the king[276] and they *earnestly desired*[277] to order and strengthen the state of the kingdom. Failure to accept the evidence of all these and of other credible witnesses of every rank is tantamount to deserving God's anger and incurring the sentence of eternal damnation. Having called them to mind, in order to demonstrate the innocence of so great a father, we shall continue our undertaking, setting down on our page that king's crimes, his evil designs and his insults to God and St Peter, so as not to allow earnest seekers of knowledge to wallow in ignorance and the darkness of error.

60 On the death of Henry III, therefore, the Roman pontiff Victor[278] (who was present when he died)[279] gave permission for that king, Henry IV, to succeed according to hereditary right, although he was still a child.[280] As Solomon bore witness, however, saying, *Woe to the land, when the king is a child and the princes feast in the morning*,[281] he was not afraid, blindly and insolently, to perpetrate whatever evil he could anywhere, to his own destruction and that of his whole kingdom. When all men reported the evidence of his youthful imperfections, however, the Roman pontiffs bore with his impudence, supposing that when he reached manhood, he could correct himself and paying no heed to what is written, that the man *who spares the rod, hates his son*.[282] For the vice is nourished and when it is not purified or plucked out while it is still a tender branch, afterwards on reaching maturity it can hardly be cut down by hand or sword. Thus indeed in the course of time he tried with all his might to place the whole Church under his arrogant heel and, by trampling her underfoot, to make her like a vile slave.[283]

61 The Roman church – who is the head and mistress of all religion and whose prerogative it is to correct all the powerful of the world

---

276 Cf. Donizo, *Vita Mathildis* I.19, p. 378 ('These women acted as mediators and friends of the king'). See T. Struve (1995) pp. 42–3; H. E. J. Cowdrey (1998) pp. 93, 96–9, 109, 129.

277 Luke 22:15.

278 Victor II (1054–7).

279 5 October 1056, Bodfeld.

280 Victor's role was magnified by adherents of the reform papacy both during his pontificate and subsequently. See W. Berges (1947) pp. 189–209; H. Beumann (1977) pp. 35–6; W. Goez (1980) pp. 11–21; I. S. Robinson (1999) pp. 26–7, 112.

281 Ecclesiastes 10:16.

282 Proverbs 13:24.

283 Cf. Gregory VII, *Registrum* I.42, pp. 64–5 ('The rulers and princes of this world ... trampling all reverence underfoot, oppress [the Church] like a vile slave').

before all others and to strengthen the waverers, as the Lord Himself commanded the apostle Peter, *when you have turned again, strengthen your brethren*[284] – did not tolerate this crime and began to exhort him by means of letters, warning and preaching. Hardened by his unfettered exercising of power, his neck could not *bear the yoke*[285] of Christ and he was evasive, twisting hither and thither; *turning over new plans in* his young *mind*,[286] he waited for a suitable time at which he could subject the Roman church to himself as he had done the rest. The exertions that he devoted to this end afterwards became apparent. For on the death of Pope Nicholas,[287] after Alexander of holy memory had secretly been put in his place,[288] madness took hold of his mind and he was not afraid to invest with his own hand the heretic Cadalus of Parma, wrongly called bishop, and to raise him up as pope.[289] But everyone abandoned him and the opponent of God could not bring into effect what he had planned. The books of father Alexander[290] bear witness to the many paternal letters by which he was admonished at that time.[291] Afterwards father Gregory, although he fled from God's will and resisted it,[292] was compelled to succeed him and, as was fitting, he sent him paternal admonitions,[293] praying and beseeching him, for the love of the eternal King, for the safety of his own position and for the relief of his own soul, to draw back and abstain from those offences, as so great a son and a member of holy Church ought, and to recognise that the King of kings *keeps watch* over him and, knowing *the counsels of hearts and those things that are hidden in the shadows*,[294]

---

284 Luke 22:32.

285 Matthew 11:29, 30.

286 Virgil, *Aeneid* 1, 657.

287 19 or 20 July 1061.

288 Paul's term (*subintroducto*) suggests secrecy: see J. Greving (1893) p. 54 n. 3; G. Meyer von Knonau (1890) pp. 220–1.

289 At the council of Basel, 28 October 1061: G. Meyer von Knonau (1890) pp. 224–5; T. Schmidt (1977) pp. 108–10, 126–7.

290 Evidently another reference to the papal register of Alexander II (above p. 302 n. 262). See H. Fuhrmann (1956) p. 301 n. 7.

291 Cf. Bonizo, *Book to a Friend* VI, above p. 217; Donizo, *Vita Mathildis* I.18, pp. 375–6 (Alexander 'in a paternal manner strove to recall the erring king').

292 Cf. Berthold, *Annales* 1073, p. 276 ('brought to the apostolic see by force'). The model is John the Deacon, *Vita Gregorii* I.44, *MPL* 75, col. 81B.

293 Cf. Gregory VII, *Registrum* I.9, p. 15 (above p. 278); *Epistolae Vagantes* 14, p. 34 (below p. 320).

294 I Corinthians 4:5.

requites each man *according to his works.*[295] He also asked him to dismiss the very wicked advisers[296] who loved their own interests rather than him,[297] since to acquiesce in the advice of such men meant nothing less than to earn the reward of death, overthrow the kingdom and wish to become *a by-word among all* [298] nations.

62 The king himself was momentarily disquieted by this and he sent a letter of supplication[299] – and, as afterwards became clear, of subterfuge – promising amendment. When this letter became public, the whole Church rejoiced, hoping that by God's grace the priestly and the royal powers would be united in cleaning up all the filth that everywhere burdened the Church. It was then decided by common counsel that because the business was so important and the cause such a godly one, Empress Agnes, his mother, should approach the king with a papal letter, in the company of the venerable bishops of Ostia and Palestrina, sent from the lord pope's side, so that he might understand the importance of his promise and definitely put an end to the evil committed in the past. The king received her with honour, together with the papal messengers; he returned to his senses, as was just, and made satisfaction to God and St Peter in all things.[300] He also promised in their hands[301] that he would most humbly bear with whatever obligations the legates imposed on him, that he would drive all simoniacs and evil and excommunicated advisers far away from him and that he would release the Church of God to be ordered and controlled according to the decrees of the canons by the advice of the pope.[302] When these and other matters were settled, they returned to the pope.

295 Proverbs 24:12.

296 The five advisers excommunicated by Alexander II in 1073: Bonizo, *Book to a Friend* VI, VII, above pp. 218, 222).

297 Cf. Gregory VII, *Registrum* II.30, p. 164 ('employ such advisers as love not their own interests but you'); *Registrum* IV.3, p. 298.

298 I Kings 9:7. Cf. Deuteronomy 28:37.

299 Henry IV, *Letter 5*, pp. 8–9. See C. Schneider (1972) pp. 57–68; H. E. J. Cowdrey (1998) pp. 95–6; I. S. Robinson (1999) pp. 130–2.

300 Spring 1074. Henry was reconciled to the Church by Gerald of Ostia and Hubert of Palestrina, 27 April in Nuremberg. See G. Meyer von Knonau (1894) pp. 377–8; O. Schumann (1912) pp. 23–8; C. Schneider (1972) pp. 73–83; H. E. J. Cowdrey (1998) pp. 98–9; I. S. Robinson (1999) pp. 132–3.

301 Cf. Gregory VII, *Epistolae Vagantes* 14, p. 36 (see below p. 320).

302 Cf. Bonizo *Book to a Friend* VII, above p. 223.

63 The king also *returned to the* same *mire*[303] in which he was accustomed to wallow, doubtless believing more in the flattery of his own
pleasures and his evil advisers than in the Christian religion. His
mother the empress was once more sent by the Roman see to correct
this.[304] After she had spent some time with him, she restored him
completely to the affections of holy mother Church. He indeed received
the[305] *seed* of *the Word* that was thrown into the field of his heart, but
according to the parable in the Gospel, while his mother sowed, *some
fell by the wayside* and was both *trodden underfoot* by passing humans
and seized by *birds; some,* falling *among thorns,* was *choked* by them
when they *sprang up* and could *not bear fruit; some* indeed, thrown *upon*
the hard surface of a stony heart and burned up by the heat of the sun,
could *have no roots.* Any intelligent person could understand that the
tread of human feet signified the advice of the wicked men whom he
made use of, the birds indeed signified the promptings of unclean
spirits, the *thorns* signified royal *riches* and *pleasures* and the *rock*[305]
indeed signified hardness of heart. The queen, however, prolonged her
stay and the pope again sent a letter so that she might be zealous in
her exhortation and in the liberation of her son.[306] He asked the king
himself to remain true to the contents of the letter that he had
formerly sent him and to the promise and the faith sworn in the hands
of the legates and especially to refrain from the simoniacal heresy for
which his spirit yearned and to keep at a distance his excommunicated
advisers, whom the apostolic see and the synod had condemned for
the sake of his own salvation and the welfare of the kingdom, lest he
fall under the same malediction.[307] The queen returned to Rome,
declaring that her son would turn towards God's justice and honour.
When soon afterwards the latter showed signs of hesitation, flattering
and suitable letters were sent to him on two occasions.[308]

64 At that time indeed all the Saxons unanimously conspired to have
him no longer as their king, since they realised that they were receiving

---

303 II Peter 2: 22.

304 The visit of April 1074 was Agnes's last to Germany: M. Black-Veldtrup (1995)
    pp. 96–7. Donizo, *Vita Mathildis* I.19, p. 376 made a similar error: hence J.
    Greving (1893) pp. 57–8 concluded that this was Paul's source.

305 /305 Luke 8:5–8; cf. Matthew 13:2–23 (parable of the sower).

306 Gregory VII, *Registrum* I.85, p. 121 (15 June 1074).

307 Gregory VII, *Registrum* II.30, pp. 163–5 (7 December 1074). Paul's allusion to the
    threat of excommunication is reminiscent of the message of December 1075
    reported in *Epistolae Vagantes* 14, p. 38 (see below p. 321).

308 Gregory VII, *Registrum* II.30, 31, pp. 163–8.

cruel treatment from him.[309] He was thus compelled to send a suppliant letter to the pope,[310] begging to be included in his prayers, so that through the pope's merits the right hand of the heavenly King might snatch him away from the horrible and fearful judgement that now hung over him, promising repeatedly that he would never again take any action towards the churches of God that could be considered blameworthy by the holy canons. Moved by his entreaties, the pope sent a letter and envoys to the Saxons[311] and he *dug around* the roots of the king, sending the baskets of his preaching in the expectation of being able to gather figs from *the fig-tree*.[312] But that place where he ought to have obtained an ample supply of moisture subsequently dried up completely; the vine that he had expected to bear plump grapes bore *wild grapes*, poor and worthless;[313] the corn, which was adorned with rather beautiful leaves, at the time of the harvest brought forth nothing but tares in an abominable mixture. He therefore advised *the king* to refrain from *having recourse to arms for the time being* until he received *envoys* from the territory of the Saxons.[314] The king, however, did not attend to the admonitions of his father's letter; he entered the land of Saxony[315] where, because of the sins of men, *much* human *blood was shed*[316] on both sides. Nevertheless, according to the *just judgement* of God, the victory was given into the hands of the king,[317] for which he ought to have abased himself under the Lord's hands, but instead, ungrateful and puffed up with the spirit of pride, he rose up against Him.[318] For all the promises that he had formerly made through his mother, through bishops and clergy, through public and private envoys, he subsequently brought to nothing in his apparent heedlessness.[319] Indeed not only did he not release the churches that he had sworn to place in the hands of the lord pope for the

309 Cf. Bonizo, *Book to a Friend* VII, above p. 233. The rebellion broke out in August 1073.

310 Paul seems here to have duplicated Henry IV, *Letter* 5, pp. 8–9, already mentioned above p. 306 and n. 299.

311 Gregory VII, *Registrum* I.39, pp. 61–2 (20 December 1073).

312 Luke 13:8.

313 Cf. Isaiah 5:2, 4.

314 *Registrum* I.39, p. 62.

315 8 June 1075: see G. Meyer von Knonau (1894) p. 499.

316 Cf. *Registrum* III.7, p. 258.

317 Battle of Homburg, 9 June 1075: see above p. 233.

318 Cf. Bonizo, *Book to a Friend* VII, above p. 234

319 Cf. *Registrum* III.10, p. 264.

purpose of their amendment, but he even conferred them by means of investiture on certain adulterers and simoniacs contrary to the decretals of the Fathers. Among these was Godfrey,[320] who had been excommunicated as an intruder in the church of Milan and whom the king invested with the church into which he had intruded like an adulterer, while Atto (whom the better part of the clergy and people had elected as their archbishop according to God)[321] dwelled with the pope.[322] He also gave away the churches of Fermo and Spoleto.[323]

65 When news of this reached the apostolic see, Pope Gregory was greatly disturbed. He began to be troubled by many anxieties since he perceived that everything that he had hoped would produce peace had turned in the opposite direction. Finally he revealed to certain honourable men some information secretly sent to him through certain envoys,[324] so that he might consider what decision he should make in this case. They all began to marvel when they investigated such promises, or rather deceptions. But lest the Roman see might seem to act in any way unjustly or hastily, it was decided that a more severe letter,[325] should be written to the king, from which he might fully understand that the Roman pastor could not forsake justice either out of fear or out of love.[326] He wrote to Beatrice and her daughter Matilda,[327] who at that time were foremost among the rulers of Italy; he wrote to the king, to the Milanese intruder[328] and to all the suffragans.[329]

---

320 Godfrey, archbishop of Milan (1071–5): see G. Schwartz (1913) pp. 80–1. His investiture (1071): above p. 214.

321 Atto, archbishop of Milan (1072): see G. Schwartz (1913) pp. 81–2; R. Abbondanza (1962) pp. 564–5. His election (6 January 1072): above p. 216.

322 Atto was ordained cardinal priest of S. Marco (but was among the twelve cardinals who deserted Gregory for the anti-pope, 1084). See R. Hüls (1977) p. 185.

323 Cf. Gregory VII, *Registrum* III.10, p. 264. In the case of Fermo Henry's candidate was probably Wolfgang (excommunicated 1079); in Spoleto, probably Rudolf. See G. Schwartz (1913) pp. 234–5, 240.

324 Cf. Henry IV, *Letter* 7, p. 10 ('I am sending to you secretly those messengers ...'). Identified as Rabbodi and Adelpreth: *Registrum* III.10, p. 267.

325 *Registrum* III.10, pp. 263–7. See G. Meyer von Knonau (1894) pp. 576–80; C. Schneider (1972) pp. 139–45; R. Schieffer (1981) pp. 134–41; H. E. J. Cowdrey (1998) pp. 132–4; I. S. Robinson (1999) pp. 140–2.

326 Perhaps an allusion to Gregory VII, *Registrum* VII.3, p. 463: 'no man could either by love or fear ... seduce me from the right path of justice'.

327 Gregory VII, *Registrum* III.5, pp. 251–2.

328 *Ibid.*, III.8, pp. 259–61 (8 December 1075) to Tedald, archbishop of Milan (1075–85). See above p. 232.

329 *Registrum* III.9, pp. 261–3 (8 December 1075).

66 Then the king, afflicted both by terror and by deep sadness, angrily considering different courses of action, summoned all his worthless advisers and brought several deceivers into his wicked presence.[330] They made very many proposals of the sort that usually deceive the human mind, reminding him of the royal honour left by his father, his freedom of action, his infinite wealth, the numbers and strength of his knights; the bishops, dukes, tyrants and princes bound to him by fealty; also the way in which the necks of the proud had been forced under his yoke and in addition the incomes of the churches delivered into his hands, together with many other matters that (as we said) seduce the minds of worldly men. Among them was the archbishop of Mainz[331] and those who served as his suffragans. When the meeting was assembled, they decided that the imperial power should send messengers everywhere, commanding all the bishops in his kingdom to appear in the king's presence. Once they were all gathered together, they were to subscribe their names to the anathema that the heretic of Mainz composed against the vicar of the blessed Peter,[332] or rather against God and His apostle. If by chance any of them, moved by feelings of reverence, wished to hold back from this proceeding, he would be deprived of all his property and his office and would be liable to the death sentence, having offended the royal majesty.[333]

67 Meanwhile, after the envoys had been sent out in all directions, there arrived from the City a certain Hugh,[334] formerly a cardinal but at that time the chief of the heretics, who had been condemned three times by the apostolic see since he had presumed to reconcile certain simoniacs[335] with a letter forged by himself, representing the persons of archbishops and bishops. He praised all that they had contrived against the lord pope and he made public other letters issued in the

---

330 The letter reached Henry 1 January 1076 in Goslar. Cf. Berthold, *Annales* 1076, p. 281 ('he at once communicated with the excommunicates [the five excommunicated advisers]').

331 Siegfried I, archbishop of Mainz (1060–84).

332 Cf. Donizo, *Vita Mathildis* I.19, p. 377 ('The audacious bishop of Mainz showed all too little fear of Christ when he cursed the pope.')

333 Cf. Gregory VII, *Epistolae Vagantes* 14, p. 38 (below p. 322); Bonizo, *Book to a Friend* VII, above p. 234. See G. Meyer von Knonau (1894) p. 617 n. 10; I. S. Robinson (1999) p. 146.

334 Hugh Candidus, cardinal priest of S. Clemente (?1049–85), cardinal bishop of Palestrina (1085–?1099). See R. Hüls (1977) pp. 111, 158–60.

335 Cf. Gregory VII, *Registrum* V.14a, c. 4, pp. 369–70 ('condemned for the third time by the apostolic see'); Bonizo, *Book to a Friend* VI, above p. 214 and n. 129.

names of all the cardinals and the senate and people, in which certain
appeals were referred to the royal presence, including a demand for a
new pope and for the rejection of the lawful pastor.[336] He also mentioned the many attacks that the pope suffered at the hands of the
Normans,[337] the neighbouring counts and also of the traitors dwelling
in the city.[338] The king rejoiced exceedingly at the sight of these letters
and received from them the stimulus that he needed to complete his
wicked task. The devilish bishops were assembled[339] and they published
an anathema against the lord pope, or rather against themselves.[340]
Envoys[341] and letters were sent by the king into Lombardy and the
March and they were commanded to subscribe their names to the
anathema that had been pronounced. They all assembled, therefore, in
Pavia[342] and subscribed the anathema because of the king's command
and even more because of their own malevolence and hatred, as the
event made clear. For as an additional demonstration of their ill will,
they took the holy Gospels and declared that henceforward they
would never accept Gregory as pope nor show him obedience.[343]
Other envoys were sent to accomplish this. The king, however, wrote
a letter to Rome, full of every shameful insult and falsehood, commanding the lord pope to vacate his throne and to relinquish his church,
calling him a perjurer, an intruder and a destroyer of the office of
king.[344] The simoniacs of Lombardy above all exerted themselves in this
enterprise. They also decided that the letter would not be delivered
before the synod, which was assembled in the Roman church,[345] could
hear it in full; and this was done.

336 These details are found in no other account. J. Greving (1893) p. 63 suggested
that they derived from the lost polemic of Bonizo 'against Hugh the schismatic':
see above p. 42.
337 Presumably the attack on Benevento by Robert Guiscard, for which he was
excommunicated in the Roman synod of Lent 1074: above p. 224.
338 Presumably an allusion to Cencius Stephani (above pp. 225–6). See D. Whitton
(1980) p. 247.
339 Council of Worms, 24 January 1076.
340 The letter subscribed by the bishops in Worms, *Die Briefe Heinrichs IV.* pp. 65–8.
341 Bishops Huzman of Speyer and Burchard of Basel, escorted by Count Eberhard
'the Bearded': G. Meyer von Knonau (1894) p. 629.
342 In Piacenza: Bonizo, *Book to a Friend* VII, above p. 234. Paul's error derives from
Donizo, *Vita Mathildis* I.19, p. 377.
343 Cf. Bonizo *Book to a Friend* VII, above p. 234.
344 Cf. Henry IV, *Letter* 11, pp. 14–15 ('I command you to come down'). The charges
of perjurer and intruder appear in the bishops' letter: above n. 340.
345 Lenten synod, 14–20 February 1076: Gregory VII, *Registrum* III.10a, pp. 268–71.

68 For, as the pope was presiding over the synod, a certain clerk of Parma[346] did not shrink from insulting the Lord God by presenting himself with that letter and he was not afraid to reveal those blasphemies before the whole Church and before the council. At the same time a portent, a sign of that iniquity and a confirmation of the future event, occurred in the city near the church of blessed Peter,[347] which filled all men's hearts with amazement. For no one could offer a suitable explanation of the event. Indeed a hen laid, in a miraculous way, an egg in which there were two remarkable signs: namely the likeness of a serpent and that of a shield, dark and exceedingly horrible. The serpent raised itself from the egg shell in three coils and tried to raise its head to the top of the egg, but stretched its tail into the area of darkness. While it was stretching out to the top of the egg, however, it was struck by a blow and its head coiled along its belly. When it was taken out of the shell, its scales could be seized and handled like any other material object. It was while all the bishops and the other participants in the synod were examining and wondering at this object, that that messenger of Antichrist arrived.

69 After the hymn was finished and the pope had sat down, being about to deliver his words of exhortation to them all, that precursor of Antichrist, who did not honour God and preferred the earthly to the heavenly empire, addressed the pope thus: 'My lord the king and all the bishops, both the Italians and those beyond the mountains, order you henceforward to relinquish the see of blessed Peter and the Roman church into which you have intruded.[348] For it is not fitting to ascend to so great an honour except by their command and by the imperial gift.' Turning to the Roman clergy, he said, 'You, brethren, are instructed to appear in the royal presence at the forthcoming feast of Pentecost[349] to receive from the hands of the king a pope and a father, because this man is no pope but is known to be *a ravenous wolf*.'[350] At these words Bishop John of Porto,[351] a man distinguished

---

346 Roland of Parma, bishop of Treviso (c. 1076–c. 1090): see G. Schwartz (1913) p. 61.

347 St Peter ad Vincula, near the Lateran basilica. Paul elaborated the miracle story found in Donizo, *Vita Mathildis* I.19, p. 377, which, according to J. Greving (1893) p. 66, 'springs directly from a folk-tale'.

348 Cf. Donizo I.19, p. 378 ('The king ... and the bishops have commanded you to leave the see that you are not worthy to possess'); Bonizo *Book to a Friend* VII, above p. 234.

349 15 May 1076. Cf. Donizo I.19, p. 378 ('at Whitsun the king will come to send a pope to Rome').

350 Genesis 49:27. Cf. Donizo I.19, p. 378 ('this man is a wolf, not a pope').

351 John II, cardinal bishop of Porto (1057–?1089), the only cardinal bishop among

for the probity of his conduct and his piety, rose impetuously and cried out in a loud voice, 'Seize him!' Then the prefect[352] sprang forward, together with the judges, knights and Roman noblemen with drawn swords, wishing to slay that great imposter there in the church of the Saviour in the presence of the lord pope. The prefect would have done it, had not the pious father fallen on the imposter, covering him with his body, while everyone was shouting for his death.[353]

70 At length, after obtaining silence with some difficulty,[354] the lord pope said, 'Sons of holy Church, do not disturb the tranquillity of our Lord God with any discord. For, according to the sequence of the divine Scriptures, there must *come times of stress*, in which *men* must *be lovers of self, lovers of money, proud, arrogant, disobedient to their parents*[355] and showing no reverence to their teachers, so that the patience of the sons of God and the demonstration of our *faith* may be *more precious than gold that is tested by the fire.*[356] The divine word cries out to us, saying, *It is necessary that temptations come;* nevertheless *woe to* him *by whom the temptation comes!* [357] In addition, to explain our situation and show how we ought to live among our enemies, it says, *Behold, I send you out as sheep in the midst of wolves; so be wise as serpents and innocent as doves.*[358] Now indeed, although the precursor of Antichrist has arisen in the Church, we have nevertheless long been under instruction both by the Lord and by the holy Fathers and thus endowed with twofold knowledge we can proceed in the footsteps of the men of former times, so that, just as the pious Fathers destroyed the serpent's cunning with their dovelike innocence and put to flight the innocence of the dove with the cunning of the serpent, so let us retain the gentleness of the bird that is without poison and let us not relinquish the wisdom of the serpent. For to exercise the mind in both these ways is not a vice, but the secret of proper discretion. We ought

---

the cardinals who deserted Gregory VII in 1084, becoming the emperor's confidant. See R. Hüls (1977) pp. 118–20.

352 Cencius, son of John Tiniosus (see above p. 225).

353 Cf. Donizo I.19, p. 378 ('he would have done it, but the kind father clung to him'); Bonizo *Book to a Friend* VII, above p. 235.

354 Bonizo *Book to a Friend* VII, above p. 235 placed the pronouncement of this papal sentence on 'the following day'. See G. Meyer von Knonau (1894) p. 636; H. E. J. Cowdrey (1998) p. 140.

355 II Timothy 3:1–2.

356 I Peter 1:7.

357 Matthew 18:7.

358 Matthew 10:16.

neither to pursue anyone with hatred nor with foolish prudence to bear with those who wish to break God's law. For *behold, the acceptable time*[359] is at hand; behold, the Lord once more walks in the spirit among men, crying out and saying, Whoever *would come after me, let him deny himself* and so forth.[360]

71 'We must, therefore, follow the Lord when He summons us to *the way and the life,*[361] if we desire to feed on the fruit of the eternal inheritance. *Through many tribulations,* as our teacher instructs us, *we must enter the kingdom of God.*[362] It is enough that we have lived hitherto in the peace of the Church, but now it is fitting that the crops of Christ, long parched, should again be watered with the blood of the saints, so that His fruit, weakened by old age, may be moistened afresh and return to its original beauty. Let us see the devil's war, which has hitherto been carried on in the dark with squalid deceptions, break out in the open field. Now is the time for Christ's recruits to fight back, raising their learned hands for the fray, so that Christ's faith, which through the devil's corruption has been scattered and abandoned throughout almost all the world, may be recognised and may be present, since the Lord God fights through us. We see of course that every day the men of this world go out to fight to destroy our salvation. They obtain no other reward for their labour than torments, nothing except hell, if we, to whom *to live is Christ and to die* for His love *is gain,*[363] for whom eternal happiness is prepared after this wretched and insubstantial life, adhere to the laws of God and our orthodox faith and ⌈do not⌉ retreat and yield to the enemy.

72 'At all events the voice of the Lord reminds us, saying, *Whoever is ashamed of me and of my words, of him will the Son of man be ashamed when He comes in His glory and the glory of the Father and of the holy angels.*[364] It ought to seem terrible to you, in that time and before so great a judgement-seat to receive a dreadful and shameful sentence for our negligence, when the Judge of all wishes to reward others for their labours. For the eternal Wisdom wishes us to be the stewards in His house so that when after a little time He comes to dwell there, He can possess a house made clean by our efforts. The priests of the Lord

---

359 II Corinthians 6:2.
360 Matthew 16:24; Luke 9:23.
361 John 14:6.
362 Acts 14:21.
363 Philippians 1:21.
364 Luke 9:26.

are exhorted to press on with this excellent work, since in the fullness of time when they have grown old in the laws of the Lord, after their fiftieth year they are commanded to become the guardians of the vessels of the Lord.[365] The vessels are indeed, as blessed Gregory says, our hearts in which we carry all our thoughts.[366] Sacred eloquence also bears witness that hearts are *the temple of the living God*,[367] which it is appropriate to clean and to adorn all the more diligently because we know that He who dwells in them is purer than all others. It is indeed written that a clean dweller seeks a clean dwelling. Again: *Come to your right mind and sin no more.*[368] And again: Behold, *I stand at the door and knock: if anyone opens, I shall come in to him and eat with him and he with me.*[369]

73 'We now see, brethren, that if we earnestly try to lift up our hearts, how our Author knocks and admonishes us so that we open to Him and close to the devil and resist his followers and confederates with all our strength, *being ready to punish every disobedience*, according to the apostle.[370] Nor must we fear even if they could prevail against us, since power is granted to them by the just Judge so that the furnace provided for our trial may quickly be consumed in ash and sparks, while we, the proven vessels, may be taken up forever into the service of the Lord. We hope indeed and we do not doubt that no *tribulation, persecution or sword*, fetters, prisons, exiles present or future, could *separate us from the love which is in Christ Jesus* [371] and His holy laws. For it is better *to die for the laws* [372] of the Lord than to give way and retreat before the attackers and destroyers of the laws, since not to oppose such men is very clearly to deny the faith of Christ.

74 'We see before our eyes and our hands the sign of the ancient serpent[373] that Almighty God showed us to make us wary and careful and to suggest what we ought to do about the son of pride who exalts himself against this holy catholic Church. Holy Scripture indeed

365 Cf. Numbers 8:25.
366 Cf. Gregory I, *Dialogi* II.2, *MPL* 66, 134A.
367 II Corinthians 6:16.
368 I Corinthians 15:34.
369 Revelation 3:20.
370 II Corinthians 10:6.
371 Romans 8:35, 39.
372 II Maccabees 7:2, 8:21.
373 Cf. Numbers 21:8. Cf. Isidore of Seville, *Quaestiones in Numeros* c. 36, *MPL* 83, col. 355A.

represents the faith of holy Church through the image of an egg,[374] in which indeed the evil are mixed up with the good until the end of the world, as none of the faithful doubts. Although they strive by frauds and deceptions to conceal themselves for a while, however, they cannot always hide because the Lord reveals them. When they burst out into the open, the fraud that was hidden is apparent to all and the holy Church of God wields the sword of vengeance against them, once they are known. This king, whose image our God wished to be represented and known by the likeness of the serpent, has hitherto been afraid and by means of his cunning words and his messages has hidden himself as though in the obscurity of a gloomy night, until he sprang out and showed what he cherished in his heart. What he has perpetrated far and wide in the churches of God would suffice to condemn him. Now, however, as you see, he is attempting to rear his head against the foundation of our faith, as it is written, *he sets his mouth against the heavens and his tongue struts through the earth.*[375] The apostle John says of him, *he was given a mouth uttering haughty and blasphemous words.*[376] Also: *the dragon swept down a third of the stars of heaven* with *his tail.*[377] The wretched man pays no heed to what the Truth Himself said to our master and the prince of the Church. *On this rock,* he said, *I shall build my church and the gates of hell will not prevail against it.*[378] Now, therefore, brethren, it is appropriate to wield the sword of vengeance and to bind and smite the enemy of God and the Church, so that the head that he is known to have reared against the foundation of the faith and of all the churches may be struck off and fall to the ground, just as in the earliest time of his pride he was told to crawl on his breast and his belly.[379] *Fear not,* as the Lord says, *little flock,* since *it is your Father's good pleasure to give you the* heavenly *kingdom.*[380] It is enough that hitherto you have restrained him and have admonished him as was fitting; but now let him know that his *conscience* is *seared.'*[381]

75 After he had concluded with these and certain other words, the

---

374 Cf. Luke 11:12. Cf. Bede, *In Lucae evangelium expositio* c. 11, *MPL* 92, col. 474BC.
375 Psalm 72:9.
376 Revelation 13:5.
377 Revelation 12:4.
378 Matthew 16:18.
379 Cf. Genesis 3:14.
380 Luke 12:32.
381 I Timothy 4:2.

great and holy synod said, 'Your judgement, most holy father, whom
the divine clemency provided to rule the world in our time, unleashes
against the blasphemous usurper, the tyrant, the renegade such a
sentence as will destroy him and provide future ages with a warning
against transgression.[382] Our duty indeed is to obey your commands
and to comply with them according to our ability and we do not desire
to make our souls more precious to us. For we willingly embrace
death, if necessary, so as not to seem to be abandoning the footsteps
of our Fathers. Why do we not give for the sake of the holy laws of our
God that which we are reluctant to lose? Draw the sword, pronounce
judgement, so that any *righteous man* may *rejoice when he sees the
vengeance* and may *bathe his hands in the blood of the sinner.'*[383] At last
with the acclamation of all it was decided that he should be deprived
of the royal office and that both the king and all his supporters should
be bound by the chains of anathema.[384] On receiving this assurance,
the lord pope with the consent and the judgement of the whole synod
pronounced the anathema in this manner.

76 The anathema which Gregory VII pronounced against King
Henry. *Blessed*[385] *Peter, prince of the apostles, incline your gracious ears to
us, we beg you, and hear me, your servant, whom you have fostered from
childhood*[386] *and have freed even to this day from the hand of the wicked,*[387]
*who hated and still hate me because of my fidelity towards you. You are my
witness and so also are my lady, the mother of God and blessed Paul, your
brother among all the saints, that your holy Roman church dragged me unwillingly to its helm* [388] *and that I did not think* it robbery to *ascend to your
see but would rather have ended my life in pilgrimage*[389] *than seize your
place by means of worldly cunning for the sake of earthly glory. So by your
grace rather than through my own works I believe that it has pleased and
continues to please you that the Christian people especially committed to you
should obey me, who have been especially appointed as your representative.
Through your grace the power of binding and loosing in heaven and on*

382 Cf. Donizo, *Vita Mathildis* I.19, p. 378 ('destroy the wicked blasphemer').
383 Psalm 57:11.
384 Cf. Donizo I.19, p. 378.
385 /385 Gregory VII, *Registrum* III.10a, pp. 270–1 (20 February 1076). Paul's variants
from the text of the papal register: H. Fuhrmann (1956) pp. 303–5.
386 See H. E. J. Cowdrey (1998) p. 28 and above p. 266.
387 Cf. Esther 14:19.
388 See above pp. 220, 277.
389 I.e. as a monk. See I. S. Robinson (1978a) pp. 34–5.

earth has been granted to me by God.[390] Relying on this trust, for the sake of the honour and defence of your Church, on behalf of Almighty God, Father, Son and Holy Spirit, through your power and authority, I deny the government of the whole kingdom of the Germans and Italy to King Henry, son of Emperor Henry, who has rebelled against your Church with unheard-of arrogance and I absolve all Christians from the bonds of any oath that they have sworn or may swear to you[391] and I forbid anyone to serve him as king. For it is fitting that he who strives to diminish the honour of your Church, should himself lose the honour that he seems to possess. And because he has scorned to obey as a Christian ought and has not returned to God, Whom he abandoned by associating with excommunicates and by rejecting the warnings that I sent him, as you yourself are a witness, for the sake of his own salvation and by separating himself from your Church and attempting to break it asunder, I bind him with the chains of anathema on your behalf so that the nations may know and acknowledge that you are Peter and that on this rock the Son of the living God has built my Church[392] and the gates of hell will not prevail against it.[385]

77 Afterwards he sent letters to various persons, publishing that same anathema and the reasons for it. We have taken care to include two of these in this present work.

Gregory,[393] bishop, servant of the servants of God, to all bishops who desire to be numbered among the sheep that Christ committed to blessed Peter, greeting and apostolic blessing. You have heard, most beloved brothers, of the new and unheard-of presumption; you have heard of the wicked babbling and audacity of the schismatics and those who blaspheme against God's name in blessed Peter; you have heard of puffed up arrogance injuring and insulting the holy and apostolic see, such as your fathers never saw nor heard and which, as all Scripture teaches, was never perpetrated by the pagans or the heretics. Even if this evil had ever been surpassed since the foundation of the Church and the spread of Christ's faith, nevertheless all the faithful must needs lament and groan at such great contempt and trampling underfoot of the apostolic, or rather the divine authority. If, therefore, you believe that the keys of the kingdom of heaven were entrusted by our Lord Jesus Christ to blessed Peter[394]

390 Cf. Matthew 16:19.

391 Cf. *Dictatus papae* c. 27: *Registrum* II.55a, p. 208: 'That [the pope] can absolve the subjects from their fidelity to the wicked'.

392 Matthew 16:18.

393 /393 Gregory VII, *Registrum* III.6, pp. 254–5 (February 1076). Paul's variations from the text of the papal register: H. Fuhrmann (1956) pp. 303–5.

394 Cf. Matthew 16:19.

and you desire the entrance to the joys of eternal life to be opened up to you by his hands, you must reflect how great a cause of grief must be the injury inflicted on him. For unless you are made companions in suffering here, wherever *your faith and hearts are proved through the dangers of temptations, there is no doubt that you are not worthy to receive a heavenly crown and glory, as sharers in the future consolation and sons of the kingdom. We ask you, beloved, that you strive earnestly to implore divine mercy either to* convert *the hearts of the impious to penitence or, by curbing their abominable counsels, to show* that *they who try to overturn the rock founded by Christ*[395] *and to violate divine privileges are senseless fools.*[393]

Gregory,[396] *bishop, servant of the servants of God, to all bishops, dukes, counts and other faithful men in the kingdom of the Germans who defend the Christian faith, greeting and apostolic blessing.*

78 *We have heard that certain men among you have doubts about the excommunication that we have imposed on the king and ask whether he was justly excommunicated and if our sentence was uttered on the authority of legal opinion with due deliberation. We have, therefore, taken care to disclose to the eyes and minds of all men, as truthfully as we could, according to the evidence of our conscience, how we were led to excommunicate him, not for the purpose of raising our voice to publish the individual reasons – which, alas! are only too well known – but rather, to answer the reservations of those who think that we laid hold of the spiritual sword rashly and following the impulses of our own passions rather than fear of God and zeal for righteousness. While we were still in the office of deacon, an improper and shameful rumour about the king's actions reached us. For the sake of the imperial dignity and out of reverence for his father and mother and also in the hope and the desire for his correction, we often admonished him by means of letters and messengers to desist from his wickedness and, remembering his most illustrious birth and his high office, to regulate his life so that his conduct was fitting for a king and – if God granted it – a future emperor.*[397] *But after we (although unworthy) came to the* office *of pope and his iniquity increased as he grew older, we felt that Almighty God would require his soul at our hands the more severely because the freedom and authority to rebuke him were given to us before all men and therefore we urged him the more*

---

395 Cf. Matthew 16:18.

396 /396 Gregory VII, *Epistolae Vagantes* 14 (*JL* 4999), pp. 32–40 (summer 1076). On the dissemination of this text in letter collections: C. Erdmann (1936) p. 12.

397 The theme of emperorship in Gregory's letters to Henry: *Registrum* II.31, III.7, pp. 165, 257. See I. S. Robinson (1999) pp. 134, 138.

anxiously, convincing, rebuking, exhorting[398] *in every way, to amend his life. After frequently sending us devout greetings by letter, excusing himself both because his time of life was unreliable and weak*[399] *and because on many occasions he had been wrongly advised and persuaded by those who controlled the court, he promised indeed in his own words that he would most readily accept our advice day after day; but nevertheless he trampled them underfoot through his deeds, as he increased his offences.*

Meanwhile we summoned to penitence certain members of his household on whose advice and through whose artifices he had contaminated bishoprics and many monasteries with the simoniac heresy, introducing for a price wolves instead of shepherds. We wished that, while there was still an opportunity for amendment, they would restore to the venerable places to which they belonged the possessions of the churches that they had received through such wicked commerce, and that they themselves through lamentation and penance would make satisfaction to God for the evil that they had done. When we learned that they scorned to take advantage of the delay granted to them to perform this and that they stubbornly remained in their usual wickedness, we rightly separated them, as sacrilegious men and servants and members of the devil, from the communion and body of the whole Church[400] *and we warned the king to expel them, as excommunicates, from his household, from his counsels and from his company. Since, however, the cause of the Saxons was meanwhile growing burdensome to the king and he perceived that the military strength of the kingdom wished for the most part to abandon him, he again sent us a suppliant letter, full of all humility, in which he declared himself most guilty towards almighty God and blessed Peter and us and he also prayed that we should strive to correct by our apostolic foresight and authority whatever wrongs he had perpetrated by his own fault in ecclesiastical matters against the justice of canon law and the decrees of the holy Fathers and in this he promised us his obedience in all things, his consent and faithful aid.*[401] *He was moreover afterwards received as a penitent by our colleagues and legates, Bishop Hubert of Palestrina and Bishop Gerald of Ostia, whom we sent to him, and he confirmed his promises in their hands by the sacred stoles that they wore about their necks.*[402] *Some time later the king did battle with the Saxons,*[403] *but such were the thanks and*

---

398 Cf. II Timothy 4:2.

399 Cf. Sallust, *Catilina* 1.4.

400 Roman synod of Lent 1075 (*Registrum* II.52a, p. 196): above p. 218 n. 162.

401 Henry IV, *Letter 5*, pp. 8–9. See above p. 306.

402 See above p. 306.

403 Homburg, 9 June 1075: above p. 308.

such the sacrifices that he offered to God for the victory that he obtained: he immediately broke the vows of improvement that he had made and, not heeding the promises that he had made to us, he received the excommunicates into his friendship and society and dragged the churches into their accustomed confusion. We were deeply grieved by this; but although his contempt for the blessings of the heavenly King had robbed us of almost all hope of correction, we nevertheless decided to make another trial of his spirit, desiring him rather to hear the voice of apostolic gentleness than to feel the effects of apostolic severity. We therefore sent him a warning letter[404] as a reminder[405] that he should not imagine that he could deceive God, who, the more abundant is His patience, the severer is His anger when He begins to judge; that he should not dishonour God by honouring himself; that he should not attempt to increase his own power, scorning God and insulting His apostle, bearing in mind that 'God resists the proud but gives grace to the humble'.[406] In addition we sent to him three religious men, his own faithful followers,[407] through whom we secretly warned him to do penance for his offences. These indeed (dreadful to relate) were well known to very many and published throughout many regions and on their account the authority of both divine and human laws bears witness and commands that not only should he be excommunicated until he made due satisfaction but also he ought to be deprived of all the honour of the kingship without hope of recovery. Finally, unless he excluded the excommunicates from his company, we could decide upon no other judgement in his case than that he should be separated from the Church in company with the excommunicates with whom he chose to associate rather than with Christ. Certainly if he wishes to accept our warnings and to correct his life, we have called and continue to call God to witness how much we should rejoice for his salvation and his honour and how lovingly we should embrace him in the bosom of holy Church as one who, since he is appointed to be a prince of the people,[408] having the government of a very extensive kingdom, ought to be the defender of catholic peace and justice. But his deeds proclaim how much he regarded our words, either written or conveyed by legates. Taking it ill that he should be held in check or rebuked by anyone, not only could he not be recalled from his previous offences to amend himself, but an even greater fury seized his mind and he did not cease until he wrecked the

404 Gregory VII, *Registrum* III.10, pp. 263–7. See above p. 309.

405 Other versions of this letter read: 'as a reminder of what he promised and to whom he promised it'.

406 I Peter 5:5.

407 Rabbodi, Adelpreth and Udalschalk: *Registrum* III.10, p. 267.

408 Cf. Isaiah 3:7.

faith in Christ of nearly *all the bishops in Italy and of as many as possible of the bishops in the German territories. He forced them to deny the obedience due to blessed Peter and to the apostolic see and the honour granted them by our Lord Jesus Christ.*[409] *Since, therefore, we saw that his iniquity was at its height, we excommunicated him according to the judgement of a synod*[410] *for the following reasons: firstly, because he refused to abstain from the company of those who were excommunicated for the sacrilege and the offence of simoniacal heresy; then because he would not even promise, let alone undertake, penance for the guilty actions of his life, having feigned* that faith *that he had promised in the hands of our legates; also because he was not afraid to rend asunder the body of Christ, that is the unity of the Church. We did this in order that, having failed to recall him to the way of salvation by mildness, we might be able with God's help to do so by means of severity; so that, if (which heaven forbid!) he should not fear even this punitive judgement, at least our own soul should not be liable to the reproach of negligence or fear.*

If, therefore, anyone thinks that this sentence was pronounced unjustly or unreasonably, if he is such a one as wishes to show his understanding of sacred rules, let him consider it with us; let him listen patiently to what not we but divine authority teaches, decrees and judges, through the harmonious voice of the holy Fathers and let him give his assent. But we do not think that any of the faithful who knows ecclesiastical laws is so possessed by this error that, even if he dares not affirm it in public, he does not assert in his heart that this action was the right one. In any case, even if (which God forbid!) we bound [him] with the bond of excommunication without sufficient cause and not entirely according to justice, nevertheless, as the holy Fathers declare, the sentence should not be rejected on that account, but absolution must be sought with all humility.

But you, dearly beloved, would not abandon God's justice because of the king's anger or because of any danger and you pay no heed to the stupidity of those who will be declared ripe for destruction for their cursing and lying.[411] *Stand firm and be strong*[412] *in the Lord, knowing that you are defending the cause of Him who, as an invincible king and eternally sublime conqueror, will judge the living and the dead,*[413] *rewarding everyone according to his deeds.*[414] *You*

---

409 In the councils of Worms and Piacenza: see above pp. 310–11.

410 Lenten synod of 1076: see above p. 317.

411 Cf. Psalm 58:13–14.

412 I Corinthians 16:13.

413 II Timothy 4:1.

414 Cf. Revelation 2:23.

also can be certain of His manifold rewards if you continue steadfast to the end, faithful and unshaken in His truth. For this reason we also unceasingly pray to God for you that He may give you the power to be strengthened by the Holy Spirit[415] in His name and that He may convert the heart of the king[416] to penitence, so that the latter may realise hereafter that we and you love him much more truly than those who now indulge and support his iniquities. If, inspired by God, he wishes to come to his senses, whatever measures he may take against us, nevertheless he will always find us prepared to receive him back into holy communion, according as your charity may counsel us.[396]

79 After the excommunication and deposition of the king, therefore, led by the Lord's grace, many noblemen and men of middling station *returned to* God *with all* their *hearts*[417] and abandoned the king. Even those who had previously conspired against the apostolic see, partly because of royal blandishments and partly because of fear and threats, were subsequently converted and composed a fitting anathema against the king. They sent suppliant envoys to the apostolic see, desiring the imposition of a penance.[418] The disciple of mercy had no wish to be satiated with the punishment of offenders and opened the bosom of holy Church to them, sending them letters of consolation so that they might be strengthened in the faith of the Lord.[419] Some of the bishops indeed, bemoaning their great crime, came barefoot to the apostolic see and remained there until the lord pope had pity on them and opened to them the hand of compassion and the bowels of piety.[420]

80 Meanwhile the Lord performed a fearful miracle before the eyes of the king and of all men and when they learned of it, many abandoned him. For after the day of his excommunication he did not shrink from coming to the Church from which he had been excluded by heaven, to celebrate the festival of Easter[421] with royal pomp and with a numerous and splendid entourage. By the king's command, therefore, a certain

415 Ephesians 3:16.

416 Cf. Ecclesiasticus 8:3.

417 Joel 2:12.

418 Cf. Bonizo, *Book to a Friend* VII, above p. 235; Bruno, *Saxonicum bellum* c. 65, p. 57; Hugh of Flavigny, *Chronicon* II, pp. 444, 459. See G. Meyer von Knonau (1894) pp. 672–3.

419 J. Greving (1893) p. 71 n. 4 suggested that Gregory VII, *Registrum* III.12, pp. 273–4 (to the archbishop of Trier and bishops of Verdun and Metz) was such a letter.

420 Udo of Trier went to Rome to submit: Lampert, *Annales* 1076, p. 263.

421 27 March 1076, Utrecht. Paul described here a 'crown-wearing': see H.-W. Klewitz (1939) pp. 93–6; C. Schneider (1972) p. 166 ('a liturgical counter-demonstration to the solemn proclamation of excommunication').

bishop,[422] if it is lawful to call him that – in reality he was a heretic and a simoniac – prepared himself to celebrate mass. At length after the reading of the Gospel the bishop went up into the pulpit to deliver the sermon to the people according to custom. Having briefly spoken of the meaning of the Gospel, being blind in his heart and of unsound mind, he immediately erupted into blasphemies against Pope Gregory, which because of their excessively horrible character it is best to pass over in silence. For it is difficult for the tongues of the detractors to refrain from stinging one who is conscious of his honesty and for the friend of righteousness to escape the taunts of the wicked. Nevertheless the vengeance that immediately followed makes clear, if it is considered carefully, how this blasphemy appeared in the eyes of God. For when the joyous Easter day was not yet over, the heavens resounded with a sudden crash of thunder and fire was seen to descend from heaven, which suddenly consumed the whole of that church and all the houses prepared for the reception of the king, turning the happiness of impious men into sorrow.[423] In truth the divine vengeance that suddenly smote that blasphemous bishop also killed him.[424] Before he breathed his last, however, he was compelled to tell the servants who made the preparations for his departure: 'I see myself snatched out of this life, bound by reins of fire, pulled by hideous ghosts. Nevertheless, go and tell the king to correct the shameful offence that he has committed against God and blessed Peter and his vicar, lest he follow me to the regions of hell.' With these words he expired. Reminded by this example, we exhort and beseech every man who reads this work to avoid the tongues of the detractors if he prefers to enjoy the company of Gregory at the resurrection rather than to suffer torments with the detractors.

81 There comes to mind the no less terrible condemnation of the bishop of Speyer.[425] *On*[426] *the very day, 24 February, indeed at the very hour in which our* Pope Gregory *began to deal with his case in the Roman synod,*[427]

---

422 William, bishop of Utrecht (1054–76). Cf. Hugh of Flavigny, *Chronicon* II, p. 458; Lampert, *Annales* 1076, p. 258. See G. Meyer von Knonau (1894) p. 661.

423 Cf. Berthold, *Annales* 1076, p. 283 '('the church, … rejected by God and St Peter, burned miraculously in an avenging fire').

424 27 April 1076. Cf. Lampert, *Annales* 1076, p. 258. See G. Meyer von Knonau (1894) pp. 669–70.

425 Henry, bishop of Speyer (1067–75).

426 /426 Bernold of St. Blasien, *De incontinentia sacerdotum* V, p. 26.

427 Cf. Gregory VII, *Registrum* II.52a, p. 196 (Lent synod 1075).

he was struck *as though with an invisible weapon and began to be ill. On the third day, 26 February, he suffered a lamentable death,*[426] having experienced a sentence no less efficacious than that with which the apostle Peter condemned Ananias and Sapphira.[428]

82 When the princes had waited for a long time for the king's conversion and waited in vain and when they saw that the kingdom fell into more dangerous disorder every day and that, lacking a head, it was falling into utter ruin, armed with the zeal of God[429] they at last held a meeting with legates of the apostolic see.[430] They most faithfully requested that the king should acquiesce in their advice[431] and recover his senses; otherwise they declared that they would no longer communicate with or obey him. He was forced by this circumstance to promise (insincerely indeed, as afterwards became apparent) that he would submit to the advice of the princes and the commands of the lord pope in all things.[432] Their advice, however, was that he should request the lord pope to come to a general conference in Augsburg on the Purification of St Mary next following,[433] so that he could settle his case there according to the laws in the hearing of the whole kingdom. The princes also sent envoys who humbly begged the lord pope to come on that day and they found him very ready to undertake the journey, as his letters, copied below, bear witness. The king, however, contrary to his promises and contrary to the advice of the princes, wished through his envoys to extort from the pope the concession that the latter should not come to Augsburg but that he should allow him to come to him in Rome, with the intention undoubtedly that he would the more easily be able to deceive the pope, the fewer of the princes of the kingdom (who had endured his trickery often enough) were present to damage his cause. The pope, therefore, did not grant his wishes, but decided, as the princes had requested, to come on the agreed day and sent the following letters to the princes

428 Acts 5:5, 10. Cf. Bernold V, pp. 25–6 ('the sentences of condemnation of our pope are of equal efficacy to those of the prince of the apostles pronounced on Ananias and Sapphira').

429 Cf. Berthold, *Annales* 1076, p. 286 ('endeavouring to have the zeal of God').

430 Sigehard, patriarch of Aquileia and Altman, bishop of Passau at the assembly of princes at Tribur, 16 October – 1 November 1076. See above p. 239 and n. 5.

431 Cf. Hugh of Flavigny, *Chronicon* II, p. 444 ('he feigned to acquiesce in their advice').

432 Henry IV, 'Promise of Oppenheim' (*Die Briefe Heinrichs IV*. p. 69). See above p. 239.

433 2 February 1077. Cf. Bernold, *Chronicon* 1076, p. 433.

of the kingdom to organise his journey.

83 *Gregory,*[434] *bishop, servant of the servants of God, to the archbishops, bishops, dukes, counts and the greater and lesser men in the kingdom of the Germans, greeting and apostolic blessing. We, the unworthy and useless servant of the prince of the apostles, have decided with the help of divine mercy to come to you and, setting aside the advice of almost all our faithful followers, to hasten our departure, so that we wish to be in Mantua on 8 January. It is indeed our will and desire that, relying on your proven hope,*[435] *we shall not hesitate with a pure and sincere intention to undergo any calamities and even bloodshed if necessary for the freedom of holy Church and the salvation of the empire. Let it be your task, therefore, to forewarn those whom your sagacity identifies as capable and dutiful towards us, to receive and serve us. Let it also be your task to secure peace throughout your territories so that nothing can hinder our fixed purpose. Whatever seems to be missing from this letter concerning the many great disputes that we have had with the king's envoys and the arguments with which we have countered those*[436] *opinions, the bearers of the letter will make known more fully. Just as we unhesitatingly believe the latter on the subject of the promises that you made through them to blessed Peter and to us, so we wish you to believe what they say to you on our behalf.*[434]

Gregory,[437] *bishop, servant of the servants of God, to all archbishops, bishops, abbots, dukes, margraves, counts and to all defending and observing the faith and teaching of Christ and blessed Peter, greeting and the benediction of the blessed apostles Peter and Paul [and] the absolution of all their sins. Such as I am, a priest and servant of the prince of the apostles, I come to you, against the will and the advice of the Romans, trusting in the mercy of almighty God and in your catholic faith, prepared to suffer death for honour*[438] *and for the salvation of your souls, just as Christ laid down His life for us. For this is the situation in which we are placed: through many tribulations we must aim for and arrive at the kingdom of God.*[439] *But as for you, my brothers whom I love and long for,*[440] *take care by all means that I can, with God's help, reach [you] and be useful to you in all things. May He bless you through*

---

434 /434 Gregory VII, *Epistolae Vagantes* 17, pp. 46–8 (*JL* 5013: December 1076?). On the dissemination of this letter: C. Erdmann (1936) p. 12.

435 The other versions read 'faith'.

436 The other versions read 'their'.

437 /437 Gregory VII, *Epistolae Vagantes* 18, pp. 48–50 (*JL* 5014: December 1076?).

438 The other versions read 'for the honour of God'.

439 Acts 14:21.

440 Philippians 4:1.

whose grace it was said to me over the body of blessed Peter on the day of my ordination,[441] '*Whatever*[442] *you bless, will be blessed and whatever you loose on earth will be loosed also in heaven.*'[437]

84 Meanwhile *the*[443] *king had no confidence in his own cause and consequently evaded a hearing* in the presence of the whole kingdom. *He secretly entered Italy* in the company of excommunicates,[444] *contrary to the command of the pope and the advice of the princes, and before the Purification of St Mary at Canossa*[445] *he met the pope, who was attempting to be in Augsburg on the aforementioned day.*[443] *He*[446] *remained there for three days*[447] *before the gate of the fortress, laying aside all the splendour of a king, wretched in appearance, barefoot and clad in woollen garments. With much lamenting he did not cease to beg for help, consolation and the forgiveness of the pope until he moved all who were present or who heard of it to such devout compassion and mercy that they interceded for him with many prayers and tears. They were all amazed indeed at the unaccustomed harshness* of the lord pope *and some of them even exclaimed that* his *conduct showed not the grave severity appropriate to a pope, but rather the cruelty and* severity[448] *of a tyrant. At last* the pope *was overcome by the earnestness of his remorse and by the fervent prayers of all who were present.* He *released him from the bonds of anathema and received him into the grace of communion and into the bosom of holy mother Church. He received from him guarantees, confirmed by the hands of the abbot of Cluny*[449] *and* the noble countesses *Matilda*[450] *and Adelaide*[451] *and other princes, bishops and laymen who seemed to be useful to* him *in this matter,*[446] in the following manner.

---

441 30 June 1073: see above p. 221.

442 A paraphrase of the eucharistic prayer in the *ordo* for episcopal ordination: see H. E. J. Cowdrey, *Epistolae vagantes* p. 51.

443 /443 Bernold, *Chronicon* 1077, p. 433.

444 Cf. Berthold, *Annales* 1077, p. 288 ('he gathered a crowd of excommunicated bishops from all sides').

445 The fortress of Matilda of Tuscany: see above p. 240 and n. 20.

446 /446 Gregory VII, *Registrum* IV.12, p. 313. The text is transposed into a third-person narrative. See H. Fuhrmann (1956) p. 303. On Henry's absolution: G. Meyer von Knonau (1894) pp. 755–62, 894–903; K.F. Morrison (1962) pp. 121–48; T. Struve (1995) pp. 44–5; H. E. J. Cowdrey (1998) pp. 155–67; I. S. Robinson (1999) pp. 160–4.

447 25–27 January 1077.

448 The papal register reads 'ferocity'.

449 Abbot Hugh I of Cluny.

450 Matilda, margravine of Tuscany.

451 Adelaide, margravine of Turin (✝1091), Henry's mother-in-law.

I,[452] *King Henry, with respect to the discontent and ill will that is felt against me by the archbishops, bishops, dukes and counts and the rest of the princes of the kingdom of the Germans and the others who adhere to them in this same discord, will do justice within the term that the lord pope fixes according to his judgement or make an agreement according to his advice, unless an obvious hindrance thwarts me or him; and when this is accomplished, I shall be ready to put it into effect. Also, if the lord Pope Gregory wishes to travel beyond the mountains or elsewhere, he will be safe from any injury to life or limbs and from capture, as far as I and those whom I can control are concerned, both he and those who are under his command or in his entourage,*[453] *when travelling thither and when tarrying there or when returning thence. He will not with my consent meet any hindrance that is against his honour and if anyone acts against him, I shall help him in good faith according to my ability.*[452]

85 After the king had received communion, the question of the kingship being, however, deferred,[454] he was absolved by the pope and departed. He paid little attention to what he had promised on oath in his reconciliation and he was not afraid to return to his usual wickedness and to give his approval to the counsels of his simoniacs against the pope. For all the simoniacs and their allies, to whose tyranny he had subjected holy mother Church and with the help of whose faction he had previously tried to rob the apostolic see of its authority – all of them, I say, returned to him now that he was reconciled. They showed no *fear* of him *on account of the wickedness that they had committed* but were rather encouraged in *their audacity.*[455] indeed he even gave them an opportunity to conspire against the pope. He and his accomplices were in a hurry to receive communion because they were well aware that according to the law of the Germans they must be deprived of their estates and their benefices if they remained excommunicate for a full year.[456] There was only a

452 /452 Gregory VII, *Registrum* IV.12a, pp. 314–15: 'The oath of Henry, king of the Germans' (28 January 1077). On the dissemination of the text: C. Erdmann (1936) p. 12. H. Fuhrmann (1956) pp. 304, 305 argued that the numerous variants demonstrated that Paul did not derive his text directly from the papal register.

453 Paul's version omits 'or those who are sent by him or who come to him from any region of the earth'.

454 Cf. Gregory VII, *Registrum* VII.14a, p. 484 (see below p. 349): 'I did not reinstate him in the kingship'; Bernold, *Chronicon* 1077, p. 433: 'the concession not of the kingship but only of communion'.

455 A quotation from Gregory VII, *Epistolae Vagantes* 19, p. 52, a letter otherwise found only in Hugh of Flavigny, *Chronicon* II, pp. 445–6.

456 Cf. Bonizo, *Book to a Friend* VIII, above p. 239. J. Greving (1893) p. 78 suggested

month left when they were reconciled. They sought communion, therefore, not for the sake of their own amendment but so that they might be reunited with the very many persons from whom they had previously been divided by the anathema. The more numerous they became, the more boldly and cruelly they could oppress holy Church with their accustomed tyranny. For immediately after their reconciliation, as I said above, they persistently returned to their wallowing-place[457] and made common cause with the simoniacs, that is with men like themselves, against the apostolic see.

86 Not long afterwards the king desired to elicit from the pope permission to exercise the kingship just as craftily as he had elicited communion.[458] He sent envoys and humbly begged the pope to permit him to be crowned in a ceremony at St John's in Monza by the bishops of Pavia[459] and Milan[460] according to the custom of earlier kings.[461] If the pope was unwilling to let the ceremony be performed by these bishops because they were excommunicate, let him at least grant this privilege by his apostolic authority to some other bishop. The king urgently sought to be crowned above all because he would then seem to have received the kingship from the Roman pontiff together with communion. The pope, however, had already had sufficient experience of his cunning and he was utterly unwilling to yield to his prayers. He was careful to remind himself indeed that he had deposed him from the kingship and released from his lordship those who had sworn fealty to him because of his many offences and especially for his disobedience and obstinacy towards the apostolic see. For this reason he ought certainly not to impose him or anyone else as king on the princes, who were free men, without their exercising the right of election. The whole kingdom held him to be guilty of so many and such serious acts of injustice that it was necessary first for him to be cleared of these, if that could indeed be achieved, and thus at last

an analogy with the Carolingian legislation punishing with the loss of property and benefices those subjects who failed for a year and a day to obey a royal command (Ansegisus, abbot of Fontenelle, *Capitularium Collectio* III.45, IV.23, 36, 74, *MGH Capitularia* 1, 430, 440, 442, 446).

457 Cf. II Peter 2:22.

458 Cf. Berthold, *Annales* 1077, p. 290 ('he wished to be crowned in Pavia according to the custom of the king of the Lombards'). See G. Meyer von Knonau (1894) pp. 769–71; J. Vogel (1983) pp. 29–32.

459 William, bishop of Pavia (1066/7–1102/3): see G. Schwartz (1913) p. 144.

460 Archbishop Tedald.

461 See above p. 73.

lawfully crowned with the consent of the whole kingdom. Despite his pretence of obedience, therefore, the king did not usurp the royal insignia at Monza. Nevertheless not long afterwards despite the lord pope's prohibition he was not afraid to take up the insignia again and to usurp the government of the kingdom that had been denied him.[462]

87 Meanwhile the date passed at which the king had undertaken to meet the princes of the kingdom in the presence of the legates of the apostolic see in Augsburg on the Purification of St Mary. The pope had intended to go there and would indeed have done so, had not the king, contrary to the general decision taken by everyone, entered Italy and frightened off those who were to escort the pope.[463] It was on that occasion in the presence of the pope and in the hearing of the whole kingdom that the king was to be cleared according to the canons of the charges against him, if he was innocent, and once cleared he could lawfully be restored to the kingship with the consent of all men. The king scorned to attend the meeting – or rather, he did not dare to attend because he had no confidence in his own cause – and he deceitfully detained the pope in Lombardy so that he should not come to the meeting.[464]

88 When the princes of the kingdom realised, therefore, that the king had shunned the meeting fixed by a general decision and that he had thereby deluded them with his customary treachery and when they learned from the most reliable reports that there was no end to his cunning either at the time of the reconciliation or thereafter, they at once held a meeting in Ulm in Swabia.[465] They resolved that henceforward they would not allow themselves to be made fools of by him or rather to be endangered by his cunning, but that they would make provision for their safety by electing a lawful prince. At that meeting in Ulm they agreed on a fuller conference[466] to meet in Forchheim on

---

462 Cf. Bernold, *Chronicon* 1077, p. 434 ('Henry, in assuming the crown in Ulm [4 June 1077], usurped the kingship that had been denied him').

463 Cf. Gregory VII, *Registrum* IV.12, p. 312 ('because of the many difficulties at this time, … an escort could not be sent to meet us').

464 Gregory VII remained in northern Italy until September 1077 in the hope of entering Germany (*Registrum* IV.23–4, pp. 334–8 of 31 May). See G. Meyer von Knonau (1900) pp. 78–81; J. Vogel (1983) pp. 23–5; H. E. J. Cowdrey (1998) pp. 167–8; I. S. Robinson (1999) p. 165.

465 Probably mid-February 1077. See G. Meyer von Knonau (1894) pp. 775–6; J. Vogel (1983) pp. 41–2; H. E. J. Cowdrey (1998) p. 168; I. S. Robinson (1999) pp. 166–7.

466 The meeting in Ulm was attended by 'few because of the harsh extremities of the winter': Berthold, *Annales* 1077, p. 291.

12 March[467] to elect a new king[468] and they also sent envoys[469] requesting the advice and help of the lord pope. When he heard of this the pope sent legates[470] to that conference, who asked the princes to delay the ordering of the kingship until the pope's arrival, if they had any hope of being able to do this without danger. He would not of course issue them with a definite command, lest he himself should rightly be held responsible for any harm that the kingdom suffered as a result of such a delay.

89 The day after the sending of the legates, however, Count Manegold,[471] a great lover of the truth, arrived. The pope, more fully informed by his report about the creation of a new king, sent another legate, namely Gregory, deacon of the Roman church,[472] to the princes of the kingdom. He compelled them by apostolic authority to await the pope's arrival. Firstly, however, that same legate was to investigate whether the king, who still remained in Lombardy, was willing to assure the safety of the assembly and to grant the lord pope safe-conduct to German territory to settle his case.[473] If the king refused to concede this, the pope commanded the legate to return to him; nor would he impose any delay on the princes in their efforts to provide for the needs of the kingdom. In imposing the burden of this legation on the legate, the pope said among other things that he had demanded this guarantee of safety from the king as a kind of trial: a promise of safety on his part would be an augury that he could be restored to the kingship, while his refusal to guarantee safety would indicate, as by divine judgement, that he could not be restored. As he spoke these words, three of the fingers of the pope's right hand suddenly appeared to be bloody up to the middle joint. Thinking that they were stained by blood flowing from his nose, he began to wipe them clean, but he

---

467 13 March, according to Berthold, *Annales* 1077, p. 291; Lampert, *Annales* 1077, p. 302.

468 Paul was alone in claiming that the purpose of organising the assembly in Forchheim was 'to elect a new king'.

469 The princes' envoy was 'our son Rapoto' (above p. 303 n. 271): Gregory VII, *Epistolae Vagantes* 19, p. 52

470 Cardinal deacon Bernard and Abbot Bernard of St Victor in Marseilles: below p. 332.

471 Manegold, count of Altshausen-Veringen (✝1104/9): see J. Kerkhoff (1964) pp. 26, 30–4, 36, 39–41, 95–6, 108–13.

472 This was probably Cardinal deacon Gregory (title church unknown, *c.* 1073–*c.* 1098): see R. Hüls (1977) p. 249.

473 Cf. Gregory VII, *Epistolae Vagantes* 19, p. 52 ('We … are striving to decide and organise [safe-conduct] with the king through our envoys').

could by no means cleanse them of the bloody spots. Hence he himself and the other wise men who observed this miracle had no doubt that this sign portended some great event.[474] Present there were Count Manegold and the venerable priest Erkinbert[475] with very many others in the castle of Canossa on the first day of Lent, which in that year fell on 1 March.[476]

90 Having received his instructions, therefore, the legate immediately hastened to the king, accompanied by the count. The king, however, scornfully refused to give the guarantee of safety that the pope demanded,[477] whereupon the legate did not delay in returning to the pope. The count made all speed to be present at the forthcoming conference in Forchheim, where the previous legates had already arrived, having been despatched by the pope only one day earlier than the count. These legates were Bernard, cardinal deacon of the holy Roman church[478] and another Bernard, the pious abbot of Marseilles,[479] the father of almost sixty monks, who also brought with him a certain excellent teacher named Christian, afterwards bishop of the city of Aversa,[480] the author of an outstanding work against Berengar of Tours.[481]

91 It seems appropriate here briefly to halt the progress of the narrative and to proclaim how faithful an adherent and propagator of apostolic teaching our Gregory had in the often mentioned Count Manegold. For he was born of the eminent and pious lineage of the

---

474 W. von Giesebrecht (1890) pp. 1076, 1154 n. 1 suggested that chapters 88–96 were based on a lost contemporary account intended to defend the legality of the anti-king's election. See above p. 76.

475 'The priest Erchinbertus' is commemorated (19 March) in the necrology of Bernold of St Blasien: R. Kuithan and J. Wollasch (1984) p. 500. J. Greving (1893) pp. 101–2 suggested that this was the friend who supplied Bernold with an eyewitness account of Forchheim. Greving argued that Bernold was the author of Paul's source, the lost account of the anti-king's election. See above p. 76.

476 Ash Wednesday 1077. But Gregory VII's letter, *Registrum* IV.13, pp. 316–17, is dated 'in Carpineto on 1 March', i.e. a few hours journey from Canossa.

477 Cf. Berthold, *Annales* 1077, p. 291 ('The king obstinately ... did not deign to guarantee the pope's security').

478 Cardinal deacon Bernard (*c*. 1073–*c*. 1083): see R. Hüls (1977) pp. 245–6.

479 Abbot Bernard of St Victor in Marseilles. See O. Schumann (1912) pp. 36–44 and above p. 303 n. 269.

480 Guitmund-Christian, monk of La Croix-St-Leufroi (near Évreux), appointed bishop of Aversa in Urban II's pontificate.

481 His work against the dialectician Berengar (†1088): *De corporis et sanguinis Christi veritate, MPL* 149, col. 1427A-1494D. See R. Somerville (1972b) pp. 70–1.

blessed Udalric, bishop of Augsburg[482] and perfectly educated in all
the observances of the Christian religion by his very wise brother,
Herman the Lame.[483] He chose a wife[484] who was, like himself, a virgin
and she bore him two sons whom he brought up during their early
years, imparting such instruction that he left behind one of them,
monogamous like himself, as his heir;[485] the other[486] was murdered
while still celibate. Although he was far away from the place, Manegold miraculously perceived through the spirit the moment of his
murder and he both lamented and rejoiced. He lamented the bitterness of his unexpected death but rejoiced at the innocence of his
unstained youth. This above all ensured the purity of his children: the
fact that this true father threatened them with disinheritance if they
were discovered to have been involved in any relations with women
other than lawful matrimony. Since the most Christian man loved the
blessed Pope Gregory exceedingly because of his just conduct, he
visited him very often so as to imitate his conduct.[487] On one occasion
in Rome he fell victim to so serious an illness that those present
despaired of his life. When the sad news reached the lord pope, he
hurried to him with the greatest sympathy and, breaking a little bread
in a cup and moistening it with wine, he offered it to the sick man as
a benediction. As soon as he tasted it, he not only experienced the
pleasure of eating it but also received the strength to rise from his bed
in perfect health. When he returned to his own land, he was not slow
in publishing everywhere the papal decrees, especially those concerning the avoidance of the offices of unchaste priests and he would not
tolerate such abominations in the clergy and the churches that especially belonged to him. The wife of a certain priest placed under his
jurisdiction, spiteful because of her separation from her husband,
threatened in the hearing of her intimates that she would bring it
about that whatever vexation she suffered in being separated from her
spouse, the count would suffer the same in being divided from his own
spouse. This is what she said and alas! God permitted her to commit

---

482 The kinship with Udalric I of Augsburg (923–73) was recorded by Manegold's
    elder brother, Herman, *Chronicon* 955, p. 114. See J. Kerkhoff (1964) p. 16.

483 Herman, monk of Reichenau (1013–54), polymath and chronicler.

484 Lietphild, last recorded in 1096: see J. Kerkhoff (1964) pp. 33, 41.

485 Wolferad, count of Altshausen-Veringen (✝ c. 1130).

486 Walter (✝10 January 1109), a casualty of the feud between the counts of Bregenz
    and Kirchberg: see J. Kerkhoff (1964) pp. 38–40, 95–6.

487 His visits to Rome: J. Kerkhoff (1964) p. 114.

so wicked a crime against her lady. For she offered delicious food mixed with poison and her feigned kindness deceived the lady, who suspected no evil. The pious count, who thus became a widower in the prime of life, could not be persuaded by the exhortations of his men to make a second marriage, saying that it seemed to him shameful and horrible that he should show himself before the tribunal of Christ on the day of judgement with two wives. He profited so much from his devout obedience to our Pope Gregory that before his death, which occurred when he was an old man, full of days, he both shone forth with the tokens of virtue and was venerable and renowned for the spirit of prophecy, as was apparent on the occasion of his son's murder.

92 It is not unfitting to join to these recollections of this count of blessed memory an account of the precious death of the blessed Cencius, prefect of the city of Rome, whose virtues we briefly described above.[488] Our Lord Jesus Christ crowned him with martyrdom because of the fidelity that he showed to the often mentioned and often to be mentioned Pope Gregory and He immediately made his tomb illustrious with twenty miracles[489] enumerated and approved in a synod.[490] For since he *had a zeal for God* and he showed a faith that was *enlightened*[491] by the pope's instruction, he was murdered by the agents of the Henrician persecution.[492]

93 When the assembly took place in Forchheim,[493] therefore, the legates made public the papal letter in which the princes of the kingdom were informed among other things how little the lord pope *rejoiced*[494] *at* the king's *promise, since* the enemies of the Church were *rather emboldened than made fearful by the presence*[494] of the king. In addition

488 Cencius, son of the Roman prefect John Tiniosus; killed in summer 1077: see above p. 294.

489 Cf. Bernold, *Chronicon* 1077, p. 434 ('More than twenty miracles occurred in a short time near his body').

490 See above p. 243 and n. 39.

491 Romans 10:2.

492 By Stephen, brother of Cencius Stephani: Bonizo, *Book to a Friend* VIII, above p. 243. Cf. Bernold, *Chronicon* 1077, p. 434 ('cruelly killed by a supporter of Henry').

493 13 March 1077. See G. Meyer von Knonau (1900) pp. 3–8, 627–38; W. Böhme (1970) pp. 65–75; W. Schlesinger (1973) pp. 61–85; W. Giese (1979) pp. 37–49; I. S. Robinson (1979) pp. 721–33; J. Vogel (1983) pp. 41–6; H. E. J. Cowdrey (1998) pp. 168–71; I. S. Robinson (1999) pp. 166–70. For the view that Paul's account was based on a lost 'official' source: above p. 76.

494 /494 Gregory VII, *Epistolae Vagantes* 19, p. 52: found in its entirety only in Hugh of Flavigny, *Chronicon* II, pp. 445–6. This was presumably the letter produced by the legates.

they said that the pope requested that the election of a new king, of which he had heard, should be deferred until his arrival, if they considered that this could be done without danger.[495] When they had performed their legation, the archbishops, bishops, dukes, margraves, counts, the greater and the lesser men,[496] expressing the reverence due to the legates, stood up one by one and made known how many insults and dangers they had already suffered or knew that they must suffer at King Henry's hands. Weeping, they began to tell the legates that on many occasions they had narrowly escaped from snares that he had set for them even as he was giving the kiss of peace, so that thereafter they could not show any faith in his oath. They also added that they had borne with him so long after his deposition not because they expected his amendment, since they utterly despaired of him, but so as to deny an opportunity for misrepresentation to certain persons, who would perhaps complain that his attempts to amend had been hindered. The whole of that day was spent in complaints of this kind and they could not enumerate half of the injuries that he had inflicted.

94 The next day they met again at the legates' lodgings and consulted them about alleviating their difficulties. They advised the legates that there would be a most dangerous and irreversible schism throughout the whole kingdom unless they united in hastening to anticipate it in that assembly, as they had already resolved to do, by setting up a new leader. The legates, however, did not forget the terms of their legation and briefly replied to this that in their opinion it would be best if, according to their legation, they could delay the appointment of a king until the arrival of the lord pope, provided this entailed no danger. On the other hand, they acknowledged that the provision of a king was a matter not subject to their counsel but to the judgement of the princes, who held the state in their hands and who could best foretell what would be damaging or beneficial to the kingdom.[497] The princes of the kingdom, therefore, being uncertain when the pope would arrive, but entirely certain that the most grave dissension and danger would ensue if they delayed, received the

---

495 Cf. Berthold, *Annales* 1077, p. 292 ('if it could be done with any precautions or artifice, they should refrain from setting up another king').

496 The assembly seems to have been attended only by the small 'deposition faction' of Henry's enemies: I. S. Robinson (1979) p. 721; H. E. J. Cowdrey (1998) p. 170; I. S. Robinson (1999) p. 167.

497 Cf. Berthold, *Annales* 1077, p. 292 ('in the last resort [the princes] were better aware of their needs and of the dangers and they might carry out what they judged to be the best course of action').

legates' leave to meet the archbishop of Mainz[498] and with particular
care they discussed among themselves what they ought to do. They
bore in mind that the pope did not compel them to delay their proceedings but that the question of a delay was left to their judgement;
that if a delay proved harmful, the blame for this would thereafter be
ascribed to them alone; moreover that they were not obliged to show
obedience to King Henry: on the contrary, they would be condemned
for transgressing the papal prohibition if they thenceforward showed
obedience to the king. For the pope had previously excommunicated
him on behalf of almighty God and St Peter and on his own behalf; he
had forbidden him the kingship and had *absolved all Christians from the
oaths that they had* already *sworn or would in future swear to him and
forbade anyone to serve him as king*.[499] Subsequently the king by means
of a false promise of amendment recovered from the pope only the
right to receive communion: he did not recover the kingship.[500]

95 When, therefore, the princes of the kingdom had very carefully
considered that (as I have already said) they were entirely independent of the power of King Henry and that they were no more obliged
to be faithful and subject to him than he was to them, as free men they
raised Duke Rudolf of the Swabians to the royal dignity.[501] In vain he
put up a strong resistance and in vain likewise he asked for an hour's
delay during which he might take counsel.[502] He was a man outstanding for his humility and suitable[503] for the royal honour in age and in
morals and they subjected themselves to him, taking the oath of
fealty.[504] He regarded the kingship not as his personal property but as
something committed to his stewardship and he rejected all hereditary
rights over it. He utterly refused to associate his son in the kingship,

---

498 The role of Siegfried of Mainz in the election: H. Thomas (1970) pp. 368–99; E.
Boshof (1978b) pp. 42–5.

499 Gregory VII, *Registrum* III.10a, p. 270: see above p. 318.

500 See above p. 328 and n. 454.

501 Rudolf's qualifications for the kingship: H. Jakobs (1973) pp. 87–115; I. S.
Robinson (1999) pp. 125–7, 168–9.

502 Cf. Gregory VII, *Registrum* VII.14a, c. 7, pp. 484–5 ('compelled to assume the
government of the kingdom'); Berthold, *Annales* 1077, p. 292. The convention that
a worthy office-holder was one who did not *seek* high office: Gregory I, *Regula
pastoralis* I.6, 10, *MPL* 77, col. 19D-20A, 23AC. See B. Weiler (2000) pp. 1–42 and
above p. 61.

503 The term 'suitable' (*idoneus*) in Gregorian political thought: Gregory VII, *Registrum* IX.3, p. 575 ('a suitable king for the honour of holy Church'). See J. Deér
(1972) pp. 54–5, 204; I. S. Robinson (1990) pp. 312–18, 372, 411.

504 Cf. Berthold, *Annales* 1077, p. 292.

most justly deciding that it was for the princes to judge, so that after his death they might make a free election, not preferring his son to any other man, but electing one whom they had found to be worthy of that high honour by virtue of his age and the dignity of his character.[505]

96 After Rudolf had been thus lawfully elected,[506] the archbishops of Mainz and Magdeburg,[507] together with their suffragans, conferred on him the royal consecration in the presence of the legates of the apostolic see and the princes of the kingdom. He had been elected, however, by the archbishops, bishops, dukes, counts, the greater and the lesser men in the assembly in Forchheim in the year of the Lord's incarnation 1077, in the fourth year of Pope Gregory, the seventh of that name, in the fifteenth indiction on 15 March. On the twelfth day after this he was consecrated in Mainz, that is *26 March, which* that year *fell in the middle of Lent.*[508] On the day of that election the snow and frost, which in that year had taken possession of the land of the Germans and of Lombardy from the feast of All Saints until that very day,[509] began to melt.[510] Certain wise men interpreted this pheno-menon thus: that God indicated to the world His assent to the election of a lawful prince by means of the dispersal of the unaccustomed cold and the restoration of more clement weather, especially since this promotion displeased no one, with the single exception of those who expected to be cast off by the lawful king for simoniacal heresy[511] and other offences, by means of which they had continuously defiled holy Church, not so much with the permission as with the active cooper-ation of the previous king. The promotion of this prince did not displease any clerk, monk or layman, except those who pined away at

505 Cf. Bruno, *Saxonicum bellum* c. 91, p. 85 ('if the son of the king was not worthy or if the people did not want him, the people should have it in their power to make whom they wished king'). See W. Schlesinger (1973) pp. 74–82; I. S. Robinson (1979) pp. 721–3, 745–50; H. Keller (1983) pp. 130–2, 145–50; U. Schmidt (1987) pp. 27–33.

506 Cf. Berthold, *Annales* 1077, p. 292 ('After this election ... had been lawfully per-formed').

507 Werner (1063–78).

508 Bernold, *Chronicon* 1077, p. 433 (Laetare Sunday, the fourth Sunday in Lent). The careful dating prompted many scholars to suggest that Paul used an official record (not extant) of Rudolf's accession. See above p. 76.

509 1 November 1076–15 March 1077. See G. Meyer von Knonau (1894) p. 750 n. 7.

510 Cf. Bernold, *Chronicon* 1077, p. 433 ('The very great snow, which covered all the land for so long that year, began to melt at the election of the new king').

511 Cf. Bernold, *Chronicon* 1077, p. 433 ('a very great uprising occurred at the instigation of the simoniac clergy').

the thought that holy Church would be administered according to the decrees of the canons and those who had no doubt that their wealth would be diminished by the suspension of the trafficking of simoniacal heresy.

97 No one could justly accuse King Rudolf and his princes of perjury, although they had sworn the oath of fealty to the king who had long since been deposed.[512] For that oath had to be observed only so long as he ruled over the kingdom. After all Christians had been absolved from that oath by the pope, because the king had been deposed and excommunicated, the oath no longer entailed the duty of subjection to him, any more than a bishop is to be obeyed by his subjects after he has been denied communion and deposed.[513] No one who accepts the legality of the decrees of the most holy Pope Gregory will deny that the Roman pontiff can depose kings from the kingship. For that apostolic man, whose decrees were dictated to him by the Holy Spirit,[514] while presiding over the apostolic see inviolably decreed that *kings shall lose their offices and shall be deprived of the communion of the* Lord's *body and blood, if they presume to scorn the commands of the apostolic see.*[515] For if the see of blessed Peter absolves and judges heavenly and spiritual things, how much more earthly and secular things, as the apostle said, *Do you not know that we are to judge angels? How much more, matters pertaining to this life!*[516] It is certainly the case that Childeric, king of the Franks was deposed by the authority of Pope Stephen because of his worthlessness and that, after he had been deposed and moreover tonsured and sent to a monastery, Pippin was substituted in the kingship.[517] Besides Henry was appointed as their

512 In Henrician propaganda Rudolf's death (1080) was represented as a divine judgement for his perjury (oath-breaking): e.g. Henry IV, *Letter* 17, p. 25; anonymous *Vita Heinrici IV* c. 4, p. 19.

513 Cf. Gregory VII, *Registrum* VIII.21, p. 554 ('Holy Church ... absolves knights from the bond of their oaths ... in the case of bishops who are deposed from the episcopal office'.)

514 Cf. Bernold, *Apologeticus* c. 3, 6, pp. 62, 66.

515 Gregory I, *Registrum* XIII.11, *MGH Epistolae* 2, 378, as paraphrased by Gregory VII, *Registrum* IV.23, 24, pp. 336, 338 (cf. *Registrum* VIII.21, p. 550). A closer parallel to Paul's version is that in 'the Swabian appendix' of the *Collection in 74 Titles* 330, ed. J. Gilchrist, p. 196. See above p. 77.

516 I Corinthians 6:3. This a fortiori argument was first used by Gregory VII, *Registrum* VIII.21, p. 550. Paul's direct source was perhaps Bernold, *Apologeticae rationes* p. 97.

517 This 'example' of Childeric III (743–51), deposed after consultation with Pope Zacharias, was first used by Gregory VII, *Registrum* IV.2, VIII.21, pp. 294, 554

king by free men according to this contract: that he should be preoccupied with judging his electors justly and governing them with
royal foresight. This contract he subsequently did not cease to violate
and to scorn, by oppressing the innocent with tyrannical cruelty and
forcing all whom he could to oppose the Christian religion. It was for
that reason, independently of the judgement of the apostolic see, that
the princes could justly reject him as king, since he scorned to fulfil
the contract that he had promised them at his election and, as it was
not fulfilled, he could not be king.[518] For he who strives not to rule his
subjects but to send them into error, can by no means be a king.[519]
What more is there to say? Surely any knight is subject to his lord by
the oath of fealty according to the contract that the latter does not
refuse him what a lord owes to a vassal. If the lord scorns to pay what
is due to the knight, will not the knight be free to decline to have him
as his lord thereafter? Entirely free, I say. No one will justly accuse
such a knight of unfaithfulness or perjury, since he will have fulfilled
all that he promised to his lord, I say, by serving as his knight as long
as he did for him what a lord owes to a vassal.[520]

98 As soon as King Rudolf was appointed king, he sent envoys to
inform the pope of his promotion. He promised him the obedience due
to him in the administration of the churches and he showed himself
much readier to obey the apostolic see than his predecessor.[521] For on
the very day of his coronation, in obedience to the prohibition of the
lord pope, he refused to receive the ministrations of a certain simoniac
subdeacon, who that day, clad in sacred vestments, processed in front
of the king, being required to read the lesson during the mass. Archbishop Siegfried of Mainz therefore removed him from the ministry of

and frequently cited by the Gregorian authors of southern Germany. The closest
parallel to Paul's version is Bernold of St Blasien, *De solutione iuramentorum* p. 148.

518 Paul's idea of the 'contract' (*pactum*) between ruler and subjects resembles that of
Manegold, *Liber ad Gebehardum* c. 47, pp. 391–2 ('when [the king] breaks the
contract by which he is elected ... he may rightly be considered to have set the
people free from the subjection that they owed'). See H. Fuhrmann (1975) pp. 21–
42; I. S. Robinson (1979) pp. 746–8; T. Reuter (1991) p. 316 n. 117.

519 Cf. Isidore of Seville, *Etymologiae* IX.3 ('he who does not correct, does not rule').
For Isidore's influence on political thought: H. H. Anton (1968) pp. 57–8; H.
Vollrath (1991) pp. 294–5; I. S. Robinson (1999) pp. 347–8.

520 The vassal's renunciation of fealty (*diffidatio*): M. Bloch (1962) pp. 227–30: F. L.
Ganshof (1964) pp. 98–101.

521 Cf. Gregory VII, *Registrum* VII.14a, pp. 484–5 (quoted by Paul below p. 349).
Bruno, *Saxonicum bellum* c. 81, p. 95 recorded Rudolf's promise of free canonical
election for bishops.

the altar and put another in his place. This caused immense ill will on the part of the simoniac and unchaste ministers of the altar against the king, who at the very moment of his promotion, in obedience to the pope's prohibition, demonstrated that he would not accept their offices by his rejection of that subdeacon. For they had not the slightest doubt that under so lawful a prince they would either lay down their office or give up their concubines and the churches that they had acquired through simony. The clergy of that city, therefore, on the very day of the royal coronation after the banquet stirred up their fellow citizens, who were enraged by wine and madness, against their bishop and the king and the other princes.[522] For a certain boy from the city, whether of his own volition or persuaded by someone else we do not know, wished to cut off part of a valuable garment worn by a vassal of the archbishop and he was at once taken prisoner by the vassal.[523] When he heard of it, the governor of the city took charge of the prisoner and then set him free, so as not to cause a riot. When the clergy heard this rumour about the boy's capture, however, although they knew that he had already been released, they were not afraid to ring the bells and with infamous commands and exhortations to arouse or rather compel the citizens to riot. The banquet being over, the king went down from the palace to the church and began to hear vespers. Meanwhile the common people in their rage, thirsting for the blood of the king and the others, tried to break into the church and the palace, but they were held in check by the king's knights, although they were unarmed.[524] For it was the custom during the days of Lent to appear in public without arms[525] and because of the riot of the citizens they could not reach the arms that they had left in their lodgings throughout the city. When vespers were over and the king had returned with the archbishop and the other princes from the church into the palace, he saw that the people in their rage would not stop their rioting but were ready to profane the Lenten season, the Lord's day, the cemetery of the church, even the mother church itself with their furious strife and that, heaping sacrilege upon sacrilege,

522 Cf. Bernold, *Chronicon* 1077, p. 433. See G. Meyer von Knonau (1900) pp. 10–11, 632–5.

523 Bruno c. 92, p. 86: a young man cut off part of the robe of 'a certain nobleman' among the courtiers, as a deliberate provocation. See H. Büttner (1973) p. 357.

524 Cf. Bernold, *Chronicon* 1077, p. 433 ('The right hand of God protected the knights of the new prince, although they were unarmed').

525 J. Greving (1893) p. 105 n. 1 interpreted this passage as evidence of 'the peace of God' movement in the German kingdom. For the earliest known examples of German peace legislation (1082–5): E. Wadle (1973) pp. 142–8.

they had conspired to cause his death and those of the bishops and all his vassals, even though they had caused them no injury. The king girded on his sword, determined to restrain their madness, but his princes did not permit him to proceed contrary to royal custom. Instead they themselves, procuring arms wherever they could, first entered the church at the king's command to pray to God, then loudly singing the *Kyrie eleison*, they left the church by the door that was under the heaviest attack. Although there were very few of them, they at once drove the immense host of their enemies into so desperate a flight that some of them flung themselves into the Rhine to their deaths, even though the king's knights pursued them little further than the cemetery of the church.[526]

99 In the year of the Lord's incarnation 1078, in the first indiction, when both kings, Henry and Rudolf, sought the help of the apostolic see, Pope Gregory VII, presiding over a general synod, decreed as follows. *Since*[527] *we perceive that the conflict and the disturbance of the kingdom every day results in the greatest damage*[528] *to holy Church, it pleases us to endeavour with all our strength so that suitable messengers, abounding both in religion and in knowledge are sent from the side of the apostolic see to that land. They will summon all the religious and the lovers of justice dwelling in the territory of the German kingdom, men of the clerical and the lay order suitable for this task and, led by the Lord's grace, either they will reach a just settlement and peace with them or they will discover the truth and be able to learn in full which party is on the side of justice so that the unjust party comes to its senses and, defended by apostolic authority, justice may gain in strength and authority. But since we are not unaware that there are some men, inspired by the devil, kindled by the flames of their tyranny, subject to avarice for filthy lucre, who desire to see discord come into being rather than peace, we decree that no person exercising power, whether king or archbishop, duke, margrave, count or knight shall ever, through any audacious or rash undertaking or through any deceit or by means of any sort of disturbance, attempt to oppose or resist our legates, so that they fail to make a settlement and peace. Whoever rashly dares (which heaven forbid!) to violate this decree of ours and attempts to deceive our legates when they go to make this peace, we bind him with the bond of anathema. We bind him by the power of the apostle not only in spirit but also in body and all the prosperity*

---

526 Cf. Bernold, *Chronicon* 1077, p. 433 ('they killed more than 100, some by the sword some by drowning').

527 /527 Gregory VII, *Registrum* V.14a, c. 6, pp. 370–1. See H. Fuhrmann (1956) pp. 304, 308, 309.

528 The register reads: 'the greatest danger and damage'.

of this life and we deny him *military victory, so that thus at least* he *may be confounded and ground down by double destruction*[529] *and grief. Enacted in Rome in the church of the Lord Saviour on 3 March in the first indiction.*[527]

100 *Gregory,*[530] *bishop, servant of the servants of God, to the archbishops, bishops, clergy, dukes, margraves,* counts *and the greater and lesser men settled in the German kingdom, except for those who are bound by canonical excommunication, greetings and apostolic blessing.*[531] *We wish you to know, most beloved brethren, that in that synod that we recently celebrated in Rome among the many other things that with God's help we accomplished concerning the state of holy Church we carefully considered the ruin and confusion of your most noble kingdom. We thought that a healthy and opportune way of restoring your peace would be to send religious legates of the apostolic see to your land, who are to urge the archbishops, bishops and religious clergy and also suitably qualified laymen to meet in a place that is accessible and convenient for both parties, so that with God's help they may make peace between you or may truly learn which party justice favours For it was decided in that synod that by the power of blessed Peter with all our efforts and in every way we should attack that party which rejects peace with haughty contempt.*[532] *And because we have learned that some men in your kingdom love strife and discord rather than peace, on behalf of almighty God and the blessed apostles Peter and Paul we forbid anyone to use any device or endeavour or violence to hinder those men from meeting to restore harmony to your kingdom* and *imposing a just and lawful settlement of this conflict at their meeting. Moreover, to suppress evil plots and unlawful enterprises, according to the judgement of the Holy Spirit and the authority of the apostolic see we anathematise anyone whatsoever, whether king or archbishop or bishop or duke or margrave or count or any person of whatever dignity or rank he may be, who presumes to disrupt this salutary ordinance in any way: anyone, that is, who makes an effort to hinder the aforesaid assembly or the settlement of so great a conflict. We also add to this anathema that whoever presumed to perpetrate this iniquity shall experience the vengeance of almighty God not only in his soul but also in his body and in all his property. In every military contest he shall have no support and obtain no triumph as long as he lives, but he shall be confounded* and ground down[533] *by double destruction so*

---

529 Cf. Jeremiah 17:18.

530 /530 Gregory VII, *Registrum* V.15, pp. 374–6 (9 March 1078). See H. Fuhrmann (1956) pp. 304, 305, 307.

531 The register adds: 'if they obey the decrees of the Roman church'.

532 The register adds: 'and which justice does not favour'.

533 The register reads: 'and overthrown by double destruction, he may become ever more worthless and be confounded'.

that thus at least he may learn to return to penitence. In fact we are sending the bearer of this letter to you for this purpose: that, together with our venerable brother, the archbishop of Trier,[534] who supports Henry, and another from the party of Rudolf, who is to be a devout bishop, suited to this task, they may settle the place and the time of the aforesaid meeting, so that our legates, whom we mentioned above, may come to us the more safely and surely and may with God's help be able to join you in accomplishing what is pleasing to Him. Given in Rome on 9 March in the first indiction.[530]

101 *Gregory,[535] bishop, servant of the servants of God, to Udo, archbishop of Trier, greetings and apostolic blessing. How great is our anxiety and how great our sadness concerning the disorder, or rather the disintegration of your kingdom, once so greatly renowned and most powerful, we believe is sufficiently evident from the general letter that we sent to you this year.[536] But because the situation seems to be developing more ruinously from day to day, concern and extreme anxiety pierce our mind ever more deeply. Hence we have taken care to hasten whatever measures seemed best at present in the shape of an intervention by our foresight and authority, which you, my brother, may learn about in the letter in which this is described in detail.[537] We therefore request and admonish your prudence, in whom we have the greatest confidence, to intervene in this case without any delay according to the sense of that letter and make known to all men, both the greater and the lesser, as far as you can, what we have decided and what has been enjoined upon you, so that with God's mercy and with the help of those who love God either we may be able to suppress entirely such fury and wild discord and (which is our greatest desire) to restore complete peace or, if men's sins prevent that from happening, we may at least deflect the accusation of negligence at a time of such great peril for our brethren. When you have communicated our advice and our decree and when you have sought replies from both sides and found sufficient certainty and agreement as to be in no doubt about the sending of our legates and when you have arranged and confirmed everything necessary to the progress of this business, such as the place, the time and certain relevant matters, however, we wish you and that brother who must join you as a mediator in this affair to come to us immediately, so that we may know what securities have been given and what hope of peace there ought to be and we may be able to send our legates to you both without danger to them and*

---

534 Udo: above p. 302 and n. 263.

535 /535 Gregory VII, *Registrum* V.16, pp. 377–8 (9 March 1078). See H. Fuhrmann (1956) pp. 304, 305–6 and n. 26, 307.

536 *Ibid.*, V.7, pp. 356–8 (30 September 1077) to Udo and his suffragans.

537 *Ibid.*, V.15: above pp. 342–3.

*without despairing of the fruits of their labour and their fatigues. It is no
hardship, brother, for you to submit to what we impose on you, since, given
the priestly rank and office that you have received in the Church, there is
nothing you can do more worthy of God,* nothing *more salutary for your
soul than to crush diabolical iniquity and deceit in this affair and with God's
help to consider measures for the salvation of so many thousands of men; and
if you should not prosper in your labours according to your wishes, nevertheless you will receive a sure reward in the eyes of Him, for whom no good
undertaking, conceived by a just and persevering will, will be regarded as
incomplete. Nevertheless, we wish you, beloved, to perform this service for us
unequivocally: that you by no means omit to come to us, even if you cannot be
accompanied by that other man whom, as we mentioned above, you are to
have as a mediator in this case. We also command you by the authority of
blessed Peter that you favour only him whom justice favours and that the clergy
and laymen whom you are able to influence on our behalf do the same.*[535]

102 *In*[538] *the year of the Lord's incarnation 1078, in the pontificate of the
lord Pope Gregory VII on 18 November in the second indiction a synod* was
assembled *in Rome in the church of the holy Saviour, in which the envoys of
Henry and Rudolf took an oath,*[539] *each on behalf of his own lord, that they
would not practise any deception to hinder the conference of the legates of the
apostolic see to be held in the German kingdom.*[538]

103 *In*[540] *the year of the Lord's incarnation 1079 in the month of February
in the second indiction and in the sixth year of the pontificate of Pope Gregory
VII the envoys of King Rudolf*[541] *denounced Henry, since, sparing no place
and no person, he destroyed religion in the lands beyond the Alps and trod it
underfoot. No one found any protection in the honour and reverence due to
their office; not only priests but even archbishops and bishops were treated
like vile slaves, placed in captivity, put in chains, in some cases slain.*[542] *Very
many members of the council therefore contended that the papal sword ought
to be unsheathed against his tyranny. The gentle pope, however, at once
dispelled this view*[540] and, bearing in mind the considerations that he

---

538 /538 *Ibid.*, VI.5b, pp. 400–1: the opening sentences of the protocol of the Roman
synod of autumn 1078.

539 The oaths: G. Meyer von Knonau (1900) pp. 163–4; H. E. J. Cowdrey (1998) p.
184; I. S. Robinson (1999) p. 183.

540 /540 Gregory VII, *Registrum* VI.17a, pp. 425, 427: extracts from the protocol of
the Roman synod of Lent 1079. See H. Fuhrmann (1956) pp. 304, 305, 306–7.

541 Bishops Altman of Passau and Herman of Metz.

542 An allusion to Archbishop Werner of Magdeburg and Bishop Adalbert of Worms,
respectively killed and captured in the battle of Mellrichstadt (1078): G. Meyer
von Knonau (1900) pp. 142–3.

included in his letter to the bishops Peter of Albano and Altman of Passau[543] concerning this business, he said: *Show[544] yourselves to be even-handed in your dealings with both parties and, as far as you are able with the help of divine grace, free from any mark of suspicion so that you may always promote the cause of righteousness rather than any party, having before you the model of our own conduct. You can bear witness that since the judgement of this great affair has been placed in the hands of blessed Peter, our sole intention has been to walk in the path of righteousness. We have not bent the integrity of the papal judgement in the interests of any party; we have yielded neither to promises nor to fear and we trust that, with God's protection, we shall never do otherwise.[544]*

104 Next *the[545] envoys of King Henry*, who denied the previously mentioned accusations that were made against him, *swore an oath* in these terms. *The envoys of my lord King Henry are to come to you within the term of the Lord's Ascension,[546] unless the legal exceptions apply: that is, death or serious illness or captivity involving no deception on their part. They are to conduct the legates of the Roman see there and back again and the lord king will be obedient to them in all things according to justice and to their judgement and he will observe all these requirements without deception, unless you order the contrary. And we swear this on the orders of* our *king, Henry. In the same way* the envoys of King *Rudolf* swore *as follows. If a conference is held according to your command in German territory at a place and time fixed by you, either our lord King Rudolf will come himself or he will send his bishops and faithful men to your presence or to that of your legates. He will be prepared to submit to the judgement that the holy Roman church decrees in the case of the kingship and he will not impede by trickery the holding of an assembly by you or by your legates. After he sees reliable news about it, he will strive to establish and confirm peace in the kingdom so that your legation can achieve peace and harmony in the kingdom. All these requirements will be observed unless you permit the contrary or unless there is a lawful impediment, namely death or serious illness or captivity involving no deception on their part.[545]*

105 Afterwards an edict of apostolic benevolence went forth, which we set down in full so that it may be evident both to the wise and to

---

543 Sent not to Altman, but to Peter of Albano's fellow legate, Bishop Udalric of Padua: see O. Schumann (1912) pp. 46–52.

544 /544 An extract from Gregory VII, *Epistolae Vagantes* 31, p. 82 (July-October 1079?). The rest of this letter to the papal legates in Germany survives only in Hugh of Flavigny, *Chronicon* II, pp. 450–1.

545 /545 A further extract from *Registrum* VI.17a, pp. 427–8: above n. 540.

546 2 May 1079.

the ignorant that our Gregory was a princely possessor of that beatitude of which the Lord says, *Blessed are the peacemakers, for they shall be called sons of God.*[547]

Gregory,[548] *bishop, servant of the servants of God, to all the archbishops [and] bishops living in the German and the Saxon kingdoms, also to all the greater and the lesser men who have not been excommunicated and are willing to be obedient, greeting and apostolic blessing. Since we know that the greatest danger to holy Church and everywhere the greatest harm to yourselves have resulted from the conflict and discord that have for so long existed among you, it has seemed to us and to our brethren assembled in a council*[549] *that we should strive with all our passion and labour, with all our power and strength so that* we *may send to your land on behalf of the apostolic see suitable* legates strong both in religion and in conscience. *They are to assemble the religious bishops, the laymen and also the lovers of peace and righteousness living in your land who are suitable for this task. Led by the Lord's grace, on a day and in a place decided by themselves and by others whom we have yet to associate with them, the legates are either to make a peace settlement or, learning the truth about those who caused so great a discord, to impose a canonical sentence. But since we are aware that some men, inspired by the devil, inflamed by the torches of his iniquity, seduced by greed, desire to bring about and see discord rather than peace, we have decreed in this synod, in the same terms as in the last, that no person, whatever his power or dignity, whether great or small, whether prince or subject, should ever boldly presume to obstruct our legates or resist them after they have reached you to make peace. Thereafter no one is to dare to attack anyone else, contrary to their prohibition, but all are to observe a true peace without any pretext or deceit up to the day that they appoint. But if any attempt through some presumptuous act to violate these decrees of ours, we bind them with the chains of anathema. We bind them by apostolic authority not only in spirit but also in body and all the prosperity of this life and we deny them military victory, so that thus at least they may be confounded and ground down by double destruction.*[548]

106 *In*[550] *the year 1080 since the Lord's incarnation and in the seventh year of the pontificate of the lord Pope Gregory VII,* in the month of March, *in the third indiction, the lord pope himself celebrated a synod in Rome in which archbishops, the bishops of various cities and also an innumerable*

547 Matthew 5:9.

548 /548 Gregory VII, *Epistolae Vagantes* 25, pp. 64–6 (late November 1078?).

549 Roman synod of November 1078: above p. 344 and nn. 538, 539.

550 /550 Gregory VII, *Registrum* VII.14a, p. 480: opening sentences of the protocol of the Roman synod of 7 March 1080.

multitude of abbots and of the various orders of clergy and laymen were present.[550] The envoys of King Rudolf and of the princes of the German kingdom arrived and presented a complaint against the tyranny of Henry in these terms. *We,*[551] *the legation of our lord King Rudolf and his princes, complain to God and St Peter, to you, father, and to this most holy council that that Henry, whom you deposed from the kingship by your apostolic authority, has tyrannically seized that very kingdom contrary to your prohibition and has laid it waste on all sides with fire, sword and plunder; he has expelled archbishops and bishops from their dioceses with irreligious cruelty and has distributed their bishoprics among his followers in the form of benefices. It was because of his tyranny that Werner of pious memory, the bishop of Magdeburg*[552] *was killed; Bishop Adalbert of Worms*[553] *is still being tortured by him as a captive contrary to the precept of the apostolic see. Many thousands of men were killed by his faction; very many churches were burned down and utterly destroyed and their relics stolen. Numberless indeed are the crimes that that Henry has committed against our princes simply because they would not obey him as king contrary to the decree of the apostolic see. Moreover the conference that you decreed should be held to discover whose cause was just and to make peace, has not taken place through the fault of Henry and his supporters.*[554] *We therefore humbly implore your clemency, for our sakes or rather for the sake of the holy Church of God, to enact the judgement decreed upon the sacrilegious attacker of churches.*[551]

107 Aroused by such tidings as these, the spirit of the man of God at once realised that the day was at hand that Mary, the blessed mother of God had indicated to him in a vision as that on which a sentence of condemnation was to be imposed on that same enemy of the Church. So as not to delay it any more, he issued the command and the prohibition, expressing his deep grief with a groan, and, as the council listened with bated breath, he burst forth with these words. *Blessed*[555]

---

551 /551 This text was printed by Melchior Goldast, *Collectio constitutionum imperialium* 1 (Frankfurt, 1613), 240, from a manuscript source independent of Paul's text. Cf. *MGH Constitutiones* 1, 555, no. 390. Its authenticity was defended by G. Meyer von Knonau (1900) p. 247 n. 21. See H. E. J. Cowdrey (1998) p. 195.

552 Werner, archbishop of Magdeburg: above n. 542.

553 Adalbert, bishop of Worms (1069–1107): above n. 542.

554 The negotiations in 1079 to hold this conference: G. Meyer von Knonau (1900) pp. 208, 210–15; O. Schumann (1912) pp. 46–52; H. E. J. Cowdrey (1998) pp. 190, 192–3; I. S. Robinson (1999) pp. 186, 190–2.

555 /555 *Registrum* VII.14a, pp. 483–7: synodal protocol of 7 March 1080 c. 7, 'the excommunication of King Henry'. The dissemination of this text: C. Erdmann (1936) p. 13; H. Fuhrmann (1956) pp. 304, 305, 307. See G. Meyer von Knonau (1900) pp. 252–6; J. Vogel (1983) pp. 189–96; H. E. J. Cowdrey (1998) pp. 196–9.

Peter, prince of the apostles, and you, blessed Paul, teacher of the Gentiles, deign, I pray, to bend your ears to me and mercifully hear me,[556] because you are disciples and lovers of the truth, help me to tell you the truth, setting aside all falsehood, which you utterly detest, so that my brethren may trust in me and may know and understand that it is because of my reliance on you, next to God and His mother, Mary, ever virgin, that I resist the wicked and the unjust, but offer help to those who are faithful to you. You know, however, that it was not in accordance with my own will that I entered holy orders;[557] it was unwillingly that I accompanied the lord Pope Gregory[558] beyond the mountains, but more unwillingly still that I returned with my lord Pope Leo[559] to your special church, in which I have served you as best I could. Afterwards it was with extreme unwillingness and with much pain and groaning and lamentation that I was placed on your throne, most unworthy as I am. This I say to you because I did not choose you, but you chose me[560] and laid on me the very heavy burden of your church. And because you have commanded me to go up to a high mountain[561] and to cry aloud and declare to the people of God their transgressions and to the sons of the Church their sins,[562] the members of the devil began to rise up against me and they presumed to lay their hands on me even to the point of bloodshed. The kings of the earth have stood up and the rulers, both secular and ecclesiastical, the courtiers and also the common people have taken counsel together against the Lord and against you, His anointed, saying, Let us burst their bonds asunder and cast away their yoke from us.[563] And they have tried in many ways to rise up against me so as to confound me utterly either by my death or by exile. Of these men Henry in particular, whom they call 'king', the son of Emperor Henry, has raised his heel against[564] your church, attempting to subject her to himself by deposing me in a conspiracy with many men, both Italians and those from beyond the mountains. Your authority resisted his arrogance[565] and your power destroyed it. He came to me in Lombardy, confused and humi-

---

556 Cf. Psalm 16:6.

557 He was presumably already in minor orders when he served Pope Gregory VI as his chaplain. See G. Miccoli (1966c) col. 296; H. E. J. Cowdrey (1998) p. 29.

558 Gregory VI (1045–6): above p. 188.

559 Leo IX: above p. 191.

560 Cf. John 15:16.

561 Isaiah 40:9.

562 Isaiah 58:1. See C. Schneider (1972) pp. 31–2.

563 Psalm 2:2–3. The significance of this text in Gregorian polemic: below c. 112, p. 355. See C. Schneider (1972) pp. 36–40; J. Vogel (1983) p. 191.

564 Cf. John 13:18. The allusion is to Judas Iscariot: see J. Vogel (1983) p. 191.

565 Cf. I Peter 5:5. See J. Vogel (1983) p. 192.

liated, seeking absolution from excommunication. Seeing his humiliation and receiving many promises from him that he would amend his life, I restored him only to communion, but I did not reinstate him in the kingship from which I had deposed him in a Roman synod; nor did I command that the fealty of the men who had sworn oaths to him or would do so in future, from which I absolved them all in that same synod, should be shown to him.[566] *I withheld* this *in order that I might do justice between him and the bishops and princes beyond the mountains, who had been resisting him in response to the command of your church, and make a peace settlement, as Henry himself promised me with an oath supported by two bishops.*[567] *Those bishops and princes beyond the mountains, however, hearing that he did not keep his promises to me and despairing of him, elected Duke Rudolf as their king, without seeking my advice, as you will bear witness.*[568] *King Rudolf hastened to send an envoy to me, declaring that he had been compelled to undertake the government of the kingdom but he was prepared to obey me in every way. In order that the truth of this would more readily be believed, he always sent the same message to me, adding that he would confirm his promises by giving as hostages his own son*[569] *and that of his vassal, Berthold.*[570] *Meanwhile Henry began to beg me to help him against Rudolf. I replied to him that I should gladly do so when I had heard the explanations of both sides so that I might know which side justice favoured. He,* however, *believed himself capable of defeating his enemy with his own military might and he treated my reply with contempt; but after he realised that he could not accomplish what he hoped, two of his adherents, the bishops of Verdun*[571] *and Osnabrück,*[572] *came to Rome and requested me in a synod on Henry's behalf to do justice to him.*[573] *Rudolf's envoys also approved of this measure. Finally, inspired, I believe, by God, I decreed in that same synod that a conference should be held beyond the mountains so that either peace would be established there or it would be known which party justice most favoured.*[574] *For, as*

---

566 The absolution at Canossa: above p. 328 and n. 454.

567 Eberhard of Naumburg and Gregory of Vercelli: see G. Meyer von Knonau (1894) p. 898.

568 Gregory VII and the election of Rudolf: I. S. Robinson (1979) pp. 724–31; J. Vogel (1983) pp. 47–52; H. E. J. Cowdrey (1998) pp. 170–1; I. S. Robinson (1999) pp. 168–9.

569 Berthold I, duke of Swabia (✝1090).

570 Berthold II, duke of Swabia, duke of Zähringen (✝1111).

571 Theoderic, bishop of Verdun (1046–89).

572 Benno II, bishop of Osnabrück (1068–88).

573 The Roman synod of 27 February–3 March 1078. See G. Meyer von Knonau (1900) pp. 98–100, 104–5, 111–12; H. E. J. Cowdrey (1998) p. 180; I. S. Robinson (1999) p. 178.

574 Gregory VII, *Registrum* V.14a, pp. 370–1: above p. 341.

you, my fathers and my lords will bear me witness, I have determined up to this very day to give help to no party except that which justice most favoured. Because I thought that the less righteous party could not wish a conference to take place in which justice was to prevail, I excommunicated and bound with anathema all persons, whether king or duke or bishop or any man who prevented the conference from taking place by some trickery. Henry, however, with his supporters, not afraid of the danger of disobedience, which is the crime of idolatry,[575] incurred excommunication by hindering the conference and bound himself in the chain of anathema; he delivered up to death a great multitude of Christians, caused the churches to be demolished and abandoned almost all the kingdom of the Germans to be laid waste. Therefore, trusting in the judgement and mercy of God and of his most pious mother, Mary ever virgin and relying on our authority, I subject Henry, whom they call king, and all his supporters to excommunication and I bind them with the chain of anathema and again I deny him the kingdom of the Germans and of Italy on behalf of almighty God and on your behalf and I withdraw from him all the royal power and dignity. I forbid any Christian to obey him as king and I absolve from their oath and promise all who have sworn or who in future swear an oath to him respecting his royal government. Henry himself, together with his supporters, will prove powerless in every military encounter and will never win a victory as long as he lives. I grant, bestow and concede on your behalf, however, that Rudolf, whom the Germans have elected as their king in their loyalty to you, may rule and defend the German kingdom[576] and on all his faithful followers I bestow (relying on your assurance) absolution from all sins[577] and your blessing in this life and in the future. For as Henry is justly cast down from the dignity of the kingship because of his pride, disobedience and falsehood, so the power and the dignity of the kingship is conceded to Rudolf because of his humility, obedience and truth. Act now, I beseech you, most holy fathers and princes, so that the whole world may know that, if you have the power to bind and loose in heaven,[578] you are also able on earth to take away and to confer, according to merit, kingdoms, duchies, principalities, marches, counties and the property of all men. You have often deprived wicked and unworthy men of patriarchates, primacies, archbishoprics and

575 Cf. I Samuel 15:23. See C. Schneider (1972) pp. 118–23; H. E. J. Cowdrey (1998) p. 516.

576 Henry was deprived of 'the kingdom of the Germans and of Italy' but Rudolf was granted only 'the German kingdom': G. Meyer von Knonau (1900) p. 254 n. 40; J. Vogel (1983) p. 193.

577 The significance of this 'absolution' see C. Erdmann (1935) pp. 156–7; I. S. Robinson (1973a) pp. 180–3; J. Vogel (1983) p. 194.

578 Cf. Matthew 16:19.

bishoprics and have given them to devout men. For if you judge spiritual matters, what can you do in secular affairs? And if you will judge the angels,[579] who rule over all haughty princes, what can you do in the case of their servants? Now let the kings and all the princes of the world learn how great you are and what you are able to perform and let them be afraid to belittle the commands of your church. Enact your judgement on the aforesaid Henry so quickly that all may know that it is not by chance but through your power that he falls and is confounded, would that it were into penitence so that his spirit may be saved in the day of the Lord![580] Enacted in Rome on 7 March in the third indiction.[555]

108 The unhappy Henry, therefore, being *delivered up to Satan,*[581] with a mad, demonic rage climbed higher and higher to the summit of wickedness. Desiring to reject the lawful pope, the new Nebuchadnezzar set up a golden statue[582] to be worshipped by the simoniacs and nicholaites in the city of Rome, which Peter and John call Babylon:[583] namely Wibert, bishop of Ravenna, who had long ago been condemned by our Gregory with a synodal judgement for his unchastity and other shameful acts.[584] A most grievous persecution was accordingly launched against the man of God and he withdrew to Salerno.[585] There he was most powerfully purified by the wormwood of divine healing in the shape of bodily infirmities[586] and he was found worthy to receive the sweet promise of heavenly consolation, namely that this purification would be effective and sufficient in perpetuity and that he need not fear any punishment after his death. Finally he attained safety from the dangers of this world as a portent of eternal salvation and – which seems exceedingly glorious – about 1 January he began to have foreknowledge that his life would end around 1 June.[587] When that time had drawn near and the pain of his last agony had begun, as the bishops and cardinals who were with him blessed

---

579 Cf. I Corinthians 6:3.

580 I Corinthians 5:5.

581 I Timothy 1:20.

582 Daniel 3:1. For this parallel see also Bernold, *De lege excommunicationis* p. 101; Gebhard of Salzburg, letter, in Hugh of Flavigny, *Chronicon* II, p. 460; Bernard, *Liber canonum* c. 29, p. 500.

583 I Peter 5:13; Revelation 16:19.

584 Cf. Gregory VII, *Registrum* V.14a, VII.14a, pp. 369, 481. See above p. 247.

585 Summer 1084: see above p. 252 and n. 58.

586 Cf. *Chronica monasterii Casinensis* III.65, p. 447.

587 Cf. the statement of Bishop Agano of Autun (*MGH SS* 5, 563) that Gregory foretold his death a week before it happened. See H. E. J. Cowdrey (1998) p. 677 n. 1.

him for his labours, his holy life and teaching, he replied, 'My most beloved brethren, I regard my labours as being of no account and I trust in only one thing: that I *have* always *loved righteousness and hated iniquity.*[588] Again when, lamenting, they expressed their fears about their situation after his departure, the pious father raised his eyes to heaven and stretched out his palms in that direction in the manner of the Ascension, saying, 'I shall ascend there and by my strenuous prayers I shall commit you to the gracious God.'

109 When moreover he was requested amidst these great perils for the faithful to designate a successor and an avenger of the Church against the aforementioned adulterer, he gave a choice of three: namely, Desiderius, cardinal and abbot of the monastery of Monte Cassino[589] and the most reverend bishops Odo of Ostia[590] and Hugh of Lyons. Odo, however, had not yet returned from Germany, where during the performance of a papal legation he consecrated the venerable Gebhard, who had become bishop of Constance[591] in his presence and with his approval, and where he had prudently taken other measures to strengthen the Church. Hugh was also carrying out the duties of government far away.[592] The pope therefore persuaded them in the meantime to elect Desiderius, since he was a neighbour, even though he would not live long. He was to be called Victor and he would not lack the semblance of victory. For during his pontificate, which was limited to four months,[593] the Lord gave a famous victory to the defenders of the apostolic see over its enemies. It was through this victory that the bishop of Würzburg, Adalbero by name, a man of notable birth, honourable in appearance and in deeds, regained his bishopric,[594] which had long been held by intruders. He was conducted back there by his venerable fellow bishops Gebhard of Constance and Herman of Metz, who themselves had lost their sees because of their

---

588 Psalm 44:8; Hebrews 1:9: see below p. 353.

589 According to the record of Gregory VII's last testament (below p. 353 n. 597) the pope's reply was: 'Elect as pontiff whomsoever of these three you can have: the bishop of Lucca [Anselm II] or the bishop of Ostia or the archbishop of Lyons'.

590 Odo I, cardinal bishop of Ostia; Pope Urban II (1088–99).

591 Gebhard III, bishop of Constance (1084–1110). Cf. Bernold, *Chronicon* 1084, p. 441. See G. Meyer von Knonau (1900) pp. 605–9; A. Becker (1964) pp. 71–4.

592 As papal legate in France: T. Schieffer (1935) pp. 91–110, 112–38; H. E. J. Cowdrey (1998) pp. 356–66.

593 Victor III, elected 24 May 1086, consecrated 9 May 1087; †16 September 1087.

594 Adalbero was briefly restored to his see as a result of the battle of Pleichfeld (north of Würzburg) 11 August 1086: G. Meyer von Knonau (1903) pp. 128–30.

fidelity towards our Gregory.⁵⁹⁵ The holy father had predicted to
Desiderius that he would not be present at his passing, even though it
was for this reason that he had visited the sick man, to remain by his
side until the end and to solemnize his funeral with the other faithful.
The prediction greatly astonished and saddened Desiderius. While he
was transfixed in amazement, wondering how he would be prevented,
the news suddenly reached him that the Normans were besieging a
fortress belonging to his monastery. Forced by the necessity of assisting his vassals, he obtained leave to depart and thus, although unwillingly, he caused the prophecy to be fulfilled.⁵⁹⁶

110 Meanwhile the blessed Pope Gregory was asked about those
whom he had excommunicated and if he wished to make any dispensations, to which he replied: '*Except*⁵⁹⁷ *for Henry the so-called king* and
Wibert the intruder in the apostolic see and all those chief personages
who either by counsel or by aid countenance their wickedness and
impiety, *I absolve and bless them all, whoever believe beyond doubt that I
possess this spiritual power in the place of* the apostles *Peter* and Paul.' *In
addition he admonished them on many subjects and gave them this command.
'On behalf of Almighty God and by the authority of the blessed apostles Peter
and Paul I command you to have no one as Roman pontiff unless he is
canonically elected and ordained by the authority of the holy Fathers.'* When
he was breathing his last, these were his final words: '*I have loved righteousness and hated iniquity,*⁵⁹⁸ *therefore I die in exile.*'⁵⁹⁷ A certain venerable
bishop is said to have contradicted him,⁵⁹⁹ saying, 'Lord, you cannot
die in exile, since, being in the place of Christ and His apostles you
have received from heaven *the nations as your heritage and the ends of the
earth as your possession.*'⁶⁰⁰ Filled with sevenfold grace, the spirit of

595 It was only in 1103–5 that Gebhard was exiled from Constance. Herman, expelled
    from Metz 1078, did not return until 1089: see G. Meyer von Knonau (1900) p.
    131; (1903) pp. 181–2, 217–18, 248.
596 According to *Chronica monasterii Casinensis* III.65, p. 447, Desiderius was present
    at Gregory's death.
597 /597 An extract from the record of Gregory VII's testament (*Briefsammlungen der
    Zeit Heinrichs IV.* p. 75). See P. E. Hübinger (1973) pp. 81–97; H. E. J. Cowdrey
    (1983) pp. 181–5; H. E. J. Cowdrey (1988) pp. 707–12; H. E. J. Cowdrey (1998) pp.
    678–80.
598 Psalm 44:8; Hebrews 1:9. This text was associated with the ceremony of anointing
    bishops and kings. On the significance of the inclusion of the reference to death in
    exile: P. E. Hübinger (1973) pp. 57–60; H. E. J. Cowdrey (1998) pp. 680–1.
599 See H. E. J. Cowdrey (1998) p. 680: the interpretation of Gregory's last words
    'manifestly caused perplexity from an early date'.
600 Psalm 2:8.

Gregory VII, who had instructed the whole world and its princes
concerning sin and righteousness and judgement, strengthened by the
heavenly food that he had recently received, took the road to heaven
and was deservedly conveyed as it were in a chariot of fire like
Elijah.[601] He wonderfully increased the happiness of his predecessor
Urban, whose feast-day that was,[602] and of all the blessed rejoicing
with Christ in heavenly glory; but on earth his departure dismayed
the pilgrim Church and filled it with mourning. His body was brought
to be buried with the blessed Matthew the evangelist,[603] concerning
the recent discovery of whose body he had written a joyful letter a few
years before.[604]

111 It seems appropriate to introduce here the foremost follower and
heir of his virtues, the blessed Anselm, bishop of the church of Lucca,[605]
who *always*[606] *made it his study before all else to imitate* him *in everything
and to differ from him in nothing at all:* consequently *whatever virtue he
possessed, he always attributed it to the other's merits.* For Gregory *was*
like *a fountain,* Anselm *like a stream that flowed from him and watered the
dry land. The former,* like *the head, governed the whole body; the latter*
worked like *the zealous hand that is joined to it. The former, like the sun,
illuminated everything; the latter, like its brightness, showed up individual
objects.*[606] When long ago Elijah was about to leave this mortal dwelling-
place, he left Elisha his mantle as the instrument of his prophetic
gift.[607] Likewise when Gregory was about to depart from this mortal
life, *he*[608] *sent* to Anselm a symbol of papal power,[609] namely *the mitre
from his head,* so that through God's help, just as Elisha inherited the
prerogative of prophecy through the mantle, Anselm might obtain

601 Cf. II Kings 2:11.

602 25 May (1085), the feast-day of Pope Urban I (223–230?).

603 The cathedral of San Matteo, Salerno. See above p. 252 and n. 61.

604 Gregory VII, *Registrum* VIII.8, pp. 526–7 (18 September 1080).

605 Anselm II, bishop of Lucca (1073–86). See C. Violante (1961) pp. 399–407; G.M.
   Fusconi (1962) pp. 26–36; H. E. J. Cowdrey (1998) pp. 303–7; K. G. Cushing
   (1998) pp. 43–63.

606 /606 An extract from the anonymous biography, *Vita Anselmi episcopi Lucensis* c.
   31, 32, p. 22.

607 Cf. II Kings 2: 13–14.

608 /608 *Vita Anselmi* c. 32, pp. 22–3.

609 P. E. Hübinger (1973) p. 77 suggested that the mitre was intended to designate
   Anselm as Gregory's successor. Anselm is named first in the list of proposed
   successors in the original record of Gregory's last testament (above n. 597). Paul
   inconsistently substituted the name of Desiderius for that of Anselm in his version
   of this list, perhaps to enhance Gregory's reputation as a prophet.

priestly excellence through the mitre. The analogy was thus far effective, that just as Elisha displayed the tokens of virtue because of Elijah's mantle, so Anselm produced great works by means of Gregory's mitre. To cite one well known instance among very many: *Ubald, the reverend prelate of the church of Mantua*[610] *had for many years been very seriously afflicted with spleen and his whole body was covered with ulcers, especially on his legs, so that he could hardly stand or even lie down or sit; he had paid large sums to physicians but was no better. When he placed that mitre where the pain was most violent, he was restored to his former health.*[608]

112 It is permissible to extract a few sentences from Anselm's treatise on the Psalms[611] and to show very clearly what a pious affection he felt towards the sanctity of his master Gregory. He writes thus in the treatise on the second Psalm. *'The kings of the earth stood by and the princes gathered together.'*[612] *The kings of the earth*, namely, the members of him who reigns over all the sons of pride,[613] have not only arrived but have also *stood by* and laid siege to the Roman church with their army[614] *and the princes* among the priests have conspired and *gathered together* against St Peter and against his vicar, Gregory[615] or rather against Him who said, *"He who touches you, touches me; he who rejects you, rejects me",*[616] to crucify the Son of God again.[617] It is indeed agreed that our head suffers through His members and is weakened through His members, as He himself said to blessed Peter, *I go to Rome to be crucified anew.*[618]

610 Bishop Hubald of Mantua: above p. 283 and n. 140.

611 This is the only surviving extract from Anselm's commentary on the Psalms. The twelfth-century bibliographer 'Anonymus Mellicensis' (Wolfger of Prüfening?) called the commentary 'an immoderate work in which [Anselm] apostrophises and attacks Wibert and Henry in appropriate places' (*De scriptoribus ecclesiasticis* c. 100, p. 89). Anselm explained the scriptural text by reference to contemporary events, using the technique that B. Smalley (1973) pp. 26–36, called 'political allegory'. See I. S. Robinson (1983) pp. 69–98.

612 Psalm 2:2. This passage was traditionally given a christological interpretation: 'the kings' signified Pontius Pilate; 'the princes', the priests who surrendered Christ to him (e.g. Cassiodorus, *Expositio in Psalmos, MPL* 70, col. 36D–37A). Anselm added a further layer of meaning: Christ signified 'St Peter and his vicar Gregory'; Pilate was Henry IV; the priests, the Henrician bishops who supported Wibert. Cf. Gregory VII, *Registrum* VII.14a, pp. 483–4, quoted by Paul above p. 348.

613 Cf. Job 41:25 (Satan 'is king over all the children of pride').

614 Henry IV's siege of Rome, 1082–4: above pp. 248–50.

615 The council of Brixen, 25 June 1080: above p. 246.

616 Luke 10:16.

617 Cf. Hebrews 6:6.

618 The apocryphal *Passio Petri et Pauli* c. 61, ed. R. A. Lipsius, *Acta apostolorum apocrypha* 1 (Leipzig, 1891) p. 171.

Does it not seem to you that they are holding a council in the house of Pilate to deliver up Christ to death, when Henry has provided so many false witnesses against the supreme pontiff, when all cry out, *He deserves death!*[619] Is not Barabbas chosen again and Christ given up to death by Pilate, when Wibert of Ravenna is elected and Pope Gregory rejected?[620] They petition for the life of a robber who is condemned by the law and condemn the righteous man through whom all are saved. Does it not seem to you that Pilate has once more *washed* his *hands* and *said, I am* free *of this man's blood;*[621] *I find no crime in Him,*[622] when Henry, feigning penitence, showed reverence to the supreme pontiff, then said to his false bishops, *Judge him by your own law?*[623]

'Furthermore: *Let us burst their bonds asunder and cast their yoke from us.*[624] "Let us crush the righteous man," they say, "since he opposes our works. For *if we let him go on thus, the Romans will come and destroy our place and our nation*";[625] that is, if Pope Gregory lives, he will send against us preachers of truth, who will scrutinise our lives and actions and snatch away the sheep of Christ from our hands; the righteous will rob us of our spoils and entrust the Church to those who will produce fruit in her.'"

We have learned how great a saint he was partly from reading about his deeds,[626] partly from the reports of the religious brethren who have borne witness that they came to his tomb from faraway, summoned by visions and were freed without delay from grave illnesses from which they had long been suffering.[627]

113 Now we think it worth the labour to show briefly how the grace or the wrath of God promoted the decrees of our Gregory against the

---

619 Matthew 26:66.

620 Wibert is similarly called 'Barabbas the thief' in a letter of Matilda of Tuscany, quoted by Hugh of Flavigny, *Chronicon* II, p. 463.

621 Matthew 27:24.

622 John 18:38.

623 John 18:31.

624 Psalm 2:3.

625 John 11:48.

626 The anonymous biography, *Vita Anselmi episcopi Lucensis* pp. 1–35. See E. Pásztor (1960) pp. 1–33; E. Pásztor (1964) pp. 91–115; E. Pásztor (1992) pp. 207–22.

627 He was buried in Mantua. On the tradition of his miracles: *Vita Anselmi* c. 34–84, pp. 23–35; Rangerius, *Vita metrica Anselmi Lucensis* V, pp. 1301–7. See P. Golinelli (1986) pp. 27–60.

avarice of Simon[628] and the lasciviousness of Nicholas[629] in our land, that is to say in Germany; how the righteous became more vigilant in guarding against the punishment of excommunication and the dreadful workers of iniquity were prevailed on to strive through the utmost efforts of penitence to escape the penalty of their transgressions. As for those heavenly deeds that, according to all the more devout Romans, have been or are being performed at his tomb,[630] we leave them to be enumerated by those who are nearer, who can more easily learn about the persons to whom these things have happened or are happening. To cite an example of the opposition to simony, the principal plague in the Church, I mention firstly William, the most reverend father of the monastery of Hirsau,[631] whose piety the writings of our Gregory reverently record.[632] Among the many who sought out his special medicine was a certain priest stained by the leprosy of simoniacal depravity, whom he received to be cured by the antidote of humility. Alas! under compulsion from his insolent monks (whose very evil custom is to care little or nothing for the sacred canons), he did not restrain him from the unlawful celebration of the mass. Thus it happened that the Saviour himself deterred him by means of a dreadful vision, when he was sitting in the presbytery after the beginning of the mass of the catechumens. When sleep overcame him, He appeared in torn garments with a countenance like that of a leper and looked at him, stunned and amazed as he was by such an apparition. 'This is how you treated me,' He said, 'when, knowing that you were a simoniac, you nevertheless presumed to undertake to celebrate the sacrament of my body and blood.' Meanwhile it was time to rise to read the Gospel and many of the brethren signified that he should be roused; but the abbot on more careful consideration shook his head, so that the vision should not be interrupted. For he realised that so deep a sleep at this time and in this place was not simply an instance of idleness. When the time for the sacrament arrived and it was then necessary to rouse him for the celebration of the mystery, he declared that he was weary and that it was impossible for him to proceed. He at once found a deputy to celebrate that mass and henceforward for the rest of his life he entirely refrained from performing the office of a priest.

---

628 Simon Magus: above p. 275 and n. 95.

629 Nicholas of Antioch (Acts 6:5), who gave his name to the offence of 'nicholaitism': above n. 97.

630 Cf. Bonizo, *Book to a Friend* IX, above p. 252.

631 William, abbot of Hirsau (1069–91).

632 Gregory VII, *Registrum* VII.24, IX.3, pp. 502–5, 573–7.

114 Hereafter examples are offered of those who prevailed against unchaste priests and their adherents.

The vision of the virgin Herluca.[633] The virgin Herluca of happy memory, whose intimate friends were visions and revelations from the Lord together with the interpretations of the apostles, made known to us in a faithful report that on one occasion while she was sitting alone in her cell, she suddenly saw the Lord Jesus coming in, accompanied by the blessed Wikterp, the former bishop of the church of Augsburg.[634] He remained standing in silence for a short while, only displaying His wounds, dripping with His blood. When her hair stood on end from the fear inspired by the strange vision, the bishop said to her, 'Sister, do you shrink from the bloody sight of the Saviour?' She said, 'Yes indeed, lord.' He said, 'Do you wish not to see Him like this any more?' She replied, 'I wish it.' 'In that case,' he said, 'do not henceforward hear the masses of the priest Richard,[635] who will not preserve the chastity appropriate to his high office.' This was the name of an unworthy priest who had charge of that church near which the virgin dedicated to God had her dwelling. Thereafter she opposed him by publicly avoiding him and by her example she encouraged the people to do the same.

115 Another vision.[636] Similarly worthy of remembrance is that vision recalled by the monk Adelbero of blessed memory, beloved of God and men, who himself suffered reproaches and threats from the enemies of our Gregory because of his obedience to his decrees. He reported that Herluca saw a vision of a certain nicholaite,[637] who through his enslavement to fleshly desires contaminated that church which is in the place called Rott. That neighbourhood, that is, the frontier of the lands of the Bavarians and the Swabians that are separated by the River Lech, was not far away from the dwellings of both the venerable old man and the blessed virgin, who deeply loved one another in Christ, since each recognised the excellent grace of God in the other. This is the story that the beloved man told of that beloved woman. The

---

633 Herluca of Epfach, ascetic and visionary (✝1127/8), whose biography Paul composed three years after her death (*Vita beatae Herlucae* pp. 168–73). The vision in c. 114 reappears in *Vita Herlucae* c. 22, p. 170.

634 Wikterp, bishop of Regensburg and Augsburg (✝749?). In Herluca's lifetime he was buried in the church of Epfach. See F. Zoepfl (1955) pp. 35–6.

635 According to *Vita Herlucae* c. 22, p. 170, 'the priest Richard of Epfach' was converted 'by the incessant chiding and reproaches of Herluca'.

636 Retold in *Vita Herlucae* c. 23, p. 170.

637 Identified in *Vita Herlucae* as 'the priest Adalbert of Rott'.

blessed Herluca was sitting one day as usual among her companions, virgins and widows, and they were busily occupied with manual work, according to their custom, when suddenly she looked out of the window and began sadly to lament and to cry out, *'Woe*, woe *to that man: it would be* better for him *if he had not been born.'*[638] A certain noble woman named Hadewiga, greatly astonished, asked her what she had seen that so moved her. She said, 'That unhappy priest of Rott has died and his soul has been carried off to hell by Satan's angels. I merely saw them passing by mocking, while the soul that accompanied them was wailing.' When the other expressed a desire that this should not be true, Herluca said, 'Send someone to inquire into the truth of the matter.' The messenger who was sent found the household mourning and ascertained that the priest had died at the same hour at which the blessed virgin had seen his spirit being carried off by evil spirits.

116 Divine vengeance also furiously struck down the wives or concubines of unchaste priests.[639] For some of them went mad and threw themselves into the fire; others went to bed quite well but were found dead in the morning without any sign of a preceding illness; the bodies of others were denied a proper burial after evil spirits tore out their souls, bore them away and stored them in their dens.

117 Moreover the wrath of God sometimes manifested itself to the unchaste while they were celebrating mass, so that at the very moment they wished to communicate, a violent whirlwind arose, upset the chalice and poured out the blood and it miraculously removed the holy bread where no human being could find it. There was such a priest in the time of Pope Gelasius II,[640] to whose care was entrusted the chasuble of our often mentioned and always to be mentioned Gregory and who once presumed to wear it at mass. We have not ourselves investigated this but we have learned for a certainty from the report of the Romans that he immediately became afflicted with the scab and recovered from it with difficulty by showing the authentic fruits of penitence.

118 How much God's grace attended those who obeyed Gregorian teaching is shown by the fourfold form of religious life reverently inaugurated in this region with the papal blessing of our Gregory and

638 Matthew 26:24.

639 On the legal status of priests' wives: J. Gaudemet (1982) pp. 8–20; H. E. J. Cowdrey (1998) pp. 550–3.

640 Gelasius II (1118–19).

happily increased: namely, that of the tonsured servants of Christ, that of the bearded brethren[641] faithfully serving them, that of virgins living the enclosed life of perpetual devotion and that of virgins governing their life according to the Rule and guarding their comings and goings.[642] There were four principal directors of these four ways of life: namely, the excellent renewer of the canonical life, Altman,[643] bishop of Lorch,[644] Udalric of blessed memory, prior of Cluny[645] and the reverend fathers William of Hirsau and Siegfried of the monastery of the holy Saviour.[646]

119 Since we have just made mention again of Cluny, as an admonition to those who preside over monasteries, we will recall two visions that our Gregory experienced there, so that those who have thus far derived advantage from his word and example, may hereafter find the contemplation of these visions no less profitable. On one occasion when he was a papal legate,[647] therefore, he had arrived in Cluny and was sitting in the chapter of the brethren while the abbot[648] presided. His spirit was raised up and he began to see Jesus in their midst, sometimes gently nodding at the abbot when he judged correctly, sometimes turning away indignantly when he chanced to pay less heed to rectitude. After the chapter had come to an end, he secretly reported this to the father and advised him to be more cautious in future. On

641 Distinguishing between the life of monks and that of *conversi* ('lay brethren'). See K. Hallinger (1956) pp. 1–104.

642 Distinguishing between the life of nuns subject to the Benedictine Rule and that of anchoresses living a life such as that of Herluca in the community of regular canons at Bernried. See H. Grundmann (1976) pp. 114–15.

643 Altman of Passau founded the houses of regular canons St Nicholas of Passau, St Florian, St Pölten, Göttweig and Rottenbuch. See J. Mois (1953) pp. 97–9; E. Boshof (1981) pp. 317–45; E. Boshof (1991) pp. 140–1.

644 A reference to the tradition, especially associated with Bishop Pilgrim of Passau (971–91), that Passau was a continuation of the former bishopric of Lorch (the ancient *Lauriacum* near the Enns estuary). Evidence of the interest of Bishop Udalric of Passau (below c. 121, p. 362) in the Lorch tradition: E. Boshof (1991) p. 145.

645 Udalric, monk of Cluny, prior of Zell (†1093) introduced the 'customs' of Cluny to Germany (in his work *Antiquiores consuetudines monasterii Cluniacensis*). See H. E. J. Cowdrey (1970) pp. 194–6; H. E. J. Cowdrey (1998) pp. 260–3 and above p. 71.

646 Siegfried, abbot of All Saints, Schaffhausen (†1096).

647 See above p. 269 and n. 65. H. E. J. Cowdrey (1978) p. 57 n. 3 placed this visit at the time of the council of Châlon-sur-Saône (1056). The first vision was also recorded by Alexander of Canterbury, *Memorials of St Anselm* pp. 213–14 (cf. above c. 17, 18, 20, pp. 269–71) and Gilo, *Vita Hugonis abbatis* I.7, p. 57. See A. Stacpoole (1967) pp. 342, 354–6.

648 Hugh I of Cluny.

another occasion he was warned by divine revelation to issue a command by apostolic authority that all persons in that place who were guilty of murder or adultery or any other offence must abstain from the office of the altar according to the decrees of the canons. After the guilty had at once made a terrified confession of their crimes, the abbot described how he had seen them in his dreams being beheaded by an angel.

120 At the conclusion of the book it is pleasant to recall the pair, admirable for their charity, bathed in the blood of martyrdom: namely, the bishops Burchard of Halberstadt[649] and Thiemo of Salzburg,[650] most powerful advocates of Gregorian doctrine. One of the two, Burchard, was very near, both in blood and in religion, to the most reverend archbishop Anno of Cologne and Werner of Magdeburg.[651] After he had long endured the most grievous burden of persecution with praiseworthy steadfastness, at last, as the day of heavenly retribution approached, he saw in a vision at night that the blessed Blasius, martyr and bishop,[652] was standing by him and promising him the glory of his companionship in blessed suffering. He was thus to find himself in dreadful straits, surrounded by a raging mob of schismatics in Goslar.[653] Mortally wounded, he survived long enough to admonish those present with admirable ardour to guard themselves from the contagion of heretics and to persevere in obedience to the catholic pope. He finally gave up the ghost amidst words of holy exhortation and prayer and was buried in the church of the apostles Peter and Paul that he himself had built from the foundations and dedicated.[654]

121 Thiemo, excellent by virtue both of his natural superiority and of his total humility and integrity, was afflicted by the frequent need to flee from the Wibertines and Henricians and finally was tortured by long captivity.[655] When he saw that his efforts could not bear fruit in

649 Burchard II, bishop of Halberstadt (1059–88).

650 Thiemo, archbishop of Salzburg (1090–1101).

651 Anno II, archbishop of Cologne (1056–75) and Archbishop Werner, of the Swabian family of Steusslingen, were the brothers of Burchard's mother: see D. Lück (1970b) pp. 31–51.

652 On the cult of St Blasius, bishop of Sebaste and martyr (✝316): above p. 125.

653 A fight between the citizens of Goslar and the bishop's vassals, 7 April 1088: L. Fenske (1977) pp. 116–17.

654 The abbey of Ilsenburg, rebuilt by Burchard c. 1085: L. Fenske (1977) pp. 128–9, 134, 136.

655 He was held captive 1097–9 by the supporters of Berchtold, Henrician archbishop of Salzburg: G. Meyer von Knonau (1904) pp. 6, 84.

his own land, he decided to travel to Jerusalem. He was intercepted on his journey by pagans[656] and, being cut in pieces limb by limb because of his unconquerable desire to acknowledge the name of Christ, he entered the heavenly Jerusalem as a glorious victor.[657] He had ordained the most reverend ordainer of this humble author, namely Udalric, bishop of Lorch or Passau and legate of the apostolic see.[658] Seven years ago, after many struggles in defence of Gregorian doctrine, according to the precepts of which he had been elected and promoted, having contended lawfully, he fell asleep in the Lord[659] in the hundred-and-fifth year of his life, leaving behind – alas, the sadness of it! – no one like himself among all the prelates of Germany. Truly, we see no one so constituted in his morals, his honourable countenance, his sober attire, his reverend authority, his gracious discourse salted with wit and everywhere ready with apt replies and possessing other privileges that we prefer rather to disguise than to arouse the vain envy of those incapable of being his equal. Nevertheless we think that it can be said with the leave of all men that nothing was more cheerful than his severity, nothing severer than his cheerfulness and his wonderful virtue of abstinence was held in check by such liveliness that it never had the odour of ostentation.

122 His special pupil, the virgin dedicated to God[660] saw heavenly visions and received insights that did much to encourage Gregorian obedience and so they ought not to be passed over in silence. For she loved a certain priest because he lived a chaste life and had received holy orders from so lawful a bishop, namely Udalric, and in his performance of the divine offices he came close to resembling that delightful and charitable man, even in the tone of his voice. It thus happened that on one occasion it seemed to her, as he celebrated the sacred mysteries, that the right hand of divine majesty appeared above him and made the canonical signs just as he did. After the death of the divine bishop, however, for our sins God *made the darkness* of foolishness *and it was the night* of arrogance *when all the beasts of the forest crept*

---

656 During the crusade of 1101 Thiemo was captured by the Turks after the ambush of the main expedition near Ereghli. See J. Riley-Smith (1986) p. 131.

657 The fact that Thiemo's death (28 September 1101) occurred soon after his capture gave rise to the traditon that he had been martyred.

658 Udalric, bishop of Passau (1092–1121). See above pp. 64, 68. For 'Lorch': above p. 360 and n. 644.

659 6 August 1121: see G. Meyer von Knonau (1909) p. 179.

660 Herluca of Epfach, according to M. Maier (1963) p. 314. But see J. Greving (1893) p. 118.

forth. The young lions roared for their prey, seeking their food from God,[661] namely, the evil spirits and, deplorable to relate, they corrupted this priest, who had hitherto been free of the pangs of lust. The virgin was informed of this in the following way. It seemed to her, when he was participating once more in the divine mysteries, that the right hand of God still appeared but that now it seemed to hang down feebly, incapable of accomplishing anything. This was revealed to the virgin by heaven. Henceforward she declined to be present at the offices of unchaste priests according to the Gregorian prohibition and directed her thoughts with faith and prayer on those to whom she could not show her bodily presence. Through the wonderful generosity of the Saviour she began to sense in her mouth that sweet taste which she had known when from time to time she had actually received communion from catholics and she rejoiced at this palpable experience of the sacraments.

123 Bishop Udalric of blessed memory loved this virgin above all the other virgins because of her innate goodness but no less because of the honourable widowhood of her holy mother and the praiseworthy virginity of her aunts, all of whom educated her in Christ. Concerning her mother, whose name was Helisea,[662] it should briefly be added that in her fervent obedience to our Gregory she was distinguished for her many virtues and her spirit of prophecy. At the time of her passage from this world she was visited by good spirits and, seeking out a suitable solitary place, she journeyed to Christ with them as her escort. Immediately on their return, her sisters found her in the likeness of Paul the first hermit,[663] with her hands stretched out to God like a suppliant. There is no doubt that the pious Creator made manifest in the dead woman how devoutly she had prayed to him while she was alive.

124 It remains for us perhaps to write down a narrative of two miracles accomplished by heaven in Salerno, one just as the blessed Gregory arrived,[664] the other shortly after he left this world. For on the first occasion that he had preached there, a certain peasant among the bystanders was prompted by an evil mind to say to himself, 'Behold the author of conflict and discord: after disturbing the whole

---

661 Psalm 103: 20–1.

662 Wife of Baldebertus (family unknown): M. Maier (1963) pp. 314, 325.

663 Paul of Thebes (✝ 341), hermit in Egypt.

664 Late June 1084: see H. E. J. Cowdrey (1998) p. 231.

world,[665] he has come to trouble this city.' When he wished to declare these thoughts aloud, he was pained to find that he had been made dumb. Compelled by necessity, he approached the man of God, fell at his feet and indicated by such signs as he could devise that he had sinned and that he repented. The pope had pity on him and blessed him, whereupon he recovered the power of speech in order to give thanks to God and to His servant. After the pope had died and was buried, in the silence of night thieves entered the church, wishing to open his tomb and to steal the papal vestments.[666] They encountered, however, a wind of such strength that all the lamps that burned in the crypt of blessed Matthew were blown out and they themselves were overtaken by madness and remained lying on the ground until they became a spectacle for the clergy and people.

665 For this theme in anti-Gregorian polemic see I. S. Robinson (1978a) pp. 95–100.
666 For similar incidents: R. Elze (1978) pp. 1–18. See H. E. J. Cowdrey (1998) p. 678.

I.

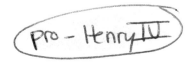

APPENDIX I: Benzo of Alba to Emperor Henry IV

Book VII

1 To his lord, Henry III, august emperor of the Romans,[1] brother Benzo, a bishop without a bishopric,[2] enfeebled in his eyes and his feet:[3] *I wait for thy salvation, O Lord.*[4] There is no man under the heavens who can say, *O Caesar*, how much you owe God for so many gracious mercies and for the granting of innumerable victories. *Offer to God,* therefore, *a sacrifice of praise and pay your vows to the Most High;*[5] for the Creator expects such recompense. And *let us lift up our hearts and hands to God in heaven,*[6] so that He will always defend you with the protection of Michael.[7] When you have hacked through the necks of the adversaries,[8] deliver us *from the nets of the fowlers.*[9] Since, my lord, you do not have the leisure to read works of history, deign at least to read this summary excerpted from the Book of the Popes.[10] For that sarabaite[11]

1 Henry IV, king of the Germans (1056–1106), emperor (1084). The usual form of his title in diplomas after the imperial coronation was 'Henry III, emperor of the Romans'. See I. S. Robinson (1999) p. 231. The chancery described him as 'Henry III' because King Henry I of the Germans (911–36) did not receive the imperial title.

2 See above p. 84.

3 Illness prevented him from attending a council of the bishops of northern Italy, June 1084: Benzo, *Ad Heinricum* VII prologue, p. 580.

4 Genesis 49:18.

5 Psalm 49:14.

6 Lamentations 3:41.

7 The Archangel Michael (Revelation 12:7). Cf. Benzo, *Ad Heinricum* VI, preface p. 500 ('just as Michael ... laid low the dragon and his followers, in the same way Saxon barbarism was put to flight by Emperor Henry').

8 Cf. Psalm 28:4.

9 Cf. Psalm 90:3; 123:7.

10 The *Liber pontificalis*: H. Leclercq (1930) col. 354–466. Cf. Benzo, *Ad Heinricum* VII.4, p. 204.

11 A monk who rejected 'the yoke of regular discipline', i.e. the stability (*stabilitas loci*) demanded by the Benedictine Rule (IV.78, LVIII.17, *CSEL* 75, 35, 136). Benzo used this word, his favourite term of abuse for Gregory VII, to stigmatise Hildebrand as a monk who left his monastery without the abbot's permission (cf. below p. 370). Gregory VII's monastic career: above pp. 60, 188, 266.

had said that it lay in his power to raise whomsoever he wished to the empire and to remove anyone whom he did not want.[12] But he is shown to be guilty of falsehood by the evidence of the Book of the Popes. There indeed we read that the appointment of pope and bishops is made and ought to be made by the hands of kings and emperors.

2 Since we wish and ought to say something about the most impious heresy of Folleprandellus,[13] it is necessary to begin briefly with earlier events. When Emperor Constantine[14] was converted to the observance of the Christian religion by divine revelation and by the worthy preaching of St Silvester,[15] he strengthened the Catholic faith *in many and various ways.*[16] After he drew those in high office in Rome and almost all the city with him to the apostolic faith, he established by edict that all should conform to one and the same profession of the sacred faith. For this reason he left his patrician[17] in Rome to defend the commonwealth and he wished the apocrisiarius[18] whom he received from the hands of the pope to be in Constantinople to maintain ecclesiastical discipline. Thus the apocrisiarius would counter anyone presuming to talk nonsense against the faith and the patrician would oppose anyone wishing to inflict an injury on the Roman church. And since the election of the pope was carried out in subterranean places for fear of the pagans,[19] he commanded that henceforward it should be celebrated solemnly in an assembly of the people in this manner. If the emperor was in a place where a Roman embassy could reach him in one or two months, the election would be delayed while His Clemency was asked by the envoy whether it pleased him to be present in person. If, however, the emperor was in a distant part of the world, on this side or the other side of the sea, the patrician should sit in state in

---

12 Benzo here attacks the Gregorian claim to depose emperors (Gregory VII, *Registrum* II.55a, *Dictatus papae* 12, p. 204) and replace them according to the principle of 'suitability' (above p. 13), as in the sentence of the papal synod of March 1080 against Henry IV and in favour of the anti-king Rudolf (above p. 350).

13 One of Benzo's contemptuous versions of the name Hildebrand, others being 'Aldeprandus' and most often 'Prandellus'. This version uses the medieval Latin adjective *follis* or *follus,* 'foolish'. For other plays on the name see above p. 87.

14 Constantine I, emperor (306–37).

15 Pope Silvester I (314–35). Cf. *Vita Silvestri I, Liber pontificalis* 1, 172–84.

16 Hebrews 1:1.

17 Benzo's conception of the patrician as the representative of the Byzantine emperor: P. E. Schramm (1929) 1, 218, 234–5. See also above pp. 56–8.

18 The envoy of the pope to the Byzantine emperor.

19 Cf. John 7:13.

place of the emperor and the election should be performed by the clergy, the senate and the people according to God's will. Finally no one was to presume to receive consecration until he obtained the imperial consent either in person or by his letter. We read that no one ever violated this command, except for Pelagius,[20] who dared not send his embassy to the emperor because of the very frequent raids of the Lombards around Rome. The emperor, learning the true facts of the case from the patrician, did not take it amiss because it was not done with evil intent. We believe, moreover, that it is not unknown to the bishops and the wise clergy how the blessed Gregory[21] was enthroned through the efforts of the patrician Germanus,[22] according to the will and the command of Emperor Maurice.[23] Whoever wishes to learn how long this lasted, might deign to read through the Book of the Popes. There he will find how secure was the imperial judgement against those who dared to break the inviolable laws of the sacred order. For in the time of the Greeks or the Franks or the Germans who gained possession of the citadel of the Roman empire,[24] the perpetrator of this sacrilege never escaped punishment. Finally Otto III,[25] whose great deeds are proclaimed throughout the whole world, punished the criminal presumption of a certain false pope[26] by mutilating his ears, tongue and nose and gouging out his eyes. O man of men, O emperor of emperors, whose nobility of spirit will be remembered forever and ever! If he was Otto the *third* and you, Emperor Henry, are Henry the *third*, then, O you two *thirds*,[27] be one in the same fellowship of law.

But let us come to the matter in hand. When our lord Emperor Henry II[28] wished to come to Rome to receive his consecration, he heard that

20 Pope Pelagius II (579–90). Cf. *Vita Pelagii II, Liber pontificalis* 1, 309.

21 Pope Gregory I (590–604).

22 Germanus, not patrician but 'prefect of the city'. Cf. John the Deacon, *Vita Gregorii I* I.44, *MPL* 75, col. 81B.

23 Emperor Maurice (582–602). On the Gregorian preoccupation with the election of Gregory I see above pp. 61–2, 220.

24 On Benzo's treatment of the theory of 'the translation of the empire' see also *Ad Heinricum* III.1, p. 266: 'Peter and Paul ... alternately conferred [the Roman empire] according to their will now on the Greeks, now on the Gauls, now on the Lombards and finally surrendered it to the Germans to be their eternal possession'. See P. E. Schramm (1929) p. 273; G. Koch (1972) p. 106.

25 Otto III, king of the Germans (983–1002), emperor (996).

26 Antipope John XVI (John Philagathos, 997–8). See above p. 56.

27 Cf. Benzo, *Ad Heinricum* III.6, p. 284: 'Benzo of Alba ... wishes for the divine Henry, most serene king, the spirit of Otto III'.

28 Henry III, king of the Germans (1039–56), emperor (1046).

three devils[29] had usurped the throne of the apostolic see. He commanded them to meet him in Sutri, but only two of them came there.
A synod was held there, over which the king presided together with
the bishops and in which both men were condemned by a just
judgement, while the third man, who fled, was struck down by the
thunderbolt of anathema. They came to Rome. On the next day a
council was assembled in the church of the prince of the apostles,[30] in
which King Henry presided in the midst of the bishops. The whole
Roman nobility was present in all its ranks, surrounded by dukes and
princes holding various offices, among whom was also Margrave
Boniface.[31] After they assembled, *they all became still and waited eagerly
in silence.*[32] Then the king said, 'Roman lords, hitherto you have been
allowed to make a wise or a foolish election, choosing whomsoever
you wished in whatever way you pleased: behold! let your election be
made in the customary manner; take whom you will from this whole
assembly.' With a single spirit and with the same purpose they
replied, 'When the royal majesty is present, the election is no longer
in our jurisdiction or according to our will. And if you happen to be
absent on a number of occasions, nevertheless you always participate
in the elevation of a pope through the office of the patrician, who is
your deputy. For the patrician is not the patrician of the pope but
rather the patrician of the emperor, to attend to the affairs of the
commonwealth. We confess, therefore, that we have gone astray and,
less than wise, we have enthroned fools and ignorant men. It belongs
to your imperial power to improve the commonwealth with laws,
adorn it with morals[33] and control this holy apostolic church with
your defending arm, so that it suffers no harm.' They then took counsel
and with the approval of the holy synod and with the commendation
of the senators and the other Roman citizens and the multitudes of
nobles and people gathered there, it was decreed that King Henry,
together with all those succeeding him in the imperial monarchy,

---

29 Benedict IX (1033–45), Silvester III (1045–6) and Gregory VI (1045–6). On the
   synod of Sutri (20 December 1046): above p. 5.

30 The synod of Rome, 23–24 December 1046, in which Benedict IX was deposed and
   Clement II elected.

31 Boniface II of Canossa, margrave of Tuscany (1030–52), father of Matilda of Tuscany: above p. 189.

32 Virgil, *Aeneid* 2.1.

33 Cf. Horace, *Epistulae* 2.1.

should become the patrician,[34] just as we read to have happened in the case of Charles.[35] Immediately a shout was raised to heaven, in which were intermingled the voices of clerks and laymen praising God. The king was then clad in a bright green mantle, invested with the patrician's ring and crowned with the golden circlet of that same office.[36] Then he was requested by all the ranks of the people on bended knees to elect according to God's will and after careful investigation such pontiffs whose teaching would purge the pestilential sickness of the Church and recall the feeble world to salvation.[37] At the king's command they all rose and sang the holy litany, shedding tears as they did so.[38] Then the king took the bishop of Bamberg[39] with his powerful right hand and caused him to sit in the apostolic seat. He was saluted by them all according to the custom and the synod was brought to an end. On the day of the Lord's Nativity the pope was *(1046-7)* consecrated and King Henry was anointed by his hands with the oil of the Holy Spirit and raised to the empire.[40] The pope was called *Clement II* Clement and deservedly so; for he was good and kind,[41] pleasing to *(1047-8)* God and men.[42] He was succeeded by the bishop of Brixen,[43] rich in *Damasus II* the knowledge of literature; but he lived in the city only twenty-three days.[44] After him the lord Leo[45] was appointed by the same emperor *Leo IX* and it seems superfluous to say anything about him, since he has his *(1048/9-* altar in the church of St Peter. *1054)*

34 According to Benzo (unlike Bonizo, *Book to a Friend* V, above p. 187) the Romans conferred the patriciate on Henry III before Clement II's election and the imperial coronation. See P. E. Schramm (1929) pp. 234–5; H. Vollrath (1974) pp. 14–18; G. Martin (1994) pp. 263–5.

35 Charles (Charlemagne), king of the Franks (768–814), emperor (800), received the title of patrician from Pope Stephen II, 754. See above p. 188.

36 On the insignia of the patrician (cf. below p. 373): P. E. Schramm (1929) pp. 232–3; P. E. Schramm (1954) p. 73; T. Struve (1988) p. 436 n. 53.

37 For this language of reform see Peter Damian, *Letter* 20, p. 201 (to Henry III): 'the golden age of David is renewed now at the very end of the world'.

38 The litany was usually part of the opening liturgy of a synod, which ended with the *Te Deum*: M. Klöckener (1980) p. 126.

39 Suidger, bishop of Bamberg (1040–7); Pope Clement II (1046–7).

40 25 December 1046. See above p. 187

41 Cf. II Maccabees 15:12.

42 Cf. I Samuel 2:26.

43 Poppo, bishop of Brixen (1039–48); Pope Damasus II (1047–8).

44 Elected 25 December 1047, consecrated 17 July 1048; †9 August 1048. See above p. 189.

45 Pope Leo IX (1048/9–54).

When the lord Leo slept the sleep of peace, there came to the emperor's court three monks, ostensibly from Rome – although they were not from Rome, for the first of them was from Tuscany, another from Burgundy, a third from Apulia, and one was called Aldeprandus,[46] the second Humbert,[47] the last Boniface[48] – and they pretended that they were performing a legation for the election of the future pastor.[49] Father Herman, archbishop of Cologne[50] said to them, 'Since you are monks, this affair does not concern you. You are runaways from St Benedict and wish to be bound by no rule.[51] If it pleases my lord the emperor, we should wait for the Romans; meanwhile let him order you to be kept under guard.' They therefore remained with that archbishop in the court without the punishment of captivity.[52] And behold! suddenly the embassy of the Romans arrived[53] and they were amazed by the deceits of the monks. It was the will of all the bishops, therefore, that the lord emperor should bind these sarabaites with an oath, according to which they themselves should never become popes nor should they intervene by any device in the election of the pope.[54]

46 Hildebrand. Cf. Bonizo, *Book to a Friend* V, above p. 194. Hildebrand's alleged Tuscan origins: above p. 262.

47 Humbert, cardinal bishop of Silva Candida (1050–61). His origins: above p. 191.

48 Presumably Boniface, cardinal bishop of Albano (?1057–?1072): see T. Schmidt (1973) p. 381; R. Hüls (1977) p. 89.

49 On Benzo's account of this legation of 1054 see T. Schmidt (1973) pp. 382–6; H. E. J. Cowdrey (1998) pp. 33–4.

50 Herman II, archbishop of Cologne (1036–56). His concern with the legation arose from his duties as imperial arch-chancellor of the Italian kingdom and arch-chancellor of the holy Roman church: D. Lück (1970a) pp. 1–50.

51 See above p. 365 n. 11.

52 In *Registrum* I.79, p. 113 Gregory VII recalled his stay in Cologne during Herman's archiepiscopate, evidently in 1047–8: see H. E. J. Cowdrey (1998) p. 29. Hence T. Schmidt (1973) p. 385: during the 1054 legation Hildebrand was Herman's guest, which Benzo chose to interpret as house-arrest.

53 The occasion was the council of Mainz, November 1054: see T. Schmidt (1973) p. 382 n. 40.

54 Cf. the letter of the bishops at the council of Worms, January 1076 (*Die Briefe Heinrichs IV*. p. 67): 'In the time of Emperor Henry ... you bound yourself by a corporeal oath never to accept the papacy yourself in the lifetime of the emperor or his son ... or to allow another to receive it without the assent and approval of the father or the son ... And still today there are, as witnesses to this oath, very many bishops who saw it then with their own eyes and heard it with their own ears.' This accusation recurs in imperial polemic. Hence W. Goez (1968) pp. 139–44 concluded that Hildebrand was indeed elected pope contrary to the terms of an oath that he had taken in 1054. T. Schmidt (1973) pp. 374–86 suggested that at Victor II's election Hildebrand (and his fellow legates) took an oath to abide by the decision of Henry III or his son in papal elections and that this was the basis of the later Henrician polemic against Gregory VII.

saraba1k

And this was done. What more is there to tell? The lord Victor[55] was elected and brought to Rome and he was received with great happiness by the whole assembly of the commonwealth in a solemn procession. The aforementioned acephalous men[56] followed him, but they were not received into the pope's secret counsels. Finally Prandellus,[57] more cunning than the others, formed links with the bankers,[58] wishing to be acceptable to the pope at least in financial matters and thus, *(simony)* whether the pope liked it or not, he went in and out like a troublesome dog, although he was excluded from the fullness of his grace.[59]

After these events, grievous to relate, our lord Emperor Henry left our earthly pilgrimage and was carried up to heaven.[60] There remained a boy king[61] with his imperial mother[62] and the Romans broke their oath and wandered from the righteous way. For after a few days had passed, the lord Victor died[63] and a new idol[64] was set up by the Romans in the church of Constantine.[65] Godfrey, who was called duke,[66] delighting in troubling the situation of the boy king,[67] took money and made an alliance with them. Prandellus, however, did not forget his association with those sarabaites[68] who were partners in his imposture and

55 Pope Victor II (1054–7), consecrated in Rome 13 April 1055.

56 I.e. monks without an abbot, living an unstable life: above p. 365 n. 11.

57 Hildebrand: see above p. 366 n. 13.

58 The allusion is to Hildebrand's dealings with the merchant and banking family of Jewish origin, the Pierleoni. Cf. Beno, *Gesta Romanae ecclesiae* II.9, p. 379 ('He filled his coffers and entrusted that money to the son of a certain Jew, recently baptised but retaining the manners of the money-changers, whom he made his familiar'). See K. Jordan (1933–4) p. 68; D. B. Zema (1944) pp. 169–75.

59 Victor II employed him as a legate: H. E. J. Cowdrey (1998) pp. 32, 35 and also above p. 200 n. 26.

60 5 October 1056.

61 Henry IV (born 11 November 1050).

62 Empress Agnes (†1077).

63 28 July 1057.

64 I.e. Pope Stephen IX (1057–8). Benzo also used this pejorative term for Nicholas II (below p. 372) and Alexander II (*Ad Heinricum* II.15, III.1, pp. 240, 270).

65 The Lateran basilica. Stephen IX was elected 2 August, consecrated 3 August. See above p. 196.

66 Godfrey 'the Bearded', duke of Upper Lotharingia, Lower Lotharingia, margrave of Tuscany (†1069). See above p. 10.

67 Twice imprisoned for rebellion against Henry III, Godfrey was reconciled to Henry IV and Empress Agnes (1056) and proved a consistent (although self-interested) supporter of the new king: E. Goez (1995) pp. 20–9; I. S. Robinson (1999) pp. 31–3, 37, 42, 49, 54–5.

68 See above p. 370 and nn. 47–8.

he entered Siena, where together with Beatrice,[69] without the knowledge of the Romans, he set up another false and worthless idol.[70] As one born in adultery,[71] he ought not to be admitted to so great a mystery. O fathers, senators, blessed ones of the eternal Father, reflect, decide and bring Prandellus to judgement. For as the truth bears witness, he is proved guilty of many offences: firstly, because the election of the pope in no way belongs to his office; then, because he confirmed on oath that he would not do so, and by doing so he has fallen into perjury;[72] furthermore, because evil was done, since he acted not together with the Romans and not in Rome but in the city of Siena, as if in a hyena's cave.[73] Finally, he bound that most wretched man by an oath to do nothing except according to his word of command. There is worse to come, that seriously vexes the heart. O heaven, O earth, why do you not show your anger? Men are insensible, if they do not demonstrate their horror at such fantastical conduct. Prandellus corrupted the Romans with much money and many perjuries and held a synod, in which he crowned his idol with a royal crown.[74] When the bishops saw this, *they became like dead men*.[75] On the lower circlet of this crown[76] the inscription could be read: 'The crown of the kingdom from the hand of God'; and on the other circlet thus: 'The diadem of the empire from the hand of St Peter'.[77] Seek out the book of Augustine *On the City of God* and learn what the dreadful hand of Emperor Pompey wrought in the case of a similar act of presumption.[78]

69 Beatrice, margravine of Tuscany (✝1076). See above p. 194.

70 Pope Nicholas II (1058–61), elected in Siena, 6 December: above p. 202 n. 37.

71 Cf. Benzo, *Ad Heinricum* I.9, pp. 174, 176 ('They say that it is a mortal sin for bastards to be placed in the office of bishop').

72 See above p. 370 and n. 54.

73 Cf. Benzo, *Ad Heinricum* VI.6, p. 562: on Henry IV's triumphal entry into Rome, 'like the hyena, [Gregory VII] wished to hide in a burial vault'. (Hyenas made their dens in graves: Pliny the Elder, *Historia naturalis* VIII.44.106.)

74 Nicholas II was crowned in the papal synod of April 1059. Benzo similarly claimed that Alexander II and Gregory VII were crowned in their synods (below pp. 374, 375). Perhaps Hildebrand performed the coronation by virtue of his new appointment as archdeacon. On this ceremony: E. Eichmann (1951) pp. 36–40; P. E. Schramm (1954) p. 63.

75 Matthew 28:4. Benzo, an eyewitness of this synod of 1059 (above p. 204), provides the earliest evidence of the crown as part of the papal insignia: H.-W. Klewitz (1941) pp. 96–8, 114.

76 The appearance of the papal crown: P. E. Schramm (1971) p. 1.

77 Cf. Isaiah 62:3. See P. E. Schramm (1954) p. 63.

78 Augustine, *De civitate Dei* XVIII.45.

Meanwhile Prandellus gave fodder to his Nicholas in the Lateran palace, like an ass in a stall.[79] The nicholaite[80] did nothing that was not ordered by the sarabaite. It is shameful to relate how many men of distinction were struck down by the madness of Prandellus through the excommunicating tongue of his frenzied herald. Anno of Cologne[81] stood up to avenge his own injury and that of others, having ascertained the fact that that man was born of an adulterous relationship. On the unanimous advice of the orthodox, he sent him a letter of excommunication and after he saw it, grieving and groaning, he departed from this life.[82]

The Romans indeed, mindful of better things, met together and promised to make amends for their sins against the boy king. They therefore sent him the mantle, the mitre, the ring and the circlet of the patrician by the hands of the bishops, the cardinals and the senators and through those who seemed to be more eminent among the people.[83] As soon as they appeared at court, however, the nobility were summoned from the whole of Italy and from the other kingdoms. For it seemed to the lady empress and to her counsellors that the gifts from Rome ought not to be received except in the presence of the foremost men of the kingdoms.[84] Meanwhile, as they waited for them, Prandellus had not forgotten his cunning; he became anxious and began to twist and turn. He sought out Richard of Capua[85] and brought him to the city on condition of paying him one thousand pounds, so that he might provide him with help in setting up the new Antichrist. What more is there to tell? Richard took the money and

79 Cf. Benzo, *Ad Heinricum* III.10, p. 298. A similar view of Hildebrand's influence over Nicholas II was presented by Beno, *Gesta Romanae ecclesiae* II.10, pp. 379–80; but see A. Michel (1953) pp. 133–61.

80 Unchaste priest: a play on the name Nicholas. See above p. 357 n. 629.

81 Anno II, archbishop of Cologne (1056–75). H.-G. Krause (1960) pp. 126–41 placed this passage in the context of the breach between papacy and imperial court in 1061. See also G. Jenal (1974) pp. 166–9; I. S. Robinson (1999) pp. 40–1.

82 Peter Damian, *Letter* 89, pp. 559–60 referred to 'a council, in which [the imperial government] condemned the pope supposedly by a synodal judgement', shortly before Nicholas's death (19/20 July 1061). See H. Zimmermann (1968) p. 148; R. Somerville (1977) pp. 157–66.

83 The Roman envoys were Count Gerard of Galeria and the abbot of S. Gregorio Magno: see above p. 206 n. 69.

84 Council of Basel, 28 October 1061: see G. Meyer von Knonau (1890) pp. 224–5; T. Schmidt (1977) pp. 108–10, 126–7.

85 Richard I, prince of Capua (✝1078). Richard's role in the election of 1061: G. Meyer von Knonau (1890) pp. 219–22; T. Schmidt (1977) p. 83.

attempted to bring the heretic of Lucca[86] to St Peter ad Vincula,[87] but the Romans resisted him with weapons of war. There was great slaughter on both sides and so the day ended. Richard, however, aided by the dark gloom of the night, advanced by another route and with bloody hands he enthroned the pope of the night and conveyed him to the Lateran palace.[88] Behold, a battle between angels and devils: while the king, together with the bishops, appointed their pope[89] justly and lawfully, Prandellus on the other hand, together with the Normans, appointed theirs simoniacally. What an appointment! This man of Lucca, called Alexander, originally invented the Pataria[90] and betrayed to enemies the secret of his lord archbishop,[91] to whom he had taken an oath. Together with his close kinsman Landulfinus,[92] he abused a certain nun. Such a man was raised over the Christian people and, what is dreadful to hear, let alone to see, he was crowned like a king in the synod.[93] *Judge rightly, you sons of men, whether indeed you speak righteousness,*[94] whether such an illusion of demons ought to reign in holy Church; whether any monk can create a pope of any kind, illegitimate, simoniac or heretical?[95] For *to do whatever one wishes with impunity, that is to be a king.*[96] Why does not the whole world rise up against the monstrous behaviour of this new Proteus[97] and the heretical wickedness of a second Arius?[98] Where are men like Herman of Cologne? Where

86 Anselm I, bishop of Lucca (1056–73); Pope Alexander II (1061–73). See above p. 206 n. 64.

87 Alexander II was enthroned during the night of 30 September–1 October in the church of St Peter ad Vincula: see above p. 206 n. 65.

88 Cf. Benzo, *Ad Heinricum* II.2, p. 198 ('Richard, girded with a bloody sword, placed [Alexander] on the throne with the same hand with which he sent three Roman noblemen to their death'). See C. Erdmann (1935) pp. 118–19.

89 Cadalus, bishop of Parma (1046–?1071); antipope 'Honorius II'. See above p. 207 n. 75.

90 The connections of Alexander (of the Milanese family of da Baggio) with the Pataria: C. Violante (1955) pp. 147–73; T. Schmidt (1977) p. 9.

91 Wido, archbishop of Milan (1045–71). According to Landulf Senior, *Historia Mediolanensis* III.5, p. 76, 'Wido himself had consecrated [Anselm] to the priesthood' and recommended him to Henry III for the bishopric of Lucca.

92 Nothing further is known about this kinsman or about this incident.

93 See above p. 372 and n. 73.

94 Psalm 57:2.

95 Cf. Benzo, *Ad Heinricum* II.4, p. 206 ('It is unheard-of throughout all the ages that the appointment of the pope should be in the hands of monks').

96 Sallust, *Bellum Iugurthinum* XXXI.26.

97 A sea-god, servant of Neptune, who often changed his shape: used here of Hildebrand.

98 The heresiarch Arius: see above p. 162.

are men like Aribo of Mainz?[99] Where are they and also those men who are not commemorated in writing? Monks and women[100] put bishops to flight, as if Hercules was in pursuit. Monks, I say, and what monks! – branded with perjury, befouled by the debauching of nuns. And these are the creators of popes, bringing disgrace on those who are the rulers of churches.

Truly, those whom Prandellus planted were grass:[101] they lived as long as he wished and went the way of all flesh[102] when he wished. Finally, when it pleased him that the man of Lucca, whom he called Alexander, should depart, he ordered Archigenes[103] to come and cut open a vein, so that through loss of blood the soul might be divorced from the body. And this was done.[104] Immediately the streets were full of running feet; money loosened the reins of generosity. Everyone had not only his purse but even his sack stuffed full of Byzantine coins,[105] so that Folleprandus might be seized, might be taken prisoner and might be dragged, as if unwilling, to the see.[106] All Rome resounds with shouts *and Queen Money confers both noble birth and beauty.*[107] The business was completed: the demon called Legion[108] was raised on high, the man in the monk's cowl was crowned; wearing the mitre, he went to the Capitol. Those who were present saw this proverb: if a servant mounts a horse, madness drives him.[109] O malady beyond all maladies, O grief beyond the griefs of death, that a sacrilegious man,

99 Aribo, archbishop of Mainz (1021–31).

100 Cf. Benzo, *Ad Heinricum* VI.4, p. 546: 'Their monks ... run here and there through all the regions, bent on doing harm; they even incite little women against [the king].' The allusion is to the rebellion of Matilda, margravine of Tuscany against Henry IV: see A. Overmann (1895) p. 152; T. Struve (1995) pp. 60–1.

101 Cf. Psalm 102:15; Isaiah 40:6.

102 Cf. I Kings 2:2.

103 A famous physician invoked by Juvenal, *Saturae* VI.236, XIII.98, XIV.252.

104 In the decree of Brixen, 1080 (*Die Briefe Heinrichs IV.* pp. 70–1) Gregory VII was accused of murdering his four predecessors. See C. Mirbt (1894) pp. 592–3.

105 Cf. Decree of Brixen, p. 71 (Gregory 'imposed himself by means of violence, deceit and money'); Wido of Ferrara, *De scismate Hildebrandi* II, p. 553 ('on the night following Alexander's death he brought out his treasure-chests and poured out much money among the Romans'). See C. Erdmann (1935) pp. 142–4.

106 A parody of the passage from John the Deacon, *Vita Gregorii* I.44, *MPL* 75, col. 81B on which Gregorian authors modelled their accounts of the election of Gregory VII. See above p. 220 and n. 4 and I. S. Robinson (1978a) pp. 31–9.

107 Horace, *Epistulae* I.6.37.

108 Cf. Mark 5:9; Luke 8:30.

109 This proverb has not be traced.

an adulterer,[110] a perjurer, a murderer, a pope-murderer besides, leprous in body and soul,[111] sorcerer,[112] sarabaite, bedecked with such pearls, becomes a citizen of Peter! And although he stank of so much dung, he despised all men and even cursed some of them. For a vessel reeks of whatever it may contain.[113] But if this blasphemer reviles any of the faithful, it is as if the devil had inflicted an injury on Michael.[114] Everyone is praised or branded with infamy according to his works,[115] for his works follow him. Truly *everyone who commits sin, is a slave to sin;*[116] he who does the work of the devil is the slave of the devil. The false monk's cowl has therefore become the heart of the devil. His curse is therefore worth nothing, since he himself is cursed and a liar, like the father of lies from the beginning.[117] That hand that clears away filth must be clean. Who does not know the rest? He was driven from the city and is rotting.[118] The devil has no blessing and there is no way that he can bless. Indeed he possesses a curse, because he is accursed. If perhaps he casts over the faithful what is his own, there is no doubt that he does them no harm. For how can the root of evil impart by inheritance what he does not possess? It is clear from conclusive proofs that the sarabaite Prandellus was not a pope, nor were they popes, those Satans whom he transformed into angels of light.[119] Whoever thinks differently about this is an enemy of the catholic faith and cannot be saved.

110 Cf. Decree of Worms (1076), *Die Briefe Heinrichs IV.* p. 68 ('cohabitation with a strange woman', i.e. Matilda of Tuscany). See H.E.J. Cowdrey (1998) pp. 300–1.

111 An allusion to the reformers' practice of associating leprosy with simony: e.g. Humbert, *Adversus simoniacos* I.16, 17, II.21, pp. 126, 128, 165.

112 Cf. Decree of Brixen, p. 72 ('openly devoted to divinations and dreams, practising necromancy with the help of a magical spirit').

113 A paraphrase of Horace, *Epistulae* I.2.69–70.

114 Cf. Revelation 12:7.

115 Cf. Revelation 14:13.

116 John 8:34.

117 Cf. John 8:44.

118 Gregory VII left Rome in June 1084: above p. 252. H. Seyffert, edition of *Ad Heinricum* pp. 9, 604 n. 138 argued that Gregory was still alive when Benzo completed his work and that the reference to 'rotting' signifies the extinction of his power (cf. Numbers 5:21, Jeremiah 13:9).

119 Cf. II Corinthians 11:14.

7
.

APPENDIX II: Bruno of Segni, The Sermon of the Venerable Bishop Bruno concerning Simoniacs[1]

1 Let us praise the saints of God, let us honour the friends of God, since He who gave them this great glory, virtue and excellence is Himself praised and magnified in them. I beg you, therefore, *Magnify the Lord with me*,[2] and on this great festival[3] of blessed Leo,[4] supreme pontiff and universal pope, let us exalt His name. *The whole world* was *plunged in evil*,[5] holiness had disappeared; righteousness had perished and truth had been buried. Iniquity reigned; avarice held dominion; Simon Magus[6] possessed the Church; bishops and priests were addicted to pleasure and fornication. Priests were not ashamed to take wives; they married openly; they contracted impious alliances and gave them legal sanction, although according to the laws they ought not to dwell in the same house as women. For the sacred canons forbid their order to live with any women, save only those who are entirely above suspicion.[7] What was worse, however, was that scarcely one was to be found among them who was not a simoniac or who had not been ordained by simoniacs. Hence even today some are to be found who, using false arguments and not understanding how the Church is administered, claim that at that time the priesthood became extinct in the Church. For they say: 'if they were all like that, that is, if they were all either simoniacs or ordained by simoniacs, where did you,

---

1 The twelfth-century scribe of the Milan codex (Biblioteca Ambrosiana Q.54) gave this work no title, but a later hand added 'Concerning the blessed Pope Leo'. The twelfth-century Wolfenbüttel codex (Helmstedt 718) gives the title used here, which fits the version of the text contained in this codex, omitting the biography of Leo IX (c. 2–9) and presenting only the discussion of the sacraments of simoniacs (c. 1, 10–16). See H. Tritz (1952) p. 298.

2 Psalm 33:4.

3 19 April.

4 Pope Leo IX (1048/9–1054).

5 I John 5:19.

6 For Simon Magus (Acts 8:9–24) see above p. 275 n. 95.

7 Cf. Council of Nicea (325) c. 3 (Dionysio-Hadriana, *MPL* 67, col. 147D; *Decretales Pseudoisidorianae* p. 258).

who are now in the priesthood, come from? From whom did you derive your orders, if not from them? There was no other source. The men who ordained you, therefore received their own orders from none other than those who were simoniacs or who had been ordained by simoniacs.' We shall reply to this later, since this question requires an extensive disputation.[8]

2 Meanwhile let us resume our discourse. Such was the Church, such were the bishops and priests, such also were the Roman pontiffs, who ought to enlighten all the rest. All *the salt* had become tasteless and there was no way of *restoring its savour;*[9] and *if the God of Hosts had not left us the seed, we should have been like Sodom and Gomorrah.*[10] In this time of crisis, therefore, the blessed Leo acceded to the apostolic see, so that this great *candle, placed on* the universal *candlestick* might *give light to all who are in the house.*[11] He was the bishop of Toul, Bruno by name,[12] of noble birth,[13] beautiful in his appearance but even more beautiful in his sanctity, well versed in literature, a master of doctrine,[14] adorned with an honourable character:[15] whatever qualifications are necessary for the episcopal order all joined together in him. Such a master was indeed needed at such a time and with such pupils. The men of religion assembled,[16] together with Emperor Henry,[17] a man most prudent in all things, and the envoys of the Romans, who were there at that time,[18] and they earnestly implored the bishop of Toul to help the Roman church, for the love of the princes of the apostles Peter and Paul and begged him not to be afraid to expose himself to danger for the sake of the Christian religion. For the men of that

---

8 Bruno's 'disputation' is found in c. 10–16 of this work (E. Sackur's edition, pp. 554–62). His central argument: 'It is clear concerning those who are ordained without simony inside the Church by simoniacs, whom they however believe to be catholics, that their ordination must be regarded as valid' (p. 561). On Bruno's discussion of simoniacal orders: L. Saltet (1907) pp. 223–4, 251–4; A. Schebler (1936) pp. 259–64.

9 Cf. Luke 14:34.

10 Isaiah 1:9; Romans 9:29.

11 Cf. Matthew 5:15.

12 Bishop of Toul (1026–51): see *Life of Pope Leo IX* I.12–II.4, above pp. 117–31.

13 Son of Hugh IV, count of Egisheim-Dagsburg: see above p. 99 and n. 16.

14 Cf. *Life of Leo IX* I.3–4, above p. 101 and n. 32.

15 Cf. Bonizo, *Book to a Friend* V, above p. 189.

16 Council of Worms, December 1048: see above p. 130.

17 Henry III, king of the Germans (1039–56), emperor (1046).

18 Including Bishop Hugh of Assisi: see *Life of Leo IX* II.4, above p. 131.

nation feared to live in this land of ours, since this meant moving from a very healthy place to a sickly one.[19] That blessed bishop, however, was afraid not of the unhealthiness of the place but of ascending to the pinnacle of so great a church. For we read that Moses did thus: when the Lord had wished to set him over the Israelite people, he said, *I beseech you, Lord, send whom you will send.*[20] At length overwhelmed by their prayers, he promised that he would do what they demanded under this condition: 'I am going to Rome and there, if the clergy and people willingly elect me as their pontiff, I shall do what you ask; otherwise, however, I shall not accept the election.'[21] They joyfully confirmed their decision and approved his condition.

In those days, however, there was in that place a certain Roman monk named Hildebrand,[22] a youth of noble qualities, of lucid mind and holy religion. The young man had gone there partly for the sake of learning, partly also so that he might enter some religious house under the Rule of St Benedict.[23] The blessed bishop summoned this man to him and, as soon as he became acquainted with his plans, his wishes and his piety, asked him to accompany him to Rome. When the young man said, 'I cannot', the bishop asked, 'Why not?' He replied, 'Because you are going to Rome to take possession of the Roman church not according to the principles of the canons but by means of the secular and royal power.' The bishop, however, as he was of a simple and most generous nature, patiently satisfied his objections, explaining everything that he wished to know.[24] In this way he imitated the example of the blessed apostle Peter, whose successor he was soon to be. For after he baptised Cornelius, a gentile and a stranger to the religion of the Jews, Peter was rebuked by the other apostles for entering the house of an uncircumcised man and he did not disdain to offer an explanation of all that he had done.[25] The bishop then came to Rome,

19 Cf. *Life* II.1, above p. 127.

20 Exodus 4:13.

21 Cf. *Life* II.4, above p. 131. See also above p. 34.

22 Hildebrand, archdeacon; Pope Gregory VII (1073–85). See above pp. 57, 190.

23 On Hildebrand's 'exile in the Lower Rhineland' see above p. 188 and n. 56. H.E.J. Cowdrey (1998) p. 29 suggested that Bruno's account was derived from Gregory's own reminiscences.

24 Bruno's version reconciles an account like that of *Life* II.4–5, above p. 131 (in which Leo himself made his election conditional) with that of Bonizo, *Book to a Friend* V, above p. 190 (in which Hildebrand persuaded Leo of the necessity of a canonical election in Rome).

25 Cf. Acts 11:2–18.

bringing that monk with him.[26] In this way he performed a service to
the blessed apostle Peter, because he brought back with him that man
by whose advice and wisdom the Roman church was henceforward to
be ruled and governed. For he was Pope Gregory VII, whose
prudence, constancy and fortitude, whose battles and labours must be
recounted in another work at another time.

Bruno was elected to the papacy by the clergy and people according
to Roman custom,[27] with great applause; then he was raised to the
throne of the blessed apostle Peter[28] – as I believe, through the
intervention of divine Providence – and his name was changed to Leo.
For *a Lion of the tribe of Judah,* from which this Leo originated, had
conquered.[29] He had become the most courageous of the beasts,[30] not
afraid to encounter anyone. His roar soon caused the earth to tremble,
terrifying the sacrilegious, disturbing the simoniacs and inflicting
wounds on the army of married priests. For this most blessed pontiff,
kindled by the fire of the Holy Spirit, was inflamed against the
simoniacs and he strengthened the ancient canons, so that the order
of the clergy would live chastely and piously.[31] Wherever it was
necessary, he condescended to grant dispensations and, imposing a
light penance, he showed mercy in the case of past sins and admonished them not to commit such offences in future. This ought not,
however, to be followed as a precedent – given that the pontiff acted
not according to his will but according to necessity[32] – unless perhaps
there is a similar case, in which the rulers of the Church are repeatedly compelled to tolerate what cannot be corrected. Who can
describe his great benevolence towards all men, his great humility, his
great clemency, how generous, how courteous, how compassionate he
was towards everyone? He became *all things to all men, that he might
win over* all men.[33] His speech was flavoured with salt and soothed the
pious and terrified the impious.

26 Cf. Gregory VII, *Registrum* VII.14a, p. 483 ('I returned ... with my lord Pope Leo');
   Bonizo *Book to a Friend* V, above p. 191.
27 Cf. Bonizo, *Book to a Friend* V, above p. 190 ('in the customary manner').
28 12 February 1049.
29 Revelation 5:5. Cf. *Life* II.8, above p. 134.
30 Cf. *De bestiis et aliis rebus* II.1, *MPL* 177, col. 56D-57D.
31 On Leo IX's reforming legislation: above pp. 6–7, 136–7, 191–2.
32 Cf. Innocent I, *Decreta* c. 55 (*JK* 303), *MPL* 67, 260.
33 I Corinthians 9:22.

3 Now, however, let us come to those works that the Lord wrought through him – not that we wish to write down everything that we have either heard about him or found in writing. The blessed Pope Gregory, whom we mentioned above, was accustomed to tell us many stories about this man (and most of what I have said so far, I remember having heard from him). He once spoke of Leo in our hearing and began to rebuke us – and me in particular, as it seemed to me, since he kept his eyes fixed on me[34] – for allowing the deeds of blessed Leo to fade into silence and not writing down what would bring glory to the Roman church and offer an example of humility to many who heard it. Since he spoke in general terms, however, and did not seem to be saying this to any one of us in particular, no one wrote down what he told us all ought to be recorded. I should not indeed have written this now, if I had not to some degree been compelled to write, as I shall demonstrate later.[35] May both these popes pardon me, because I know that in this I have offended them both.

Firstly, therefore, let us describe the wonder that, as we have heard, the power of God performed through him in the region of Gaul. For when the blessed Leo celebrated councils there[36] and many bishops were accused of simoniacal heresy, a certain man was accused among the rest, who was regarded as more suspect than the others. Since the accusation against him could not be proved by clear proofs, the pontiff adjured him to speak the truth about himself. He refused to tell the truth and tried by all means to conceal his iniquity. The blessed Leo said to him, 'If, as you claim, you are not a simoniac and if you have not sinned against the Holy Spirit, simply say, if you can, "Glory be to the Father and to the Son and to the Holy Spirit".' When he had said, 'Glory be to the Father and to the Son', although he made many attempts, he could by no means say, 'and to the Holy Spirit'. After he had very often repeated his efforts and could by no means speak aloud the name of the Holy Spirit, it was clear to all who were present that he had offended against the Holy Spirit, whose name he was unable to speak.[37] They all therefore gave thanks together to God, who had deigned to show them so novel a sign and so unheard-of a miracle.

34 Bruno's relations with Gregory VII: see above p. 89.

35 See below c. 9, p. 389.

36 Rheims (3–5 October 1049).

37 For other versions of this miracle, in which the central figure was not Leo but Hildebrand-Gregory VII, see above pp. 200, 270. In an early version of his *Dicta Anselmi* Alexander of Canterbury also ascribed this miracle to Leo IX, later changing the attribution to Hildebrand: F. S. Schmitt (1956) pp. 17–18.

Some of them were terrified by this judgement and privately came to the pope and accused themselves, opening up their consciences to him. Then the abbot of Cluny,[38] a young man of whom great hopes were entertained, was asked by the blessed Leo if he had ever had ambitions of ruling over his great abbey. As a disciple of the Truth, he replied, 'According to the flesh, I had; according to the spirit, I had not.'[39] This reply was so pleasing and seemed so praiseworthy to them all, that it was immediately inscribed on all their hearts with exceeding joy. They asked him in turn what answer he had given, so as to be able to understand his words. He, now *an old man and full of days*,[40] revered by all and loved by all, still rules with great wisdom over that same venerable monastery, a man praiseworthy in all respects, with hardly an equal and of matchless piety.[41]

4 I have heard the blessed Gregory recount another miracle of this pontiff that I think ought by no means to be omitted. He said that the blessed Leo had had a master, a wise and very devout man,[42] who entrusted a wooden goblet to him after he accepted the government of the Roman church. The venerable pontiff cherished this goblet to a remarkable degree and was accustomed to drink from it in preference to golden and silver vessels, because of his veneration for blessed Remigius, whose goblet this was said to be. It happened, however, that the goblet was carelessly set down, fell to the ground and split into two pieces. When according to his custom the blessed pontiff had ordered wine to be brought to him, the cupbearer appeared with an agitated countenance, well aware of the damage that had occurred. The pontiff said to him, 'What is wrong with you?' He replied, 'The goblet is broken.' The blessed Leo said, 'Truly broken?' The cupbearer replied, 'Broken, my lord.' 'Bring it to me,' he said. When he had brought it, the pontiff took it in his hands and, placing the pieces together, so that they fitted exactly in the way in which they had

---

38 Hugh I, abbot of Cluny (1049–1109).

39 The prelates at the council of Rheims were asked whether they had obtained their offices through simony. Different versions of Hugh's reply: Anselm of St-Remi, *Historia dedicationis* c. 14, col. 1432B; Gilo, *Vita Hugonis abbatis* I.8, p. 58; Raynald of Vézelay, *Vita Hugonis abbatis* c. 4.25, col. 903BC. See A. Kohnle (1993) pp. 69–70.

40 Genesis 35:29.

41 When Urban II consecrated the high altar at Cluny, 25 October 1095, Bruno was in his entourage. See R. Grégoire (1965) pp. 37, 109; A. Kohnle (1993) p. 124.

42 Abbot Herimar of St-Remi, Rheims (1048–71): see *Life of Leo IX* II.13, above p. 140. Desiderius, *Dialogi* III.61, pp. 1143–4 also named Gregory as his source. Other versions of this anecdote: above p. 140 n. 245.

formerly adhered to each other, he held it in his hands for a little while, then returned it sound and whole to the servant and said, 'Go and prepare a drink.' The blessed Gregory was present at this miracle and told it to us. Another man, although not a man of such great authority,[43] was also present and saw it and afterwards described it to me.

5 While the blessed Leo was in Rome, however, and had ruled the apostolic see in peace, many men came from the territory of Apulia, with their eyes gouged out, their noses cut off, their hands and feet maimed, piteously lamenting the cruelty of the Normans.[44] Thus it happened that this mildest of men, full of piety and mercy, having compassion on the immense suffering of the unfortunate people, attempted to humble the pride of that nation. He therefore assembled an army, of modest size indeed but composed of brave knights of his own nation,[45] and went to fight against the Normans.[46] He *had* indeed *a zeal for God, but* perhaps *it was not enlightened.*[47] Would that he had not gone there in person, but had only sent an army there to defend righteousness! [48] What more is there to tell? The armies of the two sides met; the many fought against the few.[49] There was enormous carnage; blood was shed on both sides. One side relied on courage, the other on numbers. The men in the former army could say, as they died, what we read that our Saviour said in His Passion: They *would have no power over* us, *unless it had been given to* them *from above.*[50] But why are the good overcome and the evil victorious? *O the depth of the riches and wisdom and knowledge of God! How unsearchable are His judgements and how inscrutable His ways!*[51] Those who fight for righteousness

---

43 Archbishop Hugh I of Besançon (1031–66) was identified as an eyewitness by *Life* II.13, above p. 140.

44 Cf. *Life* II.20, above p. 149; Bonizo, *Book to a Friend* V, above p. 192. See H. Taviani-Carozzi (1996) p. 188.

45 On the German troops in the papal army: C. Erdmann (1935) pp. 112–13; H. Taviani-Carozzi (1996) pp. 190, 192–5, 199, 206.

46 Leo IX's expedition of June 1053 against Count Humphrey of Apulia, Robert Guiscard and Richard of Aversa. See above pp. 8–9, 29, 52–3.

47 Romans 10:2.

48 An allusion to the canon law tradition that clergy should not be involved in secular warfare, which Leo IX himself had confirmed in his Council of Rheims c. 3: Anselm, *Historia dedicationis* c. 16, col. 1437B. See C. Erdmann (1935) pp. 12–16; F. Prinz (1971) pp. 5–34.

49 Battle of Civitate, 18 June 1053. See above pp. 150, 193.

50 John 19:11.

51 Romans 11:33.

are defeated; those who attack righteousness are victorious.[52] Neverthe-less the Apostle consoles us in such cases, saying, *We know that in everything God works for good with those who love Him.*[53] Whether they die or live, it is for their good. Whatever happens to them is for their good. All things work together for their good and death is more efficaci-ous for such men than life. For the death of His saints is precious in the sight of the Lord. For we must believe most firmly and in no way doubt that all who die for the sake of righteousness are placed among the martyrs.[54] May the Lord *place* them *among the princes of His people.*[55]

6 We omit much and from many examples we put together a few, since we have been ordered to write down not everything but a part of the whole. Suddenly rumours flew about, filling the earth, recoun-ting everywhere that a battle had taken place and that the knights of Christ and the army of the saints had been defeated. Then the pitiable pontiff returned to Benevento,[56] a city indeed faithful and friendly to the blessed Peter.[57] When the news of the pope's arrival was heard, the whole city rushed to meet him. Men and women, youths and virgins, old and young came, not as if in procession but with tears and lamentations. They stood bewildered and watched their coming while they were still at a distance; now the pontiff was drawing near, pre-ceded by the bishop and clergy, with sad faces and bowed heads. After the venerable pope came among them, however, and blessed them with his raised hand, shouts and mournful cries rose to heaven and the whole world resounded with weeping and lamentation. This was the procession with which he entered the city and such was the psalmody with which he came to the church. After remaining there a short time,[58] he returned to Rome and the lamentations and tears began afresh in each city on his way. Who, having originally seen him passing by with such an army, could contain his tears? Subsequently they saw him, bereft of that noble body of knights, returning only with his clergy. Arriving in Rome,[59] he hastened with all speed to the

52 This is one of the themes of Bonizo's *Book to a Friend*: see above p. 52.

53 Romans 8:28.

54 The fallen in the papal army at Civitate as martyrs: *Life of Leo IX* II.21, above p. 151 with n. 327; Bonizo, *Book to a Friend* V, above p. 193 with n. 91.

55 Psalm 112:8.

56 On 23 June 1053. See above pp. 151, 193.

57 Cf. Bonizo, *Book to a Friend* V, above p. 192 with n. 87.

58 Until 12 March 1054 (*Chronica monasterii Casinensis* II.84, p. 333).

59 On 24 or 25 March: above p. 193.

church of the blessed apostle Peter and humbly and very devoutly commended to him the souls of those who, for love of him and obedient to him even to the death, had shed their own blood in defence of righteousness, contrary to their just deserts.

While he remained there, it was revealed to him in his dreams that he must quickly depart from this world. He therefore ordered the bishops and cardinals and other clergy to be summoned to him and gently encouraged them to live chastely and to fight manfully against simoniacal heresy. He said to them, 'Know, my brethren, that after a few days I shall leave this world; for *during*[60] *this night* I, unhappy as I am and unworthy of the see of this church, entered through a vision into that other life, so that I am now weary of living in this life. I rejoice exceedingly, however, because *I saw* there *among* Christ's *martyrs those brothers* and friends of mine *who* followed me *into Apulia* and died *in defence* of righteousness. They were splendidly adorned, bearing *palms in their hands*, from which they might understand that they who thought that they had been conquered, were conquerors. And it was truly so. *Whatever is born of God overcomes the world and this is the victory that overcomes the world, our faith.*[61] They all cried out to me in a loud voice, saying, *"Come* to us, beloved, and *remain with us, because it was through you* that we have attained *this* great *glory."* But I heard others on the opposite side saying, "By no means: but you will come to us *on the third day."*[60] If I remain in this life after the third day, therefore, you will know that what I saw was not true.'[62] No one should be surprised that evil spirits wished to inspire fear in him to whom such happiness was announced in a vision; for they once dared to approach even our Lord and Saviour himself. For thus the Lord himself says: '*For the prince of this world is coming and he has no power over me.*'[63] But then Leo said, '*Go*, my brethren, *each* to your own home; but tomorrow return *to me.*'[64] All that night he prayed to the Lord, falling on his knees.

In the morning he ordered a tomb to be prepared for him.[65] The bishops and priests assembled again, as that most blessed man had commanded

60 /60 A paraphrase of Libuin, *De obitu sancti Leonis papae IX* c. 2, col. 527A.

61 I John 5:4.

62 A paraphrase of Libuin, *De obitu* c. 2, col. 527AB.

63 John 14:30.

64 Cf. Libuin, *De obitu* c. 2, col. 527B.

65 Cf. *ibid.*, c. 3, col. 527B.

them the previous day. Sitting in his bed, he said to them *as*[66] *they sat* in the church: 'Hear me, our *brethren* and fellow bishops and likewise all you who have gathered here. Above all *I command* you not to sell *the lands* of the Church and *the vines*, castles, houses and other *property of the Church* and no one is to claim *possession* of them for himself. You are not to use *oaths*. Beware of *incest*.[67] You are to do no injury to the servants of blessed Peter who come here and you are not to deceive them in business dealings. Give tithes freely of *all that you possess*.'[66] Then *turning*[68] *to the cross*, he poured out many prayers to the Lord for them all, humbly asking and praying that He might deign *to forgive them* all *their sins*. When he had done this, looking again towards heaven, he said, '*Lord Jesus Christ, good Shepherd*, who put on *the form of a servant*[69] for us and who *chose twelve apostles* for the conversion of all the nations and *said to the* blessed *apostle Peter, Whatever you bind on earth shall be bound in heaven, and whatever you loose on earth shall be loosed in heaven*,[70] I, his unworthy vicar, I earnestly pray *your* boundless *clemency* to absolve from all their sins those servants, *my brethren*, who were slain for the love of righteousness and lead them into the rest of the blessed. Absolve also, Lord, those whom I have excommunicated and convert them to the way of truth. *Destroy* simoniacal heresy[71] and *all heretical wickedness*.[68] Deign to bless and protect your faithful Beneventans, who have received me so honourably in your name and have served me so generously, and all your other faithful people; because you are God, blessed to all eternity. Amen.' After he ceased speaking, they all remained there for a short time, then *each returned to his* own *home*.

All that night, as on the previous night, he devoted to vigils and prayer.[72] On the third day, which was the last that was left in this life to the blessed Leo, the supreme pontiff, they all assembled in even

---

66 /66 A paraphrase of Libuin, *De obitu* c. 3, col. 527C–528A. A similar version is found in Bonus of Cervia, *Vita et miracula Leonis IX* II.3, p. 290. See H. Tritz (1952) p. 320. For Leo IX and the payment of tithes: above p. 137.

67 Cf. Libuin, *De obitu* c. 3, col. 527D. This command echoes the prohibition of incestuous marriages in Leo's Council of Rheims c. 11, Anselm, *Historia dedicationis* c. 16, col. 1437B; see also U.-R. Blumenthal (1976) pp. 31–2.

68 /68 A paraphrase of Libuin, *De obitu* c. 4, col. 528A–528C.

69 Philippians 2:7.

70 Matthew 16:19.

71 Cf. Libuin, *De obitu* c. 5, col. 529D.

72 Cf. *Ibid.* c. 5, col. 530A; c. 6, 530B.

greater numbers. The blessed pontiff *rose*[73] and went to *the altar* and
remained in prayer *for almost an hour*, with many tears. *Returning* from
there *to the bed*, he preached them *a short sermon*. When it was over, he
called the bishops to him, made his confession and received the body
and blood of our Lord Jesus Christ. He then lay down on his bed and
soon afterwards fell asleep in the Lord. *One of the bishops*, however, *rose
and touched him*, thinking that he was still *alive* and was sleeping.
When they realised that he had died, they immediately gathered around
him and there were great lamentations over him. The blessed pontiff
died on 19 April[73] in the reign of our Lord Jesus Christ, to whom, with
the Father and the Holy Spirit, be honour and glory forever and ever.
Amen.

7 *The*[74] *day after the death* of the blessed Leo *a certain woman arrived
from the region of Tuscany*, who, *when she climbed the steps, began to be
harassed by a demon* and to utter fearful sounds and loud screams.
When she mentioned the name of the blessed Leo, she was dragged to
his tomb by those who were present. *One of the bishops* questioned the
demon who was troubling her, *saying, 'I adjure you by Him who lives*
and reigns *to all eternity to tell us whether Pope Leo* possesses power
among the saints.' The demon replied, *'Leo*, about whom you ask, *is
truly among the saints* and has *great* power *among them* and, magician
that he is, he will *cast me out from this house*, that I have now had in my
possession for nine years and two months.' Then another wretched
woman who was there began to disparage the blessed Leo, *saying,
'Pope Leo*, who caused so many men to be killed, *will put the evil spirits
to flight!* In that *hour in which he expels the evil spirits, I shall be queen* and
shall *raise from the dead all those* whom he destroyed by his villainy!'
She had *scarcely* finished speaking when she was immediately seized *by
the demon and began to be harassed* in an extraordinary way. At once,
however, that other woman (she whom we described as having come
from the region of Tuscany) was set free. *Then all who were present* were
amazed and benumbed and *began to cry out, 'St Leo, spare us;*[74] St Leo,
pardon us and have mercy on us, for we have greatly sinned.'

At that same *hour*[75] *two lame men*, who could not walk unaided, *were
healed. On that same day* around *vespers there came* to the tomb of the
blessed man *a certain deaf and dumb man*, who in addition to this great
misfortune was gripped by a very severe palsy. As soon as *he approached*

73 /73 Cf. *ibid.*, c. 7, col. 531AC.
74 /74 Cf.*ibid.*, c. 8, col. 531D-532C.
75 /75 Cf. *ibid.*, c. 9, col. 532D.

the tomb,[75] he became sound and well and received both speech and hearing. The Lord Christ in those days performed many other miracles through the blessed Leo, so as to reveal his merits to us, His faithful.

8 I must also not pass over that miracle that the excellent man John, bishop of Porto[76] recounted to me.[77] For he said that around that time the bishop of the city of Chur[78] had come from beyond the Alps to Rome. There was in his company a certain dwarf, who was dumb from infancy and had never spoken. The bishop's servants brought him with them on the pack-horses because he was extremely trustworthy and fitted for guarding the baggage. One day while this bishop was still staying in the city, that dumb man entered the church of blessed Peter. When he saw all the crowds flocking round the grave of the blessed Leo, he also approached it. Those who stood around then understanding that he was dumb, began, as it is customary to do with such men, to communicate to him by signs that he should humble himself at the grave of the blessed man, should pour forth prayers and beseech the Saviour of all to heal him, intimating to him that this was the grave in which the blessed Leo was resting. For the fame of his virtues had spread everywhere and many who had come there from all regions were cured of various illnesses. The dumb man, therefore, approached the tomb and prostrated his whole body on the ground. After he had been lying there for a long time, overcome by fatigue, he fell asleep. Awakened soon afterwards, he got up and began to speak distinctly as if he had never suffered any impediment of the tongue. All were amazed, all rejoiced and exulted. It was not enough to hear him once: they delighted in asking him questions and hearing him speaking and replying. At last he returned to his companions, who, after hearing him speak, rejoicing exceedingly and full of amazement, brought him before the bishop. The bishop asked him how all these things had happened to him. He recounted everything in the order that it happened: he said that he had seen the blessed Leo and when he had fallen asleep before his tomb, Leo came and, placing his fingers in his mouth, loosened the tongue that had long been bound up.

---

76 John III, cardinal bishop of Porto (1087–95). See R. Hüls (1977) pp. 120–1.

77 A version of this miracle was also recorded by Desiderius, *Dialogi* III.3, p. 1145.

78 Thietmar, bishop of Chur (*c.* 1040–1070).

9 Now, however, the time urges me to explain what I have previously promised: namely, that I have not composed this work without receiving a command. For last Lent,[79] when we were in Rome and had come to church one day, the most venerable man John, bishop of Tusculum[80] came to where I was standing, in the presence of the most religious man Hubald, bishop of Sabina[81] and certain others, and said to me, 'I am sent to you as an envoy.' I stood waiting to hear what he would say to me. Then he said, 'Pope Leo commands you to give him 100,000 *solidi.*' I said, 'What are you talking about?' He said, 'I tell you truly, this is what he commands you to do'; and then he began to tell me in a methodical manner what he had seen. 'Last night, when I had fallen asleep, the blessed Leo in pontifical vestments appeared to me in a dream and said, "Go and tell the bishop of Segni to give me 100,000 *solidi.*" And when I began to reflect inwardly that you were not so rich that you could give him so great a sum of money, he read my thoughts and said, "Go and tell him to give me 100,000 or 50,000." This is his command to you: consider what reply you will make him.' Then I began anxiously to consider what this vision might mean for me and after a little while I asked the bishop if the blessed Leo had ordered me to give that money or to lend it or to pay it back; and he replied, 'No, to give it.' Then I was a little comforted; for there is a great difference between our having to to give and our having to give back. For I was afraid that I had offended him, in that I had to repay a debt. I remembered moreover that his festival used to be cele-brated in our church, but because of my own negligence the festival ceased to be celebrated there. May he pardon me, because I know that I have sinned greatly in this respect.

When I returned home from the church, however, and told this vision to our clergy, they made the same observations that had already occurred to me. For they said, 'We think that the blessed Leo required from you no money, but only that you write something that will be a fitting memorial to him. For your wealth is in your writing; and he himself seems to be in need of no other money.' It pleased me that their interpretation agreed with mine. And indeed knowledge is appropriately symbolised by money: this is also what it signifies in the

---

79 On the date of the work see above p. 93.

80 Either John III, cardinal bishop of Tusculum (*c.* 1073–*c.* 1094) or John IV, cardinal bishop of Tusculum (*ca.*1100–1119). R. Hüls (1977) p. 140 considered John III more likely.

81 Hubald, cardinal bishop of Sabina (*c.*1063–*c.*1094). See R. Hüls (1977) pp. 125–6.

Gospel in that place where our Saviour shares the talents among His servants.[82] But why does he demand 100,000 or 50,000? Of these two numbers, one is perfect but the other is imperfect. One hundred times 1000 or one thousand times 100 make 100,000. Each number, that is 100 and 1000, is perfect for this reason, that it does not have the means of increasing. For every thing is imperfect as long as it can grow to some degree. The number 100 and the number 1000 can indeed be reduced, but cannot be increased. It is therefore perfect. For when anyone is counting, after he comes to 100 or 1000, he ends there and begins to count again from one. The number 50, however, is imperfect because it is placed in the middle of 100, it does not make an end and can extend beyond itself. What was the meaning, therefore, of the blessed man's command to me to give him 50,000 *solidi*, when as it seemed both to him and to the man to whom he spoke, that I could not give 100,000, unless it was that I should begin to tell in full whatever pertains to his praise and glory? I have therefore given him 50,000 because I could not give 100,000: that is, because I could not narrate everything in full (for all the facts did not come to my attention) or because I narrated whatever I could. I pray, therefore, most blessed pontiff, that my little gift may be pleasing to you and that through your holy prayers you may obtain the remission of my debts from Jesus Christ our Saviour, who with the Father and the Holy Spirit lives and reigns, one God, forever and ever. Amen.

82 Matthew 25:15.

BIBLIOGRAPHY

Primary sources

Acta pontificum Romanorum inedita, ed. J. Pflugk-Harttung 1, 2 (Tübingen-Stuttgart, 1880)

Adam of Bremen, *Gesta Hammaburgensis ecclesiae pontificum, MGH SS rer. germ.* [2] (1917)

Altercatio inter Urbanum et Clementem, MGH Libelli 2, 169–72

Amatus of Monte Cassino, *L'Ystoire de li Normant* (Fonti per la storia d'Italia 76: Rome, 1935)

Andreas of Strumi, *Vita sancti Arialdi, MGH SS* 30/2, 1047–75

Andreas of Strumi, *Vita sancti Johannis Gualberti, MGH SS* 30/2, 1076–1104

Annales Altahenses maiores, MGH SS rer. germ. [4] (1891)

Annales Beneventani, MGH SS 3, 173–85

Annales Cavenses, MGH SS 3, 186–97

Annales Magdeburgenses, MGH SS 16, 105–96

Annales Romani, MGH SS 5, 468–80

Annales Weissenburgenses in: *Lamperti Opera, MGH SS rer. germ.* [38] (1894), pp. 9–57

Annalista Saxo, MGH SS 6, 542–777

Anonymi Chronica imperatorum Heinrico V dedicata, ed. F.-J. Schmale and I. Schmale-Ott (Ausgewählte Quellen zur deutschen Geschichte des Mittelalters 15: Darmstadt, 1972), pp. 48–120

Anonymus Haserensis (Anonymous of Hasenried), *De episcopis Eichstetensibus, MGH SS* 7, 253–66

Anonymus Mellicensis [Wolfger of Prüfening?], *De scriptoribus ecclesiasticis*, ed. E. Ettlinger, *Der sogen. Anonymus Mellicensis* (Strasbourg, 1896)

Anselm II of Lucca, *Collectio canonum*, ed. F. Thaner 1 (Innsbruck, 1906–11)

Anselm II of Lucca, *Liber contra Wibertum, MGH Libelli* 1, 517–28

Anselm of St-Remi, *Historia dedicationis ecclesiae Sancti Remigii, MPL* 142, 1415D–1440B; ed. J. M. Watterich, *Pontificum Romanorum Vitae* 1 (Leipzig, 1862), 113–27

Arnulf of Milan, *Liber gestorum recentium*, ed. C. Zey, *MGH SS rer. Germ.* 67 (Hanover, 1994)

Beno of SS. Martino e Silvestro, *Gesta Romanae ecclesiae contra Hildebrandum, MGH Libelli* 2, 369–80

Benzo of Alba, *Ad Heinricum IV. imperatorem libri VII. Sieben Bücher an Kaiser Heinrich IV.*, ed. H. Seyffert, *MGH SS rer. Germ.* 65 (Hanover, 1996)

Berengar of Tours, *Rescriptum contra Lanfrannum*, CCM 84 (Turnhout, 1988)

Bernard of Cluny, *Ordo Cluniacensis*, ed. M. Herrgott, *Vetus disciplina monastica* (Paris, 1726), pp. 133–364

Bernard of Hildesheim, *Liber canonum contra Heinricum IV*, MGH Libelli 1, 471–516

Bernold of St Blasien (of Constance), *Apollogeticus super excommunicacionem Gregorii VII*, MGH Libelli 2, 160–8

Bernold of St Blasien (of Constance), *Apologeticae rationes contra scismaticorum obiectiones*, MGH Libelli 2, 94–101

Bernold of St Blasien (of Constance), *Apologeticus*, MGH Libelli 2, 58–88

Bernold of St Blasien (of Constance), *Chronicon*, MGH SS 5, 400–67

Bernold of St Blasien (of Constance), *De damnatione schismaticorum*, MGH Libelli 2, 26–58

Bernold of St Blasien (of Constance), *De incontinentia sacerdotum*, MGH Libelli 2, 4–26

Bernold of St Blasien (of Constance), *De lege excommunicationis*, MGH Libelli 2, 101–3

Bernold of St Blasien (of Constance), *De solutione iuramentorum*, MGH Libelli 2, 146–9

Berthold of Reichenau, *Annales*, MGH SS 5, 264–326

H. Beyer (1860), *Urkundenbuch zur Geschichte der jetzt die Preußischen Regierungsbezirke Coblenz und Trier bildenden mittelrheinischen Territorien* 1 (Koblenz)

Bonizo of Sutri, *Liber ad amicum*, ed. E. Dümmler, MGH Libelli 1, 568–620

Bonizo of Sutri, *Liber ad amicum*, ed. P. Jaffé, *Monumenta Gregoriana* (*Bibliotheca rerum germanicarum* 2: Berlin, 1865), pp. 577–689

Bonizo of Sutri, *Liber de vita christiana*, ed. E. Perels (Texte zur Geschichte des römischen und kanonischen Rechts im Mittelalter 1: Berlin, 1930)

Bonus of Cervia, *Vita et miracula sancti Leonis papae noni*, ed. A. Poncelet, 'Vie et miracles du pape S. Léon IX', *Analecta Bollandiana* 25 (1906), 258–97

Briefsammlungen der Zeit Heinrichs IV., ed. C. Erdmann and N. Fickermann, MGH Die Briefe der deutschen Kaiserzeit 5 (1950)

Bruno of Merseburg, *Saxonicum bellum: Brunos Buch vom Sachsenkrieg*, MGH Deutsches Mittelalter 2 (1937)

Bruno of Segni, *Epistolae*, MGH Libelli 2, 563–5 [see also G. Fransen (1972)]

Bruno of Segni, *Libellus de symoniacis*, MGH Libelli 2, 543–62

Burchard of Worms, *Decretum*, MPL 140, 337A-1058C

Cardinalium schismaticorum scripta, MGH Libelli 2, 380–422

Casus monasterii Petrishusensis, MGH SS 20, 621–82

Chronica monasterii Casinensis. Die Chronik von Montecassino, ed. H. Hoffmann, MGH SS 34 (1980)

Chronica sancti Benedicti, MGH SS 3, 197–213

Chronicon Benedictoburanum, MGH SS 9, 210–16

Chronicon sancti Benigni Divionensis, MGH SS 7, 235–8

Chronicon Wirziburgense, MGH SS 6, 17–31

Codex Laureshamensis, ed. K. Glöckner 1: Einleitung, Regesten, Chronik (Darmstadt, 1929)

Codex Udalrici, ed. P. Jaffé, *Bibliotheca rerum germanicarum* 5 (Berlin, 1869), 17–469

Collectio in LXXIV titulos (Diversorum patrum sententie), ed. J. T. Gilchrist (Monumenta Iuris Canonici ser. B, 1: Vatican City, 1973)

Conciliorum Oecumenicorum Decreta, ed. J. A. Dossetti (third edition: Bologna, 1973)

Decretales Pseudo-Isidorianae et Capitula Angilramni, ed. P. Hinschius (Leipzig, 1863)

Desiderius of Monte Cassino, *Dialogi de miraculis sancti Benedicti*, MGH SS 30/2, 1111–51

Deusdedit, *Collectio canonum: Die Kanonessammlung des Kardinal Deusdedit*, ed. V. Wolf von Glanvell 1 (Parderborn, 1905)

Deusdedit, *Libellus contra invasores et symoniacos*, MGH Libelli 2, 292–365

Dicta Anselmi see *Memorials of Saint Anselm*

Dicta cuiusdam de discordia papae et regis, MGH Libelli 1, 454–60

Diplomata Heinrici IV: Die Urkunden Heinrichs IV., MGH Diplomata 6/1–3 (1941, 1959, 1978)

Disputatio vel defensio Paschalis papae, MGH Libelli 2, 658–66

Donizo of Canossa, *Vita Mathildis comitissae metrica*, MGH SS 12, 348–409

Ekkehard of Aura, *Chronica*, ed. F.-J. Schmale and I. Schmale-Ott (Ausgewählte Quellen zur deutschen Geschichte des Mittelalters 15: Darmstadt, 1972), pp. 124–208, 268–376

Frutolf of Michelsberg, *Chronica*, ed. F.-J. Schmale and I. Schmale-Ott (Ausgewählte Quellen zur deutschen Geschichte des Mittelalters 15, Darmstadt), pp. 48–121

Gebhard of Salzburg, *Epistola ad Herimannum Mettensem episcopum*, MGH Libelli 1, 261–79

Gerhoch of Reichersberg, *De investigatione Antichristi*, MGH Libelli 3, 304–95

Gerhoch of Reichersberg, *Opusculum de aedificio domus Dei*, MGH Libelli 3, 136–202

Gesta episcoporum Mettensium, MGH SS 10, 531–44

Gesta episcoporum Tullensium, MGH SS 8, 631–48

Gesta Treverorum, Continuatio I, MGH SS 8, 175–200

Gilo, *Vita sancti Hugonis abbatis*, ed. H. E. J. Cowdrey, 'Memorials of Abbot Hugh of Cluny (1049–1109)', *Studi Gregoriani per la storia della 'Libertas Ecclesiae'* 11 (1978), 43–109

Gregory VII, *Registrum*, MGH Epistolae selectae 2 (Berlin, 1920, 1923)

Gregory VII: *The Epistolae Vagantes of Pope Gregory VII*, ed. H. E. J. Cowdrey (Oxford, 1972)

Gundechar, *Liber pontificalis Eichstetensis*, MGH SS 7, 239–53

Heinrici III Diplomata: Die Urkunden Heinrichs III., MGH Diplomata 5 (1931)

Heinrici IV Diplomata: Die Urkunden Heinrichs IV., MGH Diplomata 6/1–3 (1941, 1959, 1978)

Henry IV, *Letters: Die Briefe Heinrichs IV., MGH Deutsches Mittelalter* 1 (Leipzig, 1937)

Herman of Reichenau, *Chronicon, MGH SS* 5, 67–133

Herrand of Halberstadt, *Epistola de causa Heinrici regis, MGH Libelli* 2, 287–91

Hildebert of le Mans, *Vita sancti Hugonis, MPL* 159, col. 857D–894A

Hugh of Flavigny, *Chronicon, MGH SS* 8, 280–502

Hugh of Fleury, *Tractatus de regia potestate et sacerdotali dignitate, MGH Libelli* 2, 465–94

Humbert of Silva Candida, *Contradictio adversus Nicetam*, ed. C. Will, *Acta et scripta* pp. 136–50

Humbert of Silva Candida, *Dialogus inter Constantinopolitanum et Romanum*, ed. C. Will, *Acta et scripta* pp. 93–126

Humbert of Silva Candida, *Epistola I ad Michaelem Cerullarium*, ed. C. Will, *Acta et scripta* pp. 65–85

Humbert of Silva Candida, *Libri tres adversus simoniacos, MGH Libelli* 1, 100–253

John of Mantua: *Iohannis Mantuani in Cantica Canticorum Tractatus*, ed. B. Bischoff and B. Taegar (Spicilegium Friburgense 19: Freiburg, 1973)

Lampert of Hersfeld, *Annales*, in: *Lamperti monachi Hersfeldensis Opera, MGH SS rer. germ.* [38] (1894), pp. 3–304

Landulf Junior de sancto Paulo, *Historia Mediolanensis* , *MGH SS* 20, 17–49

Landulf Senior, *Historia Mediolanensis, MGH SS* 8, 32–100

Lanfranc, *De corpore et sanguine Domini, MPL* 150, 407A–442D

Lanfranc, *Letters of Archbishop Lanfranc of Canterbury*, ed. H. Clover and M. Gibson (Oxford, 1979)

Liber Censuum: Le Liber censuum de l'église romaine, ed. P. Fabre and L. Duchesne, 1–3 (Bibliothèque des Ecoles françaises d'Athènes et de Rome 2. série, 6: Paris, 1886–1952)

Liber de sancti Hidulfi successoribus in Mediano monasterio, MGH SS 4, 86–92

Liber de unitate ecclesiae conservanda, MGH Libelli 2, 173–284

Liber Diurnus Romanorum pontificum. Ex unico codice Vaticano, ed. T. von Sickel (Österreichische Akademie der Wissenschaften: Vienna, 1889)

Liber pontificalis, ed. L. Duchesne, C. Vogel 1–3 (Bibliothèque des Ecoles françaises d' Athènes et de Rome 2e série: Paris, 1886–1957)

Libuin, *De obitu sancti Leonis papae IX, MPL* 143, 525B–542A

Lupus Protospatarius, *Annales, MGH SS* 5, 52–3

Manegold of Lautenbach, *Liber ad Gebehardum, MGH Libelli* 1, 308–430

Manegold of Lautenbach, *Liber contra Wolfelmum*, ed. W. Hartmann, *MGH Quellen zur Geistesgeschichte des Mittelalters* 8 (Weimar, 1972)

J. D. Mansi (ed.), *Sacrorum conciliorum nova et amplissima collectio*, 1–31 (Florence–Venice, 1759–1798)

Memorials of Saint Anselm, ed. R. W. Southern and F. S. Schmitt (London, 1969)

Orderic Vitalis, *Historia ecclesiastica*, ed. M. Chibnall, 1–6 (Oxford, 1969–80)

Orthodoxa defensio imperialis, MGH Libelli 2, 534–42

Otto of Freising, *Chronica sive Historia de duabus civitatibus*, MGH SS rer. germ [45] (1912)

Paul of Bernried, *Vita beatae Herlucae, Acta Sanctorum Aprilis* 2 (Antwerp, 1675), 552–6

Paul of Bernried, *Vita Gregorii VII papae*, ed. J. M. Watterich, *Pontificum Romanorum Vitae* 1 (Leipzig, 1862), 474–545

[Paul of Bernried and Gebhard?], *Vita prior sancti Udalrici prioris Cellensis*, MGH SS 12, 251–3

Peter Damian, *Letters: Die Briefe des Petrus Damiani*, ed. K. Reindel, MGH *Die Briefe der deutschen Kaiserzeit* 4 (Munich, 1983–93)

Petrus Crassus, *Defensio Heinrici IV*, MGH Libelli 1, 432–53

Petrus Diaconus, *De viris illustribus Casinensis coenobii*, MPL 173, col. 1003–50

Placidus of Nonantola, *Liber de honore ecclesiae*, MGH Libelli 2, 566–639

Rainald of Vézelay, *Vita sancti Hugonis abbatis*, MPL 159, 893B–906C

Ralph Glaber, *Historiae* in: *Rodolfus Glaber, Opera*, ed. J. France, N. Bulst and P. Reynolds (Oxford, 1989), pp. 2–252

Ralph Glaber, *Vita domni Willelmi abbatis*, *ibid.*, pp. 254–98

Rangerius of Lucca, *Liber de anulo et baculo*, MGH Libelli 2, 505–33

Rangerius of Lucca, *Vita metrica sancti Anselmi Lucensis episcopi*, MGH SS 30/2, 1152–1307

Regesta pontificum Romanorum, ed. P. Jaffé, revised by W. Wattenbach, S. Loewenfeld, F. Kaltenbrunner and P. Ewald, 1, 2 (second edition: Leipzig, 1885)

Rudolf of St Trond, *Gesta abbatum Trudonensium*, MGH SS 10, 213–72

Rupert of Deutz, *Chronicon sancti Laurentii Leodiensis*, MGH SS 8, 261–79

Sigebert of Gembloux, *Apologia contra eos qui calumniantur missas coniugatorum sacerdotum*, MGH Libelli 2, 436–48

Sigebert of Gembloux, *Catalogus de viris illustribus*, ed. R. Witte (Lateinische Sprache und Literatur des Mittelalters 1: Frankfurt-Berne, 1974)

Sigebert of Gembloux, *Chronica*, MGH SS 6, 268–374

Sigebert of Gembloux, *Epistola Leodicensium adversus Paschalem papam*, MGH Libelli 2, 449–64

Tractatus de investitura episcoporum, MGH Libelli 2, 495–504

Udalric of Zell, *Antiquiores consuetudines monasterii Cluniacensis*, MPL 149, 635–778

Vita Heinrici IV imperatoris, MGH SS. rer. germ. [58] (1899)

Vita Leonis IX papae, ed. J. M. Watterich, *Pontificum Romanorum Vitae* 1, 127–70; ed. M. Parisse and M. Goullet (Les Classiques de l'histoire de France au moyen âge 38, Paris, 1997)

Vita Popponis abbatis Stabulensis, MGH SS 11, 291–316

Vita sancti Anselmi episcopi Lucensis, MGH SS 12, 1–35

Vita sancti Brunonis, Acta Sanctorum Julii 4, 478–84

J. M. Watterich (ed.), *Pontificum Romanorum Vitae* 1 (Leipzig, 1862)

Wenrich of Trier, *Epistola, MGH Libelli* 1, 280–99

Wibert of Ravenna, *Decretum Wiberti vel Clementis papae, MGH Libelli* 1, 621–6

Wido of Ferrara, *De scismate Hildebrandi, MGH Libelli* 1, 529–67

Widrich, *Translatio beati Gerardi, MGH SS* 4, 505–9

Widrich, *Vita et miracula sancti Gerardi episcopi Tullensis, MGH SS* 4, 485–509

C. Will (ed.), *Acta et scripta quae de controversiis ecclesiae graecae et latinae saeculo XI composita extant* (Leipzig, 1861)

William of Apulia, *De rebus Normannorum in Sicilia, Apulia et Calabria gestis, MPL* 149, col. 1027B–1082C

William of Hirsau, *Consuetudines Hirsaugienses, MPL* 150, 927B–1146D

William of Malmesbury, *Gesta regum Anglorum* (Rerum Britannicarum Medii Aevi Scriptores 90)

Wipo, *Gesta Chuonradi II. imperatoris, MGH SS rer. germ.* [15] (1915), pp. 3–62

Secondary works

Abbondanza, R. (1962), 'Attone', *Dizionario biografico degli Italiani* 4 (Rome), 564–5

Affeldt, W. (1969), *Die weltliche Gewalt in der Paulus-Exegese* (Göttingen)

Amann, E. (1931), 'Nicolaïtes', *Dictionnaire de théologie catholique* 11, col. 499–506

Ambrosioni, A. (1988), 'Gli arcivescovi di Milano e la nuova coscienza cittadina' in *L'evoluzione delle città italiane nell' XI secolo*, ed. R. Bordone and J. Jarnut (Annali dell' Istituto storico italo-germanico 25), pp. 193–222

Amelli, A. (1903), *S. Bruno di Segni, Gregorio VII ed Enrico IV in Roma (1081–1083)* (Montecassino)

Anton, H. H. (1968), *Fürstenspiegel und Herrscherethos in der Karolingerzeit* (Bonner Historische Forschungen 32: Bonn)

Anton, H. H. (1972), 'Bonifaz von Canossa, Markgraf von Tuszien, und die Italienpolitik der frühen Salier', *Historische Zeitschrift* 214, 529–56

Anton, H. H. (1982), *Der sogenannte Traktat 'De ordinando pontifice': ein Rechtsgutachten in Zusammenhang mit der Synode von Sutri* (Bonn)

Bartlett, R. (1986), *Trial by fire and water. The medieval judicial ordeal* (Oxford)

Becker, A. (1964), *Papst Urban II.* 1 (Schriften der MGH 19/1, Stuttgart)

Benson, R. L. (1967), 'Plenitudo potestatis: evolution of a formula from Gregory IV to Gratian', *Studia Gratiana* 14, 195–217

Benz, K. J. (1977), 'Kaiser Konrad II. und die Kirche. Ein Beitrag zur Historiographie des ersten Saliers', *Zeitschrift für Kirchengeschichte* 88, 190–217

Berges, W. (1947), 'Gregor VII. und das deutsche Designationsrecht', *Studi Gregoriani* 2, 189–209

Bernard, M. (1980), 'Les offices versifiés attribués à Léon IX', *Etudes grégoriennes* 19, 89–100

Bernhardi, W. (1879), *Lothar von Supplinburg* (Jahrbücher der deutschen Geschichte, Leipzig)

Berschin, W. (1972), *Bonizo von Sutri. Leben und Werk* (Beiträge zur Geschichte und Quellenkunde des Mittelalters 2: Berlin – New York)

Berschin, W. (1987), 'Bonizone da Sutri e la stato di vita laicale. Il codice Mantova 439' in *Sant' Anselmo, Mantova e la lotta per le investiture. Atti del Convegno Internazionale di Studi (Mantova 1986)*, ed. P. Golinelli (Bologna), pp. 281–9

Beulertz, S. (1991), *Das Verbot der Laieninvestitur im Investiturstreit* (MGH Studien und Texte 2, Hanover)

Beumann, H. (1973), 'Tribur, Rom und Canossa' in *Investiturstreit und Reichsverfassung*, ed. J. Fleckenstein (Vorträge und Forschungen 17, Sigmaringen), pp. 33–60

Beumann, H. (1977), 'Reformpäpste als Reichsbischöfe in der Zeit Heinrichs III.' in *Festschrift Friedrich Hausmann*, ed. H. Ebner (Graz), pp. 21–37

Bischoff, B. (1948), 'Der Canticumkommentar des Johannes von Mantua für die Markgräfin Mathilde' in *Lebenskrafte in der abendländischen Geistesgeschichte. Dank- und Erinnerungsgabe an Walter Goetz*, ed. W. Stammler (Marburg/Lahn), pp. 24–48

Black-Veldtrup, M. (1995), *Kaiserin Agnes (1043–1077). Quellenkritische Studien* (Cologne-Weimar-Vienna)

Bloch, H. (1986), *Monte Cassino in the Middle Ages*, 1–3 (Rome)

Bloch, M. (1962), *Feudal Society* (English translation, London)

Bloch, R. (1930), 'Die Klosterpolitik Leos IX. in Deutschland, Burgund und Italien', *Archiv für Urkundenforschung* 11, 176–257

Blumenthal, U.-R. (1976), 'Ein neuer Text für das Reimser Konzil Leos IX. (1049)?', *Deutsches Archiv* 32, 23–48

Blumenthal, U.-R. (1978), *The early councils of Pope Paschal II (1100–1110)* (Pontifical Institute of Medieval Studies. Studies and Texts 43, Toronto)

Bock, R. (1909), *Die Glaubwürdigkeit der Nachrichten Bonithos von Sutri im Liber ad amicum und deren Verwertung in der neueren Geschichtsschreibung* (Historische Studien 73, Berlin)

Böhme, W. (1970), *Die deutsche Königserhebung im 10. bis 12. Jahrhundert* 1 (Göttingen)

Boglioni, P. (1985), 'Il santo e gli animali nell' alto medioevo' in *L'uomo di fronte al mondo animale nell' alto medioevo* (Settimane di Studio del Centro Italiano di Studi sull' Alto Medioevo 31: Spoleto), pp. 935–93

Borino, G. B. (1916), 'L'elezione e la deposizione di Gregorio VI', *Archivio della deputazione romana di storia patria* 39, 141–252, 295–410

Borino, G. B (1946), 'Quando e dove si fece monaco Ildebrando' in *Miscellanea G. Mercati* 5 (*Studi e Testi* 125: Vatican City), pp. 218–62

Borino, G. B (1948), 'L'arcidiaconato di Ildebrando', *Studi Gregoriani* 3, 463–516

Borino, G. B. (1952a), 'Cencio del prefetto Stefano l'attentatore di Gregorio VII', *Studi Gregoriani* 4, 373–440

Borino, G. B. (1952b), 'Note Gregoriane. 1: Ildebrando non si fece monaco a Roma', *Studi Gregoriani* 4, 441–56

Borino, G. B. (1956a), 'Il monacato e l'investitura di Anselmo vescovo di Lucca', *Studi Gregoriani* 5, 361–74

Borino, G. B. (1956b), 'Perché Gregorio VII non annunciò la sua elezione ad Enrico IV e non ne richiese il consenso', *Studi Gregoriani* 5, 313–43

Borino, G. B. (1959–61), 'I decreti di Gregorio VII contro i simoniaci e i nicolaiti sono del sinodo quaresimale del 1074', *Studi Gregoriani* 6, 277–95

Boshof, E. – H. Wolter (1976), *Rechtsgeschichtlich-diplomatische Studien zu frühmittelalterlichen Papsturkunden* (Studien und Vorarbeiten zur Germania Pontificia 6: Cologne-Vienna)

Boshof, E. (1978a), 'Lothringen, Frankreich und das Reich in der Regierungszeit Heinrichs III. ', *Rheinische Vierteljahrsblätter* 42, 63–127

Boshof, E. (1978b), 'Köln, Mainz, Trier – Die Auseinandersetzung um die Spitzenstellung im deutschen Episkopat in ottonisch-salischer Zeit', *Jahrbuch des kölnischen Geschichtsvereins* 49, 19–48

Boshof, E. (1981), 'Bischof Altmann, St. Nikola und die Kanonikerreform. Das Bistum Passau im Investiturstreit' in *Tradition und Entwicklung. Gedenkschrift für Johann Riederer*, ed. K.-H. Pollok (Schriften der Universität Passau: Passau), pp. 317–45

Boshof, E. (1986), 'Das Reich und Ungarn in der Zeit der Salier', *Ostbairische Grenzmarken* 28, 178–94

Boshof, E. (1991), 'Bischöfe und Bischofskirchen von Passau und Regensburg' in *Die Salier und das Reich*, ed. S. Weinfurter 2 (Sigmaringen), 113–54

Brakel, C. H. (1972), 'Die vom Reformpapsttum geförderten Heiligenkulte', *Studi Gregoriani* 9, 239–311

Bresslau, H. (1879, 1884), *Jahrbücher des Deutschen Reichs unter Konrad II.* (1, 2, Leipzig)

Brucker, P-P. (1889), *L'Alsace et l'église au temps du pape Saint Léon IX (Bruno d'Egisheim) 1002–1054* (two volumes: Strasbourg)

Brühl, C. (1968), *Fodrum, Gistum, Servitium regis* 1 (Cologne-Graz)

Büttner, H. (1973), 'Die Bischofsstädte von Basel bis Mainz in der Zeit des Investiturstreites' in *Investiturstreit und Reichsverfassung*, ed. J. Fleckenstein (Vorträge und Forschungen 17, Sigmaringen), pp. 351–61

Bulst, N. (1973), *Untersuchungen zu den Klosterreformen Wilhelms von Dijon (962–1031)* (Pariser Historische Studien 11: Bonn)

Bulst-Thiele, M. L. (1933), *Kaiserin Agnes* (Leipzig-Berlin)

Bur, M. (1977), *La formation du comté de Champagne (v. 950 – v. 1150)* (Nancy)

Capitani, O. (1966), *Immunità vescovili ed ecclesiologia in età 'pregregoriana' e 'gregoriana'* (Biblioteca degli Studi Medievali 3, Spoleto)

Cecchelli, C. (1947), 'Castel S. Angelo al tempo di Gregorio VII', *Studi Gregoriani* 2, 103–23

Cecchelli, C. (1951), 'Documenti per la storia antica e medioevale di Castel S. Angelo', *Archivio della società romana di storia patria* 74, 27–67

Chalandon, F. (1907), *Histoire de la domination normande en Italie et en Sicile* 1 (Paris)

Choux, J. (1957), 'Une possession des évêques de Toul en Alsace: la cour de Bergheim' in *Trois provinces de l'Est: Lorraine, Alsace, Franche-Comté*, ed. C.-E. Perrin (Strasbourg), pp. 204–11

Choux, J. (1963), 'Saint Gérard fut-il canonisé par Léon IX?', *La semaine religieuse du diocèse de Nancy et de Toul* 100, 75–9, 91–2

Classen, P. (1960), *Gerhoch von Reichersberg* (Wiesbaden)

Classen, P. (1973), 'Das Wormser Konkordat in der deutschen Verfassungsgeschichte' in *Investiturstreit und Reichsverfassung*, ed. J. Fleckenstein (Vorträge und Forschungen 17, Sigmaringen), pp. 411–60

Congar, Y. M.-J. (1968), *L'ecclésiologie du haut moyen âge* (Paris)

Constable, G. (1964), *Monastic tithes from their origins to the twelfth century* (Cambridge)

Cowdrey, H. E. J. (1966), 'Archbishop Aribert II of Milan', *History* 51, 1–15

Cowdrey, H. E. J. (1968), 'The papacy, the Patarenes and the church of Milan', *Transactions of the Royal Historical Society* fifth series 18, 25–48

Cowdrey, H. E. J. (1970), *The Cluniacs and the Gregorian reform* (Oxford)

Cowdrey, H. E. J. (1978), 'Memorials of Abbot Hugh of Cluny (1049–1109)', *Studi Gregoriani* 11, 11–175

Cowdrey, H. E. J. (1983), *The age of Abbot Desiderius: Montecassino, the papacy and the Normans in the late eleventh century* (Oxford)

Cowdrey, H. E. J. (1985), 'Martyrdom and the First Crusade' in *Crusade and Settlement: papers read at the First Conference of the Society for the Study of Crusades and the Latin East*, ed. P. W. Edbury (Cardiff), pp. 46–56

Cowdrey, H. E. J. (1988), 'Death-bed testaments' in *Fälschungen im Mittelalter* (Schriften der MGH 33/4), pp. 703–24

Cowdrey, H. E. J. (1993), 'Simon Magus in South Italy', *Anglo-Norman Studies* 15, 77–90

Cowdrey, H. E. J. (1997a), 'Pope Gregory VII and the bearing of arms' in *Montjoie: Studies in Crusade History in honour of H. E. Mayer*, ed. B. Z. Kedar, J. Riley-Smith and R. Hiestand (Aldershot), pp. 21–35

Cowdrey, H. E. J. (1997b), 'Eleventh-century reformers' views of Constantine' in *Conformity and non-conformity in Byzantium*, ed. L. Garland (Byzantinische Forschungen 24, Amsterdam), pp. 63–91

Cowdrey, H. E. J. (1998), *Pope Gregory VII (1073–1085)* (Oxford)

Cracco, G. (1974), 'Pataria, "opus" e "nomen" (tra verità e autorità)', *Rivista di storia della Chiesa in Italia* 28: 357–87

Cram, K.-G. (1955), *Iudicium belli. Zum Rechtscharakter des Krieges im deutschen Mittelalter* (Beihefte zum Archiv für Kulturgeschichte 5: Münster-Cologne)

Cushing, K. G. (1995), 'Anselm of Lucca and the doctrine of coercion: the legal impact of the schism of 1080?' *Catholic Historical Review* 81, 353–71

Cushing, K. G. (1998), *Papacy and law in the Gregorian revolution. The canonistic work of Anselm of Lucca* (Oxford)

Deér, J. (1969), *Das Papsttum und die süditalienischen Normannenstaaten 1053–1212* (Historische Texte/ Mittelalter 12, Göttingen)

Deér, J. (1972), *Papsttum und Normannen* (Studien und Quellen zur Welt Kaiser Friedrichs II., 1, Cologne-Vienna)

Dereine, C. (1946), 'Vie Commune, Règle de Saint Augustin et Chanoines Réguliers au XIe siècle', *Revue d'histoire ecclésiastique* 41, 365–406

Dereine, C. (1948), 'Le problème de la Vie Commune chez les Canonistes, d'Anselme de Lucques à Gratien', *Studi Gregoriani* 3, 287–98

Dereine, C. (1961), 'La prétendue règle de Grégoire VII pour chanoines réguliers', *Revue Bénédictine* 71, 108–18

Diener, H. (1959), 'Das Itinerar des Abtes Hugo von Cluny' in *Neue Forschungen über Cluny und die Cluniacenser*, ed. G. Tellenbach (Freiburg)

Drehmann, J. (1908), *Papst Leo IX. und die Simonie. Ein Beitrag zur Untersuchung der Vorgeschichte des Investiturstreits* (Beiträge zur Kulturgeschichte des Mittelalters und der Renaissance 2, Leipzig/Berlin)

Dressler, F. (1954), *Petrus Damiani. Leben und Werke* (Studia Anselmiana 34, Rome)

Duchesne, L. (1908), *The beginnings of the temporal sovereignty of the popes* (London)

Dümmler, E. (1876), 'Gedichte aus dem elften Jahrhundert', *Neues Archiv* 1, 175–85

Eichmann, E. (1951), *Weihe und Krönung des Papstes im Mittelalter* (Münchener Theologische Studien 3: Kanonistische Abteilung 1, Munich)

Elze, R. (1978), '*Sic transit gloria mundi.* Zum Tode des Papstes im Mittelalter', *Deutsches Archiv* 34, 1–18

Erdmann, C. (1935), *Die Entstehung des Kreuzzugsgedankens* (Forschungen zur Kirchen- und Geistesgeschichte 6: Stuttgart)

Erdmann, C. (1936), 'Die Bamberger Domschule im Investiturstreit', *Zeitschrift für bayerische Landesgeschichte* 9, 1–46

Erdmann, C. (1938), *Studien zur Briefliteratur Deutschlands im elften Jahrhundert* (Schriften der MGH 1, Leipzig)

Von Falkenhausen, V. (1967), *Untersuchungen über die byzantinische Herrschaft in Süditalien vom 9. bis zum 11. Jahrhundert* (Schriften zur Geistesgeschichte des östlichen Europa 1, Wiesbaden)

Fenske, L. (1977), *Adelsopposition und kirchliche Reformbewegung im östlichen Sachsen* (Veröffentlichungen des Max-Planck-Instituts für Geschichte 47: Göttingen)

Fichtenau, H. (1986), 'Der Mönch Hildebrand' in *Ecclesia peregrinans. Josef Lenzenweger zum 70. Geburtstag*, ed. K. Amon, B. Primetshofer, K. Rehberger, G. Winkler and R. Zinnhobler (Vienna), pp. 59–68

Fleckenstein, J. (1966), *Die Hofkapelle der deutschen Könige 2* (Schriften der MGH 16/2, Stuttgart)

Fliche, A. (1924a, 1926, 1937), *La réforme grégorienne* 1–3 (Louvain-Paris; reprinted Geneva, 1978)

Fliche, A. (1924b), 'L'élection de Grégoire VII', *Le Moyen Age* 2e sér., 26, 71–90

Flint, V. I. J. (1972), 'The chronology of the works of Honorius Augustodunensis',

Revue Bénédictine 82, 215–42

Fonseca, C. D. (1962), 'Arialdo', *Dizionario Biografico degli Italiani* 4, 135–9

Fornasari, G. (1981), *Celibato sacerdotale e 'autocoscienza' ecclesiale. Per la storia della 'nicolaitica haeresis' nell' occidente medievale* (Università degli Studi di Trieste, Facoltà di Magisterio 3. serie, 7, Udine)

Fornasari, G. (1989), 'La riforma gregoriana nel "Regnum Italiae"' in *La riforma gregoriana e l'Europa* (Studi Gregoriani 13: Rome), pp. 281–320

Fournier, P. (1915), 'Bonizo de Sutri, Urbain II et la comtesse Mathilde d'après le Liber de vita christiana de Bonizo', *Bibliothèque de l'Ecole des Chartes* 76, 265–98

Fournier, P. (1920), 'Les collections canoniques romaines de l'époque de Grégoire VII', *Mémoires de l'Institut National de France, Académie des Inscriptions et Belles-Lettres* 41, 271–396

Fransen, G. (1972), 'Réflexions sur l'étude des collections canoniques à l'occasion de l'édition d'une lettre de Bruno de Segni', *Studi Gregoriani* 9, 515–33

Frech, G. (1991), 'Die deutschen Päpste – Kontinuität und Wandel' in *Die Salier und das Reich* 2, ed. S. Weinfurter (Sigmaringen), pp. 303–32

Friedmann, A. U. (1994), *Die Beziehungen der Bistümer Worms und Speyer zu den ottonischen und salischen Königen* (Mainz)

Fuchs, F. (1986), 'Zum Anonymus Mellicensis', *Deutsches Archiv* 42, 213–26

Fuhrmann, H. (1953, 1954, 1955), 'Studien zur Geschichte mittelalterlicher Patriarchate', *Zeitschrift der Savigny-Stiftung für Rechtsgeschichte* 39, 112–76; 40, 1–84; 41, 95–183

Fuhrmann, H. (1956), 'Zur Benutzung des Registers Gregors VII. durch Paul von Bernried', *Studi Gregoriani* 5, 299–312

Fuhrmann, H. (1966), 'Konstantinische Schenkung und abendländisches Kaisertum', *Deutsches Archiv* 22, 63–178

Fuhrmann, H. (1973), 'Das Reformpapsttum und die Rechtswissenschaft' in *Investiturstreit und Reichsverfassung*, ed. J. Fleckenstein (Vorträge und Forschungen 17, Sigmaringen), pp. 175–203

Fuhrmann, H. (1975), '"Volkssouveranität" und "Herrschaftsvertrag" bei Manegold von Lautenbach' in *Festschrift für Hermann Krause*, ed. S. Gágner, H. Schlosser, W. Wiegand (Cologne-Vienna), pp. 21–42

Fuhrmann, H. (1977), 'Quod catholicus non habeatur, qui non concordat Romanae ecclesiae. Randnotizen zum Dictatus Papae' in *Festschrift für Helmut Beumann zum 65. Geburtstag*, ed. K.-U. Jäschke and R. Wenskus (Sigmaringen), pp. 263–87

Fuhrmann, H. (1984), 'Franziskus Töpsl über Paul von Bernried' in *Land und Reich, Stamm und Nation, Festgabe für Max Spindler*, ed. A. Kraus 1 (Munich), 339–53

Fuhrmann, H. (1988), 'Neues zur Biographie des Ulrich von Zell (†1093)', *Person und Gemeinschaft im Mittelalter. K. Schmid zum 65. Geburtstag*, ed. G. Althoff, D. Geuenich, O. G. Oexle and J. Wollasch (Sigmaringen), pp. 369–78

Fuhrmann, H. (1989), 'Zu den Marienwundern in der *Vita Gregorii VII papae* des Paul von Bernried' in *Ecclesia et Regnum. Beiträge zur Geschichte von Kirche, Recht und Staat im Mittelalter. Festschrift für F.-J. Schmale*, ed. D. Berg and H.-W. Goetz (Bochum), pp. 111–19

Fusconi, G. M. (1962), 'Anselmo II, vescovo di Lucca', *Biblioteca Sanctorum* 2 (Rome), cols. 26–36

Ganshof, F. L. (1952), *Feudalism* (English translation, London)

Gatto, L. (1968), *Bonizone di Sutri e il suo Liber ad amicum. Ricerche sull'età gregoriana* (Pescara)

Gaudemet, J. (1982), 'Le célibat ecclésiastique: le droit et la pratique du XIe au XIIIe siècle', *Zeitschrift der Savigny-Stiftung für Rechtsgeschichte, kanonistische Abteilung* 99, 1–31

Gawlik, A. (1970), *Intervenienten und Zeugen in den Diplomen Kaiser Heinrichs IV. (1056–1105)* (Kallmünz)

Geary, P. J. *Furta Sacra. Thefts of relics in the Central Middle Ages* (Princeton, 1978)

Giese, W. (1979), *Der Stamm der Sachsen und das Reich in ottonischer und salischer Zeit* (Wiesbaden)

von Giesebrecht, W. (1890), *Geschichte der deutschen Kaiserzeit* 3 (fifth edition, Leipzig)

Gigalski, B. (1898), *Bruno, Bischof von Segni und Abt von Monte-Cassino (1049–1123). Sein Leben und seine Schriften* (Kirchengeschichtliche Studien 3/4, Münster)

Gilchrist, J. (1965), '"Simoniaca haeresis" and the problem of orders from Leo IX to Gratian' in *Proceedings of the Second International Congress of Medieval Canon Law*, ed. S. Kuttner and J. J. Ryan (Monumenta Iuris Canonici C1), pp. 209–35

Goetz, H.-W. (1987), 'Geschichte als Argument. Historische Beweisführung und Geschichtsbewußtsein in den Streitschriften des Investiturstreits', *Historische Zeitschrift* 245, 31–69

Goez, E. (1995), *Beatrix von Canossa und Tuszien. Eine Untersuchung zur Geschichte des 11. Jahrhunderts* (Vorträge und Forschungen Sonderband 41: Sigmaringen)

Goez, E. (1996), 'Der Thronerbe als Rivale: König Konrad, Kaiser Heinrichs IV. älterer Sohn', *Historisches Jahrbuch* 116, 1–49

Goez, W. (1968), 'Zur Erhebung und ersten Absetzung Papst Gregors VII.', *Römische Quartalschrift für christliche Altertumskunde und Kirchengeschichte* 63, 117–44

Goez, W. (1970), '*Papa qui et episcopus*. Zum Selbstverständnis des Reformpapsttums im Mittelalter', *Archivum Historiae Pontificiae* 8, 7–59

Goez, W. (1973), 'Reformpapsttum, Adel und monastische Erneuerung in der Toscana' in *Investiturstreit und Reichsverfassung*, ed. J. Fleckenstein (Sigmaringen), pp. 205–39

Goez, W. (1974), 'Rainald von Como, ein Bischof des 11. Jahrhunderts zwischen Kurie und Krone' in *Historische Forschungen für Walter Schlesinger*, ed. H. Beumann (Cologne-Vienna), pp. 462–94

Goez, W. (1980), 'Gebhard I. Bischof von Eichstätt als Papst Viktor II. (ca. 1020–1057', *Fränkische Lebensbilder* 9, 11–21

Golinelli, P. (1984), *La Pataria. Lotte religiose e sociali nella Milano dell'XI secolo* (Le Origini: Storie e Cronache 5: Novara-Milan)

Golinelli, P. (1987), 'Dall' agiografia alla storia: le "Vitae" di Sant' Anselmo di Lucca' in *Sant' Anselmo, Mantova e la lotta per le investiture* (Atti del convegno internazionale di studi, Mantova: Bologna), pp. 27–60

Grégoire, R. (1965), *Bruno de Segni, exégète médiévale et théologien monastique* (Centro italiano di studi sull'alto medioevo 3, Spoleto)

Greving, J. (1893), *Pauls von Bernried Vita Gregorii VII. Papae. Ein Beitrag zur Kenntnis der Quellen und Anschauungen aus der Zeit des gregorianischen Kirchenstreites* (Kirchengeschichtliche Studien 2/1: Münster)

Gritsch, H. (1980), 'Die Pataria von Mailand (1057–1075)', *Innsbrucker Historische Studien* 3, 7–42

Grundmann, H. (1976), *Ausgewählte Aufsätze 1: Religiöse Bewegungen* (Schriften der MGH 25/1, Stuttgart)

Gussone, N. (1978), *Thron und Inthronisation des Papstes von den Anfängen bis zum 12. Jahrhundert* (Bonner historische Forschungen 41, Bonn)

Hägermann, D. (1970a), 'Zur Vorgeschichte des Pontifikats Nikolaus' II.', *ZKG* 81, 352–61

Hägermann, D. (1970b), 'Untersuchungen zum Papstwahldekret von 1059', *ZSSRG Kan. Abt.* 56, 157–93

Hageneder, O. (1978), 'Die Häresie des Ungehorsams und das Entstehen des hierokratischen Papsttums', *Römische historische Mitteilungen* 20, 29–47

Haider, P. (1979), 'Zu den Anfängen der päpstlichen Kapelle', *Mitteilungen des Instituts für österreichische Geschichtsforschung* 87, 38–70

Hallinger, K. (1950), *Gorze-Kluny. Studien zu den monastischen Lebensformen und Gegensätzen im Hochmittelalter* (Studia Anselmiana 22–3: Rome)

Hallinger, K. (1956), 'Woher kommen die Laienbrüder?', *Analecta Sacri Ordinis Cisterciensis* 12, 1–104

Halphen, L. (1907), *Etudes sur l'administration de Rome au moyen âge* (Bibliothèque de l'Ecole des Hautes Etudes 176: Paris)

Hartig, O. (1935), *Die oberbayerischen Stifte* 1 (Munich)

Haskins, H. (1929), *Studies in Medieval Culture* (New York)

Hauck, A. (1952), *Kirchengeschichte Deutschlands* (sixth edition, Leipzig)

Haverkamp, A. (1991), 'Die Städte Trier, Metz, Toul und Verdun. Religiöse Gemeinschaften im Zentralitätsgefüge einer Städtelandschaft zur Zeit der Salier', in *Die Salier und das Reich*, ed. S. Weinfurter 3 (Sigmaringen), pp. 165–90

Herberhold, F. (1934), 'Die Beziehung des Cadalus von Parma (Gegenpapst Honorius II.) zu Deutschland', *Historisches Jahrbuch* 54, 84–104

Herberhold, F. (1947), 'Die Angriffe des Cadalus von Parma (Gegenpapst Honorius II.) auf Rom in den Jahren 1062 und 1063', *Studi Gregoriani* 2, 477–503

Herlihy, D. (1958), 'The agrarian revolution in southern France and Italy, 801–1150', *Speculum* 33, 23–37

Herlihy, D. (1961), 'Church property on the European continent, 701–1200', *Speculum* 36, 81–105

Herrmann, K.-J. (1973), *Das Tuskulanerpapsttum (1012–1046)* (Päpste und Papsttum 4: Stuttgart)

Herrmann, M. (1889), 'Paul und Gebhard von Bernried und ihre Briefe an Mailänder Geistliche', *Neues Archiv* 14, 565–88

Hiley, D. (1993), *Western plainchant. A handbook* (Oxford)

Hlawitschka, E. (1969), *Die Anfänge des Hauses Habsburg-Lothringen. Genealogische Untersuchungen zur Geschichte Lothringens und des Reiches im 9., 10. und 11. Jahrhundert* (Saarbrücken)

Hlawitschka, E. (1974), 'Zwischen Tribur und Canossa', *Historisches Jahrbuch* 94, 25–45

Hoesch, H. (1970), *Die kanonischen Quellen im Werk Humberts von Moyenmoutier. Ein Beitrag zur Geschichte der vorgregorianischen Reform* (Forschungen zur kirchlichen Rechtsgeschichte und zum Kirchenrecht 10: Cologne-Vienna)

Hoffmann, H. (1963), 'Von Cluny zum Investiturstreit', *Archiv für Kulturgeschichte* 45, 165–209

Hoffmann, H. (1969), 'Die Anfänge der Normannen in Süditalien', *Quellen und Forschungen aus italienischen Archiven und Bibliotheken* 49, 95–144

Hoffmann, H. (1978), 'Langobarden, Normannen, Päpste. Zum Legitimitätsproblem in Unteritalien', *Quellen und Forschungen aus italienischen Archiven und Bibliotheken* 58, 137–80

Hofmann, H. (1933), *Der Dictatus Papae Gregors VII. Eine rechtsgeschichtliche Erklärung* (Paderborn)

Holtzmann, W. (1947), 'Laurentius von Amalfi, ein Lehrer Hildebrands', *Studi Gregoriani* 1, 207–36

Hourlier, J. (1946–1955), 'Le pape Saint Léon IX à Reims', *Travaux de l'Académie nationale de Reims* 155, 55–9

Hourlier, J. (1981), 'Anselme de Saint-Remi' in *Contribution à l'année Saint Benoît (480–1980). La Champagne bénédictine* (*Travaux de l'Académie nationale de Reims* 160: Rheims), pp. 181–261

Hübinger, P. E. (1973), *Die letzten Worte Papst Gregors VII.* (Rheinisch-Westfälische Akademie der Wissenschaften, Geisteswissenschaften, Vorträge G 185, Opladen)

Hüls, R. (1977), *Kardinäle, Klerus und Kirchen Roms 1049–1130* (Tübingen)

Humphries, M. (1999), *Communities of the Blessed. Social environment and religious change in Northern Italy, AD 200–400* (Oxford)

Hussey, J. M. (1966), 'The later Macedonians, the Comneni and the Angeli, 1025–1204' in *Cambridge Medieval History* 4/1 (Cambridge), pp. 193–249

Huygens, R. B. C. (1965), 'Bérengar de Tours, Lanfranc et Bernold de Constance', *Sacris Erudiri* 16, 355–403

Huyghebaert, N.-N. (1947), 'Saint Léon IX et la lutte contre la simonie dans le diocèse de Verdun', *Studi Gregoriani* 1, 417–32

Jakobs, H. (1961), *Die Hirsauer. Ihre Ausbreitung und Rechtsstellung im Zeitalter des Investiturstreites* (Cologne-Graz)

Jakobs, H. (1968), *Der Adel in der Klosterreform von St. Blasien* (Cologne-Graz)

Jakobs, H. (1973), 'Rudolf von Rheinfelden und die Kirchenreform' in *Investiturstreit und Reichsverfassung*, ed. J. Fleckenstein (Vorträge und Forschungen 17: Sigmaringen), pp. 87–115

Jasper, D. (1986), *Das Papstwahldekret von 1059* (Sigmaringen)

Jenal, G. (1974, 1975), *Erzbischof Anno II. von Köln (1056–75) und sein politisches Wirken* 1, 2 (Stuttgart)

Jolivet, J. (1969), *Arts du langage et théologie chez Abélard* (Paris)

Jordan, K. (1933–4), 'Zur päpstlichen Finanzgeschichte im 11. und 12. Jahrhundert', *Quellen und Forschungen aus italienischen Archiven und Bibliotheken* 25, 61–104

Jordan, K. (1954), 'Die Stellung Wiberts von Ravenna in der Publizistik des Investiturstreits', *Mitteilungen des Instituts für österreichische Geschichtsforschung* 62, 155–64

Kehr, P. (1930), 'Vier Kapitel aus der Geschichte Kaiser Heinrichs III.', *Abhandlungen der Preußischen Akademie der Wissenschaften, Jahrgang 1930, Philosophisch-historische Klasse* no. 3

Kehr, P. (1934), 'Die Belehnung der süditalienischen Normannenfürsten durch die Päpste, 1059–1192', *Abhandlungen der Akademie der Wissenschaften zu Berlin 1934, no. 1*

Keller, H. (1970), 'Die soziale und politische Verfassung Mailands in den Anfängen des kommunalen Lebens', *Historische Zeitschrift* 211, 34–64

Keller, H. (1973), 'Pataria und Stadtverfassung, Stadtgemeinde und Reform: Mailand im "Investiturstreit"' in *Investiturstreit und Reichsverfassung*, ed. J. Fleckenstein (Vorträge und Forschungen 17: Sigmaringen), pp. 321–50

Keller, H. (1977), 'Origine sociale e formazione del clero cattedrale dei secoli XI e XII nella Germania e nell' Italia settentrionale' in *Le istituzioni ecclesiastiche della 'societas christiana' dei secoli XI e XII: Diocesi, pieve e parrochie* (MIscellanea del Centro di studi medioevali 8), pp. 136–86

Keller, H. (1979), *Adelherrschaft und städtische Gesellschaft in Oberitalien 9. bis 12. Jahrhundert* (Bibliothek des Deutschen Historischen Instituts in Rom 52: Tübingen)

Keller, H. (1983), 'Schwäbische Herzöge als Thronbewerber: Hermann II. (1002), Rudolf von Rheinfelden (1077), Friedrich von Staufen (1125)', *Zeitschrift für die Geschichte des Oberrheins* 131, 123–62

Kemp, E. W. (1948), *Canonization and authority in the Western Church* (Oxford)

Kerkhoff, J. (1964), *Die Grafen von Altshausen-Veringen. Die Ausbildung der Familie zum Adelsgeschlecht und der Aufbau ihrer Herrschaft im 11. und 12. Jahrhundert* (Hohenzollerische Jahreshefte 24 [87]: Sigmaringen)

Klauser, R. (1954), 'Zur Entwicklung des Heiligsprechungsverfahrens bis zum 13. Jahrhundert', *Zeitschrift der Savigny-Stiftung für Rechtsgeschichte, Kanonistische Abteilung* 40, 85–101

Klewitz, H.-W. (1939), 'Die Festkrönungen der deutschen Könige', *Zeitschrift der Savigny-Stiftung für Rechtsgeschichte, kanonistische Abteilung* 28, 48–96

406   BIBLIOGRAPHY

Klewitz, H.-W. (1941), 'Die Krönung des Papstes', *Zeitschrift der Savigny-Stiftung für Rechtsgeschichte, kanonistische Abteilung* 30, 96–130

Klewitz, H.-W. (1957), *Reformpapsttum und Kardinalkolleg* (Darmstadt)

Klöckener, M. (1980), 'Eine liturgische Ordnung für Provinzialkonzilien aus der Karolingerzeit', *Annuarium Historiae Conciliorum* 12, 109–82

Koch, G. (1972), *Auf dem Wege zum Sacrum Imperium. Studien zur ideologischen Herrschaftsbegründung der deutschen Zentralgewalt im 11. und 12. Jahrhundert* (Forschungen zur mittelalterlichen Geschichte 20, Vienna-Cologne-Graz)

Kölmel, W. (1935), *Rom und der Kirchenstaat im 10. und 11. Jahrhundert bis in die Anfänge der Reform* (Abhandlungen zur Mittleren und Neueren Geschichte 78: Berlin)

Kohnle, A. (1993), *Abt Hugo von Cluny (1049–1109)* (Beihefte der Francia 32: Sigmaringen)

Kottje, R. (1978), 'Zur Bedeutung der Bischofsstädte für Heinrich IV.', *Historisches Jahrbuch* 97–98, 131–57

Krause, H.-G. (1960), *Das Papstwahldekret von 1059 und seine Rolle im Investiturstreit* (Studi Gregoriani 7: Rome)

Krause, H.-G. (1976), 'Über den Verfasser der Vita Leonis IX papae', *Deutsches Archiv* 32, 49–85

Krautheimer, R. (2000), *Rome. Profile of a city, 312–1308* (revised edition, Princeton)

Krimm-Beumann, J. (1977), 'Der Traktat "De investitura episcoporum" von 1109', *Deutsches Archiv* 33, 37–83

Kuithan, R. – Wollasch, J. (1984), 'Der Kalender des Chronisten Bernold', *Deutsches Archiv* 40, 478–531

Ladner, G. B. (1956), 'Two Gregorian letters on the sources and nature of Gregory VII's reform ideology', *Studi Gregoriani* 5, 221–42

Lange, K.-H. (1961), 'Die Stellung der Grafen von Northeim in der Reichsgeschichte des 11. und frühen 12. Jahrhunderts', *Niedersächsisches Jahrbuch für Landesgeschichte* 33, 1–107

Laudage, J. (1984), *Priesterbild und Reformpapsttum im 11. Jahrhundert* (Cologne-Vienna)

Leclercq, H. (1930), 'Liber pontificalis', *Dictionnaire d'archéologie chrétienne et de liturgie* 9, col. 354–466

Leclercq, J. (1947), 'Simoniaca heresis', *Studi Gregoriani* 1, 523–30

Lehmgrübner, H. (1887), *Benzo von Alba. Ein Verfechter der kaiserlichen Staatsidee unter Heinrich IV.* (Historische Untersuchungen 6: Berlin)

Lerner, F. (1931), *Kardinal Hugo Candidus* (Beiheft 22 der Historischen Zeitschrift: Munich-Berlin)

Lesne, E. (1940), *Histoire de la propriété ecclésiastique en France 5: Les écoles* (Lille)

Lewald, U. (1938), *An der Schwelle der Scholastik: Bonizo von Sutri und das Kirchenrecht seiner Tage* (Weimar)

Liebeschütz, H. (1950), *Medieval humanism in the life and writings of John of Salisbury* (Studies of the Warburg Institute 7, London)

Lindner, T. (1866), 'Benzos Panegyricus auf Heinrich IV. und der Kirchenstreit zwischen Alexander II. und Cadalus von Parma', *Forschungen zur deutschen Geschichte* 6, 497–526

Lucchesi, G. (1972), 'Per una Vita di San Pier Damiani. Componenti cronologiche e topografiche' in *San Pier Damiano nel IX centenario della morte (1072–1972)* (Cesena) 1, 13–179; 2, 13–160

Lucioni, A. (1981), '"Noviter fidelitatem imperatori iuraverat…" (Landulphi senioris Historia Mediolanensis III,29). Enrico IV o Erlembaldo?', *Annali Canossani* 1, 63–70

Lück, D. (1970a), 'Die Kölner Erzbischöfe Hermann II. und Anno II. als Erzkanzler der Römischen Kirche', *Archiv für Diplomatik* 16, 1–50

Lück, D. (1970b), 'Erzbischof Anno II. von Köln. Standesverhältnisse, verwandtschaftliche Beziehungen und Werdegang bis zur Bischofsweihe', *Annalen des historischen Vereins für den Niederrhein* 172, 7–112

Lynch, J. (1985), 'Hugh I of Cluny's sponsorship of Henry IV: its context and consequences', *Speculum* 60, 800–26

Maccarrone, M. (1974), 'La teologia del primato romano del secolo XI' in *Le istituzioni ecclesiastiche della 'societas christiana' dei secoli XI–XII: Papato, cardinalato ed episcopato (Miscellanea del Centro di Studi Medioevali* 7), pp. 21–122

Märtl, C. (1985), 'Zur Überlieferung des *Liber contra Wibertum* Anselms von Lucca', *Deutsches Archiv* 41, 192–202

Märtl, C. (1986), 'Regensburg in den geistigen Auseinandersetzungen des Investiturstreits', *Deutsches Archiv* 42, 145–91

Magistretti, M. (1897), 'Una corrispondenza Ambrosiana del secolo XII', *La Scuola Cattolica* 25, 494–504

Maier, M. (1963), 'Ein schwäbisch-bayerischer Freundeskreis Gregor VII. nach der Vita Herlucae des Paul von Bernried', *Studien und Mitteilungen zur Geschichte des Benediktinerordens* 74, 313–32

Manitius, M. (1923, 1931), *Geschichte der lateinischen Literatur des Mittelalters* 2, 3 (Handbuch der Altertumswissenschaft 9. 2/2–3, Munich)

Marchetti-Longhi, G. (1947), 'Ricerche sulla famiglia di Gregorio VII', *Studi Gregoriani* 2, 287–333

Marrou, H. I. (1950), *Histoire de l'Education dans l'Antiquité* (Paris)

Martin, E. (1900), *Histoire des diocèses de Toul, de Nancy et de Saint-Dié* 1 (Nancy)

Martin, G. (1994), 'Der salische Herrscher als *Patricius Romanorum.* Zur Einflußnahme Heinrichs III. und Heinrichs IV. auf die Besetzung der *Cathedra Petri*', *Frühmittelalterliche Studien* 28, 257–95

May, J. (1887), 'Leben Pauls von Bernried', *Neues Archiv* 12, 333–52

Mayne, R. (1954), 'East and west in 1054', *Cambridge Historical Journal* 11, 133–48

Mercati, A. (1914), 'L'autore della *Expositio in septem psalmos poenitentiales* fra le opere di S. Gregorio Magno', *Revue Bénédictine* 31, 250–7

Mertens, D. (1991), 'Vom Rhein zur Rems. Aspekte salisch-schwäbischer Geschichte' in *Die Salier und das Reich* 1, ed. S. Weinfurter (Sigmaringen), 221–51

Meyer von Knonau, G. (1890, 1894, 1900, 1903, 1904, 1907, 1909), *Jahrbücher des Deutschen Reiches unter Heinrich IV. und Heinrich V.* 1–7 (Leipzig)

Miccoli, G. (1956), 'Il problema delle ordinazioni simoniache e le sinodi lateranensi del 1060 e 1061', *Studi Gregoriani* 5, 33–81

Miccoli, G. (1960), *Pietro Igneo. Studi sull' età gregoriana* (Studi storici 40–41, Rome)

Miccoli, G. (1966a), *Chiesa gregoriana. Ricerche sulla riforma del secolo XI* (Florence)

Miccoli, G. (1966b), 'Un nuovo manoscritto del Liber de vita christiana di Bonizone di Sutri', *Studi Medievali* serie 3, 7, 371–98

Miccoli, G. (1966c), 'Gregorio VII, papa, santo', *Biblioteca sanctorum* 7 (Rome), cols. 294–379

Miccoli, G. (1970), 'Bonizone', *Dizionario biografico degli Italiani* 12 (Rome), 246–59

Michel, A. (1924), *Humbert und Kerullarios. Quellen und Studien zum Schisma des 11. Jahrhunderts* (volume 1: Paderborn)

Michel, A. (1930), 'Die Accusatio des Kanzlers Friedrich von Lothringen (Papst Stephan IX.) gegen die Griechen', *Römische Quartalschrift* 38, 153–208

Michel, A. (1935), 'Die vier Schriften des Niketas Stethatos über die Azymen', *Byzantinische Zeitschrift* 35, 308–36

Michel, A. (1940), 'Lateinische Aktenstücke und -sammlungen zum griechischen Schisma (1053/54)', *Historisches Jahrbuch* 60, 46–64

Michel, A. (1943), *Die Sentenzen des Kardinals Humbert, das erste Rechtsbuch der päpstlichen Reform* (Schriften der MGH 7: Leipzig)

Michel, A. (1948), 'Die Anfänge des Kardinals Humbert bei Bischof Bruno von Toul (Leo IX.)', *Studi Gregoriani* 3, 299–319

Michel, A. (1952–1953), 'Die Frühwerke des Kardinals Humbert über Hidulf, Deodat und Moyenmoutier', *Zeitschrift für Kirchengeschichte* 64, 225–59

Michel, A. (1953), 'Humbert und Hildebrand bei Nikolaus II (1059/61)', *Historisches Jahrbuch* 72, 133–61

Michel, A. (1954), 'Schisma und Kaiserhof im Jahre 1054: Michael Psellos' in *Collection Irénikon 1054–1954. Etudes et travaux offerts à Don Lambert Beauduin* 1 (Gembloux), 351–440

Mirbt, C. (1894), *Die Publizistik im Zeitalter Gregors VII.* (Leipzig)

Moehs, T. E. (1972), *Gregorius V., 996–999* (Päpste und Papsttum 2: Stuttgart)

Mohr, W. (1976), *Geschichte des Herzogtums Lothringen 2* (Saarbrücken)

Mois, J. (1953), *Das Stift Rottenbuch in der Kirchenreform des XI.–XII. Jahrhunderts* (Munich)

de Montclos, J. (1971), *Lanfranc et Bérenger: la controverse eucharistique du xı̇siècle* (Louvain)

Moore, R. I. (1980), 'Family, community and cult on the eve of the Gregorian reform', *Transactions of the Royal Historical Society* fifth series 30, 49–67

Morrison, K. F. (1962), 'Canossa. A revision', *Traditio* 18, 121–48

Müller, E. (1901), *Das Itinerar Kaiser Heinrichs III. (1039 bis 1056) mit besonderer Berücksichtigung seiner Urkunden* (Historische Studien 26: Berlin)

Murray, A. (1978), *Reason and society in the Middle Ages* (Oxford)

Overmann, A. (1895), *Gräfin Mathilde von Tuszien. Ihre Besitzungen. Geschichte ihres Gutes von 1125–1230 und ihre Regesten* (Innsbruck)

Pannenborg, A. (1872), *Studien zur Geschichte der Herzogin Mathilde von Canossa* (Göttingen)

Paré, G., A. Brunet and P. Tremblay (1933), *La renaissance du xii* siècle* (Paris)

Parisse, M. (1983), 'Une abbaye de femmes en Lorraine: Poussay au moyen âge', *Album amicorum. N.-N. Huyghebaert O. S. B.* (=*Sacris erudiri* 26), pp. 103–18

Parisse, M. (1984), 'L'évêque impérial dans son diocèse. L'exemple lorrain aux Xᵉ et XIᵉ siècles' in *Institutionen, Kultur und Gesellschaft im Mittelalter*, ed. L. Fenske, W. Rösener, T. Zotz (Sigmaringen), pp. 179–93

Parisse, M. (1996), 'Le peuple, l'évêque et le roi. À propos de l'élection épiscopale de Léon IX' in *Peuples du Moyen Age. Problèmes d'identification*, ed. C. Carozzi and H. Taviani-Carozzi (Séminaire Sociétés, idéologies et croyances au Moyen Age. Publications del'Université d'Aix-en-Provence), pp. 77–95

Partner, P. (1972), *The Lands of St Peter. The papal state in the Middle Ages and the early Renaissance* (London)

Pásztor, E. (1960), 'Una fonte per la storia dell' età gregoriana: la *Vita Anselmi episcopi Lucensis*', *Bullettino dell' Istituto storico italiano per il medio evo* 72, 1–33

Pásztor, E. (1964), 'Sacerdozio e regno nella *Vita Anselmi episcopi Lucensis*', *Archivum Historiae Pontificiae* 2, 91–115

Pásztor, E. (1965), 'Motivi dell'ecclesiologia di Anselmo di Lucca in margine a un sermone inedito', *Bullettino dell'Istituto storico italiano per il medio evo* 77, 45–104

Pásztor, E. (1987), 'Lotta per le investiture e "ius belli": la posizione di Anselmo di Lucca' in *Sant'Anselmo, Mantova e la lotta per le investiture*, ed. P. Golinelli (Bologna), pp. 375–421

Pásztor, E. (1992), 'La "Vita" anonima di Anselmo di Lucca: una rilettura' in *Sant' Anselmo vescovo di Lucca (1073–86) nel quadro delle trasformazioni sociali e della riforma ecclesiastica*, ed. C. Violante (Istituto storico italiano per il medio evo, Studi storici 13: Rome), pp. 207–22

Paulin, P. (1950), 'Leo IX. der Dichter und Musiker' in *Saint Léon IX, le pape alsacien*, ed. L. Sittler and P. Stintzi (Colmar), pp. 123–32

Peitz, W. M. (1911), 'Das Originalregister Gregors VII. im vatikanischen Archiv (Reg. Vat. 2)', *Sitzungsberichte der Wiener Akademie der Wissenschaften, phil.-hist. Klasse* 165 (1911), Abh. 5

Perels, E. (1931), 'Zum Kaisertum Karls des Großen in mittelalterlichen Geschichtsquellen', *Sitzungsberichte der preußischen Akademie der Wissenschaften, phil.-hist. Klasse, 1931* pp. 363–79

Petrucci, E. (1973), 'Rapporti di Leone IX con Constantinopoli', *Studi Medievali* 3 ser., 14, 733–831

Petrucci, E. (1977), *Ecclesiologia e politica di Leone IX* (Rome)

Peyer, H. C. (1955), *Stadt und Stadtpatron im mittelalterlichen Italien* (Zürich)

Picasso, G. (1989), 'Gregorio VII e la disciplina canonica: clero e vita monastica', *Studi Gregoriani* 13, 151–66

Poole, R. L. (1934), *Studies in chronology and history* (Oxford)

Prinz, F. (1971), *Klerus und Krieg im früheren Mittelalter. Untersuchungen zur Rolle der Kirche beim Aufbau der Königsherrschaft* (Stuttgart)

Ramackers, J. (1931–2), 'Analekten zur Geschichte des Reformpapsttums und der Cluniazenser', *Quellen und Forschungen aus italienischen Archiven und Bibliotheken* 23, 22–52

Reuter, T. (1991), 'Unruhestiftung, Fehde, Rebellion, Widerstand: Gewalt und Frieden in der Politik der Salierzeit' in *Die Salier und das Reich* 3, ed. S. Weinfurter and H. Seibert (Sigmaringen), pp. 297–325

Rieckenberg, H. J. (1942), 'Königsstrasse und Königsgut in liudolfingischer und frühsalischer Zeit (919–1056)', *Archiv für Urkundenforschung* 17, 32–154

Rimoldi, A. (1964), 'Erlembaldo Cotta', *Bibliotheca Sanctorum* 5, col. 3–6

Riley-Smith, J. (1986), *The First Crusade and the idea of crusading* (Philadelphia)

Robinson, I. S. (1973a), 'Gregory VII and the soldiers of Christ', *History* 58, 169–92

Robinson, I. S. (1973b), A manuscript of the "Liber de vita christiana" of Bonizo of Sutri', *Bulletin of Medieval Canon Law*, new series 3, 135–9

Robinson, I. S. (1978a), *Authority and Resistance in the Investiture Contest. The polemical literature of the eleventh century* (Manchester)

Robinson, I. S. (1978b), 'Zur Arbeitsweise Bernolds von Konstanz und seines Kreises. Untersuchungen zum Schlettstädter Codex 13', *Deutsches Archiv* 34, 51–122

Robinson, I. S. (1978c), 'Eine unbekannte Streitschrift über die Sakramente Exkommunizierten im Münchener Kodex lat. 618', *Studi Gregoriani* 11, 299–395

Robinson, I. S. (1978d), 'The friendship network of Gregory VII', *History* 63, 1–22

Robinson, I. S. (1979), 'Pope Gregory VII, the princes and the pactum, 1077–1080', *English Historical Review* 94, 721–56

Robinson, I. S. (1983), '"Political allegory" in the biblical exegesis of Bruno of Segni', *Recherches de théologie ancienne et médiévale* 50, 69–98

Robinson, I. S. (1988), 'Church and papacy' in *The Cambridge History of Medieval Political Thought c. 350–c. 1450*, ed. J. H. Burns (Cambridge), pp. 252–305

Robinson, I. S. (1990), *The Papacy 1073–1198: continuity and innovation* (Cambridge)

Robinson, I. S. (1999), *Henry IV of Germany, 1056–1106* (Cambridge)

Rörig, F. (1948), *Geblütsrecht und freie Wahl in ihrer Auswirkung auf die deutsche Geschichte* (Abhandlungen der deutschen Akademie der Wissenschaften zu Berlin, 1945/6, phil.-hist. Klasse no. 6, Berlin)

Runciman, S. (1955), *The eastern schism* (Oxford)

Ryan, J. J. (1956), *Saint Peter Damiani and his canonical sources* (Pontifical Institute of Mediaeval Studies. Studies and Texts 2: Toronto)

Sackur, E. (1892, 1894), *Die Cluniazenser in ihrer kirchlichen und allgemeingeschichtlichen Wirksamkeit bis zur Mitte des 11. Jahrhunderts* 1, 2 (Halle)

Säbekow, G. (1931), *Die päpstlichen Legationen nach Spanien und Portugal bis zum Ausgang des 12. Jahrhunderts* (Berlin)

Saltet, L. (1907), *Les réordinations: étude sur le sacrement de l'ordre* (Paris)

Santifaller, L. (1940), 'Saggio di uno elenco dei funzionari, impiegati e scrittori della cancellaria pontificia dall'inizio all' anno 1099', *Bollettino dell' Istituto storico italiano per il medio evo* 56

Saur, H. (1868), 'Studien über Bonizo', *Forschungen zur deutschen Geschichte* 8, 395–464

Schaeffer, M. (1982), 'Les abbayes Saint-Evre et Saint Mansuy aux Xe et XIe siècles', *Etudes Touloises* 27, 55–63

Schebler, A. (1936), *Die Reordinationen in der 'altkatholischen' Kirche* (Bonn)

Schetter, R. (1935), *Die Intervenienz der weltlichen und geistlichen Fürsten in den deutschen Königsurkunden von 911–1056* (dissertation, Berlin)

Schieffer, R. (1972a), 'Spirituales latrones. Zu den Hintergründen der Simonieprozesse in Deutschland zwischen 1069 und 1075', *Historisches Jahrbuch* 92, 19–60

Schieffer, R. (1972b), 'Von Mailand nach Canossa. Ein Beitrag zur Geschichte der christlichen Herrscherbusse von Theodosius der Grosse bis zu Heinrich IV.', *Deutsches Archiv* 28, 333–70

Schieffer, R. (1975), 'Hermann I., Bischof von Bamberg', *Fränkische Lebensbilder* 6, 55–76

Schieffer, R. (1981), *Die Entstehung des päpstlichen Investiturverbots für den deutschen König* (Schriften der MGH 28, Stuttgart)

Schieffer, R. (1988), 'Paul von Bernried (eigentlich: von Regensburg)', *Verfasserlexikon. Die deutsche Literatur des Mittelalters* 7, col. 359–64

Schieffer, R. (1991), 'Erzbischöfe und Bischofskirche von Köln' in *Die Salier und das Reich*, ed. S. Weinfurter 2 (Sigmaringen), pp. 1–30

Schieffer, T. (1935), *Die päpstlichen Legaten in Frankreich vom Vertrage von Meersen (870) bis zum Schisma von 1130* (Historische Studien 263: Berlin)

Schlesinger, W. (1973), 'Die Wahl Rudolfs von Schwaben zum Gegenkönig 1077 in Forchheim' in *Investiturstreit und Reichsverfassung*, ed. J. Fleckenstein (Vorträge und Forschungen 17: Sigmaringen), pp. 61–85

Schmale, F.-J. (1979a), 'Die "Absetzung" Gregors VI. in Sutri und die synodale Tradition', *Annuarium Historiae Conciliorum* 11, 55–103

Schmale, F.-J. (1979b), 'Synoden Alexanders II.', *Annuarium Historiae Conciliorum* 11, 307–38

Schmid, P. (1926), *Der Begriff der kanonischen Wahl in den Anfängen des Investiturstreits* (Stuttgart)

Schmidt, T. (1972), 'Die Kanonikerreform in Rom und Papst Alexander II. (1061–1073)', *Studi Gregoriani* 9, 199–221

Schmidt, T. (1973), 'Zu Hildebrands Eid vor Kaiser Heinrich III.', *Archivum Historiae Pontificiae* 11, 374–86

Schmidt, T. (1977), *Alexander II. und die römische Reformgruppe seiner Zeit* (Päpste und Papsttum 11: Stuttgart)

Schmidt, U. (1987), *Königswahl und Thronfolge im 12. Jahrhundert* (Cologne-Vienna)

Schmitt, F. S. (1956), 'Neue und alte Hildebrand-Anekdoten aus den *Dicta Anselmi*', *Studi Gregoriani* 5, 1–18

Schmitz, H.-G. (1975), *Kloster Prüfening im 12. Jahrhundert* (Miscellanea Bavarica Monacensia 49)

Schneider, C. (1972), *Prophetisches Sacerdotium und heilsgeschichtliches Regnum im Dialog 1073–1077* (Münstersche Mittelalter-Schriften 9: Munich)

Schneider, F. (1914), *Die Reichsverwaltung in Toscana von der Gründung des Lango-bardenreiches bis zum Ausgang der Staufer (568–1268)* 1: *Die Grundlagen* (Rome)

Schnitzer, A. (1969), 'Die selige Herluka von Bernried, Persönlichkeit und Zeitlage', *Jahrbuch des Vereins für Augsburger Bistumsgeschichte* 3, 5–15

Schramm, P. E. (1929), *Kaiser, Rom und Renovatio. Studien zur Geschichte des römischen Erneuerungsgedankens vom Ende des karolingischen Reiches bis zum Investiturstreit* (Studien der Bibliothek Warburg 17: Leipzig-Berlin)

Schramm, P. E. (1930), 'Die Ordines der mittelalterlichen Kaiserkrönung. Ein Beitrag zur Geschichte des Kaisertums', *Archiv für Urkundenforschung* 11, 285–390

Schramm, P. E. (1954, 1955, 1956), *Herrschaftszeichen und Staatssymbolik. Beiträge zu ihrer Geschichte vom 3. bis zum 16. Jahrhundert* (Schriften der MGH 13/1–3)

Schramm, P. E. (1968, 1969, 1970, 1971), *Kaiser, Könige und Päpste. Gesammelte Aufsätze zur Geschichte des Mittelalters*, 1–4 (Stuttgart)

Schreiber, G. (1948), *Gemeinschaften des Mittelalters* (Regensburg-Münster)

Schumann, O. (1912), *Die päpstlichen Legaten in Deutschland zur Zeit Heinrichs IV. und Heinrichs V. (1056–1125)* (Marburg)

Schuster, I. (1934), *La Basilica e il Monastero di S. Paolo fuori le Mura* (Turin)

Schuster, I. (1950), 'Dove Ildebrando, il futuro Gregorio VII, professò la vita monastica', *La Scuola Cattolica* 78, 52–7

Schuster, I. (1952), 'Dove Ildebrando si consacrò alla vita monastica', *Benedictina* 6, 305–7

Schwartz, G. (1913), *Die Besetzung der Bistümer Reichsitaliens unter den sächsischen und salischen Kaisern mit den Listen der Bischöfe, 951–1122* (Leipzig-Berlin)

Seibert, H. (1991), 'Libertas und Reichsabtei. Zur Klosterpolitik der salischen Herr-scher' in *Die Salier und das Reich* 2, ed. S. Weinfurter (Sigmaringen), pp. 503–69

Semmler, J. (1959), *Die Klosterreform von Siegburg. Ihre Ausbreitung und ihr Reform-programm im 11. und 12. Jahrhundert* (Rheinisches Archiv 53, Bonn)

Sepp, B. (1894), 'Paul und Gebhard, die Gründer des Klosters St. Mang', *Verhand-lungen des Historischen Vereins für die Oberpfalz* 46, 265–98

Servatius, C. (1979), *Paschalis II. (1099–1118)* (Päpste und Papsttum 14, Stuttgart)

Smalley, B. (1952), *The study of the Bible in the Middle Ages* (Oxford)

Smalley, B. (1973), *The Becket conflict and the schools. A study of intellectuals in politics* (Oxford)

Somerville, R. (1972a), *The Councils of Urban II* 1: *Decreta Claromontensia* (Annuarium Historiae Conciliorum, supplementum 1, Amsterdam)

Somerville, R. (1972b), 'The case against Berengar of Tours: a new text', *Studi Gregoriani* 9, 53–75

Somerville, R. (1972c), 'Pope Honorius II, Conrad of Hohenstaufen and Lothar III', *Archivum Historiae Pontificiae* 10, 341–6

Somerville, R. (1977), 'Cardinal Stephan of S. Grisogono' in *Law, Church and Society*, ed. K. Pennington and R. Somerville (University of Pennsylvania), pp. 157–66

Somigli, C. (1973), 'San Pier Damiano e la Pataria (Relazioni e amicizie)' in *San Pier Damiano nel IX centenario della morte (1072–1972)* 3 (Cesena), 193–206

Southern, R. W. (1953), *The making of the Middle Ages* (London)

Southern, R. W. (1970), *Western society and the Church in the Middle Ages* (Harmondsworth)

Stacpoole, A. (1967), 'Hugh of Cluny and the Hildebrandine miracle tradition', *Revue Bénédictine* 77, 341–63

Steindorff, E. (1874, 1881), *Jahrbücher des Deutschen Reiches unter Heinrich III.* 1, 2 (Leipzig)

Stevenson, J. (1998), 'Constantine, St Aldhelm and the loathly lady' in *Constantine. History, historiography and legend*, ed. S. N. C. Lieu and D. Montserrat (London), pp. 189–206

Stoob, H. (1974), 'Zur Königswahl Lothars von Sachsen im Jahre 1125' in *Historische Forschungen für Walter Schlesinger*, ed. H. Beumann (Cologne-Vienna), pp. 438–61

Struve, T. (1984), *Die Regesten des Kaiserreiches unter Heinrich IV. 1056 (1050)-1106* 1 (Regesta Imperii 3. 2, Cologne-Vienna)

Struve, T. (1985), 'Die Romreise der Kaiserin Agnes', *Historisches Jahrbuch* 105, 1–29

Struve, T. (1988), 'Kaisertum und Romgedanke in salischer Zeit', *Deutsches Archiv* 44, 424–54

Struve, T. (1995), 'Mathilde von Tuszien-Canossa und Heinrich IV.', *Historisches Jahrbuch* 115, 41–84

Taviani-Carozzi, H. (1996), 'Une bataille franco-allemande en Italie: Civitate (1053)' in *Peuples du Moyen âge: problèmes d'identification*, ed. C. Carozzi and H. Taviani-Carozzi (Aix-en-Provence), pp. 181–211

Tellenbach, G. (1988), 'Der Charakter Kaiser Heinrichs IV.' in *Person und Gemeinschaft im Mittelalter*, ed. G. Althoff, D. Greuenich, O. G. Oexle, J. Wollasch (Sigmaringen), pp. 345–67

Thomas, H. (1970), 'Erzbischof Siegfried I. von Mainz und die Tradition seiner Kirche', *Deutsches Archiv* 26, 368–99

Tondelli, L. (1952), 'Scavi archeologici a Canossa. Le tre mura di cinta', *Studi Gregoriani* 4, 365–71

Toubert, P. (1973), *Les structures du Latium médiéval. Le Latium méridional et la Sabine du IXe siècle à la fin du XII siècle* (Bibliothèque des Ecoles Françaises d'Athènes et de Rome 221: Rome)

Tritz, H. (1952), 'Die hagiographischen Quellen zur Geschichte Papst Leos IX. Eine Untersuchung ihrer Überlieferungs- und Entstehungsgeschichte', *Studi Gregoriani* 4, 191–364

Twellenkamp, M. (1991), 'Das Haus der Luxemburger' in *Die Salier und das Reich*, ed. S. Weinfurter 1 (Sigmaringen), 475–502

Ullmann, W. (1970), *The growth of papal government in the Middle Ages* (third edition, London)

Vehse, O. (1930–1), 'Benevent als Territorium des Kirchenstaates bis zum Beginn der avignonischen Epoche', *Quellen und Forschungen aus italiensichen Archiven und Bibliotheken* 22, 87–160

Villard, F. (1991), 'Primatie des Gaules et réforme grégorienne', *Bibiothèque de l'École des Chartes* 149, 421–34

Violante, C. (1955), *La Pataria milanese e la riforma ecclesiastica* 1: *Le premesse 1045–1057* (Studi storici 11–13, Rome)

Violante, C. (1961), 'Anselmo da Baggio', *Dizionario biografico degli Italiani* 3, 399–407

Violante, C. (1968), 'I laici nel movimento patarino' in *I laici nella 'societas cristiana' dei secoli XI e XII.* (Miscellanea del Centro di Studi Medioevali 5: Milan), pp. 597–687

Violante, C. (1983), 'Riflessioni storiche sul seppellimento e la traslazione di Arialdo e di Erlembaldo capi della Pataria milanese' in *Pascua Medievalia. Studies voor Prof. Dr. J. M. De Smet* (Medievalia Lovaniensia ser. 1, Studia 10), pp. 66–74

Vogel, J. (1983), *Gregor VII. und Heinrich IV. nach Canossa* (Berlin – New York)

Vollmer, F. (1957), 'Die Etichonen' in *Studien und Vorarbeiten zur Geschichte des großfränkischen und frühdeutschen Adels*, ed. G. Tellenbach (Freiburg i. Br.), pp. 137–84

Vollrath, H. (1974), 'Kaisertum und Patriziat in den Anfängen des Investiturstreits', *Zeitschrift für Kirchengeschichte* 85, 11–44

Vollrath, H. (1991), 'Konfliktwahrnehmung und Konfliktdarstellung in erzählenden Quellen des 11. Jahrhunderts' in *Die Salier und das Reich* 3, ed. S. Weinfurter and H. Seibert (Sigmaringen), pp. 279–96

Wache, W. (1936), 'Eine Sammlung von Originalbriefen des 12. Jahrhunderts im Kapitelarchiv von S. Ambrogio in Mailand', *Mitteilungen des Instituts für österreichische Geschichtsforschung* 50, 261–333

Wadle, E. (1973), 'Heinrich IV. und die deutsche Friedensbewegung' in *Investiturstreit und Reichsverfassung*, ed. J. Fleckenstein (Vorträge und Forschungen 17, Sigmaringen), pp. 141–73

Wattenbach, W., R. Holtzmann and F.-J. Schmale (1967), *Deutschlands Geschichtsquellen im Mittelalter. Die Zeit der Sachsen und Salier 2: Das Zeitalter des Investiturstreits (1050–1125)* (Cologne-Graz)

Wattenbach, W., R. Holtzmann and F.-J. Schmale (1976), *Deutschlands Geschichtsquellen im Mittelalter. Vom Tode Heinrichs V. bis zum Ende des Interregnums* 1 (Cologne-Graz)

Weiler, B. (2000), 'The *rex renitens* and the medieval ideal of kingship, ca. 900 – ca. 1250', *Viator* 31, 1–42

Weinfurter, S. (1992), *Herrschaft und Reich der Salier. Grundlinien einer Umbruchzeit* (Sigmaringen)

Weisweiler, H. (1938), 'Un manuscrit inconnu de Munich sur la querelle des investitures', *Revue d'histoire ecclésiastique* 34, 245–69

Werminghoff, A. (1902), 'Die Beschlüsse des Aachner Concils im Jahre 816', *Neues Archiv* 27, 669–71

Werner, E. (1956), *Pauperes Christi* (Leipzig)

Werner, K. F. (1968), 'Heeresorganisation und Kriegsführung im deutschen Königreich des 10. und 11. Jahrhundert' in *Ordinamenti militari in occidente nell' alto medioevo* (Settimane di studio del Centro italiano di studi sull' alto medioevo 15, Spoleto), 791–843

Werner, M. (1991), 'Der Herzog von Lothringen in salischer Zeit', in *Die Salier und das Reich* 1, ed. S. Weinfurter (Sigmaringen), pp. 367–473

Whitton, D. M. (1980), *Papal policy in Rome, 1012–1124* (D. Phil. dissertation, Oxford)

Wollasch, J. (1968), 'Die Wahl des Papstes Nikolaus II.' in *Adel und Kirche. Festschrift für Gerd Tellenbach*, ed. J. Fleckenstein and K. Schmid (Freiburg), pp. 205–20

Wollasch, J. (1971), 'Die Wahl des Papstes Nikolaus II.' in *Il monachesimo e la riforma ecclesiastica (1049–1122)* (Miscellanea del Centro di Studi Medioevali 6: Milan), pp. 54–73

Wollasch, J. (1985), 'Der Einfluß des Mönchtums auf Reich und Kirche vor dem Investiturstreit' in *Reich und Kirche vor dem Investiturstreit*, ed. K. Schmid (Sigmaringen), pp. 35–48

Zafarana, Z. (1966a), 'Ricerche sul "Liber de unitate ecclesiae conservanda"', *Studi Medievali* ser. 3, 7, 617–700

Zafarana, Z. (1966b), 'Sul "conventus" del clero romano nel maggio 1082', *Studi Medievali* ser. 3, 7, 399–403

Zema, D. B. (1944), 'The houses of Tuscany and Pierleone in the crisis of Rome in the eleventh century', *Traditio* 2, 155–75

Zielinski, H. (1984), *Der Reichsepiskopat in spätottonischer und salischer Zeit (1002–1125)* 1 (Stuttgart)

Ziese, J. (1982), *Wibert von Ravenna, der Gegenpapst Clemens III. (1084–1100)* (Päpste und Papsttum 20, Stuttgart)

Zimmermann, H. (1968), *Papstabsetzungen des Mittelalters* (Graz-Vienna-Cologne)

Zimmermann, H. (1970), 'Wurde Gregor VII. 1076 in Worms abgesetzt?', *Mitteilungen des Instituts für österreichische Geschichtsforschung* 78, 121–31

Zoepfl, F. (1955), *Das Bistum Augsburg und seine Bischöfe im Mittelalter* (Augsburg)

INDEX